ENDORSEM

MW01295447

I have known Rev. J. P. for
given Religion cannot be more than one. On that basis we are debating
with each other about Christianity and Islam. Rev. J. P. is a logically
sound man and works hard to bring unity between the Christians and
Muslims in Michigan. I wish him all success in life.

Dr. Faizur Choudhury, Hamtramck, Michigan

I have known J. P. Knight for a couple of years. His love for Muslim
people surprises me all the time. During the last few months we have
been working together debating with Muslim scholars. This book will
be a great milestone for many people around the world. A lot of our
Muslim friends will get answers to many of their questions from this
book. I am very excited about it.

Shakil Khondoker, Hamtramck, Michigan

J. P. Knight came to our West African country to conduct a conference
on Islam to the leadership of our work in this 90% Muslim nation.
At first, I was concerned that it would be redundant for the group,
given their daily life in an Islamic context. Any apprehension I had
was erased in the first few moments of the presentation. J. P. had
a strong command of the information, but more importantly, he
exhibited a heart of compassion for the Muslim world. About 40% of
the conference participants were from a Muslim background and all
were deeply affected by J. P.'s passion, insight and grace. Particularly
helpful was the discussion of the contrasting worldviews.

Randy O., Church leader

Pastor J. P. combines a scholarly mind with a pastor's heart. He took
the lead in welcoming refugees and people of all nations to our church,
and his love for them was returned.

Victoria, University ESL Instructor

Pastor J. P. has a heart for people from all different cultures. He invited
us, and He really believed and practiced what he said. He makes people
from each culture feel like one family.

Lakshmi, ESL Student

Sitting under the teachings of Dr. Knight truly changed our lives. His workshops equipped us to meet and love Hindu, Muslim, Buddhist, and other Christian believers. The refugee community around our area was deeply touched by Pastor J. P. through his visits, teaching, and prayers. Dr. Knight is a gifted and talented teacher of God's truth. His vision for churches and people from all nations must be heard!

Larry and Marsha, ESL Volunteers,
business owner & science teacher

Pastor J. P., it is hard to comprehend the impact you and your teaching have on our lives in few words. Your genuine love for people from other cultures really touched us at a personal level. Your knowledge of world religions is exceptional. You basically showed us the better alternative path, instead of the agonizing life cycle of karma.

Rao, Software Engineer

"Dr. Knight challenged my heart and my conscience. I was confronted with my apathy toward those practicing other religions and will be forever grateful for how he has changed my worldview!

Sheila, Health Care Manager

Dr. J. P. Knight's experiences with Muslims and with other faiths was enlightening. It seems like some Muslims have come to expect to be singled out and not to come into contact with Christians that are willing to engage in a positive, friendly way. To me, Christians should be one of the first to defend and protect against the mistreatment of Muslims, especially considering that they are also God's creation and He loves them.

Xavier, Salvation Army

J. P. Knight presents the subject of Islam, world religions and a Christian response with grace, candor and sensitivity. He comes qualified not only academically, having completed graduate studies in comparative religions, but experientially, having established rapport and acceptance in the Middle Eastern religious communities within Grand Rapids. J. P. is bright, warm, engaging. He is also polite.

Jim S., Church leader.

Questions Muslims
Ask Christians

Questions Muslims Ask Christians

Conversations about God and Scripture

J. P. KNIGHT

Xulon Press Elite

Xulon Press Elite
2301 Lucien Way #415
Maitland, FL 32751
407.339.4217
www.xulonpress.com

ISBN-13: 978-1-5456-1031-2
ADVANCE REVIEW COPY

To the visionary leaders of
Talk of the Town at Wayne State University
for their welcoming engagement
on matters worthy of conversation

ACKNOWLEDGMENTS

"If you find a turtle on a fence," says the African proverb, "you know it had some help." Special thanks to my family who has lived this long journey with me. Especially Pam for her endless proof-reads and many pep-talks along the way! Our sons, Jordan and Kyle, for their undying raves and our daughter Kimberly for her amazing eye for detail!

To my editor, Dr. Larry Keefauver, for his consistent optimism, competent guidance and especially for believing in the merits of this book.

To Talk of the Town, a student-led group from Wayne State University, for giving me a place in their "town" to belong, talk, listen and learn.

To Imam Dr. Sahibzadah for his long and valued friendship.

To my friend Dr. Faizur Choudhury for engaging me in spirited debates that were conducted without rancor in our mutual pursuit for truth.

To our many valued neighbors for their friendship and hospitality including Mahmoud, Sarah and their family, Saad and Hendi, Haydar, Nouhad and Ali, Helal and Mirna, Wissam and Sarah, Ahmad and Jumana and, more recently, Nisreen and her family.

To two of my mentors at GCTS, Dr. Timothy Tennent, who planted the idea for the book's Q & A format and Dr. Paul Martindale for its title.

To Glen G. and his team for generously sharing this vision.

To peer reviewers who read selected chapters and provided valuable insights, clarifications and corrections – S. Barber, S. Hyde, D. Parsons, E. Marvin, A. Elhardt, J. Davis and S. Cherry and K. Knight.

To GRIF, an incredible congregation for providing an oasis to hundreds of refugees and immigrants living in their West Michigan community.

To all the unnamed mentors who have sown wisdom into me and anonymously shaped this book.

The views in this book are mine own and do not necessarily reflect any of those mentioned.

PREFACE
Salaam!

Two growing convictions demanded the writing of this book. The first combines courtesy with common sense. Given the dynamics of a shrinking world where once-distant peoples now share neighborhoods, sit adjacently in classrooms and co-mingle on the job, **the time has come for Christians and Muslims to stop talking *about* each other and to start talking *to* each other and *with* each other.**

My wife and I moved into an Arab neighborhood that is home to many Muslims. We're amazed by how much we learn while sitting on front porches or around kitchen tables with delicious cuisine, hot tea and hospitable people! But here's the problem. For far too long we have allowed third parties to define each of us to the other. Their portrayals often leave Muslims and Christians mutually diminished and one-dimensional, making it far too easy to stay in our silos. Friendships are often sabotaged before they have a chance to start. Where's the basic human courtesy in this social form of identity theft?

> The time has come for Christians and Muslims to stop talking *about* each other and to start talking *to* each other and *with* each other."

And common sense? If I want to learn what Islam teaches, why ask another Christian, or a Hindu or Buddhist? Isn't it more reasonable to expect devout Muslims to offer more reliable answers than outsiders? And would that not apply if the shoe was on the other foot? So, it's time we talk to each other, engaging in respectful, safe and frank ongoing conversations.

But talk about what? Our conversations must land on subjects beyond sports, weather, fashion and the latest movies. Their value will be measured by our willingness to take a deep breath and delve into matters that *really* matter. Like the reality of God, the meaning of faith, the purpose of living, the basis for hope and the practice of love. Why? Because we're human!

Taking Personal Responsibility to Know Scripture

Let's move to the second conviction, this one about *exploring truth.* Given the *ultra*-serious messages contained in the Bible and the Qur'an – claims enormously relevant for our personal and societal welfare– **it is time for Muslims and Christians to stop relying on what others say about the Books we cherish and start reading them for ourselves.**

The Injeel and the Qur'an point to a Day when every person from Adam to the present – imagine! – will exit the grave with body, mind and spirit fully reintegrated to face our Maker to whom we must give an account. In light of this unnerving expectation, one question looms before us. On that day, will we feel relief or regret that, instead of informing ourselves of Scripture, we allowed fallible men to tell us what God had spoken plainly through His chosen human Messengers? This question does not deny the value of teachers and imams. But it recognizes that on ultimate matters, they serve as guides and not substitutes for God's truth. Here's a searching question for all of us: On eternal matters should I simply expect others to read these books for me and then tell me what they say? Dare we rely on group-think or "believe what *we* tell you?" Isn't it time to read these books for ourselves?

I love the way an imam living in my city, a valued friend, often answers my questions about Islam. "Read the Qur'an. Go to the Hadith for interpretation." His advice has served me well.

Does this matter? It matters because the biblical Scriptures and the Qur'an, while separated in time by many centuries, nevertheless make bold claims on common themes. They include divine creation, the nature of God, the basis of authority, the absolute certainty of final Judgment, the identity of Isa al-Masih and the way of eternal salvation. These are hardly side issues! Thankfully, Muslims and Christians will find much to agree on within each of these categories. However, we also find contradictions within them demanding a closer look. What do we do with these?

We could pretend they're not there by politely glossing over them. While well-meaning, that course of action seems irresponsible and dishonest, even bordering on malpractice. If that sounds severe, let's hear the wisdom of the Bedouin: "The biggest sin in the desert is knowing where the water is and not sharing it."[1] For example, when

> "The biggest sin in the desert is knowing where the water is and not sharing it."
> Bedouin proverb

Muslims learn in the Qur'an that belief in a triune God seals one's doom to a fiery fate, will they kindly warn their Christian neighbors of the irreversible peril awaiting them? Likewise, when Christians learn from their Bibles that there is no other Name than Messiah Jesus given under heaven by which people may be saved, will they care enough to offer *that* Savior to their Muslim acquaintances?

Here's the million-dollar question: How will Christians and Muslims steward the messages of their respective Scriptures? Will we, as spiritual co-Bedouins passing through this scorching desert towards eternal delight or irreversible woe, keep the waterholes to ourselves or will we care enough to steer our neighbors to them so they too may live?

As Muslims and Christians, why not venture out and read what the other cherished Book has to say as well as our own? I discovered that after reading a Qur'an, I understood my Muslim neighbor much more deeply than before. So Christians, read a Qur'an for yourself. Muslims, I invite you to follow suit and purchase a Bible.[2]

How I Got Your Questions

You may be curious where I go your questions. I simply asked and you kindly obliged. A doctoral project took me to the Friday Jummah prayer services at four local mosques where I was given prior permission to address the ummah. Distributing pens and paper to all present, I asked a simple question:

"If you could sit down with a devout Christian and ask any question about our beliefs or practices, what would you ask? Don't worry about offending anyone. Just be honest. Take as much time as you need. I'll wait here until you're finished and then answer your questions in a book."

Thanks to their cooperation, I received 132 questions. This book is the fruit of that project.

What I Learned at the Mosques

This project taught me how deeply Muslims ca*re about truth – especially, the big que*stions. Nearly half landed on God (including the Trinity and the nature of Jesus) and Scripture as the Table of Contents proportionately reflects. Close behind were your questions about *salvation* and *life practices* that will require a second book. Please be looking for the sequel!

The Christian community is indebted to you, for your questions open a window into Islamic perspectives and values, many of which we share. All four participating mosques welcomed me warmly while engaging me with candor.

Please receive *Questions Muslims Ask Christians—Conversations about God and Scripture* as a labor of love to Muslims living in my city and beyond, personal friends and total strangers. Your questions deserve better minds than my own. Its shortcomings invite your merciful eye. This will be a conversation in progress. Most importantly, may God most Compassionate and Glorious be magnified as we engage in this conversation.

How to Use this Book

Questions Muslims Ask Christians is organized around topics of interest exactly as they were submitted by Muslim participants. Each chapter presents a question-set beginning with a **Main Question** that is followed by **related questions** addressed later in the chapter. Each is assigned a number with a decimal to easily identify the main topic and the related question. For example, in Q2.4, the "2" identifies the chapter, "Son of God," and "4" the specific question: "What is the definition of the Son? Who is called father?"

Keys to Fruitful Conversation

Before we begin, let me introduce three principles to enrich our journey:

> When we agree, let's celebrate.
> When we disagree, let's investigate.
> In everything, let's appreciate.

Most importantly, let's agree up front that our friendship will not be contingent upon our agreement. Fair enough? My Muslim friends at Wayne State University have shown me how people can hold opposite views and remain friends.

More questions will likely arise. The Contact Information page at the end of the book will serve that purpose. Let's keep the conversation going.

For now, let's pour a fresh cup of tea, pull up a chair and begin the conversation – talking *to*, not *about* each other!

TABLE OF CONTENTS

Chapter|*Lead Question*

BOOKS OF THE BIBLE

OLD TESTAMENT 39 books		NEW TESTAMENT (Injeel) 27 books	
Section	BOOKS	Section	BOOKS
Torah of Moses (Tawrat)	Genesis	The Gospel of Jesus the Messiah	Matthew
	Exodus		Mark
	Leviticus		Luke
	Numbers		John
	Deuteronomy	The Spreading Gospel (1st 30 years)	Acts
Prophetic History (Nebi'im)	Joshua	The Gospel Applied Instructions to Congregations & Pastors	Romans
	Judges & Ruth		1 & 2 Corinthians
	1 & 2 Samuel		Galatians
	1 & 2 Kings		Ephesians
	1 & 2 Chronicles		Philippians
	Ezra		Colossians
	Nehemiah		1 & 2 Thessalonians
	Esther		1 & 2 Timothy
Writings (Ketuvim) Psalms of David (Zabur)	Job		Titus
	Psalms		Philemon
	Proverbs		Hebrews
	Ecclesiastes		James
	Song of Songs		1 & 2 Peter
Latter Prophets (Nebi'im)	Isaiah		1, 2, & 3 John
	Jeremiah		Jude
	Lamentations	The Gospel's Final Triumph	Revelation
	Ezekiel		
	Daniel		
	Hosea		
	J. P.l		
	Amos		
	Obadiah		
	Jonah		
	Micah		
	Nahum		
	Habakkuk		
	Zephaniah		
	Haggai		
	Zechariah		
	Malachi		

SURAT OF THE QUR'AN

1 Al-Fatihah, *The Opening*

2 Al-Baqarah, *The Cow*

3 Al- Imran, *The House of Imran*

4 Al-Nisa, *Women*

5 Al-Maidah, *The Table Spread*

6 Al-Anaam, *The Cattle*

7 Al-Aaraf, *The Heights*

8 Al-Anfal, *The Spoils*

9 Al Tawbah or Al-Baraah, *Repentance*

10 Yunus, *Jonah*

11 Hud, *Hud*

12 Yusuf, *Joseph*

13 Al-Raad, *The Thunder*

14 Ibrahim, *Abraham*

15 Al-Hijr, *Hijr*

16 Al-Nahl, *The Bee*

17 Al-Isra or Bani Israil, *The Night Journey*

18 Al-Kahf, *The Cave*

19 Mariam, *Mary*

20 Taha, *Ta Ha*

21 Al-Anbiya, *The Prophets*

22 Al-Hajj, *The Pilgrimage*

23 Al-Muminum, *The Believers*

24 Al-Nur, *Light*

25 Al-Furqan, *The Criterion*

26 Al-Shuara, *The Poets*

27 Al-Naml, *The Ants*

28 Al-Qasas, *The Story*

29 Al-Ankabut, *The Spider*

30 Al-Rum, *The Byzantines*

31 Luqman, *Luqman*

32 Al-Sajdah, *Prostration*

33 Al-Ahzab, *The Parties*

34 Saba, *Sheba*

35 Al-Fatir or Al-Malaika, *The Originator*

36 Yasin, *Ya Sin*

37 Al-Saffat, *Those Ranged in Ranks*

38 Sad, *Sad*

39 Al-Zumar, *The Throngs*

40 Al-Mumin or Al-Ghafir, *The Forgiver*

41 Ha Mim or Fussilat or Ha Mim Sajda, *Expounded*

42 Al-Shawra, *Counsel*

43 Al-Zkukhruf, *Gold Ornaments*

44 Al-Dukhan, *Smoke*

45 Al Jathiyah, *Upon Their Knees*

46 Al-Ahqaf, *The Sand Dunes*

47 Muhammad, *Muhammad*

48 Al-Fath, *Victory*

English titles from Seyyed Hossein Nasr (ed.), *The Study Quran* (2015)

ABBREVIATIONS FOR BOOKS
OF THE BIBLE

Alphabetical Order

OLD TESTAMENT

Abbreviation	Book	Abbreviation	Book
Amos	Amos	Judg.	Judges
1 Chron.	1 Chronicles	1 Ki.	1 Kings
2 Chron.	2 Chronicles	2 Ki.	2 Kings
Dan.	Daniel	Lam.	Lamentations
Deut.	Deuteronomy	Lev.	Leviticus
Eccles.	Ecclesiastes	Mal.	Malachi
Esth.	Esther	Mic.	Micah
Exo.	Exodus	Nah.	Nahum
Eze.	Ezekiel	Neh.	Nehemiah
Ezra	Ezra	Num.	Numbers
Gen.	Genesis	Obad.	Obadiah
Hab.	Habakkuk	Prov.	Proverbs
Hag.	Haggai	Psa.	Psalms
Hos.	Hosea	Ruth	Ruth
Isa.	Isaiah	1 Sam.	1 Samuel
Jer.	Jeremiah	2 Sam.	2 Samuel
Job	Job	Song of Sol.	Song of Solomon
Jon.	Jonah	Zech.	Zechariah
Josh.	Joshua	Zeph.	Zephaniah

NEW TESTAMENT (Injeel)

Abbreviation	Book	Abbreviation	Book
Acts	Acts	Luke	Luke
Col.	Colossians	Mark	Mark
1 Cor.	1 Corinthians	Matt.	Matthew
2 Cor.	2 Corinthians	1 Pet.	1 Peter
Eph.	Ephesians	2 Pet.	2 Peter
Gal.	Galatians	Philem.	Philemon
Heb.	Hebrews	Phil.	Philippians
Jas.	James	Rev.	Revelation
John	John	1 Thess.	1 Thessalonians
1 John	1 John	2 Thess.	2 Thessalonians
2 John	2 John	1 Tim.	1 Timothy
3 John	3 John	2 Tim.	2 Timothy
Jude	Jude	Tit.	Titus

ABBREVIATIONS

Cf.	Compare
NASB	New American Standard Bible
NET	New English Translation Bible
NIV	New International Version Bible
(p)	Peace be upon him
S.	Surah
v./vvs.	verse/verses
ASB	*Apologetics Study Bible*
Fn	Footnote
CBSB	*Cultural Background Study Bible*
RQ	Reference Quar'an
AH	*Anno Hegirae*, "Year of the Hijrah"
AD	*Anno Domini*, "Year of our Lord"

BIBLICAL NAMES IN THE QUR'AN

Biblical names in the Qur'an are listed in approximate chronological order as they appear in the Bible and the number of times they are cited (#). Arabic spellings may vary. Individuals may be referred to many more times than their names are cited.

Qur'anic Name		Biblical Name
Adam (25)	=	Adam
Iblis (11)/Shaytan (64)	=	The Devil/Satan
Qabil	=	Cain
Habil	=	Abel
Idris (2)	=	Enoch, father of Methuselah
Salih (9)	=	Methuselah, grandfather of Noah
Nuh (43)	=	Noah
Nuh's sons	=	Shem, Ham & Japheth
Ayub (4)	=	Job
Azar	=	Terah, father of Abraham
Ibrahim (69)	=	Abraham
Hagar	=	Hagar
Ismail (12)	=	Ishmael, oldest son of Abraham
Lut (27)	=	Lot, nephew of Abraham
Ishaq (17)	=	Isaac, second son of Abraham
Yaqub (16)	=	Jacob, son of Isaac
Yusuf (27)	=	Joseph, son of Jacob
Fir'aun	=	Pharaoh
Al-Aziz	=	Potiphar
Musa (136)	=	Moses
Shuaib (11)	=	Jethro, Moses' father-in-law
Harun (20)	=	Aaron, brother of Moses
Miriam?	=	Miriam, sister of Moses
Hud	=	Heber
Gideon	=	Gideon
Smameel	=	Samuel

Jahut (3)	=	Goliath, giant that David killed
Talut (2)	=	Saul, Israel's first king
Daud, Dawud (16)	=	David, Israel's second king
Sulayman (17)	=	Solomon, David's son and Israel's third king
Ilyas (2)	=	Elijah, prophet
(Elisaie) Alyasa (2)	=	Elisha, prophet
Mikaeel	=	Michael (angel)
Dhu Al-Nun/Sahib al-hut/Yunus (4)	=	Jonah, prophet swallowed by the great fish
Shia	=	Isaiah, prophet
Aramayah	=	Jeremiah, prophet/priest
Hizqeel/Dhul-kifl (2)	=	Ezekiel, prophet/priest
Uzair	=	Ezra, priest/scribe
Haman	=	Hamaan
Zakariyya (7)	=	Zachariah, John the Baptist's father; priest
Elizabeth	=	Elizabeth, Zachariah's wife
Yahya (5)	=	John the Baptizer, Messiah's forerunner
Miriam (34)	=	Mary, mother of Jesus
Jibrael	=	Gabriel, an angel sent from God
Isa (25)	=	Jesus
Al-Masih (11)	=	The Messiah (title, not a name)
(the white-garbed) Al-Hawariyyun	=	Jesus' apostles
Al-Nasara (Derived from Nazareth, Jesus' hometown or from "ansar" [helpers/servants, Al-Saff 61:14; 3:52]), RQ, 740)	=	Christian

PART 1
QUESTIONS ABOUT GOD

CHAPTER 1

MONOTHEISM

Question 1: "Do you think there is only one God?"

Q 1.1: "Why don't Christians believe in one God?"
Q 1.2: "In Islam God is one and only one. In the Orthodox Christian belief, there are three gods: God, Isa and the Spirit. This is the basic difference between the Christian and the Islam religion. How do we reconcile this?"

I t is no accident that this question appears first, given its paramount importance . What is of greater consequence in the major issues of life than entertaining right thoughts of God? They shape the choices that form our character.

> "It is impossible to keep our moral practices sound and our inward attitudes right while our idea of God is erroneous or inadequate. If we would bring back spiritual power to our lives, we must begin to think of God more nearly as He is."[1]

That right conception must begin with the right number.

Another factor pushes this question to the front. There seems to be widespread Muslim suspicion, as Q1.1 and Q1.2 suggest, that Christianity teaches some form of "tritheism," a belief in three gods.

It becomes incumbent, then, for Christians to correct that perception. So, let's begin.

EVIDENCE FOR DIVINE ONENESS

Is there one God or three? Does the Bible, from start to finish, present God as one? To find out, we will examine key passages in both of its major divisions known by Christians as the Old and New Testaments. Chapter 6 will address God's triune nature which is different from tritheism. Our aim here simply responds to your primary question with resounding clarity: *There is one God; no more and no less!*

Does the evidence of Scripture back this up beyond doubt? My goal is to lay it out before you so that you, my readers, can decide. I will endeavor to demonstrate how the Bible in its totality meets the benchmarks that one might expect of a full-orbed monotheism. To that end, let me propose an expectation-framework using three "C's:"

(1) ***Creed*** – **Is belief in one God clearly declared in a creed?**
(2) ***Conviction*** – **Is belief in one God embraced as a deeply ingrained conviction? If so, why, given the widespread polytheistic practices of Israel's surrounding nations?**
(3) ***Consistency*** – **Do the Old and New Testaments remain monotheistic through and through?**

If the answer is "yes" to these questions, it should go a long way in alleviating concerns Muslims may have about Christianity's commitment to monotheism.

Key Definitions

Throughout this chapter, you will run across these terms. Below are their brief definitions:

Monotheism: Belief in the existence of only one God who created everything ("mono" = one)
Polytheism: Belief in the existence of many gods ("poly" = many)

2

Henotheism: Worship of only one god without denying the existence of others (The sense: "I have only one father, but recognize other fathers as equally valid as mine.").

Starting with the Old Testament, I will draw out relevant passages and allow them to speak for themselves with minimal comment. From there, we will proceed similarly to the New Testament.

There is one God; no more and no less! Let's go now to the biblical testimony for verification.

C-1: CREED
*Is belief in one God stated emphatically
in the form of a creed?*

Muslim readers may be curious to discover if Christian Scriptures declare a commitment to monotheism like the Islamic Shahada did centuries later. If the biblical God is truly one, we would expect to find a categorical declaration expressed in crisp creedal form.

Part 1: Old Testament

Indeed, the biblical testimony meets this expectation with resounding clarity.

1. The Shema – Deuteronomy 6:4-5

God's oneness is categorically confessed through "the Shema," the Old Testament's irreducible creed expressed through two tightly worded statements:

"*Hear, O Israel: The LORD our God, the LORD is one.* Love the LORD your God with all your heart and with all your soul and with all your strength." (Deuteronomy 6:4-5)

"Hear, O Israel: The LORD our God, the LORD is one."
Deuteronomy 6:4-5

This magnificent creed fuses undivided Deity with wholehearted devotion.

3

Its first statement. This Creed is called "the Shema," drawn from its first Hebrew word, the command to "Listen!" It climaxes with its last word "one" (*echad*[2]), that declares a theological fact. The first half contains only four Hebrew words that translate into English like this:

"The LORD (Yahweh) | Our God | The LORD (Yahweh) | One!"
(Deuteronomy 6:4)

English Bibles translate the Hebrew personal divine name "Yahweh" in the uppercase as "the LORD." This is the ever-living "I AM" who was revealed to Moses at the burning bush (Exodus 3:13-15). That spelling distinguishes his name from his title, "Adonai," rendered "the Lord."

Muslims may see a striking resemblance with the first half of the Shahada. Like that creed,

> "The Shema is profoundly important for understanding God. . . 'We must regard it as the fullest and most significant of all the theological turning-points in the concept of deity which the Old Testament brings to our attention.'[3]

This creed declares the God of the universe to be an absolute unity. Biblical scholar Brian Edgar unpacks five of its rich overlapping meanings:

> "*God is the only Lord* – The greatest danger that the children of Israel faced was of being seduced by material things which could make them forget that the LORD is our God, the Lord alone. The primary meaning, then, is that Yahweh is the only one to be worshipped, followed, obeyed, and loved. . .Materialism tempts us to worship the creation rather than the Creator.
>
> *God is the universal ruler* – Yahweh is the only Lord for the children of Israel because he is, in fact, the only Lord; he is the universal ruler who should be worshipped by everyone. Only Israel was called into covenant relationship with God but eventually, as Zechariah prophesied, 'The LORD will be king over the whole earth. On that

day there will be one LORD [the same phrase as in the Shema], and his name the only name' (Zech. 14:9; emphasis added).

Yahweh is the unique God – Other gods are not actually gods at all and Yahweh is the unique God. The Ancient Near East was used to the idea of multiple gods with some being dominant, but the Shema challenged this when it asserted that Yahweh was the one, single, unique God and not merely one among many. Yahweh is not the head of a pantheon, like Baal of the Canaanites. . . Yahweh is not merely the best God but is the one and only God. Other gods only 'exist' as projections or fantasies.

God is undivided holiness – In Hebrew there are two words for 'one'. The word used in the Shema refers primarily to the kind of organic unity which implies an undivided inner nature. Yahweh can only be trusted to keep his word and be utterly faithful to his people if he is completely undivided in nature and if his character does not contain ambiguities, conflicts or uncertainties. Someone who is consistent in character will, for instance, behave with the same propriety and honesty when unobserved as when under scrutiny. Such an individual is a person of integrity, whole, sound and complete, just as an integer is a whole (rather than a fractional) number. God is perfectly and completely whole and undivided. This is the basis for God's holiness. . .A divided god will be morally unpredictable. Yahweh is constant.

God is the unity of the cosmos – Everything is held together by his power. He is the sustainer of the universe, the 'ground of being', the 'go-between God' who links all things, the glue of the universe, the unity of the world."[4]

Only such a God, sole Creator and universal Ruler, the one-and-only, completely whole and who holds all things together is worthy of our worship, can order human life and win over our hearts:

> "*Acknowledge and take to heart* this day that the LORD is God in heaven above and on the earth below. *There is no other.*" (Deuteronomy 4:39)

5

Its second statement. The Creed did not stop with professing the LORD as the only God, but commands the people to "love" him with their whole selves. This second part required more than the nation's commitment to a monotheistic ideal.

> "It is important that both parts of the Shema are taken together rather than separately, because only then can it be seen to emphasize both the *transcendent sovereignty of God and his loving personal nature.* It is this which makes God different from all other gods and creatures. One cannot overestimate the importance of the concept of love for understanding the Old Testament doctrine of God."[6]

This calls us to an integrated life with God as its integrating center. Loving God fully is "holistic and will engage us at every level, shaping our intellectual, moral and social lives. At its core is an exclusive commitment to a covenant relationship".[7] This call to love is heard repeatedly through the book of Deuteronomy (Deut. 6:12-15; 7:8-10; 8:11; 9:1; 10-12-13; 13:2-5; 18:9; 26:16-17).

2. The Creed's Pervasive Impact – "No God like You!" 1 Kings 8:22, 27-28; Jer. 23:23-24; Psalm 139:7-10

The Shema is the Bible's most axiomatic premise and cardinal doctrine upon which all else hinges. As its most rudimentary reality, it informs and pervades all of Scripture. For example, when the Temple was dedicated, we see God's oneness tied to his immensity in King Solomon's prayer:

> "But will God indeed dwell on the earth? Behold, *heaven and the highest heaven cannot contain You,* how much less this house which I have built! *O LORD, the God of Israel, there is no God like You* in heaven above or on earth beneath, keeping covenant and showing lovingkindness to Your servants who walk before You with all their heart...." (1 Kings 8:22, 27-30, emphasis added)[8]

And since God cannot be hemmed in, there is no room for another, as noted by John of Damascus:

> "...if there are several gods, how can one support the fact of God's being

uncircumscribed? For where there is one there cannot be another."⁹

This divine immensity not only rules out other deities. It serves to warn the sinner and comfort the believer:

> "*Am I only a God nearby,*" declares the LORD, "*and not a God far away? Who can hide in secret places so that I cannot see them?*" declares the LORD. "**Do not I fill heaven and earth?**" (Jeremiah 23:23-24)

> "*Where can I go from your Spirit Where can I flee from your presence?* If I go up to the heavens, you are there; if I make my bed in the depths, you are there. If I rise on the wings of the dawn, if I settle on the far side of the sea, even there your hand will guide me, your right hand will hold me fast." (Psalm 139:7-10)

Part 2: New Testament

As we enter the New Testament, should we brace ourselves for a departure from wholehearted commitment to the Shema? Did Jesus and the Apostles also confess monotheism unquestionably?

1. Jesus ranked the Shema as the greatest commandment (Mark 12:28-31)

Simple questions can open doors to profound truths. Such was the case when a scribe, a highly trained authority in matters of Jewish law, asked Jesus: *What is the greatest commandment?* Prior to this, the scribes had dogged Jesus, taunting him at almost every turn. Their animosity towards him boiled over at times, especially when Jesus would break one of the more than 600 legal codes. Their list of grievances was long: "Jesus, you're healing people on the Sabbath" (Mark 12:35-40), "you're eating with sinners" (Lk 5:30; 15:2), "your disciples didn't wash their hands" (Mark 15:1; 7:5), "you're claiming to have God's authority to forgive sins" (Mark 2:6) and many more!¹⁰

Yet scribes, like mullahs in Islamic societies, enjoyed great esteem from their peers. Here was one of these religious leaders, a great teacher, publicly asking Jesus a question: "What commandment is the foremost of all?" People would have been riveted, waiting to hear how Jesus would respond. He answered:

> "The foremost is, 'Hear, O Israel! *The Lord our God is one Lord;* and you shall love the Lord your God with all your heart, and with all your soul, and with all your mind, and with all your strength.' The second is this, '*You shall love your neighbor as yourself.*' There is no other commandment greater than these." (Mark 12:28-31)

And here is the stunning conclusion. The very leader who challenged Jesus was forced to concede, "You are right." The shock and awe at that very moment must have raised the question: Who was the man who could answer so brilliantly?[11]

With monotheistic clarity, Jesus turned the tide of opinion, at least with that scribe: "You are right, Teacher! You have correctly said that He is One, and there is no one else except Him. . ." (Mark 12:33 HCSB). If Jesus's monotheistic priority was convincing enough to win over a skeptical scribe, it can put to rest any second guessing we may have about it.

Next, we turn to the apostles who Jesus hand-picked to carry on his work. Will they continue his monotheistic message?

2. The Apostles Upheld the Shema in a Polytheistic-Drenched Society – 1 Corinthians 8:4-6

The apostles adamantly taught that the presence of many religions did not mean the existence of many Gods. The truth of the Shema, "No God but one," clearly resounded over the polytheistic cacophony of the Roman Empire in the first century:

> "Therefore concerning the eating of things sacrificed to idols, we know that there is no such thing as an idol in the world, and that *there is no God but one.* For even if there are so-called gods whether in heaven or on earth, as indeed there are many gods and many lords, yet for us there is but one God, the Father, from whom are all things and we exist for Him; and one Lord, Jesus Christ, by whom are all things, and we exist through Him." (1 Corinthians 8:4-6, emphasis mine)

The teaching of the apostles ensured that Christian house churches throughout the pluralistic Roman Empire became vibrant centers of monotheistic worship.

> The truth of the Shema, "No God but one," clearly resounded over the polytheistic cacophony of the Roman Empire in the first century.

3. Doxologies Celebrated One True God – 1 Timothy 1:17; Jude 24-25; 1 Timothy 6:13-16

The earliest Christian doxologies wrapped monotheistic truth in garments of praise, extoling God for his majestic glory in creation and redemption:

> "Now to the King eternal, immortal, invisible, *the only God,* be honor and glory forever and ever. Amen." (1 Timothy 1:17)

> "Now to Him who is able to keep you from stumbling, and to make you stand in the presence of His glory blameless with great joy, to *the only God our Savior, through Jesus Christ our Lord*, be glory, majesty, dominion and authority, before all time and now and forever. Amen." (Jude 24-25)

> "He who is the blessed and *only Sovereign, the King of kings and Lord of lords,* who alone possesses immortality and dwells in unapproachable light, whom no man has seen or can see. *To Him [not them] be honor and eternal dominion!* Amen." (1 Timothy 6:13-16)

Summary

Do the Scriptures pass the first monotheistic test by professing it in creedal form? The Shema, confessed in the Old Testament and reiterated in the New, easily satisfies this expectation. Israel, Jesus and the apostles unanimously and indisputably professed their belief in one God.

Let's move to C-2, conviction. How deeply was this creed believed and what made it so?

C-2: CONVICTION

Was belief in one God embraced as a deeply ingrained conviction? If so, why, given the thoroughly polytheistic practices of Israel's surrounding nations?

"Now to the King eternal, immortal, invisible, the only God, be honor and glory forever and ever. Amen."
Injeel, 1 Timothy 1:17

If the biblical God is truly one, we would expect its adherents to not only pay it lip service but tenaciously embrace it in a world awash in polytheism. Here the keyword is *stalwart*. We will look for signs of monotheistic certainty that resists idolatry's alluring traps and challenges its premises.

Part 1: Old Testament

Three evidences point to the Bible's fervent monotheism: its unmatched belief arose from an extraordinary basis that produced courageous public witness.

A. Was the Shema Creed Unique?

In the ancient world of the Bible, monotheism was anything but a foregone conclusion. The gods were geographically "bound to their territory or land."[12] Yahweh was the exception to the norm (Deuteronomy 4:32-35). No other ancient nation embraced a sustained monotheism.

> "In Old Testament times Near Eastern religions believed that gods had limited spheres of activity (2 Kings 5:17), so that the uniqueness of God was an unheard-of claim."[13]

To illustrate, the chart below pairs ancient nations with the specific deities that were thought to preside over them.

THE POLYTHEIST WORLD OF THE BIBLE		
Do not follow other gods, the gods of the peoples around you. . . (Dt 6:14)		
LOCATION Modern Locations	**REGIONAL GODS**	**BIBLICAL REFERENCES**
EGYPT	**Amon** – chief god	Jer 46:25
TYRE Lebanon	**Melqart**	
SIDON Lebanon	**Eshmun, Astarte, Reshmun, Rehaim**	
CANAAN N Israel & S Lebanon	**El** – chief god, father of the pantheon; viewed as distant. Consort with **Asherah**, goddess of fertility **Baal** – "In touch" with people; control over nature.Ruled over other gods such as **El, Yam** (Sea), **Nahar** (River), **Mot** (Death) and **Anat** (Baal's sister).	Exo 34:13-14;Deut 7:5; Jud6:25-30; 1 Ki 14:15,23; 15:13; 16:33;18:19; Isa 27:9; Jer17:2; Mic 5:14 Prophet Elijah challenged 400 prophets of Asherah (2 Ki23:4-7, 13-16).
ARAM/ SYRIA GREECE ROME	**Ashtoreth** (**Aphrodite**) – goddess of war/fertility of Greece; consort of **Baal**, associated with "**the Evening Star**," worshiped under multiple aliases; **Venus** –most prominent goddess in Mesopotamia; goddess of loveand war (Rome); **Zeus, Hermes**	Jud 2:12-13; 10:6;1 Sam 7:3-4; 12:10;31:10; 1 Ki 11:5, 33;Acts 14:11-13
ASSYRIA Iraq	*Kings incorporated names of deities* **Assur** & **Ninurta** (King Ashurbanipal); **Shulman** (King Shalmaneser); **Shamash**, sun god; **Sin**, moon god (King Sennacherib); **Adad**, "god of storm" (also worshiped in Syria)	Deut 4:19; 2 Ki 23:5, 29; Ezra 4:2
PHOENICA Lebanon	**Baal** – "lord," god of fertility/ rain. Pictured standing on a bull, a symbol of fertility/ strength **Asherah/Ashoreth**, goddesses of fertility	Jud 2:10-13

THE POLYTHEIST WORLD OF THE BIBLE		
Do not follow other gods, the gods of the peoples around you. . . (Dt 6:14)		
LOCATION Modern Locations	REGIONAL GODS	BIBLICAL REFERENCES
PHILISTIA SW Palestine coastal area [sojourners from Egypt (?)]	**Baal-Zebub** (Greek, **Belzeebub**) = "Lord of the flies" **Dagon**	Jud 16:23-24; 1 Sam 5:2-7; 2 Ki 1:1-6, 16-17; 1 Chron 10:10 Matt 12:24 (Mark 3:22; Luke 11:15)
BABYLON Iraq	**Bel**— chief deity; also Sun-god **Marduk** – his son, **Anu**, god of heaven **Nebo** – god of learning and writing; **Enlil** – god of wind; **Ninhusag** – mother goddess; **Tammuz**, fertility god; **Dagon**	Isai 46:1; Jer 50:2; 51:44 Eze 8:14
AMMON Jordan	**Milkom** – chief god, plus nine others **Molech** – demanded child sacrifice	Lev 18:21; 20:2-5; 1 Ki 11:4-7; 33; 2 Ki 23:10-13; Isa 57:9; Jer 32:35, 49; Zeph 1:5; Acts 7:43
ALL MESOPOTAMIA	**Nature Worship** – Astral deities The Sun – **Amun-Re** (Egypt); **Utu/Shamash** (Assyria); **Shemosh** (Canaan) The Moon – **Nikkal/Ningal/ Nanua; Sin** (Mesopotamia); **Yerah** (Canaan) The Stars & Constellations – those associated with **Orion**: **Sirius**, the **Dog Star**[14]	Deut 4:19; 17:3; 16:22; 1 Ki 12:31; 2 Ki 23:5; Job 31:26; Isa 1:29, 13:10; Amos 5:8

THE POLYTHEIST WORLD OF THE BIBLE		
Do not follow other gods, the gods of the peoples around you. . . (Dt 6:14)		
LOCATION Modern Locations	**REGIONAL GODS**	**BIBLICAL REFERENCES**
PERSIA Iran	*Partial list* **Ahura Mazda** – supreme god, creator of the heavens and the Earth; son of **Zurvan Anahita** – goddess of fertility, water **Asman** – god of the Sky **Bahram** – god of planets **Hvar** –Sun god **Mah (Mao)** – god of the Moon **Mithra** – god of Light, contracts, friendship; maintains cosmic order **Vata** –god of the Wind **Zam** – deified Earth	
Pre-Islamic **ARABIA** & **ABATAEA**	**Al-Ilah** – Moon god with 3 daughters: **al-Lat**, **al-Uzza** and **Manat**	

This pervasive polytheism makes the Shema, "The LORD our God, the LORD is one," all the more notable. Let's stop to consider how exceptional it truly was.

What Other Nation?

What other nation at the time of Moses could have confessed a similar creed about its deity? Could the priests of ancient Babylon declare: "Hear, O Babylonians! Bel is God, Bel alone!"? Hardly! For they also worshiped Marduk, Nebo, Anu, Enlil, Ninhusag, Tammuz and Dagon! In fact, each of the city's nine gates was dedicated to a different god.

Or had they meant "Bel is one" in a henotheistic way, i.e., "there is only one Bel among other deities" would have been equally pointless.

Could the priests of ancient Babylon have said: "Hear, O Babylonians! Bel is God, Bel alone!"? Hardly! They also worshiped Marduk, Nebo, Anu, Enlil, Ninhusag, Tammuz and Dagon!

Did anyone believe in two Bels, or Marduks, or Nebos or any of the rest? As the chart illustrates, Babylon's adherence to multiple deities was the rule rather than the exception.

What other nation? None! Monotheist confession was unique to Israel. Just as today, India touts 32-million small-g gods, the biblical world was populated by scores of deities. Was Israel's insistence of one God arrogant amid such multiplicity? How can we explain this audacious creed of only one true God and his command for exclusive devotion?

B. Basis for Unique Monotheistic Conviction
Why did Israel Alone Believe in God Alone?

Question: How can we explain Israel's strident monotheism (one God over *all*) when all the other nations embraced henotheism (one god over *us*)?

Before answering, let's consider the stakes.

The Shema was more than unique. It was daring. Your question, Muslim reader, "Do you believe in one God?" is a good starting place, but in a world crowded with gods and goddesses, it cannot stand on its own. A "yes" answer requires only a commitment to a general concept, not a particular Deity. Yet we saw that the Shema is personal, identifying this singular Deity as *Yahweh* or the LORD.

The point is that in a pluralistic environment consisting of multiple deities, a whoppingly exclusive claim will not survive for very long on miniscule attestation.

Immediately, such a statement turns heads and raises eyebrows. Answering "Do you believe in one God?" will costs nothing. Adding the name, "That sole God is Yahweh" announces to the rest "You are not!"

In religiously diverse cultures, the profession that only one all-powerful God exists– not just for me, but period! – would have been viewed skeptically as an audacity. Without supporting props, mere confession would have had little chance of surviving the cynic's logic. Even the ancient Jews of Moses' day, if left to themselves, would have fared no better. And yet, they deposited all their faith into one basket, that of Yahweh. Not a single ounce went for Bel, Marduk, Molech, Isis or any other local deity. Why? There must be an answer.

HOW CREED BECAME CONVICTION

The reason why Israel's monotheist creed became her ringing conviction, so conspicuously set forth in the Tawrat, is this: Yahweh raised the bar.

This common idiom in American society, raising the bar, originated in the high jump event in the sports world of track and field. A crossbar is placed horizontally across two standards. Each athlete attempts to "clear" the bar without dislodging it. As long as two contenders successfully do so, the bar is raised to the next notch so that each jump becomes more challenging. This continues until the highest jumper is declared the winner. According to Guinness, in 1993 a Cuban named Javier Sotomayor set the High Jump world record at, believe it or not, over 8 feet! Since no one else has matched him, Javier "set the bar." So the "bar" represents the standard and "raise the bar" the crushing height to which none except one, the champion, ever attained.

This brings us to the basis for Israel's strident belief in the existence of one God whose name was Yahweh. What path led them to that conclusion? Was it through speculation or philosophy? Neither. Something happened, and it occurred early in her history, for they professed the Shema during the time of Moses which means the Israelites had not yet entered the Promised Land.

Israel alone believed in God alone because of her unique and extraordinary experiences by which God, through unprecedented acts, raised the bar to a standard demanding such a conclusion.

Expressed another way, God *revealed* his supremacy over small-g gods before *legislating* Israel's total devotion to him. His show of power and love preceded his demand for exclusive worship. We see this vital sequence at the giving of the Ten Commandments spoken by God himself:

> "I am the LORD your God, who brought you out of the land of Egypt, out of the house of slavery. You shall have no other gods before Me." (Exodus 20:1-3)

Why should Israel worship only the LORD and none other? Because he alone, by miraculously freeing them from the house of bondage, raised the bar beyond reach of any other. Pharaoh, considered god in human form, proved no match for the LORD. Egypt, the world's dominant empire with its armies and chariots, was forced to release its grip.

God distinguished himself, building his people's confidence, in two tangible ways: his visible actions and his audible voice.

a. VISIBLE ACTS – Convinced by what they Saw

Israel's monotheistic conviction sprang directly from her firsthand experience with God's unmatched power displayed on her behalf. What she witnessed formed an outlook that underpinned everything, even her moral behavior. God said through Moses:

> Why did Israel alone believe in God alone? Because Israel alone received divine revelation that raised the bar to a standard supporting that conclusion.

> "In the future, when your son asks you, "What is the meaning of the stipulations, decrees and laws the LORD our God has commanded

you?" tell him: "We were slaves of Pharaoh in Egypt, but the LORD brought us out of Egypt with a mighty hand. *Before our eyes the LORD sent signs and wonders*—great and terrible—on Egypt and Pharaoh and his whole household. But *he brought us out from there* to bring us in and give us the land he promised on oath to our ancestors." (Deuteronomy 6:20-25)

So this explains why Israel alone believe in God alone. They were convinced by what they saw – "signs and wonders" – and what they experienced – "he brought us out from there." Signs and wonders continued to accompany them through their forty-year wilderness journey and upon entry into the land God had promised to Abraham. These continued throughout her history yet were most prominent during Israel's infancy stage as God established her faith.

Signs and Wonders Glossary

Three vivid OT terms capture God's miraculous acts:

Sign [*ot*]: [An attention-getting event] An object or event that **makes people aware** of something (Exodus 7:3; Joshua 2:17; 2 Kings 20:8-9; Palm 105:27; Jeremiah 32:20)

Wonder, Marvel [*mopet*]: Highlights the *extraordinary* **nature** of God's acts for and on behalf of his people (Exodus 7:3; Psalm 78:43; Deut 6:22; 26:8).

Wonder, Miracle, Act of God [*pele*]: Designates a mighty act of God that is *inexplicable and indescribable according to human standards* (used more in poetry and hymns and functions to *emphasize the character of God* on a general level rather than through one particular event; Exodus 15:11; Psalm 77:11, 14; 78:12; 88:10; 89:5).[15]

God convinced Israel of his sole existence in a second prominent way.

b. AUDIBLE VOICE – Convinced by what they Heard – Exodus 20:1-5; 19:4-6; Deuteronomy 8:2-4

Let's return to the giving of the Ten Commandments. In what setting were they given? Was it in a private meeting with Moses secluded on a mountain side? Or a tent in which a dozen tribal leaders sat? Neither. By divine instructions, the *entire nation* – men, women and children numbering into the hundreds of thousands – stood at the foot of a mountain on which Yahweh would descend.[16] Then it came.

> "You came near and stood at the foot of the mountain while it blazed with fire to the very heavens, with black clouds and deep darkness. *Then the LORD spoke to you out of the fire. You heard the sound of words but saw no form; there was only a voice.* He declared to you his covenant, the Ten Commandments, which he commanded you to follow and then wrote them on two stone tablets." (Deuteronomy 4:11-13)

God's own voice broke the silence with hair-raising but crystal-clear articulation. All heard the speaking God declare:

> "I am the LORD your God, who brought you out of Egypt, out of the land of slavery. You shall have no other gods before me.
> You shall not make for yourself an image in the form of anything in heaven above or on the earth beneath or in the waters below. You shall not bow down to them or worship them.
> You shall not misuse the name of the LORD your God. Remember the Sabbath day by keeping it holy. Six days you shall labor and do your work, but the seventh day is a sabbath to the LORD your God. Honor your father and your mother, so that you may live long in the land the LORD your God is giving you.
> You shall not murder.
> You shall not commit adultery. You shall not steal.
> You shall not give false testimony against your neighbor.
> You shall not covet your neighbor's house. . .wife. . .or anything that belongs to your neighbor." (Exodus 20:2-17)

How did people respond to God's direct speech? They were terrified by it, feeling certain it would kill them:

"Speak to us yourself and we will listen. But do not have God speak to us or we will die." (Exodus 20:19)

Moses later reminded them that, contrary to their fear, they survived this audible miracle:

"When you heard the voice out of the darkness, while the mountain was ablaze with fire, all the leaders of your tribes and your elders came to me. And you said, "The Lord our God has shown us his glory and his majesty, and *we have heard his voice from the fire.* Today we have seen that a person can live even if *God speaks with them.*" (Deuteronomy 5:23-24)

Previously, God had spoken directly to Moses who then repeated his message with the people. But here, instead of speaking through a prophet or even an angel, he himself addressed everyone at once, perhaps as many as a million people. "Moses joins his peers as listener. God now speaks directly to His people" (Exodus 20:1).

". . .we are face to face with the apogee or the *summon bonum* of God's will for His followers in terms of lifestyles and moral commitment? Note the sequel to the commandments: 'I have talked with you from heaven,' not from Sinai (Exodus 20:22)."[17]

So why would God break with custom by using this extraordinary means of *direct* communication to the masses? Could he not have conveyed the very same Commandments in a less dramatic way through a middleman like Moses or a group of leaders. Why include everyone? I love God's answer. To crush all doubts that he alone is God:

"To you it was shown *that you might know that the LORD, He is God; there is no other besides Him.* Out of the heavens *He let you hear His voice to discipline you;* and on earth He let you see His great fire, and you heard His words from the midst of the fire."

"Inquire from one end of the heavens to the other. Has anything been done like this great thing, or has anything been heard like it? *Has any people heard the voice of God speaking from the midst of the fire, as you have heard it, and survived?* (Deuteronomy 4:32-33; 35-36)

This spectacular miracle of divine speech, performed out-in-the-open, raised the bar even higher and inscribed itself indelibly in their memory. It was personally persuasive, "that you might know" and would later be publicly compelling in her engagement with the nations, "inquire . . . has anything been done like this great thing?"

God was creating a nation of witnesses to his sole existence and power. He did so by raising the bar to such stratospheric heights that confirmed the Creed, "The LORD your God is one." The impact of this experience is beyond calculation. Previously, they had heard how God had spoken to Abraham and the patriarchs. Now they heard it firsthand: *God spoke!* That collective experience, too public to deny and too grand to forget, would be told and re-told from one generation to the next.

Could Other gods Speak?

This begs the question. Did not these ancient deities also speak? Of course, they did! Ancient temple records provide us with considerable details describing how idols were so endowed. But first, they had to be made:

> "The primary statues of deities that dominated the temples were usually carved of wood and covered with a thin layer of gold or silver and adorned with precious stones and elegant clothing. Priests in both Mesopotamia and Egypt daily attended to the statues – washing, clothing and feeding them as though they were living gods."[18]

What endowed these objects with the capacity for speech? Temple records provide the details. Below are two examples, the first from ancient Assyria:

> "The Assyrian king Esarhaddon – The ritual that brought the image to life was referred to as the "mouth washing," which possibly paralleled the work done by a midwife to clean the breathing passage

20

of a newborn. *It required the priest to whisper into the ear of the statue and to open its eyes to see and its mouth to breathe.* The ritual states, "This statue without its mouth opened cannot smell incense, cannot eat food, nor drink water." Then the priest swore an oath that he did not make the statue." [19]

Ancient Egyptians practiced a similar ritual called:

"'Opening the Mouth and the Eyes,' which operated with different actions and beliefs, but was *performed to quicken the manufactured image into a living representation of the deity.* Similar to the Mesopotamian ritual, the priests disavowed any hand in its manufacture."[20]

"A cat fashioned out of wood will not meow."
Pakistani proverb

A Pakistani proverb puts this practice into perspective: "A cat fashioned out of wood will not meow."[21] Scripture agrees:

"Woe to him who says to wood, 'Come to life!' Or to lifeless stone, 'Wake up!' Can it give guidance? It is covered with gold and silver; *there is no breath in it."* (Habakkuk 2:19-20)

The upshot seems clear: the God who speaks is the God who lives. All others are wooden cats.

David, a man after God's own heart, saw through their outward adornment:

"Their idols are silver and gold, made by human hands. *They have mouths, but cannot speak,* eyes, but cannot see. They have *ears, but cannot hear,* noses, but cannot smell. They have hands, but cannot feel, feet, but cannot walk, *nor can they utter a sound with their throats."* (Psalm 115:4-8)

Like wooden cats, wooden gods are virtual reality, facades without breath, nothing more. No amount of "priestcraft" or magical "abracadabras" can alter essential properties. Wood is wood, God is God.

Is it fair to say that God raised the bar of speech on the field of competing deities? What judge would assign an equal score to that momentous occurrence at Mt. Sinai with the daily routines transpiring in pagan temples throughout the ancient world? Particularly is this the case when contrasting the desired *impact* of inspiring confidence in the true living God. Should we equate the rousing certainty evoked by God's imposing voice heard simultaneously by numberless listeners – terrifying to the point of begging him to stop – with the strained ears of individual supplicants for the faintest whisper coming through a deity with painted lips from a tree stump and believed to be brought to life?

Is this contest a tie? Is a heavenly auditory breakthrough that was undergirded empirically in a collective setting on par with human rituals conjured up on behalf of private supplicants? The upshot seems clear: the God who speaks is the God who lives. All others are wooden cats.

My point is not to take cheap shots at ancient idolaters acting wishfully. It's rather to show what made Israel's monotheist conviction so exceptional. That reason is simple. They alone believed in God alone because on them alone was bestowed such doubt-defying, unduplicatable empirical revelation of his sole existence.

Who else?

These inexplicable sights and sounds forced a question. After seeing Yahweh's performance on the deity-crowded world stage, it became impossible to avoid: *Who else does anything even close to this?* Moses asked it:

> "Who among the gods is like you, LORD? *Who is like you*—majestic in holiness, awesome in glory, *working wonders*?" (Exodus 15:11)

David asked it:

> "*What god is like God?. . .* You are the God who *works wonders!*"
> (Psalm 77:14 HCSB)

> "*For who in the skies above can compare with the LORD? Who is like
> the LORD* among the heavenly beings? In the council of the holy
> ones God is feared; he is more awesome than all who surround him.
> *Who is like you, LORD God Almighty?* You, LORD, are *mighty*, and
> your faithfulness surrounds you." (Psalm 89:6-8)

The answer to *Who else?*, of course, is no one. Not a single deity "is like
the LORD" in majesty, holiness, awesomeness or might. But why was
it necessary to point out his supremacy? Does God need a gold medal?
Never! Muslims agree that the Maker of the universe has no ego needs.
Statements of his unsurpassed greatness are for our benefit, not God's.
They aren't given to feed his ego but to point our faith where it belongs
– in him alone.

Does this Conviction Matter?

It meant the world to David that God was not one among many
notoriously incompetent gilded objects. He prayed to the prayer answering
God who heard his cries:

> "In the day of my trouble I shall call upon You, for *You will answer me*.
> There is *no one like You* among the gods, O LORD, Nor are there any
> works like Yours." (Psalm 86:8-10, emphasis added)

It meant the world to Hannah, a childless wife who for years suffered
the scorn of barrenness. She turned to God with tears and faith,
vowing that if God blessed her with a son, she would give him to his
service. God answered her with the birth of Samuel, one of the great
early prophets. Feel her elated soul expressing praise to the Almighty,
not only for the fact of his singularity but for the kind of God he is:

> "My heart exults in the LORD; . . . I rejoice in Your salvation. There is

no one holy like the LORD, Indeed, there is no one besides You, nor is there any rock like our God." (1 Samuel 2:1-2)

Divine interventions catapulted monotheism from cherished creed easily recited to a rousing conviction firmly grasped.

C. Monotheist Conviction Spread to Pagan Nations

Perhaps nothing reveals deep certainty as much as when someone voices an unpopular belief where it will be adamantly challenged.

First, let's step back to raise what may be a problematic question that's nagging you: Does this uneven distribution of direct revelation – seeing God's acts and hearing his voice — that overwhelmingly tilted in Israel's favor suggest that God cared more for them and less for the nations of the world?

The long answer must wait for Volume 2. For now, it's this: *Never!* The book of Genesis dispels any doubt that the nations had been on God's radar from the beginning (Gen 10; 12:1-3, etc.). So why was Israel given a feast rich in revelation– the Ten Commandments, miracles, promises, holy Scriptures and the Messiah – while the nations of the world were left with the crumbs of stargazers and spiritualists?

The answer is not because of Israel's native superiority over other nations (Deuteronomy 7:7). It was, rather, her God-given mission on the world's behalf. Carrying it out required the bedrock conviction that *only* could come from such supernatural interventions.

That brings us to our point. Without certainty, how could she fulfill this calling?

> *"You are my witnesses," declares the LORD, "that I am God.* Yes, and from ancient days I am he." (Isaiah 43:11-13)

Blessing *all* nations (Genesis 12:1-3) required Israel to pass on to others what she had received as:

"witnesses to the existence of God, to his uniqueness, holiness, power, and love. When they failed to acknowledge his uniqueness and holiness and turned to polytheism, he sent them into captivity, as he had warned, for they had failed in their witness and had given opportunity for the enemies of God to blaspheme."[22]

David, a man after God's own heart, prayed passionately for this to be realized:

"Let them know that you, whose name is the LORD — that you alone are the Most High over all the earth." (Psalm 83:18)

"All nations whom You have made shall come and worship before You, O LORD, and they shall glorify Your name. For You are great and do wondrous deeds; You alone are God." (Psalm 86:8-10, emphasis added)

Desiring to be known by all the families of the world, God never overlooked those born outside of Abraham's descendants. He desires for all to know who he is:

"I am the LORD, and there is no other; Besides Me there is no God. *I will gird you, though you have not known Me*; that men may know from the rising to the setting of the sun that there is no one besides Me. I am the LORD, and there is no other." (Isaiah 45:5-6)

Obviously, the Creator of all people desires to be known and served universally. Isn't it reasonable that one *true* God would perform acts so extraordinary to make his reality evident? We've already seen how God achieved that through his miraculous sights and sound. It didn't stop with those. God kept raising the bar.

a. God Raised the Bar of Wisdom among Nations through his Laws

"See, I have taught you *decrees and laws* as the LORD my God commanded me, . . . *Observe them carefully, for this will show your wisdom and understanding to the nations,* who will hear about all these decrees and say, "Surely this great nation is a wise and understanding people. . . *And what other nation is so great as to have such righteous decrees and laws as this body of laws I am setting before you today?"* (Deuteronomy 4:5-6, 8; see 5:33; 6:2)

b. God Raised the Bar of Prophecy by Challenging False Deities to Predict Future Events

God alone sees the future with the same 20/20 vision as the past, a capacity that set a high bar for the surrounding mini-deities to clear. Prophets drove home how unique this connection was by way of direct challenge.

All the nations gather together and the peoples assemble. *Which of their gods foretold this and proclaimed to us the former things? Let them bring in their witnesses to prove they were right,* so that others may hear and say, "It is true." (Isaiah 43:9-10)

"Declare and set forth your case; Indeed, let them consult together. *Who has announced this from of old? Who has long since declared it? Is it not I, the LORD?* And there is no other God besides Me, A righteous God and a Savior; There is none except Me." (Isaiah 45:21)

"Thus says the LORD, . . . the Lord of hosts: 'I am the first and I am the last, And there is no God besides Me. 'Who is like Me? Let him proclaim and declare it; Yes, let him recount it to Me in order,

. . .*And let them declare to them the things that are coming and the events that are going to take place."* (Isaiah 44:6)

God conveys his sole divine authority precisely here. The living God, the Everlasting One, is without peer. Go to Chapter 7 for more on ways in which God's Word is proven. A list of fulfilled predictions to verify this claim can be found in Question 9.1.

Witnessing to the living God before polytheistic kings and neighbors required more than personal conviction. It took courage.

The Old Testament provides many examples such as Prophet Elijah confronting the prophets of Baal (1 Kings 18).

c. God Raised the Bar among Idolaters by Empowering Daring Testimony

Daniel 3 introduces us to three promising young men who show do-or-die conviction under unthinkable pressure. While Judah was exiled in Babylon, a pagan king set up an outlandish image of himself and issued this order:

> "'Nations and peoples of every language, this is what you are commanded to do: As soon as you hear the sound of the horn, flute, zither, lyre, harp, pipe and all kinds of music, you must fall down and worship the image of gold that King Nebuchadnezzar has set up. Whoever does not fall down and worship will immediately be thrown into a blazing furnace." (Daniel 3:4-7)

Three young Hebrews – Shadrack, Meschek, and Abednego – refused to participate in this national idolization. The king's astrologers saw them ignore the order and informed the king of their defiance. Enraged, the king summoned them and gave them one last chance. "There's no god who can rescue from my hand," he said. What happened next? Would they save their skin or show do-or-die conviction? They answered:

> "King Nebuchadnezzar, we do not need to defend ourselves before you in this matter. If we are thrown into the blazing furnace, the *God we serve is able to deliver us from it,* and he will deliver us from Your Majesty's hand. *But even if he does not, we want you to know, Your Majesty, that we will not serve your gods or worship the image of gold you have set up.*" (Daniel 3:16-18)

These men signed their own death sentences by choosing costly martyrdom over safe idolatry. The enraged king had them bound with thick ropes and hurled into a blazing furnace to be burned alive. When he peered into the incinerator, two things shocked him. First, none of them was harmed by the scorching flames. They walked around in the furnace as if strolling through a park. Impossible! Moreover, they were joined by a fourth man who the pagan monarch identified as "a son of the gods," an expression found in excavations (Ras Sharma, Syria) referring to a member of the court of the gods (likely the pre-incarnate Christ). The king extinguished the furnace, released the young men and issued a surprising decree:

> "'Blessed be the God of Shadrach, Meshach and Abednego, who has sent His angel and *delivered His servants who put their trust in Him*, violating the king's command, and yielded up their bodies so as not to serve or worship any god except their own God. . . . *there is no other god who is able to deliver in this way*." (Daniel 3:28-29)

The young men's courageous choice to not give-in under pressure was no irrational leap of faith. It was predicated on a certainty owing to the true God who revealed himself in history through his saving acts, clear speaking, righteous laws, wisdom for life and keeper of promises.

Summary

What was the cumulative effect of all these divine interventions? Monotheism set ablaze, ever-burning within the biblical soul. Nothing was more certain. It was the constant rudimentary reality. What the true God declared clearly, he demonstrated convincingly.

Part 2: New Testament Conviction

Will the Injeel continue in this deeply ingrained belief in one God and defend it in a world of alternatives?

Jesus – Hearing God through living for his approval alone (John 5:44)

Jesus exposed a deep monotheistic conviction while solving a huge mystery. Have you ever wondered why so often the smartest people in the room are the most tone-deaf to God's voice, blind to his actions and oblivious to his presence? Scripture is to them what milk is to the lactose intolerant. Why is this so? Jesus answers:

> "How can you believe, when you receive glory from one another and
> you do not seek the glory that is from the one God?" (John 5:44)

In other words, one's capacity to receive divine revelation, says Jesus, has nothing to do with IQ, ethnic background, religious training or social position.

The timing of this lesson is key, coming just moments after Jesus healed a cripple of 38 years. Society's most learned scholars were present. Seeing the before and after, they should have celebrated the man's new wholeness. Instead they went into a huff, scolding him who, for the first time in four decades, toted his bed instead of being stuck to it!

Jesus saw the root of their outrage which wasn't Sabbath day violation. It was the search for acceptance in the eyes of their peers. So how can smart people be so dumb about spiritual matters? Placing human approval above the applause of "the one and only God." It blunts the edge of reason, blinds spiritual perception, and creates predictable religious clones. Most tragic, from Jesus' day up until now, it blinds people to God's greatest revelation.

How about the apostles? Was monotheism just a doctrine of convenience to which they paid lip-service or their passionate conviction?

Apostles – You call yourself a 'monotheist?' Prove it! – James 2:19-20

Touting monotheism without a life of obedience mimics demons rather than saints.

> **"You believe that God is one. You do well; the demons also believe,
> and shudder.** But are you willing to recognize, you foolish fellow,
> that faith without works is useless?" (James 2:19-20)

Authentic monotheistic belief requires more than lip-service. The devil himself can profess God's oneness, but that does not make him a saint. He will never submit to anyone but himself. Monotheism's authenticating badge is submission to God expressing itself in humble readiness to follow him.

Overcoming Secret Idolatry – 1 John 5:21; 2:15-17

Even for believers, avoiding idolatry is an ongoing battle. The absence of shrines or statues of worship in our homes exempts no one from the hidden idols lurking from within the heart. Daily the alluring idolizations of sex, power and greed bombard us. A church Father, Augustine, hit the nail on the head with this definition:

> "Idolatry is worshiping anything that ought to be used, or using anything that is meant to be worshiped."[23]

How can anyone swim against that constant undertow that removes God from first place in our lives? The holy Injeel arms us with two effective countermeasures, one defensive and the other offensive. The first tactic calls for vigilance:

> "Little children, *guard yourselves from idols.*" (1 John 5:21)

> *Do not be idolaters*, as some of them were; as it is written, 'The people sat down to eat and drink, and stood up to play.' Therefore, my beloved, *flee from idolatry.*" (1 Corinthians 10:6-7, 14)

"Guarding" involves separating healthy pleasure from dark forces lurking beneath the guise of innocence. "Fleeing" means to distance ourselves, to stop flirting and get out! We must heed these defensive measures but they are not enough. Who wants to play constant defense? Life is more than avoidance! Playing offense is better because it taps the springs of our soul by a higher connection:

> "Do not love the world or anything in the world. If anyone loves the world, love for the Father is not in them. For everything in the

world—the lust of the flesh, the lust of the eyes, and the pride of life—comes not from the Father but from the world. The world and its desires pass away, but whoever does the will of God lives forever." (1 John 2:15-17)

This measure fights our fiery passion for forbidden things with the consuming fire ignited by the proximity of God's purifying presence. How so? By putting God first. Each day before booting up our computers and Smart Phones we can draw from his Word and find power to resist those inner idols.

In summary, biblical monotheism is more than a tidy creed. It is a conviction born of personal testimony of God's supernatural intervention resulting in gratitude that lies at the heart of worship.

The Apostles Courageously Speak Up – Acts 17:16-30

The apostles demonstrated deep monotheistic conviction by their responses to audiences who were hostile to it. Let's take one example. During NT times, Athens, Greece was the "Gods R Us" of the ancient world. It was a city "aesthetically magnificent and culturally sophisticated, but morally decadent and spiritually deceived or dead." When the Apostle Paul visited there, how did he respond to their rampant practices? Did he throw up his hands and sigh, *What's the use?* or brush it off with *Who cares?* The Injeel reports:

> "While Paul was waiting for them in Athens, he was *greatly distressed* [*paroxyno*] to see that the city was *full of idols* [lit., "under the sway of"]. So he reasoned in the synagogue with both Jews and God-fearing Greeks, as well as in the marketplace day by day with those who happened to be there. A group of Epicurean and Stoic philosophers began to debate with him. " (Acts 17:16-1)

Paul exploded with two emotions: grief and zeal.[25] Upon seeing this smothering blanket of idolatry over the city, he felt p*aroxyno*, a term used for God's reaction to idolatry[26], particularly on the part of Israel. It is often translated in English as "provoked the Lord God to anger" and described Israel as "an obstinate people . . . who continually

31

'provoke' me to my very face (Exodus 34:14). Scripture sometimes refers to this feeling as "jealousy." At first, that confuses us – *God jealous?* Kidding, right? Applied to God, jealousy applies only in a restricted sense:

> "Now jealousy is a resentment of rivals, and whether it is good or evil depends on whether the rival has any business to be there. To be jealous of someone who threatens to outshine us in beauty, brains or sport is sinful, because we cannot claim a monopoly of talent in those areas. If, on the other hand, a third party enters a marriage, the jealousy of the injured person, who is being displaced, is righteous, because the intruder has no right to be there. It is the same with God, who says 'I am the LORD, that is my name? I will not give my glory to another or praise to idols' (Isaiah 42:8)."[27]

Seeing these "third parties" intrude where they did not belong, Paul was overcome by a jealous grief over the loss of divine glory, not to mention the idolaters themselves who struggled "under the sway of" false gods. Importantly, he did not sink into passive pity! He spoke up, turning godly emotion into courageous persuasion.

> ". . . we should not think that *the divine being* is like gold or silver or stone—*an image made by human design and skill.* In the past God overlooked such ignorance, but now he commands all people everywhere to repent." (Acts 17:29-30)

> "We are bringing you good news, telling you to turn from these worthless things to the living God, who made the heavens and the earth and the sea and everything in them." (Acts 14:15)

Bold testimony like this provides us with clear evidence of monotheist commitment. The apostle also offered these idolaters with an escape route. He joined the sobering message of divine judgment with the healing medicine of divine mercy. That was more than bravery. It was godly caring!

Summary

Stronger evidences for monotheistic conviction than a willingness to challenge the prevailing idolatrous belief systems in a pluralist society would be hard to find.

C-3: CONSISTENCY

Do the Old and New Testaments remain monotheistic through and through?

Third, if the biblical God is truly one, we expect its testimony to be *consistent* through and through. Specifically, this expectation hones in on two important questions.

First, will biblical monotheism be *resilient* in the face of spiritual decline among those who champion it? Is there truly a difference between God's constant reality and the fluctuating faith held by those embracing it? Will it prove itself durable or fragile?

Second, will monotheistic faith that was heard loud and clear throughout the Old Testament trail off into some kind of deviant tritheism in the New (Injeel)?

Overview of the Bible

The books of the **Old Testament (OT)** can be grouped into three large sections in the Hebrew Bible: the *Torah* of Moses (Tawrat), the *Nebi'm* (Prophets) and the *Ketuvim* (Writings) commonly referred to as "the Psalms" of David, its largest book.

The **New Testament (NT) books** or Injeel announces the arrival and ministry of the Messiah, Jesus of Nazareth, who was born four centuries after the last OT prophet, Malachi. It includes the history of the growth of the early Church under the teaching of the apostles.

1. TORAH (Law) of Moses (Tawrat) → 2. NEBI'IM (Former & Latter Prophets) → 3. KETUVIM (Writings, Wisdom); Zabur of David → 4. NEW TESTAMENT (Injeel)

Especially in light of the long span of time, geography and multiple human authors involved, will both Testaments consistently remain monotheistic from first to last?

Part 1: Old Testament

We might call this monotheism's Resilience Test. What happens when Israel, the standard-bearer of monotheistic faith, breaks the covenant by falling into polytheistic practice? What happens when saints flounder? If faith collapses, will their one God disappear with it?

Can Monotheism Survive Apostasy?

To answer this question, we will listen to Scriptures' threefold perspective on it: its historical fact, its causes and cure and its impact on monotheism.

A. Historical Fact: Israel Broke God's Covenant

That Israel violated the Shema and broke the covenant is a recorded biblical fact echoed in the Qur'an (Al-Baqara 2:83, 92-94, 100; Al-Maida 5:12-13, 70, etc.). This tragedy occurred long after the death of Moses in the late sixth century B.C. After receiving blessings beyond anyone's wildest dreams, Israel forsook the true God and lapsed into widespread idolatry. Will monotheist reality come to an end through its denial by the very people called to champion it?

When people of faith exchanged their God for false ones, or more accurately, supplemented belief in Yahweh with local deities, God sent prophets to warn them and to call them back. They condemned false worship, warning Israel to resist their allure (Jeremiah 25:6; 2 Kings 17:38-39; 2 Samuel 7:22; 1 Chronicles 17:20; Isaiah 37:19; 19:4; 35:15; Jonah 2:8).

The prophets were God's mouthpieces calling Israel back from idolatry to himself. While pulling no punches, they reflected the heart as well as the truth of God. One of these was Jeremiah. His courageous straight talk proved himself as Israel's true friend and they tried to kill him for it. Called the weeping prophet, preaching during Israel's apostasy, Jeremiah's tears were not for his own plight but over his nation's famine of soul and the fate awaiting it. His warnings fell on deaf ears among a people with dead hearts. Israel preferred false prophets who tickled their ears over Jeremiah's call for repentance. From top to bottom – king, priests and people –all were attuned to the sanguine preachers of "peace and safety." For that, they paid dearly.

B. God's Message to Apostate Israel

What message did God deliver to Israel before, during and after her apostasy? From Jeremiah, God's mouthpiece, we can distill these six crucial truths.

(1)   *I cherish the memory of your early devotion*

"'I remember the devotion of your youth, how as a bride you loved me and followed me through the wilderness, through a land not sown. Israel was holy to the LORD, the firstfruits of his harvest." (Jeremiah 2:1-3)

(2)   *In your material prosperity you forgot Me*

"They followed worthless idols and became worthless themselves. They did not ask, 'Where is the LORD, who brought us up out of Egypt and led us through the barren wilderness, . . . I brought you into a fertile land to eat its fruit and rich produce. But you came and defiled my land and made my inheritance detestable. The priests did not ask, 'Where is the LORD?' Those who deal with the law did not know me; the leaders rebelled against me. The prophets prophesied by Baal, following worthless idols." (Jeremiah 2:5-8)

Thanksgiving is a function of memory. Israel stopped counting her blessings when she forgot where they came from. She ignored Moses' commands to "remember" and "not forget" the One to whom she owed her existence (Deuteronomy 8:2, 11, etc.)

(3) *You swapped the Fountain of Life for leaky cisterns*

"*Has a nation ever changed its gods?* (Yet they are not gods at all.) But *my people have exchanged their glorious God for worthless idols. Be appalled* at this, you heavens, and shudder with great horror," declares the LORD. "My people have committed *two sins:* They have *forsaken me,* the spring of living water, and have *dug their own cisterns,* broken cisterns that cannot hold water." (Jeremiah 2:11-13)

Forgetting the treasures from her past, Israel did the unthinkable. She traded off her glorious treasure for hollow trinkets.

(4) Your threefold rejection (God, truth and faith) tripled your predicament (paranoia, desperation and grasping at straws)

> "Do not learn the ways of the nations or be terrified by signs in the heavens, though the nations are terrified by them. For the practices of the peoples are worthless; "Like a scarecrow in a cucumber field, their idols cannot speak; they must be carried, because they cannot walk. Do not fear them; they can do no harm nor can they do any good." (Jeremiah 10:1-3, 5)

While continuing to pay lip-service to monotheistic belief they behaved as though God was absent. Rather than reaching up in faith to the Proven One, in their panic they grasped at straws in the form of false gods.

(5) You lost your land because you left your Lord

> "I am the LORD, the God of all mankind. Is anything too hard for me? Therefore this is what the LORD says: *I am about to give this city [Jerusalem] into the hands of the Babylonians* and to Nebuchadnezzar king of Babylon, who will capture it. The Babylonians who are attacking this city will come in and set it on fire; they will burn it down, along with the houses where the people aroused my anger by burning incense on the roofs to Baal and by pouring out drink offerings to other gods." (Jeremiah 32:27-29)

True to his Word, in 586 B.C. the Babylonian armies carted off the upper- classes of Judah's population to Babylon. Jerusalem was destroyed and Israel out of the land. Is this destruction the end of the story? To stop here would be an injustice.
God spoke again through Jeremiah.

(6) I am not finished with you! My last word is not doom and gloom.

> "This is what the LORD says: "*When seventy years are completed for Babylon, I will come to you and fulfill my good promise to bring you back to this place.* For I know the plans I have for you," declares the LORD, "plans to prosper you and not to harm you, plans to give you hope and a future." (Jeremiah 29:10-11)

> ". . . I will be found by you," declares the Lord, "and will bring you back from captivity. I will gather you from all the nations and places where I have banished you," declares the Lord, "and will bring you back to the place from which I carried you into exile." (Jeremiah 29:13-14)

God's eternal purpose still stood. His severe discipline through her eviction and exile served its purpose of ridding her of idolatry. Even during severe punishment, "The LORD does not despise his captive people" (Psalm 69:33).

Fulfillment of Jeremiah's prediction came in 539 BC, when the Persians overthrew the Babylonian empire. Cyrus the Great issued this edict:

> "The Lord, the God of heaven, has given me all the kingdoms of the earth and he has appointed me to build a temple for him at Jerusalem in Judah. Any of his people among you may go up to Jerusalem in Judah and build the temple of the Lord, the God of Israel, the God who is in Jerusalem, and may their God be with them." (Ezra 1:2-4; cf. 6:2-5)

Not only does this edict confirm the accuracy of the biblical record, it reveals the amazing depth of character of one and the same God, holy and just as well as full of mercy!

C. The Test: Can Monotheism Survive?

Did Israel's apostasy call monotheism into question? Can it bounce back after such a radical loss of faith? Did this catastrophic fall from grace undermine or in any way compromise the Bible's commitment to monotheism? What happens to God when his people abandon him?

1. Monotheistic Consistency Prevailed Over Human Failure – Psalm 110:4; Malachi 3:6-7

Israel, thanks to God's mercy upon the repentant, regained her faith! Her loss was severe, but only temporary.

> "The LORD has sworn and will not change his mind. . ." (Psalm 110:4)

> "*I the LORD do not change. So you, the descendants of Jacob, are not destroyed.* Ever since the time of your ancestors you have turned away from my decrees and have not kept them. Return to me, and I will return to you," says the LORD Almighty." (Malachi 3:6-7)

2. Israel's Apostasy Provides 4 Arguments for Monotheism – Isaiah 43:10; 45:4-5; 46:12-13

First, Israel's lapse confirmed God's independent existence. God needs no one to exist. Divine oneness is sustained even when its belief is compromised. Since the reality of God preceded the idea of God, he cannot be believed in or out of existence. The great I AM is absolute. God through Isaiah made this clear:

> "...*though you [Israel] do not acknowledge me. I am the LORD, and there is no other*" (Isaiah 45:4-5). "Before me no god was formed, nor will there be one after me." (Isaiah 43:10)

Second, Israel's lapse could not sabotage God's saving purpose. Remarkably,

> "*What I have said, that I will bring about; what I have planned, that I will do.* Listen to me, you stubborn-hearted, you who are now far from my righteousness. I am bringing my righteousness near, it is not far away; and *my salvation will not be delayed.* I will grant salvation to

Zion, my splendor to Israel." (Isaiah 46:12-13)

Third, Israel's lapse was not final for all Israel. God preserved a faithful remnant. This not only reinforces consistency but, in the case of Israel, fixed its reality all the more. Israel's return to Jerusalem from her 70-year excursion in Babylon was more than a geographic relocation. For a holy remnant, it became spiritual renewal. Nehemiah 9 provides a moving episode of national repentance in solemn assembly upon their return. Ezra read the entire Book of the Law, (Deuteronomy from the Tawrat). It pierced their hearts and produced confession and repentance.

Fourth, while God can be abandoned, he can never be eliminated. Oliver Wendell Holmes got it right: "No one has succeeded in getting rid of God."[34] Like truth itself, the living God isn't going anywhere.

> "Truth is tough. It will not break, like a bubble, at a touch; nay, you may kick it about all day like a football, and it will still be round and full at evening."[35]

The lesson? Monotheism is no fragile reality that's subject to human whims. It is the unchanging fundamental reality behind all existence, capable of surviving the dips of human unbelief. Israel's apostasy, rather than calling it into question, proved it.

Part 2: New Testament Consistency

Does the Injeel remain monotheistic through and through or will it trail off into a deviant tritheism? Does the Bible begin in the Old Testament with Yahweh and somehow arrive in the New Testament with three new Gods? Did God-swapping occur between the Testaments like a man going to bed with Susie and waking up with Sally? Some of my Muslim friends see it that way, all the more reason to look to the Scriptures themselves to find out.

In addition to the previous NT citations, let us consider the following.

1. The Injeel Testifies to God's Unchanging Nature – Acts, James and Hebrews

God's reality is unchanging and has no need of human propping up. For God is our generous Benefactor; never our lucky beneficiary:

> "*The God who made the world* and everything in it is the Lord of heaven and earth and does not live in temples built by human hands. And *he is not served by human hands, as if he needed anything.* Rather, he himself gives everyone life and breath and everything else." (Acts 17:24-25)

> "Every good and perfect gift is from above, coming down from the *Father of the heavenly lights, who does not change like shifting shadows.*" (James 1:17)

> "In the beginning, Lord, you laid the foundations of the earth, and the heavens are the work of your hands. They will perish, but you remain; they will all wear out like a garment. . . But you remain the same, and your years will never end." (Hebrews 1:10-12)

2. Worship of One God will Resound throughout Eternity – Revelation 4:11; 22:1-4

We find the ultimate evidence for monotheistic consistency in the Injeel's final book, Revelation:

> "You are worthy, our Lord and God, to receive glory and honor and power, for you created all things, and by your will they were created and have their being." (Revelation 4:11)

Like a movie trailer previewing the next blockbuster, finally the last biblical book shows a vivid preview of heavenly worship. It culminates the story of redemption with rousing worship. But will it be monotheistic?

> "Then he showed me a river of the water of life, clear as crystal, coming

from *the throne of God and of the Lamb,* in the middle of its street. On either side of the river was the tree of life, bearing twelve kinds of fruit, yielding its fruit every month; and the leaves of the tree were for the healing of the nations. There will no longer be any curse; and *the throne of God and of the Lamb* will be in it, and *His* bond-servants will serve *Him*; they will see *His* face, and *His* name will be on their foreheads." (Revelation 22:1-4)

Key details in this passage deserve our close attention. Noted scholar Michael Brown highlights them for us:

"We come to the end of the book [of Revelation], and in a real sense, the end of the story. Revelation 22:1 speaks of "the river of the water of life as clear as crystal, flowing from the throne of God and of the Lamb. Mark those words carefully: the throne of God and of the Lamb. And now look at these astounding verses: 'The throne of God and of the Lamb will be in the city [i.e., the New Jerusalem], and his servants will serve him. They will see his face and his name will be on their foreheads' (22:3-4).

"What an incredible description! There is one throne for God and the Lamb (not two thrones), and his servants (not their servants) will serve him (not them) and see his face (not their faces).

"One throne, one God, and one face. This is profound, glorious, monotheistic truth at its best. Our God is complex and unique! And so the angel exhorts John in Revelation 22:9, "Worship God!" not "Worship gods." Perish the thought. The one God of Abraham and Moses is the one God of Peter and Paul."[36]

From first to last, the Bible's message never wavers. There is one God; no more and no less!

Conclusion

Your question, *Do you believe in one God?*, ranked first. I pray, Muslim reader, that any previous doubts you have entertained on the matter can be set aside on the basis of Scripture. It satisfies all three expectations for a full-orbed monotheism– creed, conviction and consistency. Creeds confess it crisply, miraculous interventions turned verbal assent into bedrock conviction and its restored testimony survived catastrophic human fickleness proving its durability. The New Testament never deviates – Jesus elevated it, the apostles pressed it upon the Church, and the Bible's final book, Revelation, previewed heavenly worshipers bowing before a majestic throne occupied by one God.

From first to last, the Bible's message never wavers: *There is one God; no more and no less!*

CHAPTER 2

SON OF GOD

Question 2: "Why do Christians think that Jesus is the Son of God, not just a prophet? There is no evidence that God ever married Mary! Mary became pregnant and it was a miracle. This is very shameful and sinful."

Q 2.1: "We believe that God was not born and never gave birth to a son or daughter! Do you believe the same?"
Q 2.2: "When you say that Jesus was the Son of God, doesn't that mean Isa was sired and had a date of birth?
Q 2.3: "Where did Jesus (pbuh) say in the Bible that He is the Son of God???"
Q 2.4: "What is the definition of the Son? Who is called father?"

This question-set about the Son of God deserves priority attention, so let's jump right in. The rumor that Christians believe some kind of marital union to have occurred between God and Mary is widely accepted by Muslims known by this author. I appreciate the candor of your questions that shows your desire to protect God's honor.

Oddly enough, this news of marital union on the part of God catches Christians completely off guard! Hearing this, we might say something like, "What? That's a new one. Where did you hear that? How unthinkable!"

So let's clarify this right up front: **God never entered into marital union with Mary!** The very idea is repugnant to Christians. It stands diametrically opposed to God's majesty and supremely defames his character. On top of that, it is a baseless rumor.

Why does the Qur'an take offense to Jesus' sonship? We'll start there and then present seven core teachings about the Son of God in the Injeel.

PART I: The Son of God Considered Scandalous by the Qur'an

The Qur'an's stance on any belief that Jesus was God's Son sends no mixed messages. It's the height of perversity. "The Christians say that the Messiah is the son of God. Those are words from their mouths. . .God curse them! How they are perverted!" (Al-Tawbah 9:30 Nasr). This unrelenting recoil throughout the Qur'an stems from an understanding that Christians teach some kind of marital act of begetting between God and Mary. If true, the Qur'an to its credit never minces words:

> "The disbelievers say, 'The Lord of Mercy has offspring.' How terrible is this thing you assert: it almost causes the heavens to be torn apart, the earth to split asunder, the mountains to crumble to pieces, that they attribute offspring to the Lord of Mercy. It does not befit the Lord of Mercy [to have offspring]. . ." (Mariam 19:88-93[1] Kaleem)

Abdallah Yousuf Ali calls it "stupendous blasphemy:"

> "The belief in Allah begetting a son is not a question merely of words or of speculative thought. It is a stupendous blasphemy against Allah. It lowers Allah to the level of an animal."[2]

Repeatedly the Qur'an echoes this revulsion.[3] The question is: "Who is the offspring in mind—Isa or pre-Islamic pagan deities?" The following *aya*, along with traditional commentary, makes it clear:

> "It is not befitting to (the majesty of) Allah that He should beget a son. Glory be to him!" (Al-Maryam 19:35)

Ali's comment leaves no doubt as to the target of criticism:

> "Begetting a son is a physical act depending on the needs of men's animal nature ... It is derogation from the glory of God–in fact it is blasphemy–to say that God begets sons, like a man or an animal. The Christian doctrine is here emphatically repudiated. If words have any meaning, it would mean an attribution of God of a material nature, and of the lower animal functions of sex. In a spiritual sense, we are all children of God."[4]

To beget blurs the lines between Creator and creature, thus erasing God's incomparable distinction:

> "Say, 'He is God the One, God the eternal. He begot no one nor was He begotten. No one is comparable to Him." (Al-Iklas 112:1-4, Kaleem)

The Qur'an condemns any scenario of a procreating God, a sentiment shared by Christians everywhere!

In summary, the Qur'an condemns any scenario of a procreating God, a denunciation echoed by Christians with a resounding Amen. Muslim readers will have to help me understand the basis supporting these charges of sexual involvement. All I find is accusation without demonstration. I invite your response.

Now let's turn to the Injeel. What does it teach about the Son of God?

PART II: The Son of God Presented Holy by the Injeel – Seven Core Teachings

The Injeel does in fact call Isa al-Masih the "Son of God" – 124 times, to be exact. But what does that mean and not mean? The following facts can be demonstrated from the Injeel:

1. *Its Nature* – Jesus' sonship is a spiritual rather than a biological reality.

2. *Its Origin* – God himself, not the apostles or the church, first conferred on Jesus the title "Son of God." Thus, it came as an early divine revelation rather than a late theological development.

3. *Jesus' Awareness* – From an early age, Jesus habitually addressed God as his Father, indicating his awareness of unique filial kinship.

4. *It's First Opposition* – The first attempt to question Jesus' divine Sonship came from Satan.

5. *Its Meaning* – The Son of God is properly understood against the ancient Scripture's rich tapestry rather than the travesties parodied in Greek legends. It proclaims Jesus as God's Messiah and King.

6. *Its Validation* – Jesus' divine Sonship was proven by his resurrection from the dead.

7. *Its Personal Relevance* – God's eternal Son gave his life in death for human sin. God raised him as proof of his Sonship, his authority to forgive sins and to give eternal life to all who believe (1 John 5:12).

> The Sonship of Jesus is a spiritual rather than a biological reality.

In this chapter, please don't be confused by its structure. I will integrate your specific questions with these seven core teachings from the Injeel. Let's turn now to the first two.

Q – 2.1: "We believe that God was not born and never gave birth to a son or daughter! Do you believe the same?"

Q – 2.2: "When you say that Jesus was the Son of God, doesn't that mean Isa was sired and had a date of birth?

CORE TEACHING 1: Its Nature – The Sonship of Jesus is a spiritual rather than a biological reality.

How can the title Son of God possibly avoid the charge of a shameful marital arrangement that your questions imply? Support in the Injeel for the spiritual nature of Jesus' sonship (rather than any type of physical begetting) begins at his miraculous conception. Jesus was born of a virgin mother through a miracle by the Holy Spirit. God never had a wife or consort, including Mary! Nor did God ever "beget" any sons or daughters. The very suggestion offends all Christians.

So how was Jesus conceived? The Injeel presents only two complementary accounts, one from Mary, the other from Joseph, her fiancé at the time. These tell a much different story, one consistent with Mary's chastity and God's majesty.

Mary's Story – Jesus' Mother

Angel Gabriel to Mary: "The Holy Spirit will come on you, and the power of the Most High will overshadow you. So the holy one to be born will be called the Son of God."

"Now in the sixth month, the angel Gabriel was sent from God to a town of Galilee named Nazareth, to a virgin legally promised in marriage to a man named Joseph of the house of David. And the name of the virgin was Mary. And he came to her and said, "Greetings, favored one! The Lord is with you."

But she was greatly perplexed at the statement, and was pondering what sort of greeting this might be. And the angel said to her, 'Do not be afraid, Mary, for you have found favor with God.

And behold, you will conceive in the womb and will give birth to a son, and you will call his name Jesus.'

32 'This one will be great, and he will be called *the Son of the Most High,* and the Lord God will give him the throne of his father David. And he will reign over the house of Jacob forever, and of his kingdom there will be no end.'

And Mary said to the angel, 'How will this be, since I have not had sexual relations with a man?'

35 And the angel answered and said to her, "The *Holy Spirit will come upon you, and the power of the Most High will overshadow you. Therefore also the one to be born will be called holy, the Son of God.*

And behold, your relative Elizabeth—she also has conceived a son in her old age [John the Baptist], and this is the sixth month for her who was called barren. For nothing will be impossible with God.'

So Mary said, 'Behold, the Lord's female slave! May it happen to me according to your word." And the angel departed from her.'" (Luke 1:26-38)

This narrative twice refers to Jesus as the "Son of God" (verses 32, 35). I draw your attention to the word "holy" to describe baby Jesus, a term always associated with God. So, as you read Mary's account, do you find any hints of marital relations between her and God?

Joseph's Story – Mary's Fiancé

For obvious reasons, Joseph, Mary's fiancé, was directly impacted by her unexpected pregnancy. News that his wife-to-be was pregnant must have been devastating! Had this developing child been his, it would have been shameful enough. But such was impossible – he knew they had been chaste. So what were his options? Just walk away? Would he believe Mary's explanation about an angelic visit or consider it a wild tale like something out of a tabloid? Matthew faithfully records his reaction:

> "His [unborn Jesus] mother Mary had been betrothed to Joseph, but before they came together, she was found to be pregnant by the Holy Spirit. So Joseph her husband, being righteous and not wanting to disgrace her, intended to divorce her secretly. But as he was considering these things, behold, an angel of the Lord appeared to him in a dream, saying,
>
> 'Joseph, son of David, do not be afraid to take Mary as your wife, for what has been conceived in her is from the Holy Spirit. And she will give birth to a son, and *you will call his name 'Jesus,' because he will save his people from their sins.'*
> Now all this happened in order that what was spoken by the Lord through the prophet [Isaiah] would be fulfilled, saying, 'Behold, the virgin will become pregnant and will give birth to a son, and they will call his name *Emmanuel*," which is translated, *"God*

with us."

And Joseph, when he woke up from sleep, did as the angel of the Lord commanded him, and he took his wife and did not have sexual relations with her until she gave birth to a son. And he called his name Jesus." (Matthew 1:18-25 Lexham)

While the title "Son of God" is not mentioned, its equivalent, "Immanuel," literally "God with us," draws from ancient prophecy (Isaiah 7:14). Again, as you read this narrative from Joseph's perspective, do you find anything that suggests illicit divine-human sexual involvement?

Two Observations

First, these are the Injeel's only accounts of how Isa al-Masih was conceived. Clearly, there was no marital union or sex involved by God or anyone else, including the visiting angel or Joseph. Instead, we find a miracle in which the Holy Spirit conceived a holy Child. Exonerating both God's majesty and Mary's chastity, these accounts make any accusation of vulgar impropriety baseless. Instead, they strike wonder into those reflecting on a miraculous act appropriate to a Being for whom "nothing is impossible."

Second, these passages integrate the miracle of Jesus' virgin birth into the whole biblical story. As such, it is not to be read isolated from the larger plotline. It culminated what had gone before and launched what was yet to follow. The Qur'an correctly places great emphasis on Jesus' Virgin Birth. The earlier Books tell us why. **This one-of-a-kind birth is far more than an accident of nature but a milestone on a long divine plan.** It linked back to David's royal throne (Lk 1:32) and to Prophet Isaiah's prediction (Isaiah 7:14). It set in motion God's larger purpose.

That grand purpose was captured in the baby's name. In that culture names were typically chosen by the father and would highlight a prominent feature of the child. Here, however, it was not Joseph but God making the call, choosing a name to encapsulate the child's identity, ancient prophecies and divine mission.

"You will call his name *Jesus*' (the Greek form of Joshua (Yeshua), meaning *"the LORD saves!"*

Why *this* name, "Jesus?" The angel answers: "because he will save his people from their sins." This Son named Jesus is God's answer for the primal human condition.

> "The manifold profound troubles in human life have their root in the one trouble of man's relationship with God."[5]

This plan involved Mary but it was not about her. She was part of something monumentally more than her wedding plans or personal reputation. Compensating for the gossip behind her back and her public shame was the delivery to earth of the Son she bore, one who would answer humanity's fundamental deficit – the need for peace with God through his forgiveness.

Her son would impact world history like none other. Millions of lives, mine included, have experienced a depth of transforming love never thought possible (see Epilogue).

We have established two key truths about the Son of God:

1. **His divine sonship refers to a spiritual rather than biological reality brought about by the Holy Spirit.**

2. **The Son of God came to answer humanity's root problem, the brokenness caused by sin and our need for a Savior.**

Let's now address your concerns pertaining to divine "begetting."

Q 2.1: "We believe that God was not born and never gave birth to a son or daughter! Do you believe the same?"

Q 2.2: "When you say that Jesus was the Son of God, doesn't that mean Isa was sired and had a date of birth?

These two questions express legitimate concern about God's "begetting" and can be put to rest by a biblical understanding of "beget" as it relates to Jesus. Again, Christians agree with Muslims that any conception of God as himself begotten from another source or committing an act of begetting would imply "stupendous blasphemy[6]." That understanding is foreign to the Injeel in reference to Jesus. The good thing is that this offense is based on a confusion that is easily cleared up. "Begotten" is an unfortunate and misleading translation of the Greek word "monogenes." Even in translations such as the New King James rendering it "only begotten" it always means: *one-of-a-kind – a unique, special, chosen, close or precious one.* Never is it understood "sired!" God forbid!

The best lexicons confirm that *monogenes* describes someone who is "one of a kind:"

> . . . pertaining to what is unique in the sense of being the only one of the same kind or class—"unique, only." . . . 'he [God] gave his only Son' (John 3:16); . . . 'God sent his only Son' (1 John 4:9).[7]

The *Baker Dictionary* reinforces this meaning: "The word traditionally translated 'only-begotten' does not carry the idea of birth at all. Literally it means 'only one of its kind,' 'unique.'" M. Anderson elaborates:

"The word monogenes which is translated 'only begotten' in the King James version in John 3:16 appears 9 times in the New Testament: 3 times in Luke (7:12, 8:42 and 9:38) and 4 times in John as a designation of Jesus' relationship to God (1:14, 18; 3:16, 18), in 1 John 4:9 and in Heb 11:17 (of Isaac). According to the *Exegetical Dictionary of the NT* the word *monogenes* means: 'only, one of a kind, unique (derived from *monos* and *genos*).' This basic meaning is found in *Plato Ti 92c* (of the heaven); *Wisdom* 7:22 (of the Spirit of Wisdom); *Cornutus Theologia Graeca* 27 [49:13] (of this one and only world).

> "The word traditionally translated 'only-begotten' does not carry the idea of birth at all. Literally it means 'only one of its kind,' 'unique.'"
> *The Bakers Dictionary*

'Unique' is the actual meaning of monogenes as can be seen in

Hebrews 11:17, where it is used of Isaac (Gen 21:12). The word here means only (son) of his kind. Abraham in fact had already begotten Ishmael and later had six other sons . . . 'The/his only son' is the clear meaning of the phrase with monogenes in John 3:16,18 and 1 John 4:9. The expression indicates Jesus' unique personality, in relation to the Father, and mission. According to John 1:14,18 the Logos [the Word of God] is the 'Only One' from the Father and therefore in his nature is the only revealer of the Father." [8]

Applied to Jesus, **monogenes** means there is no one else like him. This sense of the word agrees with the Qur'an in presenting Jesus as the only person who was born without a human father.

The 'Son' points to a Spiritual Reality

The definition of the Son is not restricted to a literal and physical meaning. Michael Brown, a respected authority in Semitic languages explains:

". . .Any student of the Semitic languages knows that the word son (Hebrew, *ben*; Aramaic, *bar*; Arabic, *ibn*) has many different meanings. It can refer to literal offspring (such as one's physical son or distant descendant) as well as to metaphorical offspring (such as "the sons of the prophets," meaning the disciples of the prophets). When applied to the Israelite king, it means "son" by divine adoption (e.g., 2 Sam. 7:14: "I will be his father, and he will be my son") . . ."[9]

M. Anderson concurs, stressing its figurative sense:

"The use of expressions such as 'son of ' or 'father of ' or 'mother of ' is universal. Most people would have heard the expression 'Mother of all battles' used by the Iraqi leader Saddam Hussein. What does that expression mean? Are we to understand that if there is a 'mother of battles' then there must also be a 'father of battles' and if they join together they will produce baby battles? Of course not! In the Qur'an itself we read the expression 'Mother of the Book' (Q. 13:39). Does that mean that there is a 'Father of the Book' and 'Sons of the Book' somewhere? Of course not. Muslims believe that the expression 'Mother of the Book' refers to the heavenly origin of the Qur'an and that the earthly copy of the Qur'an is the visible expression of the invisible 'Mother of the Book.'"[10]

This understanding of *monogenes* combined with the metaphorical use of "son" removes the offense, thus exonerating the Injeel from committing slander of a God who begets or was begotten.

Q 2.3: "Where did Jesus (*pbuh*) say in the Bible that He is the Son of God?"

This question about Jesus' claim as the Son of God is critical. Did he really believe and embrace this relationship or did others pin this distinction on him as a novelty imported much later from Roman paganism? We will take you to passages where Jesus explicitly claims to have this unique relationship. Let's begin, however, at a different place: Who declared Jesus to be the Son of God in the first place? Was it the apostles? Or Paul? Or even Jesus? None of the above! This leads us to the second fact of Jesus' divine Sonship.

CORE TEACHING 2: *Its Origin* – God himself, not the church, first conferred the title Son of God on Jesus.

Jesus did claim to have this uniquely privileged relationship as God's only Son, but he was not the first to say so. If he had, it might have meant little more than vaunted self-delusion. Which testimony carries greater weight: someone who says "God is my father" or a God who says "He is my son"? In Jesus' case, it was God who first came out with it. What difference does that make? It is night and day! Something fundamental is at play.

Anytime ordinary persons claim to have special friendship with a well-known public figure or high-ranking official, we might raise an eyebrow. Are they just trying to impress us? Which is more convincing? If I say "I know President Obama" (I don't) or if President Obama says, "I know J. P. Knight"? The answer is obvious. In the case of the latter, we hear it differently. Why so? Because the testimony by the greater party always carries more weight than that of the lesser party.

Let me illustrate. A summer day in 1960 placed me in the presence of a man of national fame. For an American nine-year old boy in the sixties, the game of baseball was huge! My father took our family to Kansas City, Missouri where he attended a conference. While he attended meetings, my older brother, sister and I roamed the lobby of the famous Muehlebach Hotel. By chance, two professional baseball teams also lodged there, the Boston Red Sox and the New York Yankees! They had come to play the then KC Athletics. My brother and I thought we were in heaven. The best is yet to come!

One morning the three of us stepped onto an elevator and who was standing there but the Red Sox legend, Ted Williams, arguably one of the greatest hitters of all times! He was to baseball what today's Argentinian Lionel Messi is to soccer or Pakistani Azhar Ali to cricket. This was Williams' final season and we three nobodies are sharing the same space with him! Those ten seconds with his undivided attention felt like an ascent into Paradise. His impressively athletic frame was softened by a warm smile that I still remember. We got his autograph and he even stooped down to kiss the cheek of my sister that almost sent her to the floor in a fainting spell.

This story has a point. Today, with a little cleverness, I could spin a convincing tale about my close friendship with the great baseball legend Ted Williams. "Oh yes, Ted and our family go back all the way to the sixties. Yeah, we've had a few ups and downs (on the elevator), but he just kisses my sister on the cheek and everything's good." Baseball enthusiasts would be so impressed by my long association with the legendary slugger. But my clever manipulation of facts would hardly reflect reality! If Ted Williams could be brought back to life and asked about me, he would say, J. P. *who?*, instantly exposing my conceit as the big fat lie it truly is. It would collapse under the weightier testimony of the greater figure!

This common human tendency – inflating one's importance by name-dropping celebrities – I'll call the "Ted Williams Syndrome."

Now to your question asking where *Jesus* claimed to be God's Son. As important as that is, given this "syndrome," the place to start is with the testimony of the greater Party who, in this case, is Almighty God!

All it will take to either disavow or validate such a claim is to hear from the greater witness. To find out, we go to three scenarios.

Scene 1: Who announced to the virgin Mary via Gabriel that the baby conceived in her by the Holy Spirit was the "Son of the Most High" (Injeel, Luke 1:33). It was God himself.

Scene 2: Fast-forward thirty years when Jesus began his public ministry at the baptism waters of the Jordan River.

> "At that time Jesus came from Nazareth in Galilee and was baptized by John [Yahya] in the Jordan. Just as Jesus was coming up out of the water, he saw heaven being torn open and the Spirit descending on him like a dove. And a voice came from heaven: 'You are my Son, whom I love; with you I am well pleased.'" (Injeel, Mark 1:9-11)

The first to identify Jesus as God's Son was not his disciples, not Paul, nor even Jesus. It was God himself! The manner by which God made this claim conveyed far more than a formal title. The heavenly voice addressed Jesus directly, affirming his true identity, special love and his Father's joy. We can imagine the surge of jubilation that must have come over Jesus upon hearing those words! If any inklings of doubt about this filial kinship existed before, they were gone! God the Father himself said it: "You are my son! And I'm delighted with you!"

> The first to identify Jesus as God's Son was not his disciples, not Paul, nor even Jesus himself. It was God!

Scene 3: Jumping ahead two and a half years, we come to an even more dramatic event. Jesus had for the most part withdrawn from the crowds. His soaring popularity has made it difficult to move about in public. But he also desired privacy with the Twelve (apostles) to prepare them for the ordeal he (and they) were about to face in Jerusalem. Jesus took three of his apostles – Peter, James and John – to a mountain to pray. As you read this pronouncement of Jesus' Sonship made on that mountainside, let's pay close attention to who is making it, remembering the "syndrome" that we learned from the story of Ted Williams.

> "Jesus took with him Peter, James and John the brother of James, and led them up a high mountain by themselves. There he was transfigured before them. His face shone like the sun, and his clothes became as white as the light.
>
> Just then there appeared before them Moses and Elijah, talking with Jesus.
>
> Peter said to Jesus, 'Lord, it is good for us to be here. If you wish, I will put up three shelters—one for you, one for Moses and one for Elijah.' While he was still speaking, a bright cloud covered them, and a voice from the cloud said, '*This is my Son, whom I love; with him I am well pleased. Listen to him!*'
>
> When the disciples heard this, they fell facedown to the ground, terrified. But Jesus came and touched them. 'Get up,' he said. 'Don't be afraid.' When they looked up, they saw no one except Jesus." (Matthew 17:1-13, emphasis added)

In this scene, God again singles out Jesus as his Son, but this time in a manner that the three apostles would never forget.[11] Five key features set it apart.

(1) *Outward Radiant Flash* – Earlier at his baptism, the sign marking out Jesus as the Son of God and "Chosen One" came from outside himself (see Jn 1:32), the heavenly descent of the Holy Spirit resting upon him. Now, nearly three years later, the three men surrounding Jesus in a time of prayer fixed upon him as he became "transfigured"[12] before them. His appearance was radically altered so that "his face shone like the sun, and his clothes became as white as the light." What is the significance of this? This confirming sign was not a coming down on Jesus from the outside, but a coming out from within him and breaking through his flesh. Jesus' eternal nature, previously concealed beneath his humanity, now suddenly flashed to the fore.

> "His clothes also become 'white as light', not because of a light shining on him from the outside but because of the light shining out of him

from the inside."[13]

This metamorphosis was truly a breaking through:

> "...the heavenly glory of His nature, which was still concealed under
> His earthly appearance (and during His conflict with the kingdom
> of darkness), now broke forth."[14]

(2) *Visitors from the Ancient Past* – Two leading figures from biblical history, Moses and Elijah, long gone from this earth, appeared and talked with Jesus. Early in his ministry, Jesus said, "I have come to fulfill the law and the prophets" (Matthew 5:17). Moses represents the Books of the Law (Tawrat) including the Ten Commandments and Elijah all the prophets. Their joint appearance with Jesus underscored God's unfolding and unified revelation that was now culminating with Jesus!

(3) *God's Enveloping Presence* – A "bright cloud" covers them. This reminisces the time of Moses when God filled the tabernacle with his manifested glory (Tawrat, Exodus 40:34-38. See Son of Man section in Chapter 5).

(4) *God's Audible Testimony* – At Jesus' baptism, you recall, God had addressed Jesus directly: "*You* are my Son." Now, however, God tells the apostles, "*This* is. . ." Two striking features are noteworthy:. (a) Three men heard the same unmistakable identification declared: *Jesus is the Son of God!* Hearing it simultaneously rules out the possibility of private hallucinations. (b) The Speaker was God himself! Not only was the relationship clearly made, it expressed God's delight with his Son: "This is my Son, whom I love; with him I am well pleased."

(5) *Jesus, God's Final Word* – The two prophets, Moses and Elijah, suddenly vanish and leave Jesus standing alone. Immediately following their disappearance, all three men hear a resonant divine command: "Listen to him!" Strikingly, this order presents the sole standing Figure as not only the divine Son, but also the one whom Moses said to expect centuries earlier: "the prophet like me from your own brothers. You

must listen to him!" (Tawrat, Deuteronomy 18:15 HCSB). In other words, the long history of biblical revelation reached its summit in the One revealed as Son of God.

In this third scenario, Jesus' designation as the Son of God came from the Father, not himself. The phenomena accompanying it overwhelmed all three apostles, reducing them to awestruck silence.

Summary

The Injeel's designation of Jesus as "God's Son" started with God the Father, not with Jesus himself. Three separate announcements, beginning with the angel to Mary at Jesus' conception, to Jesus at his baptism and, finally, to his apostles while praying on a mountain make one thing clear about the Son of God. It did not emerge from a man with "Ted Williams Syndrome." It originated with God.

Now to your question. Did Jesus call God his Father?

CORE TEACHING 3: Jesus' Awareness – From an early age, Jesus habitually addressed God as his Father, indicating his awareness of unique filial kinship.

Did Jesus ever call God "My Father?" Was he aware that he was God's Son? Jesus fully acknowledged God as his Father and addressed him as such. Out of many instances, we will highlight two occasions that make his awareness clear.

Scene 1. Evidence that Jesus was cognizant that God was his Father surfaces during his childhood. Around age twelve, Jesus' parents traveled to the city of Jerusalem. On the way home, panic erupted when they realized that Jesus was not with them. They made a beeline back to the city in search for the "lost child," one they expected to be frantically looking for them! How shocked they were to find him sitting in the Temple area fully composed and engaging with biblical scholars on matters of Scripture.[15] Only the parents are upset; the child is unfazed:

"When his parents saw him, they were astonished. His mother said to him, 'Son, why have you treated us like this? Your father and I have been anxiously searching for you.'"

At this moment, we hear our first clue of Jesus' awareness. Mary's anxious inquiry to Jesus over his seeming disregard for "your father and I" got what was to her an inscrutable answer:

"Why were you searching for me?" he asked. *Didn't you know I had to be in my Father's house?'* But they did not understand what he was saying to them. (Luke 2:48-50)

"*My* Father's house?" Was Jesus confused? Wasn't the home of his legal father located up in Nazareth? There was no confusion. Mary's adolescent son knew who his true Father was.. This admission, coupled with the natural manner in which he spoke, caught them off-guard.

> "Why were you searching for me?" he asked. "Didn't you know I had to be in my Father's house?"
> Jesus in the Temple, age 12

Was this a childish fantasy? After all, Jesus was only twelve. If this mother-son conversation from the Temple courts was our only example of Jesus' awareness of his divine Sonship, some might think so. Jesus had not yet reached maturity. The next example removes that possibility.

Scene 2. At the end of his life on earth we see the most touching example when Jesus acknowledged God as his Father. The occasion arose when he was the most helpless. Just before his arrest, Jesus began his dark night of agony. During this crucible, Jesus fully acknowledged God to be his father in the starkest of terms. To *Pater,* the term of respect, Jesus joined *Abba*:

"'My soul is overwhelmed with sorrow to the point of death,' he said to them. 'Stay here and keep watch.' Going a little farther, he fell to the ground and prayed that if possible the hour might pass from him. '*Abba, Father,*' he said, 'everything is possible for you. Take this cup from me. Yet not what I will, but what you will.'" (Injeel, Mark 14:34-36)

"Abba" was the intimate term used by children with their own fathers and translated, "Papa." Addressing God in this way is important for several reasons. It removed any doubt whether or not Jesus was aware of his unique filial kinship with God. It also underscores that for Jesus, Son of God was more than a formal title but a uniquely deep and intimate kinship.

A Controversial Claim

Addressing Almighty God as "Father," however, was not Jesus' invention. It had preceded him in the earlier sacred Books. We find numerous references to God as Father throughout Scripture (Tawrat, Deuteronomy 32:6; Prophets Isaiah 63:16; 64:8; Jeremiah 3:19; 31:9; Malachi 1:6; 2:10; 1 Chronicles 29:10; Zabur, Psalm 103:13; Proverbs 3:12).[16] If that is so, why did Jesus' use of this term stir up controversy with Jewish scholars who would have been familiar with those passages? The Injeel says "...the Jews were seeking all the more to kill Him, because He was ... calling God His own Father, making Himself equal with God" (John 5:18).

This riled them up because it showed that he regarded himself to be *uniquely* related to God. Rather than addressing God as "Our Father," as he taught his disciples to pray, Jesus addressed him as "My Father." Further, he claimed to be one with the Father (John 10:30, 38; 14:10-11), being privy to his inner knowledge (Matt 11:27; *John* 5:20, 10:15; Lk 10:21022), even having seen the Father (John 6:46) and sharing his Father's glory (John 17:11f)! These claims, without removing Jesus' subordinate position as Son to the Father, placed him equally in the same category as God.[17]

Jesus unquestionably acknowledged God to be his Father.

CORE TEACHING 4: Its First Opposition – The first attempt to question Jesus' divine Sonship came from Satan.

We saw that God himself was first to call Jesus his Son. Who was the first one to challenge it? Immediately on the heels of his baptism, the Spirit led Jesus into a nearby desert to fast from food and public life. And this fast was not like those during Ramadan. For 40 days, Jesus ate nothing, day *or* night! After nearly six weeks when Jesus is famished and alone, he hears another voice. Out of nowhere a visitor appears, showing up in the guise of an old friend who was so concerned over the starved and lonely Son of God. This visitor got right down to business:

> "*If you are the Son of God,* tell these stones to become bread." (Matthew 4:3)

"*If* you are the Son of God?" Did not God declare just prior to his fast, "You *are* My Son?"

On the face of it, the logic made perfect sense: the divine Son who possesses limitless power finds himself hungry in his human condition. Why not turn a dry stone into a delicious loaf of bread? Just say the word. Yet Jesus declined. He saw through the insinuation, "if " you are the Son of God. Jesus immediately recognized his "friend." Tipped off by the insinuating "if " that contradicted God's prior declaration, this was the same ancient voice who whispered a question to our first parents in the Garden, "Did God really say?" (Tawrat, Genesis 3:1). Jesus saw through his feigned concern for the Son in his hunger, spotting him as the Father of Lies exploiting his vulnerability.[18] Always crafty, ever twisting God's life-giving Word into an instrument of death, the satanic design maligned God's goodness, thwarted his good purposes and pit his creature against him. That ploy had worked on Adam, but would fail on Jesus. Jesus countered him with Scripture:

> "It is written: 'Man shall not live on bread alone, but on every word that comes from the mouth of God.'" (Matthew 4:4, a citation from Tawrat, Deuteronomy 8:3)

Satan returned a second time, this time quoting Scripture to plant a doubt that Jesus was God's Son:

"Then the devil took him to the holy city and had him stand on the highest point of the temple. 'If you are the Son of God,' he said, 'throw yourself down. For it is written:

'He will command his angels concerning you, and they will lift you up in their hands, so that you will not strike your foot against a stone.'" (Matthew 4:5-6. Citation of Zabur, Psa 91)

The Devil cited Psalm 91 to Jesus, a passage promising God's protection to David. His endgame was clear: to cause Jesus to abort his mission. He craftily hid a murderous plot under a tantalizing garment. What better way to convince the world of his divine Sonship by taking a suicide dive from the peak of the Temple in broad daylight and then caught by angels in mid-air?

The ability to quote Scripture, obviously, is no proof of sainthood. Even the Devil can pull it off, but always twists it to oppose God's ends. What a slimy creature! Pulling biblical verses out of their contexts or substituting this or that word are dead giveaways. Jesus knew who he was, the Son of God, and had nothing to prove. He turned the tactic of his adversary into a weapon against him:

> Jesus answered him, "It is also written: 'Do not put the Lord your God to the test.'" (Matthew 4:7)

Round Two went to Jesus who underscored to his opponent that he underestimated the one he was messing with.[19]

The attempt to undermine the veracity of the claim, "You are my Son" that God spoke directly to Jesus originated with Satan, the Father of Lies.

Q 2.4: "What is the definition of the Son? Who is called father?"

Your request for definitions is wise. Two people can use the same words and come away with opposite meanings. Comprehension across cultures relies on clear definitions. We have already disavowed any association of Son of God from physical procreation or divine "begetting." Now we're ready to offer a biblical definition.

CORE TEACHING 5: *Its Meaning* – The Son of God is properly understood against the ancient Scripture's rich tapestry rather than the travesties parodied in Greek legends. It proclaims Jesus as God's Messiah and King.

The Old Testament is the lens through which we see the full picture of divine sonship. It used the title "son(s) of God" in a way that bore no resemblance to pagan mythology, so common after the spread of Hellenism through Alexander the Great. These were metaphorical "sons of God," meaning they were subordinate to God and received special care. It applied to three separate groups, **none of whom involved physical begetting:** (1) Members of the *heavenly court,* the angels who are often called 'sons of the gods.' As Yahweh's creatures they are quite subordinate to him."[21] (2) *God's people*, chosen by God and the object of his care and love (Exodus 4:22f). (3) *The Davidic king.* The relationship of God to the Davidic kings was one of a Father to a Son. Taken together, New Testament scholar, Martin Hegel, reminds us that:

> . . .no recipients of the title, "son of God" or "begotten" one, "were literally sons of God, as if the Lord consorted with a goddess who then gave birth, the way the gods and goddesses did in pagan mythology."[22]

Jesus the Son of God

All previous lines from the Old Testament converge upon Jesus the Son as on no other human being. Its clearest proclamation in distilled form awaited the end of Jesus' ministry when Jesus raised **this question to his apostles.**

> "Who do you say I am?' Simon Peter answered, **'You are the Messiah, the Son of the living God.'** Jesus replied, 'Blessed are you, Simon son of Jonah, for this was not revealed to you by flesh and blood, but by my Father in heaven.'" (Matthew 16:13-16)

For two reasons, Jesus called Peter "blessed." He got the right answer and received it from above. The living God himself, through the mouth of a fisherman, unveiled Jesus as both his Messiah and Son. Jesus' divine Sonship is a "fundamentally a Messianic concept" (F. F. Bruce). Two titles, "Son of God" and "Messiah," take us back to God's covenant promise made to King David roughly a thousand years before Jesus' birth. How did it all begin? It's a remarkable story. Get ready for a history lesson here. It will take some effort but will be worth it. You might want to pour yourself a cup of coffee or tea. Specifically, the Messiah would reign as the final and quintessential King. Unlike his royal predecessors, Jesus combined his royal position with willing sacrifice.

Son of God – A Royal Title Beginning with King David

Backstory – Who is King?

A major debate in Israel's early history centered around the pros and cons of having a human king ruling over her. It arose during the period of the judges when the twelve tribes spread out geographically over the land and held together by their common covenant with God. The people wanted a king who could conscript an army to defend themselves against military attacks. Other nations had kings, so why not Israel? The problem was theological. Israel already had a king!

> "The LORD reigns, let the earth be glad!" (Psalm 97:1).

> "Who is he, the King of glory? The LORD Almighty – He is the King of glory!" (Psalm 24:10)

God alone was Israel's king and had defended her at every turn. Prophet Samuel warned them that monarchies would introduce practices unfitting for the people of God. So what happened? **A monarchy was established, but without God abdicating his Sovereign throne.** He would continue to rule over his people through a human king, defending them and fostering peace and justice. It was to David, Israel's second king, that the terms of monarchy were spelled out.

Davidic Kings Adopted as God's Sons

As his forty-year reign drew to a close, God made this promise to David:

> "I took you from the pasture, from following the sheep, to be ruler over My people Israel. . . .The LORD will make a house for you. When your days are complete and you lie down with your fathers, I will raise up your descendant after you, who will come forth from you, and I will establish his kingdom. . .

> "*I will be a father to him and he will be a son to Me;* when he commits iniquity, I will correct him with the rod of men and the strokes of the sons of men, but My lovingkindness shall not depart from him. . .. Your *house and your kingdom shall endure before Me forever; your throne shall be established forever.*" Nathan reported to David all the words of this entire *revelation.*" (2 Samuel 7:8-15, 17; Psalm 89:4)

What do we learn from this?

First, David's lasting dynasty came through a divine plan rather than human ambition. It involved David, but as a "revelation" (v 17), it paved the way forward to fulfill a larger masterplan (for David's response, see verses 27-28).

Second, God promised on oath that David's dynasty would never end (cf. Deut. 17:14- 15).[23] Initially, this seems odd in that David was the Israel's second king. Why not award this lasting dynasty to his predecessor, King Saul, who possessed all the markings of royalty. His towering figure intimidated his subjects (1 Sam. 10:23) and he possessed strong natural instincts as commander-in-chief. That compelling persona, however, could not compensate for his two disqualifying deficiencies – his ancestral line and serious moral flaws. King Saul was from the tribe of Benjamin while the Tawrat made it clear that the "scepter shall not depart from [the tribe of] Judah" (Genesis 49:10). And then there was Saul's pattern of disobedience.[24]

> "The LORD has torn the kingdom of Israel from you [Saul] today

and has given it to one of your neighbors—to one better than you."
(1 Samuel 15:28 NIV)

Both qualities absent in Saul were abundantly present in David who hailed from Judah and earned the reputation as "the man after God's own heart" (Acts 13:22):

> "The LORD, the God of Israel, chose me from my whole family to be king over Israel forever. He chose Judah as leader, and *from the tribe of Judah* he chose my family, and from my father's sons he was pleased to make me king over all Israel." (1 Chronicles 28:4)

Third, God established a unique fatherly relationship with David that extended to each succeeding heir to the throne: "I will be a father to him and he will be a son to Me." Each king ("Son") would reign in a subordinate position to God as "Father" to rule Israel according to God's laws. In other words, "the ruler is God, and it is he who determines the nation's laws, as well as the people's direction—politically, militarily, and economically."[25] Ruling by the laws of Moses required the king to know them well (Deuteronomy 16:16-17; 17:16-20). As the Father, God would keep a watchful eye of protection over the king to ensure his promise of a perpetual dynasty.

Fourth, God's revelation to David acknowledged faults that human kings were bound to bring to the royal office. This recognition stipulated measures to keep kings in line. If a king should flagrantly disregard the sacred law, his privileged sonship would not shield him from divine correction. The Father would not coddle the son. Their special relationship called for their obedience and his caring discipline. If necessary, God would "correct him with a rod." These expectations countered any king's assumed exemption, "I can do as I please" by an indulgent Father that says, "My boy can do no wrong." Importantly, this discipline, however severe, was the proof of God's faithful love:

> "My son, do not make light of the Lord's discipline, and do not lose heart when he rebukes you, because the Lord disciplines the one he loves, and he chastens everyone he accepts as his son." (Hebrews

12:5)

Scriptures weave together four essentials about David's dynasty that ultimately lead us to Jesus.

A. Divine Adoptions were Solemnized on Inauguration Day

Every new inauguration ritualized the king's "adoption," solemnly reminding each ascendant to the crown of the true King's identity.

'You are My Son, Today I have begotten You." (Psalm 2:6-7)

Kings became sons of God through spiritual means, not physical. His role as "son" was to be obedient to the Father. His inauguration included the act of anointing with oil, empowering him to rule in God's stead. Oil symbolized the Spirit's enabling to equip the king to serve as God's agent-son. Kings were often called "the LORD's anointed" to mark them as far more than a political figure but occupying a sacred office (1 Samuel 24:5-6; Psalm 18:50; 20:6).

Sonship materialized, then, through an adoptive act by the agency of the Spirit to which the anointing oil symbolized. This adoptive agency of the Spirit renders sonship to be completely free of physical cause and effect. Connecting two terms, "anointing" with "monogenes," in reference to OT royalty throws additional light on the non-physical aspect of "begetting:"

> "Furthermore, it is to be noted that in the New Testament the verb 'to beget (*gennao*) (become the father of)' is used to describe the relationship between God the Father and the Son only in quotations of Ps. 2:7 (Acts 13:33 and Hebrews 1:5, 5:5). In the Old Testament the reference was to the earthly king who on the day of his assumption of the high office was said to have been "begotten" by God. In Acts 13:33 the quotation is applied to the resurrection of the Lord Jesus. It is nowhere applied to the birth of the Lord Jesus.[26]

B. David's Dynasty Promised on Oath to Never End

God made this amazing promise of perpetuity to David:

> "I will maintain my love to him forever, and *my covenant with him will never fail. I will establish his line forever, his throne as long as the heavens endure.*" (Psalm 89:28)

This promise staggers our minds. God certainly knew that all of David's descendants would not show David's heart for God. Nevertheless, God swore by his own holiness:

> "If his sons forsake my law and do not follow my statutes, if they violate my decrees and fail to keep my commands, I will punish their sin with the rod, their iniquity with flogging; *but I will not take my love from him, nor will I ever betray my faithfulness. I will not violate my covenant or alter what my lips have uttered.* Once for all, *I have sworn by my holiness*—and I will not lie to David— that *his line will continue forever and his throne endure before me like the sun;* it will be established forever like the moon, the faithful witness in the sky." (Psalm 89:28-37)

God's sworn promise to David's permanent dynasty anticipated severe testing in its distant future that no one at the time could see coming. The dynasty continued from David's forty-year reign from about 1000-960 B.C. and that of Solomon his son, (ruling another 40 years from 960-920 B.C.). More importantly, it survived two catastrophic threats. The first severe test came as civil uprising when ten tribes split-off to become the Northern Kingdom ("Israel"). That left the Southern Kingdom with only two tribes, Judah to which David belonged and Benjamin.

Later, God's sworn promise of a perpetual dynasty was put to an even greater test when royal "sons" stop listening to the true King as "Father." All the Northern kings of Israel and most of Judah's in the South led their nations away from Yahweh into idolatry. They closed their ears to God's messengers such as Jeremiah, the "weeping prophet," who alerted them of God's imminent judgment. God had warned David that he would not tolerate a rogue dynasty (2 Samuel 7:15). God's rod of punishment turned out to match the severity of the prophet's prediction. The Babylonians invaded and destroyed the City of Jerusalem in 586 BC, deporting its population 700 miles away to Babylon.

But what about David's dynasty? Would it survive? Every indication pointed to its fatal collapse. Nebuchadnezzar snatched the sitting King Jehoiachin and appointed his twenty-one-year-old uncle as king, renaming him Zedekiah. His reign would last a mere 11 years. In vain, the people looked to him for protection. He proved useless against the invading armies. Later, prophet Ezekiel sugar-coated nothing, wailing to show that God took no pleasure in the sword. The Fall of Jerusalem was tragic enough (1 Kings 25; 2 Chronicles 36:15-20). The demise of the dynasty would be the last nail in Israel's coffin.

> "'Shall we rejoice in the scepter of my royal son? The sword despises every such stick." (Eze 21:10)

The Babylonian sword would sever the Judean scepter. We should pay close attention to the triple-message God delivered to the king. First, God says, "Your time is up!"

> "'You profane and wicked *prince of Israel*, whose day has come, whose time of *punishment has reached its climax*. . ." (Ezekiel 21:25)

Second, God made a distinction between the wicked king and the royal throne. He ordered him to remove the very symbol of his authority:

> "This is what the Sovereign LORD says: *Take off the turban, remove the crown*. . ." (Ezekiel 21:25)

Thankfully, the King has two sons! The dynasty will last!

> ". . .it [the sword] is against my people; *it is against all the princes of Israel*. They are thrown to the sword." (Eze 21:12)

Sacred history records what happened:

> "The Babylonian army pursued the king [Zedekiah] and overtook

him in the plains of Jericho. All his soldiers were separated from him and scattered, and he was captured. He was taken to the king of Babylon at Riblah, where sentence was pronounced on him. *They killed the sons of Zedekiah before his eyes. Then they put out his eyes, bound him with bronze shackles and took him to Babylon.*" (2 Kings 25:6-7)

Zedekiah did evil as did the people so that "in the end the LORD thrust them from his presence" (2 Kings 24:20).

God himself confronts the people with the perish-the-thought question of "what if ?":

"'Testing will surely come. And what if even the scepter, which the sword despises, does not continue?' declares the Sovereign Lord." (Ezekiel 21:13)

Will the dynasty survive? It seemed to come to an end with this last king. Here is a just a glimmer, a hint that the fate of the crown will not go the way of the man currently wearing it. That ominous "what if" question seems to just hang in midair. What now? The king is out. The princes are dead. What if it doesn't continue! What would that say about the promise God made on oath to David: "your throne shall be established forever" (2 Samuel 7:15)?

Most stunning of all, God's third message is one of hope, announcing God's rightful king:

"The crown will not be restored until he to whom it *rightfully belongs* shall come; to him I will give it.' (Ezekiel 21:27-28, emphasis mine)

This points to the Messiah to appear in the last days.

"David my servant [who] will be their prince forever" (Ezekiel 37:25; see Hosea 3:4-5).

C. Prophets Foretold the Arrival of a Son Greater than David Ruling over a Kingdom Greater than Israel

During this long dark period of Israel's apostasy and exile, God raised up prophets to stoke the embers of hope. Peering far beyond the immediate horizons, they saw another king who would resume the defunct dynasty. Like them, he would hail from Davidic lineage called "God's Son," but with a dramatic shift. This new heir would be more than a son by adoption. They fixed on a quintessential Son, someone far greater than David who would inaugurate a kingdom far greater than Israel!

One of the most comprehensive descriptions came through the prophet Isaiah seven-hundred years prior to Jesus' birth.

Divine Son given Divine Titles – Like his reigning predecessors, this heir to the throne would descend from David's human lineage. Unlike them, he will come from heaven, the eternal Son of God by nature, not by adoption.

> "For to us a child is born, to us a son is given, and the government will be on his shoulders. And he will be called Wonderful Counselor, Mighty God, Everlasting Father, Prince of Peace." (Isaiah 9:6)

First, consider the stature of this King. As great as David was, this Son would be infinitely greater! So who is this Child-King? These titles far surpassed those conferred on David or his heirs, or to prophets or priests. And they did not originate in the Injeel or the Greek translation of the Old Testament. They come from the Hebrew Bible!

> "Who is "el gibbor" ("el" – God; "gibbor" – strong one, hero, warrior), "mighty God," a title reserved for God alone (Isaiah 10:21)? The text says what it says, and there is no way to get around this profound fact: No Davidic king could bring to reality the full meaning of these words except Jesus the Messiah. It is the Hebrew Bible itself that indicates that the Davidic Messiah would be the "Son of God" in a unique way, even bearing divine qualities and in a real sense being divine.

Once again, it is only through Jesus the Messiah that all the varied pieces of the puzzle fit together. Far from being idolatrous, the

New Testament doctrine of the Son of God is the culmination of the dream of Israel's prophets and psalmists, the fulfillment of the Hebrew Scriptures, the hope of mankind."[27]

Second, consider the scope of his kingdom. While David had expanded Israel's borders, the rule of this new King would reach far beyond national Israel.

"Of the greatness of his government and peace there will be no end. He will reign on David's throne and over his kingdom, establishing and upholding it with justice and righteousness from that time on and forever. The zeal of the Lord Almighty will accomplish this." (Isaiah 9:7)

Who is this reigning king? Other prophets filled in the gaps. The Holy Spirit showed them specific details about this coming king which they meticulously penned on sacred parchment for future generations. His profile began to emerge portraying both the external circumstances surrounding his life and character. These features of recognition would signal his arrival to ensure that he would not be missed. Below is a partial list of what these ancient prophets saw:

"The Lord Himself will give you a sign: Behold, a virgin will be with child and bear a son, and she will call His name Immanuel." Prophet Isaiah 7:14 (NKJV), seven centuries before Jesus' birth

Birthplace in Bethlehem – Seven centuries preceding Jesus' birth, God announced the location of his birthplace.

"But you, Bethlehem Ephrathah, though you are small among the clans of Judah, out of you will come for me one who will be ruler over Israel, whose origins are from of old, from ancient times." (Micah 5:2)

Born of a Virgin – The question of how a "child to be born" of a woman could at the same time possess divine names? We have seen already that since Jesus was God's spiritual Son rather than biological, it ruled out inappropriate relations. Still, it meant that he could not come through a man, but only through a virgin! God spoke through Isaiah:

> "The Lord Himself will give you a sign: Behold, a virgin will be with child and bear a son, and she will call His name Immanuel." (Isaiah 7:14)

We have already heard the angel Gabriel's answer to Mary's perplexity at its announcement:

> "How can this be, since I am a virgin?" The angel answered and said to her, "The Holy Spirit will come upon you, and the power of the Most High will overshadow you; and for that reason the holy Child shall be called the Son of God." (Luke 1:34-35)

Such is no pagan legend!

> And the doctrine of the virgin birth is not some borrowed, pagan myth. Rather, it explains how the eternal Son of God could enter our world as a "divine human." His origins were both earthly and heavenly, as the angel Gabriel announced to Miriam, the Messiah's mother: "The Holy Spirit will come upon you, and the power of the Most High will overshadow you. So the holy one to be born will be called the Son of God" (Luke 1:35).[28]

Humble Roots in Galilee – While the Messiah would be born in Bethlehem, the royal city of David located on the outskirts of Jerusalem, he would not grow up there. Rather, he would be raised in Galilee, the marginalized North, in the humble village of Nazareth.

> "But there will be no more gloom for her who was in anguish; in earlier times He treated the land of Zebulun and the land of Naphtali with contempt, but later on He shall make it glorious, by the way of the sea, on the other side of Jordan, *Galilee of the Gentiles.* The people

who walk in darkness will see a great light; *Those who live in a dark land, The light will shine on them.*" (Isaiah 9:1-2)

Jewish leaders in Jerusalem called it "Galilee of the Gentiles" because of its mixed population of Jews, half-Jews and pagans. Such, however, was according to God's plan. What people despise, God prizes. He was not ashamed to place the Light of the world in its darkest corner. Galilee became the headquarters for Jesus' ministry until making his final trip to Jerusalem.

Light to the Nations – The realm of this King would not be national, restricted to Israel, but universal. His righteous rule will not be confined to Israel!

> "Of the greatness of his government and peace there will be no end. He will reign on David's throne and over his kingdom, establishing and upholding it with justice and righteousness from that time on and forever." (Isaiah 9:8)

> "It is too small a thing for you to be my servant to restore the tribes of Jacob and bring back those of Israel I have kept. I will also make you a light for the Gentiles, that my salvation may reach to the ends of the earth." (Isaiah 49:6)

> The Injeel began with an introduction: "This is the genealogy of Jesus the Messiah the son of David, the son of Abraham. . . ."
> Matthew 1:1

Prophetic Summary – Look Ahead!

Ancient prophets alerted succeeding generations of a coming kingdom that would be universal in scope, righteous in character and everlasting in duration.

- **A King is coming who will be far greater than David.**
- **He will inaugurate a kingdom that is far greater than Israel.**

D. Jesus was God's Greater Son Announced in the Injeel

Four centuries of silence passed since Prophet Malachi penned the Old Testament's final message announcing the coming One. Had God forgotten his promise to David? It must have seemed so. Finally, the Injeel breaks the silence with its opening announcement.

> "This is the genealogy of Jesus the Messiah the son of David, the son of Abraham. . . ." (Matthew 1:1)

This genealogy of God's Messiah links the birth of Jesus to the royal line of David.[29] God's promises that were made a millennium earlier to David are finally being fulfilled! Light has pierced the darkness. Jesus' kingdom will stretch to include **all nations**. You can follow this theme through Matthew's outline:

> Part 1: Presentation of the King (1:1-4:1)
> Part 2: Proclamation of the King (4:12-7:29)
> Part 3: Power of the King (8:1-11:1)
> Part 4: Progressive Rejection of the King (11:2-16:12)
> Part 5: Preparation of the King's Disciples (16:13-20:28)
> Part 6: Presentation and Rejection of the King (20:29-27:66)
> Part 7: Proof of the King (28-1-20) [30]

Wrap-up

God alone is King who reigns through the royal line of David, human kings who are charged with listening and obeying him as sons to a father. These sons are now superseded by a Divine Son whose obedience will be perfect.

A huge problem ensued. This Messiah was rejected by Jewish leaders, the very ones who eventually conspired to send him to the Cross. Would their rejection send him the way of Zedekiah, the last Judean king, stripping Jesus of his royalty and shattering his claims to be God's unique Son?

CORE TEACHING 6: *Its Validation* – **Jesus' divine Sonship was proven by his resurrection from the dead.**

Let's review. Jesus' identity as the Son of God was first declared verbally, starting with the angel Gabriel's announcement to Mary that "the holy child will be called the Son of God" (Luke 1:35). Next came Jesus' baptism where a voice from heaven addressed Jesus directly, "You are my beloved Son; with you I am well-pleased!" Finally, it was heard by three of Jesus' closest companions who accompanied him in prayer, witnesses who also gazed upon his hidden sublimity made manifest through his transformed body: "This is My Son. Listen to Him!"

To be taken seriously, the audacious title Son of God demanded matching proof. What happened to drive this identity home even more deeply for the apostles, something moving it beyond an audacious claim to a certain fact, one they would declare to their deaths? The God of bold speech is also the God of stunning performance. The final answer to the question of Jesus' identity came without a single word. It was stated with power, making it news – *very* good news:

> ". . . the *gospel of God*, which He promised beforehand through His prophets in the holy Scriptures, concerning *His Son*, who was born of a *descendant of David* according to the flesh, who was *declared the Son of God with power by the resurrection from the dead*, according to the Spirit of holiness, Jesus Christ our Lord. . . . (Romans 1:3)

Jesus was declared the Son of God, not with verbal argument but visual persuasion. On the third day, he burst the chains of death and met with his followers, plus some skeptics, repeatedly over a forty-day period. During those times, he provided one proof after another that he was alive. What did this say about him? The earliest sermon after his resurrection announced the impact:

> "God has made this Jesus, whom you crucified, both Lord and Messiah" (Acts 2:36).[31]

Divine revelation reached its summit, providing humanity with the *aya* to top all *ayat*. That crowning miracle solidified Jesus' claims. He was in fact everything he said he was. It disclosed his identity beyond reasonable doubt.

The Apostles proclaimed Jesus as the "Son of God" to the most strident monotheists without being accused of

> The Apostles proclaimed Jesus as the "Son of God" to the most strident monotheists without being accused of pagan legend.

pagan legend.

Did the twelve apostles themselves believe in Jesus' divine Sonship, or was it a doctrine that was added later? Some uncritically view this teaching as the Church's invention borrowed from pagan legends that developed over time. That view overlooks two factors – when Jesus was first proclaimed the Son of God and to whom.

Within two months after Jesus ascended into heaven, the apostles preached their first message to devout Jews in Jerusalem, the heart of Judaism, in Acts 2:25-36. It directly links Jesus' death and resurrection as fulfilment of ancient promises made to King David. Son of God terminology figured central in their message:

> "Brethren, sons of Abraham's family, . . .to us the message of this salvation has been sent. For those who live in Jerusalem, and their rulers, recognizing neither Him nor the utterances of the prophets which are read every Sabbath, fulfilled these by condemning Him. And though they found no ground for putting Him to death, they asked Pilate that He be executed.

> When they had carried out all that was written concerning Him, they took Him down from the cross and laid Him in a tomb." (Acts 13:26-29)

Let's pause for a moment. In this audience were Jewish leaders who had rejected Jesus as Messiah and conspired his execution. They did not see this coming:

> "But God raised Him from the dead; and for many days He appeared to those who came up with Him from Galilee to Jerusalem, the very ones who are now His witnesses to the people.

Why didn't these pious Jews protest the apostles' message, "You are My Son; today I have begotten You"? We expect to hear charges of blasphemy for associating God with a female consort or goddess. And yet not a peep. Why? They heard it through scriptural filters. Familiar with God's promises to David's dynasty of a Son-Messiah.

And we preach to you the good news of the promise made to the fathers, that God has fulfilled this promise to our children in that He raised up Jesus, as it is also written in the second Psalm, '*You are My Son; today I have begotten You.*'

As for the fact that He raised Him up from the dead, no longer to return to decay, He has spoken in this way: '*I will give you the holy and sure blessings of David.*' Therefore He also says in another Psalm, '*You will not allow Your Holy One to undergo decay.*'

For David, after he had served the purpose of God in his own generation, fell asleep [died], and was laid among his fathers and underwent decay; but He whom God raised did not undergo decay.

Therefore let it be known to you, brethren, that through Him forgiveness of sins is proclaimed to you, and through Him everyone who believes is freed from all things, from which you could not be freed through the Law of Moses." (Acts 13:30-39 [Psalm 16:10])

Why didn't these pious Jews protest the apostles' message, "You are My Son; today I have begotten You"? We expect to hear charges of blasphemy for associating God with a female consort or goddess. And yet not a peep. Why? They heard it through scriptural filters. Familiar with God's promises to David's dynasty of a Son-Messiah, they did not associate it with pagan legend.[32] Many resisted their message, of course, but not for that reason. These audiences interpreted Son of God title against David's Royal Line, avoiding wrong connotations.

They also knew that David's prophecy written nearly 1,000 years earlier, "You will not allow Your Holy One to undergo decay," could not refer to David whose tomb holding his decomposed body was within walking distance![33] It could point to only one Figure, the One whom David had addressed as "Lord" (Psalm 110:1). Here is proof that the final and consummate King had come! Jesus' resurrection removed all doubt: God's promise had been fulfilled![34]

Belief in the divine Sonship of Jesus was not the product of late theological development. This extensive historical section prepares us for a final question surrounding Jesus' Sonship: Does it matter today?

CORE TEACHING 7: God's eternal Son gave his life in death for

human sin. God raised him as proof of his Sonship, his authority to forgive sins and to give eternal life to all who believe (1 John 5:12).

Only an eternal Being can impart eternal life. Having borne our sins and conquered the grave, all who receive the Son will receive forgiveness of sins, spiritual adoption and eternal life:

> "God has given us eternal life, and this life is in his Son. Whoever has the Son has life; whoever does not have the Son of God does not have life. I write these things to you who believe in the name of the Son of God so that you may know that you have eternal life." (1 John 5:12-13)

As a result, we have God's own assurance of life. Jesus' disciples become children of God through him.[35]

Summary

This chapter has shown that the basis for condemnation of the Son of God in the Qur'an – that it denotes a biological reality – has no relevance to the Injeel's account. It was, indeed, embedded in God's oath to King David of a perpetual dynasty and future kingdom without borders. God himself was the first to vocally affirm it and Satan the first to challenge it. Jesus proved an awareness of his Sonship starting at an early age and continuing into adulthood. Finally, this unique kinship was supernaturally validated by his resurrection from death and, as the eternal Son is uniquely able to impart eternal life.

> "Jesus is called the Son of God because he came forth from God the Father, because he was born to a young Jewish virgin, because he had an intimate and unique relationship with his Father, and because he was the Davidic king."[36]

CHAPTER 3

JESUS' TWO NATURES

Question 3: How can a human be God?

Q 3.1: "How do Christians explain the dual divinity and humanity of Christ? How does the Bible say it?"

Deification, the supreme folly that turns human heroes into divine beings, has a catch. It only works in Hollywood. Who wouldn't want to be Superman? Only in Tinsel Town can an ordinary Clark Kent become stronger than a locomotive and faster than a speeding bullet. It's time for a reality check. Thankfully, deification has no place in the New Testament.

People, under no circumstances, can become God. God alone is eternal; all creatures are finite. Human creatures have the same chance of merging with their Creator as marble statues with the artists who sculpted them. This scarcely requires elaboration except for the unfounded accusation that Christians believe otherwise when it comes to Isa al-Masih. Yusef Ali is but one of many to say so:

> People, under no circumstances, can become God.

The idea that Jesus is divine is a product

of human embellishment and excessive adulation that evolved over time. The first Christians initially believed that He was a prophet, nothing more, but later got carried away. They turned a great Prophet into a God-man! The Qur'an corrects this misguided and offensive teaching.[1]

The Qur'an itself conflates Jesus' deity with deification and then charges Christians with shirk:

"They do blaspheme who say: 'Allah is Christ the son of Mary.' But said Christ: 'O Children of Israel! Worship Allah, my Lord and your Lord.' Whoever joins other gods with Allah- Allah will forbid him the Garden..." (Al-Tin 5:76)

> Deeply rooted in the soil of first-century Judaism, the apostles were diehard monotheists. As such, elevating a man into the Godhead or making him a second God were out of the question.

Question 1 has already shown the Tawrat's adamant antipathy towards any form of creature-worship, human or otherwise. But what will the Injeel say? Will it continue that hard stance against deification or soften it to make an exception for Jesus? Was Jesus a human caterpillar who morphed into a divine butterfly? We cannot afford to dodge this question.

DID EARLY CHRISTIANS TURN JESUS INTO GOD?

Many lines of evidence rule out any possibility that Jesus' deity was the product of hero worship. I will mention just two.

Evidence 1: Belief in Jesus' deity sprouted in the soil of first-century Judaism.

The environment in which Jesus and his apostles lived would have nixed any exalted-Man notion of Jesus. One of the reasons for this is that the Scriptures – the Tawrat, Prophets and Zabur – were ingrained in them. Deeply rooted in the soil of first-century Judaism, the apostles were diehard monotheists.

As such, elevating a man into the Godhead or making him a second God were out of the question. Two cultural hallmarks support this.

Premium Value of Childhood Religious Education

First-century Judaism placed enormous value on religious education, particularly for boys. The Jewish historian, Josephus (late 1st century A.D.), indicates that religious learning was taken most seriously: 'Above all we pride ourselves on the education of our children.'[2]

> "The Jerusalem Talmud states that before A.D. 70, 480 synagogues existed in Jerusalem, each with its own bet sepher and bet Talmud (Megillah 3:1)."[3]

Schooling for children progressed through stages. Early education was the responsibility of the father:

> "Since the Talmud specifies that "the father must teach him" (i.e., the son), we may confidently assume that Joseph, Jesus' earthly [step-] father, was responsible for fulfilling this task."[4]

At age 10, instruction expanded beyond the home to more formal studies:

> "Up to the start of their teen years, youths attended elementary school, an institution attached to the synagogue. The earliest years were spent in the bet sepher, where the reading of the written law was taught.
>
> Around the age of 13, gifted and diligent pupils might continue their studies in their spare time at bet midrash, "house of study." These 'academies' were conducted by teachers of the law, some of considerable repute (e.g. Hillel and Shammai)."[5]

This educational process instilled monotheistic belief and immunized the community against encroachments against it.

Jewish Education was founded upon the Shema

The Shema creed introduced in Chapter 1 stated:

> "Hear, O Israel! The LORD, the LORD your God, the LORD is one! You shall love him with all of your heart. . ." (Deuteronomy 6:4).

This creed formed the crux of the covenant with God through Moses at the time God gave the Ten Commandments.[6] To love the living God who displayed his power (Deuteronomy 4:35) and lavished his grace (Deut. 7:6-9) meant, among other things, that **Israel must abhor all other gods which are fraudulent (Deut. 11:16-17) and loathe their detestable practices (Deut. 12:31; 18:9-11).** It also formed the core of this childhood education:

> "The biblical curriculum for the earliest phase of schooling (bet sepher) seems to have consisted in the Shema (Deuteronomy 6:4-9; 11:13-21), the law of tzitzit (or zizith, Numbers 15:37-41), the Hallel (Psalm 113-118), the Creation Story (Genesis 1-5), and the essence of the Levitical Law (Leviticus 1-8)." [7]

> "Jewish boys were taught this biblical passage [Deuteronomy 6] as soon as they can speak. The roots in which Jesus grew up were far more than mental assent to the one God. The Shema was the core and foundation of his faith."[8]

In his masterful work, *Our Father Abraham*, Wilson adds these key features of the Shema:

(1) It is located in the book of Deuteronomy, which in Jesus's day was the most widely circulated and popular book of the Pentateuch [Tawrat].

(2) It reinforced obedience with rewards and the consequences of disobedience with punishments (Deuteronomy 11:13-21).

(3) With 613 individual statutes of the Torah from which to choose, Jesus explicitly ranked it as Number One, calling it the "greatest commandment" (Mark 12:28-34; Matthew 22:34-40).[9]

Importantly, education reinforced strict adherence to the *Shema* at a young age.

The point is this. **Monotheism that was so deeply ingrained in the mindset of Jesus and his followers was non-negotiable.** Such an environment virtually guarantees a visceral reaction by Jesus' apostles against turning Jesus of Nazareth from a mere Clark Kent into a divine Superman. So the thinking of Jesus' disciples was shaped by OT Scriptures which were fiercely monotheistic.

Will Moses' hardline intolerance against deifying creatures in the Tawrat slacken off in the Injeel? Not a bit!

Evidence 2: The Injeel's Zero-Tolerance of Idolizing People

Another line of evidence shows an instinctive abhorrence throughout the Injeel towards any tendencies towards deifying the man Jesus.

3 Case Studies

The Injeel introduces several examples of men who were wrongfully worshipped.

Exhibit A: King Herod Agrippa

King Herod was a godless monarch renown for political cunning and ruthless cruelty. Having recently murdered one of Jesus' apostles, James, the brother of John, he hoped now to gain more curry with his Jewish audience who had applauded the murder.

> "Then Herod went from Judea to Caesarea and stayed there. He had been quarreling with the people of Tyre and Sidon; they now joined together and sought an audience with him...

On the appointed day Herod, wearing his royal robes, sat on his throne and delivered a public address to the people.

They shouted, 'This is the voice of a god, not of a man.' Immediately, because Herod did not give praise to God, an angel of the Lord struck him down, and he was eaten by worms and died. But the word of God continued to spread and flourish." (Acts 12:20-25)

Why would the audience shower such praise to this human king? It must have been quite a speech! Actually, it wasn't. Josephus, the first-century historian, provides a clue. This event occurred during the games held in honor of Caesar. King Herod's attire enhanced the moment:

"Clad in a garment woven completely of silver so that its texture was indeed wondrous, he entered the theatre at daybreak. There the silver, illumined by the touch of the first rays of the sun, was wondrously radiant and by its glitter inspired fear and awe in those who gazed intently upon it."[10]

The audience, riveted to this shimmering, larger-than-life figure, obviously went overboard: "The voice of a god, not of a man." A proper response to such over-the-top accolades? How about "Don't get carried away! I'm just a man." Instead, the pompous peacock said "Thank you" and was met with an immediate reality check:

"Instantly, an angel of the Lord struck Herod . . . he was consumed with worms." (Acts 12:23)

The judgment of God was immediate because God will not share his glory with another.

"This passage teaches us that Herod Agrippa's demise graphically portrays the truth that those who usurp God's place will face his swift and certain judgment and will by no means thwart the advance of his mission."[11]

King Herod shows us the wrong response to excessive honor when elevated to a divine pedestal. What, then, is the right way? Let's turn now to observe the disciples of Jesus when showered with similar accolades.

Exhibit B: Simon Peter

Simon Peter, highly esteemed by the early Christian community, had some notable firsts. With God's help, he was first to recognize Jesus' true identity as God's Messiah. He courageously delivered the first sermon of Jesus' resurrection just ten days after he had ascended into heaven to a massive audience in which stood Jesus' executioners. Afterwards, 3,000 Jews believed and were baptized. On top of these notable firsts, God performed healing miracles through Peter in Jesus' name. What a portfolio!

Did this reputation go to his head? One day, a Roman centurion by the name of Cornelius received a vision in which God told him to bring Peter into his home. One problem was that Peter, a strict Jew, would not step foot into a Gentile home. Miraculously, Peter agrees (Acts 10:9-16). One small part of this unfolding drama will tell us much about the character of this leader:

> "And on the next day he [Peter] got up and went away with them, and some of the brethren from Joppa accompanied him. On the following day he entered Caesarea. Now Cornelius was waiting for them and had called together his relatives and close friends.
>
> "When Peter entered, Cornelius met him, and fell at his feet and worshiped him. But Peter raised him up, saying, 'Stand up; I too am just a man.'" (Acts 10:24-26)

Peter instantly recoiled, wasting no time disavowing any accolades of being anything more than human. As a model of restraint, he showed zero tolerance for fawning adulation.

Exhibit C: Paul and Barnabas at Lystra

God was performing extraordinary miracles through Paul and Barnabas among people from pagan backgrounds in cities where superstition was rampant. As a result, people attempted to worship them.

"In Lystra there sat a man who was lame. He had been that way from birth and had never walked. He listened to Paul as he was speaking. Paul looked directly at him, saw that he had faith to be healed and called out, 'Stand up on your feet!' At that, the man jumped up and began to walk.

When the crowd saw what Paul had done, they shouted in the Lycaonian language, 'The gods have come down to us in human form!' Barnabas they called 'Zeus,' and Paul they called 'Hermes' because he was the chief speaker. The priest of Zeus, whose temple was just outside the city, brought bulls and wreaths to the city gates because he and the crowd wanted to offer sacrifices to them."

How will they respond? Say "Thank you!" like Herod or "Stop it!" like Peter?

"But when the apostles Barnabas and Paul heard of this, they tore their clothes and rushed out into the crowd, shouting: 'Friends, why are you doing this? We too are only human, like you. We are bringing you good news, telling you to turn from these worthless things to the living God, who made the heavens and the earth and the sea and everything in them. In the past, he let all nations go their own way. Yet he has not left himself without testimony: He has shown kindness by giving you rain from heaven and crops in their seasons; he provides you with plenty of food and fills your hearts with joy.'"

Even with these words, they had difficulty keeping the crowd from sacrificing to them." (Acts 14:12-15, emphasis added)

Paul and Barnabas claimed that they were merely human vessels of divine power, nothing more. But they didn't stop with disavowal. Neither did they condemn the superstitious idolaters who acted out of ignorance. Instead, they offered them an alternative by telling them about the true and living God.

Conclusion

So to your question on how a human can be God, it is impossible. The biblical writers under the guidance of the Holy Spirit, show revulsion to human aggrandizement. **Their message was clear: men cannot become God – including Jesus, Mary's son!**

But this presents us with a conundrum! The same Injeel presents us with Jesus as one having two natures, divine as well as human. If man cannot become God, how can that be? How do we explain the fact that strict monotheists can make a lone exception in the case of Jesus Christ? And why does Jesus, a Jew by birth, permit it?

Q 3.1: "How do Christians explain the dual divinity and humanity of Christ? How does the Bible say it?"

The outlandish fantasy of human deification is one thing; the holy miracle of divine incarnation quite another. Having dismissed the former, we are ready to consider the latter. Not only is it monotheist-compatible; it is breathtaking Good News for the human race. Something has been done for us that we could never do for ourselves. God broke a boundary that we could not cross to repair a broken world that we could not mend:

> The outlandish fantasy of human deification is one thing; the holy miracle of divine incarnation quite another.

> "Scripture indicates that there is nothing in us that can bridge the chasm between the creature and the Creator. We have no ladder to climb to heaven. The citizens of Babel, who tried to build a tower to heaven, found they were unable to do it. God's face is hidden to us unless he chooses to disclose it to us, and he has revealed his face to us in the person of Jesus Christ, the Son of God and the Word of God. Never settle for a secondhand picture of God."[12]

But how is incarnation possible? This is a reasonable question. If I were a Muslim encountering a Christian, my first question would be how is it possible that the Almighty Creator could become a man, a physical creature? Divine incarnation? **Can a mountain be squeezed into a shoebox?** If so, would it still be a mountain? Its apparent absurdity is implied in the question.

How wise is your question, "How does the Bible say it?" Of foremost importance is, *What says Scripture?* You're starting your search in the right place! Have you ever noticed that the only exercise some people get is jumping to conclusions? They hear just a crumb of information and make a whole cake out of it! Let's take a different approach and go directly to three weighty Scriptures to find out how they describe Jesus' two natures. I invite you to spend a few moments acquainting yourself with each one. They address your question head-on. Each discusses different facets about the dual nature of Jesus.

> Divine incarnation? Can a mountain be squeezed into a shoebox? If so, would it still be a mountain? Its apparent absurdity is implied in the question.

How the Injeel Describes Jesus' Two Natures

Earlier in Chapter 2 we read the Injeel's only two passages about Jesus' Virgin Birth. These historical accounts are told with artless simplicity that are free of legendary embellishment. They help us better understand how Jesus inherited his dual natures. So if you missed them, I encourage you to go back and read them. It is impossible for me to read these without being moved by a God so simultaneously mighty and good!

In addition to those historical narratives, the Injeel presents three theological summaries about Jesus' dual nature. I am not asking for your agreement, but your close observation. Those should never be confused. Even though they may contradict Islamic doctrines or cause unintended offense, we provide them because of a conviction that the right of Muslims to gaze upon the Injeel's full portrait of Jesus Christ equals that of Christians. That you can draw your own conclusions goes without saying.

A word to the wise. The more careful we are with our observations, the more accurate we will be with our interpretations. And the better our interpretations, the more fair-minded will be our evaluations. This process is the opposite of jumping to conclusions.

What to Observe

As you read each passage, what should you be looking for? Let me suggest four core questions:

1. Was Jesus really human? What words describe his humanity?

2. Did Jesus share God's nature? What terms are used to express it?

3. Which is the correct sequence?

   Option A: A man became God (human deification)
   Option B: A member of the Godhead became man (divine incarnation)

4. How does this miracle benefit people?

You may wish to use a pad to jot down your observations.

Passage #1: John 1:1-18 CJB

"In the beginning was the Word, and the Word was with God, and the Word was God. [2] He was with God in the beginning. [3] All things came to be through him, and without him nothing made had being. [4] In him was life, and the life was the light of mankind. [5] The light shines in the darkness, and the darkness has not suppressed it.

[6] There was a man sent from God whose name was John. [7] He came to be a testimony, to bear witness concerning the light; so that through him, everyone might put his trust in God and be faithful to him. [8] He himself was not that light; no, he came to bear witness concerning the light.

[9] This was the true light, which gives light to everyone entering the world. [10] He was in the world — the world came to be through him —yet the world did not know him. [11]

He came to his own homeland, yet his own people did not receive him. [12] But to as many as did receive him, to those who put their trust in his person and power, he gave the right to become children of God, [13] not because of bloodline, physical impulse or human intention, but because of God.

[14] The Word became a human being and lived with us, and we saw his Sh'khinah [glory], the Sh'khinah [glory] of the Father's only Son, full of grace and truth·

[15] John witnessed concerning him when he cried out, "This is the man I was talking about when I said, 'The one coming after me has come to rank ahead of me, because he existed before me.'" [16] We have all received from his fullness, yes, grace upon grace· [17] For the Torah was given through Moses; grace and truth came through Jesus the Messiah·

[18] No one has ever seen God; but the only and unique Son, who is identical with God and is at the Father's side — he has made him known."

Passage #2: Philippians 2:5-11

"Have this attitude in yourselves which was also in Christ Jesus, who, although He existed in the form of God, did not regard equality with God a thing to be grasped, but emptied Himself, taking the form of a bond-servant, and being made in the likeness of men. Being found in appearance as a man, He humbled Himself by becoming obedient to the point of death, even death on a cross.

For this reason also, God highly exalted Him, and bestowed on Him the name which is above every name, so that at the name of Jesus every knee will bow, of those who are in heaven and on earth and under the earth, and that every tongue will confess that Jesus Christ is Lord, to the glory of God the Father."

Passage #3: Hebrews 1:1-4; 2:9-10, 14-18 (NRSV)

"Long ago God spoke to our ancestors in many and various ways by the prophets, but in these last days he has spoken to us by a Son, whom he appointed heir of all things, through whom he also created the worlds. He is the reflection of God's glory and the exact imprint of God's very being, and he sustains all things by his powerful word. When he had made purification for sins, he sat down at the right hand of the Majesty on high, having become as much superior to angels as the name he has inherited is more excellent than theirs. (Heb 1:1-4)

But we do see Jesus, who for a little while was made lower than the angels, now crowned with glory and honor because of the suffering of death, so that by the grace of God he might taste death for everyone. It was fitting that God, for whom and through whom all things exist, in bringing many children to glory, should make the pioneer of their salvation perfect through sufferings. (Heb 2:9-10)

Since, therefore, the children share flesh and blood, he himself likewise shared the same things, so that through death he might destroy the one who has the power of death, that is, the devil, and free those who all their lives were held in slavery by the fear of death. For it is clear that he did not come to help angels, but the descendants of Abraham. Therefore he had to become like his brothers and sisters in every respect, so that he might be a merciful and faithful high priest in the service of God, to make a sacrifice of atonement for the sins of the people. Because he himself was tested by what he suffered, he is able to help those who are being tested." (Heb 2:14-18)

Your Observations

So what did you discover? Again, this is not about agreement or disagreement. I would love reading your observations on the four big questions.[13] Let me share mine.

THE 4 BIG QUESTIONS

1. Was Jesus really human? What words describe his humanity?

<u>John 1:14</u>: (1) The term used here for Jesus' humanity is *sarx*, literally, "flesh." It could not be plainer. It means fully human, emphasizing "frail creatures, mere flesh, in comparison to their majestic Creator."[14] There is nothing angelic about its properties.

(2) Jesus' humanity was created, what he "became" (v 14), not what he always was. As a condition that he acquired at a point in time, it was not part of his original nature. (3) Jesus "made his dwelling among us" further drives home how he co-mingled with other humans who were already present. In other words, Jesus entered into our world with both feet as a man among human beings. So, yes, Jesus became a bona fide man.

<u>Philippians 2:</u> (1) This passage describes Jesus' humanity using two parallel phrases. The first, "being born in human likeness" (*ginomai anthropos homoiinia*) highlights his entrance into the human race through birth resulting in a human life that manifested those human properties. The second phrase, "being found in human form" (*erisko anthropos skema*) extends that thought. That is, the condition into which Jesus was born was exactly what people actually discovered him to be: human, like them. When people referred to him, they said, "I met a man;" not, "I met an angel or quasi-human." (2) Jesus' humanity was created and began at birth, in contrast with his previous uncreated existence. (3) Jesus' humanity imposed new limitations on himself, even mortality, "to the point of death." (4) Becoming human like us was for Jesus a choice he made. It reflected an "attitude" or inner disposition of submission to God rather than self-promotion. So the answer is yes, Jesus became true man.

<u>Hebrews 1 and 2</u> – Four key elements point to Jesus' humanity. (1) He "shared flesh and blood," plainly referring to the human nature he "shared" with us. That is, his knowledge of humanity came through participation and not by distance learning or reading a book, *What*

People are Like. (2) "He himself likewise shared the same things" deepen his human experience by fully participating, identifying and engaging with the human family. He truly belonged by becoming just like them. (3) "He *had* to become like his brothers in every respect" (emphasis mine). Experiencing the full range of human experience was necessary for his mission: (4) Jesus' human condition was a voluntary step down from a prior status, having a definite starting point when he was "*made* lower than angels (emphasis mine)" by doing so. Again, our answer is yes.

2. Did Jesus share God's nature? What terms are used to express it?

John 1:1-2: Jesus' divine nature is set forth with utmost care and precision as the "Word of God." Verses 1 and 2 highlight four attributes in terms of time, personal distinction and essence. He was: (1) Co-eternal with God ("in the beginning was the Word" (also v 2). The pre-incarnate Word always accompanied God. Never was there a time that God existed without his Word. It was uncreated.

(2) Distinct from God ("with God," referring to the Father). (3) Shared the nature of God ("was God" [*theos en ho logos*]). (4) The pre-incarnate Word shared in the creation of all things (1:2). Verse 18 shows how the Word's unique attributes uniquely qualify him as God's full and true revelation on earth. The Word alone performed this incarnate act, not the entire Godhead. Otherwise, this miracle would have left a divine vacancy in heaven, an absurdity.

Philippians 2: Jesus' divine nature is not drawn by the mere fact of his pre-existence, but by two realities expressed about him during that period of time: his status and his attitude towards it. He was "in the form of God," pointing to his divine likeness. To this was added that he shared "equality with God," a phrase explicitly affirming his divine status. Equally remarkable was his attitude whereby he "emptied himself" of his exalted position, voluntarily relinquishing what was rightfully his because he "did not regard equality with God a thing to be grasped." His pre-incarnate disposition in heaven was necessary to make his physical destination on earth. Again, the answer is *yes*.

Hebrews 1:1-4: (1) Two vivid phrases describe Jesus' divine nature: (a) "the reflection of God's glory," means he literally manifested the divine Presence in a form that could be humanly perceived and (b) "the exact imprint of God's very being" presents Jesus as the replica of the Father or "who is just like what God really is."[15] (2) Jesus, an agent of creation, highlights his pre-incarnate presence with God before the world was formed. The absolute monotheism of the Injeel prohibits a second god. Will the Son who shared divine space violate God's unity or impose something foreign to God? Verse 3 answers with a resounding *No!* (3) Jesus entered our world not as a substitute for God but as "the exact representation of His nature," crisply revealing his God's character with 20/20 clarity. Such is impossible for any mere mortal. His divine nature qualified him to reveal God faithfully, reliably and infallibly without reducing, replacing or ousting him! (4) Given these credentials, Jesus' revelation of God surpasses the prophets. While both spoke with divine authority, Hebrews 1:1-2 makes a contrast. After centuries of the coming and going of one prophet after another faithfully delivering God's messages in bits and pieces, God spoke at last through his Son with unprecedented totality and finality.

Because Jesus reflected "the radiance of His [God's] glory," his sojourn on earth made the attributes of the invisible God conspicuous. The Son displayed publicly what previously had been privy to the angelic realm. This explains why a stroll through the pages of the Injeel will bring the reader to a strange awareness that that every place Jesus stepped became an epiphany, an eruption of divine glory. While often veiled by his human shell, its flashes are impossible to ignore. So again the text demands a *yes* answer.

3. Which is the correct sequence?

Option A: **A man became God (human deification)**
Option B: **A member of the Godhead became man (divine incarnation)**

John 1:14: Option B, divine incarnation. Option A would have required it to say, "the flesh [man] became the Word [God]" and not, as it says, "the Word became flesh." Thus, it began with God on the side of eternity. By definition, this is incarnation and not deification.[16]

Philippians 2: Option B, divine incarnation. Option A would have reversed the direction of Jesus' journey. Instead of starting from the divine realm and descending to earth as presented here, Jesus would have had to ascend from human nature into the divine. The heart of this passage, however, focuses as much on Jesus' mental attitude as it does about his change of address. In that regard, Option A would have portrayed Jesus as a restless man, one discontented with his humble station in life, who pursued more for himself – grandeur, autonomy, recognition and unrestrained self-mastery. Such a portrait is polar opposite of this Jesus.

Hebrews 1 and 2: Option B, Divine incarnation. Option A would have placed the ladder on the ground of human muck to climb to more blissful environs. It is doubtful that one who was "superior to angels" would have agreed to be "made lower than the angels." What happened here was clearly Option B.

The Son, the eternal co-Creator for whom mortality had been foreign, saw us, and taking note of our frailty and mortality, chose to make it his own and "partook of the same."

Let's move to our final Big Question.

4. How does this miracle benefit people?

John 1 – The incarnation benefits humanity in two overlapping ways. (1) It corrects our optical problem, showing us what we cannot see: "No one has ever seen God" (v 18). When the eternal Word pitched his tent among mankind as a man, "we *saw* his *Sh'khinah* [glory]," that "of the Father's only Son, full of grace and truth" (v 14). By this, "he [the Son] has made him [the Father] known" (v 18), lit. "led him out," i.e. made conspicuously noticeable. The illumination of Scriptural truth became crisp illustration through an embodied life. Jesus alone, as the eternal Logos, was able to pull this off, bringing earth-bound people a picture of God that was reliable in content, comprehensible in form and compelling in moral force.

(2) The incarnation removes our distance problem, bringing closeness to God where our sinfulness had imposed distance: "As many as did receive him, to those who put their trust in his person and power, he gave the right to become children of God" (v 12). This right of spiritual adoption is offered to all without natural pedigree: "not because of bloodline, physical impulse or human intention, but because of God" (v 13). Instead, it comes from God's "grace and truth through Jesus the Messiah" (v. 17)!

Philippians 2 – Jesus redefined success and rerouted the path to find it. Where conventional wisdom searches for it on the ladder of self-promotion, Jesus carved out a better path by "descending into greatness" in the service of others.

Specifically, the one aspect of Jesus' life called out for imitation here is his *attitude*: "have the same mindset that was in Christ Jesus" (v 5). Such an orientation provides the antidote to frittering our energies in trivialities by the Greater Pursuit as Jesus taught elsewhere:

> "So do not worry, saying, 'What shall we eat?' or 'What shall we drink?' or 'What shall we wear?' For the pagans **run after** all these things, and your heavenly Father knows that you need them. But seek first his kingdom and his righteousness, and all these things will be given to you as well." (Matthew 6:32-33)

The Jesus attitude of true significance is the readiness to improve the lot of others, an orientation marked by open hands. It counters the grasping hands of Adam, our first ancestor, for whom even Paradise wasn't enough. He wanted more. Tightly grasping at what was not his, he listened to the Evil One, and by his over-reach slid down the slippery slope. We've all been there. Jesus became his counterpart, reversing the curse by opening his hands, foregoing his divine rights and finally receiving the highest honor.

Hebrews 1 & 2 – Jesus' incarnation benefits us in both the here-and-now and the hereafter. (1) *Firsthand Experience with Our Common*

Challenges. Though by *nature* he was "much superior to angels" (Heb 1:4), by *choice* he was "made lower" than them (Heb 2:9). In doing so, he identified with us in our struggles since he was "made like us in all things." He became a "propitiation for the sins of the people," for whom he is a "merciful and faithful high priest in things pertaining to God."

(2) *Champion over Our Common Enemy.* Jesus demonstrated power over our greatest enemy – death! No person has ever overcome the power of death. But Jesus did! He became the author of our salvation. He suffered sin's penalty for humanity when he "tasted death for everyone" and overcame it when he rose from the grave and ascended into heaven. He liberates those who trust in him from the tyranny of fear, looking forward to the Day when he will bring them into his heavenly glory.

NINE FINE-TUNING QUESTIONS (FTQ'S)

You've raised *the* crucial question regarding the dual divinity and humanity of Christ: "How does the Bible say it?" Hopefully, your close attention to these three foundational Scriptures have helped to answer it.

I was struck by the interest level surrounding Jesus' nature you have shown by the variety of your questions. These move us beyond "the Big Four" to what I've grouped together as nine Fine-Tuning Questions" (FTQ's).

1. Did two natures really coexist in Jesus? Wouldn't that form a contradiction?
2. Does the incarnation violate God's immutability, causing his nature to change?
3. How did each nature (divine and human) relate to each other?
4. Did the addition of humanity to the eternal Word form a new partnership with God or create two gods?
5. Do the "Word of God" and the "Son" of God mean the same thing?
6. Does the incarnation limit Almighty God?

7. Did Jesus' humanity mean that he had sin?
8. Isn't Jesus' incarnation the same as Hindu avatars like Rama and Krishna?
9. Why was it necessary for two natures to unite in Jesus?

FTQ 1: Did two natures really coexist in Jesus? Wouldn't that form a contradiction?

Who hasn't wrestled with these questions! My good friend Kahlil brought home to me the challenge of grasping Jesus' two natures. Sitting at a table in Starbucks, we read John 1:1-18 together about God's eternal Word becoming flesh. He showed me how ludicrous this sounded. Taking a sheet of paper, he drew a line down the middle. Over the left column he wrote "God," and over the right, "Man." Then he asked me to describe the defining qualities and attributes appropriate for each which he listed. Under God, of course, he wrote words like infinity, immortality, immensity, etc. In the right column he wrote finite, ignorant, weak, and so forth. The incompatibilities between the two columns became obvious.

His point was well-taken. Since God cannot be contained something must give. By inserting infinite deity into limited humanity, the incarnation becomes an exploding balloon. For this fusion to work, it would require each part to lose its defining properties. Knowing Kahlil well as a reputable young man with gifted intelligence and philosophical training, I could not simply dismiss his protest. What can we say?

It is admittedly mind-boggling. Kahlil is correct. From our three-dimensional vantage point, conceptions in divine mysteries have all appearances of contradiction. And yet, it is presented to us as a historical fact of biblical revelation: "the [eternal] Word became [in history] flesh, and lived among us" (John 1:14). How do we reconcile the revelation with the logic?

In the following FTQ's, I hope to throw light on this important question.

> "Jesus possesses all the properties that are essential to a human being, and Jesus possesses all the properties that are essential to deity."
>
> Ronald Nash

FTQ 2: Did the incarnation alter God's nature, violating his immutability?

Adding humanity to the eternal Word did not alter divine nature which is immutable, an attribute that includes the eternal Word. The incarnation united these two natures in one person, the person of Christ, so that each remained intact, not forming a compound of one nature. The Word condescended to wrap itself in human form while retaining both natures.

> "In saying that the Word 'was incarnate' we assert . . . that the Word, in a manner indescribable and inconceivable, united personally . . . to himself flesh animated with a reasonable soul, and thus became man and was called the Son of Man." [18]

> "The natures which were brought together to form a true unity were different; but out of both is one Christ and one son. We do not mean that the difference of the natures is annihilated by reason of this union. [19]

Scientists use the term "immiscible" to describe liquids that are incapable of mixing with other liquids or attaining homogeneity. For instance, oil and water poured into a glass container and shaken up will settle into two separate layers. The opposite are those liquids that, when mixed, lose their peculiar properties. For example, milk and orange juice poured into a blender and stirred make a smoothie. Each element is obliterated so that the two become a new homogenized liquid.

Jesus' deity and humanity, while united, are immiscible. That is, just as oil, when mixed with water, doesn't cease to be oil and water does not lose its properties, so in the incarnation the uncreated Word did not cease being divine and the humanity received from his mother never ceased to be human. Both natures are retained. The incarnation, then, is not a mixing but a uniting. Jesus kept both natures fully intact.

FTQ 3: How did each nature (divine and human) relate to the other?

Let's address this in two ways: in terms of Jesus' two natures and then briefly in the interpersonal relationship between the Father and Son.

Jesus' Dual Nature

As seen above, the miracle of incarnation united two natures without altering either. The eternal Word did not cease to exist nor change in character by the addition of humanity.

> "Each nature performs its proper functions in communion with the other; the Word performs what pertains to the Word, the flesh what pertains to the flesh. The one is resplendent with miracles, the other submits to insults. The Word withdraws not from his equality with the Father's glory; the flesh does not desert the nature of our kind. . . And so it does not belong to the same nature to say 'I and the Father are one' and "The Father is greater than I' (John 10:30; 14:28)."[20]

In light of John 1:1, 14, the two natures of Jesus' incarnate state may be summarized like this:

> "Jesus possesses all the properties that are essential to a human being, and Jesus possesses all the properties that are essential to deity."[21]

FTQ 4: Did the addition of humanity to the eternal Word form a new partnership with God or create two gods?

Christians agree with Muslims: God is partnerless! And that partnership with deity amounts to polytheism – the creation of "two gods." And yet many, if not most, Muslims view Jesus' divine nature as created through partnership.

In the miracle of the incarnation, an entirely new creation was formed in the womb of a virgin by the power of the Holy Spirit.

First, partnerships require multiple parties who form a new relationship. These come in all forms like colleagues, spouses, associates, companions, teammates, helpers and sidekicks. Thirty-nine years ago when my wife and I said "I do" to each other, we entered partnership. Marriage, like all partnerships, share one common element: multiple parties.

Jesus' incarnation, by contrast, involved only one party, the eternal Word as the second Person of the triune Godhead who merged with a separate *nature*. To qualify as partnership, Jesus would have had to merge with a second party, mistakenly believed to be God. But the incarnation occurred when the divine Word partook of human *nature* and not a second party. Literally, "the Word became *flesh* (Jn 1:14). Had it said, "the Word became God," Christianity would be sunk in partnership and justly condemned as polytheistic. As we saw in Big Question 3, that scenario describes human deification, the fusion of man into the Godhead, both base and baseless. But Christianity has always taught the opposite:

> "The Scripture does not say 'the Word united himself to the person of a man,' but 'the Word was made flesh.' And that means precisely this, that he became partaker of flesh and blood, just as we do, and made our body his own. He was born of a woman; but he did not cast aside his being God. . . He assumed our flesh; but he continued to be what he was." [23]

No living person can enter the eternal Godhead to form a partnership. *Partnership* moves from bottom-up where an existing man is believed to join the Godhead. *Incarnation* came top-down when, by the power of the Holy Spirit upon order of the Father, God's heavenly and eternal Word entered our race through the sacred womb of a humble virgin. Partnership is travesty, incarnation mystery.

Second, and closely related, the incarnation formed a new creation altogether. We would be seriously mistaken to think the man Jesus, at some time during his life, merged with God. With utmost care and clarity, the Bible describes Jesus' birth as the formation of an entirely new person rather than a refashioning of someone already alive. The eternal Word wrapped itself in human flesh to become a *new* creation: Jesus of Nazareth. Ancient church fathers seriously weighed in on this:

"The mode of incarnation was full of significance: Instead of bringing with Him a body from heaven, the Lord made a new thing from the Virgin Mary, and put this on."[22]

"Deity and Manhood, by their inexpressible and inexplicable concurrence into unity, have produced for us the one Lord and Son Jesus Christ."[24]

One can only imagine the impact of God in the totality of his almighty, all-present being forcing himself into any living mortal. An exploding balloon comes to mind! Kahlil's objection was made on the basis of uniting infinity with an existing mortal. Had God united with Jesus in that way, uniting with him during his human life, it would indeed have squeezed a mountain into a shoebox. But Jesus was deity before he became man. He never was not Deity! How different was the holy genesis from the chaste virgin! Without it, the fusion of two natures would have constituted the absurd ascendency of a man and earned the wrath of shirk!

Third, partnership multiplies the number of gods by inserting an outsider into the Godhead; the incarnation preserved God's absolute unity, protected its inner- distinctions from contradiction and achieved God's purpose of salvation. The incarnation introduced nothing created into God but someone divine into the human race – the arrival of a Savior predicted by prophets centuries earlier. Such was the work of one God whose one nature was shared by the Father, the Son (Word) and the Spirit to achieve one purpose: rescue his creation from its bondage to evil. Remaining distinct in personhood, each worked in perfect tandem towards that goal. Jesus the Son revealed God to us as Father. We enlarge this emphasis elsewhere, but wish simply to show their consistency with monotheism and interpersonal compatibility:

"In no way does the incarnate Word violate the Shema [Deut. 6:4]. It unveils the interpersonal distinctions eternally coexisting within it (John 1:1-2). The Father designs each act and wills it and shares in the spiritual emotion consequent on it – in a word, does it, while the

actual execution is the Word's. There is no contradiction in terms here; the brain does an act, which a member executes, for example."[25]

This union of the second Person of the Godhead with human **nature** was no illicit partnership as would have been the case of merging two separate **beings.**

FTQ 5: Do the "Word of God" and the "Son" of God mean the same thing?

Almost. Their meanings overlap. As two expressions of divine revelation, yes, they are identical. In terms of bringing a full disclosure of the character of God, they are complementary. Let's take these one at a time. Two verses in John 1 show how both titles underscore Jesus' unique revelation of God:

> John 1:1 – "In the beginning was *the Word,* and the Word was with God, and the Word was fully God. . . The Word became flesh and lived among us, and *we have seen his glory. . .*" (emphasis added)

> John 1:18 – "No one has ever seen God. The *only one [Son]*, him- self God, who is in *closest fellowship with the Father, has made God known.*" (emphasis added)

Together these perfectly capture God's character for our benefit. God's embodied Word allows us to "see his glory" and the Son, having basked in eternal fellowship with the Father, is the more suitable to "make God known." There is so much overlap, but let me hazard a fine distinction: one emphasizes glory, the other personality.

"Just as the word is the expression of the speaker's thought, so the son is the manifestation of the father's character. As Word and Son, Jesus reveals the nature of God."
John T. Seamans

"The title 'Son of God' is the same as the title 'Word of God'. Both refer to the One who is the visible expression of the invisible God, not only when

He became incarnate and was given the name Jesus, but in His essential being throughout eternity."[26]

In terms of producing a full-orbed disclosure of God's character and purposes, the Word and the Son are complementary, each contributing something distinctive to our understanding of God. When verse 18 speaks of "the only one, himself God," it translates *monogenes* from which refers to the chosen Son without overtones of begetting (see Q2.2). But consider the complementary nature of these two terms:

"The Qur'an actually speaks of Jesus as 'the Word of God' or 'Word from God.' In Arabic, the prepositions 'of ' and 'from' signify the same genus. Thus 'Word of God' and 'Son of God' are identical in meaning. Just as the word is the expression of the speaker's thought, so the son is the manifestation of the father's character. As Word and Son, Jesus reveals the nature of God."[27]

What relationship exists between God and his Word?

"God does speak to men. He speaks through his Word, as I do. Where were my words before they came from my mouth? In my brain or in my thoughts? But if you cut open my head, you will not find them there. *In some mysterious way I and my words are the same.* Whatever my word does, whether pleasing you or annoying you, you can say that I am doing them. *So whatever the Word of God does, God himself is doing it.* In the same manner, the Father and Son are one. Whoever looks at the Son sees the Father."[28]

Together, the Word of God and the Son of God make Jesus the supreme revelation of God. A fuller divine self-disclosure is not possible.

"The title 'Son of God' does not apply only to Jesus in His human form. The 'Son of God' existed with the Father from eternity. This is why the Bible describes not only the Father as 'the First and the Last', but the 'Son of God' also (Revelation 1:17).

The 'Son of God' who is the 'Word of God' existed with the Father from eternity. He is the knowable God. He is called the 'Word of God' because the word reveals the hidden thoughts of a person. The word written or uttered is the visible expression of the invisible thoughts." [29]

FTQ 6: Did the incarnation limit Almighty God? (See Chapter 4)

The incarnation limits God only in the minds of those who deny his divine sovereignty by reducing him to the size of their religious traditions. The great Black preacher, Dr. Tony Evans, made this astute observation: "God is not who you think He is. He is who He says He is." Let's trust what he says.

> "If God can speak through human language, Arabic, why not through human personality? Which is the greater revelation? A book, or a life?"
>
> John T. Seamans

Great question. Let's address it on three levels – God's Being, his revelation and transcendence.

First, no, the incarnation subtracted nothing from the Almighty. Deity changes not, growing larger or becoming smaller. So in regard to his Being, words like "limit" and "God" never belong in the same sentence. The incarnation did nothing to modify God's changeless nature. Remember, only "the Word became flesh," not the Father who remained on his heavenly throne during Jesus' sojourn on earth. Nor during that time did the eternal Word ever cease being the Word. Manhood was added, not deity subtracted.

Second, in regard to humanity's access to the knowledge of God, the incarnation, rather than restricting it, actually did just the opposite. It dramatically expanded its range by unveiling what had been previously hidden from view. Thanks to this miracle, "we have seen his glory, full of grace and truth" (John 1:14).

Is this form of communication something we really want to protest?

"If God can speak through human language, Arabic, why not through human personality? Which is the greater revelation? A book, or a life?" [30]

106

The incarnation did, however, impose one limitation. By its very physicality and proximity, the Word's living embodiment in residence among men restricts the latitude of human speculation and the credibility of guesswork pertaining to God's character, purposes and will. Its sheer plainness of form and public display of unprecedented power – both moral goodness and creative sway – render man's common excuses of divine ignorance flimsy at best.

Let's consider the incarnation's third level of impact – God's majesty.

Is the Incarnation an Affront to God's Transcendence?

Some assert that the Sovereign Ruler of the universe would never stoop to become a mere man. It's below His dignity, they say.

The real issue here is not one of divine capacity, something we can agree is unlimited. The better question is: *Did the incarnation, an action requiring divine condescension, remove God from the height of his divine majesty as sovereign over all?*

To help us understand this, consider two human figures.

Albert Einstein

Consider the brilliant physicist, Albert Einstein. Let's pretend that one morning a second-grade teacher at an elementary school called in sick. The principal desperately searched for a substitute but with no success. He discovered to his delight that the famous Einstein happened to be in town visiting his sister. The principal has a crazy idea. He telephoned the scientist and said: "Dr. Einstein, we're honored to have you in our city. But we're desperate and I have a big favor to ask. A class of second graders is without a teacher today. Would give an hour of your time to teach them how to subtract?" To the principal's surprise, the eminent physicist jumped at the challenge. Thirty minutes later, he stood before a room full of high-pitched bundles of curiosity. Even for this mental giant, his wheels spun to create an on-the-spot effective lesson plan. The scientist did not disappoint. The children learned how to subtract.

In this scenario, would Einstein have succeeded by imparting to these eight-year-olds his latest thoughts on the theory of relativity? Of course, not. Success with these munchkins demanded that he meet them on their level by restricting himself to just a fraction of his vast intellect. He became less so they could become more.

More to the point, by choosing to limit his subject to basic subtraction did Einstein diminish his stellar reputation? Quite the contrary! His action showed the kind of person he was – a giant soul as well as a first-rate mind.

If a genius can taper the range of his intellect to benefit others without diminishing his identity or reputation, by what logic could Almighty God not do the same?

Why must we conclude that God's self-imposed limitation of privilege for the salvation of humanity make him any less in stature or call his Divinity into question? Why should we assume such a choice alters who he is rather than enlarges what we know of him?

Maybe there is a better example, a closer match to the divine Word's self-diminishment.

Mother Teresa

Consider the life of a young Albanian woman, Agnes Bojahbiu. Reaching age eighteen, she exchanged her life in the home of her prosperous family for a convent to devote herself to a life of prayer and service for seventeen years. While there, she learned of the indignities suffered by those living in the slums of Calcutta, India. Her heart went out to them. Soon, God called her to go to that massive city. Finally, she relinquished all the familiar conveniences afforded her in her convent and moved to the slums where she founded the Missionaries of Mercy. For nearly 50 years, she devoted herself to "wholehearted and free service to the poorest of the poor." Agnes Bojahbiu became known as Mother Theresa.

> "The impression of Jesus which the Gospels give is not so much one of deity reduced as of divine capacities restrained."
>
> J. I. Packer

By giving up her privileged station in life, did she cease being Agnes Bojahbiu? Who was she? When asked that question, her answer is revealing:

'By blood, I am Albanian. By citizenship, an Indian. By faith, I am a Catholic nun. As to my calling, I belong to the world. As to my heart, I belong entirely to the Heart of Jesus.'[31]

Both the scientist and the missionary kept their statures fully intact, unfazed by relinquishing their privileges for others. Far from diminishing themselves, their prominence increased and influence shined all the brighter.

"The impression of Jesus which the Gospels give is not so much one of deity reduced as of divine capacities restrained."[32]

FTQ 7: Did Jesus' humanity imply that he had sin?

Not at all, although it is natural to assume so. Given sin's universality, being human is commonly equated with being sinful. Wherever people live, sin always follows. But such was not always the case.

Like Adam, Jesus entered the world as a pure and morally spotless man. Also, both men's uprightness remained unproven until a time of testing from the Evil One. So the short answer to your question is that Jesus' humanity only made sin *possible* as a moral choice, but thankfully not inevitable.

Jesus, the Word who "became flesh" (Jn 1:14) assumed human nature with all of its limitations and freedoms, minus sin (see Q5.1, #1 and Q5.2, sign #5).

"He did not become partaker of our sins because he entered into fellowship with human infirmities. He assumed the form of a servant without the stain of sin, making the human properties greater, but not detracting from the divine."[33]

So becoming human does not imply that Jesus had sin.

FTQ 8: Isn't Jesus' incarnation the same as Hindu avatars like Rama and Krishna?

My good Bangladeshi Muslim friends dismiss the Christian teaching of Jesus' incarnation by equating it with the avatars of Hindu mythology. This association is logical, given their interactions in their country's religious populations (roughly 90% Muslim, 9% Hindu, .06% Buddhist and .03% Christian).[34]

But are they the same? In his classic work, *The Crown of Hinduism*, J. N. Farquhar who was known for his love for the people of India and his comprehensive grasp of their literature, wrote, "The belief that God actually appeared as a man, was born, and lived and died among men" is a fact found throughout sacred literature and heard in conversations with Hindu people.[35] Lumping Jesus' incarnation with their avatars overlooks four striking contrasts:

First, the divine incarnation in Jesus was a one-time occurrence. Hindu incarnations are repetitive.

Second, in Jesus we find an incarnation of God. Hindu avatars were humans who were then thought to become deified. It took centuries after their death for this to occur.

> "Rama, Krishna, and Gautama the Buddha, as they appear in the earliest literature, are men, and men only, indeed, are as far from being incarnations as any men could possibly be. Rama and Krishna are not even religious leaders in any sense: they are but kings and warriors; and it was *only some three hundred years after their appearance in literature that the belief arose that they were incarnations.*
>
> [Buddha's] system was determinedly opposed to the ideas that lie behind incarnation. To have the thought of himself as an incarnate god would have been revolting to him; and it was *at least five hundred years after his death* before his followers dared associate his name with the doctrine of the one living God."[36]

Third, Jesus' incarnation is actual history; Hindu avatars are clearly mythological.

"Every Indian incarnation story is a myth. Philosophic Hinduism is independent of history...Hindus are keenly conscious of this fact."[37]

Through Jesus' words and deeds, his incarnation as "Immanuel, God with us" was often immediately recognized.

"Those who knew Jesus best declared that in Him they had seen God revealed...Where in the history of mankind can we find anything resembling this, that men who had eaten and drunk with their Master should glorify him, not only as the revealer of God, but as the Prince of life, as the Redeemer and Judge of the world, as the living power of its existence, and that a choir of Jews and Gentiles, Greeks and Barbarians, wise and foolish, should along with them immediately confess that out of the fullness of this one man they have received grace for grace?"[38]

Fourth, and perhaps most important, Jesus' humanity was real and not imaginary. Unlike the avatars thought to incarnate Shiva or Krishna, etc., those are not truly human but only *appear* so. Even their *humanity* was an illusion!

"In the case of every Indian incarnation, the humanity assumed by the god is unreal. His human body is but a disguise; his human weakness and emotion are assumed; his limitations are but a pretense...There is never the idea that the incarnate God was confined to human conditions or limited to the powers of human nature. In the Gita all the stress is laid on the divinity of Krishna: he has a man-like form, but he is never conceived as a true man. He is always the god concealed in the seemingly human form."[39]

The same conceptions apply to Gautama, Siva and Rama whose human limitations, while believed necessary for the good of humanity, are called "a piece of deceit," "only sport" (*lila*), "the great master of the unreal," "mere acting."[40]

Was the humanity of Jesus a deception? Do either the Injeel or the Qur'an depict his humanity as a ruse? The Injeel defends his full and complete humanity as much as his deity. The Qur'an, while denying his divinity, it never calls his humanity into question. In fact, the earliest Christological heresy was not a denial of his deity, but of his humanity. Arising late in the first century, it argued that Jesus only *seemed* human ("Docetism", lit. "seems like"). They overlaid their view of Jesus with avatar-doctrine. The Injeel rebutted that view in the strongest possible terms:

> "Dear friends, do not believe every spirit, but test the spirits to see whether they are from God, because many false prophets have gone out into the world. This is how you can recognize the Spirit of God: Every spirit that acknowledges that *Jesus Christ has come in the flesh is from God*, but every spirit that does not acknowledge Jesus is not from God. *This is the spirit of the antichrist...*" (1 John 4:1-3)

FTQ 9: Why was it necessary for two natures to unite in Jesus?

The union of Jesus' two natures was necessary to fulfill his role as Mediator between God and humanity:

> "For there is one God and one mediator between God and mankind, the man [*anthropos*, "human," not *andros*, "male"] Christ Jesus, who gave himself as a ransom for all people." (1 Timothy 2:5-6)

An effective mediator must fully understand both parties being represented. The "man Christ Jesus" is better translated "human being," pointing to human nature rather than gender. The one representing us in the presence of the Almighty need not resort to guesswork about what we face (see Hebrews 4:15-16). There was nothing artificial about his humanity:

> "We must look upon Christ as a real historic figure, a real man, not a magical prodigy. He shared in the life of limited man, the life of His age and the life of His land. The limitations of His consciousness was no limitation of His moral power but its exercise."[41]

Why did God go to such enormous lengths?

"The Gospel Christ is the Being Who came down to earth and lived our life and was possessed of a frame like ours. He became Man in order to show the relationship man was to hold to God and by His death and resurrection He can put any man into that relationship. Jesus Christ is the last word in human nature."[42]

Conclusion

My goal has been to present this truth in its Scriptural simplicity, beauty and power. As the Injeel witnesses, "Thanks be to God for his indescribable Gift!"

Is the incarnation really scandalous? The God who spoke the cosmos into existence never asks permission nor apologizes for his revelation.

"If God is truly sovereign, can he not choose to become a man and reveal himself in person? Who are we to deny Him that right?"[44]

Yes, we often stammer in our attempts to capture this marvelous miracle. Through it we have found a God of grace and truth who freely acted for the welfare of all.

"For you know the grace of our Lord Jesus Christ, that though he *was rich*, yet for your sake he *became poor*, so that you through his poverty might become rich." (2 Cor 8:9, emphasis added)

CHAPTER 4

JESUS' HUMAN LIMITATIONS

Question 4: "Why is Isa a god or a son of god if he is a human being like us?"

Q4.1: "According to the Bible, someone called Jesus *(pb*uh) a good teacher. Jesus replied by saying, 'Why do you call me good? The good is only one God.' How do you say Jesus is God?"

Q 4.2: "How do you say that Jesus is God but we can't see anything in the Bible that says that? All we can see is that he always says 'Father' and 'I have no power, but all my power comes from my Father.'"

Q 4:3: If all three members of the trinity were God, wouldn't each member know what the others knew? When Jesus was asked about when the end of the world would come, why did he say he didn't know, only his Father did?

Q 4.4: How can Jesus be a part of god when he prays to God himself?

Q 4.5: If Jesus was divine, then why did he fast and pray?

Q 4.6: When Jesus prayed, to whom did he pray? Himself?

Q 4.7: Did Jesus tell us "Pray to me, fast to me. . .I'm God. . .?"

Th ese probing questions of clarification follow naturally after the previous discussion on the incarnation. They capture the interest of both Muslims and Christians. We saw previously that Jesus behaved like a human being because his humanity was real and that his dual nature was necessary for Him to fulfill His role as Messiah and Mediator, the One who bridged the gap between God and humankind. Your questions force us to grapple with how to reconcile Jesus' human limitations with his deity. Do they require us to call his divine nature into question?

Same Nature, yet Subordinate

> Do Jesus' human limitations require us to call his divine nature into question?

How are we to understand such statements as "the Father is greater than I?" What is important to learn here is the interpersonal structure of the Godhead and the hierarchical relationships within it. Specifically, Jesus placed his submission to the Father on full exhibit while retaining his kindred nature with him. The focus here is on his position within the Trinity, not his divine nature. This upholds the absolute unity of God in one Godhead.

Nabeel Qureshi offered this helpful comparison. If I compare myself with President Obama by saying, "He is greater than I,' is this correct? *Yes*, in the sense that he has a much higher office or role than me. But is he more of a human being than me? No. But his role is higher than I."[1] Similarly, Jesus shared the Father's divine nature while calling his Father "God" because of his subordinate position.

Q 4.1: "According to the Bible, someone called Jesus (*pbuh*) a good teacher. Jesus replied by saying, 'Why do you call me good? The good is only one God.' How do you say Jesus is God?"

It is easy to understand why this admission by Jesus poses a serious problem to anyone who contends for his divine nature! These words sound more appropriate coming from our next-door neighbor than a divine Being. And yet Jesus did, in fact, say them:

"A certain ruler asked him, 'Good teacher, what must I do to inherit eternal life?'

'Why do you call me good?' Jesus answered. 'No one is good—except God alone. You know the commandments: 'You shall not commit adultery, you shall not murder, you shall not steal, you shall not give false testimony, honor your father and mother.'

'All these I have kept since I was a boy,' he said. When Jesus heard this, he said to him, 'You still lack one thing. Sell everything you have and give to the poor, and you will have treasure in heaven. Then come, follow me.' When he heard this, he became very sad, because he was very wealthy." (Luke 18:18-23)

What are we to make of this? It sounds exactly as your question suggests, that Jesus is making a clear disclaimer that he is good and, by his own logic, that he is God.

Anytime we come across a statement in a single literary work that is totally out of sync and completely at odds with everything else, it catches our attention and forces us to take a closer look. For the person in search of a certain outcome for the purpose of challenging Jesus' deity, such a quotable verse would serve them well. But such bias would blind them to the obvious fact that the human authors of the New Testament were not dummies. Left to their own devices, they could have left out a statement they heard Jesus make, anticipating how it might be yanked out and used against Jesus. The Holy Spirit who inspired them what to write, however, was not so concerned. Others who sincerely desire to understand who Jesus is and who invest the time will come to see that this contradiction is only apparent.

For starters, this statement was made by Jesus in a one-on-one conversation. Conversations are not lectures. Lectures typically dispense general truths in a manner more appropriate for general audiences. Conversations pinpoint issues that are pertinent to a specific matter at hand often involving one individual, in this case, a rich young ruler of a synagogue's governing body.

Ignoring the immediate context obscures its meaning and too easily creates a contradiction where there is none.

No counselor worth his or her salt would dispense the same advice to all their patients. That was the error made by Prophet Job's (Ayub's) counselors in his grievous suffering. Their platitudes completely missed the mark of their sick patient! Let's not miss the point. For Jesus to make a one-of-a-kind statement to a particular individual should neither surprise nor alarm us.

To correct a specific problem that was ailing a man, Jesus uncovered it and offered a solution. While his issue was personal, it illustrated a more widespread human malady of spiritual pride. Luke 18 is all about humility. Note the progression: (a) a humility-parable, (b) a humility-talk, (c) humility on display and then (d) humility's absence.

Jesus began with a story. Parables, stories that illustrate a truth, often take aim at a certain type of people. This one was no exception. Jesus directed it to "those who were confident of their own righteousness and looked down on everyone else" (Luke 18:9).

> "Two men went up to the temple to pray, one a Pharisee and the other a tax collector. The Pharisee stood by himself and prayed: 'God, I thank you that I am not like other people—robbers, evil-doers, adulterers—or even like this tax collector. I fast twice a week and give a tenth of all I get.'
>
> But the tax collector stood at a distance. He would not even look up to heaven, but beat his breast and said, 'God, have mercy on me, a sinner.'" (Luke 18:10-13)

Jesus then applied the truth: "I tell you that this man, rather than the other, went home justified before God" (Luke 18:14). Looking into the faces of his audience, Jesus brought the point home:

> "For all those who exalt themselves will be humbled, and those who humble themselves will be exalted" (Luke 18:15).

Next, as people crowded around Jesus, parents brought their little children for Jesus to bless them. His disciples would have none of it! "Scram, kids! Jesus has more important things on his agenda than babysitting." Jesus overheard it and became indignant, but not with the children (Mark 10:14)!

"But Jesus called the children to him and said, 'Let the little children come to me, and do not hinder them, for *the kingdom of God belongs to such as these.*'" (Luke 18:16)

To whom does the kingdom of God belong? To those who exhibit certain childlike characteristics. These little people who Jesus welcomed to sit on his lap pictured the hallmarks of kingdom citizens: full trust, spontaneous joy, hearts bursting with gratitude and completely free from religious pride! So what kind of people will enter God's eternal kingdom?

"Truly I tell you, anyone who will not receive the kingdom of God like a little child will never enter it" (Luke 18:16).

Here Jesus clearly taught that God's kingdom is not an award to be earned but a gift to be gladly received as a child takes a gift from a loving father.

Immediately following, we meet our young man, a member of the governing body at a local synagogue. He asks Jesus: "Good teacher, what must I do to inherit eternal life," that is, to share the life in the world to come, the kingdom of God? Jesus perceived a quality of superficiality in the man, evidenced first by calling Jesus, who he does not even know, "good," and later surfacing in appraising himself as righteous.

"The title showed the speaker's charm, perhaps too much of compliment, and too little penetration of thought; for the word 'good' is a profound depth. . ."[2]

True goodness implies an "unlimited range of moral activity and in that sense belongs only to God." What is goodness?

"It must be constantly reexamined, or it becomes mere respectability. . . 'Good people,' so-called, are not usually adventurous: they are more often circumspect and perhaps censorious. Many 'good people' are good only in what they refrain from doing: they think that goodness originated in the era of Queen Victoria rather than in the holiness of God. The Pharisees were good, but their goodness became locked against the thrusts of God, and therefore hardened into an ethic and a ritual. Continuing to be selfish, it festered; and they helped to crucify Jesus."

"Our goodness is only partly good. We condemn fleshliness, as is right; but we do not often condemn legalized avarice or the standardization of man's mind. How goodness needs to be scrutinized!

"To say that none is good save God does not necessarily express a low view of human nature. It is a realistic view; but because God has visited man in Jesus Christ and still visits man in the Holy Spirit, it is a hope-filled view. It rebukes our notion that by moving the furniture we can change the soul." "Why do we call Jesus good? Only God is good, yet men will always call Jesus good. Who then is Jesus?"[3]

Jesus answered this man on his own terms. First, he ascribed only to God the quality of absolute "good" and then prescribed obedience to the commandments, what he must "do," as the doorway into eternal life. Jesus selected only four of the ten commands, those dealing with loving the neighbor. The young man's response, "I've done all that," echoed the bragging Pharisee in Jesus' parable rather than the humble tax-collector.

"He may have abstained from sin outwardly, but his response to the next demand of Jesus show that he neither loves God completely nor his neighbor entirely."[4]

Jesus exposed his superficial religious pride about loving his neighbor with his command: "Sell off your estate, give it away and come and follow me." The man became sad and left.

Jesus then said, "How hard it is for the rich to enter the kingdom of God" (Luke 18:24). Those within earshot of this whole back-and-forth asked: "Who then can be saved?" Jesus answered, "What is impossible with man is possible with God" (Luke 18:27).

Here's the point. Jesus was not making a theological statement about himself, but uncovering a spiritual condition of a man.

This is followed by two more Jesus encounters, not with the self-assured religionists, but with two unlikely candidates for blessings in the kingdom of God: a blind beggar's desperate plea, "Jesus, Son of David, have mercy on me" (Luke 18:35-43) and a shady tax collector who has amassed his wealth by cheating others (Lk 19:1-10). Unlike the ruler, both seized onto the kingdom like a child receiving an ice-cream cone.

Q 4:3: "If all three members of the trinity were God, wouldn't each member know what the others knew? When Jesus was asked about when the end of the world would come, why did he say he didn't know, only his Father did?"

Indeed, Jesus' admission of ignorance about the exact date of his return amazes us! Before we impulsively dismiss his deity on this basis, we should examine the context of his statement. Again, anytime we come across a statement in Scripture that seems contradictory or out of place, our first response is examine its setting. This is sound interpretive practice. Let's read it in context:

> *"But of that day and hour no one knows, not even the angels of heaven, nor the Son, but the Father alone.* For the coming of the Son of Man will be just like the days of Noah. For as in those days before the flood they were eating and drinking, marrying and giving in marriage, until the day that Noah entered the ark, and they did not understand until the flood came and took them all away; so will the coming of the Son of Man be." (Matthew 24:35-39)

What are we to make of this? Does it call his divine nature into question?[5] It is admittedly baffling in light of the extent of his knowledge. Over and over we see Jesus knowing what could not be known through normal human faculties. He saw the secrets lurking in human hearts (God is called the "heart-knower")[6] and predict future events as though they happened yesterday (the Fall of Jerusalem decades in advance, even his own death when everyone else denied it). Never do we find him trapped by the wiles of his enemies nor caught off guard. So what is behind his admission, "Only the Father knows?"

The Context of "I Don't Know" in Matthew 24:4-31

Jesus applies four striking claims to himself in this passage that force us to reconsider dismissing his deity.

Jesus' Claims

1. His Range of Knowledge – Recalls the Ancient Past and Predicts the Distant Future

First, in Matthew 24:4, Jesus begins to answer the disciples' questions about the signs that would precede his future coming. He describes the perilous turbulence and tribulation on earth during the last days. He gives detail after detail of the end times with matter-of-fact familiarity. In verse 37, he described the days of Noah at the time of the Flood from 3,000 years earlier. His description of these events are told as if they happened yesterday. These verses demonstrate the range of his knowledge. The point is that Jesus spoke with firsthand knowledge of the ancient past and the distant future, a divine attribute (Isaiah 44:7-8).

2. Authority over the Angelic Realm

Next, Jesus pivots from the earth's dreadful darkness to action in the heavens, pointing ahead to his glorious return.

"Then will appear the sign of the Son of Man in heaven. And then all the peoples of the earth will mourn when they see *the Son of Man coming on the clouds of heaven, with power and great glory.*

And he will send his angels with a loud trumpet call, and they will gather his elect from the four winds, from one end of the heavens to the other." (Matthew 24:30-31)

Since when does a person tell angels what to do? Yet Jesus orders them to "go," and they go. How remarkable is this? Who else, other than Almighty God, has such authority?

Since when does a person tell angels what to do? Yet Jesus orders them to "go," and they go. How remarkable is this? Please consider the significant place angels have in Scripture:

- Angels belonged exclusively to God, often identified as the "angel of the LORD" (Genesis 22:15; Numbers 22:22; Judges 6:22, Matthew 1:24, 2:13, etc.).
- Angels worship God in His presence (Luke 1:19; Revelation 7:11) for his works of creation (Job 38:4-7; Psalm 148:1, etc.), for his kingdom (Psalm 103:19-21; Revelation 11:15) and his salvation (Isaiah 44:23; 49:19; Luke 2:13-14; 15:10; Hebrews 1:6).
- Angels are God's "servants" (Psalm 103:20), who are sent to reveal his will to prophets and people (Isaiah 40:3-5; Daniel 8:15-16; Zechariah 1:8-10).
- Angels possessed supernatural powers to do God's bidding as "his [God's] ministering spirits sent out to serve" (Hebrews 1:6). They were not to be trifled with. For example, when two angels rescued Abraham's nephew, Lot, from the wicked city of Sodom they stopped a gang rape by striking the assailants with blindness (Genesis 19:10- 11). If a person of faith was visited by an angel, the first words they would hear was "Fear not," as in the case of Zacharias, the father of John the Baptizer (Yahya) (Luke 1:11-13).
- Angels carry out God's judgments on earth (Genesis 19:13, 24-25; Exodus 12:23; Acts 12:18-23). They will accompany Jesus when he returns to judge (Matthew 16:27; 25:31; Mark 8:38; 1 Thessalonians 3:13; 2 Thessalonians 1:7).
- Angels must never be worshipped (Matthew 4:9-10; Revelation 22:8-9; Romans 1:25; Colossians 2:18).
- Angels are commanded to worship Jesus (Hebrews 1:5-13). They served Jesus, not vice versa. They cared for his needs at critical times during his earthly sojourn (Matthew 4:11; Luke 22:43) and they stood ready to protect him from crucifixion even though he refused their help (Matthew 26:53).

But Jesus commands angels! This presents us with a crucial question. *What is Jesus' relationship to these creatures possessing such extraordinary power?* The answer becomes most evident by this significant contrast:

Notice that now Jesus does not say, he will send "God's" angels but "his" angels, those belonging to him as the Son of Man. He orders angels to "go" and they go. Who else, other than Almighty God, wields that kind of authority?

Jesus informs us when the final day arrives, that he, "the Son of Man," will dispatch these celestial creatures to prepare for that last Hour: "he will send out *his* angels..." Who then has highest authority? Angels, prophets or Jesus?

Angels command prophets what to preach and they obey them.

Jesus commands angels what to do and they obey him.

Jesus made this claim for himself because he knew who he was and that from eternity past and future, "all God's angels must worship him [Jesus]" (Hebrews 1:6). This second clue provides insight into Jesus' view of his position. He placed the angelic realm beneath himself, not above him.

3. His Word is Final

Scriptures often contrast fleeting human lives with the God's everlasting Word. Immediately on the heels of this section, Jesus says this about his own teachings:

"Heaven and earth will pass away, but My words will not pass away." (Matthew 24:35)

Whose word carries this level of authority? First Jesus calls the angels his own and now the Word of God as his own.

"Heaven and earth will pass away, but My words will not pass away." Jesus, Matthew 24:35

123

4. His Transcendent Identity – The Son of Man

Jesus foretells history's final Day when he will descend from heaven on the clouds with incomparable power that Daniel prophesied (Dan 7:13-14). Doesn't only Yahweh ride on the clouds?[7] He identifies himself as that Son of Man coming in glory. This transcendent Figure as far more than a man with clay feet. Chapter 5 elaborates on the Son of Man.

What Can We Say?

The sum total of these four claims made by Jesus – I possess knowledge of the ancient past and distant future, have command over angels, speak imperishable truth and am the divine Figure introduced in Daniel 7 – say much about his self-understanding. Together they point to someone assuming an identity that far exceeds any prophet.

And yet, tucked in the middle of this, we hear Jesus admit: "only the Father knows." So it is fair to ask why Jesus was left in the dark regarding the exact day of his return.

This combination of Jesus' exalted self-identity with his startling admission evokes curiosity, forcing us to look beyond our simplistic categories for him.

Insights into Jesus' Nature

1) *Complexity of Jesus' Nature* – Promising to return on "clouds of glory" while admitting "I don't know" regarding a detail about it is logically consistent with his dual nature.

2) *Totality of Jesus' Submission* – Jesus did not know the answer to the question because he came to obey the Father. By his own admission, he did nothing on his own initiative (John 5:30), including both his miracles (John 5:17, 19-24; 10:37-38) and his teaching:

> "My teaching is not mine, but His who sent me." (John 7:16; see John 12:49-50)

> "For I did not speak on my own, but the Father who sent me com-

manded me to say all that I have spoken. I know that his command leads to eternal life. So whatever I say is just what the Father has told me to say." (John 12:49-50)

It is clear that Jesus was content with the role of God's revealer to man and not his replacement! Anyone responsible to represent another must forego certain personal freedoms. Such a task precludes them doing their own thing or making a name for themselves. As the revealer of Another, Jesus was not about self-promotion. His default-mode was just the opposite, subordinating himself to the Nth degree before the One who sent him. Jesus held nothing back! And that included being willing to forego the full range of his knowledge.

Such limitation was not permanent. After Jesus had risen from the grave, so did the limitations connected with it. Then when his disciples asked him a second time when the End would come, instead of answering "only the Father knows," he said, "it is not for you to know" (Acts 1:6). This suggests that his previous human limitations that were part and parcel to his mission in the world, now having been fully completed with his death, were removed.

This agrees with the Qur'an's designation of Isa as "the Sign of the last hour, or knows when the last hour will be" (Al-Zukhruf 43:61, RQ).

3) Expression of Divine Wisdom – The Father's withholding of this information from his Son and then the Son from his disciples had nothing to do with Jesus' nature. His mission on earth was never to be a first-century Wikipedia, answering curiosities on non-essentials. The human appetite for irrelevant information is insatiable. On the essentials, however, Jesus held nothing back. That need-to-know came in verse 44:

> Rather than a contradiction, divine majesty and human frailty converged in Jesus as a revelation showing the infinite lengths to which God went to rescue us from ourselves.

"So **you also must be ready**, because the Son of Man will come at an hour when you do not expect him." (Matt. 24:44)

That is relevant knowledge! Not days and times but our perpetual readiness! Had the Father divulged the exact date to the Son, it would have been utterly useless. God never wastes words.

4) Measure of Sacrificial Love – Jesus' admission says far more about his willingness to put others first than it does about any deficiency thought to undermine his divine identity. Acknowledging one's limited knowledge can just as easily express personal choice as prove identity. Distinguishing Jesus' unlimited knowledge by virtue of his divine nature from his limited knowledge as his own choice. This vital distinction guards us against hasty denigration – "Obviously, He's not divine" – to a new elevation – "Look at the extent of His sacrifice!" Without forfeiting his divine nature, he set aside his own considerable privileges for the greater good. What grace!

> "For you know the grace of our Lord Jesus Christ, that though He was rich, yet for your sake He became poor, so that you through His poverty might become rich." (Injeel, 2 Corinthians 8:9)

By making himself less Jesus displayed the greater character of love. This explains how Jesus could admit that the Father knew something that the Son did not.

The answer might be summed up this way. Jesus' omniscience arose from his unchanging deity, its temporary suspension from his voluntary entrance into humanity for its redemption! One expressed the full capacities belonging to his transcendent nature while the other his courageous moral choices of self-sacrifice. Rather than a contradiction, divine majesty and human frailty converged in Jesus as a revelation showing the infinite lengths to which God went to rescue us from ourselves.

Jesus' Prayer-Life Question-Set

Q 4.4: How can Jesus be a part of god when he prays to God himself?
Q 4.5: If Jesus was divine, then why did he fast and pray?
Q 4.6: When Jesus prayed, to whom did he pray? Himself?
Q 4.7: Did Jesus tell us "Pray to me, fast to me. . .I'm God. . .?"

These questions present us with an apparent absurdity by fusing what appears to be two conflicting claims: that Jesus prayed and yet was divine. Since God doesn't pray to himself, how can Jesus be "a part of god" since he prayed? Before answering, let's take a fresh look at Jesus' payer life to see if we find any keys for solving this mystery.

Key #1: Jesus prayed during his life on earth.

Jesus was certainly a man of prayer. It was his habit, one could say, his instinct. Prayer was not for show. Most of his prayers, in fact, were prayed privately, away from distractions:

> "After He had sent the crowds away, *He went up on the mountain by Himself to pray*; and when it was evening, He was there alone." (Matthew 14:23; also Mark 6:46)

> "In the early morning, while it was still dark, Jesus got up, left the house, and *went away to a secluded place, and was praying there.*" (Mark 1:35 NASB)

Sometimes he prayed all night long when faced with choices of great consequence. When he selected the Twelve Apostles, "he went off to the mountain to pray, and he spent the whole night in prayer to God" (Luke 6:12-13).

Jesus also prayed in the presence of others. He prayed before meals (Mark 6:41), in the company of his disciples at the Last Supper (Mark 14:22), with two of his followers before breaking bread (Luke 24:50). On one occasion, he took his inner-circle away to a place for special prayer (Luke 9:28).

Key #2: Jesus prayed like no one else.

How did Jesus not pray? Did he offer formal and ritualized prayers? No. Practice meditation to probe his inner self? No. Pray eloquently with impressive words? No. Tap into spiritual powers with magical mantras like shamans? No. Babble on and on repeating the same words? No. Pray facing the Temple? No. Pray like anyone else in his day? No. How, then, did Jesus pray?

Prayer was as natural for Jesus as a private conversation between two soul-mates. It did not follow a script. He prayed personally, sometimes with gut-wrenching tears and other times with jubilant joy. One thing was certain. Jesus prayed as if someone was listening. For example,

> "During the days of Jesus' life on earth, he offered up prayers and petitions with *fervent cries and tears* to the one who could save him from death, and he was heard because of his reverent submission. Son though he was, he learned obedience from what he suffered . . ." (Hebrews 5:5-7)

In fact, so remarkable were Jesus' prayers that the only request made by his disciples was "Lord, teach us to pray!" (Luke 11:1), not "teach us how to heal the sick or to preach." It was as though they said, "Lord, your prayers are not only heard but answered. We want to pray with that kind of intimate connection to God."

What was his secret? Why was Jesus alone so freed up in the presence of God? That uniqueness in prayer signaled one thing: his unique relationship with God.

Key #3: Jesus always addressed God in prayer as his Father.

Jesus prayed as he did because of his close relationship with God the Father. While learning methods of prayer are not wrong, prayer was not a matter of learning proper techniques, physical motions and memorizations. There is no evidence that anyone taught him to pray so naturally. He prayed that way because it *was* natural. Intimacy expressed something else: kinship.

This inside knowledge was privy only to Jesus: "No one knows who the Son is except the Father" and "no one knows who the Father is except the Son" (Lk 10:22). Known to Jesus alone, it had to be imparted. So Jesus taught his disciples, "When you pray, say: Father. . ." (Lk 11:2). His prayers were personal rather than generic. What made it so was that, for Jesus, prayer was Father-Son communication.

Jesus' composure in prayer during his time on earth is explained by "the only Son, who is close to the Father's heart" (John 1:18), a kinship that preceded his coming to earth.

Prayer's primary ingredient, according to Jesus, was recognizing the One receiving it. This is illustrated in a conversation between Jesus and a Samaritan woman. She brought up the ancient dispute between Jews and Samaritans over the right place of worship:

> "Our ancestors worshiped on this mountain, but you Jews claim that the place where we must worship is in Jerusalem." (John 4:20)

Jesus gently corrected her by supplying what she had omitted: a direct object! Prayer for her was about where it happens; for Jesus, to Whom it is addressed:

> "Woman," Jesus replied, "believe me, a time is coming when you will worship *the Father* neither on this mountain nor in Jerusalem.
>
> . . .Yet a time is coming and has now come when the true worshipers will worship *the Father* in the Spirit and in truth, for they are the kind of worshipers *the Father* seeks. God is spirit, and his worshipers must worship in the Spirit and in truth." (John 4:21-24)

Acceptable worship is not about this or that place or method. It is about *Who*! And Jesus revealed that Who as the Father.

The second factor about Jesus' prayer-life is less familiar, but must be factored in as well.

Key #4: Jesus' prayer life was ongoing, occurring before, during and after his coming to earth.

Prayer for Jesus was not confined to his days on earth. He prayed even before assuming manhood in the world. This key underscores both the fact of his pre-existence as the eternal Word (Jn 1:1) and the quality of his relationship with the Father during that time.

Prayer, to Jesus, was two-way conversation with his Father. It began before he entered our world and continued *after* leaving it.

The earliest on record is in the Injeel, Hebrews 10:4-7. It records their parting conversation while still together in heaven prior to his entrance into the world, making this their final exchange before his birth in Bethlehem. Christ is speaking and addresses God the Father as "you:"

> "Therefore, when Christ came into the world, he said: "Sacrifice and offering you did not desire, but **a body you prepared for me;** with burnt offerings and sin offerings you were not pleased.
>
> Then I said, 'Here I am—it is written about me in the scroll— **I have come to do your will, my God.'**" (Hebrews 10:4-7)

Among other things, we learn two important lessons from this pre-incarnate prayer. First, the Son's submission to the Father reaches back to eternity past and was not confined to the period of his humanity. This attitude of deference to the Father, unbroken throughout Jesus' earthly life, did not start once he became man. Here we see it beforehand in his willingness to assume "the body You prepared for me," one soon to be formed by the Spirit in the womb of Mary. What does that tell us? It points to an attitude of readiness to obey that was permanent rather than occasional. In the end, of course, Christ's birth in Bethlehem became the historical piece. And yet, what chances would the Son have arrived at his destination of Bethlehem without his earlier disposition – "Here I am. I have come to do your will, my God"?

Back to your question, does this prayer undermine Jesus' deity or underscore it? I welcome your feedback. Please continue reading.

Jesus continued to pray *after* ascending back to heaven. Shortly before leaving this world, he prayed: "And now, Father, glorify me in your presence with the glory I had with you before the world began." (John 17:5) The next key will highlight his prayers upon reentering his former glory with his Father.

Key #5: Jesus never requested his believers to pray for him. Instead, he is the One praying for believers. Today he sits at God's right-hand interceding for them and invites them to pray to the Father in his name.

Today, Jesus continues to intercede from his exalted place with the Father:

> ". . .because Jesus lives forever, he has a permanent priesthood. Therefore he is able to save completely those who come to God through him, because *he always lives to intercede for them.* Such a high priest truly meets our need—one who is holy, blameless, pure, set apart from sinners, exalted above the heavens." (Hebrews 7:24-26)

> "Christ Jesus who died—more than that, who was raised to life— *is at the right hand of God and is also interceding for us.*" (Romans 8:34)

> "For we do not have a high priest who is unable to empathize with our weaknesses, but we have one who has been tempted in every way, just as we are—yet he did not sin. *Let us then approach God's throne of grace with confidence, so that we may receive mercy and find grace to help us in our time of need.*" (Hebrews 4:15-16)

Jesus gave his disciples the authority to pray in his name:

> "And I will do whatever you ask in my name, so that the Father may be glorified in the Son. You may ask me for anything in my name, and I will do it." (John 14:14-15)

What authority! To pray in Jesus' name means to pray with his authority and to ask God the Father to act in such a way because we come in his Son's name. It means to ask according to the will of God, not a magic formula to get anything we want.

In summary, we learn from the Injeel that Jesus prayed before, during and after his life on earth. We also learned that during his human life, his prayers displayed an exceptional naturalness that resulted from his close relationship.

Now back to your question. How can we square two seemingly incompatible claims: that Jesus was divine and that he prayed? Perhaps these interpretive keys from his prayer-life will point us in the right direction.

Lessons and Insights

> God's triune nature removes the absurdity of prayer in the life of Jesus. Interpersonal distinctions within the one Godhead make dialogue between them authentic, thus erasing the apparent farce.

First, God's triune nature removes the absurdity of prayer in the life of Jesus. Interpersonal distinctions within the one Godhead make dialogue between them authentic, thus erasing the apparent farce.

Jesus' prayers were never addressed to Himself. That would have been pointless. When he prayed, it was to the Father.

Second, prayer was as natural for Jesus on earth as it had been in heaven. Rather than challenging his deity, his prayers illustrated the eternal kinship out of which they emerged. Normal interaction in the Father's immediate company during his timeless preexistence simply continued (John 1:1; 17:24; Heb 10:4-7). And why not? Should it really surprise us that their intimate connection would continue? Why should they suddenly stop talking? That would have been abnormal. *Prayer was natural.*

Jesus' prayer-life on earth illustrated an unbroken fellowship within the eternal Godhead.

The warm and intimate interaction between the Father and the Son continued on earth what had always been in heaven.

Third, this close connection without interruption underscores why Jesus left heaven for earth in the first place and highlights a striking contrast. Prior to entering our world, Adam and Jesus both enjoyed close fellowship with God, basking in his immediate presence. Later, each of them vacated that sacred proximity, but for entirely different reasons. Adam's was banishment for disobeying God, resulting in divine judgment. Jesus was sent for mission, demonstrating divine love. What changed for Jesus was only his environment, not his fellowship. Adam forfeited not only his physical proximity, but compatibility. For Jesus, the presence of God meant rest. For Adam, it spelled fear, sending him into hiding. Jesus left heaven on good terms. Fellowship with God was never severed, thus ongoing prayer was natural.

> "The Father loves me ... The one who sent me is with me; he has not
> left me alone, for I always do what pleases him." (John 8:29)

Where Adam alienated himself from God, Jesus made reconciliation on his behalf. Jesus was the best thing that ever happened to Adam and his race.

Fourth, Jesus' prayer-life shows that his humanity was not a sham. Like you and me, he faced challenges that were painfully real. He carried no Exemption Card that gave him a special pass from heartache. Even as the Son of God, he was granted no shortcuts of divine privilege and spared nothing (Hebrews 5:7). As such, Jesus became our merciful go-between with the Father, interceding on behalf of all who call upon him.

Fifth, Jesus' prayers expressed familiarity and intimate kinship with the Father without usurping his authority. Conversations with his heavenly Father boldly acknowledged his kindred nature while humbly recognizing his Father's supreme position. This takes us to the next chapter.

CHAPTER 5

JESUS' DEITY

Question 5: "Jesus didn't say anywhere in the Bible 'I am a god.' He says he is a messenger of Allah."

Q 5.1: "When did Jesus claim to be divine?
Q 5.2: "On what basis do Christians believe that Jesus (*pbuh*) is divine?"
Q 5.3: "In the Bible we see a lot of people who did more miracles than Jesus, but no one says they are God. Why?"

The Qur'an repeatedly denies the divinity of Jesus, making this excellent question-set inevitable. One ayah states that anyone who accepts Jesus' deity is an unbeliever:

> "They indeed have disbelieved who say, 'God is the Messiah, son of Mary'" (Al-Maidah 5:17; see also 4:157, 171-172; 5:72, 75, 116; 9:30-31).

The same Surah answers why this is so. It commits the sin of exaggeration, transgressing the boundary of truth:

> "Say: 'O People of the Book! [Christians] exceed *not in your religion* the bounds (of what is proper), *trespassing beyond the truth* ....'" (Al-Maidah

5:77). *Christ, the son of Mary, was no more than a Messenger*; many were the Messengers that passed away before him. His mother was a woman of truth. They had both to eat their (daily) food." (Al-Maidah 5:75-79)

Youssef Ali explains:

"Excess means that truth is sometimes concealed. . .and Allah's name is dishonored by blasphemies or . . . that good (or even bad) men are deified and worshipped."[1]

An Imam in Metro Chicago helped me understand. Some students from a Christian university and I visited the Friday service at his mosque. Afterwards he graciously met with us to answer our questions. He was cordial, courteous and candid. Why did he reject Jesus' deity?

> "If Jesus is God and Muslims do not worship him, then Muslims are in trouble.
> If Jesus is not God and Christians worship him, then Christians are in trouble."
> Dr. Faizur Choudhury

"I'm a logical man. Muslims highly esteem Prophet Jesus (pbuh). But a man cannot be God. Calling Jesus deity is not an honor to him. That would be like someone calling me a doctor even though I'm no M.D. Instead of flattering me, the exaggeration would make me feel shame because I cannot live up to what they say and it would prove how little they know of me."

His point is well-taken. Sooner or later, overblown titles flame-out like comets, bringing shame to the very ones intended for honor. How humiliating when the truth finally surfaces. Mice must know they aren't lions, despite the raves of their starstruck relatives. The imam sincerely believes this is what Christians are doing to Prophet Isa. That sword, of course, cuts both ways. Roaring lions also know themselves to be far more awesome than tiny rodents. Shaming is bi-directional, coming just as easily through belittling as by exaggeration.

We can all agree that praise must fit its recipient. Faizur, a good Muslim friend from Bangladesh, said it like this:

"If Jesus is God and Muslims do not worship him, then Muslims are in trouble. If Jesus is not God and Christians worship him, then Christians are in trouble."

In light of these cautions, he clarified our tension and set the right tone:

"So the misunderstanding between the Christians and the Muslims is not an enmity, but it is a love affair. They are trying to save each other from hell fire. But it is a matter of great sorrow that both of us cannot be correct at the same time! If one group is right, then the other group is definitely wrong!"[2]

The mutual goal of "trying to save each other" elevates this discussion from an adversarial debate to the higher ground of the prophetic appeal, "come, let us reason together." In that spirit, let us proceed.

Each of your four questions pinpoints an integral aspect of Jesus' deity and illustrates its multifaceted nature. They will provide structure for this chapter to which I will add a question of my own:

Introduction: Why Jesus Would *Never* Proclaim "I am God"
Part 1: The Declaration of Jesus' Deity (Q-5)
Part 2: The Presentation of Jesus' Deity (Q-5.1)
Part 3: The Logic of Jesus' Deity – Why I Believe (Q-5.2)
Part 4: Jesus Distinguished from Miracle Workers (Q-5.3)
Part 5: Author's Question: Why does the Qur'an Elevate Isa in the Prophetic Line?

INTRODUCTION
Three Words Jesus would Never
Say in Public: "I am God"

Question 5: "He didn't say anywhere in the Bible 'I am a god.' He says he is a 'messenger of Allah.'"

"Jesus, are you God?" Can you imagine Jesus being asked that question in a public setting, especially by one of his Jewish peers? It never came up in the Injeel. And if it had, would Jesus have answered either Yes *or* No? Not likely.

Muslims often quickly point out that Jesus was not as explicit in claiming his deity as we Christians want to believe. Your question makes sense: If Jesus was God, why didn't he say so? Let's consider this possibility: Are there good reasons for us to avoid making a hasty conclusion that the absence of Jesus' explicit public announcements reflect his private beliefs about himself? Could his *not* answering have been the wiser choice?

Reasons for Jesus' Reluctance

At least two good reasons prevented Jesus from publicly announcing his deity.

Backfire effect. Jesus the Truth would never lie but that does not mean that he would ignore his own teaching. "Do not throw your pearls to pigs" (Matthew 7:6), meaning that we must be discreet in the dispensing of truth. Otherwise, he says, the pigs will "trample them under their feet, and turn and tear you to pieces." In other words, a message intended for good would surely backfire.

Let's pretend that Jesus stood before a first-century Jewish audience and just came out with it: "I am divine!" Would anyone have fallen down to worship him? More likely, they would have thrown him off a cliff. Could it be, Muslim reader, that it is this criterion of proof – the demand for an explicit public announcement – that calls for closer scrutiny even before we delve into the subject of Jesus' deity itself?

Oddly, the ones pushing that envelope of full disclosure were Jesus' enemies. The devil, in fact, tempted him to do just that – come out with it dramatically – by leaping off the top of the temple. The public spectacle of a band of angels catching Jesus in mid-air would, so it was pitched, win him instant notoriety as the divine Son of God. Later, "impure spirits" commonly blabbed Jesus' divine identity only to be

137

immediately silenced at his command (Mark 1:34; 3:11-12; 5:7, etc.). His refusal to publicize his deity certainly did not mean his denial of it. Nor was he afraid of reprisals. Jesus waited for the right time.

Absurd Conclusions. Another good reason Jesus refrained is that the naked assertion, "I am God," would have opened the door to countless absurdities. Can you imagine the flurry of disastrous conclusions such an announcement would have drawn?

- ***Jesus is a second God***
- ***Jesus came to replace God***
- ***Jesus became a partner with God***

Those are just the tip of the iceberg.

Muslims submitted many excellent questions about Jesus' deity that, for the most part, asked for reasons to warrant its belief. Surprisingly, one question was missing: "When you Christians say, 'Jesus is God,' what exactly do you mean?" Rather than mounting a defense for *why we believe* Jesus is God, our conversation might be better served on a foundation of *what we understand* by it.

As with any doctrine, basic clarity should come first. Otherwise, how can we decide whether to accept it as true or reject it as false? Many have rejected Jesus Christ to their peril because of liabilities in the misinformation circulating about him. So before rushing in to either accept or reject his deity, our first priority is allowing Jesus himself to clarify its meaning. Parts 1 and 2 in this chapter aim to inform as much as to persuade.

We begin by listening to what Jesus said about himself. Are there indications that he believed himself to share in the divine nature?

PART 1: THE DECLARATION OF JESUS' DEITY
His Exalted Claims

While never openly proclaiming, "I am God," Jesus made explicit statements catapulting him far above what is possible for the human realm and that well-exceed the prophetic vocation. Taken together, these were tantamount to asserting his deity.

1. Jesus considered himself morally and spiritually perfect.

The first indication that Jesus claimed to be divine is his belief in his own moral and spiritual perfection. The starting point for this line of evidence is God's unique holy nature.

"God is the Holy One" (Habakkuk 3:3), the moral exception, separate from evil and absolutely pure. Holiness is his exclusive attribute, for "you *alone* are holy" (Revelation 15:4) and quintessential quality: "*Holy, holy, holy* is the LORD Almighty" (Isaiah 6:3). People, not God, behave badly.

> A life lived completely free of sin would place him in a category well-above humanity in general and prophets in particular.

We begin here because any moral deviation by Jesus, even a single lapse, would disqualify his claim. Conversely, a life lived completely free of sin would place him in a category well-above humanity in general and, as we will see, prophets in particular.

Did Jesus regard himself without sin? This is a valid question, for we never hear him say, "I am sinless."[3] But did he think so? Four evidences confirm this.

Evidence 1: No trace of Jesus acknowledging his own guilt. First, Jesus taught his disciples that they should pray, "Forgive us our sins" (Luke 11:4) and regularly insisted that others repent. And yet where do we find Jesus confessing, repenting or asking forgiveness for *his* sins? Such instances do not exist. The significance of this absence is heightened by his familiarity with the Ten Commandments. Raised in a pious home and "born under the law" (Galatians 4:4), he was taught to revere and observe them. That knowledge of God's moral Standard did not affect him as it did most others, feeling conflicted by the gap between their agreement with it and actual practice of it (Romans 7:7, 10). With Jesus we find no such compunction.

What self-aware human being has never approached Almighty God with contrition: "God, it's me again. *Again!* I messed up. Lord, have mercy on me. Give me strength to overcome?" The Injeel answers, only "one," Jesus the Messiah!

Evidence 2: Claimed a life of unbroken obedience. For anyone to assume a totally sinlessness life is remarkable, even bordering on preposterous. Jesus didn't hesitate to make bold statements inferring such as indicated by these three instances.

First, Jesus showed that he had nothing to hide:

> "*Can any of you prove me guilty of sin?* If I am telling the truth, why don't you believe me? Whoever belongs to God hears what God says. The reason you do not hear is that you do not belong to God." (John 8:45-47)

How daring! Only public figures with a clean conscience would put themselves at risk by inviting their enemies to examine them for incriminating evidence. Jesus had nothing to hide, no skeletons in his closet, no titillating scandals dogging him. But this absence of "dirt" only scratches the surface.

Second, going deeper, towards the end of his thirty-three years on earth, he said:

> "...The prince of this world [Satan] is coming. *He has no hold over me,* but he comes so that the world may learn that *I love the Father and do exactly what my Father has commanded me.*" (John 14:30-31)

Jesus made two remarkable claims here. First, he connected his total adherence to God with his freedom from Satan's clutches. The Hebrew idiom, "has no hold over me," is frequently used in "has no claim on me."[4] In this passage Jesus is saying, "Satan. . .has no point in my personality on which he can fasten."[5] Why doesn't he?

"It is Jesus' lack of sin – 'I do exactly what my Father has commanded me' – which he gives as the reason why there is nothing in him which allows Satan to claim any legal rights."[6]

He could then say, "I love the Father and do exactly what my Father has commanded me."

Third, Jesus' claim to a sin-free life was only half the picture, his abstinence from vice. While exceptional, it hardly explains the broad attraction of his character causing people to believe in him. The world has known many a "holy man" retreating from the world in social isolation. Jesus was not that. He was far more than squeaky clean, a man evil-free with a hollow soul. What people found so compelling were not the vices he avoided, but the good he consistently did:

"'I always **do** the things that are pleasing to Him.' As He spoke these things, many came to believe in Him." (John 8:28-29)

Jesus came to "do" what pleased God rather than to "not do" what displeased him. His deeds were rooted in the Fount of love whom he consistently pleased. The results were astounding! The Father's love overflowed through his obedience like a healing stream into broken society. Note his word "always"[7] and its effect upon his audience. They "believed in him." And why not? Matching his spectacular miracles was a lifestyle equally stupendous in holiness. Here was a miracle-worker and more: *the* moral exception to this biblical teaching:

"Indeed, there is no one on earth who is righteous, no one who does what is right and never sins." (Ecclesiastes 7:20)

"The LORD looks down from heaven on all mankind to see if there are any who understand, any who seek God. All have turned away, all have become corrupt; *there is no one who does good, not even one.*" (Psalm 14:2-3; 53:1-6)

"The LORD looks down from heaven on all mankind to see if there are any who understand, any who seek God. All have turned away, all have become corrupt; there is no one who does good, not even one."
Psalm 14:2-3; 53:1-6

The Injeel concurred, even lumping Abraham's family into the mix:

"There is no difference between Jew and Gentile, for *all have sinned and fall short of the glory of God*" (Romans 3:22-23).

As people revering the Ten Commandments, they knew what sin was and was not. They distinguished innocent mistakes from willful violations. They knew that losing my wallet is a mistake; taking yours is a sin. Or that desiring to own property is acceptable; desiring to own what is yours is coveting. They also recognized that all people have not only made mistakes but are guilty of sin. None is morally perfect.

Evidence 3: Jesus self-identified as the LORD's promised Righteous Servant who actively and unceasingly listened to God. The OT promised the coming of one who would break the sinful pattern. I will mention two such predictions beginning with the Servant of the LORD.[8] Israel who was chosen to be God's servant had become "deaf" to his word in their rebellion (Isaiah 42:8). Another Servant took their place who would listen and obey.

"The Sovereign LORD has given me a well-instructed tongue, to know the word that sustains the weary. He wakens me morning by morning, *wakens my ear to listen* like one being instructed. *The Sovereign Lord has opened my ears; I have not been rebellious, I have not turned away.*" (Isaiah 50:4-5)

Jesus fulfilled this role by attentively listening and with unhesitating compliance. He would not falter.

The second OT prediction was for the holy Messiah, a "righteous Branch:"

". . .the days are coming, says the LORD, when I will raise up for David *a righteous Branch.*" (Jer 23:5 RSV; see Isaiah 11:1; Zechariah 6:12)

This "Branch,"[9] a shoot or sprout from David's family tree and marked out as the LORD's "Servant" (Zechariah 3:8), would distinguish himself as righteous. Most striking was his name:

"Now this is *his name* by which he will be called: 'The LORD our Righteousness.'" (Jeremiah 25:6).

Again in Jeremiah 33:15-16 that name expands to *"The LORD our Righteous Savior* [who] will *do* what is just and right" (Jeremiah 33:15-16). Who is this? It is not all of David's posterity but points to a single "sprout," a specific Person on it.

This individual is given a name describing his nature, "the LORD our Righteous Savior!" How can a divine name be given to any mere mortal? Bundled into this single individual would be God, righteousness and salvation. Moving forward, what name was given by God to the son of Mary? *"Jesus," or* **Yeshua**, *meaning "the LORD saves!"* His life bore out these OT predictions. Every day, "morning by morning," Jesus woke up having a listening ear to the Father and who met him because he was not "rebellious" or ever "turned away." Jesus always "did what is just and right."

Evidence 4: Jesus never had a morally transforming experience that made him sinless because he was holy by nature. Another strong indicator of Jesus' sinlessness was the nature out of which it arose. Since Jesus was human like everyone else, how could he live above evil at all times and places? The answer came through the angel Gabriel's announcement to Mary. Her son, conceived not by man but through the Holy Spirit, would be called the "the holy One" (Lk. 1:35). From day one, Jesus conducted his life accordingly without deviating even once in word, thought or deed. That is because he was *essentially* the "holy One" and "Righteous One" (Acts 3:14). Never was it necessary for him to be made that way, replacing his defiled heart with an upright one.

Weren't Prophets Sinless?

What about God's prophets? Did they not think of themselves as sinless? Noah did not (Genesis 9:20; Hud 11:47). Abraham did not (Genesis 20:1-18; Ibrahim 14:41). Moses did not (Numbers 20:8-13; Al-Qasas 28:16). David did not (Psalms 32 and 51; Sad 38:24). John the Baptist did not (Matthew 3:13-14). Isaiah did not (Isaiah 6).[10]

While upright and uncompromising spokesmen for God, none claimed moral perfection. Even Moses was barred from entering the Promised Land, allowed only to glimpse it from the summit of Mt. Nebo. Why so?

> ". . . *you broke faith with me* in the presence of the Israelites at the waters of Meribah Kadesh in the Desert of Zin and because *you did not uphold my holiness among the Israelites.* Therefore, you will see the land only from a distance; you will not enter the land I am giving to the people of Israel." (Deuteronomy 32:51-52)

David, too, a man after God's own heart, confessed: "For I know my transgressions, and my sin is always before me" (Psalm 51:3-4).

Obviously, the Bible does not scrub the sins of its leaders from its archives. Why is this so? God does not want us to place our faith in men, including his prophets, but in the supreme subject of their prophecies: the sinless Savior.

In a world plagued by sin, Jesus claimed to be the Moral Exception. This was tantamount to claiming deity for himself. He *was* holy.

But he does not stop there. His next claim raises the bar another notch.

2. Jesus claimed God's authority to forgive sins.

The second evidence that Jesus believed himself to be divine is by taking upon himself the power to forgive the sins of others, a right belonging to God alone. This claim provoked a major fuss:

> "And they came, bringing to Him a paralytic, carried by four men. Being unable to get to Him because of the crowd, they removed the roof above Him; and when they had dug an opening, they let down the pallet on which the paralytic was lying. And *Jesus seeing their faith* said to the paralytic, 'Son, your sins are forgiven.'

But some of the scribes were sitting there and reasoning in their hearts, 'Why does this man speak that way? *He is blaspheming; who can forgive sins but God alone?'* Immediately Jesus, aware in His spirit that they were reasoning that way within themselves, said to them, 'Why are you reasoning about these things in your hearts? Which is easier, to say to the paralytic, "Your sins are forgiven"; or to say, "Get up, and pick up your pallet and walk"?

But *so that you may know that the Son of Man has authority on earth to forgive sins*'—He said to the paralytic, 'I say to you, get up, pick up your pallet and go home.' And he got up and immediately picked up the pallet and went out in the sight of everyone, so that they were all amazed and were glorifying God, saying, 'We have never seen anything like this.'" (Injeel, Mark 2:2-12)[11]

Jesus' critics were correct in their belief that only God can forgive sins. While sinful acts usually affect other people, they are first and foremost against God. Some people mistake sin for karma, a violation of an abstract universal law. Karma is believed to be an impersonal Force, thus incapable of being offended. Laws feel nothing. Sin is personal because God is a Being, not an impersonal Force. It is not against law but the law-*Giver*. David acknowledged this in his confession:

"*Against you [God], you only, have I sinned* and done what is evil *in your sight;* so you are right in your verdict and justified when you judge." (Psalm 51:4; see 2 Samuel 12:13; Genesis 20:6; 39:9; Luke 15:18)

Since sin is against God, the choice whether to remove offenses and place offenders back on good terms is his.

"*I, even I, am he who blots out your transgressions,* for my own sake, and remembers your sins no more." (Isaiah 43:25)

The decision to grant or withhold forgiveness rests entirely with God. That God's nature is both merciful[12] and righteous is beyond question. The Old Testament is filled with examples of his forgiving actions. But when his kind overtures were persistently rejected, we find instances when God withheld mercy and forbade pity (Ezekiel 8:18)![13]

What had rankled the religious leaders is that Jesus claimed that right of selection for himself. He told *that* man, "*You* are forgiven." What are we to make of this? Was he encroaching into God's exclusive domain? Let's consider:

First, the religious leaders believed Jesus was playing God. This was nothing less than blasphemy. How could he pretend to know God's verdict in this specific case?

Second, it matters who says what. The credentials of the speaker will either validate or invalidate their pronouncements. I could walk into a cancer ward and declare everyone cancer-free. As a layman in the field of medicine, my sunny prognosis offers little hope for improvement. On the other hand, an oncologist after performing thorough tests who pronounced his patients cancer-free could be trusted. Who says what matters. Here the spokesperson was Jesus. Did it make any difference and how can we know?

Third, the bolder the claim, the weightier the evidence is required to back it up. Huge claims like this one – declaring a man guilt-free in God's eyes – call for substantial evidence. But how could anyone prove a spiritual miracle, that the man's sins were actually forgiven? How could anyone know if Jesus' words bounced off the ceiling or infused fresh spiritual vitality to the man's soul? Was this man's guilt truly removed or did he just feel better under an illusion of forgiveness?

Now it starts getting good.

Fourth, Jesus certified a spiritual miracle that was impossible to see with a physical miracle that was impossible to deny. He backed up his colossal declaration with colossal demonstration. Where are his accusers now? They are hushed. Everyone present got the message: If Jesus could do *this*, he certainly could do *that*! If his command prevailed over an invalid's physical deformity, why call into question his pronouncement of spiritual restoration?

146

Reactions to Jesus split between outrage and praise. Where his opponents saw blasphemy, the people saw *Immanuel*, God with us! A cripple returned home walking uprightly in body *and* in spirit, swift on his feet and secure in his soul!

> "This amazed everyone and they praised God, saying, 'We have never seen anything like this!'" (Mark 2:12)

Jesus keeps raising the bar.

3. Jesus called himself "the Son of Man."

The third evidence Jesus believed in his divine nature is by calling himself "the Son of Man." On *eighty* separate occasions (not counting their parallels), Jesus took this enigmatic title for himself.[14] It became his calling card. With such frequent use, he was obviously making a statement about himself, but what was it – his deity, his humanity or both?[15] On its face, one might think Jesus used "Son of *Man*" to draw attention to his humanity while reserving "Son of *God*" to assert his deity. Sounds logical enough. Some digging into the Old Testament and Jesus actual sayings, however, demand a different conclusion.

While the subject is vast, our question here is narrow: Did Jesus apply this phrase to himself as some kind of magnificent human being or as a majestic heavenly one? To find out, let's begin with the Old Testament.

The Son of Man in the Old Testament (OT)

The OT uses the "son of man" in both its human and exalted senses.[16]

1. Human Beings. "Son of man" can describe a human being or humanity as a whole, stressing weakness and frailty (Num 23:19; Job 25:6; Psa 8:5; Isa 51:12; Dan 8:17). Most notable in this category is Ezekiel, a young aristocratic priest from Jerusalem who was among the first wave of exiles to Babylon (597 BC). In his fifth year there, he received a vision of God's glorious throne, collapsing "fell facedown" like a corpse until being touched by One who said:

"*Son of man*, stand up on your feet and I will speak to you. . .*Son of man,* I am sending you to the Israelites, to a rebellious nation that has rebelled against me. . .And you, *son of man*, do not be afraid of them.. ." (Ezekiel 2:1, 3, 6)

Over the course of twenty-two years while faithfully preaching to the exiles, God addressed him "son of man" ninety-two times, clearly noting his creaturely dependence in contrast to "the glory of the LORD" (Eze 1:28; 3:12, 23; 10:4, 18, etc.).

2.   *A Heavenly Being.* At the opposite end of the spectrum, Daniel, also a prophet in Babylon, saw "one like a Son of Man" who approached God's throne:

"As I looked, "thrones were set in place, and the Ancient of Days took his seat. His clothing was as white as snow; the hair of his head was white like wool. His throne was flaming with fire, and its wheels were all ablaze. A river of fire was flowing, coming out from before him.

Thousands upon thousands attended him; ten thousand times ten thousand stood before him.

The court was seated, and the books were opened." (Daniel 7:9-10)

"As I looked on, in the night vision, *one like a Son of Man* was coming with the clouds of heaven; he reached the Everlasting One and was presented to him. Dominion, glory, and kingship were given to him. All peoples and nations of every language must serve him. His dominion is an everlasting dominion that shall not pass away, and his kingship, one that shall not be destroyed. . . and all rulers will worship and obey him." (Daniel 7:13-14, 27)

Who is this Son of Man? Clearly, he is not "God" in the sense of encompassing the total Godhead, for he is a separate being who approached the enthroned Eternal One – a distinction, by the way, that Jesus would later repeatedly emphasize. At the same time, this "one like a Son of Man" is presented as more than just an outstanding person.

Four traits and capacities mark him as someone above human limitation:

From Heaven. This Son of Man, unlike Ezekiel, emerged out of heaven and not from the earth. While the prophet's *calling* came from heaven, he ministered as an earthling to earthlings. Daniel's heavenly "one *like* a Son of Man" was not from earth, and yet bore human resemblance and was not yet made man as he was still in his pre-incarnate state.[17] His transcendent existence preceded his human appearance.

Appeared with Clouds. Daniel foresaw this Son of Man "coming with[18] the clouds." Is this a weather forecast predicting his Second Coming to occur on an overcast day? No! Throughout the Old Testament, "the cloud is the garment or dwelling-place of deity, the symbol of its presence in the midst of the people."[19] The OT provides numerous examples when God's power and glory came near to his people through the sudden formation of a cloud.

> "As Moses went into the tent, *the pillar of cloud would come down and stay at the entrance, while the LORD spoke with Moses.* Whenever the people saw the pillar of cloud standing at the entrance to the tent, they all stood and worshiped, each at the entrance to their tent. The LORD would speak to Moses face to face, as one speaks to a friend." (Exodus 33:9-11; cf. 13:21; Nu 12:5)

What mortal survives the unshielded appearance before God's throne, that majestic perch cordoned off by rivers of fire and innumerable angelic hosts?

"Then *the LORD came down in the cloud* and stood there with him and proclaimed his name, the LORD. And he passed in front of Moses, proclaiming, "The LORD, the LORD, the compassionate and gracious God, slow to anger, abounding in love and faithfulness. . .' Moses bowed to the ground at once and worshiped." (Exodus 34:5-8; see also Exo 16:10; 24:16-18)

"When the priests withdrew from the Holy Place, *the cloud filled the temple of the LORD.* 11 And the priests *could not perform their service because of the cloud,* for the glory of the LORD filled his temple." (1 Kings 8:10-11)[20]

When God descended among persons, a cloud enveloped him since no mortal can see God and live. This association with clouds tags the Son of Man as one possessing divine power and glory.

Stood before the Almighty. What mortal survives the unshielded appearance before God's throne, that majestic perch cordoned off by rivers of fire and innumerable angelic hosts? Recall Ezekiel glimpsing that splendor from afar: his legs gave out and he fell on his face (Eze 2:1)! Daniel's Son of Man entered that very Presence, and he did so "as is!" What does this say about him? While separate in Being from the Everlasting One, he was compatible in nature. Significantly, his first "coming" moved horizontally from the clouds into that Presence long before his glorious descent at the end of the age.

> "'You are from below, I am from above; you are of this world, I am not of this world.'"
> Jesus, John 8:23-24

King with an everlasting kingdom. Ezekiel brought God's *message* to the nation of Israel. The "one like a Son of Man" would bring God's *kingdom* to all nations of the world. His kingdom was spiritual, one derived not through military might or confined to national borders. In the dramatic build-up of Daniel 1-7, his dominion will alone have standing power, displacing all others. Daniel 2 anticipated this, symbolizing this invincible kingdom:[21]

[God's Interpretation of King Nebuchadnezzar's dream, v. 34] "In the time of those kings, *the God of heaven will set up a kingdom that will never be destroyed,* nor will it be left to another people. *It will crush all those kingdoms and bring them to an end, but it will itself endure forever.* This is the meaning of the vision of the rock cut out of a mountain, but *not by human hands*—a rock that broke the iron, the bronze, the clay, the silver and the gold to pieces." (Daniel 2:34, 44-45)

Not only would his kingdom last. It would surpass previous empires geographically and ethically. Daniel 2 and 7 present their empires as bestial – *like* a lion, *like* a bear, *like* a leopard in their ferocity – while his, "*like* the Son of *Man*," would be humane! Theirs ravaged humanity, his would restore it. The kingdom of God would outlast, out-reach and out-love every authority.

"No one has seen the Father except the one who is from God; only he has seen the Father."
Jesus, John 6:46

OT Summary

The OT presents the son of man in both senses, a human creature and a heavenly Figure with human appearance. With this background, we are ready to hear from Jesus.

Jesus as the Son of Man
Finite, Transcendent or Both?

Did Jesus apply this title to himself as a finite human being like Ezekiel or as the transcendent Figure in Daniel's vision? One of the first things we notice is that each time Jesus spoke of the Son of Man he used the definite article, "the." By doing so, he singled out just one. The definite article cannot describe indefinite objects or persons. For example, it would sound strange for me to say, "I am *the* man" when the world is populated by billions of others. When God addressed Ezekiel, it was always as "son of man" without the definite article. He was one among many. Jesus had a *specific* person in mind, one without peer. Was it the transcendent Figure seen in Daniel's vision?

The surest way to find out is to see if Jesus applied the four transcendent traits of Daniel's Son of Man to himself. Specifically, did he (a) come from heaven, (b) enter the divine Presence, (c) appear with clouds, and (d) reign as King over a kingdom that is humane, universal and eternal? If not, we can only conclude that he viewed himself as a prophet only, like Ezekiel.

(a) *Heavenly Being.* Jesus plainly identified himself as the Son of Man who had come from heaven. He said,

> "No one has ever gone into heaven except the one who *came from heaven—the Son of Man.*" (John 3:13; see also 6:62, 67 and 7:28-29)

> "'You are from below, *I am from above*; you are of this world, *I am not of this world.'*" (John 8:23-24; cf. v 14)

(b) *Co-existent with God.* Jesus claimed to have co-existed in the very presence of his Father. He said,

> "No one has seen the Father except the one who is from God; only he has seen the Father." (John 6:46)

> "*I am telling you what I have seen in the Father's presence . . . I know him.* If I said I did not, I would be a liar. . ." (John 8:38, 55)

This prayer shows Jesus anticipating the return to the Father's presence that he had already experienced:

> "And now, Father, glorify me in your presence with the glory I had with you before the world began." (John 17:5; 11)

(c) *Appears in Clouds.* Twice Jesus was suddenly enveloped by a cloud to mark him as God's manifest presence. While praying on a mountain in the company of three apostles, a cloud appeared as both a sign of and shield from the majestic glory that was his:

> "he was transfigured before them. His face shone like the sun, and his clothes became as white as the light. . .a *bright cloud covered them*, and a voice from the cloud said, 'This is my Son, whom I love; with him I am well pleased. Listen to him!' When the disciples heard this, they fell facedown to the ground, terrified." (Matthew 17:1-11)

Again at his ascension back to heaven, they saw him disappear in clouds to enter his enthroned glory at God's right hand (Acts 2).

Jesus identified himself as the future Son of Man descending in clouds of glory and enthroned with God. In Matthew 25:31, he points to the day when "the Son of Man comes in *his* glory" (emphasis added). Glory, we should note, is reserved for Almighty God and thus off-limits to creatures, even apostles and prophets. "I am the LORD; that is my name! I will not yield my glory to another or my praise to idols" (Isaiah 42:8).

(d) King of Kings. Finally, at his trial the Jewish high priest demanded of him on oath to testify exactly who he was: "Are you the Messiah, the Son of the Blessed One?" Jesus cinched it explicitly and his answer got him crucified:

> "*I am*; and you will see the Son of Man *seated at the right hand of the Power, and coming with the clouds of heaven.*'"

The court-in-session clearly got the message.

> "Then the high priest tore his clothes and said, 'Why do we still need witnesses? *You have heard his blasphemy!* What is your decision?' All of them condemned him as deserving death." (Mark 14:61-65 NRSV)

Their charge of blasphemy confirmed the divine status of the Son of Man. Jesus could have stopped at "Yes, I am," but went beyond it (see also Matthew 19:28; 24:30; 25:31). His added words touched a nerve with the men on this tribunal. By claiming to be the Son of Man, Jesus informed them who would someday sit in the judgment seat:

> "Jesus said, in effect, to his accusers that the day would come when the situation would be reversed. Now he was standing before their tribunal being tried. The day would come when they – his judges – would stand before his tribunal, and he, the heavenly Son of Man, would fill the role of eschatological judge."[22]

Jesus viewed himself as the King reigning over a kingdom that would be humane, universal and eternal. If the Son of Man was Jesus' calling card, the kingdom of God was his manifesto. Just as in Daniel's vision, world empires took after the bestial character of their kings, so the kingdom of God would bear the imprint of "One like a Son of *Man*" who now in Jesus had become *actual* man. It comes as no surprise that Jesus' ministry launched on this buoyant keynote:

> "Jesus went throughout Galilee . . . *proclaiming the good news of the kingdom, and healing* every disease and sickness among the people." (Matthew 4:23)

> "The Son of Man did not come to be served, but to serve, and to give His life a ransom for many."
> Jesus,
> Matthew 20:28 HCSB

This kingdom unfolded with a beginning, middle and end.

Beginning – Emphasized the Son of Man's spiritual power and authority while beset by human limitations, humility and service. It dovetails with descriptions of the "Servant of the Lord" from Isaiah 42:1-4 and 53:2. Cf. Isaiah 61:1-3.

> Divine privileges removed. "Foxes have dens and birds have nests, but *the Son of Man has no place to lay his head.*" (Matthew 8:20; Lk 9:58)

> Humane. ". . . the Son of Man did not come to be served, but to serve, and to give his life as a ransom for many." (Matthew 20:28; Mk 10:45)

> Divine Prerogatives. ". . . the Son of Man is Lord of the Sabbath" (Matthew 12:8; Matt 12:8; Mk 2:28; Luke 6:5). ". . . the Son of Man has authority on earth to forgive sins." (Matthew 9:6)

> Proof that God's kingdom is present. "But if it is by the Spirit of God that I drive out demons, then the kingdom of God has come upon you." (Matthew 12:28; Lk 11:20)

Middle – Emphasized the Son of Man's rejection, suffering, death and vindication through resurrection and ascension. Dovetails with the Servant of the Lord from Isaiah 49:4-5; 52:13-53:12.

> Derided – "*The Son of Man came eating and drinking,* and they say, 'Here is a glutton and a drunkard, a friend of tax collectors and sinners.'" (Matthew 11:19)

Rejected. "*The Son of Man must suffer* many things and be rejected by the elders, the chief priests and the teachers of the law, and that he must be killed and after three days rise again." (Mark 8:31; Lk 9:22; etc.)

Turning Point. "The hour has come. Look, *the Son of Man* is delivered into the hands of sinners! Rise! Let us go! Here comes my betrayer!" (Mark 14:42)

Path to Glory. "*The hour has come for the Son of Man to be glorified.* Very truly I tell you, unless a kernel of wheat falls to the ground and dies, it remains only a single seed. But if it dies, it produces many seeds." (John 12:23-24; see 13:31)

Authority over All Nations. "*All authority in heaven and on earth has been given to me.* Therefore go and make disciples of **all nations**. . ." (Matthew 28:18-19; see Isaiah 49:6)

Going & Growing. "And this *gospel of the kingdom* will be preached in the whole world as a *testimony to all nations*, and then *the end will come.*" (Matthew 24:14)

Enthroned at God's Right Hand. "He was taken up before their very eyes, and a cloud hid him from their sight." (Acts 1:9)

End – Emphasized the Son of Man's universal reign. Jesus is King over a kingdom with staying power to finally displace pagan world empires. Dovetails with Isaiah 49:7; 52:13; 60:18-22.

Kingdom Fullness. "For as lightning that comes from the east is *visible* even in the west, *so will be the coming of the Son of Man.*[28] (Matt 24:30)

Sober Division of Humanity. "Then will appear *the sign of the Son of Man in heaven.* And then all the peoples of the earth will mourn when they see the Son of Man *coming on the clouds of heaven*, with power and great glory. And he will send his angels with a loud trumpet call, and they will *gather his elect from the four winds, from one end of the heavens to the other.*" (Matthew 24:30-31; Mk 13:26; Lk 21:27)

Kingdom Consummated. "The kingdoms of the world has become the kingdom of our Lord and of his Christ, and he shall reign for ever and ever." (Revelation 11:15)

In summary, Jesus' identification as the majestic and glorious Son of Man is indisputable. Out of that identity comes the next role, further attesting his divine nature.

4. Jesus claimed to Preside over the Final Judgment

Next, Jesus claimed to preside over the Final Judgment at the end of history:

"The Father ... has given him [Jesus] authority to judge because he is the Son of Man." (John 5:30; see vv 25, 27)

"... *the Father judges no one, but has entrusted all judgment to the Son."* (verse 22)

His jurisdiction encompasses both the human population of individuals and the community of nations.

"When *the Son of Man comes in his glory*, and all the angels with him, *he will sit on his glorious throne.* All the nations will be gathered before him, and *he will separate the people one from another* as a shepherd separates the sheep from the goats." (Matthew 25:31-32)

"What good will it be for someone to gain the whole world, yet forfeit their soul? Or what can anyone give in exchange for their soul? For *the Son of Man* is going to come in his Father's glory with his angels, and *then he will reward each person according to what they have done."* (Matthew 16:26-27; see Mark 8:37-38; Lk 9:26)

This is no trivial matter. Christianity and Islam share a core belief that human history advances towards a Day of Reckoning. The OT declares that "God will bring every deed into judgment" (Ecclesiastes 12:14). The NT continues, "The secrets of hearts will be brought to light" (Romans 2:16).[23] The Qur'an warns, "Each soul is paid in full for what it did, and He [Allah] is best Aware of what they do" (Al-Zumar 39:70). Its urgency is heightened in that "it is appointed for people to die once, and after this, judgment" (Hebrews 9:27 HCSB), making each verdict final with no second chances. Any subject with greater relevance seems inconceivable.

THE JUDGMENT THRONE
A Position for God or Man?

The numerical magnitude of the Judgment demands the transcendence of its Judge.

At the end of history, who will render just verdicts to every person to have walked the planet, assigning each one to an eternal fate? Who but God is capable of performing this herculean task? Given humanity's countless souls, not to mention their interior motives and the local behavioral standards between this place and that by which to measure acceptable behaviors, who else could it be?

A mathematical conundrum. The Judgment's staggering numerical magnitude demands a transcendent Judge. Consider the math. In 2017 the world population was estimated to have reached 7.5 billion people. How long would it take to adjudicate them? By devoting a mere five seconds to each, this caseload would require 625 million hours or roughly 71,000 years non-stop. This, however, only factors our current population, just one-seventh of the 108 billion persons estimated to have ever lived.[24] Now adjudication jumps to 9 billion continuous hours spread over 1 million years. What, then, do these staggering figures tell us? They show that Jesus either preposterously mistook himself to preside over the Last Judgment or that he is far more than a man. Prophets might adjudicate local cases, but the statistical marvel of universal judgment will require a presiding Deity.

Scriptural Witness. The Old Testament consistently identifies the Judge as God himself:

> "Arise, O God, judge the earth! For it is You who possess all the nations!" (Psalm 82:8 NASB)

> "Rise up, O Judge of the earth, Render recompense to the proud. . .How long shall the wicked exult?" (Psalm 94:2-3 NASB)

Why only God? Two divine attributes rule out human judges.

a. Who God is

God is righteous and always acts congruently with his nature. Abraham knew it: "Will not the Judge of all the earth do right?" (Genesis 18:26). Moses knew it: "For the LORD your God is God of gods and Lord of lords, the great God, mighty and awesome, who *shows no partiality and accepts no bribes*" (Tawrat, Deuteronomy 10:17). David knew it: "The LORD reigns forever; he has established his throne for judgment. He *rules the world in righteousness and judges the peoples with equity*" (Psalm 9:8). And so did every biblical prophet.

Such a God earns our trust. We are confident his judgments will be right because of who he is. He will be free from outside pressure and will deliver verdicts without prejudice or any liability known to undermine the halls of justice.

b. What God Sees

God sees what people overlook.

> "Man does not see what the LORD sees, for man sees what is visible, but *the LORD sees the heart.*" (1 Samuel 16:7)

> "The heart is deceitful above all things and beyond cure. Who can understand it? *I the LORD search the heart and examine the mind, to reward each person according to their conduct,* according to what *their deeds deserve.*" (Jeremiah 17:9-10; see Psalm 7:9-11)

> "For *the word of God* is alive and active. Sharper than any double-edged sword, it *penetrates even to dividing soul and spirit, joints and marrow; it judges the thoughts and attitudes of the heart. Nothing in all creation is hidden from God's sight. Everything is uncovered and laid bare before the eyes of him to whom we must give account.*" (Injeel, Hebrews 4:12-13)

Despite the daunting mathematics of world judgment and the OT passages assigning God as Judge, Jesus still claimed that role for himself!

Jesus knew his divinity qualified him to render justice for all. For the very attributes ensuring God's perfect justice belonged equally to him.

He would judge as the Son of Man. Jesus would execute judgement as this Figure that we have already seen to be transcendent: "The Father . . . has given him [Jesus] authority to judge because he is the Son of Man" (John 5:30; see vv 25, 27).

He would judge as the Messiah. Prophets foretold of the just judgments of the coming Messiah:: "He will *not judge by what he sees with his eyes*, or decide by what *he hears with his ears*; but *with righteousness he will judge* the needy, *with justice he will give decisions* for the poor of the earth" (Isaiah 11:3-4; see Micah 4:3).

He would judge as the Word of God. Jesus would judge as "the Word" who "was made flesh and lived among us" (John 1:1, 14). That dual nature as the God-Man will endow his judgments with two essential capacities: empathy with mankind through his personal experience and full knowledge of everyone's words, deeds and secrets through his omniscience: ". . . *the Word of God judges the thoughts and attitudes of the heart. Nothing in all creation is hidden from God's sight.* Everything is *uncovered* and *laid bare before the eyes of him to whom we must give account*" (Injeel, Hebrews 4:12-13). Jesus knew what was *in* man even while on earth (Jn 2:24- 25; Jer 17:10; Jn 6:64; 9:4; 12:25; 1 Cor 4:5; S. 3:48-49; 52; 5:110, 112; 19:19, 20, 24, 30-33).

But how can humanity's Savior also become its Judge? People will be held responsible for their own choices to God's saving work through the sacrifice of his Son. **Refusal of his gifts will establish the basis of justice at Jesus' second coming.**

"If I had not done among them the works no one else did, they would not be guilty of sin. As it is, they have seen, and yet they have hated both me and my Father." (John 15:24)

Christ's "works" revealed God's nature of love and made saving faith in him possible:

"For God so loved the world that he gave his one and only Son, that whoever believes in him shall not perish but have eternal life. *For God did not send his Son into the world to condemn the world, but to save the world through him."* (John 3:16-17)

> "Christ comes to judge the world 'as little as the sun comes to throw a shadow. Judgment like the shadow is the natural consequence."
> Holtzmann

But those same works achieved more:

"Whoever believes in him is not condemned, but whoever does not believe stands condemned already because they have not believed in the name of God's one and only Son." [25]

> A rejection of God's living revelation is a rejection of God himself.

"This is the verdict: Light has come into the world, but people loved darkness instead of light because their deeds were evil. Everyone who does evil hates the light, and will not come into the light for fear that their deeds will be exposed. But whoever lives by the truth comes into the light, so that it may be seen plainly that what they have done has been done in the sight of God." (Injeel, John 3:16-21)

These verses unravel for us "the paradox that Jesus both came to judge and did not come to judge. Why would anyone reject the Son who performed awesome works and spoke the truth? "Because the Son was the light (Jn 1:9; 8:12; 9:5) that exposed mankind's true spiritual condition and need for salvation."[26]

His coming gives men the opportunity of salvation and challenges them to a decision. To refuse His good gift is to be judged."[27] In other words, neither God nor fate condemns no one. People choose for themselves. Jesus came to bring salvation but judgment must follow.

> "Christ comes to judge the world 'as little as the sun comes to throw a shadow. Judgment like the shadow is the natural consequence."[28]

Conclusion

Our response to Jesus Christ in this life will determine his response to us in the next.[29]

> "If anyone is ashamed of me and my words in this adulterous and sinful generation, *the Son of Man* will be ashamed of them when he comes in his Father's glory with the holy angels." (Mark 8:38; Matt 16:27, Lk 12:8-9

> "Be always on the watch, . . . that you may be able to stand before the Son of Man." (Luke 21:36)

That is because a rejection of God's living revelation is a rejection of God himself.

> "The culpable unbelief that counted the offer of Christ's grace as nothing will be condemned. By rejecting grace in this life, one already judges oneself, receives according to one's works, and can even condemn oneself for all eternity by rejecting the Spirit of love."[30]

Next, Jesus reverses the focus of his existence from the future to the distant past.

5. Jesus claimed a preexistent life.

The next evidence that Jesus claimed divinity was how he spoke of the eternal world as though he had been there personally.

We need not repeat what has already been noted under the Son of Man. Two additional factors deserve our attention.

Jesus' disarming manner. Jesus on occasion described the heavenly realm or life on "the Other Side." That in itself is not particularly noteworthy. Other founders of world religions have done the same. Unlike Jesus, however, for access to their knowledge, they resorted to third-parties (angels, shamans, etc.) or out-of-body experiences such as divination, spiritism, rituals, trances, visions or "enlightenment."[31] Not so with Jesus. We never see him entranced in an altered state, receiving heavenly messages through any of these avenues. He described heaven naturally, much like a son telling his mother about his day at school or a husband relating his day at the office.

Why so? How do we explain that difference from the religious founders? The following disarming statements give us a clue:

> "The seventy-two returned with joy and said, 'Lord, even the demons submit to us in your name.' He replied, 'I **saw** Satan fall like lightning from heaven.'" (Luke 10:18)

Jesus' listeners must have done a double-take. He saw Lucifer booted from heaven at the dawn of history? At another time, he described what happened in heaven whenever lost people would accept God's Truth and come home:

> "The one who comes from above is above all; the one who is from the earth belongs to the earth, and speaks as one from the earth. The one who comes from heaven is above all. He testifies to what he has seen and heard, ..."
> Jesus, John 3:31-32

> "*I tell you* that in the same way there will be *more rejoicing in heaven over one sinner who repents than over ninety-nine righteous persons who do not need to repent.*'" (Luke 15:7)

These mini-glimpses into the unseen world catch us off-guard by their candid simplicity. How did his emphatic, "I tell you. . ." come across so naturally? Jesus shared his secret:

> "The one who comes from heaven is above all. *He testifies to what he has seen and heard . . .*" (John 3:31-32)

These statements about heaven arose from Jesus' memory, not conjured through trance.[32]

> "Very truly I tell you," Jesus answered, "before Abraham was born, I AM [*Ego eimi*]!" At this, they picked up stones to stone him . . ."
>
> Jesus, John 8:58

Jesus' claims of timelessness. Jesus said he had personally seen Abraham even though the patriarch had lived 2000 years before him:

> "Your father Abraham rejoiced at the thought of seeing my day; he saw it and was glad."

> "You are not yet fifty years old," they said to him, "and you have seen Abraham!"

> "Very truly I tell you," Jesus answered, *"before Abraham was born, I AM [Ego eimi]!"* At this, they picked up stones to stone him . . ." (John 8:58)

Hearing this claim rankled his opponents. They thought he was claiming equality with God.

But let's step back for a moment. Does Jesus' preexistence necessarily indicate his divinity? Muslims, Sunni and Shia alike, have countered that "all prophets preceded Abraham, but that doesn't make them God!"[33] Is the preexistence of prophets taught in the Qur'an? If so, I missed it. Our Scriptures say just the opposite, emphasizing that prophets are like Elijah, "a human being, even as we are" (James 5:17) and nothing more. The larger point about Jesus' preexistence is that for purposes of salvation, origins matter. Who can impart the gift of everlasting life except someone who is himself an eternal Being (John

6:27)? His own eligibility for that role rested on his pre-existence as the Son of Man on whom "God the Father has set his seal of approval" (John 6:62 alluding to Daniel 7:14).

Even Muslims who argue the pre-existence of prophets never ascribe them with divine status. By contrast, the preexistence of Jesus was associated with his divinity above the human realm.

6. Jesus assumed a position of final authority that no prophet would dare take.

Another strong line of evidence that Jesus considered himself divine came in the form of statements he made positing absolute authority in *himself,* claims far exceeding the authority of prophets.

a. His Teaching – "Heaven and earth will pass away, but My words will not pass away" (Matthew 24:35).[34]

Prophets of God, of course, also spoke with divine authority. But Jesus enshrined his words with finality that placed them beyond abrogation. We see this in some of the idioms and choice of words he used such as "truly I say to you." Biblical prophets usually began, "Thus says the LORD." By contrast, Jesus uttered what no prophet would dare say: "*I* say to you. . ." or "*I* tell you the truth." In his longest message, for example, notice this refrain: "You have heard . . . *But I say to you* . . . ."

> "When Jesus had finished saying these things, the crowds were amazed at his teaching, because he taught as one who had authority, and not as their teachers of the law." Jesus, Matthew 7:28-29

Murder (the sixth commandment). "*You have heard* that the ancients were told, 'You shall not commit murder' . . . *But I say* to you that everyone who is angry with his brother shall be guilty. . . ." (Matt. 7:21-22)

Committing Adultery (the seventh commandment). "*You have heard* that it was said, 'You shall not commit adultery'; *but I say* to you that everyone who looks at a woman with

164

lust for her has already committed adultery with her in his heart." (verses 27-28)

Taking Revenge. "*You have heard* that it was said, 'An eye for an eye, and a tooth for a tooth.' *But I say* to you, do not resist an evil person; but whoever slaps you on your right cheek, turn the other to him also." (verses 38-39)

Treating Enemies. "*You have heard* that it was said, 'You shall love your neighbor and hate your enemy.' *But I say* to you, love your enemies and pray for those who persecute you, so that you may be sons of your Father who is in heaven." (verses 43-45)

Those listening took note:[35] "When Jesus had finished saying these things, *the crowds were amazed at his teaching,* because *he taught as one who had authority, and not as their teachers of the law*" (Matt 7:28-29. See also Matt 22:33, 46; Mk 1:22, 27; Lk 4:32).

b. *His Name* – Jesus taught his followers to invoke his own name in prayer and ministry.

> How many times did Moses, Elijah, David or any prophet instruct the Israelites to speak in his name? Zero. They knew God's power resided in Yahweh's name, not theirs.
>
> How often did Jesus instruct the disciples to act in his name? Yet Jesus said, "I will do whatever you ask in my name, so that the Father may be glorified in the Son. You may ask me for anything in my name, and I will do it."
>
> John 14:13-14

"*I will do whatever you ask in my name,* so that the Father may be glorified in the Son. You may ask me for anything *in my name,* and I will do it." (John 14:13-14)

"Again, truly I tell you that if two of you on earth agree about anything they ask for, it will be done for them by my Father in heaven. For where two or three gather *in my name,* there am I with them." (Matthew 18:20)

How many times did Moses, Elijah, David or any prophet instruct the Israelites to speak in their respective names? Zero. They knew Divine power resided in *Yahweh's* name, not theirs. How often did Jesus instruct the disciples to act in his name?

> "The Messiah will suffer and rise from the dead on the third day, and repentance for the forgiveness of sins will be preached *in his name* to all nations, beginning at Jerusalem." (Luke 24:46-47)

> "Yet to all who did receive him, to those who believed *in his name*, he gave the right to become children of God." (John 1:12)

> "The seventy-two returned with joy and said, "Lord, even the demons submit to us *in your name*." (Luke 10:17)

> Jesus performed many other signs in the presence of his disciples, which are not recorded in this book. But these are written that you may believe that Jesus is the Messiah, the Son of God, and that by believing you may have life *in his name*." (John 20:31)

If *this* prediction failed to materialize, Jesus' previous claims must be dismissed as delusional. But if they played out, it forces us to reconsider all he claimed to be.

> "Truly I tell you, anyone who gives you a cup of water *in my name* because you belong to the Messiah will certainly not lose their reward." (Mark 9:41)

The point becomes obvious:

> "The significance which the prophets attached to the name of Jahveh [Yahweh] is transferred by the Savior Himself to His own name as being the Messiah."[37]

c. *His Demands and Rewards* – Jesus called people to a lifetime of full devotion "for my sake" or "on my account" with the promise of blessings or consequences accordingly.

"You must be on your guard. You will be handed over to the local councils and flogged in the synagogues. *On account of me* you will stand before governors and kings as witnesses to them." (Mark 13:9)

"And everyone who has left houses or brothers or sisters or father or mother or wife or children or fields *for my sake* will receive a hundred times as much and will inherit eternal life." (Matthew 19:29)

Speaking like this placed himself at the center of religious devotion as no biblical prophet would dare. Anyone other than Jesus making such statements would be considered creepy. Jesus required extreme sacrifices with the promise of eternal rewards. These sayings from the earliest tradition are of supreme importance:

"Then he called the crowd to him along with his disciples and said: "Whoever wants to be *my disciple must deny themselves and take up their cross and follow me.* For whoever wants to save their life will lose it, but whoever *loses their life for me* and for the gospel will save it." (Mark 8:34-35; see Matthew 10:39; 16:24-25; Luke 9:23-24; 14:27; 17:33)

Jesus scaled back the public presentation of his deity to align it with the divine pattern prefiguring it, namely, the OT tabernacle.

"Blessed are you when people insult you, persecute you and falsely say all kinds of evil against you *because of me.* Rejoice and be glad, because great is your reward in heaven. . ." (Matthew 5:11-12)

"'Truly I tell you,' Jesus replied, 'no one who has left home or brothers or sisters or mother or father or children or fields *for me and the gospel* will fail to receive a hundred times as much in this present age: homes, brothers, sisters, mothers, children and fields—along with persecutions—and in the age to come eternal life.'" (Mark 10:29-30)

"They will seize you and persecute you. They will hand you over to synagogues and put you in prison, and you will be brought before kings and governors, and *all on account of my name.* And so *you will bear testimony to me.*"

"Everyone will hate you *because of me*. But not a hair of your head will perish. Stand firm, and you will win life. (Luke 21:12, 17-19; see Matt 24:9; Mark 13:3)

"They will treat you this way *because of my name . . . .*" (John 15:20)

What is this but to claim equality with God? Jesus substituted "for me" instead of the prophet's 'for the Lord's name's sake.' Argyle writes,

"Who is this who calls upon men to sacrifice their lives for His sake? In the OT the prophets and psalmists emphasize their oracles with the words 'for the Lord's sake' or more frequently 'for his name's sake'; but Jesus deliberately substitutes 'for my sake.'

8. Jesus claimed to be God's Mirror Image on Earth

Philip said to Him, "Lord, show us the Father, and it is enough for us."

Jesus said to him, "Have I been so long with you, and yet you have not come to know Me, Philip? **He who has seen Me has seen the Father;** how can you say, 'Show us the Father'? Do you not believe that I am in the Father, and the Father is in Me? (John 14:8-11)

Jesus' response to Philip's request must have baffled everyone sitting in the Upper Room that night. Did we hear that right? "Show us the Father" and, in effect, "You're looking at him!"

Was Jesus doubling the number of Deities? Far from it! Everyone in that room grew up reciting the Shema, knowing there are "no other gods." Robert Clyde Johnson in his classic book, *The Meaning of Christ*, calls this Christianity's "optical problem."

"If in looking to Jesus our attention is diverted from God, we have blundered on one side. Or if we attempt to "see God" without looking to Jesus, we have blundered on the other. To blunder on either side is to see without seeing [cf. Matthew 13:13]."

How can we avoid either of these blunders? Johnson draws an analogy of a greenhouse in which one looks through glass at a garden.

"Optically it is possible to do either of two things. We may focus upon the window. If we do so, we see the garden; but it is only a confused mass of color pointlessly framed by the window. If, however, we focus upon the garden, we not only see the garden clearly, and appreciate it fully, but we also see the window as it should be seen. **The function of a window is transparency; and the more transparent it is the more perfectly it fulfills its reason for being.** It is when we see through a window that we see a window as it is intended to be seen."

How does this relate to Jesus?

"It is in much the same way that we must look to Jesus Christ when we seek to fathom his meaning. It must be axiomatic that God is God. If our concern with this man Jesus in any way distorts this fact, we have bumbled into the optical fallacy and violated the basic conviction of the Christian faith, that there is one God.

Yet, if the New Testament is right in its claim that "God was in Christ," we may, and we must, turn to this man with complete and final concern. It must be, however, a looking "through" Jesus to see God, as we would look through a window to see a garden."[1]

Jesus was God's revelation, not his replacement.[2] His answer to Philip's question echoed his earlier public claim: "The one who sees Me sees Him who sent Me" (John 12:45; cf. 16:28). That is, the One *seen* (Jesus) precisely portrays the One *believed* (God the Father). For "The one who believes in Me believes not in Me, but in Him who sent Me" (John 12:44). In other words, our trust in Jesus does not pull us away from God, but to him. It affirms monotheistic truth, respects its complexity and focuses our vision to one supreme God.

Muslim reader, while Jesus' bold claim might strike you as flagrant self-aggrandizement, actually it was just the opposite. It was another way of saying, "This isn't about me!" The grand subject of his life was God the Father about whom he transparently displayed.

This word picture must not be pressed unduly. For "the greenhouse window" which exhibited a clear view of God was far more than a piece of glass serving that purpose. It *itself* was the divine Word (Jn 1:1-2; 14). Were it not, it would cease as God's infallible revelation, for no created thing can reveal him. Jesus' avowal to Philip was a bold claim to his divine nature.

9.   Jesus claimed that he would be killed at the hands of his enemies by God's will, raised back to life on the third day and his death would provide redemption for humanity. (See Chapter 9)

We come finally to the last piece of evidence that Jesus believed himself divine. Here it came in the form of a near-future prediction:

> "Listen! We are going up to Jerusalem. *The Son of Man* will be handed over to the chief priests and scribes, and *they will condemn Him to death*. Then they will hand Him over to the Gentiles to be mocked, flogged, and crucified, and *He will be resurrected on the third day*." (Matthew 20:17-19 HCSB)

Of all Jesus' predictions, this one was by far the most daring. Coming just months before his death, it was no safe end-of-the-age forecast, one he made while fully aware his listeners would not be around to verify it. But it was more than daring.

It was also Jesus' most critical claim, the linchpin holding together all the of evidence for his deity. If *this* prediction failed to materialize, Jesus' previous claims must be dismissed as delusional. But if they played out, it forces us to reconsider all he claimed to be.

A doctor from a psychiatric ward recently told of patients who would say, "Doctor, I am God" or "I'm the Son of God. I have power to give eternal life!" His impulse to reply, "No, you're not. You're crazy," was, of course, left unsaid. He continued. "Had that patient, however, followed up his outrageous claim with: 'Next week I will be killed and three days later come back to life. You will see me again,' I would suddenly pay very close attention."

> If *this* prediction failed to materialize, Jesus' previous claims must be dismissed as delusional. But if they played out, it forces us to reconsider all he claimed to be.

If this prediction failed to materialize, Jesus' previous claims must be dismissed as delusional. But if they played out, it forces us to reconsider all he claimed to be.

- The holy One, morally and spiritually perfect
- Authority to forgive sins
- The future Son of Man returning in clouds of glory
- The judge of the human race past and present
- Pre-existed with God in heavenly glory
- Authority centered in himself, elevating his name above any prophet
- God's mirror image on earth

What kind of man would make such claims? While never hearing Jesus say, "I am God," can the person making such declarations be saying anything less? C. S. Lewis, a former Oxford atheist, aptly observed:

> "I am trying here to prevent anyone saying the really foolish thing that people often say about Him: 'I'm ready to accept Jesus as a great moral teacher, but I don't accept His claim to be God.' That is the one thing we must not say. A man who said the sort of things Jesus said would not be a great moral teacher. He would either be a lunatic — on a level with the man who says he is a poached egg — or else he would be the Devil of Hell. You must make your choice. Either this man was, and is, the Son of God: or else a madman or something worse. You can shut Him up for a fool, you can spit at Him and kill Him as a demon; or you can fall at His feet and call Him Lord and God. But let us not come with any patronizing nonsense about His being a great human teacher. He has not left that open to us. He did not intend to."[38]

We will return to the *question* of Jesus' resurrection. Now that we have seen what Jesus claimed for himself, we are ready to turn our attention to *how* he said it, that is, his presentation.

PART 2: THE PRESENTATION OF JESUS' DEITY

Question 5.1: "When did Jesus claim to be divine?"

How did Jesus openly present his deity in a manner that maximized faith and minimized unnecessary havoc, the latter being a certain consequence that a bare assertion, "I am God," would have caused. He did so through two effective ways. He scaled back its presentation to conform to an earlier divine pattern and yet he made it too obvious to deny.

1. Jesus Scaled Back his Disclosure to Fit God's Pattern

Jesus scaled back the public presentation of his deity to align with the divine pattern prefiguring it, namely, the OT tabernacle. That prototype takes us back to the time of the wilderness wanderings after the Israelites left Egypt. God commanded Moses:

> "Build a sanctuary for me ... Make this tabernacle and all the furnishings exactly like the pattern I will show you." (Exodus 25:8-9; 40; cf. Heb 8:5)

Why would a God who exists outside of creation, who calls heaven his throne and earth his footstool, order Moses to do such a thing – construct for him a dwelling-place on earth, one built to his exact blueprints? It's baffling! This was not Moses requesting it, but God commanding it!

God's stated reason for this command provides us with more than clarity. It gives us hope: *"that I will dwell among them"* (Exodus 25:8). God almighty is not only holy and separate but *personal* and gracious. So much so that he chose to place himself *with* his people – stubborn and prone to selfishness as they are – in a "tabernacle," a word taken from the verb "to dwell." Thus, it was often called the "Tent of Meeting" (Exo 27:21; Lev 24:3, etc.) emphasizing the direct encounter that would occur between the God of heaven and his people on earth.

> "The tabernacle is the place where God and man can be closest to each other. Here God meets with His people (Exodus 29:42-43).[43]

This sanctuary built in the wilderness was the precursor to the Jerusalem Temple built centuries later by King Solomon and then again by King Herod.

How does this OT tabernacle shape the way that Jesus publicly presented his deity? Since God specified tabernacle's exact "pattern," a term designating it as a "type" of something else, clues to answering its application to Jesus can be found by paying attention to its structure. The Bible lays out enormous detail about the building, its furnishings, priesthood and sacrifices but for now we will zero in on two prominent features.

Animal Hides on the Outside, Gold Within

Let's begin on the outside. Its covering was a "tent" consisting of animal hides or badger skins sewn together. It was rough to the touch and nothing notable to see (Ex 26:14).

Stepping inside, one entered another world altogether. Inside was the "Dwelling Place" itself where the people would meet God. It was divided into two sections. The larger outer area was the **"Holy Place"** illuminated by a *golden lampstand*[39] and furnished with an *altar of incense*[40] and the *table of showbread* (Ex 25:30) holding the *Bread of the Presence.*

The smaller innermost chamber was called the **"Most Holy Place"** or **"Holy of Holies."** In contrast to the outer sanctuary where priests performed daily rituals, this room was so holy that only one person, the *High Priest*, could enter, and then only once annually on the Day of Atonement.

Blocking entry to this inner chamber hung a thick curtain, a **"veil"**41 placed as a protective shield to prevent anyone from a direct perilous encounter with God. This barrier was embroidered of finely twisted linen of blue, purple and scarlet yarn (Ex 26:1) and hung on gold hooks attached to posts made out of gold-plated acacia wood (Ex 26:32).

Such was God's pattern given to Moses. Other nations surrounding Israel also built temples to their gods, even with inner chambers, but with one striking difference. Sitting in their inner chambers was an image of their god. Here *no* such statue was present! Instead, we find two furnishings: a *Mercy Seat* of pure gold symbolizing God's throne and beneath it the *Ark of the covenant* overlaid with pure gold that held objects of remembrance such as the stone tablets of the Law. In this place, the High Priest confessed national sins of the people from the previous year while sprinkling the blood of a sacrificial animal on the Mercy Seat. God's holy judgment transformed into grace and mercy.42 He spoke from above the Mercy Seat where sin was removed and friendship with His people restored (Exodus 25:21-22).

This sanctuary was completed according to God's blueprint. Why *this* arrangement placing tacky hides on the exterior that concealed rather than displayed God's majestic beauty? It seems counterintuitive. One would think God's Temple would be arrayed with an eye-catching façade featuring artistic ornamentation to make his glorious splendor conspicuous. Would not that magnify Yahweh's name to the nations? Not really because it would miss out on the greatest revelation manifested inside: God's glory.

The sanctuary was associated with divine "glory." Once the tabernacle was completed,

> "The cloud covered the Tent of Meeting, and the glory of the LORD filled the tabernacle" (Exodus 40:34).

This descending fullness of glory reoccurred later at the completion of the Jerusalem Temple (2 Chron 7:1-3). What exactly is the *"glory [kabod]* of the LORD?"* Is it simply a general term for his splendor? It's meaning is more precise. It denotes the *visible manifestation of his Presence*. It was synonymous with "Shekinah," a word for "dwelling" (Lev 17:4; Nu 16:9, 17:13, etc.) and in Jewish tradition was sometimes substituted for God's name.45 No one can directly see God's face and live. Yet, the people needed assurance that his Presence was with them. What they could see was his "glory," always visible.44 In the days of Moses, it also appeared through a pillar of cloud by day and fire by night and rested at the center of the Israelite camp. It reminded them of God's Presence and their covenant obligation to him.46

The Modern readers may read this dismissively as a primitive institution that humanity has outgrown. By doing so, we may throw out the proverbial baby with the bathwater. While its rituals have become obsolete, the tabernacle conveys fundamental realities with enduring value about God and humanity.

Mrs. Charles Cowan in her spiritual classic, *Streams in the Desert*, captured the significance of this pattern:

> "The very tabernacle of God was covered with badgers' skins and goats' hair; one would not think there would be any glory there. The Shekinah of God was manifest under that kind of covering."47

Indeed, rough hides on the outside subtracted nothing from the divine glory on the inside. The "tent" was clearly distinguished from God's "dwelling place" inside it (Nu 3:25; Exo 26:7; 35:11, etc.). The glory of his Presence was not perceived in the ordinary covering itself but through the divine-human fellowship revealed within.

The tabernacle's dual composition of animal hides and pure gold helps us gain a better theological understanding of Jesus' nature, but also how that nature would express itself through his demeanor. That is, neither part ruled-out the other.

Let's move on. Though the tabernacle was a collapsible structure made to be quickly moved from one place to another until replaced by the stone Temple in Jerusalem, its significance was long-range. The Tawrat does not jump suddenly from the pattern given to Moses to the New Testament. Let's proceed to the intermediate stage.

Anticipated by God's Prophets. The structural pattern God gave to Moses was projected onto the living portrait drawn by God's prophets. Prophet Isaiah foretold the coming Messiah who would embody the same complexity of the tent-shrouded, glory-filled tabernacle. From the outside, what would people see? An ordinary man who:

> "sprouted up like a twig before God, like a root out of dry ground"

> "no beauty or majesty to attract us to him, nothing in his appearance that we should desire him" (Isaiah 53:2).

The same pattern God gave to Moses was projected onto the living portrait drawn by the prophets. The Messiah would enter human society in plain clothes. Concealed under his human shell, however, would be "Immanuel, God *with us*" (Isaiah 7:14; 9:6). God's actual Presence, his Shekinah-glory, would visibly move into local neighborhoods. It would be free of outwardly impressive marks of glitzy celebrity, handsome V.I.P.s or stiff royalty. So homespun, local folks would say things like "Is this not the carpenter's son?" (Matt 13:55).

Moses' pattern and the prophet's portrait merged fully embodied in Jesus, "the Word made flesh."

> "The Word [divine, glorious, eternal] became flesh [human] and made his dwelling [lit. *skene*, "tabernacled"] among us. We have seen his glory [*Shekinah*], the *glory* of the one and only Son, who came from the Father, full of grace and truth." (John 1:14)

When Jesus arrived on the scene, what did people see? The Samaritan woman said, "I saw a man" (John 4:29, 39). Nothing was recorded about his looks. Yet in him resided the sanctuary (tabernacle), the locus of God's presence on earth. What the OT tabernacle provided the people of Israel – "What other nation has a God so near?" – Jesus as the Word incarnate provided the world.

"The tabernacle is the principal bridgehead in the OT to the doctrine of the Incarnation. God, who once dwelt among His people in an edifice, now dwells among us in Jesus Christ."[48]

The force of this second and greater Tabernacle in John 1:14 is *fullness* and *finality*. The same divine Presence concealed long ago under badger skins now resided fully in the Lord Jesus Christ!

"All the ways of tabernacling of God in Israel had been transitory or incomplete: all are fulfilled and superseded by the Word-made-flesh and dwelling among us.' That is the great point. What had been hinted at and even realized in a dim, imperfect fashion earlier was perfectly fulfilled in the Word made flesh."[49]

Humanity did not erase divinity from Jesus any more than animal skins removed God's glory from the first tabernacle. As Augustine wrote,

"Man was added to Him, God was not lost to Him."[50]

"He emptied Himself not by losing what he was, but by taking to Him what He was not."[51]

Muslims' excellent question, "Where did Jesus say *I am God. Worship me?*" is partially answered here in the OT tabernacle typifying it. God's glory would not be seen through outward accoutrements of splendor. Jesus refused to just come out with it—*I am God! Worship me!* Flaunting it would have turned God's holy Shekinah into a circus.

This pattern explains why Jesus rejected the Devil's ploy at the start of his ministry: "Jump off the Temple Tower. Make a big splash. Seize the headlines!" Flamboyancy is the way of the world. Jesus' way was chosen for him by his Father and he followed it to the letter.

"My chosen One in whom I delight. "He will not shout or cry out, or raise his voice in the streets" (Isaiah 42:2).

He chose the prototype covered in badger skins. In appearance, he was little distinguished from other men. Nothing on the outside marked him off as eminent. While understating his deity, Jesus never undermined it. Here was God made flesh.

But How?

Jesus composite nature begs the question: How could the concealed Deity of Jesus of Nazareth, whose glory lay hidden beneath a shell of ordinary humanity, possibly break through so that people could see for themselves and believe him? More bluntly asked, **how could a man who ate, slept and answered the call of nature ever convince anyone of his true identity as the eternal divine Word?**

2. Jesus Made his Deity too Obvious to Deny

Jesus performed his first miracle at a wedding in Cana, Galilee. It introduced a pattern of cause and effect:

> "What Jesus did here in Cana of Galilee was the first of *the signs* through which *he revealed his glory; and his disciples believed in him.*" (John 2:11)

What occurred here? Jesus made his deity too obvious to deny. To "reveal" means to uncover something that is present while hidden from view. Here at his first miracle, a stunning one at that, Jesus uncovered his "glory," placing his invisible divine Presence before the eyes of men and women. This was an epiphany, but one of objective substance rather than a mere flash of insight. By this, he engendered recognition and effected faith in his divine nature. Over the next three years, we see this pattern of cause and effect, sign and belief, expand into three sequential stages.

STAGES IN HIS PRESENTATION OF DEITY

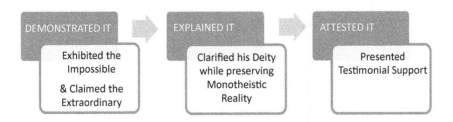

DEMONSTRATED IT	EXPLAINED IT	ATTESTED IT
Exhibited the Impossible & Claimed the Extraordinary	Clarified his Deity while preserving Monotheistic Reality	Presented Testimonial Support

STAGE 1: Demonstrated It – Jesus exhibited the impossible and claimed the extraordinary.

Jesus did not just say, *I am the Bread of life.* First, he borrowed a boy's lunch basket containing five loaves of bread and two fish and with it fed 5,000 hungry people (John 6:27, 35, 41, 51). He showed them before he told them.

> The miracles of Jesus strained conventional thinking and forced new conclusions about God. What had first been considered too illogical to believe suddenly became too irrational to deny.

Jesus did not just say, *I am the Light of the world.* First, he met an adult man who had been blind since birth (John 9:25) and gave him perfect vision. He showed them before he told them.

Jesus did not just say, *the Son of Man is Lord of the Sabbath.* On a Sabbath Day, he ordered a cripple for 38 years to stand up, pick up his bedroll and go home. And he did! He showed them before he told them.

Jesus did not just say, *I am the resurrection and the life.* Standing alongside mourners at the tomb of a beloved young man four days dead, he called him by name and shouted, "Come out!" That evening they *all* dined together in the formerly deceased man's home (John 11:25-26, 43-44). He showed them before he told them.

Jesus made his deity too obvious to deny. The point is this. Instead of announcing himself as God, he did things in front of people that only God could do. When I first met my beautiful wife-to-be, did she have to inform me, "I am a woman?" Of course not! Stating the obvious was not necessary.[52]

Those who argue that Jesus never said, "I am God," are correct only in the most literal sense. He never *said* those words. But they overlook that his *works* spoke volumes! If Michelangelo had never said, "I am an artist," would later generations debate the issue? His masterpieces spoke for themselves. Jesus was not "the Word made *words,*" giving the world a book of essays. He was "the Word made *flesh*" (John 1:14), planting the Presence of the living God with us that we might see his divine glory (John 1:14b), thankfully, in veiled form that does not blow us off the planet.

This reality of Jesus as the *living* Word explains why the earliest controversies surrounding his deity did not happen in seminary classrooms. They occurred on life's playing field, usually at the tail-end of supernatural acts that, by the way, had three notable characteristics. They were *humane* – people got better. They were *unprecedented* – completely over-the-top! And they were *undeniable* – performed out in the open.

What did Stage 1 accomplish? The miracles of Jesus strained conventional thinking and forced new conclusions about God. What had first been considered too illogical to believe suddenly became too irrational to deny. This put Jesus' opponents at a disadvantage. How tough it must have been to discredit his divine claims while the happy recipients of his divine power stood before them – now seeing colors and shapes, now leaping high in the air, now freed from demonic slavery. How unnerving! For example,

"They summoned the man who had been blind. 'Give glory to God by telling the truth,' they said. "We know this man [Jesus] is a sinner.'

He replied, 'Whether he is a sinner or not, I don't know. One thing I do know. *I was blind but now I see!* . . .'

Then they hurled insults at him and said, 'You are this fellow's disciple! We are disciples of Moses! We know that God spoke to Moses, but as for this fellow, we don't even know where he comes from.'

The man answered, 'Now that is remarkable! You don't know where he comes from, yet he opened my eyes. We know that God does not listen to sinners. He listens to the godly person who does his will. Nobody has ever heard of opening the eyes of a man born blind. If this man were not from God, he could do nothing.'

My hunch is that many Christians like myself have not followed Jesus' example of providing explanatory caveats, perhaps adding to Muslim confusion about his deity in relation to monotheism.

To this they replied, 'You were steeped in sin at birth; how dare you lecture us!" And they threw him out.'" (John 9:24-25, 28-34)

The Light of the world had come! The blind began to see while the religious leaders became blind. Each miracle opened a window into Jesus' Shekinah, rays of glory that had gone previously undetected beneath his tent of flesh.

STAGE 2: Explained It – Jesus preserved monotheistic reality by clarifying his divine nature

In John 5:1-8, Jesus healed a lame man who for 38 years had been disabled. Because it occurred on the Sabbath Day, it precipitated a firestorm of questions, challenges and accusations of blasphemy. This became one of the first occasions in which we find Jesus embroiled in a controversy concerning his deity.

> "So, because Jesus was doing these things on the Sabbath, the Jewish leaders began to persecute him. *In his defense Jesus said to them*, 'My Father is always at his work to this very day, and I too am working.' For this reason they tried all the more to kill him; *not only was he breaking the Sabbath, but he was even calling God his own Father, making himself equal with God.*" (1 John 5:16-18)

Jesus commendably did not shy away from controversy. I love these words: "he gave them this answer!" Jesus bent over backwards to explain what his claims did and did not mean.[53] My hunch is that many Christians like myself have not followed Jesus' example of providing explanatory caveats, perhaps adding to Muslim confusion about his deity in relation to monotheism.

He stood his ground, defended his claim *and* clarified what he meant. His answer in John 5:19-30 provides Christians with an excellent example of patient explanation and unflinching conviction.

Stage 2 preempted his audience of absurd conclusions:

I am not a second God. There is only one Godhead with one final authority in it: the Father!

I did not come to replace God, but to fully reveal him.

I never became God's partner, for as the Son I share the Father's nature without obliterating the distinction between us.

But it did more than avoid absurdity. It set forth three positive realities on the nature of God. Answering the "equality with God" charge, Jesus clarified what it did and did not mean.

"I am not a second God." Jesus preserved monotheistic reality while clarifying the inner relationship between the Father and Son. He called God his Father and conveyed three core truths about their kinship. They were (a) one in nature (see John 1:1,18) and thus not two Gods, (b) distinct in Person (they constantly interacted) [54] yet (c) unequal in authority. That is, they shared equal nature but not equal position. Without question, Jesus says the Father's *place* is higher than his own. He instructed the Son and not the other way around. Chapter 3 has already presented these connections and need not be repeated.

> Jesus insisted that divine truth cannot be determined at the ballot-box.

"I came to reveal God, not replace him." He established the basis for trusting his revelation of God. Two factors qualified Jesus as God's supreme revelation.

Submission – The Son's full submission to the Father protected his portrayal of him from personal ego. Often Christians, in defending Jesus' deity, have over-claimed his position in the Godhead. This exaggeration is exactly what Jesus avoided here. His authority on earth did not mean autonomy from heaven. *Everything* the Father willed the Son promptly executed. The Son never played solo, but always acted in concert with his Father. *Two moved and spoke as one.* Only because of that, Jesus could say,

"He who believes in *Me*, does not believe in *Me* but in *Him* who sent Me. He who sees *Me* sees the *One* who sent *Me*." (John 12:44)

In fact, all who love Jesus also love the Father. It is impossible to love Jesus and hate the Father, for he is the Father come in the flesh.

> "Jesus spoke with the confidence of being commissioned by the Father, not with the arrogance of self-assertion."[55]

Concrete Actions – With vivid clarity, Jesus' brought to the world stage the God whom no man can see. His proximity to the Father, thanks to his kindred nature as the Son, gave him direct and immediate access to him.

> *"No one has seen the Father except the one who is from God;* only he has seen the Father." (John 6:46)

Thus, what he saw in private he enacted in public:

> "The Son ... can do only what *he sees his Father doing, because whatever the Father does the Son also does."* (Jn 5:19; see 4:34; 5:30; 8:28; 12:50; 15:10)

What the Father creates, the Son executed. Jesus' miracles lifted the curtain into the glory of God's grace and power.

"I never became God's partner." Eternal kinship between the Father and Son made partnership unnecessary, excluding it altogether. Even the statement, "the Father loves the Son. . ." (John 5:20a; see Jn 1:18), is not the language of Master-to-slave or partner to partner. By describing the inner-workings between the Father and Son in terms of kinship – closeness, trust and intimacy – Jesus does more than simply dismiss error.[56]

He is saying that his revelation of God is of maximum value because of their closest possible relation.

So in the Explanation Stage of presenting his Deity, Jesus combined three factors: his total submission, his concrete action and their shared kinship. Together these achieved what no prophet could produce: an unsurpassable and final[l] revelation of God.[57] Jesus'

Sonship, transcending both metaphor and biological reality, describes an eternal relationship with the Father made possible through their shared nature. His complete submission to the Father further ensured that what we see in Jesus is exactly what the Father is like.

Jesus easily could have stopped with Stage 2. After all, His miracles were too obvious to deny and his clarifications affirmed his divine kinship with God while preserving monotheist reality and honor. But he adds one more layer of evidence to solidify his claim.

STAGE 3: Attested It – Jesus presented credible witnesses who vouched for his authority and Identity (John 5:30-47)

Divine truth is not up for a vote. Many rejected Jesus on the basis of religious tradition or, what might be called, the prevailing majority opinion. Jesus insisted that divine truth cannot be determined at the ballot-box.

> Jesus' opponents appealed to wide support for their ideas; Jesus rested his case on higher authority.

"*I do not accept glory from human beings*, but I know you. I know that you do not have the love of God in your hearts. I have come in my Father's name, and you do not accept me; but if someone else comes in his own name, you will accept him. *How can you believe since you accept glory from one another but do not seek the glory that comes from the only God?*" (John 5:31-47)

In effect, Jesus said, "You don't let God be God." His opponents appealed to wide support for their ideas; Jesus rested his case on higher authority.

Credible Testimonies Attested Jesus' Claims

There is nothing wrong with multiple witnesses *per se*. Biblical law required multiple witnesses to establish truth by which to render just verdicts (Deut.

> One ounce of credible testimony weighs more than a pound of human opinions!

17:6; 19:15). To satisfy the law, Jesus chose five witnesses to attest his claims, but not just *any* five. He was selective, aware that **trustworthy testimony to divine realities must come from God**. An ounce of credible testimony outweighs a pound of human opinions! No wonder he refused to "accept glory from human beings" (John 5:41). Had he let human opinion shape him, he would have become a political Messiah rather than a crucified and risen Savior. Nor would he permit testimonies from jinn or demonic entities (Mark 3:7-12). Finally, he even withdrew his *own* testimony (John 5:31; see 8:13), not because it lacked truth but for "the Jewish principle that self-witness was illegitimate on its own."[58]

Five Divine Witnesses

In John 5:31-47, Jesus called on five witnesses to testify on his behalf, all sharing one thing in common. Each spoke with God's authority.

> "I have ***testimony*** weightier than that of [1] ***John*** [*Yahya*]. For the works that the Father has given me to finish—[2] the very *works* that I am doing—testify that the Father has sent me. And [3] ***the Father*** who sent me has himself testified concerning me. You have never heard his voice nor seen his form, nor does his word dwell in you, for you do not believe the one he sent. You study the Scriptures diligently because you think that in them you have eternal life. These are the very [4] ***Scriptures*** that testify about me, yet you refuse to come to me to have life. "But do not think I will accuse you before the Father. Your accuser is Moses, on whom your hopes are set. If you believed [5] ***Moses***, you would believe me, for he wrote about me. But since you do not believe what he wrote, how are you going to believe what I say?"" (John 5:31-47)

Briefly noted, these witnesses are:

1. God's Messenger: John the Baptizer, Forerunner to the Messiah. The testimony of John the Baptist (*Yahya*) was huge.

> "There was a man sent from God whose name was John. He came as a witness to that light." (Jn 1:6)

Widely recognized as the Messiah's forerunner, John publicly testified that Jesus is "the Lord" (Jn 1:23). That John himself preached as the prophet who had been pre-announced by earlier prophets (Mal 3:1) obligated people to hear what God said through him. He attested that Jesus was the "true Light" (Jn 1:9), the "Lamb of God," and "God's Chosen One" (Jn 1:23, 29, 34, 36). Jesus often endorsed his testimony as here:

"There is another who *testifies in my favor,* and I know that his testimony about me is true. 'You have sent to John and he has *testified to the truth.* . . I mention it that you may be saved." (John 5:32-33).

Authorities at the Jerusalem Temple sent priests to spy on John. To them he boldly proclaimed Jesus. Despite John's eminent reputation, he was unworthy to "untie the straps" of Jesus' sandals; he "surpassed me because he was before me" (Jn 1:15). Jesus was more than a prophet, said John, and they should have listened. Through his testimony, scores believed in Jesus.

"They [those baptized by John] said, 'Though John never performed a sign, *all that John said about this man was true.'* And in that place many believed in Jesus." (John 10:40-42)

2. God's Miracles. Even more convincing than John's testimony was that of Jesus' public miracles. Performed with such frequency, they provided a strong basis for belief in him and became a stalwart defense against his opponents. They "speak for me" (John 10:25), offering convincing evidence for his claims.[59]

"'Why then do you accuse me of blasphemy because I said, "I am God's Son"? *Do not believe me unless I do the works of my Father.* But if I do them, even though you do not believe me, *believe the works, that you may know and understand that the Father is in me, and I in the Father.'"* (John 10:36-39)

Out of the scores of Jesus' miracles (Jn 20:30), seven were distinguished as "signs" (*semeion*) and given special significance. The idea of a sign is that it points beyond itself to something greater. In Jesus' case, they attested to his divine glory as the divine Word made flesh. These seven are: Jesus (1) turned water into wine (Jn 2:1-11); (2) healed an official's son (Jn 4:43-54); (3) healed a paralytic (Jn 5:1-15; (4) fed thousands (Jn 6:1-14); walked on the sea (Jn 16-21); cured a blind man (Jn 9:1-41); and (7) raised Lazarus from the dead (Jn 11:1-41). These herculean signs gave clinching testimony to Christ's claims of divine glory and marked him out as the Messiah, the One for whom the world awaited.

3. God Himself. God, who is incorporeal Spirit having no form, became visibly prominent through the public miracles performed by the Son. In this way, the unseen Father vouched for the Son.

> "And *the Father who sent me has himself testified concerning me.* You have never heard his voice nor seen his form, nor does his word dwell in you, for you do not believe *the one he sent."* (John 5:37)

How did the Father testify on the Son's behalf?[60] If the Father was not involved, the Son could not do miracles. For *the Father was "in him" doing the works* (Jn 14:11). By committing the performance of those works to the Son (Jn 4:34; 5:36; 9:3; 10:37; 17:4), they signaled the Father at one with him. Referring to the Father, Athanasius (ca. 296-373 A.D.), an early Church leader, noted:

> "For just as, though invisible, he is known through the works of creation; so, having become man, and being in the body unseen, it may be known *from his works that he who can do these things is not man, but the power and Word of God."*[61]

4. God's Scriptures. The Messiah's coming was copiously predicted throughout the three main sections of Scripture: the Torah, prophets and Psalms.[62] How was it possible that those so steeped in Scripture to miss Jesus? They missed him by putting God's revelation in the place of God, turning it into an end in itself, a fetish, an object of worship, an idol and turned the living God into a dead letter. They missed the living One to whom it pointed. Scriptural witness included the sufferings of Christ (Jn 3:14-15; 12:14-15; 19:24, 28, 34).

"You study the Scriptures diligently because you think that in them you have eternal life. These are the very Scriptures that testify about me, yet you refuse to come to me to have life" (John 5:39).

5. *God's Law-Giver.* A belief in the revelation given to Moses would have led them to a belief in Christ (see Luke 16:29-31; Cf. Deuteronomy 18:15 with John 6:14; 7:40-41).

SUMMARY

How did Jesus publicly present his deity? Rather than flaunting it through public announcements, he scaled back its disclosure to fit the divine pattern given to Moses and earlier prophets. Then he let his actions precede his claims. First, he showed them. Then he told them. Finally, he backed it up with credible witnesses. All combined, he made it too obvious to deny.

PART 3: THE LOGIC OF JESUS' DEITY
Why I Believe

Q 5.2: On what basis do Christians believe that Jesus (*pbuh*) is divine?

Reasons for my personal belief in the deity of Jesus draw on comprehensive support rather than one strand of evidence. The subtitle, "Why I Believe," hints at a factor that is difficult to capture on paper. The path to belief includes logic, as the title suggests, but surpasses it. I did not reach that conclusion by first sitting down and thinking it out. That came afterwards. God alone knows God and only God can make himself known to mortals. It was God who led the earliest Christians to arrive there through what they knew in Scripture and what they saw. They, in turn, under the Spirit's leadership, recorded these things so that those in later times may read and follow suit.

What influences one's recognition of divine truth and what prevents it? We are but recipients of God's revelation of himself and how each of us comes to believe involves mystery. The same divine

Spirit who first inspired sacred Scripture also illuminates us within – our mind, affections and will.

Neither our belief nor unbelief in Jesus' deity can be explained by human reasoning alone. The passage below explains that behind its rejection is its distortion by the Adversary.

> "The god of this age has blinded the minds of unbelievers, so that they cannot see the light of the gospel that displays the glory of Christ, who is the image of God." (2 Corinthians 4:4)

Christians and Muslims have a common enemy and it is not each other! Thankfully, God does not leave us helplessly groping for truth in our blindness.

> "For *God*, who said, 'Let light shine out of darkness,' *made his light shine in our hearts to give us the light of the knowledge of God's glory displayed in the face of Christ*." (2 Corinthians 4:6)

While acknowledging our foe, we need not yield to him! He cannot wield sovereign power over us. We prevail by the Word of God.

God himself awakens us to the "glory of Christ" by means of his choosing. It may be through his Word, the lifestyle of one of his followers, or even a dream allowing us to recognize a quality that marks Jesus differently than our previous perceptions.

Christians and Muslims have a common enemy and it is not each other!

God helps us see who Jesus is and our desperate need for him. And, of course, God does not lead us to Jesus initially and leave us there at the threshold. Initial dawning enables constant deepening. The following evidences of Jesus' deity have emerged out of years of being drawn into a deepening knowledge of blessed Scripture.

This section introduces biblical signposts pointing to the divine nature of Jesus of Nazareth. In addition to Jesus' own declarations noted earlier, let us add seven more signs, clues and manifestations attesting to his deity.

1. ITS DESCRIPTION – Jesus' deity is presented with precision, theological propriety and personal appeal.

Sources matter, so let us begin with indications of credibility found in our pipeline of information. What we learn from the Injeel about Jesus' divine nature rings true both in description and tone. Chapter 7 will expand on this, but the paragraph below from 1 John 1:1-4 merits our close attention:

> "What was from the beginning, what we have *heard*, what we have *seen* with our eyes, what we have *looked at* and *touched* with our hands, concerning the Word of Life— and the life was manifested, and we have *seen* and *testify* and *proclaim* to you the eternal life, which was with the Father and was manifested to us— what we have *seen* and *heard* we proclaim to you also, so that you too may have fellowship with us; and indeed our fellowship is with the Father, and with His Son Jesus Christ.
>
> These things we write, so that our joy [together] may be made complete." (1 John 1:1-4, emphasis added)

This poignant paragraph unveils Jesus al-Masih as God's very Word of Life and eternal Son. Four striking traits commend its trustworthiness:

a) *Eyewitnesses* – "heard . . . seen with our eyes . . . touched with our hands"

Our information comes to us through firsthand eyewitnesses who occupied front-row seats to all that Jesus said and did over a three-year period. Rumor and hearsay had no place in the Injeel's record of Jesus' life. Their reporting was observation-based, passing on to others what they themselves had first seen, heard and touched. Note the repeated references to their multi-sensory direct experience.

b) *Joint testimony* – "*we* have heard . . . *we* have seen . . . *we* have touched . . . ."

Adding to its empirical plausibility is collective corroboration. Note the repetition of the plural "we." Our information did not originate with a solo observer reporting "*I* saw, *I* heard, *I* touched. . ." Individual accounts were corroborated by others who also witnessed them. This protected the story against private exaggeration or unwarranted innovation. One may suspect that this was herd-think, the power of peer-pressure if not for the fact that each of them paid the ultimate price for their report. These joint witnesses testify to the relevant facts surrounding key events with remarkable consistency.

c) *Monotheistic commitment* – "the eternal life, which was with the Father and was manifested to us"

These reporters were strident monotheists. The living Word who became historically manifested in time "was from the beginning," that is, eternally present in the Godhead. For them, it could be no other way. The apostles as Scripture-revering Jews would have taken every precaution against inflaming God's wrath by turning a human being into a divine Superman. Yet they had no qualms to "proclaim to you the eternal life, which was with the Father. . ."

> The apostles as Scripture-revering Jews would have taken every precaution against inflaming God's wrath by turning a human being into a divine Superman.

d) *Noble Intentions* – "that you may have fellowship with us"

Their invitation to outsiders is winsome and infused with the warmth of a welcoming God. Their aim is clearly not to win a contest but to enlarge a fellowship. As such, their appeal shifted from logical persuasion to personal invitation: "so that you too may have fellowship with us . . . that our joy may be made complete."

Clarity of mind is one thing; goodness of heart another. We find in these sources a nobility of soul. They've found a good thing and are eager for others to share in it. I especially appreciate this, for that outsider looking in was once me. My name found its way on their invitation list. As God's enduring Word, this door remains open. Every name in the Muslim world is found there as a standing invitation into this fellowship!

2. GOD'S RIGHTEOUS CHARACTER – Jesus was sin-free in everyday life from cradle to grave

When people observed the moral character of Jesus, they saw God's holiness lived out. And what they saw confirmed rather than contradicted his divine nature. Since God is holy, Jesus' divine nature is contingent upon his sinlessness.

Was Jesus without sin? We already discussed what he himself said about it. While fitting, his testimony is yet incomplete. This subject calls for broader voices. Jesus' critics appealed to this, "Here you are, appearing as your own witness; your testimony is not valid" (Injeel, John 8:13). Volunteering as a prison chaplain years ago, I commonly heard convicted thieves, pedophiles, and even murderers assert their innocence by rationalizing their crimes. The question is whether others will back up their claim. Let's listen to the wider testimonies.

Jesus' Character References

Testimony of John the Baptist [Yahya], Jesus' Forerunner

"The next day John the Baptist [Yahya] saw Jesus coming to him and said, '*Behold, the Lamb of God* who takes away the sin of the world!'" (John 1:29; see v 35)

By calling Jesus this title, John bore witness to his unassailable character.[63] Jewish law required sacrificial lambs to be without blemish.

Testimony of the Apostles

Jesus' most qualified character witnesses were those closest to him, his apostles. If anyone had the inside scoop on his moral character, they did. Three years at his side provided them with plenty opportunities to observe his moral patterns. They saw him under intense pressure and hostility. They watched him mingle with the opposite sex, how he responded to needy people, often marginalized, when he was physically tapped out. What would they find? Did he, like so many public figures, post body guards to protect his reputation as he engaged in trysts and shady deals? How often was damage control required to hide his scandals?

Apostle John – Jesus' moral character was a stark contrast to all others:

> "If *we claim to be without sin, we deceive ourselves* and the truth is not in us. . . If *we claim we have not sinned, we make him out to be a liar* and his word is not in us." (1 John 1:8, 10)

> "You know that He [Jesus] appeared in order to take away sins; and *in Him there is no sin.*" (1 John 3:5)

John called Jesus "the Righteous One" (1 John 2:1), who like God was the Moral Exception. His personal purity was in step with his world mission.

Apostle Peter, the Fisherman – Testified to three relevant facts:

First, Jesus was condemned in a court of religious law despite his known innocence. This injustice contrasted his divine holiness with the capacity of self-righteous people to commit heinous evil..[64]

> "You [God] will not let your *Holy One* see decay . . . You [*religious* people] disowned *the Holy and Righteous One* and asked that a murderer be released to you." (Acts 2:27; 3:14)

Second, Jesus lived without sin in the crucible of severe and brutal testing. Despite his innocence, hostility against him took the form of mob rejection, verbal slander and grueling physical torture. And yet Jesus kept his cool by a singular focus upon his Father who sent him for that purpose. That goal was you and me. As a life-pattern, Jesus was exemplary.

> ". . . Christ also suffered *for you*, leaving you an example for you to

follow in His steps, who *committed no sin, nor was any deceit found in His mouth;* and while being reviled, *He did not revile in return;* while suffering, He *uttered no threats, but kept entrusting Himself to Him who judges righteously;* and He Himself *bore our sins in His body* on the cross, so that *we might die to sin and live to righteousness;* for by His wounds you were healed." (1 Peter 2:21-25)

Third, Jesus' innocent sufferings were not wasted.

"Christ *suffered once* for sins – *the righteous for the unrighteous* – to *bring you to God*." (1 Peter 3:18)

Jesus' non-stop obedience from cradle to grave culminated in righteousness in its rarest form: "suffered once for sins;" its benefits, however, fan out to the widest number (the "unrighteous") for the highest cause ("bring you to God").

Judas Iscariot – Even the one who betrayed Jesus with a kiss testified:

"Judas felt remorse and returned the thirty pieces of silver to the chief priests and elders, saying, 'I have sinned by betraying *innocent blood.'*" (Matthew 27:4)

Apostle Paul – Testified on the authority of Scripture that on Judgment Day, no man will be able to bear the punishment for another because all are sinners. There is one exception.

"God made *Him [Jesus] who knew no sin* to be sin [offering] *on our behalf,* so that *we might become the righteousness of God in Him.*" (2 Corinthians 5:21)

Because he was without sin, God accepted Jesus' death as our substitute for our vice that we may take on his virtue.

Testimonies from Outside Jesus' Circle

Author, Injeel's Book of Hebrews – Jesus encountered the full range of the devil's arsenal. Yet not once did he deviate from his mission or cave in to worldly allurements.

> "For since *He Himself [Jesus] was tempted in that which He has suffered*, He is able to come to the aid of those who are tempted." (Hebrews 2:17-18)

> "For we do not have a high priest who cannot sympathize with our weaknesses, but One who *has been tempted in all things as we are, yet without sin*. Therefore let us draw near with confidence to the throne of grace, so that we may receive mercy and find grace to help in time of need." (Hebrews 4:15-16)

Testimony of Jesus' Enemies

Religious Leaders. Even Jesus' adversaries admitted his spotless reputation. By their flattery to "trap him in his words," they admitted to having nothing to pin on him:

> "Teacher, we know that you are a *man of integrity* and that you teach the way of God in accordance with the truth. *You aren't swayed by others*, because you pay no attention to who they are. Tell us then, what is your opinion...?" (Matthew 22:16)

Pilate & King Herod. Testified to Jesus' innocence after cross-examination:

> "...Having examined Him before you, *I have found no guilt in this man* regarding the charges which you make against Him. No, nor has *Herod*, for he sent Him back to us; and behold, *nothing deserving death has been done by Him*.'" (Luke 23:13-15)

> "Pilate said to them, 'Why, *what evil has He done?*' But they shouted all the more, 'Crucify Him!'" (Mark 15:13; Matt 27:23)

"I find *no guilt in Him*." (John 18:38; 19:4)

Pilate's Wife. Testified that Jesus' innocence was confirmed through her dream:

> "While he was sitting on the judgment seat, his wife sent him a message, saying, *'Have nothing to do with that righteous Man;* for last night I suffered greatly in a dream because of Him.'" (Matthew 27:19)

Roman Executioner at Jesus' Crucifixion

> "Now when the centurion saw what had happened, he began praising God, saying, *'Certainly this man was innocent.'*" (Luke 23:13-16, 47)

This impressive range of testimony vouched for Jesus' moral perfection. This remarkable consensus reveals a person having a nature that is more than human. Like no other,

> "His life was a unique, moral miracle."[65]

3. MORE THAN A PROPHET – Signs Placing Jesus above Prophets

That Jesus filled the honorable role as prophet in the Injeel is beyond question (Mk 1:32; 3:28; Lk 13:31f; *4:24f; Jn* 5:46, etc.). The Qur'an concurs, along with the adamant caveat that Jesus was a prophet and no more (Al-Nisa 4:171; Al-Zukhruf 43:59, etc.).

How can we sort out these differing acclaims for Jesus? Was he prophet-plus (i.e. also deity) or prophet-only? The question naturally leads Christians and Muslims to pay close attention to his attributes. Why so? Because anything or anyone's essential traits, behaviors or characteristics provide us with a set of clues by which to define them. Dogs, for example, don't grow feathers and birds do*n't grow fu*r. To date, there is no record of a barking cat. Everything behaves according to its attributes.

That matchup of identity and attributes makes the Injeel's book of Hebrews so relevant to our question. Its opening paragraph compares the attributes of Jesus as God's Son (see Chapter 2) with those of God's messengers, his prophets. Through these striking contrasts, it provides further evidence for Jesus' **deity.**

TEN SIGNS JESUS WAS
MORE THAN A PROPHET
Hebrews 1:1-4

"After God spoke long ago in various portions and in various ways to our ancestors through the prophets, in these last days he has spoken to us in a son, whom he appointed heir of all things, and through whom he created the world.

The Son is the radiance of his glory and the representation of his essence, and he sustains all things by his powerful word, and so when he had accomplished cleansing for sins, he sat down at the right hand of the Majesty on high. Thus he became so far better than the angels as he has inherited a name superior to theirs." (Hebrews 1:1-4 NET)

1. *Superior Capacity for Revealing God.* God's messages given to each prophet was fragmentary and distributed among others in "various portions" [*polumeros,* "many parts"]. Each received a unique portion of the whole in God's unfolding revelation throughout the OT period.

The Son expressed God's nature and purposes fully. Two factors explain this initial contrast. First, he fulfilled the sum-total of OT predictions which were about him. We need not belabor this matter here (See Chapter 9, "Sources of the Injeel"). Second, the Son's vivid portrayal of God drew from an eternal relationship with the Father, reaching all the way back in time before creation.

"but in these last days he [God] has spoken to us by a Son, ... through whom he also created the worlds." (Hebrews 1:3 NRSV)

Never was there a time when the Son was absent from the presence of God. This advantage gave Jesus a more personal, intimate and complete portrayal of the nature of God.

2. *Superior Mode of Reception.* Prophets received messages from God in "various ways" (*polutropos*, "many ways") including angelic visits, dreams, visions, the Urim and Thummim, etc. (see Numbers 12:6-8). Regardless of which mode was used, in all cases the message originated from outside of themselves via an intermediary. In Jesus' life, by contrast, these external modes of delivery are missing entirely. The reason for this omission is explained next.

3. *Superior in Nature.* Prophets were only human. Elijah, for example, endowed with enormous power was, nevertheless, "a human being, even as we are" (James 5:17). While the Spirit breathed God's messages into them, they did not possess God's own character. The Son, however, was:

> "the reflection [*apaugasma*, "radiance"] of God's glory and the exact imprint [*charaktēr*, "impression; stamp"] of God's very being..." (Hebrews 1:2 NRSV)

As the Son, Jesus not only delivered God's messages but radiated his character. He was Light of Light, the effulgence or brightness of God's glory. "The sun is never seen without effulgence [radiance], nor the Father without the Son." Contrasted with prophets, we see that:

> "Ezekiel portrayed the glory of God, but Christ reflected it (1:3). Isaiah expounded the nature of God as holy, righteous and merciful, but Christ manifested it (1:3). Jeremiah described the power of God, but Christ displayed it (1:3). He far surpassed the best of prophets of earlier times..." [3]

Not only was Jesus the beam of God's radiance. Another term distinguished him as "the exact imprint of God's very being."

> "All the attributes of God became visible in him. The stamp vividly

presents the picture of an image or superscription on a coin or medal. It exactly and perfectly matches the picture on the die. The verbal form of the word used here (*charaktēr*) means 'to engrave'. In other words, if man wants to see God he must look to Christ."

Jesus' revelation of God, then, was not simply audible, restricted to his teachings, but conspicuously visible. His nature explains why none of the intermediary methods given to prophets were not necessary in his case. "Christ is the ultimate Word of God...God spoke to us in one who has the character – that He is Son."

4. *Superior in Life-giving Power.* Prophets' words carried divine power to guide people in the ways of God. The Son matched that capacity but supplemented it with the power to create life by his commands.

> "God has spoken to us through his Son through whom he made the universe" (1:2)... "In the beginning, Lord [the Son], you laid the foundation of the earth, and the heavens are the works of your hands."' (Hebrews 1:10)

Jesus' words brought what was not into being and, by the same word, what was broken restored to vibrant health. The Son, then, "was no mere Galilean preacher. He shared actively in the creative work of Almighty God."

5. *Superior in Moral Character.* Prophets, while upstanding men in society, confessed their own sins (see earlier discussion). Jesus was holy by nature at his birth (Luke 1:35), a moral attribute from which he never deviated. Not even once! His humanity was as real as yours and mine; yet sin was absent. Moreover, he passionately lived to please his Father and share his joy:

> "But about the Son he says, ... You have loved righteousness and hated wickedness; therefore God, your God, has set you above your companions by anointing you with the oil of joy." (Hebrews 1:9)

This moral attribute was a requirement for his life mission as One "who makes people holy" (Heb 2:11). Only a holy being can make others holy.

6. ***Superior Change-Agent.*** Prophets effected change by informing people of God's nature and pointing them to the right path. Moses did so for Israel by erecting the tabernacle or "tent of meeting" according to divine plan. It became the place where ongoing animal sacrifices were made by which to restore fellowship with God. Other prophets such as Isaiah foretold of a future sin-bearing Messiah (Isaiah 53). All pointed to Jesus' who effected change by his ultimate one-time sacrifice for human sin.

> "When he had made purification for sins, he sat down at the right hand of the Majesty on high..." (Hebrews 1:3-4 NRSV)

Christ's posture, "he sat down" emphasizes the completion of his saving work, a contrast to the repetitive labor of OT priests in the Temple:

> "The priest stood because his task was never complete. He could never hope to bring it to the moment of final achievement. Only Christ's sacrifice could be eternally effective. He sat down to indicate that the work was finished. On that day when he bore our sins in his own body, he cried, 'It is finished.'

As a result, the people were enabled to enter into the presence of God without dying, (Deut 5:26; Lev 16:1–34). How then did Jesus bring spiritual renewal and moral change?

> "...when he gave himself up on the cross Jesus shed his blood once for all at a single point in time. No repetition of this saving act will ever be necessary, nor can anything that we do serve to procure our own salvation. Christ is God's unrepeatable sacrificial provision for the greatest problem of mankind—sin."

7. ***Superior over the Angels.*** When the Son entered the world as a baby, God commanded, "Let all God's angels worship him" (Heb 2:6).

In obedience, they filled the Bethlehem sky (Luke 2: 9, 13-14). This divine command placed Jesus not only above prophets themselves, but the heavenly agents sent to inform them. How striking that these emissaries, endowed with supernatural power and authority, were ordered to bow their knee to Jesus.

8. *Superior Death.* Prophets are mortal and their tombs shrine-like as devotees of successive generations travel long distances to venerate them with costly adornment. In silence, each lies there permanently until the Day of Resurrection. While their messages endure, their passing brings an end to their prophetic office.

What a contrast with the Son. The Son still speaks because the Son still lives.

> "...Because Jesus lives forever, he has a permanent priesthood. Therefore he is able to save completely those who come to God through him, because he always lives to intercede for them." (Heb 7:24-25)

As Savior and Mediator, Christ never retired. He holds his office permanently.

His ongoing priesthood rests "on the basis of the power of an indestructible life" (Heb 7:16). Even the universe will "perish and wear out like a garment." [Yet] it is said of the Son:

> "But you remain the same, and your years will never end" (Heb 1:11-12).

9. *Superior Authority.* Prophetic authority resided in their divine words. Jesus' authority rested in his divine status as the Son of God coupled with his accomplishment won through his suffering and humiliation.

> "But we do see Jesus, who was made lower than the angels for a little while, now crowned with glory and honor because he suffered death, so that by the grace of God he might taste death for everyone." (Heb 2:9-10)

"To which of the angels did God ever say, 'Sit at my right hand until I make your enemies a footstool for your feet'?'" (Heb 2:13)

Conclusion

By comparing their respective attributes, what have we learned about the prophets and the Son?

10. ***Superior Place in Line.*** God, who spoke to people "in the past" through prophets has spoken in a new way through his Son "in these last days." Jesus appeared at the very end of the prophetic line, concluding one epoch in biblical history and starting another. In Jesus, God's eternal purposes were realized in history to which the earlier prophets faithfully testified.

"What kind of
man is this?"
Matthew 8:27

The Son Distinguished from Prophets – Jesus is more than a prophet. He clearly is not identified here as one more prophet, or God's final prophet or "seal of the prophets." He came as the Messiah, the Son of God as the grand Object of their predictions.

Muslim reader, if you have observed Jesus in action on the pages of the Injeel, it's likely you will echo a question raised by those on the scene: "What kind of man is this?" (Matthew 8:27). Exactly. "What kind," a query into Jesus' type, class or species made necessary by observing his unique attributes on display. I hope this short passage from Hebrews helps answer such an inquiry.

"Hebrews introduces us to a Christ whose perfect sinless nature is a
unique revelation, whose sacrifice is alone effective for our salvation,
and whose authority in heaven and on earth is without rival."

Continuing along this theme of divine attributes, let us continue.

4. PERFORMED GOD'S WORKS – Jesus did what only God could do.

Jesus was directly involved in the awesome works attributed to Deity including God's work in creation (John 1:3; Col. 1:16, etc.), in forgiving the sinful (Luke 7:48 and Mark 2:5 respectively), of salvation (John 3:16ff, etc.), of judgment (John 5:22; 2 Tim. 4:1, etc.) and so forth.

One of the strongest evidences attesting Jesus' deity was the miracles he performed.[67] Do these tag him as a divine Being? While some prophets also performed miracles on occasion, Jesus did so frequently, purposefully and judicially.

A. Frequency – Miracles were Jesus everyday acts

Miracles, wonders and signs attested who Jesus was (Acts 2:22).

> *"If Jesus was a supernatural being, then one should not find his acts shocking.* Jesus exercised absolute power over nature, wrought miracles, gave sight to the blind, caused the deaf to hear, hushed winds, and raised the dead. *He was the omnipotent God."*[68]

Some people imagine that he only performed a few miracles here and there. The Injeel tells a very different story. They were integral to who he was. His ministry began with a flurry of healing power:

> "Jesus *went* throughout Galilee, *teaching* in their synagogues, *proclaiming* the good news of the kingdom, and *healing every disease and sickness among the people.*" (Matthew 4:23)

> "News about him spread all over Syria, and people brought to him all who were ill with various diseases, those suffering severe pain, the demon-possessed, those having seizures, and the paralyzed; and he healed them." (Matthew 4:24-25)

These continued with such frequency that they became a "characteristic activity"[69] as denoted by one of the terms often used to describe them (*ergon* or "works"), signifying the character of the one performing them.[70]

In reference to Christ (Jn 5:36; 7:3, 21; 10:25, 32-33, 38; 14:11-12; 15:24; 17:4), his miraculous "works" were consistent with who he was, normal manifestations of a supernatural being.

> "Any person's attributes determine their actions. Jesus was no exception. Who he was preceded and explained what he did, and what he did was in every way consistent with who he was."[71]

B. Public –Jesus' miracles were usually performed out in the open, making their denial possible only on the basis of willful blindness rather than empirical evidence.

Jesus' miracles were witnessed firsthand by people crowded in streets, in synagogues, in houses and out in open country. No one, not even his enemies, could logically deny their occurrence. Here are two examples:

Fed 5,000 Hungry People from One Boy's Picnic Basket

> "Jesus, seeing that a large crowd was coming to Him, said to Philip, 'Where are we to buy bread, so that these may eat?' . . . One of His disciples, Andrew, Simon Peter's brother, said to Him, 'There is a lad here who has five barley loaves and two fish, but what are these for so many people?'
>
> Jesus said, 'Have the people sit down.' Now there was much grass in the place. So the men sat down, in number about five thousand. Jesus then took the loaves, and having given thanks, He distributed to those who were seated; likewise also of the fish as much as they wanted.

Jesus was a prophet, but more. Prophets infallibly *declared* God's Word to be heard and heeded. Jesus as the living Word came wrapped in flesh to perfectly reveal the Father's glory, casting a transforming vision (John 1:14).

> When they were filled, He said to His disciples, 'Gather up the leftover fragments so that nothing will be lost.' So they gathered them

up, and filled twelve baskets with fragments from the five barley loaves which were left over by those who had eaten." (John 6:5-14)

Brought Dead People Back to Life

"So when Jesus came, He found that *Lazarus had already been in the tomb four days.* Now Bethany was near Jerusalem, about two miles off; and many of the Jews had come to Martha and Mary, to console them concerning their brother.... Martha said to Jesus, 'Lord, if You had been here, my brother would not have died...'

When He had said these things, He cried out with a loud voice, 'Lazarus, come forth.' The man who had died came forth, bound hand and foot with wrappings, and his face was wrapped around with a cloth. Jesus said to them, 'Unbind him, and let him go.'" (John 11:43-44)

C. Enormous Range – The scope of Jesus' miracles displayed the creative power of his Divine Word.

The scope of Jesus' power matched that of the omnipotent Creator. By his command, he restored physical health to human bodies, was able to alter what we call scientific laws and wielded authority over the unseen powers of the demonic world. Nothing lay beyond his reach. While humanly confined to a body of flesh, he often defied those limits. For example,

"When it was evening, the boat was in the middle of the sea, and Jesus was alone on the land. Seeing them straining at the oars, for the wind was against them, at about the fourth watch of the night He came to them, *walking on the sea;* and He intended to pass by them. But when they saw Him walking on the sea, they supposed that it was a ghost, and cried out; for they all saw Him and were terrified. But immediately He spoke with them and said to them, 'Take

Who is this? Even the wind and the waves obey him!'"
Mark 4:35-41

206

courage; it is I, do not be afraid.' Then He got into the boat with them, and the wind stopped; and they were utterly astonished. . . ." (Mark 6:47-51, cf. Matthew 14:22-27; John 6:15-21)

D. Purposeful – Jesus' miracles were signs pointing beyond themselves.

Jesus' miracles were not for shock value. They served to manifest the works of the Creator. Justin Martyr, after exploring many philosophies before becoming a Christian and was later martyred in Rome between A.D. 163 and 167, wrote to a Jewish skeptic:

> "Jesus was manifested to your race and healed those who were from birth physically maimed and deaf and lame, causing one to leap and another to hear and a third to see at his word. And he raised the dead and gave them life and by his actions *challenged the men of his time to recognize him.*"[72]

The New Testament, like the Old, used a rich vocabulary to describe Jesus' miracles.[73] One of these, as previously mentioned, "sign" (*semeion*), points beyond the spectacular act to something greater. By performing a "sign," Jesus highlighted one aspect of his divine glory, that is, confirming a claim. These were typically followed with professions of belief by many of the spectators (Jn 2:11; 4:53; 6:66, 69; 9:38; 11:48)[74].

What greater purposes did Jesus' miracles serve?

> *a. Jesus' Miracles proclaimed the overthrow of Satan's kingdom and the inauguration of God's.*

Every healing, exorcism and act of forgiveness demonstrated that the long reign of the Evil One is being dismantled. God's rule is breaking in right here, right now! Jesus explained: "But if it is by the Spirit of God that I drive out demons, then the kingdom of God has come upon you." (Matthew 12:28; Lk 11:20)

Who is this? Even the wind and the waves obey him!'"
Mark 4:35-41

"The miracles are a means of confirming the message that the kingdom of God is now being established with power! God is establishing his rule through Christ, and proving it with the miraculous power which Jesus exercises over the forces of nature, over the spirit world, and over death and disease."[75]

b. Miracles pointed to Jesus' deity so that people may believe in him.

> "The only Christ for whom there is a shred of evidence is a miraculous figure making stupendous claims."
>
> C. S. Lewis

Miracles illustrated Jesus' divine power. As "signs," they pointed to realities beyond themselves. His first miracle recorded in the Injeel occurred at a wedding in Cana of Galilee. The hosts of the event were in a panic because the wine had run out. Jesus took charge by ordering the servants to fill the large jars with water, dip a ladle into it and take it to the host. Taking a sip, he raved over its quality. Please pay attention to its three final words:

> "What Jesus did here in Cana of Galilee was the first of the signs through which he *revealed his glory*; and his disciples believed in him." (John 2:11)

This "first of the signs" pointed beyond the miraculous beverage, lifting the shade into Jesus' divine identity. Yes, this man *is* "Mary's son," but more! This is a Lion and not a mouse.

> "The Word became flesh and made his dwelling among us. We have *seen his glory*, the glory of the one and only Son, who came from the Father, full of grace and truth." (John 1:14)

Miracles were windows through which his divine glory shined out so that seeing-is-believing people can believe in him (see John 11:4, 40). They continued throughout his life (Luke 9:28-32; Matt 17:1-2; Mark 9:2-3; Acts 9:3; 22:6; 26:13; 2 Peter 1:17).

c. Miracles forced questions about Jesus' identity

i. "Who can calm raging seas?"

The Old Testament answers:

> *"He [The LORD] stilled the storm to a whisper; the waves of the sea were hushed. They were glad when it drew calm, and he guided them to their desired haven. Let them give thanks to the LORD for his unfailing love and his wonderful deeds for mankind."* (Psalm 107:30-31)

But then we get to the New Testament and this happens:

> "That day when evening came, he said to his disciples, 'Let us go over to the other side.' Leaving the crowd behind, they took him along, just as he was, in the boat. . .A furious squall came up, and the waves broke over the boat, so that it was nearly swamped. Jesus was in the stern, sleeping on a cushion. The disciples woke him and said to him, 'Teacher, don't you care if we drown?' He got up, *rebuked the wind and said to the waves, 'Quiet! Be still!' Then the wind died down and it was completely calm.*
>
> He said to his disciples, 'Why are you so afraid? Do you still have no faith?' They were terrified and asked each other, *Who is this? Even the wind and the waves obey him!*" (Mark 4:35-41)

The apostles' fear shifted from one terror to another. First, "We're drowning!" and then, "Who is this in the boat with us?"

ii. "Are you the One, the Messiah?"

> "When John [Yahya], who was in prison, heard about the deeds of the Messiah, he sent his disciples to ask him, *'Are you the one who is to come,* or should we expect someone else?'" (Injeel, Matthew 11:2-3)

Why did John ask that? "The One" what? Where did he get the idea that "one" was coming? And why does he want to know with certainty? Because John was stuck in prison for confronting King Herod for his immorality. Jesus answered John with neither "Yes, I am" or "No, I'm not." Instead, he let his actions speak for themselves:

> "'Go back and report to John what you hear and see: *The blind receive sight, the lame walk, those who have leprosy*

The "Jesus" they thought they knew was too small; puny faith got them puny results.

are cleansed, the deaf hear, the dead are raised, and the good news is proclaimed to the poor. Blessed is anyone who does not stumble on account of me.'" (Matthew 11:4-6)

What an answer. Miracles were the Messiah's business card. Some, however, took offense at Jesus. The evidence of miracles were not enough to cinch it for many who rejected Jesus.

iii. Questions from the Offended – Jesus' Hometown

As an adult, Jesus' return to his hometown of Nazareth created quite a stir. The folks there knew him only as the carpenter and Mary's son. That was no surprise since it wasn't until he was around age 30 when he began performing miracles. Now word had gotten around and his reputation as a miracle worker spread like wildfire. After hearing him teach in their synagogue questions really began to percolate:

> "'Where did this man get these things?' they asked. 'What's this wisdom that has been given him?'
>
> 'What are these remarkable miracles he is performing?'
>
> 'Isn't this the carpenter? Isn't this Mary's son and the brother of James, Joseph, Judas and Simon? Aren't his sisters here with us?'" (Mark 6:1-5)

Sadly, they forfeited what could have been because "they took offense at him" (v 6). Why were they offended? The "Jesus" they thought they knew was too small; puny faith got them puny results.

Even today, Jesus' miracles as signs of divine power not only validate his claim of deity but also provide an unshakable basis for trusting him as Savior:

> "*Jesus performed many other signs* in the presence of his disciples, which are not recorded in this book. But these are written that you may believe that *Jesus is the Messiah, the Son of God, and that by believing you may have life in his name.*" (John 20:30-31)
>
> "To *all* who did receive him, to those who believed in his name, *he gave the right to become children of God*— children born not of natural descent, nor of human decision or a husband's will, *but born*

of God." (John 1:12-13)

God gave these convincing signs for a reason: that we may be "born of God" through believing in the eternal Messiah who gives eternal life.

"The only Christ for whom there is a shred of evidence is a miraculous figure making stupendous claims." -C. S. Lewis[76]

5. RECEIVED GOD'S TITLES – To Jesus were ascribed divine names and titles.

Another line of evidence for Jesus' divine nature is the rich variety of divine titles and names ascribed to him. These reflect the multifaceted nature of his Messiahship as Prophet, Priest and King.

Titles of Divine Authority

"**Lord**" – In the Old Testament, LORD (*Yahweh*, the I AM) was God's name revealed to Moses (Exo 3:14). "Lord" (*Adonai*), means "master" or "owner." While sometimes referring only to men or angels (Exodus 34:23), it was often used in connection with God, "Adonai YHWH" (Gen 15:2), showing absolute authority as "The LORD of lords" (Deut 10:17; Psa 136:3). As such, God is the "Lord of all the earth" (Josh 3:11, 13; Psa 97:5; Zech 4:14; 6:5). See Matt 7:21; Lk 1:43; 2:11; 6:46; Jn 3:13; 6:68; 20:28; Acts 2:25; Rom 10:9, 13 (cf. Isa 28:16); 1 Cor 2:8; 3:5; 12:3; 2 Cor 4:5; Phil 2:11; Col 3:23; 1 Thess 4:16-17; 2 Pt 1:11; Rev 19:16

"**Chief Shepherd**" – (*al-Hadi*, the Guide) A well-known name for God throughout the Old Testament: Gen 49:24; Psa 80:1. He **leads** (Psa 23:2-3; Isa 40:11), **provides** (Psa 23:1, 5-6; Gen 48:15; Hos 4:16; Mic 7:14), **protects** (Psa 28:9; Gen 49:23-24), **rescues lost sheep** (Jer 31:10; Psa 119:176; Isa 53:6; Eze 34:11-16) and **judges** (Eze 34:17-22; Jer 23:1; Zech 10:2-3; 11:16). **For Jesus:**

"The deity of Jesus was invented in A.D. 325 at the Council of Nicaea." How surprising to hear this secular dogma in light of the abundant evidence that his deity was believed and preached from the very beginning of the Christian Church.

Matt 2:6 (Mic 5:2); Matt 18:12-14; 25:32-46; Jn 10:11-16; 1 Pet 2:25; 5:4; Heb 13:20

"Judge" – In the Old Testament, final responsibility for judgment is assigned to God (Gen 18:25). For Jesus in the NT, see Matthew 16:27; 25:31-33; Mk 8:38; Lk 9:26; Jn 5:27; Acts 17:31; Rom 2:16; 2 Cor 5:10

"Prince" – Acts 5:31

"King of kings, Lord of lords" – (*al-Malek*) Upon his return, Jesus will rule over the nations. In the Old Testament: Psa 2:7-9; Dan 7:13-14. For Jesus, see Matt 19:28; 25:31-32; Rom 15:12; 1 Cor 15:25; Phil 2:9-10; Rev 1:5; 12:5; 17:14; 19:11-16 (cf. Deut 10:17; Psalm 136:3)

"God" – Jn 1:1; 20:28; Phil 2:6; Tit 2:10, 13

Titles of Divine Character
"Righteous One" – Acts 3:14; (see Jer 23:6; 33:15-16; Acts 7:52; 22:14)

"The Amen" – 2 Cor 1:20; Rev 3:14 ("the Truth" [al- Haq], Jn 14:6)

"True Light" – (*al-Nur*) Isa 9:2; Lk 2:32; Jn 1:3-9; 3:19-21; 8:12; 12:46

"The Word" (*Logos*) – Jn 1:1, 14

Titles of Timelessness and Immutability

"Alpha and Omega" (First and last letters of the Greek alphabet); Isa 41:4; Rev 1:7-8; 21:6; 22:13-16 (*al-awal and al-akher*)

"Living One" – Jn 5:26; 11:25; Rev 1:18

(*Al-baeth*, **the Resurrection**, Jn 11:25-26)

Firstborn from the Dead – Rev 1:5

Messianic Titles & of Salvation

"Lion of Judah" – Rev 5:5 (see Gen 49:9-10)

"Son of David" – Matt 1:1; 15:22; 21:9; 20:30-31

"Root & Offspring of David" – Rev 22:16

"King of the Jews" – Matt 2:1-2; 27:37

"Son of God" – Matt 3:17; 4:3, 6; 8:28-34; 14:33; 16:13-20; 17:1-8; 26:57-66; 27:54; Luke 24:54; 1 Jn 5:20; Rom 1:2-4

"Immanuel" – "God with us" – Matt 1:23; Isa 7:14; 8:8

"The Prophet" – Matt 21; Jn 6:14; 7:40

"The Rock" – 1 Cor 10:4; see Isa 8:14; 28:16; Romans 9:32-33; 1 Peter 2:8

"Messiah," "Savior"– Tit 2:13; Lk 2:11

"Jesus" – Matt 1:21

"Man of Sorrows" – Isa 53:3

"Passover Lamb" – 1 Cor 5:7

"Deliverer" & "Redeemer" – Isa 59:20; Rom 11:26

Author and Finisher of Salvation – Heb 2:10; 5:9; 12:2

Titles as Mediator between God and Humanity

"Mediator" – 1 Tim 2:5

"High Priest" – Heb 3:1; 2:17; 6:20

"Son of Man" – Matt 11:19; Lk 5:24; 19:10; Jn 3:13; 6:35; Acts 7:56; Rev 1:13

7. **WORSHIPED AS GOD – Worship was given to Jesus and he received it.**

No one would argue that Jesus' words and actions profoundly affected everyone who came into contact with him. But did people during his lifetime go so far as to worship him? The question here is not *if* Jesus was divine, but was he worshipped as such by his generation?

Today's intelligentsia generally denies it, pushing the worship of Jesus to a later century. "The deity of Jesus," they say, "was invented in A.D. 325 at the Council of Nicaea." To support that position, they appeal to the process of gradual embellishment of religious founders that does in fact occur in other religions. Correctly, they note that this progression of turning great mortals into gods can only occur with the passing of many generations, even centuries.

The Buddha, for example, adamantly disavowed any identification with deity for himself or even divine inspiration for his teachings – a known fact Theravada Buddhists celebrate. Yet later generations of Buddhists padded his memory and conferred on him divine status.

Today's comparative religion courses routinely project that same tendency to Jesus in Christianity. What does this prove? Only that sophisticated elites are not immune to blindly accepting unsupportable dogmas and perpetrating them onto the historically naïve.

Does the evidence show that Jesus' deity was believed and preached from the very beginning of the Christian Church? Did they worship him as God and, if so, did he receive it?

Biblical Examples of Jesus-Worship

It should not surprise us so much that people who knew Jesus worshipped him.[77] Truly remarkable is that he never rebuked them for it! Chapter 3 presented examples of the Injeel's zero tolerance of excessive human veneration. Jesus, however, was the only exception. Even in an environment that abhorred deification, Jesus, Jewish monotheist among others, received rather than rejected their homage.[78]

The daily exposure to all Jesus said and did, how did his first followers respond to him? As strident Jews, their response was remarkable. They did what was appropriate for Deity. They worshipped him as God.

1. **A Beggar when cured of Blindness** – We have already noted this healing miracle. It concludes:

   > "Jesus said, 'Do you believe in the Son of Man?' He answered, 'Who is He, Lord, that I may believe in Him?' Jesus said to him, 'You have both seen Him, and He is the one who is talking with you.' And he said, *'Lord, I believe.' And he worshiped Him.*" (John 9:6-12; 35-38)

We see no evidence of Jesus' objection.

2. **Jesus' Apostles after Witnessing His Power over Nature**

"When they got into the boat, the wind stopped. And those who were in the boat *worshiped Him*, saying, '*You are certainly God's Son!*'" (Matthew 14:33)

Jesus did not silence them.

3. "Doubting Thomas" after Seeing him Alive

The grizzly spectacle of Jesus' crucifixion jettisoned the apostle Thomas' faith, so much so that the jubilant reports of Jesus' resurrection from the other disciples left his skepticism unfazed.

"Thomas said to them, '*Unless I see* in His hands the imprint of the nails, and put my finger into the place of the nails, and put my hand into His side, *I will not believe.*'"

A week later, something happened that reversed his stubborn doubt:

"After eight days His disciples were again inside, and Thomas with them. Jesus came, the doors having been shut, and stood in their midst and said, 'Peace be with you.' Then He said to Thomas, 'Reach here with your finger, and see My hands; and reach here your hand and put it into My side; and do not be unbelieving, but believing.'

Thomas answered and said to Him, '*My Lord and my God!*'" (John 20:24-28)

Even with this explicit profession of deity, Jesus did not reprimand him.

Is it possible that instead of expressing deity, Thomas, shocked by what he saw, simply engaged in profanity, "My God!" My friend Faizur contended that Thomas simply reacted like someone suddenly involved in an automobile accident. Besides the obvious fact that Faizur himself could not truly believe his own explanation (since he denies Jesus died in the first place), he misses two points. The words "to Him," that is, "Jesus," indicate that Thomas was not merely expelling expletives but addressing the One standing before him with a fresh burst of recognition.

Secondly, afterwards Thomas the doubter became Thomas the martyr who carried the message of Jesus' deity to India for which he died by a Brahman sword.

4. Angels Worshiped Jesus by God's Command

"And when He again brings the firstborn into the world, God says, 'And *let all the angels of God worship Him.*'" (Hebrews 1:6; See Revelation 5:11-12; 7:9-10)

5. The Apostles at his Ascension to Heaven

"And He led them out as far as Bethany, and He lifted up His hands and blessed them. While He was blessing them, He parted from them and was carried up into heaven. *And they, after worshiping Him, returned to Jerusalem with great joy,* and were continually in the temple praising God." (Luke 24:41, 52)

Since Jesus was worshiped continually from NT times, how could a church council be thought to have invented his deity 300 years later?

Historian Philip Schaff summarizes that in the NT itself:

"Christ was the object of worship, prayer, and praise from the very beginning, as must be inferred from such passages of the New Testament as John 20:28; Acts 7:59-60; 9:14, 21; 1 Corinthians 1:2; Philippians 2:10; Hebrews 1:6; John 5:13-15; Revelation 5:6-13." [79]

Historical Evidence of Early Jesus Worship

Beyond the Injeel we also find strong documentary evidence attesting the worship of Jesus long before 325 A.D. Pagan emperor, Pliny (the Younger) from Bithynia (NW Turkey), wrote Emperor Trajan in **112 A.D.** requesting counsel regarding Christians he had arrested. What was their crime? **They refused to worship the image of Caesar.** The Emperor wrote:

"On an appointed day they had been accustomed to meet before daybreak, and to *recite a hymn antiphonally to Christ, as to a god,* and to bind themselves by an oath, not for the commission of any crime but to abstain from theft, robbery, adultery and breach of faith. . ." [80]

Again, Schaff adds several ancient testimonies attesting to belief in Jesus' deity:

Gloria in Excelsis which was the daily morning hymn of the Eastern Church as early as the second century; 'Tersanatus;' from the *Hymn of Clement* of Alexandria to the divine Logos (*Paedagogus,* III. 12); From the statements of Origin (*Contra Celsum,* VIII.67) and Eusebius (*Hist. Eccl.* c. v. 28); and many other testimonies; Christ was believed to be divine, and adored as divine.

The Ante-Nicene rules of faith as they are found in the writings of Irenaeus, Origin, Tertullian, Cyprian, etc. are in essential agreement among themselves and with the Apostles' Creed, as it appears, first in the fourth century, especially at Rome and Aquileia (cf. *Rufinus, De symbol*). They all confess the divine-human character of Christ as the chief object of the Christian faith, but in the form of facts, and in simple, popular style, not in the form of doctrinal or logical statement." [81]

In other words, since Jesus was worshiped continually from NT times, how could a church council be thought to have invented his deity 300 years later? Schaff concludes:

"The Nicene Creed is much more explicit and dogmatic in consequence of the preceding contest with heresy; but *the substance of the faith is the same in the Nicene and Apostles' Creeds.*" [82]

Summary and Brief Time Out

These staggering claims about Jesus bring us to a final question: Are they *strong* or are they *arrogant?* These are often confused.

Let's recall the Chicago imam's caution against excessively honoring Jesus, producing the opposite effect by setting him up for failure and cause him embarrassment. His concern, however, assumes that Jesus' claim to deity is not only strong, which it is, but arrogant, which it is not. There's a world of difference between the two. Arrogance, according to Webster, is:

Does ascribing deity to Jesus amount to bold truth or exaggerated arrogance? We should never conflate the two.

"The act of making *undue claims* in an overbearing manner; that species of

217

pride which consists in *exorbitant claims of rank, dignity, estimation, or power,* or which exalts the worth or importance of the person to an *undue degree."*

By contrast, big claims people make can also be true. When Tiger Woods the famous golf pro asserts that he won the PGA Masters Tournament in Augusta, Georgia four times, he is not exaggerating. It is both huge and accurate, coming out on top in 1997, 2001, 2002 and 2005. Had I made that claim as a hacker golfer, however, that statement would prove arrogant and bring me well-deserved embarrassment. Before considering Jesus, please consider this fable:

> The Jesus men carried into the tomb was the same Jesus God carried out.

A caterpillar with an inferiority complex had an annoying habit of bragging to compensate for it. One day he laid it on thick. Strutting up to his friend the cricket, he said, "Hey, I'm a grasshopper."

The cricket knew him well. Suppressing the urge to say, "Have you looked at your legs lately?" he softened the blow. "You know, I've always seen you more of a crawler than a jumper."

The caterpillar raised his voice. "Listen to me! I am a grasshopper."

"C'mon, you're just a worm," said the cricket.

This went back and forth until finally the cricket had all he could take. He searched and found a small twig and lifted it as high off the ground as he could, almost an inch. Breaking into a grin, he said, "Okay, Mr. Grasshopper, jump over this!"

Turning beet red, his friend turned and inched away until wrapping himself in a fallen leaf.

I wrote this fable to illustrate the absolute truth behind the imam's concern at the Chicago mosque. Arrogance always ends with a blush, a shameful fate from which he wanted to spare Jesus. Determining if Jesus' claims to deity consisted of bold truth or hyped arrogance leads us to our last piece of evidence.

7. CONQUERED MAN'S GREATEST ENEMY – Jesus alone overcame the power of death.

Was Jesus or his followers like the arrogant caterpillar, hyping his importance? His enemies thought so. Hearing him call God his Father and making the old patriarch Abraham his contemporary was brazen and over-the-top! To them, Jesus was a worm with a grasshopper complex. Like the cricket, they'd had all they could take and were determined to bring him down to size. John 2 records their verbal exchange which I will take liberty to paraphrase:

> Leaders: "You make yourself God's equal, claim to be the mighty Messiah and the Son of God. Prove it! How high can you jump?"
>
> Jesus: "How high can I jump? Destroy this temple and I will raise it in three days!" (John 2:19).

In the background stood the majestic Jerusalem Temple built by King Herod with its massive stones and ornate columns. Looking at each other, they rolled their eyes like the cricket. They asked Jesus,

> "It took forty-six years to build this temple, and will You raise it up in three days?"

Jesus had another temple in mind:

> "He was speaking of *the temple of His body*. So when He was *raised from the dead,* His disciples remembered that He said this." (John 2:21)

His resurrection from the dead proved that sin's deathly effects have indeed been reversed, providing an abiding hope for all who believe in him!

"For as in Adam all die, so also in Christ all will be made alive."

Injeel,
1 Corinthians 15:20-22

Did Jesus' life end in infamy?

After his public crucifixion, two disciples removed his bludgeoned corpse from the cross, wrapping it tightly in a linen shroud with spices. With utmost care they laid it on a stone slab in a tomb. Upon the request of Jewish leaders, the magistrates posted guards to secure the entrance with an immovable stone to make doubly sure no one could steal the body. Despite these precautions to keep the body in – armed guards, the massive stone, his snug shroud – on the third day he broke out. The very same Jesus carried in by men was the Jesus lifted out by

God. Over the next 40 days he was seen alive, eating, teaching and interacting with his followers as well as showing himself to previous skeptics like his brother James who thought him crazy.

Seven weeks later, they all watched Jesus soar triumphantly into heaven to sit at God's right hand:

> ". . . [Jesus] was declared the Son of God with power by the resurrection from the dead, according to the Spirit of holiness, Jesus Christ our Lord. . . ." (Romans 1:1-3)

What does this prove? Jesus' victory over the grave and ascension into heaven prove he was no caterpillar with a grasshopper complex. Nor was he a mouse imagining himself a lion. Praise and worship befit him, allaying the Imam's concern of shaming him.

Is our contemplation of this subject just a historical curiosity? Or a contest of "who's right?" between Christians and Muslims? Or could it stand for something more? It beckons us all to ponder anew his earlier claim:

> "I am the resurrection and the life; he who believes in Me will live even if he dies" (John 11:24).

His resurrection from the dead proved that sin's deathly effects have indeed been reversed, providing an abiding hope for all who believe in him!

> "For as in Adam all die, so also in Christ all will be made alive." (1 Corinthians 15:20-22

PART 4: Jesus Distinguished from Miracle Workers

Question 5.3: "In the Bible we see a lot of people who did more miracles than Jesus, but no one says they are God. Why?"

You may review Part 3 for a larger discussion of Jesus' miracles. Your question correctly points to Biblical instances where God performed miracles through different people. As to the identity of those who did more of them than Jesus, I am unclear who you have in mind (see chart8[3] below). Yet your larger point is valid that performing miracles by itself endows no one with divinity!

MIRACLES IN THE BIBLE	
Person	**Miracles Performed**
Jesus	106+
Moses	27
Paul (Saul)	15+
Elisha	15
Simon Peter	12+
Elijah	10
Philip, the deacon	7+
Stephen, martyr	2+
Noah, Joshua, Gideon, Samson, Samuel, Isaiah, Daniel	2 each
Enoch, Lot, Solomon, Zechariah (father of John Baptist), Mary (mother of Jesus), John (son of Zebedee), Ananias	1 each

For the sake of argument, even if one of these men named in the chart performed more miracles than Jesus, what would that prove? Certainly not their divinity nor even their godliness. Jesus warned of false Messiahs who would perform many signs and wonders in the last days (Matthew 23:24). The "man of lawlessness" appearing at the end of the age is one case in point:

". . . the one whose coming is in accord with the activity of Satan, with *all power and signs and false wonders, and with all the deception of wickedness* for those who perish, because they did not receive the love of the truth so as to be saved." (2 Thessalonians 2:9-10)

Like Moses (Tawrat, Deuteronomy 13:1-3), Jesus warned against false prophets performing magic and miracles. On Judgment Day, many miracle workers will be in for a big surprise when Jesus tells them: "I never knew you" (Matthew 7:21-23). The Bible is clear. Miracles alone cannot prove moral goodness, much less divinity!

PART 5: Author's Question:
Why does the Qur'an Elevate Isa in the Prophetic Line?

Having responded to your questions about Jesus' deity, I would like to raise one question and welcome your thoughtful responses. As previously noted, the Qur'an affirms Jesus as God's messenger and no more. At the same time, five separate surahs (Al- Imran 3, Al-Nisa 4, Al-Maidah 5, Mariam 19, and Al-Zukhruf 43) ascribe to Jesus titles, attributes and actions elevating him to a category of supremacy.[84]

According to the Qur'an, no other prophet but Isa was:

a "seed" of a woman (Al- Imran 3:36), himself a word from Allah (Al- Imran 3:39, 45) in existence before it was cast into his mother (Al Nisa 4:171), highly exalted in this world and the hereafter (Al- Imran 3:45), named as brought near to Allah (Al- Imran 3:45), raised up to be with Allah and is with Allah now (Al- Imran 3:55; Al Nisa 4:158),

spoke as an infant in the cradle (Al- Imran 3:46, 55; Al-Maidah 5:110; Miriam 19:30), a prophet from birth (Miriam 19:30), created life (Al- Imran 3:49; Al-Maidah 5:110), healed the sick (Al- Imran 3:49) – even a man born blind and a leper (Al-Maidah 5:110); gave life to the dead (Al- Imran 3:49; Al-Maidah 5:110),

told hidden things (Al- Imran 3:49), confirmed a book (Al- Imran 3:50), confirmed the Tawrat as guidance and admonition (Al- Maidah 5:131), permitted formerly forbidden things (Al- Imran 3:50), commanded obedience in the context of a straight path (Al-

Imran 3:50; Al-Zukhruf 43:63),

sensed disbelief in people (Al- Imran 3:52), was a spirit from

Allah (Al Nisa 4:171), a witness on the Day of Judgment (Al Nisa

4:159), was aided by the Holy Spirit (Al-Maidah 5:110), spoke *af-*

ter his death implying that he was alive after his death (Al-Maidah

5:117),

was sinless (Miriam 19:19), born of a virgin (Miriam 19:20),

was a sign (Miriam 19:21), was blessed (Miriam 19:19), pronounced

peace upon himself (Miriam 19:19), was himself a proverb (Al-

Zukhruf 43:59) and a sign of the last hour, knowing when it will be

(Al-Zukhruf 43:61).

Given these unique capacities, titles and names the Qur'an ascribes

to Jesus that elevate him above all others in the prophetic succession,

can you help us understand the basis upon which we should view him

only as a prophet?

CHAPTER 6

TRINITY

Question 6: "The concept of Trinity, how does it make sense?"

Q 6.1: I never understood the concept of Trinity. I believe it should be simple. One God in three persons? What does that mean?
Q 6.2: "Is the doctrine of the trinity in the Bible?"
Q 6.3: "Is trinity an innovation in Christianity?"

AIDS FOR A BETTER UNDERSTANDING

Making sense of God's triune nature begins with a proper approach. Before delving into it, here are four guiding principles that may help.

1. Right Attitude – Tune my heart to the Subject at hand

The study of God is holy ground and calls for spiritual and mental attunement. Jesus linked our capacity to discern if a teaching is from God with our willingness to obey.

> "Anyone who chooses to do the will of God will find out whether my teaching comes from God or whether I speak on my own." (John 7:17)

Later, he enlarged on this:

> "Then Judas (not Judas Iscariot) said, 'But, Lord, why do you intend to show yourself to us and not to the world?' Jesus replied, 'Anyone

who loves me will obey my teaching. My Father will love them, and we will come to them and make our home with them. Anyone who does not love me will not obey my teaching.'" (John 14:22-24)

God honors those who search for him. That attitude describes many devout Muslims I know.

The sacred Being must never become to us a clinical object. We approach the subject of God not as medical students examining a cadaver, but men and women seeking knowledge of the One to whom we owe our existence, from whom life pulsates, and about whom Jesus prayed that we have more than textbook knowledge:

"This is eternal life, that they may know You, the only true God, and Jesus Christ whom You have sent" (John 17:4).

2. Right Request – Ask God to show you

God is our only reliable source of wisdom, insight and knowledge about himself.

"For who among men knows the thoughts of a man except the spirit of the man which is in him? Even so the thoughts of God no one knows except the Spirit of God." (1 Corinthians 2:11)

"Then Jesus opened their minds to understand the Scriptures" (Luke 24:45)

Ask God to show you who he is, to unveil the truth about himself so that you may know, worship and love him. He promises, "You will seek me and find me when you seek me with all your heart" (Jeremiah 29:13). God heard this man's humble prayer:

As finite creatures incapable of forecasting tomorrow's events, why are we stumped over being stumped when comprehending the nature of a God "whose greatness no one can fathom" (Psalm 145:3)?

"O God, I am unworthy of the least of Thy favors. I freely acknowledge my need for understanding. I pray for Thy favor to rest upon my life, but know it cannot unless I so live that You can bless me with Thy Presence. Help me, O God; guide me; strengthen me; open my understanding of Thy mind, will, and way. In return, I promise to serve Thee more faithfully and effectively."[1]

3. Right Text – Meet God in Scripture

The best way to gain understanding of God's triune reality will not come by asking Christians but by diligently searching his Word. Reading the Tawrat, Zabur and Injeel firsthand will solve most of the difficulties surrounding God's nature.

> "Scripture is where the key to the interpretation of life really is. . . It is the clue to the reality given to us by the One who created reality."[2]

Maybe you had school teachers like mine. If we complained with something like, "This is too hard. I don't get it," they would often ask, "Did you read the chapter?" That usually tipped them off if we were serious about learning or just making excuses.

4. Right Expectation–Accept limits to your knowledge of God

Accepting limits to our knowledge of God demonstrates contentment with the range of God's self-revelation. It makes sense for obvious reasons.

> "We will never pour the ocean of God's truth into the teacups of our minds or completely encapsulate truth in our neat little formulations about God."[3]

Relish mystery. God is a wise Revealer and not a "tell all." The holy Injeel didn't take its cues from the *National Inquirer*, a tabloid divulging inappropriate and ill-gotten information on people for public consumption to the detriment of all. God made boundaries for good reason. Human attempts to break through them have no value except to feed human pride (Colossians 2:8, 18)! By delighting in the revelation itself we will promote God's Name and avoid useless guessing or bland insults ("the Big Man upstairs").

Who wants a God we fully understand? "If you understand God, it's not God," wrote Augustine.[4] As finite creatures incapable of forecasting tomorrow's events, why are we stumped over being stumped when comprehending the nature of a God "whose greatness no one can fathom" (Psalm 145:3)? The Injeel exalts God for his unfathomable qualities:

> "Oh, the depth of the riches both of the wisdom and knowledge of God! How unsearchable are His judgments and unfathomable His ways! For who has known the mind of the Lord, or who became His counselor?" (Romans 11:33-36)

It is essential to keep ourselves within the limits of Scripture.

The Trinity is not a doctrine of sport with winners who "figure it out" and losers who don't.

5. Right Optimism – Delve fully into God's vast disclosure of himself.

Accepting these limits might tempt us to view God as stingy with his self-revelation like a miser is with his money. Quite the opposite!

> "The secret things belong to the LORD our God, but the things revealed belong to us and to our sons [and daughters] forever, that we may observe all the words of this law [instruction]." (Tawrat, Deuteronomy 29:29)

While God first imparted "things revealed" to Israel alone through Moses, he did not stop there. As a non-Jew, how thankful I am to possess this knowledge! God has made ancient mysteries, long hidden from the wider world, plain through the gospel! Muslims are not excluded from the full range of "things revealed" for themselves, not merely for clarity's sake but to learn God's full blueprint for life and peace.

5. Right On-Ramp

Start with Jesus![5] Did his apostles enter a city proclaiming, "God is Triune. Believe or else?" Far from it! They spoke of Jesus, the one Scriptures had foretold as God's gift of peace to a world alienated by sin. Starting with the Trinity is premature, like teaching trigonometry to kindergarteners. **A growing understanding of God's triune nature comes after meeting Jesus, not before.** It is a most enriching monotheism to learn *in its time*.

Occasionally, a Muslim I hardly know will pepper me with questions about the Trinity. Honestly, going there right off the bat is usually not in anyone's best interest. People normally come to know God's Triune nature after meeting Jesus, not before. Starting with Jesus will not divert attention from the one true God. He is the lens through whom we see the beautiful perfection of God's unity, complex and yet without division.

John Subhan, a Muslim who came to embrace the Trinity, explains:

> "I did not accept the doctrine of the Trinity as a result of some satisfactory explanation of it offered by some Christian teacher, but it was the doctrine which came to possess me. The belief in God as Triune is inevitable as a result of Christian experience...The change in the life of a believer which it produced in consequence of accepting Christ as his Savior brings him to an entirely new relationship with God, wherein his experience of God's redemptive love corresponds to the objective revelation of God as the Father, the Son and the Holy Spirit."[6]

Two Guarantees

Making sense of the Trinity then starts with the right approach. Begin with the right attitude, the right request, the right Text, the right expectation and the right on-ramp. If you do, I will guarantee two things. First, your knowledge of God will grow fuller and richer. He will impart fresh insights to you and enlarge your heart. Second, you will discover the Muslim offense to the Christian Trinity to be a false scandal. Let me explain.

A FALSE SCANDAL

My "aha" moment came the week of 9-11. At that time, I was pastoring an international church in West Michigan. Three days after the New York City attack, I attended the Friday Jumuah Prayer service with permission of the imam, a personal friend. My purpose was to convey sentiments from our Christian community and to extend an invitation to a friendship dinner. My remarks were brief:

> "We don't hold you responsible for what happened on Tuesday. We will pray for your protection against any reprisals and our women will be happy to assist your wives with shopping if they don't want to go out in public. Finally, we would be honored for the Muslim community to be our guests for a meal this Sunday at 1:30 p.m."

It was well received and led to a memorable dinner. As I was exiting the mosque that Friday, a young man, maybe thirty, followed me into the parking lot. His demeanor was immaculate – full beard, hair and eyebrows all trimmed to precision. More importantly, he delivered a message to me with matching precision:

> "You have done a favor to the Muslim community today. May I ask you for one more? On the day of Judgment when you stand before almighty Allah, before he sends you into the flames of Hell for your polytheistic belief in the trinity, will you declare to him this message: that today I witnessed to you that the only pure monotheism is found in the Noble Qur'an of Islam?"

His blunt message got my attention and earned my respect. While his words stung, they caused me to take a closer look at the Qur'an's pronouncement upon the fate of those who believe in the Trinity. He was exactly right (The Feast, Al-Maidah 5:73).

So why respect a young man who brashly consigned me to hell? Was not this hate speech? Not at all. He acted as a faithful steward of his sacred Book. Good for him! To his mind, he was jarring me awake from my slumbering delusion. Although a "person of the Book," my belief in the triune God made me, for all practical purposes, a *kafir* (unbeliever). He did me a service by opening the door of repentance before it's too late. Better to sting now than to burn later. Let's give him credit.

Did his *dawah* (preaching) produce its intended result? Did I repent? No, but it forced me to take a closer look at the trinity that was in the crosshairs of the Qur'an.[7] That led me to a new discovery. Previously, I had just assumed the Qur'an's trinity to be one and the same with the Trinity formulated from the pages of the Injeel and embraced by Christians. I could not have been more wrong.

Two Trinities Compared
Are They the Same?

The Qur'an condemns the trinity as an unworthy portrayal of God. Such is common knowledge. *One question jumps to the foreground. Does the Qur'an have the Injeel's Trinity in mind?* To find out, we will compare seven attributes of each of them: number (of God), members included, logic, consistency, capacity, inner-concord and reality. Hopefully, by laying bare each of their core elements, we'll discover if they describe the same or entirely different trinities.

1. NUMBER – God is three versus God is one

QUR'AN'S TRINITY: Denies Divine Oneness – "Allah is one of three"

The Qur'an's most devastating criticism of the trinity is that it is a tritheism of three gods, Allah plus two.

> "They do blaspheme who say: '*Allah is one of three in a trinity:*' *for there is no god except One God.* If they desist not from their word (of blasphemy), verily a grievous penalty will befall the blasphemers among them." (Al-Maidah 5:73)

"People of the book, do not exaggerate in your religion, and only say the truth about Allah. Truly the Messiah, Isa son of Miriam is Allah's messenger and his word which he sent down on Mariam, and a spirit from him. So believe in Allah and his messengers and *do not say, 'Three.' Stop it. It is better for you. Allah is one god."* (Al-Nisa 4:170 RQ)

INJEEL'S TRINITY: Affirms the Shema, God is one!

The Injeel never strays from the fundamental creed of the Shema in Deuteronomy 6:4. When Jesus was asked by a religious leader which of all the commandments was most important, he cited this creed. God is not three, a tri-theism, but a tri-unity. Polytheism is illogical, offensive, pagan and idolatrous. This was addressed in Chapter 1.

The Qur'an's initial criticism of the Trinity is mitigated by the Injeel's strict commitment to the *Shema*, a clear affirmation of divine oneness.

2. MEMBERS – Allah, Jesus and Mary versus Father, Son (Word) and Holy Spirit

QUR'AN'S TRINITY: God, Mary and Jesus

The trinity of the Qur'an is composed of God, Mary and Jesus.

"Allah said, 'Isa son of Mariam, did you tell the people: *Take me and my mother as two gods in addition to Allah?*[8] He said, 'May you be glorified. I could not say what I have no right to say. If I had said that, you would have known. You know what is in my soul, and I do not know what is in your soul.[9] You know what is unseen.'" (Al-Maidah 5:116 RQ; see 70-72)[10]

How was this understood by ancient Islamic commentaries? Baidhawi, Jalaluddin and Yahya identified the three as "Father, Mother, and

Son."[11] This interpretation was also espoused by *Ibn Kathir* along with the *Tafsir al-Jalalayn*:

> "So believe in Allah and His Messengers. Do not say, '*Three gods: Allah, Isa and his mother.*' It is better that you stop saying these things. Affirming the Divine Unity [is] better. Allah is only One God. He is too Glorious to have a son!"[12]

INJEEL'S TRINITY: Father, the Son (Word) and the Holy Spirit

> "We believe that there is one God, eternally existent in three persons: Father, Son and Holy Spirit." [13]

What about Mary? God chose Mary to be the mother of his promised Messiah, never a member of the Godhead. Mary knew herself to be the favored recipient of high honor and sacred responsibility. Never could she imagine herself as an object of worship, but a most grateful recipient of divine blessings. Listen to her in the early days of her pregnancy with Jesus:

> "My soul exalts the Lord, And my spirit has rejoiced in God my Savior. For He has had regard for *the humble state of His bond- slave*; For behold, from this time on all generations will count me blessed. For *the Mighty One has done great things for me*; And holy is His name." (Luke 1:46-55)

Mary deserves our honor but never our worship, making this second trinitarian criticism another mismatch with the biblical Trinity.

3. LOGIC – Late Additions versus Eternally Coexisting Members

QUR'AN'S TRINITY: Mathematical Contradiction – "1 + 1 + 1 = 1?"

This criticism was expressed by a young Bangladeshi man who was eager to challenge the trinity as a mathematical contradiction. His reasoning seems widespread among Muslims. Our exchange went like this:

> "Christians are tri-theists. You believe in three gods."
>
> "No," I said, "we believe in one God consisting of three persons: the Father, the Son (Word) and Holy Spirit."
>
> "How can that be? Do you believe the Father is God?" "Yes." "Do you believe the Son is God?" "Yes." "Do you believe the Spirit is God?" "Yes."
>
> "So the Father is one. The Son is one. And the Spirit is one. One plus one plus one equals three! You believe in three gods!"

My attempts to present clarifying Scriptures were silenced. The young man had made his point.

INJEEL'S TRINITY: Three eternally co-existing Persons rules out the addition of later arrivals. Nothing created can be added to God.

How can "one" be compatible with "three" in relation to God? Is the Bible confused? Does this leave us at an impasse – God must be either singular or plural? It is not as ludicrous as it first sounds. It can be explained by logic and, more importantly, by Scripture.

Let's begin with logic. Is the Trinity a mathematical contradiction? My young friend certainly thought so. He saw a contradiction by putting God's singularity at odds with his complexity. In his youthful zeal he made the mistake of using "plus" to describe Trinity: "One plus one plus one equals three." This common error refashions the true God of three eternally co-existent members into something else: one original God to whom two more were added. Had that been the case, it would indeed total three gods, a logical absurdity.

My guess is that if the young man saw a centipede crawling across the floor on dozens of legs, he would have no problem recognizing it as a single insect rather than a contradiction of nature, some kind of original worm onto which legs were later tacked. Yet plurality within one Godhead posed to him a logical contradiction because he understood it to be exactly that – something else becoming affixed to God. He was right to dismiss this contorted "trinity" by augmentation.

The young man might profit from the wise counsel of Ravi Zacharias, a renowned defender of the Christian message. He cautioned Christians against making snap judgments about the dogmas of other religions that appear at first glance far-fetched:

> "If you can make any major world religion look ludicrous, chances are, you haven't understood it."[14]

Many Muslims will concur with that sage advice and approach this subject with a more investigative attitude that seeks understanding. By reading the Injeel for themselves, they will find it to be fully aware that nothing can be added to God, ever! And that its Godhead is an everlasting and permanent reality, not the product of accumulation.

Thinking himself as a defender of pure monotheism, the young man seemed to border on monolatry, worshiping a number rather than one supreme God. He refused me the opportunity to open the Scriptures to show him how one God has revealed himself through three distinct beings. The sound of three immediately set off the alarm of contradiction. But was it?

A Contradiction?

> The Almighty Creator who fashioned a universe of such intricate complexity can be no less than what he has made.

"A contradiction" writes Douglas Blount, "involves saying something that is both true and false at the same time and in the same way."[15] For example, "If the shirt I am wearing today is solid blue but I say it's yellow with green stripes, that is a contradiction. The same shirt must be one or the other color and pattern, not both." Blount elaborates:

> "Christians affirm that in one way God is one and in another way He is three. And in so doing they do not contradict themselves.[16]

A century earlier, A. M. Hills expressed the same thought:

"We need not at all be disturbed by the Unitarian sneer, at our worshiping 'three God's': *God is not three in the same sense that He is one.*"

An analogy may help us understand this logic.

"If I say God is one in being and three in persons, that is not a contradiction because there is a difference between a human being and a person. A "human being" is the quality that makes you *what* you are, that is, human. A "person" is the quality that makes you *who* you are, that is, you.

So if someone asks me, "Who are you?" and I say "I'm a human being," that is a wrong answer. All of us are human beings. A human being is *what* I am. Rather, I say "I am J. P." That is *who* I am.

What is God? God is one *what*, only one divine Being. Unlike us, there are three *whos*, the Father, the Son and the Spirit. All exist eternally."[17]

Obviously, this explanation does not remove mystery, but it does eliminate contradiction. God is not three in the same sense that he is one.

Next, Christians and Muslims agree that God is one. The question then is whether God's unity is simple or complex.

"Oneness can describe a single-cell ameba, double-bodied insect, a dual-system cow, or a complex unity of material, spiritual, intelligence, moral, emotional multisystem human being that is capable of creating and expressing himself in an intricately complex universe?" The Creator cannot be less than the highest order of creatures. Unity goes beyond simple oneness. It contains an internal compatibility out of which can emerge various outward manifestations without violating its oneness."[18]

Why should we think of God as anything *but* complex? The Almighty Creator who fashioned a universe of such intricate complexity can be no less than what he has made. Plurality and complexity within one Godhead is even taught in the Old Testament.

Let's proceed to Scripture in resolving how "one" can be compatible with "three." It uses two terms for "one," *echad* and *yachid*. In the *Shema* quoted earlier in Deuteronomy 6, "The LORD our God, the LORD is *one*," uses *echad*. What did it convey?

> "It is a definition of God which denies every form of deism and polytheism and at the same time declares him to be more than absolute unity.... the word that is used in this passage (echad) always means *one in connection with others.*"[19]

Echad describes a single reality having multiple components. For example, we go to the institution of marriage in Genesis 2:24:

> "Then the Lord God made the rib [lit. side] He had taken from the man into a woman and brought her to the man. And the man said: This one, at last, is bone of my bone and flesh of my flesh; this one will be called "woman," for she was taken from man. This is why a man leaves his father and mother and bonds with his wife, and they become *one flesh.*" (HCSB)

In marriage, we are to understand that one plus one equals "one flesh" and that "one" obviously refers to something more profound than mere singularity (see also Exodus 36:13, 18; 2 Samuel 7:23).

No unity can exist without internal distinctions and we must avoid obliterating them. The one God is infinitely more than a monad.

Yachid, on the other hand, denotes one and one alone. It is fitting, for example, in John 11:34 to refer to "one and only child" or in Jeremiah 6:26, to "mourn as if an only child." God, however, referring to himself, used *echad*, the plural form of one. "If God wanted to say, 'I am one and one alone,' he would have said '*yachid*.' If plural, he would use '*echad*.'"[20] "It stresses unity while recognizing diversity within that oneness."[21] For more examples of plurality within the one God in the Old Testament, please see Question 6.3.

Certainly, both Muslims and Christians must vigilantly guard monotheism in our increasingly idolatrous society. But we must also guard the inner plurality within the one Godhead. No unity can exist without internal distinctions and we must avoid obliterating them. The one God is infinitely more than a monad.

Since the members of the Godhead co-existed eternally in the Injeel, thus removing "plus" from the vocabulary of Deity, makes this third criticism of mathematical contradiction inapplicable.

4. GOD'S NATURE – Changing versus Changeless

QUR'AN'S TRINITY: God's nature changes as new partners are added.

In contrast to the true God who is "eternal and absolute" God (Al-Iklas or Tawhid 112:1-4), this trinitarian god undergoes change. "Joining gods with Allah" (Al-Anaam 6:23) alters God's nature, thus denying his immutability. It forms and re-forms by the addition of outside partners, swelling with each merger.

This trinity resembles a vocal trio in which soprano, baritone and bass singers gather from different locations to perform at a music hall, awaiting completion once all three of them arrive. Starting as a soloist, it grows into a duet until, *finally*, it becomes a full trio (whew!). Applied to Deity, any god-in-the-making is dead on arrival and earns the Qur'an's condemnation:

> "Allah forgives not that **partners should be set up with him**; but he forgives anything else, to whom he pleases; to **set up partners with Allah** is to devise a sin most heinous indeed." (Al-Nisa 4:48)

Whether this criticism takes aim at supposed partnerships with Allah that arose with other gods (Al-Anaam 6:21-24) or with human beings who were imagined subsuming into deity (Al-Maidah 5:70-72), the flawed logic remains that God underwent change. That's the criticism.

INJEEL'S TRINITY: Changeless Godhead of three Co-Eternal Members

The biblical Trinity answers the previous criticism. Since "I the LORD do not change" (Malachi 3:6), there can be no latecomers to the Godhead. The eternal God who exists "from vanishing point to vanishing point" remains the same.

> "God never differs from Himself. The concept of a growing or developing God is not found in the Scriptures. God cannot change for the better. Since He is perfectly holy, He has never been less holy than He is now and can never be holier than He is and has always been. Neither can God change for the worse.
>
> The immutability of God appears in its most perfect beauty when viewed against the mutability of men. *In God no change is possible; in men change is impossible to escape.* Neither the man is fixed nor his world, but he and it are in constant flux. Each man appears for a little while to laugh and weep, to work and play, and then to go to make room for those who shall follow in the never-ending cycle."[22]

Why would Scripture need to introduce latecomers into the Godhead when the Tawrat placed all three members actively working in tandem in its Creation account? That's a fair question. In Genesis 1-2 which describes the Cosmos coming into existence, we hear the voice of the Father, see the creating acts of the Word (Son) and the animation of the life-giving Spirit (Genesis 2:7). Yet these are absent from the inventory of species produced on each of the six creative days. Why so? Because both the Word and the Spirit are inseparable from God. Neither belonged to created life but instead were credited with its formation. The Injeel in John 1:1-3 underscores this Creator-creature distinction:

> ". . . the Word was with God, and the Word was God. He was with God in the beginning. *Through him all things were made; without him nothing was made that has been made.*" (John 1:1-3)

Rather than lumping them in with the created world, both the Word and the Spirit were directly involved in creating it by the will of the Father. Creation itself lets us glimpse at three uncreated Agents who were not only united in creative artistry but in sharing an uncreated nature. There's no hint of addition by succession.

Two Essential Attributes of Each Member

An unchanging God means each member of the Godhead must share two essential attributes: inherent and intrinsic belonging.

Inherent belonging denotes that which "belongs by nature" as opposed to being added (like an annex on a building complex). It emphasizes "permanent existence."[23] To say that each Member of the Trinity inherently belongs means that each has always been present in and essential to God.

Intrinsic belonging emphasizes place, referring to that which is "interior, inward, private or secret: belonging to the inmost constitution of a thing; not merely apparent." In relation to God, this points us to what has always been present, yet largely hidden in secret. I relish this aspect of private place, something akin to what the Psalmist described as "the secret place of the Most High" (Psalm 91:1). What was hidden away could surface without altering its eternal essence. This Most High God foretold of a day when his Word, tightly concealed in that most cherished place "in the bosom of the Father" (John 1:18), protected deep in "the secret place of Your presence from the conspiracies of man," a "shelter from the strife of tongues" (Psalm 31:20), would be sent out! Leaving those protections, he would enter the created realm, exposed to a place infected by sin where men do indeed conspire and the strife of tongues are everyday occurrences.

But does not the Father-Son relationship suggest a temporal sequence that contradicts this, making Jesus a late-comer? Question 2.2 raised this issue: "When you say that Jesus was the Son of God, doesn't that mean Isa was sired and had a date of birth? It is a good question. This has been partly answered in the Question 3.1 which presented three passages showing Jesus' eternal pre-existence (John 1:1-3). I would encourage revisiting that discussion. In addition, please consider:

"The two terms [father and son] are completely reciprocal. A man does not become a father until the precise moment when the son is born. Indeed, one cannot occur without the other precisely because the terms are inherently relational.

In reference to God, however, it refers to *an eternal relationship without any temporal beginning,* which is why Jesus prayed in the Garden of Gethsemane, 'Father, glorify me in your presence with the glory I had with you before the world began' (John 17:5).

Thus, the terms signify an eternal, co-equal relationship, 'that all may honor the Son just as they honor the Father.'" (John 5:23)[24]

The Qur'an's fourth criticism that the act of trinity-making imposes change on the Godhead has something else in mind than the unchanging Trinity of the Injeel.

5. GOD'S CAPACITY – Insufficient versus All-Sufficient

QUR'AN'S TRINITY: A Deficient God Required a Partner – Jesus was added to *Help* God Out

Compared to the true God who has a name Self-Sufficient (*al-ghani*),[25] the Qur'anic trinity displays incompleteness and incompetence. Beset by limitations, this deity must solicit assistance from outside himself to rule the world, much like an employer posting a "Help Wanted" sign.

"Say 'Praise belongs to God, who *has no child nor partner in His rule. He is not so weak as to need a protector. Proclaim His limitless greatness!*'" (Al-Isra or Bani Israil 17:111)

According to this view, God does not need total replacement, only augmentation. Without naming him, this Surah identifies Jesus as God's partner who came to his aid. That partnership exposes trinitarian deficiency before the one true Sufficient Trustee:

"Allah is one god. May he be glorified **above having a boy**. Everything in the heavens and the earth is his. **Allah is a sufficient trustee.** The Messiah will not disdain to be a servant of Allah." (Al-Nisa 4:170-171 The Reference Qur'an)

This alleged partnership diminishes God's magnitude and amplitude. Instead of filling the gaps, plus becomes minus; more equals less:

"God said, 'Do not take **two gods**' – for **He is the One God** – 'I alone am the One that you should hold in awe.'" (Al-Nahl 16:51 See Al-Maidah 5:116.)

Two heresies arose in tandem, one spawning the other. The first error turned the man Jesus (and his mother!) into God, thus requiring the second concoction: a "trinity" to incorporate these new additions!

"People of the Book, do not go to excess in your religion, and do not say anything about God except the truth: the **Messiah, Jesus, son of Mary, was nothing more than a messenger of God**, His word directed to Mary, and a spirit from Him. So believe in God and His messengers and **do not speak of a 'Trinity'** – stop [this], that is better for you – **God is only one God**, He is far above having a son, everything in the heavens and earth belongs to Him and He is the best one to trust." (Al-Nisa 4:171 Kaleem)

As we saw in Chapter 3, this divinization of Jesus was believed to have evolved either by: the act of divine begetting[26] or by excessive embellishment over time. To accommodate this aggrandizement, God must move over to make room for two newcomers, Mary and Jesus (Maidah 5:116)! Either of these paths forms a partnership with Allah that will incur God's wrath.

"If anyone **associates others with God**, God will forbid him from the Garden, and Hell will be his home." (Al-Maidah 5:72 Kaleem)

These twin heresies sink side-by-side in the same quicksand.

INJEEL'S TRINITY: Fully Complete, Freely Loving

God is all-sufficient, eternally complete, self-contained and has never needed anything.

> **"Whatever God is, and all that God is, He is in Himself**. . .To admit the existence of a need in God is to admit incompleteness in the divine Being. **Need is a creature-word and cannot be spoken of the Creator."**[27]

The Old Testament made this clear, "The LORD is the everlasting God, the Creator of the ends of the earth. **He will not grow tired or weary**" (Isaiah 40:28). The Injeel follows suit. It debunks any notion of God needing outside help as delusional:

> "The God who made the world and everything in it is the Lord of heaven and earth . . . And *he is not served by human hands, as if he needed anything.* Rather, he himself gives everyone life and breath and everything else." (Acts 17:24-25)

The Bible also teaches that God that "God is love" (1 John 4:8). While intended to be understood as a description of character rather than a definition of deity, that statement designates love as God's overriding disposition precisely because it describes *what God is in himself.*

Does it Matter?

You may be weighing the relevance of this topic. Does it matter in any meaningful way that the self-sufficient God of love is also triune? Muslims agree with Jews and Christians in denying the eternality of the Cosmos. In our estimation, the universe had a date of birth, so to speak, when God called it into being. We also agree that God existed prior to Creation. Does it really matter if God existed utterly alone or as a tri-personal Being? It matters a great deal.[28]

If love was the core of his Being and yet no one but himself was present, who could God love? Who were the subjects of his affection before anything existed? None of us would dare call Deity a narcissist, but it is hard to escape how love could be an essential attribute of a divine Monad. To whom could it express love prior to creation? Wouldn't that make divine love contingent on something outside of himself, something God *needed*, rather than an attribute? A triune God, on the other hand, suffered no such limitation. A community of three Persons as Father, Son and Spirit could and did express and reciprocate love *prior to* creation. Jesus prayed that his disciples to know this eternal love:

> "Father, I want those you have given me to be with me where I am, and to see my glory, the glory you have given me because **you loved me before the creation of the world.**" (John 17:24)

Creation, then, emerged as the free act of God's overflowing love rather than necessitated by anything lacking in God.

> "God has a **voluntary relation** to everything He has made, but He **has no necessary relation to anything outside of Himself.** His interest in His creatures arises from His sovereign good pleasure, not from any need those creatures can supply nor from any completeness they can bring to Him who is complete in Himself."[29]

How do we know the meaning of love? What better model than in God himself, the Trinity?

> "The Bible introduces love as an interpersonal quality requiring a subject-object relationship that is available in the Trinity because of the Father-Son relationship through the Holy Spirit. **The trinitarian God is complete in his love relationship without reference to his creation. The Father loves the Son before the creation of the world** (John 17:24). **The infinite personal medium through whom this love is communicated is the Holy Spirit,** and he is the one who pours the love of God in our hearts as well (Romans 5:5)."[30]

Absolute tawhid, then, implies divine limitation and represents, as noted by Timothy Tennent, that this is the most profound difference between the Christian and Muslim conceptions of God:

"The Muslim doctrine of monotheism (tawhid) protects God's otherness at the high cost of sacrificing the relational aspect of God's nature as expressed in the Trinity. In this respect, the two doctrines are utterly incompatible."[31]

God's triune nature overcomes this limitation:

"No true worship of God is possible without the qualities of transcendence and immanence existing together in him. **He is worthy of worship** only because he is **transcendent**; we can truly relate to him in worship only because he is close to us (**immanent**)!"[32]

God is ever above us in the *Father*, was God *with* us in his Son and even now is God in us through the Spirit. His trinitarian nature enables God to be near us while retaining his majestic transcendence.

"Trinitarianism reveals that, even apart from creation, God's very nature is relational. To abandon the doctrine of the trinity risks a form of monotheism that can easily drift toward cold austerity and a legalistic relationship with the living God, because God is not regarded as being relational."[33]

Since God brought us into being through his free act of love, the motive behind the act is pure and unmixed by compulsion. The triune God does not expose divine *need* but the *free exercise* of his abundant love!

Does the Trinity Limit God's Presence?

Khalil, a devoted Muslim friend and I sat together one night on the front porch of a mutual friend. He wanted to discuss with me about the triune nature of God. While sipping tea, he asked: "**If Jesus is God, doesn't that impose a limitation on God?**" Khalil's concern was valid (see Chapter 3, FTQ 6). He wanted to protect the doctrine of divine omnipresence which seems to fly in the face of incarnation by concentrating God into one person. My answer included that God, without giving up the heights of his transcendence, sent Jesus down from heaven so that through him we may reach God through him. Khalil provided this insight:

244

"It's like the Apple Store located in California's Silicon Valley. It's too far away for me to visit. But Apple has a branch office in a mall near my house. I can't reach the California store by myself, but I can the local branch. In the same way, God is too far away. Jesus, like that branch office, gets me to God from anywhere."

While not embracing the Trinity, he started to grasp its reality. Rather than limiting God, it expanded his access. A.W. Tozer would have agreed:

"We need never shout across the spaces to an absent God. He is nearer than our own soul, closer than our most secret thoughts."[34]

God needs no partners because he was complete from eternity. Rather than an obstacle to faith, the triune nature of God is a means to it.

The Qur'an's fifth criticism of the trinity, divine limitation, does not apply to its earlier counterpart in the Injeel.

6. GOD'S UNISON – A Fighting Pantheon versus Harmonious Godhead

QUR'AN'S TRINITY: Plagued by internal conflict between its members.

The Qur'an's trinity points to a group of petty gods competing for human allegiance:

"Then how can you be so deluded? . . . Nor is there any God beside Him – if there were, **each god would have taken his creation aside and tried to overcome the others.** May God be exalted above what they describe!" (Al-Muminun 23:91-93 Kaleem)

This describes members of the pagan pantheon, not the biblical Triunity. Its gods and goddesses were notorious for petty backbiting, jealousy, and scornful behavior. The Qur'an's got it right. Any collection of deities presiding over humanity, even a "trinity" of competing members, spells disaster for the human race as each mini-god vies for allegiance. Pure worship degenerates, plunging the ummah into a proliferation of religious sects destined for perpetual conflict.

The Qur'an has it right here. Pure worship concentrates itself on the one incomparable God rather than picking and choosing from a smorgasbord of deities. Al-Iklas 112:1-4 highlights such purity of worship:

> "In the name of God, the Lord of Mercy, the Giver of Mercy: Say, 'He is God the One, God the eternal. **He begot no one nor was He begotten. No one is comparable to Him.**" (Kaleem)

Prophet Muhammad (p) attached extreme importance to this *Surah*, as noted by the translator:

> "'Ikhlas' [fidelity; sincerity] conveys the meaning of sincerity in one's religion and total dedication to the One true God. Because of the importance of this theme in Islam, the Prophet said that this Surah, despite its brevity, was equal to one-third of the Qur'an."[35]

INJEEL'S TRINITY: Undivided Community elicits Unselfish Love

What about the triune God of the Injeel? Will we find rivalry between its members and division among its worshipers? Quite the contrary. The God we meet there displays one heart, performs one work and proclaims one truth.

A. One Heart – United in love

Above the sour notes heard from pantheon insiders, Jesus strikes harmonious chords in describing his relationship with his Father:

> "The Father loves the Son ..." (John 5:20; see Jn 3:35; 10:17; 15:9; 17:24) and "I love the Father and do exactly what my Father has commanded me." (John 14:31; 15:10)

Their loving concord is total and perpetual, a constant attribute rather than fickle puppy-love or fleeting passion. Memories flooding Jesus' mind must have delighted him: "Father, you loved me before the creation of the world" (John 17:24). What a durable kinship.

The Father delights to glory in his Son and his Son cannot say enough good about his Father. This is more than the absence of conflict. They are so tight that, according to Jesus, "The one who loves me will be loved by my Father. . ." (John 14:21). And "whoever accepts me accepts the one who sent me" (John 13:20). "... that all may honor the Son just as they honor the Father. Whoever does not honor the Son does not honor the Father who sent him" (John 5:23). Shared honor eliminates competition between them.

What about the third person of the Holy Spirit? Reciprocating praise going back and forth among the Trinity also includes the Spirit. Sometimes he is even called the *Spirit of God* (Ps 106:33; 1 Cor 2:14; Phil 3:3; 1 Jn 4:2) and in other places the *Spirit of the Son* or *of Christ* (Isa 61:1; Jn 1:33; 14:16-17, 26; Acts 10:38; Ro 8:9). By doing so, that is, taking the names of the Father and the Son, demonstrates a deferential relation to both members without losing his own identity.

Love reigns in the Godhead. Plurality subtracts nothing from "God is love." Rather than inciting conflict, it heals division and creates community:

> "...Divine oneness is not aloof solitary isolation. It expresses inner concord between the Father, the Son and the Holy Spirit who is credited with cosmos in creation, harmony in family, symmetry in beauty, consistency in scientific law and compatibility in law-abiding society. Rather than inciting conflict, it heals all that it touches.

Scripture shows the unity of God. Out of that, we have cosmos and not chaos. We have a pattern for family and not isolation. We find a model for marriage as two mysteriously become one flesh without sacrificing individuality."

B. One Work – Together in Action

In the pantheon, each god or goddess acted autonomously. Behaving like adult toddlers in a nursery, it was all about Athena, or Zeus, or Apollo or whoever, each edging the others out.

But, one may ask, isn't that what Jesus did? *He* healed the sick, *he* calmed the seas, *he* cleansed the lepers and *he* entered the fray against hostile opponents, right? Jesus himself answered.

> "...It is the Father, living in me, who is doing his work ...." (John 14:10-11; see Jn 5:36)

> "Very truly I tell you, the Son can do nothing by himself; he can do only what he sees his Father doing, because whatever the Father does the Son also does." (John 5:17-20)

Jesus did not act on his own initiative. He claimed that his miraculous works formed a perfect match on earth with those of his Father who indwelt him (Jn 14:10-11, 20; 10:38; 17:21-23).

Their efforts involved more than the two of them. Just as the Son worked jointly with the Father, he worked in tandem with the Spirit. We see this immediately following a dramatic deliverance, one that set a bound man gloriously free. People were astonished by his instant transformation. Yet Jesus' opponents credited this miracle to the work of the Devil! While confronting their sacrilege, Jesus revealed that he was not acting alone:

> "If it is **by the Spirit of God** that I drive out demons, then the kingdom of God has come upon you. . ." (Matthew 12:22-23)

Jesus identified the responsible party: the Spirit of God. Unlike Athena, Apollo or Zeus, Jesus was not about Me, Me, Me. "*I* drive out the demons." This was his pattern. He shared the credit with the full Godhead! **The *Father* through the *Spirit* performed extraordinary works through the *Son*.**

Someone observed, "In the biblical Trinity all three members work complementarily towards the same goals of Creation and salvation.

God acts as a unity in all His deeds." True. They think, act and operate in perfect sync. This includes God's work of *creation* (Gen 1:1-3; Psa 33:6; 104:30; Jn 1:3-4; Colossians 1:16), all of *Christ's ministry* (Jn 3:34; Acts 10:38) and of *salvation* (1 Peter 1:2; 2 Cor 1:22-23; Titus 3:4-6).

> "'The outward works of the Trinity are indivisible.' Why is there something rather than nothing? Because God the Father created all things in and through the Son in the Spirit. Why is there good news rather than no news (silence)? Because God the Father has reconciled the world to himself in Christ through the Spirit. . .'"

C. One Truth – Consensus in Message

What about doctrinal teaching? Will three members confuse us with mixed messages, each one slanting it differently? Not at all. Here's why. Whenever Jesus taught, people fastened onto every word, blown away by his poignant wisdom and noticeable authority. One question inevitably percolated from the crowds: "How did this man get such learning without having been taught?" Here was Jesus' opportunity to wax eloquent, stick out his chest and put on airs. He did none of that. Instead, he encapsulated his answer in three short words: *Not my own!* He pointed above to his Father: 'My teaching is not my own. It comes from the one who sent me'" (John 7:15-16; 14:24). *Herein lies the chief reason we never hear mixed messages coming from the Trinity. It is the absence of ego.*

What a contrast, Jesus observed, to teachers making a name for themselves who "teach on their own [i.e. accountable to none] for their own glory" (John 7:18).

Will this pattern of consensus linking the Father and Son extend to the Holy Spirit? Jesus doesn't stop at his kinship with the Father (Jn 14:6). The apostles were anxious because he was about to leave them. He knew their thoughts. *Who will teach us, guide us and comfort us after he ascends to heaven?* Jesus also knew that later on they would need additional guidance that, at the time, lay beyond their capacity to receive: "I have much more to say to you, more than you can now bear" (Jn 16:12). He alleviated their fears with this promise:

> "If you love me, keep my commands. And I will ask the Father, and

he will give you **another Advocate** [of the same kind as himself]
to help you and be with you forever— **the Spirit of truth**." (John
14:16-17)

Jesus had previously identified himself as *"the* truth" (John 14:6), or
truth personified. Now, though, he attaches that distinguished title
to his replacement, the Holy Spirit (John 16:13). Did he fear that the
one next-in-line might usurp his role by challenging his teachings?
And once the Spirit arrived on the scene, would he swap-out Jesus'
instruction with material of his own?

Jesus answers these concerns in three ways. First, he informs them how
the Spirit had *already* been present with Jesus and speaking through
his teachings: "The Spirit gives life; the flesh counts for nothing. The words
I have spoken to you—they are full of the Spirit and life." (John 6:63)

Second, Jesus informed them that once he ascended to heaven, the
Spirit-teacher would build on his foundation, not start over with
a new one:

> "The Holy Spirit, whom the Father will send in my name, will teach
> you all things and will *remind you of everything I have said to you*."
> (John 14:26)

> "When the Advocate comes, whom I will send to you from the
> Father—the Spirit of truth who goes
> out from the Father—*he will testify
> about me*." (John 15:26)

> "No created thing
> can be the revelation
> of God. The very fact
> of its creatureliness
> would make that utterly
> impossible." Karl Barth

Third, the same three words, *not my
own*, that Jesus had used to summarize
his own teachings would apply equally
to the Spirit's:

> "When he, the Spirit of truth, comes, he
> will guide you into all the truth. He will *not speak on his own; he will
> speak only what he hears,* and he will tell you what is yet to come. *He
> will glorify me because it is from me that he will receive* what he will
> make known to you." (John 16:12-14)

Never does the Spirit compete with the Son. His primary role was to point people *towards* Jesus. Proof of this is seen in the way by which it is only through the Spirit anyone can confess 'Jesus is Lord' (1 Cor 12:3).

So what does all this mean? **It confirms that the Trinity speaks with one voice that leads us into all truth** (John 15:26-16:15). Divine plurality in the Godhead subtracts nothing from perfect agreement. Nowhere three-way tug-of-wars exist between its members, each contradicting the rest and directing a confused humanity down conflicting paths. Instead, a seamless message roots itself in one God with three likeminded members. This beautiful truth — one heart, one work and one voice – caps off the Trinity's contrast to the pathetic spectacle of a conflicting pantheon.

The Qur'an's sixth trinitarian criticism that a plurality of members competing for human allegiance will fracture the ummah contrasts the undivided concord exhibited between members of the biblical Trinity. Again, it must have a different "trinity" in mind.

7. GOD'S REALITY – Man-made folly versus Divine revelation with eternal reward

QUR'AN'S TRINITY: Human Invention Ending in Disaster

The trinity rejected by al-Qur'an is man-made (Al-Muminun 23:117), a con- struct of the mind rather than revelation from God.

> "They **set aside part of the sustenance** We give them, for [idols] about which **they have no true knowledge**.[40] By God! You will be questioned about your **false inventions**." (Al-Nahl 16:56)

"Who could be more wicked than someone who *invents lies against God or denies His revelations*?" (Al-Yunus 10:17 Kaleem)

"They worship alongside God things that *can neither harm nor benefit them*, and say, 'These are our intercessors with God.' . . . Glory be to Him! He is

"We cannot say that 'God is love' and also say that 'God is solitary' or, in this solitary sense, that 'God is one.' Entire transcendence is in the end a blank agnosticism."
Kenneth Cragg

far above *the partner-gods they associate with Him*!" (Al-Yunus 10:18 Kaleem)

As a mental construct and nothing more, this trinity lacks substance and value. Old Testament prophets agree. Those who craft idols of wood and gold "are only human beings" (Isaiah 44:11) whose products "can profit nothing" (Isaiah 44:10). Unfortunately, by the time their worthlessness is discovered it will be too late!

> "*On the Day We gather them all together, We shall say to those who associate partners with God,* 'Stay in your place, you and your partner-gods.' Then We shall separate them, and their partner-gods will say, 'It was not us you worshipped – God is witness enough between us and you – we had no idea that you worship us.' *Every soul will realize, then and there, what it did in the past.* They will be returned to God, their rightful Lord, and *their invented [gods] will desert them.*" (Yunus 10:28-9 Kaleem)

INJEEL'S TRINITY: God's Revelation Leading to Eternal Life

The NT is under no illusion that any person can know God on his own, much less reach him. For God is both *incomparable*, "there is none like me" (Isaiah 46:5, 9)[41] and *transcendent*. Job (*Ayub*) agonizing in his suffering lamented, "*The Almighty – we cannot reach Him – He is exalted in power!*" (*Job 37:23 HCSB*).[42]

Muhammad's (p) shift away from a reliance upon Christ's death towards the law of human merit reintroduced a system of human failure and shame, the very thing from which Christ's blood has rescued us.

Since God exists beyond our reason and out of our reach, Marty Parson aptly wrote,

"*God is bounded, so that only God can reveal God.* No created thing can be the revelation of God. The very fact of its creatureliness would make that utterly impossible."[43]

ALMIGHTY GOD, CREATOR

◀――――――――――――――――▶

CREATION

How can any creature from beneath the line say anything with certainty about the One above it "whose heaven is my throne and the earth is my footstool"?[44] Even the most rudimentary information we know of him must come down from his side, not up from ours.

For this doctrine of God's transcendence to be of any value to people, it is necessary for God to cross the boundary in a form comprehensible to human beings. Bishop Kenneth Cragg, a scholar with deep affection for Muslim people, wrote:

> "We cannot say that 'God is love' and also say that 'God is solitary' or, in this solitary sense, that 'God is one.' **Entire transcendence is in the end a blank agnosticism.**"[45]

What does this have to do with the Trinity? The Trinity made possible what these factors made impossible. Jesus' entering our world as the eternal Word penetrated the dividing wall. He brought God into view, out into the open through his signs, teachings and lifestyle. By doing so, Jesus made belief in **biblical Trinity not only possible but inescapable.**

For the first time, God raised our horizons that we might see "above the line." For what purpose? Jesus had more in mind than lifting the veil for us to peer into heaven's mysteries (as great as that is). Listen to his final recorded prayer:

> "Now this is *eternal life: that they know you [Father], the only true God,* and Jesus Christ, whom you have sent." John 17:4

What kind of knowledge of God is Jesus requesting? Not that "they know *about* You [God]," but "know *You*, the only true God!" Does it matter? Jesus certainly thought so, equating this personal knowledge with "eternal life!" He links this life-giving relationship with belief in "Jesus Christ, whom You have sent."

The Qur'an's seventh criticism of the trinity as a manufactured invention promising disastrous ends has no correlation with its NT counterpart. Rather than a short-lived fantasy, God's triune structure placed his eternal salvation within reach.

Let's summarize this lengthy comparison between the trinities presented by our Books. The table below distills their contrasts and comparisons.

Summary

Let's return to our original question of first importance – Is the trinity condemned by the Qur'an one and the same with that of the Injeel? A comparison of their respective attributes clearly describes two entirely different deities. The chart below distills their contrasts.

TWO TRINITIES AT A GLANCE

	QUR'AN	INJEEL
NUMBER	Tritheistic *"Allah is one of three"*	Monotheistic *One Godhead*
MEMBERS	Father, Mary & Jesus	Father, Son & Holy Spirit
LOGIC	Mathematical Contradiction 1+1+1=1	Eternal Union without Addition
CONSISTENCY	Evolving	Changeless
CAPACITY	Insufficient *Needs Help*	All-Sufficient *Freely Gives*
INTERPERSONAL RELATIONS	Pantheon in Conflict	Model Community *One Heart,* *Work & Message*
REALITY	Human Invention *Ends in Disaster*	Divine Revelation *Leading to Life Eternal*

Call to Repent?

We come now to the Qur'an's remedial action for the adherents of its disastrously flawed trinity. Here it initially struck me as odd. In light of our preceding comparisons, of chief importance is that its target is not the biblical Trinity. And yet, we hear:

> The trinity scorned by the Qur'an bears no resemblance with the Triune God worshipped by Christians, not by a long shot!

> "They do blaspheme who say: Allah is one of three in a trinity: for there is no god except One God. If they desist not from their word (of blasphemy), verily a grievous penalty will befall the blasphemers among them." (Al-Maidah 5:73)

Those who repent and turn to God are offered forgiveness:

> "Why do they not turn to God and ask His forgiveness, when God is most forgiving, most merciful?" (Al-Maidah 5:74 Kaleem)

To whom might this be addressed? Who is being summoned to repent of this trinity? Apparently, Christians. As a voracious reader and one who travels the world, I have yet to come across a single Christian, past or present, in a book or on a bus or on a plane, who held to even one of those outrageous theologies. Christians can no more repent of doctrines they never believed than law-abiding citizens can return money they never stole.

If not Christians, then, who might justifiably be called to repentance? During time, did other groups conflate notions of trinity with the deification of creatures? The answer is *yes*.

Muslims often tell me about pre-Islamic Arabia, called *Jahiliyyah*, the time of ignorance. This period characterized as the "darkness of idolatry" was believed to have stemmed from the departure from the worship of the one God by the sons of Ishmael. Idolatry flourished in Arabia.[46]

What kind of god presided during this period? Maybe a deity with a "complex form of neo-animism" offering a variety of "divine and semi-divine intermediaries who stood between the creator god and his creation." The creator god was called Allah, a contraction of *al-ilah*, meaning simply "the god."[47] This was the reigning high god but, as such, beyond the reach of ordinary people. When times were tough, people consulted other deities closer to home who "acted as Allah's intercessors."[48] At the top of these lesser deities were Allah's three daughter8s, *Allat* ("the goddess"), *al-Uzza* ("the mighty"), and *Manat* (the goddess of fate).

> "These divine mediators were not only represented in the Ka'ba, they
> had their own individual shrines throughout the Arabian Peninsula.
> *Alat* in the city of Ta'if; *al-Uzza* in Nakhlah; and *Manat* in Qudayd.
> It was to them that the Arabs prayed when they needed rain, when
> their children were ill, when they entered into battle or embarked on
> a journey deep into the treacherous desert abodes of the Jinn. . ."[49]

Conflating these three goddesses with the biblical Trinity would be natural for any Muslim. As we have seen, this pre-Islamic "trinity" bears zero resemblance with it. Moreover, the following passage identifies those associating with Allah as "jinn" and "sons and daughters," obviously not aimed at Jesus the Son of God.

> "Yet they made **the jinn** partners with God, though He created them,
> and without any true knowledge **they attribute sons and daughters
> to Him**." (Al-Anaam 6:100-101 Kaleem)

FIVE CONCLUSIONS

What have we learned from this cursory comparison of these two trinities? For this author, it has been eye-opening, enough to draw the following five conclusions and implications.

1. First, the trinity scorned by the Qur'an bears no resemblance with the Injeel's Triune God worshipped by Christians, not by a long shot! Not even one of the Qur'an's seven trinitarian criticisms applies to the Biblical Trinity. I do not doubt that it accurately describes a trinity somewhere. All we can say with certainty is that it is *not* the triune God of Christianity.

2. Christians agree with Muslims that the trinity condemned by the Qur'an deserves the trashing it receives. Its criticisms expose it as a monstrosity, an invention calling for immediate dismissal and visceral disdain as an explicit denial of monotheism.

3. Third, only a fraction of Christians and Muslims are aware of these core differences, thus wrongly assume that references to our respective circles refer to the same reality. That assumption gridlocks meaningful conversation on the subject. We tend to avoid the topic, talk past each other, or worse, engage in a war of words. If a comprehension meter existed, it would be stuck at zero. There must be a better way!

4. Fourth, if by a fair comparison Muslims can concede that the Qur'an's "trinity" bears no similarity with that of the Injeel and Christians that the Qur'an is justified in denouncing it, then what prevents us from downgrading this dispute from the category of scandal to one of misidentification?
What is to be gained by this? For starters, truth. This mutual recognition will require neither Muslims nor Christians to relinquish theological real estate. Further, it will put us on the same side as co-combatants fighting against a common enemy, the fraudulent imposter-trinity. Together, we will humbly and diligently seek the living God who alone merits our praise. Last, downgrading this controversy should go far in loosening our aforementioned gridlock. Conversations will be better informed, more authentic and less combative. Now we can focus on real differences and dismiss *false* ones!

5. Fifth, since the scandal is false, so is the need for Christian repentance. Remember the young man at the mosque's parking lot telling me to repent? No wonder he was so adamant! The prism through which he "saw" polytheism in the holy Trinity of the Injeel was the distorted trinity of the Qur'an that, no doubt, arose in part from the brazen idolatries of ancient Arabia. His zeal, however, was brash because it was uninformed. Zeal fueled by ignorance easily radicalizes into the red zone. He blundered twice, first by his assumption and then by his inaction. He uncritically swallowed what he was taught about the Trinity. Then he failed to invest the time to read the Injeel for himself to investigate what it actually said. Had he done so, he would have learned that what is needed is not Christian repentance of the Trinity but Islam's recovery of it.

For Christians Readers

Where do these conclusions leave everyday Muslims and Christians? Studying the distorted trinity in the Qur'an helps people like me to better appreciate why Muslims recoil at the term! Christians can be more relaxed when challenged from the Qur'an on the subject since it clearly has another one in mind.

"Should we expect the God who created calculus to be simple?" Abdu Murray

Questions for Muslims to ask yourselves
Muslim reader, I've endeavored here to provide a basic understanding of the Christian Trinity and, hopefully, make it less confusing. It's a lot of information to sort out. The following questions might help you reflect and process it:

- Have I ever compared these two trinities? Has this chapter dispelled any confusion about the Christian trinity?
- Has any new information caused me to change in how I think and feel about the God of the Bible? Has it removed any of its stigma for me?
- Do my previous arguments against the Trinity still hold up?
- Do any of the specific qualities describing the Trinity in the chart's righthand column catch me by surprise? Offend me? Make me curious?
- Would belief in this God compromise my commitment to his absolute oneness? If so, how exactly?
- Could the Injeel's original trinity become a restore-point for the flawed one roundly and rightly condemned by the Qur'an?
- Since God is the only reliable authority about himself, would I be open to a simple prayer, something like this: *God, I want to worship you in spirit and in truth. Would you show me who you are? If you do, I will make you the Lord and Master of my life.*

A Final Thought

Muslim reader, before leaving this question, I invite you to consider the looking-glass through which the Triune God has for so long been seen. The following story may help.

We once owned a bigger-than-life Golden Retriever dog, ninety-fivepounds of drooling love. Dietrich was a tail-wagging, family-friendly, loveable pet. A few years ago, four children from West Africa stayed with us for a month while their parents made a trip overseas. In their country, dogs typically were vicious watchdogs, not affectionate pets. I'll never forget the day when these three boys and their sister arrived at our front door with their little suitcases. Dietrich greeted them with his tail happily wagging. *Oh boy! New playmates!* They did not see a new playmate. They saw a monster that devoured African children. *Frankenstein! Run for your life!* One of them actually did. They refused to enter the house until the beast was in the back yard. Slowly their fears gave way to affection.

Why were they afraid of a harmless furball? They saw him through their old lenses, an outdated reality. How did their monster become their playmate? By getting to know Dietrich for who he was. I am hopeful that by taking a fresh look at the triune God through the Injeel's lens, Muslims will discover a God unsurpassed in beauty, holiness and grace who is majestically exalted and graciously near.

> Divine innovation is stricted to God's works, never his essential attributes.

Q 6.1: "I never understood the concept of Trinity. I believe it should be simple. One God in three persons? What does that mean?"

You are right to think that we should not complicate God unnecessarily by forcing human ideas into divine Scriptures. Your guileless question deserves two responses. First, while avoiding needless complexity, neither should we over-simplify the Maker of heaven and earth! A friend of mine and gifted teacher, Abdu Murray, put this question in perspective: "Should we expect the God who created calculus to be simple?"

Even when describing human beings, does "simple" do anyone justice? If I call my wife "simple," would she feel flattered or insulted? So why call God simple? An Arab proverb reminds us that some realities lie beyond simple explanations: "Not being able to prove something is no proof it doesn't exist."

Second, I believe God welcomes your sincere question because his self-revelation achieved the clarity you desire. Oddly enough, the biblical Trinity actually *clarified*, not muddled, our view of God. So vivid its unveiling, it condemned every idolatrous pretense about God as human puffery. Rest assured. The Son's revelation of the Father by the Spirit mixed holy mystery with gracious simplicity. Without it, God would remain forever aloof, hidden and unknown to us.

Question 6.2: "Is trinity an innovation in Christianity?"

No. Innovation describes new things, products and ideas. Divine innovation is restricted to God's works, never his essential attributes. The triune God revealed in the New Testament is the same God of the Old. Though God himself never changes, we must never imagine the ever-living One to preside over his world in a static or same-ish fashion:

> "There is a mutation of state, but not in nature, or intrinsic attributes
> or divine personality."[50]

The Creator of the universe is the consummate innovator, the brainchild of every living thing. He declared, *I make all things new!* Yet God's triune nature cannot be an innovation, for it describes One who is complete from all eternity — who he is, was and always will be. Divine innovation pertains only to his works, not his being.

Yet we glorify God for his miraculous innovation. *What is impossible with man is possible with God!* Combined with his unchanging character, his life-giving activity in our decaying world bolsters our confidence. Evil and death do not have the last word. For instance, when we are faced with catastrophic loss, his *"mercies are new every morning"* (Lam 3:23). When Israel broke the prized covenant resulting in her spiritual and physical demise, God promised a *"new"* one (Jer 31:31), far superior to the first, this time offering not only to Israel but all people *"new hearts"* (Eze 11:19; 18:18; 36:26) that are animated by a *"new spirit"* (Rom 7:6). Jesus returned from the dead to mediate this *new covenant* (Heb 12:24; 1 Cor 11:25; 2 Cor. 3:6; Heb. 8:8; 9:15). By trusting in his triumph over sin and death, anyone may obtain *new birth into a living hope* (1 Pet 1:3), a *newness of life* (Ro 6:4), becoming a *new creation* (2 Cor 5:17; Gal. 6:16; Eph 2:10). By his death and ascension to God's right hand, Jesus opened up a *new and living way* (Heb 10:20) into God's holy Presence by which the weakest believer may pray bold prayers. Finally, followers of Jesus anticipate an arrival in heaven, also called the *new heavens and a new earth* (Isa. 66:17; 2 Pet 3:13; Rev 21:1).

So, yes, the good and living God constantly innovates for our good. Yet he himself never changes. The Alpha and the Omega is not in a state of flux. The God who breathed life into Adam and who will oversee the Son of Man descending on clouds of glory is one and the same. From Tawrat to Injeel, we encounter one God.

Q 6.3: Is the doctrine of the Trinity in the Bible?

The doctrine of the Trinity is in the Bible, but not the term itself. This omission does not invalidate its reality any more than the absence of "Tawheed" in the Qur'an lessens Islamic belief in monotheism. These terms help Christians and Muslims explain God's nature.[51]

How does the Bible present the one, unchanging and eternal God as a triune Being?

Trinity Revealed Increasingly in the Biblical Story

God never *became* triune. He has always been that way. Yet his self-revelation to humanity did not come all at once. The Sovereign Creator chooses how and when to make himself known.

God's Being is forever fixed while his self-revelation to humanity is progressive, unfolding over time. His immutable essence and ongoing disclosure are commonly confused. But more disclosure is not the same as a changing identity. For instance, when God revealed his personal name, "Yahweh," to Moses at the burning bush, did Moses think God suddenly became Yahweh right then and there? Of course not. Always existing, the Sovereign God knew when, where and to whom he would divulge more information about himself. This was considerate, coming to us in proportion to our readiness to receive it. It was as though God placed his thumb over the end of the hose of revelation, governing its flow throughout the biblical narrative. How fitting for the Ancient of Days! This pacing should surprise no one.

> "Before me no god was formed, nor will there be one after me. I, even I, am the LORD, and apart from me there is no savior." (Isaiah 43:11)

A. Implicit Evidence for the Trinity in the Old Testament (Tawrat)

Truly new in the Injeel is not the Trinity, but our fuller knowledge of it. NT scholar D. A. Carson explains:

> "God himself, progressively revealed across the sweep of the Old Testament literature, is now simultaneously more clearly disclosed and, precisely because of that revelation, more mysterious: he is one God but not solitary, three 'persons' who clearly interact with one another and with his creatures yet still but one God, the triune God."[52]

What had been hidden in God became more fully revealed when "the Word became flesh and lived among us" (John 1:14). The precise timing was divinely determined, for "in the fullness of time, God sent his Son, born of a woman" (Galatians 4:4). The Old Testament had to prepare the way.

Let's begin with God's names.

i. GOD'S NAMES – Two Principal Names for God in the Old Testament: *Yahweh Elohim*

The Torah presents evidence of complexity within the Godhead, even in the names for God. In the biblical world names express reality.

> "The Hebrew language is peculiarly expressive, and its names of

objects are not arbitrary signs, but significant of their nature and properties, or of some remarkable circumstance connected with their history (see Genesis 17:5; 32:28; Matthew 1:21). In conformity with this feature of the language, *the names of God were expressive of himself, and were chosen by him for this purpose.*"[53]

Christian theologian and Hebrew scholar, Benjamin Field, brings out what is implicit about the divine names.

> "The two principal names which are applied to deity in the Old Testament are *Yahweh* ("LORD") and *Elohim* ("God"). The former is God's proper [personal] name, and clearly applies to the divine essence. This name is always singular, and may be rendered, 'He who exists." This is the name that God revealed to Moses. The other name, . . . *Elohim*, is plural."

ii. Singular and Plural – Precise Grammar Clarifies God's Name and Removes Contradiction

Why is the name *Yahweh*, which refers to his essence, always singular? Plainly to express the unity of the divine essence. Why is the other, *Elohim*, plural? As clearly to note a plurality of persons in the Godhead.

Hundreds of passages combine these two names of God to express his divine nature — *Yahweh Elohim* translated 'the LORD[54] God' (Exodus 20:2, 5; Deuteronomy 6:3, 4, 5; Isaiah 42:5). This double name is the one which God has ordinarily assumed in addressing mankind.

Are singular and plural names for God a contradiction?

> "Now, as there must be fitness and propriety and the language of God, there must be a sense in which he is both singular and plural — plural in persons, his name is *Elohim*; singular in essence, for his name is *Yahweh*. If the Trinity were false, the names would be contradictory; if the Trinity be true, the genius of the language is consistent, and the names appropriate."

> "Everyone knows that verbs and pronouns should agree in number with the leading noun. Yet *Elohim*, though plural, is almost invariably constructed with verbs and pronouns in the singular, as in Genesis 1:1, 'Elohim created;' the agent is plural, the verb singular."

"And this strange form of expression is used by Moses above 500 times. It is not as if the grammar had been unformed, and necessitated such an idiom; it was that the writer, actuated by an inspiring influence [the Holy Spirit], has selected a mode of speech denoting an undoubted plurality in the agents, while there was perfect unity in the action."

iii. In the OT, God acts as Creator (Father), Word (Son) and Holy Spirit

In a few remarkable instances, Elohim is combined with plural verbs and pronouns. Genesis 1:26: *"Elohim* said, 'let us make man in our image.'"[55]

If the language is proper, there must be a plurality of persons in the Godhead, and each person must be related to us as our Creator. In harmony with this, the Son and the Holy Spirit are set forth in other parts of the sacred volume as united in the act of creation.

"Then the LORD God formed a man from the dust of the ground and breathed into his nostrils the *breath of life* [the Spirit], and the man became a living being". (Genesis 2:7)

"The *Spirit of God* has made me, And the *breath* of the Almighty gives me life." (Job 33:4)

"All things came into being through Him [Jesus, the *Word* of God], and apart from Him nothing came into being that has come into being." (John 1:3)

On some occasions, the singular name, *Yahweh*, is united with plural verbs and pronouns.

"As soon as Jesus was baptized, he went up out of the water. At that moment heaven was opened, and he saw the Spirit of God descending like a dove and alighting on him. And a voice from heaven [Father] said, 'This is my Son, whom I love; with him I am well pleased.'" (Matthew 3:13-17)

Genesis 11:6, 7, which obviously contains solemn intercourse of divine persons: "*Yahweh* said, '. . .let us go down.'"

Isaiah 6:3,8, where both the singular and plural pronouns, "Whom shall I send?" and "who will go for us?" refer to the one true and only God, "The LORD of hosts."

Thus by the very names in which God is revealed to man, . . .we are taught the great mystery of godliness – the fact of a plurality of persons in the essential unity the Godhead.[56]

OT References to the Son and the Spirit

Many passages in the Old Testament speak distinctly of the Son and the Spirit:

Of the Son:

"I will surely tell of the decree of the Lord: He said to Me, 'You are My **Son**, Today I have begotten You.

"Do homage to the *Son*, that He not become angry, and you perish in the way, For His wrath may soon be kindled. How blessed are all who take refuge in Him!" (Psalm 2:7, 12)

Of the Spirit:

"The earth was formless and void, and darkness was over the surface of the deep, and *the Spirit of God* was moving over the surface of the waters." (Genesis 1:2)

"Then the LORD said, *'My Spirit* shall not strive with man forever, because he also is flesh; nevertheless his days shall be one hundred and twenty years.' (Genesis 6:3)

"Teach me to do Your will, For You are my God; Let *Your good Spirit* lead me on level ground. For the sake of Your name, O LORD, revive me." (Psalm 143:10-11)

"It will come about after this That *I will pour out My Spirit* on all mankind; And your sons and daughters will prophesy, Your old men will dream dreams, Your young men will see visions. Even on the male and female servants *I will pour out My Spirit* in those days." (Joel 2:28)

"This is the Word of the LORD to Zerubbabel saying, 'Not by might nor by power, but by *My Spirit,' says the LORD* of hosts." (Zechariah 4:6)

With this OT background, let's proceed to the Injeel.

B. Explicit Evidence of the Trinity in the Injeel

As stated above, what was implicit in the Old Testament became explicit in the New. Below are clear examples of the three Persons of the Godhead.

Baptism of Jesus – The Father's Voice, the Son's human presence, the Spirit's visible descent

"As soon as Jesus was baptized, he went up out of the water. At that moment heaven was opened, and he saw the *Spirit of God* descending like a dove and alighting on him. And a voice from heaven *[Father]* said, 'This is my *Son*, whom I love; with him I am well pleased.'" (Matthew 3:13-17)

"As soon as Jesus was baptized, he went up out of the water. At that moment heaven was opened, and he saw the Spirit of God descending like a dove and alighting on him. And a voice from heaven [Father] said, 'This is my Son, whom I love; with him I am well pleased.'" (Matthew 3:13-17)

Baptism of Christians

The "name" into which believers are baptized is singular even though it represents three distinct Persons.

"And Jesus came up and spoke to them, saying, 'All authority has been given to Me in heaven and on earth. Go therefore and make disciples of all the nations, baptizing them in the name[57] of the Father and the Son and the Holy Spirit, teaching them to observe all that I commanded you; and lo, I am with you always, even to the end of the age.'" (Matthew 28:19)

Benedictions

"The grace of the *Lord Jesus Christ*, and the love of *God*, and the fellowship of the *Holy Spirit*, be with you all." (2 Corinthians 13:14)

Prayer – ". . .where the glorious Three are addressed in prayer, as the united fountain of grace and love" (Fields)

We pray to *God* (Creator and Father) through *Jesus our Mediator* (Word/Son), by the *Holy Spirit* present in us.

". . .for through *Him [Jesus]* we both have our access in one *Spirit* to the *Father*." (Ephesians 2:18)

A PERSONAL NOTE – *Is This a Waste of Time?*

> A triune God can stoop to enter humanity without vacating his heavenly throne or dropping an inch from his transcendent heights.

I want to wrap-up this lengthy chapter on a personal note. Some of my Christian friends who regularly interact with Muslims say that I'm wasting my time discussing the Trinity with them. They contend that your interest in it isn't genuine and that you only bring it up as a talking point for argument. My own experience confirms this, not always, but in most cases. Why then proceed? For this simple reason.

If the God of the universe has scripturally revealed himself to us tri-personally, then everyone from disinterested listener, argumentative opponent to ardent seeker has the right to such knowledge. That the biblical Trinity has a rival Qur'anic alternative is not beside the point. Quite the contrary. The poisonous distortions justifying its dismissal is all the more reason for serious Muslims to examine the original version. So Muslim reader, wherever you fall on the spectrum of interest, this chapter has been provided as my honest attempt to answer your questions in four parts:

- Aids to help you better understand the Trinity
- A fair comparison of our trinities as a platform for evaluation and discussion
- Disavowal that the Injeel's Trinity is a novelty
- Biblical examples rooting the Trinity deeply in both Testaments, Old and New

Why does trinitarian monotheism matter to me? Why do I even care if my Muslims neighbors have a correct understanding of it? They already embrace the most thoroughgoing monotheism in tawhid. Does not tawhid's simplicity make it the preferred option over the Trinity with its added layer of complexity?

The answer seems straightforward. "Preferred option?" Is God's nature settled by personal preference like choosing between Coke and Pepsi? Muslims and Christians both know better.

We can agree that God's reality – as he has shown himself in Scripture – must override theological descriptions made about him. If that reality is interpersonal, it suggests that God made us, at least to some degree, to encounter as well as understand him. Knowing God moves us beyond defining him.

Christians sometimes feel put on the spot when asked by Muslims to define the Trinity and explain its intricate mysteries. Definitions have their place, precisely spelling out what something is, marking out its attributes and fixing its properties. The downside is their limited range. They do a better job answering *What's this?* than *Who's that?*

Take my wife, for example (not physically, please). I know her intimately, but can I define her? Not very well, for she is infinitely more than a what. Forty years of marriage have taught me how there remain depths to her that I have yet to plumb. Just when I think I have her figured out, a new situation arises that forces something deep within her to bubble to the surface. As a who, she continues to defy the very definitions I thought circumscribed her. So no, I cannot define her but would gladly introduce her to you so that you may delight in knowing her too.

The point is, if our definitions of human beings don't cut it, how much less of the divine Being! But here's the bright spot. If defining the triune God as a *what* gives Christians a brain-freeze, introducing him as a *who* becomes a golden opportunity! Here's why.

The Triune God is not a problem with God, but a solution to a problem with us. Our tragic separation from God found its remedy in a tri-personal God capable of entering our world without vacating his heavenly throne. The Father loved the world to the point that he gave his one and only Son, so that everyone who believes in him will receive eternal life. They will be born from above by God's Spirit. I shudder to think where I'd be without the one God revealed as sublime love and generous grace in the Father, the Son (Word) and the Holy Spirit. Human salvation rests squarely upon divine Trinity.

This subject is not a waste of time for another reason. To justify their rejection of the Trinity, Islamic apologists must repackage it in a way that contradicts monotheism and defies logic. One must keep in mind that this repackaged version, typically composed of piecemealed Bible passages, is their creation, a reproduction that no one outside of their own circles takes seriously. Whether intentional or not, their misrepresentations tragically rob sincere Muslims of knowing the unmade God through whom salvation comes.

Rather than a product of personal preference, the biblical Trinity glorifies God alone. God the Father above us gave the world His Son to be God with us in life, for us in death and in us by the miracle of new birth through the Holy Spirit. What a subject worth our time!

PART 2

QUESTIONS ABOUT
SACRED BOOKS

CHAPTER 7

CREDIBILITY OF THE INJEEL

Question 7: "The Gospels were written decades after his death. How can anyone assume their accuracy?"

Q 7.1: "Why has the Bible been rewritten in so many ways and how come it never states the same things each time it's written? Isn't the original good enough or do men know better how to guide than God?"

Q 7.2: How come the Bible changes such as there are different ones?

W hat a timely question zeroing in on the accuracy of the Gospel accounts, especially in today's climate of biblical skepticism. It is also commonplace for modern readers who are unfamiliar with ancient documents to raise concerns about time-periods existing between historical events and their written records. So let's get right to it.

You correctly point out that decades stand between the death of Jesus and the written records.

33 A.D.	Jesus Dies
48-64 A.D.	Paul's Letters
50-66 A.D.	Gospel of Matthew, Mark & Luke

| 52-62 A.D. | Acts |
| 92-100 A.D. | Gospel of John (the last written down) |

All of the Injeel (New Testament [NT]) was written in the first century, within sixty years of Christ's death. At the time of their composition, eyewitnesses to Jesus' teachings and miracles were still alive and could easily verify or challenge these written accounts. So this early date provides one of the myriad of reasons to assume their accuracy. For more on the importance of early dating, see reason 4 below.

WHY THE INJEEL CAN BE TRUSTED

From the many grounds supporting the Injeel's trustworthiness, I have selected six. The Injeel: (1) Produces life change; (2) Claims to be God's Word spoken through men; (3) Authenticates its claim of divine origins by passing a stringent test; (4) Presents telltale signs that its authors provided reliable historical information; (5) Dispels doubt that the Apostles sincerely believed their message; (6) Corroborates its narrative with independent verification. I will conclude by asking a question about your question: On the basis of the Qur'an's testimony, how can you as a Muslim cast doubt on the Injeel's reliability? Please indulge me as I begin with my own journey.

1. Evidence of Life Change – My First "Bible"

My belief in the Injeel's message began not by reading its contents, but by watching the lives of those through whom I learned it. The Injeel refers to such persons as the first Bible that people will read: "... *you are a letter of Christ*, ... written not with ink but with the Spirit of the living God, not on tablets of stone but on tablets of human hearts" (Injeel, 2 Corinthians 3:3).

Blessed with a godly heritage, the first Injeel I read was the remarkable lives of parents and grandparents, God's living books, upon whose lives he penned his character of love and light. Despite their imperfections, they became a legible living preview of what I would later read in text.

Of special note was my maternal grandmother who infected her grandchildren with a reverence for Scripture. Widowed young, she lived with us for extended periods of time. Her daily routine included devoting an uninterrupted time period with her grandchildren for biblical memorization.

The process was simple and effective. While she sat on a sofa with an open Bible, we gathered at her knees with childlike wonder. She would select a key chapter and recite to us the first verse.[1] We echoed it back to her exactly as she said it, even with voice inflection. Once we could repeat the whole verse without help, she would proceed to verse two. After repeating both verses perfectly, she would introduce the next verse until the entire chapter could be quoted from memory.

It went something like this. "Today we are going to begin with the 'Love chapter' (Injeel, 1 Corinthians 13) or the 'Faith Chapter' (Injeel, Hebrews 11) or Psalm 19, the great passage about Divine Revelation, and so on. One fruit of this exercise was a healthy respect for context and flow of the biblical story. I tell you this for two reasons. First, like devout Muslims I know, Scripture holds a revered place not simply by giving it a prominent place on our shelves but a formative role in our lives. Second, and more to the point, biblical education was not achieved through distant learning. It was done up close, enough that the teacher's life could lend credibility to the subject being taught. Young Timothy was instructed to:

> "continue in what you have learned and have become convinced of, because *you know those from whom you learned it,* and how from infancy you have known the Holy Scriptures. . ." (2 Tim 3:14-15; see 1:4-5)

That daily drill from a loving grandmother inculcated in me a deep reverence towards the large collection of Books consisting of the Torah, Prophets, Psalms and Gospel that we bind in a single volume called the Bible. It also instilled trust in the Scriptures' veracity that would withstand periods of plaguing doubts that are a normal part of growing

The Bible does not shy away from boldly asserting itself as God's message to people.

up. Moreover, it aided me to counter vicious attacks against biblical revelation from the secular academy.

Of course, exemplary lives cannot of themselves make the Injeel trustworthy. But the lifestyle of those surrounding my early heritage were foundational in establishing my trust in the credibility of the Scripture they professed to believe.

2. The Injeel Claims to be God's Words Spoken through Men

My second reason for trusting the Bible's accuracy of which the Injeel is a part is the claim it makes for itself as God's Word. Over 2,500 times the Bible declares, "Thus says the Lord." As an integral part of Scripture, the Injeel attributes its message to God. Obviously, that assertion does not make it so, but the claim itself distinguishes the Bible from the scriptures of major world religions in the first century and earlier.

Wait a minute! All scriptures of the world claim to be the Word of God, do they not? One might think so, but such is not the case. Gary DeLashmutt reminds us: "One of the best kept secrets is the fact that very few 'scriptures' even claim to be God's revealed Word."[2] A research project of my own bore this out.[3] Drawing from the ancient scriptures of classical Hinduism, Buddhism and Confucianism, I found no corollary to the oft-repeated Biblical words, "thus says the LORD." Only in those religions that were offshoots of the Judeo-Christian faith appearing *afterwards* do we hear those claims of divine inspiration echoed. The Bible, however, does not shy away from boldly asserting itself as God's message to people. A few examples will illustrate this extraordinary claim.

The Bible's Unique Claims as God's Word

Moses in the Tawrat

> "When *the LORD finished speaking to Moses* on Mount Sinai, he gave him the two tablets of the covenant law, *the tablets of stone inscribed by the finger of God.*" (Exodus 31:18)

"These are *the commandments the LORD proclaimed in a loud voice* to your whole assembly there on the mountain... Then *he wrote them on two stone tablets and gave them to me.*" (Deuteronomy 5:22)

All scriptures of the world claim to be the Word of God, do they not? One might think so, but such is not the case.

"Do not add to what I command you and do not subtract from it, but keep *the commands of the LORD your God that I give you.*" (Deuteronomy 4:2)

"*Man does not live on bread alone but on every word that comes from the mouth of the LORD.* " (Deuteronomy 8:2-3)

Fifty times in Scripture we read, "God said" in the form of direct address to men and women. Noah is but one of dozens of examples:

"*God said to Noah,* "I am going to put an end to all people, for the earth is filled with violence because of them." (Genesis 6:16)

Another 259 times we read "the LORD said" such as in the case of Abraham upon the death of his father, Terah:

"*The LORD had said to Abram,* "Go from your country, your people and your father's household to the land I will show you." (Genesis 12:1 NIV)

Moses wrote down the words of God in the first five books: Genesis, Exodus, Leviticus, Numbers and Deuteronomy. When he died, would God continue speaking?

The Prophets

As we move to the long period of God's prophets, we first note that all of them confirmed the five books of Moses as God's very Word. Never did they challenge its history or its commands.

But did God speak through them as well? Indeed, he did. The manner in which prophets received their messages is telling. Coming as "the word of the LORD" (*davar Yahweh*) removed any guesswork in the prophet's mind. Here is a small sampling:

> "*The word of the LORD came to Jeremiah* in the thirteenth year of the reign of Josiah son of Amon king of Judah. . . *The word of the LORD came to me*, saying, "Before I formed you in the womb I knew you, before you were born I set you apart; I appointed you as a prophet to the nations." (Jeremiah 1:4-9)

> ". . . in the land of the Babylonians. There *the word of the LORD came to Ezekiel* the hand of the LORD was on him." (Ezekiel 1:3)

> "*The word of the LORD came to Jonah* son of Amittai: "Go to the great city of Nineveh and preach against it, because its wickedness has come up before me." (Jonah 1:1-2)

> "In the eighth month of the second year of Darius, *the word of the LORD came to the prophet Zechariah* son of Berekiah, the son of Iddo" (Zechariah 1:1-3)

"All Scripture is inspired by God [theopneusos, "God-breathed"] and profitable for teaching, for reproof, for correction, for training in righteousness; so that the man of God may be adequate, equipped for every good work."
Injeel, 2 Timothy 3:16-17

David in the Zabur

David, as shepherd and king, passionately loved and honored the divine words of the Torah. The Zabur opens in Psalm 1 describing the truly happy and blessed people as those "whose delight is in the law of the LORD, who meditates on his law day and night" (Psalm 1:2). The Bible's longest chapter, Psalm 119, bears eloquent testimony to the transformative power of God's Word. A thousand times David testifies,

"The Holy Spirit supernaturally motivated and superintended the prophetic and apostolic recipients of revelation in the entire process of writing their scriptural books."
Gordon R. Lewis

"As for God, his way is perfect: *The LORD's word is flawless*; he shields all who take refuge in him." (Psalm 18:30)

But did God speak to David? His last words dismiss any doubts:

"*The Spirit of the LORD spoke through me*; his word was on my tongue." (2 Samuel 23:2)

Moving ahead to the Injeel, let's begin with Jesus.

Jesus in the Injeel

Jesus was born about 400 years after Prophet Malachi, the last Old Testament literary prophet (with a book bearing his name). Did he regard the Old Testament to carry binding divine authority?

"Do not think that I have come to abolish the *Law [of Moses]* or the *Prophets; I have not come to abolish them but to fulfill them.* For truly I tell you, until heaven and earth disappear, not the smallest letter, *not the least stroke of a pen, will by any means disappear from the Law until everything is accomplished.*" (Matthew 5:17-18)

> "Everything must be fulfilled that is written about me in the Law of Moses, the Prophets and the Psalms."
> Jesus, Luke 24:44

"...the *Scripture cannot be broken.*" (John 10:35 NKJV)

"This is what I told you while I was still with you: *Everything must be fulfilled* that is written about me in *the Law of Moses, the Prophets and the Psalms.*" (Luke 24:44)

Jesus viewed his own words as having binding Scriptural authority:

"Heaven and earth will pass away, but *my words will never pass away.*" (Mark 13:31)

Let's go now to Jesus' apostles, who by the Holy Spirit are responsible for the written record of the Injeel.

The Apostles

The apostles' attitude towards Scripture is of utmost importance since each of the Injeel's twenty-seven books traces back to them. Like their Master, they unanimously view Scripture as originating with God and not man:

> "But know this first of all, that no prophecy of Scripture is a matter of one's own interpretation, for *no prophecy was ever made by an act of human will, but men moved by the Holy Spirit spoke from God.*" (2 Peter 1:20-21)

> "No prophecy was ever made by an act of human will, but men moved by the Holy Spirit spoke from God."
> (2 Peter 1:20-21)

In another place,

> "*All Scripture is inspired by God* [*theopneusos*, "God-breathed"] and profitable for teaching, for reproof, for correction, for training in righteousness; so that the man of God may be adequate, equipped for every good work." (2 Timothy 3:16-17)

Divine Inspiration

What does 'inspired by God' mean? We may hear a speech or watch a movie that moves us emotionally and call it inspiring. In 2 Timothy 3:16 it is used in a different way. The term literally means "God-breathed" or "breathed into by God." To call the Bible inspired by God means:

> "The Holy Spirit supernaturally motivated and superintended the prophetic and apostolic recipients of revelation in the entire process of writing their scriptural books."[4]

Rabbinical teaching underscored this divine process:

> "*The Spirit of God rested on and in the prophets and spoke through them,*

so that their words did not come from themselves but from the mouth of God; they spoke and wrote in the Holy Spirit. The early church was in entire agreement with this view."[5]

Scriptural inspiration meant to the apostles, then, something far more than human emotion. It conveyed divine origin and authority and summoned man's obedience. If from God, we can trust its reliability. But how much of the Bible is inspired?

Range of inspiration. Inspiration covers *all* Scripture. A Muslim recently asked me an unusual question: "What does the Red Bible say?" We had been discussing a passage in the Fourth Gospel penned by John, one of the apostles. I was confused until he explained that he was referring not to a separate Bible with a red cover, but to Jesus' words which are often printed in red ink. Once clarified, he said,

"If Jesus didn't say it, then it cannot be God's inspired Word in the Injeel. Others, just humans, wrote it."

So to my friend, all the words in black originated with the apostle John and lacked divine authority while those in red from the mouth of Jesus came from God. This understanding led him to limit the range of divine inspiration.

The answer is found in the Holy Spirit who first inspired the writings of Moses and the Prophets in the Old Testament, and then who anointed Jesus at his baptism. That same Spirit guided the apostles in producing a faithful account of all Jesus did and said. How do we know this?

Jesus explicitly endorsed this ongoing work of the Spirit. Before leaving the apostles, he assured them that when the Holy Spirit would come, he would speak through them with the *same authority as himself*:

"But *when he, the Spirit of truth, comes, he will guide you into all the truth.* He will not speak on his own; he will speak only what he hears, and he will tell you what is yet to come. He will glorify me because *it is from me that he will receive what he will make known to you.*" (John 16:13-14; see also 14:26 and 15:26-27)

The color of ink will not matter because inspiration is the operation of one and the same Holy Spirit. What applies to one part of Scripture applies to all. Therefore, thanks to the Spirit, every part, whether printed in black ink or red, can be equally trusted as from God.

Most people are under-impressed by the Bible's claim to be God's Word because they err in assuming that all religious writings made the same claim. Nevertheless, it remains one of the Bible's distinguishing features.

These passages clearly invest Scripture with divine origin through the Holy Spirit, making faith in them a possibility and obedience to them an expectation.

The next line of evidence for trusting the Injeel will take us from this significant claim to an extraordinary test by which to authenticate it. Claiming divine origin is one thing; proving it, quite another.

3. The Injeel authenticates its claim of divine origin by passing a stringent test.

One of the most compelling reasons to trust the New Testament message is its passing grade on the biblical test for authenticating divine messages. For that test, we go to the Old Testament.

Why was this necessary? In Moses' day, well over 1000 years before Jesus, the young nation of Israel was surrounded by nations that sought divine knowledge or guidance by resorting to sorcerers and diviners. These avenues were strictly off-limits to Israel (Lev 19:31). But there were also men *within Israel* who dared speaking in Yahweh's name (the LORD) even though God had not spoken. Often their messages conflicted with those previously given to Moses. Making matters worse, many of them used miraculous powers, obviously not from God, that seemed to validate their message.

> "A prophet who presumes to speak in my name anything I have not commanded, or a prophet who speaks in the name of other gods, is to be put to death."
> Tawrat of Moses,
> Deuteronomy 18:19

Confused by this, the people appealed to Moses for guidance on how they might know which prophets to take seriously (e.g. Deut. 13:2). Moses gave them two criteria by which to spot pretenders. We can refer to this as "The Prophet Test."

The Prophet Test

The Prophet Test underscored the premium value that God placed on his Word! It was not to be trifled with and getting a passing grade was often a matter of life and death.

Two Benchmarks of the Divine Word

Two standards were put in place to authenticate a divine message: doctrinal congruence and predictive accuracy.

Benchmark #1: Loyalty to God's Covenant

A prophet's authenticity was either proven or disproven by his faithfulness to God's covenant, the Ten Commandments.

"A prophet who presumes to speak in my name anything I have not commanded, or *a prophet who speaks in the name of other gods, is to be put to death.*" (Deuteronomy 18:19)

"My [God's] word that goes out from my mouth: It will not return to me empty, but will accomplish what I desire and achieve the purpose for which I sent it."
Prophet Isaiah 55:10-11

"If there arises among you a prophet or a dreamer of dreams, and he gives you a *sign or a wonder*, and the sign or the wonder comes to pass, of which he spoke to you, saying, *'Let us go after other gods'—which you have not known—'and let us serve them,'* you shall not listen to the words of that prophet or that dreamer of dreams, for *the LORD your God is testing you to know whether you love the LORD your God with all your heart and with all your soul.*

283

But that prophet or that dreamer of dreams *shall be put to death*, because *he has spoken in order to turn you away from the LORD your God*, who brought you out of the land of Egypt and redeemed you from the house of bondage, *to entice you from the way* in which the LORD your God commanded you to walk. So you shall put away the evil from your midst." (Deuteronomy 13:1-5 NKJV)

Any spokesperson for God in ancient Israel should think twice before saying "God told me."

Benchmark #2: Fulfillment of Prediction

Second, a prophet's authenticity was proven or disproven by the outcome of his prediction. Meeting this challenge was as convincing for the people as it was difficult for the prophet, for as the saying goes: "Everyone has perfect hindsight; God has perfect foresight." In this case of failed prediction, the prophet was not to be killed but simply ignored. This benchmark was necessary, as Prophet Ezekiel later showed: "False prophets wait in vain for fulfillment of their visions" (Ezekiel 13:6).

"You may say to yourselves,'How can we know when a message has not been spokenby the LORD?' If what aprophet proclaims in thename of the LORD does nottake place or come true, that is a message the LORD has not spoken. That prophet has spoken presumptuously, so do not be alarmed."
Tawrat, Deuteronomy 18:20-22

"You may say to yourselves, 'How can we know when a message has not been spoken by the LORD?' If what a prophet proclaims in the name of the LORD does not take place or come true, that is a message the LORD has not spoken. That prophet has spoken presumptuously, so do not be alarmed." Tawrat, Deuteronomy 18:20-22

One is struck by the simplicity of these benchmarks. Spotting false prophets over time was relatively easy, requiring no special erudition. Covenant loyalty could be easily seen by the speaker's compliance to the Ten Commandments, an objective behavioral standard known by all Israel. For that, no sorcerers were necessary to sort out the meaning of an esoteric message, no clever riddles had to be solved and no ponderously complicated oracles demanded interpretation. The second benchmark was equally clear. One had only to connect the front end of a prophet's prediction with the back end of historical fulfilment. The only exceptions were those that awaited their fulfillment centuries later. In such cases, the value of preserving written Scripture for future generations cannot be overestimated.

> "I am God, and there is none like me. I make known the end from the beginning, from ancient times, what is still to come. I say, 'My purpose will stand, and I will do all that I please.'"
> Prophet Isaiah 46:9-10

Supernatural Range of Prophetic Knowledge

The predictive role of biblical prophets was concisely defined by a twelfth-century Christian monk, Peter the Venerable:

> "*A prophet is one who discloses to mortal men matters unknown* either from the past or the present or the future, taught not by human understanding but *inspired by the Spirit of God.*"[7]

Why would anyone imagine they could fill this role? The ability to see the distant past and unknown future with the same 20/20 vision as the present required the "eyes" of One who exists outside of time. Someone like this:

> "A prophet is one who discloses to mortal men matters unknown either from the past or the present or the future, taught not by human understanding but inspired by the Spirit of God."
> Peter the Venerable, twelfth century

"I am God, and there is none like me. *I make known the end from the beginning,* from ancient times, what is still to come. I say, '*My purpose will stand, and I will do all that I please.*'" (Isaiah 46:9-10)

Without a direct connection to such a Being, who would dare say this?

> "I am God, and there is none like me. I make known the end from the beginning, from ancient times, what is still to come. I say, 'My purpose will stand, and I will do all that I please.'" Prophet Isaiah 46:9-10

Prophetic Time Dimensions

The prophetic Word required supernatural power over three dimensions: past, present and future.

Past – An example of prophetic knowledge of past events is Moses who was not present when God created the heavens and the earth, yet by the Spirit he wrote Genesis 1-2.

> God promised Hagar, "As for Ishmael, I have heard you; behold, I have blessed him and will make him fruitful and multiply him greatly. He shall father twelve princes, and I will make him into a great nation."
> Tawrat, Genesis 17:20

Present – Prophecies in the present time were sometimes necessary when evil deeds had been done in secret that became supernaturally known to Moses (e.g., Numbers 16:31-31, 46 etc.).[8]

Future – Our interest is prophecy's future aspect since the events of the Gospel still lay far in the distance at the time of the prophets' writing. Within this group are (a) prophecies of *near-future* events (e.g., that the Jews would be exiled in Babylon for a specific duration of 70 years (Jeremiah 29:10-14) or the destruction of Babylon by the Persians (Isaiah 21:1-10; Jeremiah 50:1-3; 51:41-43) and (b) prophecies occurring in the *distant* future. Throughout the Old Testament many were proven true by the fulfillment of their predictions: Noah, Jacob, Joseph, Samuel, David, Isaiah, Elijah, Elisha and others.

Two Types of Future Prophecy

Finally, within this category of *future* prophecy are two types: those whose predictions pertained to *specific* individuals or nations and others to *universal* events that affect all people.[9] Our chief concern is with the latter type, yet the former deserves our notice.

Type 1: Examples of Prophecies pertaining to Individuals or Nations

Prophet Jonah to Nineveh – Jonah prophesied not only *about* ancient Nineveh, Assyria's capital city, but directly *to* its citizens (Jonah 1:2, 15, 17; Al-Saffat 37:138-48; Al-Anbiya 21:87). His message was met with extraordinary success.

Prophecy about Ishmael to Hagar – A notable example of prophecy to a specific *person* was Hagar, Sarah's mistress. When she fled into the desert in a dire situation, God promised her that she would become the mother of Abraham's son Ishmael and innumerable descendants:

> "The LORD has listened to your affliction." (Genesis 16:11) Then the angel of the LORD told her... *'I will increase your descendants so much that they will be too numerous to count. . . You are now pregnant* and *you will give birth to a son.* You shall name him Ishmael, for the LORD has heard of your misery.' So Hagar bore Abram a son, and Abram gave the name Ishmael ...." (Genesis 16:9-12, 15-16)

God later promised Hagar that Ishmael's descendants would become a great nation:

> "As for Ishmael, I have heard you; behold, *I have blessed him and will make him fruitful and multiply him greatly.* He shall *father twelve princes, and I will make him into a great nation"* (Genesis 17:20).

Did God keep his promise to Hagar? We read in the book of Genesis how God not only gave her a son as he promised, but twelve princes.

"Revelation is the manifestation of God Himself in His action, and it is accompanied by Inspiration which declares the meaning of what God is doing. . .Revelation comes in a closed series of Events; Inspiration declares the meaning of those events at the time and after. . ."

A. G. Herbert

287

"These are the names of the *sons of Ishmael*, listed in the order of their birth: Nebaioth the firstborn of Ishmael, Kedar, Adbeel, Mibsam, Mishma, Dumah, Massa, Hadad, Tema, Jetur, Naphish and Kedemah. . . . and these are the names of the twelve tribal rulers according to their settlements and camps. . . His descendants settled in the area from Havilah to Shur, near the eastern border of Egypt, as you go toward Ashur." (Genesis 25:12-16, 18)

The next type of prophecies impinges on your question about the Injeel's veracity.

Type 2: Prophecies Pertaining Universally to All Humanity

The second type, prophecies pertaining universally, point to salvation for the human race. They include the coming Messiah, his miracles and his death and resurrection.[10] These found their historical fulfillment in the Injeel and have become the foremost reason many people place their confidence in its unique divine message. Why so?

Why this Test Works

What makes this Prophet Test so effective in verifying or disqualifying spokespersons for God? The answer, deserving our utmost attention, begins not with the human prophet but with the divine nature as a God of truth. God is undeviatingly faithful to his Word (1 Sam. 15:29; Heb 6:18; Titus 1:2 etc.). If not, or if he spoke carelessly or capriciously, this test would prove nothing of prophetic authenticity. Its compelling value stems directly from the character of the Promise-Maker. Remember, this is the Creator who powerfully *spoke* everything into existence. His quickening formative speech continued well-past the dawn of creation. He states:

"As the rain and the snow come down from heaven, and do not return to it without watering the earth and making it bud and flourish, so that it yields seed for the sower and bread for the eater, *so is my word that goes out from my mouth: It will not return to me empty, but will accomplish what I desire and achieve the purpose for which I sent it.*" (Isaiah 55:10-11)

Unlike weathermen who see gathering clouds and predict rain, God's forecasts were more than predictions. They did more than announce the future; they determined it, "accomplishing" his will and "achieving" his purpose. At Creation, God looked into the formless void and issued commands that burst forth a magnificent universe teeming with life. Should it surprise us if, after his pristine world became ravaged by sin, that the Creator would again speak life-giving words to heal, redeem and restore it? This should surprise no one if the God of creation and of redemption is one and the same.

The Prophet Test actually works because God never exaggerates outcomes and makes no promises that he fails to keep. A plethora of evidence in Chapter 11 (Table, "Sources for Jesus in the Injeel") will validate this statement:

> "That prophecies were no idle proclamations is evidenced by the number that were fulfilled."[20]

These show how daring God's Word can be, declaring future events with bold specificity and actually bringing them about.

Proof is in the Pudding

"As the rain and the snow come down from heaven, and do not return to it without watering the earth and making it bud and flourish, . . . so is my word that goes out from my mouth: It will not return to me empty but will accomplish what I desire and achieve the purpose for which I sent it."
Prophet Isaiah 55:10-11t

Perhaps you've heard the expression, *the proof is in the pudding*, probably first spoken when a cook excited hungry guests with the promise of a tasty meal. Upon hearing, one of them mumbled, "The proof is in the pudding." In other words, "We'll see about that!" Today people use this in response to big promises of all kinds. It means, "Maybe so, maybe not. We'll wait and see."

The Prophet Test is the Scriptural counterpart to the proof-is-in-the-pudding. The proof of prophethood was in the pudding of fulfillment. Future

289

events foretold in "the Name of the LORD," must await their actual happening. Until then, the prophet's reputation was on the line.

One thing going for this biblical Test was the ease in which it could be verified. No specialist was needed to interpret its results. Let's say one of my neighbors publicly insulted me and in a rage I said to him, "God told me that by next Tuesday your dog will get rabies and have to be put down." Did God really say that? By the following Wednesday morning everyone present would know. It wouldn't take a crystal ball to discover that my statement arose from human malice rather than divine inspiration.

Let's consider a more serious example. Jesus, around A.D. 30, predicted with tears the total destruction of Jerusalem and its Temple within one generation. Why? Because, like the City's forefathers had killed God's prophets, its present religious leaders rejected him as the Messiah-King (Luke 19:41-44; 13:34-35). The Prophet Test proved Jesus' prediction to be from God and not out of a personal vendetta when, in 70 A.D. Roman armies thoroughly demolished the Holy City, just as he said. The front end of his prediction paired with the far end of its historical fulfillment.

What makes this symmetry so striking between Scripture's prophetic predictions and their historical fulfillment is how they occurred over a 1400-year period involving about forty authors writing from different world areas. This bears eloquent testimony to the influence of the Holy Spirit acting as editor-in-chief, ultimately concentrating a wide range of ancient predictions on a single Figure, Jesus the Messiah.

Does the Injeel Pass the Prophet Test?

What would it take for the Injeel to receive a passing grade? It must meet both benchmarks of doctrinal loyalty to previous Scriptures and historically fulfill prophetic promises. Its doctrinal alignment will be presented in Chapters 10 and 11. Let's focus on the second benchmark.

Here's the million-dollar question. Will the Injeel's Jesus story form a match with the centuries of inspired prophecies preceding him? Or captured more vividly: Is the Gospel sewn integrally into the fabric of Scripture or has it been stuck onto the Old Testament garment like a patch, an unsightly distraction that doesn't belong? The Injeel's opening line clues us in by introducing Jesus like this:

"This is the genealogy of Jesus the Messiah the son of David, the son of Abraham..." (Matthew 1:1)

A few observations are in order.

First, this opening line announces the arrival of Jesus as the Messiah who belongs to two crucial family lineages. His genealogy links Jesus to Abraham through whose "seed" God promised to spread blessing to the whole world (Genesis 12:1-3; 22:17-18). It then fasts-forward to King David to whom God promised an everlasting royal lineage that culminates with the Messiah-King (1 Samuel 7; Isaiah 9:1-7). In other words, Jesus is presented in a way that signals to us that the single fabric of God's story, stretching back over two thousand years, is not coming unraveled but is unfolding. The divine Tailor is stitching together the final touches onto the ancient Garment.

Second, the Injeel's terminology used to introduce God's Word shifted dramatically from that of the Old Testament. You may recall how the OT often introduced a divine message with the phrase: "the word of the LORD came to [prophet's name]. . ."[14] However, once the New Testament arrived, *never* again is it heard. In its place, Jesus[15] and later his apostles[16] use *"It is written"* (77 total NT instances) and *"It is fulfilled."* Matthew alone cites the Old Testament fifty-seven times, often using the formula "It is written" (14 times) and "It is fulfilled" (8 times).

> Matthew's Gospel account cites the Torah of Moses, the Prophets and the Zabur fifty-seven times, often using the formula "It is written" (14 times) or "to fulfill" (8 times).

This sudden shift of terms tips us off that all that Jesus said and did fulfilled the "word of the LORD" previously spoken. It was the high watermark of divine history. Jesus knew it. The hands on God's clock of revelation had reached the hour.

"Jesus came into Galilee, preaching the gospel of God, and saying, *"The time is fulfilled, and the kingdom of God is at hand*; repent and believe in the gospel." (Mark 1:14-15, emphasis added)

Jesus deliberately paired the front end of the prophets' predictions with himself at the back end of historical fulfillment. On thirty-one separate occasions, he explicitly matched his actions and teachings with the previous "word of the Lord!" At his first sermon in the Nazareth synagogue, he read Isaiah 61, a Messianic prophecy, and said: *"Today this Scripture is fulfilled in your hearing"* (Luke 4:6-21). Jesus clearly believed the Scriptures pointed to him and his mission. Another example:

"Now *all this took place to fulfill what was spoken by the Lord through the prophet. . ."* (Matthew 1:22, emphasis added)

"All this" encompasses the totality of Jesus' ministry. Even his healing ministry was seen in this light. After restoring a sick woman to health,

"*This was to fulfill* what was spoken through Isaiah the prophet: "He Himself took our infirmities and carried away our diseases." (Matthew 8:17, emphasis added)

Because the Gospel historically fulfilled the "word of the LORD" previously spoken, Jesus was keenly aware that the hands on God's clock of revelation had reached that hour. He preached: "The time is fulfilled, and the kingdom of God is at hand; repent and believe in the gospel." (Mark 1:14-15)

Every detail of the Gospel flows out of the Old Testament. Ancient prophets not only predicted the Messiah, but the simultaneous appearance of a forerunner to prepare people for his arrival. His message would be to-the-point: *The Promised One we've been waiting for has arrived, so prepare to meet him!* The city would buzz with excitement. Thanks to him, no one need miss the Messiah. The question is, how would anyone recognize the forerunner? Would he himself have a forerunner or just show up in downtown Jerusalem and start preaching? No and no.

The Gospel finally brought the long prophetic waiting period to a glorious end!

Messiah Jesus' forerunner was John the Baptizer (*Yahya*) and he did not preach in Jerusalem's inner-city. He preached in the unpopulated, to say the least, Judean wilderness. How then can we explain John's immense popularity – "the whole city went out to hear him" – since he preached in a deserted area?

"*As it is written* in Isaiah the prophet: "I will send my messenger ahead of you, who will prepare your way"— *a voice of one calling in the wilderness,* 'Prepare the way for the Lord, make straight paths for him.'" (Mark 1:1-3 citing Isaiah 40:3; Malachi 3:1)

John's enormous fame in Jerusalem can be traced back to Prophet Isaiah.

What the Shift Says about the Bible

What does this shift from the OT "word of the LORD" to the NT "it is fulfilled" teach us about the Injeel's relationship to the Torah, Prophets and Zabur? It shouts loud and clear: This Gospel of Jesus is no patch! It is tightly sewn into every divine Word previously spoken! Declaration has become revelation; audible Word matches visible Event. Three lessons must not be missed.

The Injeel was not starting something new, but finishing something ancient.

First, the Injeel was not starting something new, but finishing something ancient. Rather than introducing novelties, it tied directly to ancient promises, thus validating the whole. Words that "went forth from the mouth of God" through the lips of prophets were not empty promises.

Second, the Gospel brought the long prophetic waiting period to a glorious end. The Injeel is the sequel to and culmination of the

Tawrat of Moses, all the Prophets, the Zabur of Dawud and then, finally, to John the Baptizer (Yahya).

Third, the Old and New Testaments, though containing a vast library, belong together as one Book. The Christian Bible comes bound as a single volume for the simple reason that it all sprang from one Source, tells one story, and aims at one goal. For this reason, Scripture itself is the staple diet of healthy Christian faith. By immersing ourselves in "the *whole* counsel of God" we discover that its immense diversity does not erase its grand unity. No wonder it's been called the "symphony of Scripture."

Without the New Testament, the Old would be incomplete, still missing its Messiah. But a New Testament without the Old would leave us with a rootless Messiah, missing the promises anchoring him to the larger biblical story by which to identify him. Metaphorically, he'd just be a patch on an old garment. Such was not the case. The Injeel passed the Prophet Test.

> The Old and New Testaments, though containing a vast library, belong together as one Book.

Time Out

Let's call a brief time-out. Before advancing to the next line of evidence for the Injeel, let's pause long enough for Muslims and Christians to think together about what was, to me, a surprising discovery.

Through conversations, discussions and debates with Muslims, two realities quickly surface. The first is common knowledge. Muslims and Christians both believe our Book came from God and carries divine authority. Nothing new there. The second caught me by surprise. Each of us arrives at that conclusion by using a different yardstick by which to authenticate divine speech. The greatest contrast between our cherished Books is not what I often hear – namely, that one Book is corrupted and the other flawless. Far more critical is the contrasting criterion by which to test God's Word. If in doubt, just put this question (expressed in two ways) to your Christian and Muslim friends and it will become clear:

> How do you know a message comes from God? That is, by what means does God verify that he has spoken?

When we engage each other about our Books, it typically plays out where each of us defends our Book on the basis of our own checklist of authenticating standards. By doing so, we end up at an impasse by applying the criteria of one to invalidate the other without paying much attention to the criteria themselves. Typically, we dispute over historical discrepancies between our Books without addressing deeper questions about what qualified them as God's Word in the first place.

> Christians are not embarrassed that God's Word had a beginning. One aspect of Scripture that we relish is not its eternality but imperishability! "The grass withers, the flower fades, but the word of our God stands forever."
> Prophet Isaiah 40:7-8

Not until *common* benchmarks are in place, however, will we arrive at any real conclusions. Here's why.

Would we expect a 250-pound bodybuilder to win a beauty pageant because of his physical prowess? He may insist that what made him the champion in one arena – say, the bench-press competition— should count in another that measured poise and physical beauty. The absurdity is obvious. His only shot at being crowned is if *he* could set the standards. Yet, contestants don't make the rules. Judges do. After losing the crown, he may protest by saying, "But I can lift an elephant!" to which the judge will reply, "That doesn't matter here. How do you look in an evening gown?"

Gleaning useful logic from this unlikely scenario might lead us to more fruitful discussions. Could we agree on two goals? First, let's see if we can apply the same set of criteria to both Books. Second, let's doggedly and prayerfully pursue the answer to: What says the Judge? If we find that God has already established a means by which to authenticate his Word, can we resist the temptation to substitute it with our own? Most Muslims I know would agree with this wisdom from the Injeel:

"It is not the one who commends *himself* who is approved, but the one *the Lord* commends" (2 Cor 10:18).

Muslim reader, we value your insights on this question because you take Scripture seriously. On what basis does either the Qur'an or Islamic authorities declare that God has spoken? We'd love hearing from you!

Let's wrap-up this lengthy section. As Christians, our chief concern began with who put the standards in place verifying an authentic "word of the LORD." That search led us to the "Prophet Test," pairing what men *said* with what God *did*. Specifically, the Injeel, we found, receives a passing grade on both counts of *doctrinal coherence* with the Old Testament and *historical fulfillment of prophetic prediction*. While not a stand-alone, it is a huge signpost pointing to the divine origin of the Injeel's Jesus Message. Making it so is its objectivity. Anyone willing to look will be able to see the connections. Importantly, by its early introduction in the Tawrat – all the way back to Moses' day – the Prophet Test served future generations by providing the means to verify all subsequent messages spoken through Prophets, the Zabur and the Injeel.

4. The Injeel shows signs of historical accuracy.

Another reason I trust the Injeel are the host of strong indicators that its authors got their facts right. I'll identify four of these: early dating, reliance on eyewitness testimonies, Luke's notable example and their impressive apostolic qualifications.

a. Early Date of Composition Lends Credence to its Accuracy

History is central to the Gospel, making the early date of composition more crucial.

"The events of the Gospel were recorded within the lifetime of several of those who claimed to have observed them."[29]

Does historical accuracy matter? Would not the teachings of Jesus remain relevant even if the Gospel's supernatural elements were legendary? F. F. Bruce answers well:

> "This argument sounds plausible, and it may be applicable to some religions. It might be held, for example that the ethics of Confucianism have an independent value quite apart from the story of the life of Confucius himself...But the argument can be applied to the New Testament only if we ignore the real essence of Christianity. *For the Christian gospel is not primarily a code of ethics or a metaphysical system; it is first and foremost good news,* and as such it was proclaimed by the earliest preachers...Christianity as a way of life depends upon the acceptance of Christianity as good news. *And this good news is intimately bound up with the historical order,* for it tells how for the world's redemption God entered into history, the eternal came into time, the kingdom of heaven invaded the realm of earth, in the great events of the incarnation, crucifixion, an resurrection of Jesus the Christ. The first recorded words of our Lord's public preaching in Galilee are: 'The time is fulfilled, and the kingdom of God has drawn near; repent and believe the good news.'"[30]

> "For the Christian gospel is not primarily a code of ethics or a metaphysical system; it is first and foremost good news, and as such it was proclaimed by the earliest preachers. .. And this good news is intimately bound up with the historical order."
>
> F. F. Bruce

Since Christianity's beliefs rest on historical events, it goes without saying that the credibility of those reporting them is of premium value. Bruce continues:

> "That Christianity has its roots in history is emphasized in the Church's earliest creeds, which fix the *supreme revelation of God at a particular point in time,* when 'Jesus Christ, His only Son our Lord . . . suffered under Pontius Pilate'. This *historical 'once-forall-ness' of Christianity,* which distinguishes it from those religious and philosophical systems which are not specially related to any

particular time, *makes the reliability of the writings which purport to record this revelation a question of first-rate importance.*"[31]

The notion that reports increase with accuracy over time, placing greater distance from the occurrences being recalled, is counterintuitive and suspect.[32] There is no substitute for reliable reporters to capture what happened locally and make it widely known. Many so-called "histories" of Jesus appeared much later that introduced details about Jesus' life that contradicted these earliest firsthand accounts. **The Injeel's record is by far the earliest and most informed. Why should anyone trust later ones written by absentees?**

While divine truth is eternal, its revelation to human beings is not. Those later writers who discount the value of historical accuracy tend to see the Gospel as *views* rather than *news*. But its views cannot be separated from its news.

b. Eyewitness Testimony Provided a More Authentic and Lively Record

Only an eyewitness – in this case, Peter – could provide information this valuable:

> "For we did not follow cleverly devised stories when we told you about the coming of our Lord Jesus Christ in power, but we were eyewitnesses of his majesty. He received honor and glory from God the Father when the voice came to him from the Majestic Glory, saying, "This is my Son, whom I love; with him I am well pleased." We ourselves heard this voice that came from heaven when we were with him on the sacred mountain." (2 Peter 1:16-18)

Ancient historians regarded eyewitness testimony as the most reliable:

> "The ancient historians – such as Thucydides, Polybius, Josephus, and Tacitus – were convinced that *true history could be written only while events were still within living memory,* and they valued as their sources the *oral reports of direct experience of the events by involved participants* in them. Ideally, the historian himself should have been a participant in the events he narrates

...but, since he could not have been at all the events he recounts or in all the places he describes, the historian had also to *rely on eyewitnesses whose living voices he could hear and whom he could question himself: 'Autopsy [eyewitness testimony] was the essential means to reach back into the past.*"[33]

"The standards set by Thucydides and Polybius were historiographic best practice, to which other historians aspired or at least paid lip-service. *Good historians were highly critical of those who relied largely on written sources.*"[34]

Given that background, how well does the Injeel's account of Jesus fare? Let's examine Luke, one of the four Gospel witnesses.

c. Case in Point – Luke's Account Bore Marks of Historical Credibility

Two of the 27 books of the New Testament were penned by a physician named Luke.

Volume 1: LUKE – History of JESUS
Volume 2: ACTS – History of the CHURCH's first thirty years
directed by the Holy Spirit

These companion volumes chronicle the life of Jesus (Luke) and the growth of the early church (Acts). How much can we trust these?

MARKS OF HISTORICAL CREDIBILITY IN LUKE

Luke opens his account of the Gospel like this:

"Inasmuch as many have undertaken to compile an account of the things accomplished among us, just as they were *handed down to us* by those who from the beginning were *eyewitnesses* and servants of the word, it seemed fitting for me as well, having *investigated everything carefully from the beginning,* to write it out for you *in consecutive order,* most excellent Theophilus; so *that you may know the exact truth* about the things you have been taught." (Luke 1:1-4 emphasis added)

Details Pointing to Luke's Credibility

Luke's humility. Rather than composing literature of his own invention to make a name for himself, his record of Jesus was "just as they were handed down to us."

Luke's sources. Three qualities commended those he consulted:

> *Firsthand* – "those who . . . were *eyewitnesses*." The most reliable reports of historical events are from those in closest proximity to it.
>
> *Comprehensive* – "were handed down to us by those who *from the beginning* were eyewitnesses." These were not late-comers, but those who had accompanied Jesus from the start.
>
> *"Servants of the word"* – reverence for Scripture, placing God's truth over themselves to which they were subject.

Luke's Scriptural connection. He "compiled an account of the things 'accomplished' among us," demonstrating how Jesus completed earlier Scriptures.

Luke's chronological presentation: "to write it out for you in consecutive order."

Luke's habitual accuracy. Luke strives for accuracy: "so that you may know the exact truth about the things that you have been taught." He examined the key moments of Jesus' life and teaching: "having investigated everything carefully from the beginning." F. F. Bruce observed:

> "Accuracy is a habit of mind, and we know from happy (or unhappy) experience that some people are habitually accurate just as others can be depended upon to be inaccurate. Luke's record entitles him to be regarded as a writer of habitual accuracy."[35]

And yet some have questioned Luke's credibility and deserve our attention.

Luke On Trial – Passes Rigorous Scrutiny

Since Luke was not part of the original Twelve apostles, liberal scholars once questioned his accuracy[36] One such scholar was Sir William Ramsay, a renowned archaeologist who taught Classical Archaeology at Oxford University who had studied under the famous liberal German historical schools in the mid-nineteenth century. Known for its scholarship, this school taught that the New Testament was not a historical document. Like his professors, Ramsay was certain that "Luke was a terrible historian." But to his credit, he set out to prove his premise by visiting the ancient cities in Asia Minor mentioned in the Book of Acts.

Ramsay was in for a surprise. Instead of confirming his skepticism, he found in the cities where Paul traveled key historical figures in correct time sequence as well as proper local titles of government officials. For example, in **Thessalonica** he uncovered "politarchs;" in **Ephesus**, "temple wardens;" in **Cyprus**, "proconsuls;" in **Malta**, the "first man of the island;" and in **Abila** (NW of Damascus), Greek inscriptions of "Lysanius the tetrarch" (AD 14 – 29). These demonstrated Luke's attention to detail. Along with other discoveries, they opened his eyes and reversed his initial skepticism:

> "Luke's history is unsurpassed in respect of its trustworthiness. . .Luke is a historian of the first rank; not merely are his statements of fact trustworthy. . .this author should be placed along with the very greatest historians."
>
> Sir William Ramsay, classical archaeologist, Oxford University

"I began with a mind unfavorable to it [Injeel, Acts], for the ingenuity and apparent completeness of the Tubingen theory had at one time quite convinced me. It did not then in my line of life to investigate the subject minutely; but more recently I found myself often brought into contact with the Book of Acts as an authority for the topography, antiquities, and society of Asia Minor. **It was gradually borne in upon me that in various details the narrative showed marvelous truth.**"[37]

William Ramsay, the renowned skeptic finally weighed in:

"Luke's history is unsurpassed in respect of its trustworthiness. . .Luke is a historian of the first rank; not merely are his statements of fact trustworthy. . .this author should be placed along with the very greatest historians."[38]

Let's probe a little deeper. Can we trust Luke's sources? He drew from existing Gospel accounts already circulating at the time of his writing and identified as "the servants of the Word," referring primarily to the other apostles. How reliable are they and do we have good reasons to trust them?

Seven More Reasons to Believe the Apostles' Message

Were the apostles trustworthy "servants of the Word?" All four Gospel accounts – Matthew, Mark, Luke and John – show their direct hand. Why should we trust their accounts of Jesus? The following seven factors lend them considerable credibility.

Jesus chose them. The apostles were not volunteers. Jesus first called many individuals to follow him so that he could place them under observation before making his selection as apostles. Later, after an all-night prayer vigil, Jesus handpicked the Twelve from this larger group (Matthew 10:2-4; Luke 6:12-16; See Mark 1:17; 3:13; Matthew 9:9; 10:2-4).

Jesus placed rigorous demands on their calling to which they agreed. Jesus' claim on their lives was total, calling them to follow him by leaving behind their vocations and homes (Matthew 9:9).

They shadowed Jesus for three years. An apostle's first role was to "be with" Jesus. As his future witnesses, Jesus kept them constantly at his side to give them a close-up view of every detail of his ministry.

"He appointed twelve that they might be with him and that he might send them out to preach and to have authority to drive out demons." (Mark 3:14)

In addition, qualifying as one of "the Twelve" required them to accompany him throughout the entire three- year period beginning with his baptism at the Jordan River until his final ascension (Acts 1:21-22). They saw everything from start to finish. Who could be more reliable to get his story right?

They imitated Jesus' way of life, duplicated his miracles and continued his teachings. The apostles were trainees rather than casual followers. While Jesus remained with them, he sent them out and gave them authority to preach, heal, raise the dead, cleanse lepers and cast out demons in his Name (Matthew 10:1, 5; Mark 3:14). Battle tested men naturally pay close attention to their commander, raising their attentiveness to heightened levels. Their knowledge of Jesus' power and authority came through watching him command it and exercising it themselves in his Name. How successful was this training? Even those opposing the Jesus movement could not help but notice Jesus' imprint on their lives:

> "When they saw the courage of Peter and John and realized that they were unschooled, ordinary men, they were astonished and *they took note that these men had been with Jesus.*" (Acts 4:13)

Jesus commissioned them for a global mission. After conquering death, Jesus authorized and tasked the apostles with a global mission:

> "All authority in heaven and on earth has been given to me. Therefore go and make disciples of all nations, baptizing them in the name of the Father and of the Son and of the Holy Spirit, and teaching them to obey everything I have commanded you." (Matthew 28:18-20)

This responsibility of passing on Jesus' way of life to all nations for future generations was placed in their hands. Doing so required an accurate and permanent written record of all Jesus taught and did.

After leaving them, Jesus sent the Holy Spirit to ensure accurate recall of everything he taught and did. Jesus sent the Holy Spirit to the apostles to *continue* his ministry rather than replace it.

> "But the Advocate, the Holy Spirit, whom the Father will send in my

name, will teach you all things and will **remind you of everything I have said to you.**" (John 14:26)

"But when he, the Spirit of truth, comes, he will *guide you into all the truth*. He will not speak on his own; he will speak only what he hears, and he will tell you what is yet to come. He will glorify me because *it is from me that he will receive what he will make known to you.*" (John 16:13-14)

Jesus forewarned them of severe backlash awaiting them. Jesus never sugar-coated the consequences of their witness. He warned them of the hatred they would receive because of him, sometimes even from their own families (Matt 10:22). He then sent them out "as sheep among wolves" and instructed them to "be wise as serpents and innocent as doves" (Matthew 10:16). Those who hated Jesus would hate them as well, for servants are not greater than their master. Rather than focusing on the backlash they will trust God who would reward their faithful service (Matthew 10:40-4 and Matthew 10:32-33).

Summary

Spending three years with Jesus in his school of discipleship was no small investment! Given these demands, is there any good reason to distrust them as "servants of the Word?"

Still, one more question needs answering: After Jesus left them, did they go the distance?

5. Final proof the apostles believed the Gospel they preached

Three Muslim friends and I sat in a university café enjoying a fabulous hamburger. Our conversation landed on the topic of Jesus' crucifixion, specifically the events leading up to it. I described for them his arrest when his apostles all fled the scene and

> "I could never trust a New Testament that was written by men who ditched Prophet Jesus (p) on the very night he was arrested!"
>
> Khalil, a friend

Peter denied him later that same night. I was not prepared for Khalil's visceral reaction:

"What? They fled the scene? How shameful! I could never trust a New Testament that was written by men who ditched Prophet Jesus (p) on the very night he was arrested!"

There was logic to his passion. Any group claiming to speak for God about truth they refuse to die for should never be taken seriously. **On that night, the apostles lost more than their courage; they lost their credibility!**

My friends schooled me on a contrasting story. They compared the cowardice of Jesus' apostles to the courage of the followers of Imam Ali. In the most uneven battle against a formidable enemy, these brave soldiers believed in their leader so much that despite their certain death, they fought with him at his side. It was a riveting account of bravery and sacrifice for a cause beyond their personal welfare. Their sacrifices left an enduring legacy. The conversation quickly circled back to the shaky authors who wrote the Injeel. Again, Khalil asked:

"How can we trust a single word of what they wrote if they didn't believe it enough to die for it? They denied him! When their belief was tested, they ran?" Why should anyone trust them?"

His brutally honest questions raise an unavoidable factor in evaluating the Injeel's trustworthiness. While a comparison of the deaths of Jesus and Imam Ali (p) is not between apples and apples,[39] yet one contrast remains. The original ambassadors of the Gospel message could not stand up for it when put under pressure. If *they* won't fight for it, why should *anyone* take the Gospel seriously?

There is, however, a compelling reason to do exactly that. Should we dismiss the Gospel because its authors failed to believe in it with their lives?

Before taking that drastic step, please consider two factors. First, they swallowed their pride by permanently recording their failure rather omitting it to save face. Informing their readers of their unflattering action says much about the honesty of their report.

Second, and of much greater importance, their behavior that night could not have constituted a rejection of the Gospel. At the time, there was as yet no Gospel to reject. The "game" wasn't over. Friday was still halftime. Darkness still prevailed. The second half had yet to be. Friday's defeat without Sunday's victory was nothing to shout about! What could they possibly preach? *He's dead! He's dead!?* What kind of gospel is that? The second half had yet to be played. Sunday's arrival brought the game-changer. Early morning visitors to his tomb heard the final score: "Don't be alarmed. You are looking for Jesus of Nazareth, who was crucified. He isn't here! He is risen from the dead!" (Mk 16:6 NLT). That same one who freely surrendered his innocent life in death was taken back up again never to return. When Sunday's empty Tomb reversed Friday's horrific Cross, the apostles had a treasure in their sole possession worth taking to the world.

I can understand Khalil's immediate reaction towards the apostles and their message. Staying with them to the end, however, will bring to light why we can believe every bit of their Jesus story.

50-Day Gospel

You may find it surprising, but even on resurrection Sunday the Gospel story remained incomplete! *So, when was it finished?*

The Gospel of Jesus Christ was one divine miracle enacted through four momentous events unfolding over a fifty-day period.

Day 1: Friday, Jesus died
Day 3: Sunday, Jesus rose from the grave
Day 40: Jesus ascended into heaven
Day 50: The Holy Spirit descended upon all of Jesus' believers

Each divine action was integral to the Gospel. On each of these four days, the God of the universe acted mightily on behalf of humankind! Specifically,

Day 1: Day of Supreme Love – God in love gave his Son to bear the awful punishment owed us for our sins, wiping them out to bring us near to God.

Day 3: Day of Triumph – God proved his power over death by raising Jesus up. God triumphed over his enemies who gloated over defeating Jesus when, in fact, they played into God's plan. Because Jesus rose from the grave, assuring all who trust him as Savior and Lord are assured of eternal hope.

Day 40: Day of Exaltation – Having perfectly obeyed to the point of death on the Cross, all authority in heaven and earth was given to Jesus. As Victor over the Devil, death and sin, he ascended to heaven as the exalted Lord and Messiah to sit down at God's right-hand making intercession for us.

> A fair evaluation of the apostles' belief in the Gospel message must consider their performance once that Gospel was complete.

Day 50: Day of Indwelling – God sent the Holy Spirit to indwell believers, imparting new life, adopting them as his children and forming them into one fellowship called the Church whose mission is to make Christlike disciples in all nations until Jesus returns!

These four actions, while separated in time over seven weeks, are singular in producing one gospel of salvation.

So were the apostles deeply convinced of the Gospel they preached? A fair answer must factor in their performance once it was completed. To do so, we must fast-forward fifty days and beyond from Day 1.

CASE STUDY: PETER – *The Difference 50 Days Made*

Notice the dramatic change in Peter's witness from Day 1 to Day 50:

Day 1, Friday in Jerusalem at Jesus' interrogation – In a courtyard around a campfire, a teenage girl asked Peter "You aren't one of this man's disciples too, are you?" Dumbstruck with fear, he cowered, answering, "I am not" (John 18:17). As Jesus predicted, Peter denied him three times that night![40]

Day 50, Jerusalem, the Holy Spirit was poured out on all Jesus' followers– Peter publicly proclaims the Gospel to thousands.

> "Then Peter *stood up* with the Eleven, *raised his voice and addressed the crowd:*
>
> 'Fellow Israelites, listen to this: Jesus of Nazareth was a man accredited by God to you by miracles, wonders and signs, which God did among you through him, as you yourselves know. This man was handed over to you by God's deliberate plan and foreknowledge; and you, with the help of wicked men, put him to death by nailing him to the cross. But God raised him from the dead, freeing him from the agony of death, because it was impossible for death to keep its hold on him." (Acts 2:22-24)
>
> "*God has raised this Jesus to life, and we are all witnesses of it. Exalted to the right hand of God,* he has received from the Father the promised Holy Spirit and has poured out what you now see and hear." (Acts 2:32-33)
>
> "Therefore let all Israel be assured of this: *God has made this Jesus, whom you crucified, both Lord and Messiah.*" (Acts 2:36)
>
> "*Repent and be baptized, every one of you, in the name of Jesus Christ* for the forgiveness of your sins. And you will receive the gift of the Holy Spirit." (Acts 2:38)

This begs the question. How can a man's witness go from cowardly silence before a teenybopper to a powerful preacher before thousands over a mere seven-week period? The answer is simple. *Peter and the Twelve now have a full Gospel to tell with the power given by the Holy Spirit to tell it.*

Peter's transformation does not end there. Weeks later he and John, another apostle, remain in Jerusalem, the site of Jesus' crucifixion. Tensions still hung over the same religious authorities who had condemned Jesus to death who now issued a gag order banning the apostles from preaching the message of Jesus' resurrection. The apostles ignored it and were hauled into court. What will Peter and John do now? Will they kowtow to their intimidation? Addressing them, they said:

"We must obey God rather than human beings! The God of our ancestors raised Jesus from the dead—whom you killed by hanging him on a cross. God exalted him to his own right hand as Prince and Savior that he might bring Israel to repentance and forgive their sins. We are witnesses of these things, and so is the Holy Spirit, whom God has given to those who obey him.'" (Acts 5:29-30)

"It is not circular when claims are made that are verifiable outside the document. This is possible because the Bible makes historical and geographical statements that are verifiable independently."
Paul D Feinberg

For their bold witness they paid dearly.

"When they heard this, they were furious and wanted to put them to death. *They called the apostles in and had them flogged.* Then they ordered them not to speak in the name of Jesus, and let them go." (Acts 5:33)

At this point, we might expect Peter and John to cave to pressure, suck their thumb in self-pity or retaliate with threats. Instead, they kept preaching with a fresh burst of joy!

"The apostles left the Sanhedrin, *rejoicing because they had been counted worthy of suffering disgrace for the Name.* Day after day, in the temple courts and from house to house, they never stopped teaching and proclaiming the good news that Jesus is the Messiah." (Acts 5:41-42)

Muslim reader, once the Gospel was complete, the men who authored the Injeel could not be silenced. Never again do they flee in fear. They proclaimed the truth boldly at great personal cost. King Herod later arrested Apostle James and ordered his execution with a sword (Acts 12:1-4). Peter would be impaled and crucified upside down in Rome. According to tradition, all but one of the apostles paid the ultimate price for that message. Not one of them backpedaled under pressure or disavowed their message when their necks were on the line.

Why do I trust the Injeel? Because its authors paid the ultimate price for preaching it. Rather than fair-weather followers, they earned a martyrs' crown.

Let's summarize. So far, we've answered your question with evidences from within the Christian Faith – personal testimony, the Bible's own claims for itself along with the means by which to authenticate them, and positive signs supporting apostolic trustworthiness. As much weight as these internal evidences carry, let's look beyond them to independent verification from outside the Bible.

6. Independent Sources Corroborate the Injeel's Historical Events – Science and History Interface with Biblical People, Places and Events

This line of evidence for the Injeel's accuracy draws from sources from outside Christianity that corroborate biblical individuals and events. Its findings offset the circular argument stating its message is trustworthy simply by claiming to be God's Word.

> "It is not circular when claims are made that are verifiable outside the document. This is possible because the Bible makes historical and geographical statements that are verifiable independently."[41]

Scientific investigation, of course, cannot prove theological truths (e.g. God's existence). Since biblical teachings involve actual events as opposed to legendary tales or timeless platitudes, *anyone,* regardless of religious heritage, can investigate its material aspects. Geography attests to the trustworthiness of Scripture. Writing for *National Geographic*, Jean-Pierre Isbouts said, "The Bible is a superbly geographic narrative."[42] That narrative takes us to multiple countries and cities all over the Middle East including Egypt, Babylon (modern Iraq) and Persia (Iran). People leave traces behind so that much can be verified or discredited by today's scientific advances.

I subscribe to *National Geographic* (NG) magazine mostly for its maps. As I write this, two favorites are spread out in front of me: "Early Civilizations in the Middle East" and "Lands of the Bible Today with Descriptive Notes."[43] The NG, a non-religious journal, looks at the world through a secular lens and often takes positions that are contrary to biblical creation. Yet a good map knows no bias. The "Lands of the Bible" map covers the entire Middle East, using blue ink to identify locations of biblical events that through archaeological excavations have been explored. These references underscore the Bible's connection to real history. Our current neighbors grew up in Basra, Iraq. Looking at the map, that's just a mere inch away from Ur of the Chaldees, Abraham's hometown!

SCIENTIFIC ADVANCEMENTS SUPPORT BIBLICAL INTEGRITY

You've probably heard, "Everyone knows the Bible is full of mistakes and fairy tales." A prevailing assumption has seeped into our collective mindset giving the impression that the Bible has more holes than Swiss cheese. This may come as a surprise, but hard science is one of Scripture's closest allies.

Have you ever experienced a spiritual meltdown, maybe that pushed your faith in God to the brink of collapsing? Or perhaps a crisis less severe, still acutely painful, that forced you to grapple with disturbing questions about your faith? If so, you're not alone. During my late twenties, my faith nearly tanked. While outwardly going through the motions, inwardly I had the nagging feeling that the truths I had learned as a child could no longer withstand historical scrutiny.

> "Nothing is so firmly believed as that which has once been doubted."
>
> Alexander B. Bruce

Serious questions hounded me that I could not shake loose. What precipitated this turmoil was my dive into biblical "higher criticism" during graduate school. Their teaching originated in Europe, primarily Germany, during the nineteenth century and cast doubt upon Christianity's most rudimentary foundations. Complicating matters was how this chipping away of my faith came from universities deemed *Christian.* As a result, my youthful vibrancy gradually ebbed away until my "faith tank" hovered on "E." What if these scholars were right, that the key events recorded in the Old and New Testaments never really happened but were composed long after the fact? Would it matter if Patriarchal history was fictitious, that Abraham never actually lived? Or if Moses and the exodus from Egypt was a riveting story lacking factual basis? Biggest of all, what if Jesus never returned from real death, but only resuscitated from near death, then dying again later – a scenario that would make his resurrection a complete hoax? The Injeel itself answers: "if Christ has not been raised, your faith is futile; you are still in your sins" (1 Cor 15:17). It matters. If Jesus died and rose again, we have solid hope. If not, we sink in despair. Alone with these doubts, I prayed desperately:

> "O God, my faith in your Word has taken a hit. I'm barely hanging on. Nagging doubts are bigger than rallying certainties. If there's solid ground to stand on, please show me. I'm not asking for any surge of emotion, just solid truth. Amen."

Six months later, my young wife and I were on a plane to Jerusalem for a six-week course[44] on the geography of the Holy Land hosted by the Biblical Archaeology Society. In the mornings we listened to scholarly lectures and the afternoons visited "tells.[45]" For a week, we traced the life of Moses while camping in the Sinai Desert (Negev). For two weeks we participated in an archaeological dig at the City of David[46] where Herod's Temple[47] once proudly stood. For another week, we traced the steps of Jesus in Galilee on the ruins of ancient synagogues where he taught. Being exposed to these locations and venues allowed us to travel back in time.

What benefit did I gain? On the minus side, I did not find the ark of the Covenant. The plus side made up for it.

That archaeological experience became the catalyst by which God answered my prayer. It can be captured in four words: "The rocks cry out!" And what do they shout? *"The Bible – all the way from Noah, Abraham and Moses to Jesus – is rooted in history, not legend!"*

Thanks to archaeology, the land of the Bible from 2,000 BC to AD 33 is filled with historic markers testifying to God's gracious and mighty activity. These epochal events were enacted on that tiny land-bridge between three continents. Its landscape, stretching from the wooded city of Dan in the North to dusty Beersheba in the South, matched what I read on the sacred pages of the Torah, Prophets, Zabur and Injeel. Squaring the empirical with the literary augmented my faith and heightened my attentiveness. The Bible was the textbook and the land its commentary. That journey taught me a great lesson:

"Nothing is so firmly believed as that which has once been doubted."[48]

The God of the universe stooped to the cries of one young man.

How Archaeological Science Aids Biblical Studies

Biblical archaeology will not prove spiritual realities such as the existence of God. Yet its value is enormous for the Good News of Jesus the Messiah whose message rests upon historical events. Biblical scholar, Walter C. Kaiser, Jr., explains its threefold purpose:

"Archaeological discoveries have vindicated the existence of individuals, groups of people and places that were once thought to be made up by the biblical writers."
Dr. Walter Kaiser, renowned scholar

1. To supply cultural, epigraphic, and artifactual materials that provide the background for accurately interpreting the Bible,

2. To anchor the events of the biblical text in the history and geography of the times, and

3.   To build confidence in the revelation of God where the truths of Scripture impinge on historical events.[49]

He concluded, "Archaeological discoveries have vindicated the existence of individuals, groups of people and places that were once thought to be made up by the biblical writers." These are plentiful![50] Consider the following:

Biblical People, Places and Events Corroborated by Archaeology

TAYLOR PRISM
Discovered: 1830 in Mosul, Iraq
Biblical connection – Confirms Assyrian King Sennacherib's military campaign c. 701 BC recorded in 2 Kings 18:1319:37; 2 Chronicles 32:1-12; Isaiah 36-38

SARGON INSCRIPTION

Discovered: 1843 in Khorsabad Iraq
Biblical connection – Confirms existence of Sargon, King of Assyria in Isaiah 20:1 and his conquering of Samaria recorded in 2 Kings 17:23-24. Khorsahad, the present name of Dur-Sharrukin, capital in the time of Sargon II.

BLACK OBELISK
Discovered: 1846 at Nimrud, Iraq
Biblical connection – Pictures Israel's King Jehu (BC 841) on his knees bowing before the Assyrian king Shalmaneser III along with an Assyrian report that he brought hefty sums of tribute This is the oldest known picture of an ancient Israelite and corroborates Israel's King Jehu's identity in 2 Kings 9.

LACHISH RELIEFS

Discovered: 1847 at the Sennacherib's palace in Nineveh (modern Mosul), Iraq
Biblical connection: Confirms the destruction of the city of Lachish, Judah. These stone panels celebrate the Assyrian destruction of Lachish (near Jerusalem) in 701 B.C. It pictures Assyrian soldiers impaling its

citizens who became POWs. This confirms 2 Kings 18:13-17. This palace art shows soldiers peeling off skin of captives and taking head-counts in the piles of the beheaded victims, etc. King Sennacherib destroyed 46 Jewish cities. After filling a plain with enemy corpses, he said, "I cut off their testicles, and tear out their privates like seeds of a cucumber." (Miller, 269). A culture of grisly terrorism helps explain Prophet Jonah's reluctance to preach God's message of repentance to the Assyrians in Nineveh (Miller).

EPIC OF GILGAMESH
Discovered: 1853 in Mosul, Iraq
Biblical connection – The first extra-biblical find that is consistent with the Great Flood recorded in Genesis 6-7. (ABS)

KING HEZEKIAH'S TUNNEL
Discovered: 1867 in Jerusalem
Biblical connection: Built prior to the Assyrian invasion of Judah (701 BC) to channel waters of the Gihon Spring into Jerusalem. It still stands today, confirming 2 Kings 19:35; 2 Kings 20:20.

ASSYRIAN KING TIGLATH-PILEASER III

Discovered: 1879 at Nimrud, Iraq
Biblical connection: Inscriptions found that corroborate 2 Kings 15:29.

THE CYRUS CYLINDER

Discovered: 1879 at Babylon, Iraq
Biblical connection: Contains a decree from the Persian king Cyrus that correlates with Ezra 1:1-3, 6:3; 2 Chronicles 36:23; Isaiah 44:28. "A nine-inch-long clay cylinder, dating from 536 BC, confirms the Bible's report that the Persian king Cyrus freed the Jews" to return home and rebuild their Temple (Miller, 128).

MOABITE STONE (MESHA STELE)

Discovered: 1886 at Dibon in Transjordan (20 miles east of the Dead Sea)

Biblical connection: Contains the Annals of King Mesha of Moab. It confirms Israel's kings in 2 Kings 3:5 and references "the land of Omri," a powerful Israeli king (885 BC) and his wicked son, Ahab (BC 874).

WELD-BLUNDELL PRISM
Discovered: 1922 at Babylon, Iraq
Biblical connection: Contains a list of Sumerian kings that ruled before and after the Great Flood; those that pre-dated the Flood are attributed enormous life spans reminiscent of, though greater than, the life spans of pre-flood inhabitants of the Bible. (ABS)

THE GEDELIAH SEAL

Discovered: 1935 at Lachish, Israel (Tel ed-Duweir)
Biblical connection: Corroborates King Nebuchadnezzar's appointment of Gedeliah to oversee those left behind after destroying Jerusalem in 2 Kings 25:22.

LACHISH LETTERS

Discovered: 1935 at Lachish
Biblical connection: Written records of communications on broken pieces of pottery between the city of Lachish and the king in Jerusalem shortly before the time Nebuchadnezzar attacked Jerusalem 605-587 BC. Archaeologists found the officer's notes among the layers of charred remains by the main gate (Miller, 201). This rubble attests to the massive and catastrophic destruction of Jerusalem by the Babylonians in 586 BC. and Jewish exile to Babylon recorded in 2 Kings 25:8-10; Jeremiah 39:8; 2 Chronicles 36:17-20.

DEIR ALLA INSCRIPTION

Discovered: 1967 at Deir Alla, Jordan
Biblical connection: Plaster text confirms "the vision of Balaam, son of Beor" between 840 – 760 BC recorded in Numbers 22-24.

KETEF HINNOM AMULETS
Discovered: 1979 at Jerusalem
Biblical connection – God's Name "Yahweh." Contains the Hebrew text of Numbers 6:24-26 and Deuteronomy 9:7. "This is the oldest instance to date of the Hebrew text of the Old Testament from 7th-6th

century BC. A silver scroll amulet was found with the name 'Yahweh' dated to the 7th century BC" (Kaiser, *Hard Sayings*).

SEAL OF BARUCH, JEREMIAH'S SCRIBE

Discovered: 1970's at Jerusalem

Biblical connection: A dry plug of clay used as an impression of Jeremiah's professional seal, contains the name of his assistant. It reads "Belonging to Baruch, son of Neriah, the scribe," just as the Bible identifies him in Jeremiah 36:4.

Indeed, the rocks cry out!

Two Lessons from Archaeology

That archaeological study did more than simply rebuild my faith in the Bible's message. It taught me two unexpected lessons.

First, by visiting biblical lands I learned to read ancient texts with more humility. Specifically, it cautioned me against my tendency to think I know more about a given situation than those who were present and wrote what they saw. Passages in the Injeel that previously presented themselves as obvious contradictions, I learned, are not contradictions at all. Let me give you one example. In Matthew 27:5 Judas, Jesus' betrayer, was filled with remorse and "went away and hanged himself." But then Acts 1:18 tells us:

> "Judas. . .bought a field; there he fell headlong, his body burst open and all his intestines spilled out. Everyone in Jerusalem heard about this, so they called that field in their language Akeldama, that is, Field of Blood." (Acts 1:18-19)

> "Archaeological discoveries have vindicated the existence of individuals, groups of people and places that were once thought to be made up by the biblical writers."
> Dr. Walter Kaiser, renowned scholar

So which was it? Did he hang himself or leap to his death from a Judean cliff? Our study in Jerusalem took us to some cliffs just outside of the City. There we saw trees growing near the top jutting out horizontally from the semi-rocky side. A grown man's weight could easily

317

have snapped such a tree from its roots, precipitating a fall sufficient to rupture his innards.

We learned that some contradictions are only apparent. In this case, both eyewitness accounts are correct. The point is that we should not read an ancient text assuming we know more than those present. That would be what **C.S. Lewis would call "chronological snobbery," a common vice we would be wise to avoid.**

Second, archaeology taught me to be more skeptical about unfounded accusations made by biblical skeptics. Biblical archaeology counters much popular but unwarranted skepticism. Where hard sciences quietly undergird Scripture, untested ideologies noisily undermine it. I'm using ideology in the sense of a culture's prevailing assumptions. Projecting an aura of scientific endorsement, their premises are often feeling-based. As such, they have limited lifespans because new discoveries of hard evidence have a way of catching up with them, eventually exposing their assumptions as unfounded. One of those long-running fabrications is that the places, people and events in the Sacred Books are legendary rather than true history. Below are just a few examples of how unscientific many of the early claims against biblical history turned out to be.

THE ROCKS CRY OUT	
Old Accusations Debunked by Later Discoveries	
ALLEGED ERRORS **Scholars Once Said**	**LATER DISCOVERIES** **Archaeology Confirmed Scripture**
"Abraham never lived; his home city of Ur was a myth"	ABRAHAM – Ur, flourishing city 2000 BC. Relics displayed in British Museum
"Sodom and Gomorrah were fictions"	EBLA TABLETS discovered in TEL MARDIKH near Aleppo, Syria mentions Sodom & Gomorrah
"The Ten Commandments given to Moses were written centuries later. Writing was not yet invented and Moses was illiterate."	HAMMURABI CODE[51] from 1700 BC; ESHNUNNA from 1950 BC; HITTITE SUZERAINTY TREATIES from 15th century BC. Ebla tablets from 2100 BC cite names of kings mentioned in Genesis 14; also RAS SHAMRA TABLETS from 1400 BC. All of these confirm writing to exist very early.
"Prophet Daniel was mistaken that Belshazzar was reigning in Babylon on the night the Medes and Persians invaded." "Two inscriptions prove him wrong by naming Nabonidus as the last king of Neo-Babylon. Daniel's prophecy is a late forgery and ignorant of the facts." "Herodotus also, writing in the 5th century BC, does not mention Belshazzar."	CYLINDER OF NABONIDUS discovered in 1854 at Ur, Iraq confirms Daniel 5:1-30; 7:1; 8:1 identifying Belshazzar as Babylon's last king. It reads: "However, the first inscription is a prayer of Nabonidus for his son Belshazzar. The second relates that Nabonidus spent much of his reign at Tema in Arabia. These, then, explain why Belshazzar was reigning and why he could only offer Daniel the third highest position in the kingdom – a dramatic confirmation of the historicity of the Bible." (Toby Jepson)
"The Bible's message was passed on orally. It cannot be reliable."	THE DEAD SEA SCROLLS discovered in 1948 included copies of all the Books of Moses, Prophets and Zabur except one (Esther) that were 1,000 years older than our oldest scrolls. "Hidden for nearly 2,000 years in a cave beside the Dead Sea is a nearly complete copy of Isaiah. Written on leather about 100 years before Jesus' time, it's the oldest copy of [Prophet] Isaiah yet discovered...." *This momentous discovery confirmed the reliability of the transmission process and accuracy of the later texts from which the Bible was translated.*" (Miller, 183)
"Luke 18:35 contradicts Mark 10:46" – Was Jesus entering or leaving Jericho?	Excavations reveal two Jericho's side by side.[52] Original Hebrew Jericho (Mark's Gospel) and Newly rebuilt Roman Jericho (Luke's Gospel)

THE ROCKS CRY OUT
Old Accusations Debunked by Later Discoveries

ALLEGED ERRORS Scholars Once Said	LATER DISCOVERIES Archaeology Confirmed Scripture
"Jesus was not crucified." [53]	SKELETON OF YOHANAN discovered in 1968 at Jerusalem gives us the only known remains of a crucifixion victim. It closely corroborates the Biblical description of Jesus' death. ANNALS OF TACITUS (c. 60-c.120). Tacitus, one of the most important Roman historians, recorded Nero's persecution of the Christians (AD 64). In 112 he wrote: "But all the endeavors of men, all the emperor's largesse and the propitiations of the gods, did not suffice to allay the scandal or banish the belief that the fire [the great fire of Rome, summer AD 64] had been ordered. And so, to get rid of this rumor, Nero set up as the culprits and punished with the utmost refinement of cruelty a class hated for their abominations, who are commonly called Christians. **Christus, whom their name is derived, was executed at the hands of the procurator Pontius Pilate in the reign of Tiberius. . ..**"[54] Caiaphas, the High Priest presided over Jesus' trial and played a key role in his conviction which led to his crucifixion." OSSUARIES OF CAIAPHAS discovered in 1990 just outside Jerusalem supports the identity of this High Priest. Of the 12 ossuaries ("bone chests") discovered, two bore the name of "Joseph, son of Caiaphas," dating to the 1ˢᵗ century AD. One of them contained elegant carvings befitting the honor given to someone with in this position. It is probably the same High Priest who tried Jesus." (Kaiser, *Hard Sayings*)
"There is no pool of Bethesda where Jesus healed a cripple. John reports that Jesus heals a man at this pool, describing it as having five porticoes (Jn 5:1-15). This proves John's inaccuracy."	THE POOL OF SILOAM discovered in 2004 at Jerusalem is the site of Jesus' miracle recorded in John 9:1-11. This site had long been in dispute until then. Forty feet underground, archaeologists discovered a pool with five porticoes, and the description of the surrounding area matches John's description.
"Luke in the Book of Acts invented ancient names and titles." Lysanius, Tetrarch of Abilene (Lk 3:1). Scholars questioned Luke's credibility since the only Lysanius known for centuries was a ruler of Chalcis who ruled from 40–36 BC. .	LYSANIUS INSCRIPTION dating to be in the time of Tiberius, who ruled from 14–37 A.D., was found recording a temple dedication which names Lysanius as the "tetrarch of Abila" near Damascus. This matches well with Luke's account.[55]

THE ROCKS CRY OUT	
Old Accusations Debunked by Later Discoveries	
ALLEGED ERRORS Scholars Once Said	**LATER DISCOVERIES** Archaeology Confirmed Scripture
"Gallio, Proconsul of Achaea, before whom Paul was brought in Acts 18:12-17 never existed."	DEPHI OR GALLIO INSCRIPTION discovered in 1905 at the Temple of Apollo in Delphi, Greece corroborates Luke's account. In one of the nine fragments of a letter written by Roman Emperor Claudius he states, "Lucius Junios Gallio, my friend, and the proconsul of Achaia . . ." Historians date the inscription to 52 A.D. which corresponds to the time of the apostle's stay in AD 51. [56]
Erastus. "Erastus, named the Corinthian city treasurer who became a coworker of Paul (Acts 19:22, Rom 16:23) – never existed."	Archaeologists excavating a Corinthian theatre in 1928 discovered an inscription: "Erastus in return for his aedilship[57] laid the pavement at his own expense." The pavement was laid in 50 A.D. The designation of treasurer describes the work of a Corinthian aedile.
Plubius. "Luke was wrong in the Injeel, Acts 28:7, by giving Plubius, the chief man on the Island of Malta, the title, "first man of the island." Scholars questioned this strange title and deemed it unhistorical.	SERGIUS PAULUS INSCRIPTION discovered in 1877 at Paphos, Cyprus confirms the existence of Sergius Paulus, proconsul of Cyprus who was encountered by Paul and Barnabas in Acts 13:7. Inscriptions have recently been discovered on the island that indeed gives Plubius the title of "first man."
	"In all, Luke names thirty-two countries, fifty-four cities, and nine islands without error." 58 William Ramsay

Is this long litany of archeological support really necessary? I offer it for two reasons. First, to show that the events of Scripture do not come to us unsubstantiated. They were real happenings in a real world and are now corroborated from sources outside the Bible itself. Hard science truly is Christianity's greatest ally.

Secondly, I bring it to your attention because often in our discussions of Christian belief, a Muslim will ask a question like this: "Show me where the Bible says so-and-so." When I show them, their default response is "But the Injeel can't be trusted." When probed as to why, their answer often reveals an unknowing dependence upon nineteenth century liberal Christianity whose ideas have been debunked by scientific discoveries. Their old accusations, "That never happened," are much easier to repeat than to demonstrate. Conveniently supporting their skepticism at the time, they no longer hold water. By dismissing the cumulative weight of testimony in support of biblical integrity causes one to miss the Gospel message. It also puts them on the wrong side of science. What ancient book comes close to having equal attestation? The stones will cry out. History cannot be erased.

Preservation – Did the God who inspired Scripture also preserve it for future generations?

Did God faithfully inspire the authors to write the New Testament and then decide to withdraw himself from the process of preserving it for future generations? How solid is the manuscript evidence for the Injeel? Anyone wondering about the integrity of NT manuscripts would benefit from a recently released documentary, "Fragments of Truth." It tackles these questions:

- Have the Gospels been doctored to push a theological agenda?
- Has Jesus been misquoted?
- How good are the manuscripts upon which the New Testament is based?
- Have the texts been deliberately changed?

Widely recognized biblical scholar Dr. Craig Evans challenges the claim head-on that the Gospels were "doctored" by later generations. He travels the globe to track down the most ancient New Testament manuscripts. Along with other scholars, they highlight groundbreaking new evidence, demonstrating that "the case for the reliability of the New Testament manuscripts is stronger than ever."

Earlier studies arrived at the same conclusion. Manuscript evidence for the NT is impressive. Those unschooled in ancient manuscripts, upon learning about the interval between the Injeel's first-century authors and today's earliest available manuscripts, conclude that it discredits the integrity of the New Testament.

> "Yet no classical scholar would listen to an argument that the authenticity of *Herodotus or Thucydides* is in doubt because the earliest MSS of their works which are of any use to us are *over 1,300 years later than the originals.*"[59]

Evidence for accurate transmission is abundant.

> "From the time the Old and New Testament texts were written down, Hebrew and later Christian scribes maintained rigorous and meticulous methods of replacing old, worn copies with fresh, new ones."

Have you ever played the Whispers game in which, according to Wikipedia, players stand in line and the first player whispers a message into the ear of the second person who repeats it to the third, and so on. Finally, the last person announces to everyone the message in its final version. Compared to the original message, it bears little resemblance. The point is how original messages get lost in their retelling. Some have tried to use this game to show how the original message of the New Testament became distorted beyond recognition.

> "The transmission of the New Testament textual tradition is characterized by an extremely impressive degree of tenacity. . . . It is precisely the overwhelming mass of the New Testament textual tradition, . . .(1 Timothy 1:10) which provides an assurance of certainty in establishing the original text."
> Bruce Metzger

Can such an analogy apply to the NT manuscripts? It breaks down in the case of the biblical documents for one reason: **manuscript longevity.** Those using this analogy mistakenly assume that ancient biblical documents lasted only as long as today's well-used books, ten or maybe twenty years. By comparison, Steven Collins, a veteran scholar of ancient texts and artifacts, says:

> "On average, manuscripts (MSS) did last for a long time: **clay tablets** (basically, forever!), **papyrus** (200-300 years), **parchment** (300-500 years).

> Because documents lasted for so long, 1,000 years could easily be spanned by only two or three generations of MSS. Thus, the idea that hundreds of 'generations' of copying biblical texts obscured the original meanings is simply an urban myth!"

What this means is that this reduces the number of links in the message chain. Furthermore, simultaneous manuscripts prevent error by their ability to correct a mistake of a copyist.

A leading authority on classical texts, F. G. Kenyon, wrote:

> "The interval then between the dates of original composition and the earliest extant evidence becomes so small as to be in fact negligible, and the last foundation for any doubt that the Scriptures have come down to us substantially as they were written has now been removed. *Both the authenticity and the general integrity of the books of the New Testament may be regarded as finally established.*"[60]

By ancient standards, this is extraordinary as seen in the chart below and noted by classical scholar F. F. Bruce.[61]

MANUSCRIPT COMPARISON
The Injeel & Great Works of Ancient History

Ancient Work	Date Composed	Manuscripts Available Today	Years between Date Composed & Our Earliest MSS
Caesar, Gallic War	58-50 BC	9 or 10 good copies	900 yrs
Livy, Roman History	59 BC- AD 17	35 (20 of consequence	400 yrs (one mss from Books iii-iv)
Tacitus, *Histories* (14 books)	AD 100	4 ½	800 yrs
Annals (16 books)		10	800 yrs
Dialogos de Oratoribus, Agricola, Germanta		1	900 yrs
The History of Thucydides	c. 460-400 BC	8	1300 yrs
History of Herodotus	c. 488-428 BC		1300 yrs
The Injeel			
Fragments, papyri,	AD 48-64 – Paul's letters	Over 5,000 mss	Papyrus fragments:
codices and allusions	AD 50-66 – Gospels	Excellent codices:	40 -100 yrs
and quotations from the	of Matthew, Mark &	*Codex Vaticanus*	250 yrs
earliest church fathers	Luke AD 92-100 –	*Codex Sinaiticus*	350 yrs
(AD 90-160)	Gospel of John	*Codex Alexandrinus*	400 yrs
		Codex Bezae containing Gospels and Acts in both Greek/Latin	400 yrs

Two of the most respected NT textual scholars of the last century are Kurt Aland of Germany and Bruce Metzger (USA). Aland noted, regarding the tenacity of the NT texts:

"The transmission of the New Testament textual tradition is characterized by an extremely impressive degree of tenacity. Once a reading occurs, it will persist with obstinacy. *It is precisely the overwhelming mass of the New Testament textual tradition, . . .(1 Timothy 1:10) which provides an assurance of certainty in establishing the original text.* Even apart from the lectionaries. . .there is still *the evidence of approximately 3,200 manuscripts of the New Testament text,* not to mention the early versions and the patristic quotations – we can be certain that among these there is still a group of witnesses, which preserves the original form of the text, despite the pervasive authority of ecclesiastical tradition and the prestige of the later text."[62]

Dr. Metzger, toward the end of his life, was asked whether his study of the New Testament had impacted his personal Christian faith. He replied,

"Oh. . . it has increased the basis of my personal faith to see the firmness with which these materials have come down to us, with a *multiplicity of copies,* some of which are very, very ancient. . .I've asked questions all my life, I've dug into the text, I've studied this thoroughly, and *today I know with confidence that my trust in Jesus has been well placed. . . . Very well placed.*

"The thousands of early manuscripts provide us with a *remarkable consistency on the cardinal doctrines of Christianity.* Also, if a later copyist made a mistake on a detail, the other manuscripts help NT scholars to correct it." [63]

So why do I trust the Injeel? As the culmination of all Scripture, it alone offers a message of hope that produces life-change, claims divine authority for itself, authenticates that authority, was transmitted through credible authors and receives independent corroboration.

How is it possible for Muslims to deny the Injeel's accuracy without impugning the testimony of the Qur'an?

Questioning Your Question

Question 7: "The Gospels were written decades after his death. How can anyone assume their accuracy?"

Having answered your question regarding the Injeel's accuracy, let me respectfully pose this question about your question. **On the basis of the Qur'an's testimony, how can you as a Muslim question the Injeel's accuracy?** It explicitly confirms both the Injeel and the Qur'an to be the inerrant Word of God (Al-Baqarah 2:136; AlImran 3:3; Al-Maidah 5:47-55), thus beyond human alteration (Al-Anaam 6:34; Yunus 10:64). On that basis, it is confusing to hear devout Muslims call the Injeel's integrity into question. How is that possible without impugning the Qur'an's testimony?

This difficulty comes out of my own journey. Twenty years ago I purchased a Qur'an and read it for the first time. I wanted to find out what it had to say about Jesus. How pleased I was to learn that the primary source about Jesus for *Muslims* was the Old and New Testaments. From that first journey through the Qur'an, my eyes were opened!

The Qur'an taught five positive truths relating to the earlier Scriptures:

1. The Tawrat, Injeel and the Qur'an originated from one Source.

One of the first things I learned from the Qur'an about Jesus was the reliability of the source material about him. It points to the primary source for Muslims about who Jesus was: the Books of Moses, Prophets, Psalms and the Injeel.

> "Say you: "We believe in God, and in that which has been sent down on us [the Qur'an] and sent down on Abraham, Ishmael, Isaac and Jacob, and the Tribes, and that which was given to *Moses* and *Jesus* and *the Prophets,* of their Lord [that is, the Bible]; *we make no division between any of them,* and to Him we surrender." (Al-Baqarah 2:136)

This remarkable passage portrays the Bible and the Qur'an not as two swords clashing against each other, but more like two sacred vines sprouting from a single Source, the one God. In other words, the literary record recited by the Prophet of Mecca and those that were first written about the Christ of Nazareth share a common origin. If I read it correctly, the Qur'an is abundantly clear: *"When it comes to divine revelation, don't be selective because all of it comes from the same God."*

What does this organic unity mean? It seems to clearly affirm that together, all these Books belong equally on the path of divine revelation. That blanket stamp of approval is followed with a strict warning against tearing apart what God has joined together. How then can anyone pick-and-choose, pitting one part against another so that divine revelation becomes nothing more than a smorgasbord of personal favorites? Can anyone – Jew, Christian or Muslim – break the chain of God's interlocking revelation by deleting some parts and accepting others? If so, Muslims should beware. If God's revelation forms an organic whole, what prevents the repudiation of the earlier Books from imperiling the Last? Can you chop down the Trunk without killing the Branch?

2. Muslim Obedience Requires Belief in the Earlier Scriptures

It came as a surprise to learn that the Qur'an tells Muslims to believe, not only the Book sent down to His Messenger, but "the Book He sent down before."

> If God's revelation forms an organic whole, what prevents the repudiation of the earlier Books from imperiling the Last? Can you chop down the Trunk without killing the Branch?

"O you who believe! Believe in God and His Messenger, and the Book He sent down upon His Messenger, and the Book[64] He sent down before. Whosoever does not believe in God and His angels and His Books and His messengers and the Last Day has wandered far astray." (Al-Nisa 4:136, Nasr)

Is not belief in "the Book He [Allah] sent down before" at minimum a reference to the Injeel? That concurs with Al-Ankabut 29:46:

"Dispute not with the People of the Book [Christians] save in the fairer [kind] manner, except for those of them that do wrong; and say, 'We believe in what has been sent down to us [the Qur'an], and what has been sent down to you [the Bible]; our God and your God is One, and to Him we have surrendered." (Al-Ankabut 29:46)

According to this, Muslims believe what has been sent down to the Christians, i.e. the Injeel. From that belief should follow obedience. The logic here seems clear. From the premise of common belief in all — "no division" existing between the earlier Books and the Qur'an — follows common obedience to all – our God and your God is One, and to Him we have surrendered." Does not "surrender" entail obedience to God's Word in all of its unfolding installments?

3. The Injil was deemed accurate when the Qur'an was given

In addition to repeated instances in which the Qur'an confirms the Injil (2:41, 89, 91, 97, 101; 3:3, 81; 4:47; 5:48; 6:92; 35:31; 46:12, 13), ayat explicitly testify to its accuracy at the time Muhammad (p) received them. Al-Maidah 5:47, 66, 68 plainly validates the Injeel at the time of the Qur'an:

"So let the people of the Injil judge by what Allah has revealed in it. Whoever does not judge by what Allah has revealed are unbelievers" (5:47, RQ).

"Had they [the people of the Book] observed the Torah and the Gospel and that which was sent down to them from their Lord, they would surely have received nourishment from above them and from beneath their feet" (66, Nasr)

"People of the Book, you have no foundation unless you uphold the Tawrah and Injil and what was revealed to you by your Lord" (68 RQ)."

Do not these passages commend the Injeel to be (a) a reliable criterion of judgment by which to guide Christians (5:47), (b) a means of Christian prosperity by obeying it (5:66), (c) a Book whose origin was divine, "sent down to them from their Lord" (5:66) and (d) a source capable of establishing Christians with a solid "foundation" (5:68)? Endorsements this plain seem to make charges of corruption a glaring contradiction. The Injeel we find in the Qur'an suffered no liability. Its continuing validity as a thoroughly reliable divine text is affirmed throughout.

4. Man is Not Stronger than God

The Qur'an unfailingly declares God's power to preserve his Word. In Yunus 10:64: *"No change can there be in the words of Allah."* Al-Anaam 6:34 echoes: "There is *none who can alter the words of Allah.*" Al-Kahf 18:26 concurs: "And recite (and teach) what has been revealed to thee of the Book of thy Lord: none can change His Words, and none wilt thou find as a refuge other than Him." This guarantee of durability resounds in Al-Anaam 6:115:

> *"Perfected is the Word of the Lord* in truth and justice. *There is nothing that can change His words.* He is the hearer and the knower."

This testimony seems highly problematic. If "nothing can change his words," when you accuse men of later corrupting the original Injeel, are you saying that man is stronger than God or that he cannot preserve his Word? Does he not invest both perfection and preservation to his Word in all the Books, not only Itself?

One could argue that this aya refer only to the Qur'an. "The word 'Qur'an,' however, is used many times in its pages. In this aya it says *"the Word (kalam) of the Lord,"* without confining it to the Qur'an."[65] Further, it confirms that the Tawrat, Zabur and Injil are also the Word of the Lord. Al-Nisa 4:163, for example, makes no distinction between the Revelation sent to Muhammad (p) and that of the earlier Books:

"Verily, We have sent the revelation to you (O Muhammad (p)) as We sent the Revelation to Nuh (Noah) and the Prophets after him: We also sent the Revelation to Ibrahim (Abraham) . . . Isa (Jesus) . . . and to Dawud (David) we gave the Zabur (Psalms)." (Kahn)

Similarly, In Al-Imran 3:48, Allah himself taught the Tawrat and the Injeel directly to Isa.

Since God's Word cannot be changed, what prevents Muslims from trusting the Injeel?

5. Ask the Christians

When in doubt, Muhammad (p) taught Muslims to consult Jews and Christians. Christians offer Muslims clarifications regarding matters in the Bible:

> "If thou wert in doubt as to what We have revealed unto thee, *then ask those who have been reading the Book from before thee:* the Truth hath indeed come to thee from thy Lord: so be in no wise of those in doubt." (Yunus 10:95 Ali)

Why would the Qur'an instruct Muslims to take their Bible-related questions to Christians for clarification if their Book was inaccurate or misleading? The answer seems obvious: it wouldn't.

Taken together, these five positive statements powerfully attest to the Qur'an's unqualified support of the earlier Books.

A Confusing Double Message?

Muslim reader, your Book's endorsement of ours leaves us with a choice between two testimonies: your Book's consistent affirmations or your traditions' unanimous denials. Which testimony deserves our trust?

Initially, I wondered if this choice may be sectarian driven, restricted to the Sunni tradition. Would Shi'as answer differently? Do both Islamic traditions (a) affirm the perpetual infallibility of God's revelation starting with the Earlier Books or that (b) men prevailed over God by corrupting his Word? The editor of the famous *Najhul- Balagha* wrote:

> "Shi'ism respects all prophets of Allah without exception, but believes that as a result of the passage of time their holy books have become mixed with kinds *of superstitio*ns and have suffered various forms of deviation. A living witness to this fact is the unjust and childish qualities mentioned in these books about Allah and His prophets."[66]

Clearly, Shi'as land on option b: God's Word can "become mixed with superstition." They join their Sunni brothers in their admission that God's Word can indeed suffer human corruption and that man can prevail over God.

An Eye-Opener at a Mosque

Soon after 9-11, leaders from our Muslim community invited the public to an event at a mosque for introducing Islam. It was well-attended and cordial in tone. I joined about thirty others in one of the workshops on Islamic beliefs taught by a devout Muslim physician. He read to us verses from the Qur'an describing the Injeel. **Everyone was amazed that the Qur'an gave such a positive view of the New Testament.** He spoke glowingly of Jesus and the Injeel. The class seemed happy. Then someone asked what seemed to be a question with an obvious answer: **"Is the Injeel in the Qur'an referring to the same New Testament that Christians read today?"**

His answer went something like this: "Yes, it refers to the original New Testament! Or course, its many translations are confusing with all their differences and are not endorsed by the Quran. In fact, we regard the Qur'an to be the word of God only in the original Arabic. Once translated into another language, it becomes an interpretation."

I was confused. He seemed to be saying that just as Islam recognizes only the Qur'an in its original Arabic but not in other languages, it also recognizes the Injeel in the original Greek but not modern translations. Fortunately, I happened to have my Greek New Testament with me that day. Holding it up, I asked a follow-up question: "So then, am I hearing you correctly that the Injeel endorsed by the Qur'an is the Greek NT from which all modern translations are made?"

His answer was quick and emphatic: "Oh no! The Greek New Testament was the product of the later church." The class was over. I left the room with those words ringing in my ears. "A product of the later church?!" So men prevailed over God?

When did the Injeel become corrupt?

We are grateful for Muslim attempts to resolve this dilemma for us. Sometimes to defend the Qur'an from endorsing corrupt Books, they explain for us that errors crept into the Injeel after the seventh century when the Qur'an was revealed to the Prophet (p). If so, that's extremely good news for Muslims. All Bible translations are based on ancient manuscripts pre-dating Muhammad (p) by many centuries. Therefore, Muslim reader, you can purchase a Bible today knowing that it is just as corruption-free now as when the Qur'an endorsed it. All Bible translations are based on the earliest ancient manuscripts pre-dating Muhammad (p) by many centuries. None depend on manuscripts as late as the seventh century! Today anyone can purchase a reputable Bible translation with full assurance that it is corruption-free!

Q 7.1: "Why has the Bible been rewritten in so many ways and how come it never states the same things each time it's written? Isn't the original good enough or do men know better how to guide than God?"

Generalities are difficult to answer intelligently or in a helpful way. Exactly which instances of change in the updated versions of the Bible do you find troubling? I could be wrong, but my hunch is that this is either your assumption or something you've heard another person say. Regardless, your basic question is valid about what might justify altering the unchanging Word of God.

> Bible translations are not about *upgrading* God's unfailing message, but offering it to a global audience in which over 7,000 languages are spoken.

"Forever, O LORD, Your word is settled in heaven. Your faithfulness continues throughout all generations" (Psalm 119:89).

Faithful Bible translators agree with you that the "original is good enough." So why do we do it? **Bible translations are not about** *upgrading* **God's unfailing message, but offering it to a global audience in which over 7,000 languages are spoken.** Why their passion for this? "God so loved the world" – not just language specialists fluent in the biblical languages of Hebrew, Greek and Aramaic– "that he gave his only Son, that whoever trusts in him will not perish but have eternal life." Bible translators employ painstaking measures to faithfully "rewrite" its message for new audiences without changing its meaning.

Some people have it backwards. We don't change God's Word. It changes us!

> "The word of God is alive and active. Sharper than any double-edged sword, it penetrates even to dividing soul and spirit, joints and marrow; it judges the thoughts and attitudes of the heart. Nothing in all creation is hidden from God's sight. Everything is uncovered and laid bare before the eyes of him to whom we must give account." (Hebrews 4:12-13)

The Merits of Bible Translations

What justifies the arduous work of Bible translation? Four realities motivate translators in this ongoing task:

- The message of the Bible was written in Hebrew, Aramaic and Greek.
- There are roughly 6,500 languages spoken in the world today.
- The message of the Good News is for everyone.
- Without translation, the vast majority of the world will miss out.

These translators recognize the Bible's unique role in the world:

> "The Bible, one of the oldest and most popular books of all time. But is it just a book? Or is it much more than that? . . . We believe the

Bible is literally God's Word to us, and we think everyone deserves to hear it in a language that they clearly understand. . .

"When people finally get the Bible in their own language, lives are often changed in amazing ways. We've seen people freed from addictions, saved from violent lifestyles, and rescued from some very dark corners in their own hearts. Men and women have found forgiveness for past wrongs. And relationships have been restored, each by the truth and wisdom of God's Word.

"But the most important thing about the Bible, the thing that makes translation so crucial, is that it leads people to Jesus Christ and a right relation with God. That's why Wycliffe exists. . .no matter what it takes, we won't stop until all people have the Bible in a language they can understand. Inability to read Hebrew, Greek or Aramaic should not deprive anyone of the Word of God which first came to us in those ancient languages. **God does not play favorites with nations and their languages. This is why we keep translating the Bible.**"[68]

A God of goodness and justice rightly demands universal access to His Good News. For that reason alone, He still calls competent men and women who ably capture His message of love and grace for every linguistic niche of the vast human family. Everyone deserves to hear and comprehend the Bible's message of hope, peace and forgiveness.

Can God speak to us in our mother tongue. Yes! African Kwame Bediako explains why Scripture in his vernacular language is so vital:

"In matters of religion, no language speaks to the heart, mind and innermost feelings as does our mother-tongue. The achievement of Christianity with regard to this all-important place of language and religion is truly unique. For Christianity is, among all religions, the most culturally translatable, hence the most truly universal, being able to be at home in every cultural context without injury to its essential character.

"For a scriptural religion rooting religious authority in a particular collection of sacred writings, this achievement is remarkable. Its

explanation must lie with Christianity's refusal of a 'sacred' language.
. .Each of us with the Bible and our mother tongue can truly claim to hear God speaking to us in our own language.

"The importance of this fact is theological. The Christian belief that the Bible in the vernacular remains in every respect the word of God, has its basis and what took place on the day of Pentecost, when the Holy Spirit, through the first Christian witnesses, spoke at one and the same time to people 'who had come from every country in the world' (Acts 2:5 GN), each in his own language, causing them to 'hear the great things that God had done in Jesus Christ' (Acts 2:1-12). Hearing the Word of God in our own language is not to be sneered at and left to illiterates; it is essential if we seriously seek growth in our understanding of Jesus Christ."[69]

God can speak to each of us in our mother tongue. His perfect language does not come to humanity in the form of a book or new translation but embodied in a real Person.

Variation between Translations

Variations between the translations are a matter of style and not substance. Viable translations must pass two tests: faithful to its original source and comprehensible to the audience. *Biblica*, a resource for biblical studies, says:

Variations between the translations are a matter of style and not substance.

"Each translation has the power to transform your life. Though the cadence and the terminology may differ, the voice of God can speak to you through each one. Then the question remains: how will you respond to God's voice as He speaks to you from the pages of this life-changing book?"[70]

CHAPTER 8

THE INJEEL'S CONSISTENT MESSAGE

Question 8 – The Qur'an says to read the Injeel. Yet, the message of Jesus is given by Matthew, Mark and so forth. Whose do you read?

Q 8.1: How many prophets are there in Christianity?
Q 8.2: Who is Paul? Why was his contribution in Christianity more than Jesus and the disciples?

Confusion over "four gospels" is perhaps inevitable. Thank you for providing the opportunity to clarify it. I'll begin by answering your question directly about personal choice. I read all four Evangelists with equal benefit because together they present a comprehensive portrait of one Jesus, one Gospel and one salvation. The number one conveys simplicity, but that should never be confused with simplistic! A Gospel of divine origin will surely come with a richness befitting its fourfold presentation. Five things deserve noting.

1. "Gospels" – A Simple Error with a Simple Correction

"Gospels" in the plural is a misleading misnomer that easily leads to false conclusions for which Muslims are not to blame. Though unintended, it implies the existence of more than one Gospel and reflects the imprecise way in which we Christians often speak. Similarly, we may say, "Matthew's Gospel" or "Mark's" Gospel" etc. While we insiders know what we mean, it leaves others scratching their heads. Our apologies are in order.

The New Testament itself suffers no such imprecision. There are not four competing "Gospels" but only one that's observed by multiple eyewitnesses and faithfully recorded by Matthew, Mark, Luke and John.

These four accounts are united first by their core message – the final arrival, life, death and resurrection of Jesus Messiah as the prophets' consummate fulfilment. Greek titles of the four Evangelists underscore their singular message. They are written this way:

> "Gospels" in the plural is a misleading misnomer that easily leads to false conclusions for which Muslims are not to blame.

KATA MATTHEW = "According to Matthew"
KATA MARKON = "According to Mark"
KATA LUKE = "According to Luke"
KATA JOHN = "According to John"

This language emphasizes one common subject, not four. Had it wanted to say instead, "Matthew's Gospel" or "Luke's Gospel" and so forth, it would have used the Greek genitive of possession misleading readers to attribute ownership to each of the four, suggesting each author had his own separate gospel message! **Such would have quartered the Church into four sects, each appealing to its own authority.** Thankfully, such wasn't the case.

2. The Gospel is News and not Views

The word "gospel" is translated from the Greek term *euangelion*, literally "good news." What made it "news" was its proclamation of actual events occurring, not in a world of make-believe. "The good news of Jesus is only good if it's true.[4]" Making it "good" was what it produced. What were those newsworthy watershed events? God's eternal Word entered our world in human flesh and is summarized in the earliest recorded living tradition, even preceding the writing of our four Gospel accounts:

> "**By this gospel you are saved**, if you hold firmly to the word [message] I preached to you. Otherwise, you have believed in vain. "For *I delivered to you* as of first importance *what I also received, that Christ died for our sins according to the Scriptures, and that He was buried, and that He was raised on the third day according to the Scriptures,* and that He appeared to Cephas, then to the twelve. After that He appeared to more than five hundred brethren at one time, most of whom remain until now, but some have fallen asleep; then He appeared to James, then to all the apostles; and last of all, as to one untimely born, He appeared to me also." (1 Corinthians 15:2-8)

Which leads us to the third observation.

3. The Gospel Came in Power before it Came in Print

Jesus and the apostles preached the gospel before a single word of it was written on papyrus or parchment:

> "Jesus came to Galilee, preaching the gospel of the kingdom of God, and saying, 'The time is fulfilled, and the kingdom of God is at hand. Repent, and believe in the gospel.'" (Mark 1:14-15 NKJV)

> "For I am not ashamed of the gospel, because it is the power of God that brings salvation to everyone who believes: first to the Jew, then to the Gentile. For in the gospel the righteousness of God is revealed. . ." (Romans 1:16-17)

That people's lives underwent immediate change is amply illustrated in the Book of Acts. Reading it is like turning the pages of a photo album. It illustrates one life after another hearing the Good News, embracing with repentance and belief to discover its transforming power. The point here is that most of these occurred *before* a single New Testament book was written. The Gospel is not the Book but God at work through Jesus the Messiah.

4. One Gospel Unanimously Report Core Events – Apostle Certified!

Public events reported by multiple witnesses nearly always contain variations without anyone calling the main events into question. Reputable eyewitnesses will highlight the incident(s) so that, despite variation of minor details between them, readers will recognize the same event being described. Since the Gospel narrates the life of one man over a three-year period, some variation on non-essentials is expected, along with an unwavering commitment to accurately report what happened. Agreement on the core is vital to its survival and must be faithfully preserved.

All four authors wrote with apostolic authority. A key consideration for certifying authoritative texts was their connection to Jesus' apostles. Why is this important? It underscores the credibility of eyewitness testimony. An apostle had been personally chosen by Jesus himself to accompany him throughout his ministry from start to finish (see Chapter 7). Since the apostles must carry on the ministry after Jesus was gone, their role cannot be exaggerated.

Early church fathers often referred to the canonical gospels as "handed down from the Apostles."[1] Each apostle testified to what he saw and experienced. Rest assured that **the four canonical gospel accounts provide the church a reliable living memory of the life of Jesus.**

> Rest assured that the four canonical gospel accounts provide the church a reliable living memory of the life of Jesus.

5. Four Accounts Better than One

The Holy Spirit arranged the New Testament with one fourfold Gospel for good reasons. We will highlight three benefits of having multiple witnesses.

Advantages of Multiple Accounts

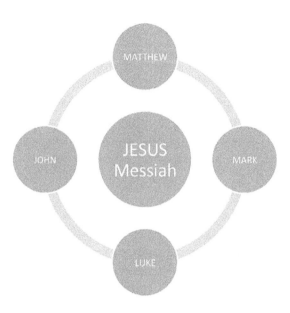

(a) FAR REACHING – One Gospel for ALL Nations

First, four unique witnesses underscore the Gospel's universal provision by extending the target audience beyond Judaism. To no country or group does God say "You are unimportant." Irenaeus, a church father writing in about 180 A.D., ties the four canonical accounts to the Gospel's universal appeal:

> "For as there are four quarters of the earth in which we are, and four universal winds, and as the Church is disbursed over all the earth, and the Gospel is the pillar and base of the church and the breath of life, so it is natural that it should have four pillars, breathing immortality from every quarter and kindling the life of men anew. Whence it is manifest that the Word, the architect of all things, who sits upon the cherubim and holds all things together, having been manifested to men, has given us the Gospel in fourfold form, but held together by one Spirit."[2]

The presentation of four witnesses, at the risk of being accused of contradiction, points to a bigger truth. God desires the salvation of all (2 Peter 2:9). The Gospel goes to all the world and not only favored nations.

This goal of reaching all nations is not at the expense of building one Church on one common Gospel. Four canonical Gospel accounts have always been an essential part of the unity of the Church. Oscar Cullmann, a prominent NT scholar, explained why:

> "The unity of the one divine Gospel is hidden in the human plurality of the four gospels. It remains a challenge to find it in its full richness. The early Church already confessed that they are held together by one Spirit. Every effort therefore to reduce this unity into uniformity was bound to fail because the greatness and uniqueness of the Christ event cannot be expressed by just one witness."[4]

(b) COMPLETE – A Fuller Portrayal of Jesus

The four authors complete each other rather than compete with each other. Multiplicity adds to rather than takes from the Gospel's singularity. Multiple voices enhance it. A quartet provides harmony and nuance that a soloist cannot.

Mark Strauss, a noted authority on this subject, states: "Each of the four gospels – Matthew Mark, Luke and John – paints a unique portrait of Jesus. They show us the same Jesus but portray him from different perspectives."[5] He succinctly identifies those four unique portraits:

Isn't a song, whether performed by a soloist or a quartet, still the same song?

1. **Matthew presents Jesus as the Jewish Messiah**, the fulfillment of Old Testament hopes.
2. **Mark portrays him as the suffering Son of God**, who offers himself as a sacrifice for sins.

3. Luke's Jesus is the Savior for all people, who brings salvation to all nations and people groups.

4. In John, Jesus is the eternal Son of God, the self-revelation of God the Father.

Having four gospels gives us a deeper, more profound understanding of who Jesus is and what he did."

They truly provide us with four angles of one Person:

"No one Gospel writer gives us the whole story. The four complementary accounts mesh seamlessly with one another and resonate harmoniously with countless promises and prophecies from cover to cover of the Bible."[5]

While each Evangelist brings a unique perspective, they all share one purpose:

"...the preservation of Jesus' life, teaching, and miraculous works so that all who read may acknowledge him as Lord and Savior."[3]

That purpose has not changed through the centuries (John 20:30-31).

(c) HUMAN IMPACT – More Testimonies of Changed Lives

I hate to think of the scores of personal testimonies that would have escaped us had any of the four Gospel accounts went missing! Consider for a moment how we cannot seem to get enough of the people we admire. Take the bachelor who finds himself in love. At the very mention of her name, his ears perk up. Outside the romantic realm, our curiosities are piqued by certain persons of interest, whether notable historical figures, parents or an esteemed ancestor, or spiritual leader. What did they achieve? What ideas drove their courageous actions? Our appetite to learn all we can about them is insatiable.

Thankfully, then, we are not limited to just one account of the Gospel! I'm glad we have four and would have welcomed ten had God so ordered. I cannot hear enough testimonial record of Jesus Christ down through the ages! As David Hume praised its value:

"There is no species of reasoning more common, more useful, and even necessary to human life, than that which is derived from the testimony of men [sic] and the reports of eyewitnesses and spectators."[6]

But this raises a question. Did the apostles' personal involvement with Jesus cloud their objectivity and undermine the accuracy of their historical accounts? Not at all. A noted authority of ancient historical texts wrote:

"In all four Gospels we have a history of Jesus only in the form of testimony, the testimony of *involved participants* who responded in the face to the disclosure of God in these events. In testimony fact and interpretation are inextricable; in this testimony empirical sight and spiritual perception are inseparable. *If this history was in fact the disclosure of God, then to have the report of some uncommitted observer would not take us nearer the historical truth but further from it."*[7]

Jesus' multiple participating witnesses did more than validate their message. **Numerous unique voices featuring one Gospel simply illustrated the range of those he personally touched.**

> Minor variations are a staple of multiple eyewitness accounts. This applies to Matthew, Mark, Luke and John. "Perfect sameness would suggest their falsifying rather than attesting trustworthiness."
>
> C. S. Lewis

6. Minor Variations between the Four Accounts Pinpoints Faith where it Belongs

Multiple reports by eyewitnesses are normative for public events. No one comes to a conclusion that the event never occurred on the basis of varying details each one provides. There is a difference between variation and contradiction. Readers recognize the main feature being reported. To paraphrase C. S. Lewis, an Oxford scholar of ancient literature, the minor contradictions (e.g. how many times the rooster crowed) give it the paradoxical twist that only real things have. *Minor variations are a staple of multiple eyewitness accounts.* This applies to Matthew, Mark, Luke and John. "Perfect sameness would suggest their falsifying rather than attesting trustworthiness."[8] Noted scholar Darrell L. Bock explains:

> "Assessing trustworthiness means understanding history's complexity. Differences in accounts do not necessarily equal contradiction nor does subsequent reflection mean a denial of history. *Events can be viewed from different angles or perspectives without forfeiting historicity.* Thus the differences in the four Gospels enrich our appreciation of Jesus by giving us four perspectives on Him – *Jesus in four dimensions, so to speak. . .Trustworthiness simply affirms that the assessed account is an accurate portrayal of what took place and a credible explanation of what emerged, not that it is the only way the events in question were seen.*"[9]

Divine Scripture deserves to be read as such. We must humble ourselves, remembering that we do not critique God's Word but that it critiques us. Most importantly, variation on the core events about Jesus that define the Gospel — his life, death and resurrection – do not exist. On these we find undeviating agreement.

Q 8.1: How many prophets are there in Christianity?

By my reckoning (take with a grain of salt), there is a total of fifty-one.[10]

(1) Out of the forty-nine prophets mentioned in the Old Testament, twenty-nine are named. The most well-known of these serving prior to the Monarchy (starting with King Saul) are Samuel, Elijah, Elisha and Micaiah. Add to that 16 literary prophets whose books are included in the biblical canon (see Introduction).

(2) Six prophets are identified in the Injeel: John the Baptist, Simeon (Luke 2:25-35), Zechariah, father to John the Baptist

(Luke 1:67), Judas [not Jesus' betrayer] and Silas (Acts 15:32) and Agabus (Acts 11:27-28; 21:10).

A well-educated imam in Chicago pointed out what he saw as a moral deficiency in the Bible by pointing to the misbehavior of a prophet: "Prophet Solomon had a harem of females numbering into the hundreds." He was correct about the behavior. The Bible, however, presents Solomon as a king and not a prophet. Even as a king his flagrant defiance during his later years incurred divine judgment upon his family. So what exactly is a biblical prophet? In Question 7 we described the prophet's predictive role. Far more was involved. A prophet:

> "functions as *God's spokesperson and is commissioned by him to deliver his word* ... The prophet of God is typically characterized as one who acts as a *mouthpiece for God* and communicates God's word *either to an individual or to a nation.*"[11]

Q 8.2: "Who is Paul? Why was his contribution in Christianity more than Jesus and the disciples?"

Thank you for asking about the apostle Paul's identity and influence on Christianity. Forgive me if I'm reading into your question, but it hints that his "contribution" was unwarranted, *exceeding* that of "Jesus and the disciples." Certainly, others would agree, pitting Paul against his predecessors and villainizing him as the usurper-in-chief of pristine Christianity founded by Jesus and the original Twelve. The merits of this estimate deserve our careful attention.

Your twofold question wisely prioritizes Paul's identity before assessing his contributions. We'll take them one at a time.

PAUL THE MAN

Paul's personal story is timely in today's world, offering anyone caught in the shackles of radicalism with a way out. Paul was such a person.

First, have you ever formed a negative opinion about someone you didn't know, only to meet and find them to be opposite from how you had sized them up? One of my college classmates we'll call Ron fits that description. If anyone had it all together, it was this well-dressed rich kid who exuded confidence, intelligence, and eloquence. And yet, he wrapped those attractive qualities in that peculiar brand of conceit relishing in the put-down of others. Ron had issues, among them zero capacity to care about anyone but himself. I admit to harboring ill-feelings towards him, even picturing in my mind the spectacle of him reduced a few notches.

In prayer one day, God checked my attitude: "J. P., are you thinking like me? Didn't I teach you to 'Love your enemies, bless them who curse you, do good to them who hate you?'" I confessed, "God, forgive me, but I hate this guy. Loving him is impossible.! I can't. I'll need help!" A few days later I was sitting in a campus office and who dropped by, but Ron! Though greeting him with civility, frankly he was the last guy I wanted to see. Upon reflection, God seemed to be teaching me that he's less interested in our feelings than our choices. Then something weird happened. Out of nowhere these words came out of my mouth: "Ron, we hardly know each other. Would you mind telling me a little about yourself?"

What followed was most surprising. He did just that. Off came his protective armor, and he opened up about a past. I could not have been more wrong about Mr. Confidence. I learned of a family of brokenness, leaving him scarred, miserable and bitter. That day was a turning-point. We never became buddies, but through this knowledge he was no longer my enemy.

Most Muslims I know look at Paul of Tarsus with the same repugnance that I once harbored towards Ron. His name is almost synonymous to Iblis. And for good reason. They are taught that Paul created Christianity as we now know it, polluting its original purity established by Jesus and the Twelve apostles by

> Muslims are taught that Paul polluted Christianity's original purity that was established by Jesus and the Twelve apostles by importing ideas into it from the pagan world. Is that a fair estimate of Paul?

importing in ideas from the pagan world.[1] That accusation became widespread in Islamic culture through *The Gospel of Barnabas* (see Chapter 9) and more recently popularized by Reza Aslan's *Zealot: The Life and Times of Jesus of Nazareth*.[13] Earlier still, the Jews residing in Arabia at the time of Muhammad (p) were Judaizers, fierce opponents of Paul as noted in a historical study of Islam's origins by an Iraqi scholar.[14] But were these fair estimates of Paul?

My goal is to let him Paul tell his own story the way Ron did with me. Then you can decide for yourself.

Paul's Life in Three Phases

Paul's life falls into three distinct chapters: his life before meeting Jesus, his personal encounter with Jesus, and after meeting Jesus. On the surface, the answer of Paul's identity shifts according to which stage of life we meet him. One thing remained constant. Paul *always* championed God's cause as he understood it. What shifted was his understanding.

Phase 1: Saul, Monotheism's Radical Champion (A.D. 30 – 35)

We first meet Paul, then named Saul, in Jerusalem as monotheism's chief defender and ultra-zealous crusader. The memory of Jesus' death and the rumors of his resurrection still hung in the air like a putrid odor to some and a fragrant perfume to others. Allied with the Sanhedrin, the high court who had recently convicted Jesus, Paul is on a rampage against the budding Jesus movement. He enters the story as a willing accomplice in the execution of Stephen, a Jesus-follower who dared to proclaim him in his now ascended glory. This launched him on an all-out attack on Christians in an effort to eliminate their message, fully convinced that he was pleasing God with every brutal arrest.

---

[1] For a well-documented historical survey of Islamic views of Paul, both positive and negative, see Muhammad Bilal, "Muslim Perspectives on St. Paul" (Feb 9, 2020) at https://bliis.org/research/saint-paul-islam/. Positive assessments include Ibn Ishaq, Ahmad al-Ya'qubi, Ibn al-Jawzi, Ibn Kathir, Qurtubi, Ibn 'Asakir and Shawkani.

"Now Saul, still *breathing threats and murder against the disciples of the Lord*, went to the high priest, and asked for letters from him to the synagogues at Damascus, so that if he found any belonging to the Way, both men and women, he might bring them bound to Jerusalem." (Acts 8:1-2)

Later, after turning to Christ, Paul did not conceal his past. By his own words we learn a lot about him. His testimony before Jewish accusers reveal his birthplace, education and religious zeal as an official agent to stop the Jesus movement:

"I am a Jew, born in Tarsus of Cilicia, but brought up in this city, educated under Gamaliel, strictly according to the law of our fathers, being zealous for God just as you all are today. I persecuted this Way to the death, binding and putting both men and women into prisons, as also the high priest and all the Council of the elders can testify. From them I also received letters to the brethren and started off for Damascus in order to bring even those who were there to Jerusalem as prisoners to be punished." (Acts 22:3-5)

In sworn testimony, Paul told King Herod Agrippa II how as a Pharisee he unleashed hostility towards followers of Jesus:

"So then, all Jews know my manner of life from my youth up, which from the beginning was spent among my own nation and at Jerusalem; since they have known about me for a long time, if they are willing to testify, that *I lived as a Pharisee according to the strictest sect of our religion.* . . .

"So then, I thought to myself[15] that *I had to do many things hostile to the name of Jesus of Nazareth.* And this is just what I did in Jerusalem; not only did *I lock up many of the saints in prisons,* having received authority from the chief priests, but also *when they were being put to death I cast my vote against them.* And as I punished them often in all the synagogues, *I tried to force them to blaspheme; and being furiously enraged at them, I kept pursuing them even to foreign cities.*" (Acts 26:4-5, 9-10)

Who is Paul? The man we meet in this phase of his life is:

- Named "Saul," an ethnic Jew from the tribe of Benjamin (Saul is the name of the first Jewish king of this tribe)
- Born a Roman citizen of Tarsus, an influential city in eastern Turkey with large university, but raised in Jerusalem
- Trade – Tentmaker
- Education – Schooled in Jerusalem under Rabbi Gamaliel, a widely reputable teacher of the Torah, Prophets and Psalms and grandson of the famous Hillel
- Jewish sect – Pharisee, top defenders of Scripture who practice the commandments to the letter
- Agent of the Jewish Sanhedrin, the supreme tribunal council
- View of Jesus – Heretic and Messianic imposter; opposed his teachings, claims of deity and atoning death
- Deep convictions – Zealous monotheist; brimming with confidence before God and man (Philippians 3:4-6)
- Relationship to Christians – Public Enemy #1

Saul's hostile pursuit was about to come to an end.

Phase 2: Paul the Proud Crusader brought to his Knees (c. A.D. 35)

Saul was stopped in his tracks. While in hot pursuit of Christians, the zealous pursuer discovered what it feels like to be hunted by a far more formidable power:

> "As I was journeying to Damascus with the authority and commission of the chief priests, at midday, O King, I saw on the way a light from heaven, brighter than the sun, shining all around me and those who were journeying with me. And when we had all fallen to the ground, I heard a voice saying to me in the Hebrew dialect, "Saul, Saul, why are you persecuting Me? It is hard for you to kick against the goads.'
>
> And I said, 'Who are You, Lord?'

And the Lord said, 'I am Jesus whom you are persecuting.'"
(Acts 26:12-15)

The answer to Saul's inquiry into the identity of the One who just pinned him and those with him to the ground must have come as a shock: "I am Jesus whom you are persecuting." We can only guess the thoughts flooding his mind that went from incredulity to self-preservation. *Jesus of Nazareth who we crucified?! He's alive? followed closely by, He knows the hunt I've been on, terrorizing his followers. I'm a gonner!*

Jesus, however, had other plans for Saul. He ordered him:

> "But get up and stand on your feet; for this purpose I have appeared to you, to *appoint you a minister and a witness* not only to the things which you have seen, but also to the things in which I will appear to you; rescuing you from the Jewish people and from the Gentiles, *to whom I am sending you, to open their eyes so that they may turn from darkness to light and from the dominion of Satan to God, that they may receive forgiveness of sins and an inheritance* among those who have been sanctified by faith in Me." (Acts 26:16-18, emphasis mine)[16]

Suddenly, something clicked in the mind of this highly trained biblical scholar. God's original promise to Abraham that all nations would be blessed (Genesis 12:3) was being fulfilled! And now God was calling the least likely candidate, Saul of Tarsus, to usher the nations into his family of blessing! No longer would he be Saul. Paul, his new name, would be symbolic of even more radical changes ahead.

Phase 3: Ambassador of Love (c. A.D. 35-64)

That Damascus Road experience was transforming. Saul the self-righteous persecutor became Paul the humble recipient of God's grace. As an expert in Scripture, he came to realize that what had just taken place involved him but was not about him. It was just one part, a single piece of an ancient plan. What had happened to him fulfilled God's ancient promises of the Messiah who now had died, rose, appeared to Paul and commissioned him as his ambassador to all nations:

> "So, King Agrippa, I did not prove disobedient to the heavenly vision, but kept declaring both to those of Damascus first, and also at Jerusalem and then throughout all the region of Judea, and even to the Gentiles, that they should repent and turn to God, performing deeds appropriate to repentance. . .
>
> "I stand to this day testifying both to small and great, stating nothing but what the Prophets and Moses[17] said was going to take place; that the Christ was to suffer, and that by reason of His resurrection from the dead He would be the first to proclaim light both to the Jewish people and to the Gentiles." (vv. 19-23)

Phase 1 introduced us to a man who, in today's terms, would be called a religious terrorist bent on inflicting harm in God's name. What a contrast to the man we meet in Phase 3. What new motivation overcame his hatred and propelled him forward?

> "Christ's love compels us, because we are convinced that one died for all, and therefore all died. And he died for all, that those who live should no longer live for themselves but for him who died for them and was raised again." (2 Corinthians 5:14-15)

Paul would crisscross the ancient world, announcing in Jewish synagogues and Gentile markets and auditoriums everywhere that the One who was promised to come in the Tawrat of Moses and all the Prophets had arrived. Jesus is that man, crucified, buried and risen!

Would it stick? Given Paul's past, that's a fair question. Three decades of biographical experience prove the genuineness of his about-face on the Damascus Road. Four profound changes illustrate the *new* man of Phase 3.

Personal Revolution

So revolutionary for Paul was his internal change. Jesus' appearance overturned his previously prized religious trophy case of his own achievements, shiny medals of honor proving his right-standing before God. Paul once boasted of his religious inventory:

> "If someone else thinks they have reasons to put confidence in the flesh, I have more: circumcised on the eighth day, of the people of Israel, of the tribe of Benjamin, a Hebrew of Hebrews; in regard to the law, a Pharisee; as for zeal, persecuting the church; as for righteousness based on the law, faultless." (Philippians 3:4-5)

The Jesus revolution was not about switching religions, replacing one inventory of religious merit with another. It was instead a transformation of the heart with an entirely new basis of trust. Paul described it this way:

> "But whatever were gains to me I now consider loss for the sake of Christ. What is more, I consider everything a loss because of the surpassing worth of knowing Christ Jesus my Lord, for whose sake I have lost all things. I consider them garbage, that I may gain Christ and be found in him, not having a righteousness of my own that comes from the law, but that which is through faith in Christ— the righteousness that comes from God on the basis of faith." (Philippians 3:6-9)

This revolution, replacing human achievement with divine gift, stripped Paul of his old boasts.

Overwhelming Gratitude

> "I thank Christ Jesus our Lord, who has given me strength, that he considered me trustworthy, appointing me to his service. Even though I was once a blasphemer and a persecutor and a violent man, I was shown mercy because I acted in ignorance and unbelief. The grace of our Lord was poured out on me abundantly, along with the faith and love that are in Christ Jesus." (1 Timothy 1:12-13)

Global-Trotting Ambassador

> "We are therefore Christ's ambassadors, as though God were making his appeal through us. We implore you on Christ's behalf: Be reconciled to God. God made him who had no sin to be sin for us, so that in him we might become the righteousness of God." (2 Corinthians 5:20-21)

Unstoppable Martyr

Paul suffered severely for his message. His final letter, 2 Timothy, written from prison became his last will and testament. Paul, like Jesus, carried no grudges. He was faithful to the end (see below).

I hope this overview of Paul's life answers your first question, "Who is Paul?" Let's go now to your second question about the relative merits of his contribution to Christianity.

PAUL'S CONTRIBUTIONS TO CHRISTIANITY

Christian teaching forbids us from comparing the relative value of Christian leaders. Measuring one servant of God against another is considered childish, incites envy or pride, and disrupts Christian fellowship.[18] All of them are servants of God. So let's not go there.

Far more important than answering "Who's the best or contributed the most?" is "Did their individual contributions serve one purpose and message?" In other words, was Paul on the same page as Jesus and the Twelve?

> The common practice of pitting Paul and his gospel message against that of Jesus' apostles is overblown and deserves a closer look.

Did Paul Compete with Jesus' Twelve Apostles?

The common practice of pitting Paul and his gospel message against that of Jesus' apostles is overblown and deserves a closer look. For example, *The Gospel of Barnabas* states,

> "Dearly beloved, the great and wonderful God hath during these past

days visited us by his prophet Jesus Christ in great mercy of teaching and miracles, by reason whereof many, being deceived of Satan, under pretense of piety, are preaching most impious doctrine, calling Jesus son of God. Repudiating the circumcision ordained of God for ever, and permitting every unclean mean: among whom also Paul hath been deceived . . . Therefore beware of every one that preacheth unto you new doctrine contrary to that which I write, that ye may be saved eternally."[19]

According to the editor of this work,

". . .the discontinuity between the historical Jesus and the Christ of the Church became so great that any unity between them is scarcely recognizable."[20]

Reza Aslan echoed this sentiment in *Zealot*:

"Why does Paul go to such lengths not only to break free from the authority of the leaders in Jerusalem, but to denigrate and dismiss them as irrelevant or worse? Because Paul's views about Jesus are so extreme . . . [He] advances an altogether new doctrine that would have been utterly unrecognizable to the person [Jesus] upon whom he claims it is based."[21]

Zealot demonstrates Aslan's skill as a creative writer, one superbly able to produce a page-turner on par with *The Da Vinci Code*. Readers with only a superficial knowledge of the New Testament might fall for his guise of historical scholarship. His ability to combine selected citations to fit preconceived conclusions is impressive. Yet a more informed response to his theories might respond similarly to an astronomer watching amateurs turning random stars into constellations. In the present case, four realities undermine the likelihood that Paul bucked the authority of the original Twelve or attempted to introduce doctrinal novelty about Jesus: Paul and the Twelve (1) shared the same apostolic credentials, (2) proclaimed the same gospel message, (3) vigorously promoted one fellowship and (4) served under one final authority.

Paul and the Twelve Apostles
Differences, Yes. But Divided?

1. One Basis of Apostleship – The Twelve and Paul Established their Credentials on the Same Grounds

The basis for apostolic authority was threefold.

Eyewitness testimony of Jesus

The original Twelve were required to have participated in Jesus' ministry from the start and witnessed his resurrection. The reason behind this demand is obvious. As witnesses, they must speak from firsthand conviction, not secondhand hearsay. Consider the replacement of Judas:

> "It is necessary to choose one of the men who have been with us the whole time the Lord Jesus was living among us, beginning from John's baptism to the time when Jesus was taken up from us. For one of these must become a witness with us of his resurrection." (Acts 1:20-22)

Let's not ignore this last emphasis: "must become a witness with us of his resurrection." That miracle would be the linchpin holding the Gospel together. Jesus, once dead, is alive. The first public sermon climaxed with this declaration: "This Jesus God raised up again, to which we are all witnesses" (Acts 2:32, etc.).

Some have argued that Paul lacked this qualification. The historical record tells a different story. As we saw above, he met Jesus face-to-face as the risen Messiah and Son of God. But did he really? To use an idiom, the proof was in the pudding. That encounter reversed his direction as a violent predator of Christians to become an ardent apologist and tireless ambassador to the gentile world for his King. This was no invention. Like the Twelve, Paul justly testified, asking bluntly, "Am I not an apostle? Have I not seen Jesus our Lord?" (2 Corinthians 9:1; see Galatians 1:11-12, 16).

Commissioned by the Risen Christ as his ambassadors to the nations

Just before ascending into heaven, Jesus commissioned the original Twelve with this mission:

> "All authority in heaven and on earth has been given to me [Jesus]. Therefore go and make disciples of all nations. . ." (Matt. 28:18-19)

Like them, Paul was a chosen, not a self-appointed apostle. Two features of his calling lend it credibility. First, Jesus himself chose and sent him out to do a specific mission:

> "I am sending you to them to open their [Gentiles] eyes and turn them from darkness to light, and from the power of Satan to God, so that they may receive forgiveness of sins and a place among those who are sanctified by faith in me." (Acts 26:17-18)

Second, Paul's calling was not given to him *alone*, but was confirmed by the larger Christian community. Ananias, a devout Christian leader living in Damascus, expected the unconverted Saul to arrive from Jerusalem for the purpose of arresting Christians. Through a vision, Jesus himself informed him of Saul's radical reversal:

> "This man is my chosen instrument to proclaim my name to the Gentiles and their kings and to the people of Israel. I will show him how much he must suffer for my name." (Acts 9:15)

Suffered for their obedience

On multiple occasions, Jesus warned the Twelve that they would suffer for their witness (Matt. 10:16, 22, 40-42; See Chapter 7, "Apostles Qualified as Servants of the Word"). What about Paul? As a late comer, would he be exempt?

> "I have . . . been in prison more frequently, been flogged more severely, and been exposed to death again and again. Five times I received from the Jews the forty lashes minus one. Three times I was beaten with rods, once I was pelted with stones, three times I was shipwrecked, I spent a night and a day in the open sea, I have been constantly on the

move. I have been in danger from rivers, in danger from bandits, in danger from my fellow Jews, in danger from Gentiles; in danger in the city, in danger in the country, in danger at sea; and in danger from false believers. I have labored and toiled and have often gone without sleep; I have known hunger and thirst and have often gone without food; I have been cold and naked." (2 Corinthians 11:23-27)

Paul's single aim was spreading the good news of Jesus and he allowed no obstacle to stop him. His farewell speech to his dear Christian brothers bear the marks of the apostolic heartbeat:

"I only know that in every city the Holy Spirit warns me that prison and hardships are facing me. However, I consider my life worth nothing to me; my only aim is to finish the race and complete the task the Lord Jesus has given me—the task of testifying to the good news of God's grace." (Acts 20:23-24)

As Paul saw his life reaching its conclusion, he could easily have whined that he had done his fair share! Paul finally landed in a Roman prison (Acts 27-28) where, according to strong tradition, he was martyred. From there he wrote his last will and testament in his letter to Timothy, his son in the faith. There is not an ounce of self-pity:

"And of this gospel I was appointed a herald and an apostle and a teacher. That is why I am suffering as I am. Yet this is no cause for shame, because I know whom I have believed, and am convinced that he is able to guard what I have entrusted to him until that day." (2 Timothy 1:11-12; see 2:9; 4:6-8)

Like the Twelve, then, Paul met all three apostolic credentials.

2. One Message – The Apostles and Paul Proclaimed the Same Truth

Did Paul introduce doctrinal novelties about Jesus and salvation that prevailed over the teachings of the original Twelve? Was he a charlatan with proclivities to heretical exaggeration and personal aggrandizement? Most importantly, didn't he pollute the church's pure monotheism with ideas from the pagan world? Do these charges asserted by the Gospel of Barnabas and Reza Aslan have support?.[22]

Four evidences from a careful reading of the biblical story pose formidable challenges to these accusations.

First, Paul took action to ensure that his message was the same as that of the Twelve. As he began his ministry, he made a special trip to Jerusalem. For what purpose?

> "Then after fourteen years I went up again to Jerusalem with Barnabas, taking Titus along with me. I went up because of a revelation and set before them (though privately before those who seemed influential) the gospel that I proclaim among the Gentiles, in order to make sure I was not running or had not run in vain." (Galatians 2:2-3 ESV)

Paul set up a private meeting with the Twelve for the expressed purpose of comparing his Gospel message with theirs. Does that sound like the shenanigan of a charlatan? His goal was unifying, not divisive. Notice the action he did *not* take: calling a public theological conference! Their private meeting distanced them from the "cameras" and grandstanders. Why go to all this trouble? He answered later: "so that the truth of the gospel might be preserved for you" (Galatians 2:5 ESV). In other words, Paul confirmed that the message he "proclaimed among the Gentiles" was the same as what the original Apostles delivered to the Jews. Each of them taught the same core message wherever the Lord sent them.

A second clue challenges the charge that Paul's message prevailed over that of the Twelve. His critics ignore Paul's incredible debt to the apostles, for they filled in the gaps for him and he was not too proud to receive it. They passed on to him critical information from their firsthand experiences with Jesus throughout their three-year apprenticeship. They supplied what he lacked. Evidence of his dependence upon them surfaces throughout his letters to churches. One example, to the church in Corinth he wrote:

"I want to remind you of the gospel I preached to you ... For what I received I passed on to you as of first importance: that Christ died for our sins according to the Scriptures, that he was buried, that he was raised on the third day according to the Scriptures. . ." (1 Corinthians 15:1-4)

The narrative of saving events – Jesus' death, burial and resurrection – that Paul "passed on" to the churches was first "received" from the eyewitnesses present. Paul never trivialized this information but counted it "of first importance." This debunks the caricature of Paul as a one-man show. Together, between the Twelve and Paul, we have but one Injeel bound as seamless revelation.

A third hint of agreement between Paul and the Twelve is how they perceived him. Did they view him as a false apostle peddling a rival gospel? Peter, a leading voice among the Twelve, wrote:

"Bear in mind that our Lord's patience means salvation, just as our dear brother Paul also wrote you with the wisdom that God gave him. He writes the same way in all his letters, speaking in them of these matters. His letters contain some things that are hard to understand, which ignorant and unstable people distort, as they do the other Scriptures, to their own destruction." (2 Peter 3:15-16)

Calling Paul a "dear brother" corrects the accusation of resentment towards him. Attributing his writings to a divine source, "the wisdom that God gave him," mitigates concerns that his Letters were regarded as self-originated. Further, associating his writings with "the other Scriptures" clearly points to their divine authority. As with other Scripture, responsibility for their abuse lays not with the author but with people. So yes, they believed, as can we that the Holy Spirit actively spoke through Paul's Letters making them and us beneficiaries of God's message and not Paul's.

A fourth evidence counters his critics most serious allegation that Paul polluted Christianity's pristine monotheism with a mixture of heresies borrowed from pagan idolatry. Actually, the reverse was true. Paul hated idolatry, even before his Jesus-encounter. No, it was the polytheists who threw off the shackles of their false worship to embrace the true God preached by Paul.

Consider Thessalonica, home of the Emperor cult (Act 17:7) in which Caesar worship was the expectation. Pressure to give in to small-g gods was enormous. Statues of deities wielded sentimental attachment as a family duty. There as elsewhere, Paul fearlessly announced Jesus, not Caesar, as the promised Messiah, true Savior and King (Acts 17:2-3). Who imported ideas from whom – Paul from the pagans or the pagans from Paul?

> "When you received the word of God, which you heard from us, you accepted it not as a human word, but as it actually is, the Word of God...*You turned to God from idols to serve the living and true God* ... and to wait for his Son from heaven, whom he raised from the dead—Jesus, who rescues us from the coming wrath." (1 Thess 1:8-10)

Through Paul, a fallen society heard the inconvenient truth that idolatry and immorality are inexcusable and judgment is coming plus one more indispensable truth. In his former days he had force-fed people a plate of cold monotheism. Now he gave them the living God who had sent the true Savior to bring them repentance, forgiveness and eternal life.

Herein lies Paul's chief contribution to Christianity. *He exported its Gospel message beyond Israel into an idolatrous Empire without importing its pagan superstitions back into it.* Thanks to his ministry, idolaters found a saving alternative.

A fifth and final hint shows how Paul's most revolutionary message in the first century was not "new truth" about which the Twelve were ignorant.

> ". . . the mystery [secret] of Christ [Messiah], which was not made known to people in other generations as it has now been revealed by the Spirit to God's holy apostles and prophets. This mystery is that

through *the gospel the Gentiles are heirs together with Israel, members together of one body, and sharers together in the promise in Christ Jesus.*" (Ephesians 3:4-6, emphasis mine)

For centuries this "secret" awaited its disclosure. It had been building and building, lying dormant in the soil of the Books of Moses and the prophets. It was well worth the wait. Through the Messiah, God's special privileges reserved for Israel would open up to believers from every nation on earth. Exclusion would end, giving way to inclusion on the basis of faith.

Was this secret given only to Paul but not the apostles? No, for Jesus had already unpacked it for the Twelve on the evening of his resurrection (Luke 24:44-47). Like Jesus, Paul rooted it in the earlier Books. Paul's enormous contribution, then, was now to crack open the secret that had been building and building for centuries. As "the apostle to the nations," he activated it at large in major cities throughout the Empire. Again, Paul and the Twelve preached but one message.

3. One Fellowship – Separated by Diverse Assignments, United by a Common Lord

Paul wrote:

> "When they saw that I had been entrusted with the gospel to the uncircumcised [Gentiles], just as Peter had been entrusted with the gospel to the circumcised [Jews] (for he who worked through Peter for his apostolic ministry to the circumcised worked also through me for mine to the Gentiles), and when James and Cephas and John, who seemed to be pillars, perceived the grace that was given to me, *they gave the right hand of fellowship to Barnabas and me, that we should go to the Gentiles and they to the circumcised.*" (Galatians 2:7-9 ESV, emphasis mine)

Paul and the Twelve, entrusted with different assignments, belonged to one fellowship. Unity outshines uniformity by its capacity to blend people with diverse personalities, temperaments and backgrounds. Here we see the old guard – Peter, James and John – extend the "right hand of fellowship" to newbies – Paul and Barnabas. Through them all, God does a mighty work!

4. One Authority–The Apostles and Paul Placed Final Authority in Gospel Truth, not Infallibility of Church Leaders

A controversy in one of the congregations has led some to see a rupture between Paul and the Twelve. Some readers may say, for instance, "Okay, I see what you're saying but it's not the whole story. You've skipped over the rift between Paul and the Twelve evidenced first by how he denigrated them and then a sharp confrontation over a doctrinal dispute." Missed here are two important lessons on authority in doctrinal matters

First, final authority in the Christian faith rests with the truth of Jesus the Messiah and not the human messenger who delivers it. That message demands its messengers to adhere to its precepts and conform to its lifestyle. This brings us to an early confrontation between Paul and Peter. Does it indicate estrangement between Paul and the Twelve? Let's take a look.

Whenever the gospel message becomes distorted through false teaching, true freedom suffers. This was occurring in the Galatian church as false teachers were poisoning the gospel. Young believers began losing their newfound joy and freedom in Christ. The mistake that many such as Aslan Reza[24] make with Paul is to misidentify the perpetrators of these errors as the other apostles. If not the Twelve, then who were they?

> "Yet because of false brothers secretly brought in—who slipped in to spy out our freedom that we have in Christ Jesus, so that they might bring us into slavery— to them we did not yield in submission even for a moment, so that the truth of the gospel might be preserved for you. And from those who seemed to be influential (what they were makes no difference to me; God shows no partiality)—those, I say,

who seemed influential added nothing to me." (Galatians 2:4-6 ESV)

Paul's dispute here was not with the Twelve at all, but with "false brothers secretly brought in." These stealth pretenders *"seemed* to be influential," made so by acting like big shots who heavy-handedly intimidated the young Christians. Their goal was to distort the one Gospel that was unanimously believed by the apostolic circle to which Paul now belonged.

The second lesson we learn about final authority is that no one, not even an apostle, is above the Truth. It must be "preached" not only in word but in action! Paul indeed clashed with Peter, but not over doctrinal *belief* (see Peter's defense, Acts 15:10-11) but Peter's *practice*. Peter had failed to *act* according to the truth of salvation by grace for both circumcised Jews and uncircumcised Gentiles. It should have created an inclusive fellowship lived out daily at mealtimes, a rarity in the first century. Kosher Jews and their non-kosher counterparts did not eat together. Christ, who ate with sinners and tax collectors, changed that. This new norm set the stage for a sharp confrontation.

> "But when Cephas [Peter] came to Antioch, I opposed him to his face, because he stood condemned. For before certain men came from James, he was eating with the Gentiles; but when they came he drew back and separated himself, fearing the circumcision party. And the rest of the Jews acted hypocritically along with him, so that even Barnabas was led astray by their hypocrisy. But when I saw that their conduct was not in step with the truth of the gospel, I said to Cephas before them all, 'If you, though a Jew, live like a Gentile and not like a Jew, how can you force the Gentiles to live like Jews?' (Galatians 2:11-14)

How did Peter compromise the truth? Not in his teaching, but his behavior. As we see in their exchange, hypocrisy and fear of what others think of us can cause us to act in ways that contradict the liberating truth of the Gospel. Unfortunately, such kowtowing still happens with too many Christians.

> "We ourselves are Jews by birth and not Gentile sinners; yet we know that a person is not justified by works of the law [e.g. circumcision]

but through faith in Jesus Christ, so we also have believed in Christ Jesus, in order to be justified by faith in Christ and not by works of the law, because by works of the law no one will be justified." (Galatians 2:11-16 ESV)

If a doctrinal rift ensued from this clash involving Peter and the apostles with Paul, why would Peter later recognize Paul's epistles as divinely inspired and warn against distorting them (2 Peter 3:14-18)?

Paul versus Jesus – Was Paul's contribution more than Jesus?

Your question why Paul's "contribution in Christianity was more than Jesus" gives me pause. Was it not Jesus, the object of Paul's hostility, who prevailed over Paul, stopped him in his tracks, seized him against his will, reshaped him into his battle-tested servant and finally adorned him with a martyr's crown by Nero's sword?

Contributions made by Jesus, not only to Christianity, but to our entire planet could fill volumes. To name a few:

- The centerpiece of the Gospel is Jesus. Without his life, death and resurrection there would be no Injeel.
- Had Jesus not come, who today would have even heard of Paul? Our knowledge of him is a tribute to the greater work of Jesus Messiah, the Risen One. Were Paul's contributions "more than Christ's"? Paul knew better:

"I will not venture to speak of anything except what *Christ has accomplished through me* in leading the Gentiles to obey God by what I have said and done— by the power of signs and wonders, through the power of the Spirit of God. So ffrom Jerusalem all the way around to Illyricum, I have fully proclaimed the gospel of Christ." (Ro 15:17-19))

- Jesus out-lived, out-loved and out-died all others. If imitation is the greatest form of flattery, Paul yielded supremacy to Jesus by saying: "Imitate me as I imitate Christ."
- Paul died as a martyr for Jesus; Jesus as the Savior for all.

But didn't Paul write more books in the Injeel making his contribution greater? William Barclay observed:

"Jesus never wrote on paper; He left no printed book; instead He wrote his message upon men, and these men were the apostles."[25]

E. F. Harrison adds, "These disciples were the product of the Lord. They bore his stamp."[26]

The apostle Paul was proof.

CHAPTER 9

COMPETING GOSPELS

Question 9: "Why wasn't *The Gospel of Barnabas* considered part of the Bible when he was a disciple? It is consistent with the teachings of the Qur'an."

Q 9:1: Why has the history of Isa (Jesus) changed and we [Muslims] believe different facts from the Christians?

The immense popularity of *The Gospel of Barnabas* (GB) in the Muslim world calls for a close look at its teachings and evaluate its claim as the original Injeel.

Several years ago I visited the Arab International Festival in Dearborn, Michigan. In a large tent, the Muslim Student Association had a book table displaying an attractive assortment of literature. There I was greeted by a female university student who saw my curiosity, politely extended a warm greeting and expressed her keen interest in the history of Prophet Jesus. Handing me a copy of *The Gospel of Barnabas,* she glowingly shared how it had answered many of her questions. I thanked her and asked if she had read the Injeel. She replied,

"The GB actually was the original Injeel. Barnabas, one of the original Twelve apostles, was an eyewitness. He provided a more reliable record of Jesus than the four New Testament gospels that were written much later and filled with confusing contradictions."

The book she highly praised I had seen sitting on bookshelves in stores and mosques. To form my own opinion, I had recently purchased a copy that I had just finished reading.[1] The young woman at the book table was right. Its claim for itself is clearly stated in its opening line:

"The True Gospel of Jesus, called Christ, a new Prophet sent by God to the world: according to the description of Barnabas his apostle."[2]

It went on to say that this "true Gospel" is "the most accurate detailed portrayal of Jesus' life and ministry in existence today."[3] I can understand her enthusiasm. To say it "is consistent with the teachings of the Qur'an" is an understatement. As I read it carefully, I got the sense that its author had a Qur'an sitting in front of him as he wrote it. Here is an Injeel in lockstep with the Qur'an.

Before examining its major teachings, readers may wonder why, if the GB is the original gospel, do Christians around the world use the New Testament instead, most of them unaware of the GB.

Why the New Testament Prevailed over the GB

How did the world end up with the Son of God of the New Testament and not this Prophet of the GB? It answers:

"Dearly beloved, the great and wonderful God hath during these past days visited us by his prophet Jesus Christ in great mercy of teaching and miracles, by reason whereof many, being deceived of Satan, under pretense of piety, are preaching most impious doctrine, calling Jesus son of God, Repudiating [sic] the circumcision ordained of God forever..."[4]

How bold! I was mesmerized. I couldn't stop.

"With the conversion of Paul, a new period opened in Christian Theology. . .The theory of redemption was the child of his brain, a belief entirely unknown to the disciples of Jesus. Paul's theory involved the deification of Jesus."[5]

Such convictions don't change overnight. How was Paul able to take the church on a detour into a new brand of Christianity? According to the GB, it began with a sharp rift over the issue of circumcision between Barnabas, one of Jesus' apostles, and Paul:

"According to Aristides, one of the earliest apologists, the worship of the early Christians was more purely monotheistic even than of the Jews.

"As recorded in the Acts, Barnabas represented those who had become personal disciples of Jesus, and Paul co-operated [sic] with them for some time. But finally they fell out. Paul wanted to give up the Commandment given through Abraham regarding circumcision. Barnabas and the other personal disciples disagreed. The following sentences in the [book of] Acts[6] give a hint of the rift: certain men which came down from Judaea taught the brethren, and said, 'Except ye be circumcised after the manner [of] Moses, ye cannot be saved.'" Xv

After this rift [between Paul and Barnabas], there was a parting of Jews. In the Acts, Barnabas disappears after the rift, because the recording of the Acts of the Apostles was done by the followers of Paul.

Because of Paul's compromise with Roman beliefs and legends, Pauline Christian[s] grew in number and grew in strength. . .The followers of Barnabas never developed a central organization. . .These Christians incurred the wrath of [the] church and systematic effort was made to destroy them and to obliterate all traces of their existence, including books and Churches."[7]

In other words, a fraudulent New Testament won the day over the GB because men prevailed over the Word of God.[8] The GB went underground not because it was less true but outnumbered. The sheer numerical success of Paul's heretical brand of Christianity gave him the upper-hand to eradicate the original Gospel from memory. Power won; truth lost. So for 2,000 years, the Church of Jesus Christ has followed the wrong Gospel.

Is it the true Gospel as it claims to be? An examination into its teachings may throw some light on that question.

PART 1: TEACHINGS OF THE GOSPEL OF BARNABAS

The veracity of the GB neither proves nor disproves the Qur'an. It could be false and the Qur'an still be true. Its contradictions in the main are not with the Qur'an at all, but with the New Testament. If it is truly the original Injeel, it exposes the New Testament as a colossal fabrication and explodes the foundations of the Christian faith. Is this melodramatic? Consider its view of Jesus.

Who is Jesus?

The Gospel of Barnabas informs its readers that:

1. *Jesus is not God or the Son of God.* The original Twelve honored Jesus as a prophet but never worshiped him as deity (pp 169, 228). Jesus himself adamantly denied that he was God or the Son of God (p 169).
2. *Jesus was the forerunner to the world's true Savior and Messiah, Prophet Muhammad (p).* Jesus submitted to the greater Messenger who would arrive 600 years later. He announces the Prophet's arrival, magnifies his position and even identifies him by name. John the Baptist's relation to Jesus in the New Testament is precisely mirrored in Jesus' relation to Muhammad (p) in the GB. He was unworthy to stoop down and untie the sandals of the greater one (pp 50, 89, 104, 106, 178, 214-15).

3. *Jesus made circumcision a requirement for salvation.* Jesus said, "Leave fear to him that hath not circumcised his foreskin, for he is deprived of paradise" (p 11).

4. *Jesus received a Book (the Injeel) from the angel Gabriel (pp 8, 62,182).*[9] Jesus was not himself the eternal Word of God but the recipient of a physical Book, the Injeel.

5. *Jesus was a sinful man with moral shortcomings.* Jesus suffered for his own misbehaviors, not those of others. His pain came in the form of a poor reputation because the world would believe the "illusion of infamy" that he was the Son of God (pp 121, 128). His shame brought him anxiety because "I have not served God so faithfully as I was bound to do" (p 208). While deserving hell for his sins in allowing others to mistake him as God, Jesus received the merit of God, spared punishment because he finally told the truth by denying he was the Messiah and confessing that Muhammad (p) was (p 208).

6. *Jesus warned of the coming of a dangerous heretic.* A man named Paul would enter the Christian ranks and pollute Christianity with pagan heresies: the Trinity, Jesus' deity, the Son of God, and a crucified Savior whose death would atone for the sins of humanity. Such deceptions would continue until corrected by Muhammad (p) (pp 121, 128, 228).

7. *Jesus was condemned to die for identifying Ishmael, not Isaac, as the son of Abraham's sacrifice.* Jesus swore under oath that the son whom Abraham was willing to slay was Ishmael, not Isaac. For that, the presiding Jewish High Priest called him an "Ishmaelite." Fury was set ablaze among the Jews encircling Jesus. They picked up stones to kill him, but he suddenly vanished so that the stones struck the accusers bringing the death toll to 1000 Jews (pp. 214-15).

8. *Jesus was miraculously rescued from death.* He avoided arrest by taking stealthlike maneuvers to evade his executioners. Cringing in fear, Jesus hid in a house (150, 220, 225, 229). God sent three angels in a last-minute rescue operation to snatch him from danger, carrying him through a window to heaven.

9. *The cross that was intended for Jesus held his Betrayer.* While Jesus was rescued from crucifixion. Judas did not fare so well. His nefarious plan backfired. Allah caused him to look and sound exactly like

Jesus. Fooled into thinking him to be Jesus, the executioners crucified Judas, sealing for himself the fate he had intended for Jesus (pp. 178, 221, 225).[10] As he hung on the cross, Judas cried out,

> "God, why has thou forsaken me, seeing the malefactor [Jesus] has escaped and I die unjustly?" (225)

10. Jesus' stupendous rescue corrected the New Testament crucifixion story in two ways:
    - It "Preserved the righteousness of God" who couldn't let his prophet be killed. How could God be just and his prophet impaled?
    - It confirmed the Earlier Books. Old Testament Scripture decreed his safety (225). During his rescue, Gabriel cited a Bible verse to Jesus from Psalm 91 (11). Little did he know, perhaps, that this very passage was used by Satan during Jesus' temptations in an effort to lure him away from his mission of suffering to gain instant notoriety for himself.[11]

11. *The Gospel was the good news that Jesus escaped the cross while the Traitor got his due.* Jesus was saved from death, not humanity through his death. Expressed another way, it was good news for Jesus, but for no one else.

12. *At the end of time, Jesus will return to earth to Islamacize the world in preparation for the Day of Judgment.*

No Christian or Muslim can possibly read this profile of Jesus without being confronted by its glaring contradictions with the New Testament Jesus.[12] One thing is certain: these two "Gospels" present irreconcilable accounts of both the facts and significance of Jesus. Choosing both is logically impossible.

Does the GB Agree with the Qur'an?

While the GB overtly supports Islam's view of Jesus, there are places in which it contradicts the Qur'an.

MESSIAH – The Gospel of Barnabas committed *its most obvious* blunder by identifying the Messiah as Muhammad (p) while, for the Qur'an, it is Jesus (AlImran 3:45). And this is no slip, a one-time mistake.

MARRIAGE – The GB supports monogamy (ch 115) while the Qur'an permits up to four wives (Al-Nisa 4:3; Al-Marij 70:30) in addition to female slaves.

BIRTHPANGS – Of less significance, Mary, says the GB, birthed Jesus painlessly (GB, ch 3) where the Qur'an states she experienced normal birth pangs (Miriam 19:22-23). It was his conception that was supernatural. Christians agree.

THE HEAVENS – More significant to Islamic cosmology, the GB has nine different heavens (ch 178), whereas the Qur'an only seven (Al-Isra 17:44).

> The Gospel of Barnabas committed its most obvious blunder by identifying the Messiah as Muhammad (p) while, for the Qur'an, it is Jesus (Aali Imran 3:45). And this is no slip, a one-time mistake. Its repetition proved how its author truly believed it. This error alone instantly discredits its claim as the original Injeel.

PART 2: GB'S CLAIM OF ORIGINALITY
Original Injeel or Late Forgery?

Is the GB the infallible Injeel that God sent down to Jesus and recorded by one of the original twelve apostles named Barnabas? Claims this remarkable, even revolutionary, call for close analysis by Christians and Muslims alike. Those defending the authenticity of the GB must honestly face the issues raised in this and the preceding sections. In light of these, could this "gospel" have been the work of one of Jesus' original Twelve followers? Please consider:

Highly Suspicious Mistakes for a First-Century Eyewitness

Confused Identity. The GB states that Jesus was "born under Pontius Pilate." But any of the Twelve surely would have known that Jesus was born under Herod the Great who reigned from 37-4 BC but suffered under Pontius Pilate who ruled from 26-36 AD, that is, after Jesus had already reached adulthood.

Unfamiliar with the Geography of Jesus' Land. A geographical blunder exposes this author as a stranger to the land of Jesus. Jesus' home town of Nazareth sat on a hillside and not a seaport.

> "Jesus went to the sea of Galilee, and having embarked on a ship sailed to his city of Nazareth.... Having arrived at the city of Nazareth the seamen spread through the city all that Jesus wrought (did)...(then) Jesus went up to Capernaum" (paras.20-21).

Ignorant of the Meaning of Messiah. Why does Barnabas not understand that "Messiah" (Hebrew) and "Christ" (Greek) are synonymous terms and refer to the same person, "the Anointed One"?

> "Dearly beloved the great and wonderful God hath during these past days visited us by his prophet Jesus <u>Christ</u> in great mercy of teaching and miracles... (2)

> Jesus confessed, and said the truth: 'I am not the Messiah.'" (ch 42)[13]

How could Jesus be "Christ" while denying that he is "Messiah?" Was Jesus ignorant of its meaning?

Absence of Manuscript Evidence. If GB was the original first century Gospel, why does its earliest manuscript not appear until the fourteenth? The oldest copies are written in Italian and Spanish and these are dated from the fifteenth century AD or later.[14]

> If GB is the original firstcentury Gospel, why does its earliest manuscript not appear until the fourteenth?

Confused over the Dispute between Paul and Barnabas. According to the GB, the controversy igniting the dispute between Paul and Barnabas was over whether or not the Jewish rite of circumcision was required for salvation. Paul answered that it did not while "Barnabas and the other personal disciples disagreed"(p. xv). Where is the evidence for that? The Injeel tells a very different story.

Barnabas never attacked Paul! He was the one who welcomed, nurtured, and trained Paul as young convert! It's true that a later dispute arose between them, but it had nothing to do with theology or the rite of circumcision. It was a personal matter involving Barnabas' cousin, Mark (Acts 15:36-41). There are strong indications that these great leaders resolved the issue and were reconciled as suggested by 2 Timothy 4:11. Paul and Barnabas were lifelong comrades.

The Wrong Barnabas. The author, placing himself among the original Twelve apostles, commits an embarrassing mistake. The GB's apostolic list includes the following:

> "Andrew, Peter, Barnabas, who wrote this, Matthew the publican, John, James, Thaddaeus, Judas, Bartholomew, Philip, James, and Judas Iscariot."

Four New Testament rosters identify the Twelve apostles by name: Peter, Andrew, brothers James and John, Philip, Bartholomew, Thomas, Matthew, James son of Alphaeus, Thaddaeus, Simon the *Zealot* and Judas Iscariot (Matthew 10:2-4; Mark 3:13-19; Luke 6:14-16; Acts 1:13). Barnabas is not found on a single one. So how did the GB get the wrong man?

The GB confuses its author with another Barnabas who was called an "apostle" (Acts 14:14), but *not* as one of the original Twelve who Jesus hand-picked to accompany him. This Barnabas appears much later, *after* Jesus ascended back to heaven.[15] He comes from the island of Cyprus near Turkey and accompanied Paul years later when the church officially sent them out for missionary service (Acts 13:2-3). Since this Barnabas wasn't around to record the life of Jesus, he must be ruled out as an eyewitness.

This proves that GB's author either knowingly lied when he included himself among the Twelve or, more probably, made an ignorant mistake. Either way, he discredits himself and anything he has to say about Jesus.

Glaring Anachronisms. The GB introduces several obvious anachronisms. These denote "an act of attributing a custom, event, or object to a period to which it does not belong" (Oxford). When readers of history spot one, three words instantly come to their minds: "That can't be!" For example, let's say you're reading Sirat Rasul Allah, a biography of Muhammad (p) by the famous Ibn Ishaq(AD 704 /AH 85-150's). Halfway through, you come to this sentence:

"After his companions left, he quickly entered their conversation on his Apple MacBook so that he could recall it accurately at a later time."

You know instantly "That can't be! This book is not eighth-century literature at all!" In fact, you're dead sure that it originated after 2006 when MacBooks came on the market. The problem with anachronisms is that they go undetected unless readers know better.

The GB claims to have been written by a contemporary of Jesus who died around AD 30. So it should be free of inventions that were introduced at a later date. Its author, however, introduced practices and objects that were not invented until centuries after the time of Jesus. These push the GB far later than the first to at least the fourteenth century. Here are a few examples:

- *Wine Barrels.* The GB mentions wine being stored in wooden wine- casks (para.152). This practice was common in medieval Europe. In first-century Palestine, however, wine was stored either in skins (Matthew 9:17) or clay pots (John 2). By taking a common practice from the author's time period and imposing it into first-century Palestine causes us to say "that can't be."
- *Year of Jubilee every 100 Y*ears. According to the Tawrat, Leviticus 25:10- 13, the Jubilee Year always came every 50 years. Yet the GB renumbers the cycle to every 100 years:

"The Jubilee will change from every 100 years to every day during the reign of the Messiah."[16]

The only time when the Jubilee Year changed from 50 to 100 years, and then only briefly was when Pope Boniface VIII in 1300 AD declared Jubilee to occur each 100 years in an effort to raise finances to build the Vatican. He was mistaken. His successor, Pope Clement VI corrected this in 1343 AD when the Vatican project ran out of money. The only time in history when Jubilee was thought to last 100 years was this 43-year period between 13001343 AD. This begs the question, could the confusion of the Pope explain the confusion of the GB?[17] Again, "That can't be!"

- *Cites the Poet Dante's 'Divine Comedy.'* Can a first-century author cite a fourteenth-century poet, one who lived about the same time as Pope Boniface? One of Dante's books of poetry was *Divine Comedy*. It describes the ascent through nine heavens to reach paradise, the tenth. Many passages in the GB show how its author relied on Dante's work. Consider the following in which the author speaks of nine heavens and says that paradise is greater than the sum of all[18]:

"Paradise is so great that no man can measure it. Verily I say unto thee that the heavens are <u>nine</u>, among which are set the planets, that are distant one from another five hundred years' journey for a man . . . and Verily I say unto thee that paradise is greater than all the earth and heavens together." (para.178).

"That can't be."

- *Dependence on later accounts of Jesus' Death by Basilides and 'Seth.'* The explanation of Jesus' death in Al-Nisa 4:156 echoes the illusion stories of Basilides and "Seth," anti-Christian Gnostical teachers from the second and third centuries. Anyone named Barnabas in the Injeel would have already died by the time this teacher invented his story. That can't be.

Honest Mistakes or Deliberate Fraud?

Those historical and geographical mistakes expose obvious fallacies that raise suspicions about the author's range of knowledge. But was this foul play? Now we move to the issue of ethics and basic honesty. More troubling than mistaken details are evidences of deliberate manipulation.

Yusseff's Dishonesty. The critical edition of the English translation of the GB was published in 1907. Its translators, Longsdale and Laura Ragg, wrote an introduction disclaiming the GB as a first-century eyewitness account of Jesus.

"Against the supposition that the Gospel of Barnabas ever existed in

Arabic we must set the argument from the total silence about such a Gospel in the polemical literature of the Moslems. This has been admirably catalogued by Steinschneider in his monograph on the subject.'[19]

...The many Muslim writers who wrote books who would no doubt have referred to such a work had it been in existence such as Ibn Hasm (d. 456 A.Injeel.), Ibn Taimiyyah (d. 728 A.Injeel.), Abu'l-Fadl al-Su'udi (wrote 942 A.Injeel.), and Hajji Khalifah (d. 1067 A.Injeel.). But not one of them, or anyone else, ever refers to it between the seventh and fifteenth centuries when Muslims and Christians were in heated debate."[20]

When the Raggs' work was republished in 2001, the editor, M. A. Yuseff, retained the reputable translation but conveniently omitted their introduction and replaced it with his own that provided "evidence" for its veracity, along with his notes and commentary.

Egregious Use of Scripture – Author "Cooked the Books" to Make them Fit

How does the author manage to recreate his "new and improved" Jesus? Reaching that goal required him to radically revise both the eyewitness accounts of Jesus' life and their foundational Old Testament predictions supporting him.

By taking bits and pieces from the original Injeel, GB spins a completely new Jesus story. The author's exegetical method is nothing short of stunning. By deftly dipping his hand into unrelated biblical texts and fusing them into a tight montage of lively vignettes, he laced them together to create a grand portrait – not of Jesus, but of the preeminent Prophet.

Page after page, the author retrofits earlier Scriptures to make them fit snugly with the Qur'an. In the table below, notice how his slight edits produce whopping changes of meaning.

THE GOSPEL OF BARNABAS	
Indications of Deliberate Manipulation	
The Gospel According to the Bible	**The Gospel According to GB**
God calls Jesus "My Son"	**God calls Jesus "My Servant"**
""This is My <u>Son</u>, whom I have chosen" (Lk 9:35). God's words to Jesus' apostles when Jesus' body transfigured	• "Behold My <u>Servant</u>, in whom I am wellpleased" (GB, 47)
Jesus Fulfills the Law	**Jesus Obeys the Law**
• Jesus came to "<u>fulfill</u> the law" (Matt 5:17) • Ritual washing (Mk 7:1-8; 14-15)	• Jesus came to "<u>obey</u> [observe] the law" • Ritual washing: "No one will make prayer pleasing to God if he be not washed, but will burden his soul with sin like to idolatry." (GB, 41; see 88)
Jesus Far Mightier than John the Baptist	**Muhammad (p) Far Mightier than Jesus**
John the Baptist about Jesus: "After me One is coming who is mightier than I, and I am not fit to stoop down and untie the thong of His sandals." (Mk 1:7)	Jesus about Muhammad (p): "I am not worthy to untie his hosen" (GB, 104)
Jesus: "I am the Messiah"	**Jesus: "Muhammad (p) is the Messiah"**
• Samaritan Woman to Jesus: "I know that Messiah is coming. . . when that One comes, He will declare all things to us." • Jesus' answer: "I who speak to you am He." (Jn 4:25-6)	• Samaritan Woman to Jesus: "O Lord, perchance thou are the Messiah." Jesus answer: "I am indeed sent to the house of Israel as a prophet of salvation; but <u>after me</u> shall come the messiah, sent of God to all the world." (GB, 89) • ". . . the Messiah that we should expect to meet is not even an Israelite but an Ishmaelite, and not Jesus but Muhammad (p)!"

378

THE GOSPEL OF BARNABAS	
Indications of Deliberate Manipulation	
The Gospel According to the Bible	The Gospel According to GB
Jesus faced his death with courage	**Jesus avoided dying as a coward**
They were on their way up to Jerusalem, with Jesus leading the way, and the disciples were astonished, while those who followed were afraid. Again he took the Twelve aside and told them what was going to happen to him. "We are going up to Jerusalem," he said, "and the Son of Man will be delivered over to the chief priests and the teachers of the law. They will condemn him to death and will hand him over to the Gentiles, who will mock him and spit on him, flog him and kill him. Three days later he will rise." (Mk 10:32-34)	• Jesus said, "I fled because I knew that a host of devils is preparing for me that which in a short time ye shall see. For, there shall rise against me the chief priests with the elders of the people, and shall wrest authority to kill me from the Roman governor. . .Moreover, I shall be sold and betrayed by one of my disciples. . ." (GB) • The disciples wept because they couldn't find Jesus. That is because he was hiding in fear. (GB, 150)
Jesus viewed his Death as God's Plan	**Jesus viewed his Rescue as God's Plan**
"Now My soul has become troubled; and what shall I say, 'Father, save Me from this hour'? But for this purpose I came to this hour. Father, glorify Your name." (Jn 12:27-28)	"For God shall save me from their hands, and shall take me out of the world." (GB, 150)

These citations clearly reveal these misrepresentations to have been deliberate rather than accidental. A historian's honest mistakes are one thing, intentional fabrications quite another. His sly methodology to recreate Jesus exposes his true character and motivation – to deceive his readers who were probably unacquainted with the New Testament. The GB is the product of a schemer. Yet all schemers leave loose ends. In pulling off his deception, the author hit a major snag. Since the New Testament was rooted in earlier Scriptures, his GB was headed for a major compatibility crisis. How was it going to look against the plethora of Old Testament texts? He knew full well how it would look. It would appear sham and manufactured, like welding luxury Cadillac fenders to a measly Volkswagen body. His new Jesus must look genuine, not fake. What can he do with all those old prophecies about Jesus? Overcoming this embarrassment was going to require a creative solution: a modified Tawrat to fit his modified Injeel!

For Barnabas, this posed no problem. By putting words in the mouth of Jesus, he invents the idea that the Jews corrupted the OT and that the original "Book" no longer exists. **Just as he had charged Paul with usurping the Injeel, he charges the Jews with changing the Tawrat, Prophets and Psalms!** His "true gospel" quotes from that "original Old Testament" that conveniently he alone possesses!

Which brings us to GB's colossal scandal.

Who is Muhammad (p)?

The GB stripped Messiahship from Jesus its rightful heir and awarded it to Muhammad (p). How did the author pull off this coup? By a devious sleight-of-hand. He took Messianic prophecies that had long been fulfilled in Jesus, and then re-routed them to the Prophet (p)! So who was Muhammad (p)? According to the GB:

The GB stripped Messiahship from Jesus its rightful heir and awarded it to Muhammad (p). How did the author pull off this coup? By a devious sleight-of-hand. He took Messianic prophecies that had long been fulfilled in Jesus, and then re-routed them to the Prophet (p)!

1. *Muhammad (p) was "the seed of the woman" in Genesis 3:15 who was destined by God to someday "crush the head of the Serpent."* "The world awaits the joy of his coming!" (46) [Note: When this prophecy was made, "the world" was populated by only two persons, Adam and Eve.]

2. *Muhammad (p) was the chosen "seed of Abraham" passing through Ishmael's lineage (48).* When Jesus' Twelve Apostles protested by appealing to Scriptures explicitly tracing the lineage through Isaac, Jesus became angry and upbraided them. Then he denied Scriptural infallibility: "Moses wrote it not, nor Joshua, but rather our rabbis, who fear not God" (49-50).

3. *Muhammad (p) was "the prophet like Moses from among your brethren"* (Deuteronomy 18:18) on the mistaken basis that Moses was an Arab (225);

4. *Muhammad (p) was God's chosen One, predestined from eternity, the desire of the nations.* In fact, at the Last Judgment, three witnesses will come forward to exonerate Muhammad (p): Moses, David and Jesus (62).

If not so tragic, these bizarre misattributions would be laughable.

Summary

We've covered much material and drawn conclusions. Let's review: The GB is riddled with mistakes that were not made innocently. The GB was a hoax. Its author was clever, but culpable. To pull off his scheme, he used two simple, but highly effective, tactics. First, he redrafted the New Testament to make it comply with the Qur'an. Then he redrafted the Old Testament to make it comply with his Injeel.

But the author could not have foreseen the fate of his literary invention.

PART THREE: How GB was Blindsided

This author could never have seen it coming. He had no idea that in 1947 a shepherd, Muhammad edh-Dhib and his cousin, would stroll through the arid wilderness near the Dead Sea. One of them would throw a rock up onto a steep hillside. It disappeared in a cave but landed with an odd sound. Instead of the normal thud, it went "tink." What was that? Hurrying up the rugged hill to find out, they reach a cave. Peeking in, they discover some pottery jars, some broken and others intact. Hoping these contained gold, they discovered eleven leather scrolls bundled in cloth. They had no idea of the treasure before them. Two were complete copies of the OT book of prophet Isaiah. There would be more. Little did they know that located in that cave and in ten others surrounding it would sit even more clay jars containing a massive collection of ancient scrolls and manuscripts – 600 complete books or fragments – that would come to be regarded as the greatest archaeological discovery in biblical studies, popularly known as "the Dead Sea Scrolls" (DSS).

Thanks to the dry desert climate, these jars housed complete and partial copies of manuscripts from all thirty-nine Old Testament books except Esther! What do the DSS have to do with the GB's accusation that the original Old Testament had later been corrupted by Jewish rabbis?

Prior to this discovery, the oldest Old Testament manuscripts ("Masoretic Text") dated from the tenth and eleventh centuries AD. That long span of time spawned skepticism among some biblical critics who tried to discredit the OT by accusing Jewish rabbis of text-tampering. Christians were also accused of manipulating OT texts to make them conform to their view of Jesus, much like the author of the GB redrafted the Injeel to fit the Qur'an. Passages such as Isaiah 53 were singled out for suspicion because they explicitly described the willing act of one innocent Messiah to lay down his life for the sins and transgressions of humanity. No way, so it was thought, could it have come from the pen of anyone writing many centuries prior to Jesus' birth! Christians must have added it later to support Jesus' crucifixion. Other OT passages lending support of Christian doctrines about Jesus such as his virgin birth and deity were also suspected of modification.

Did the authors of the Injeel tamper with Old Testament passages to make them support Christian beliefs? The early date of the OT books found in those jars settled the matter. Using modern dating methods, the near-unanimous opinion of scholars say these scrolls originated in the time period from 250-200 BC.[21] That period predates Christianity by more than two centuries. But that does not rule out the possibility of Christian tinkering in the centuries that followed.

The moment of truth came when comparing the content of these ninth-century AD scrolls with their earlier DSS counterparts dated over a 1,000 years earlier. Would they be contradictory or compatible? Astonishingly, both in its content and its inclusion, the "overall agreement between them is striking."[22]

> "Scholars were surprised to find that there was very little difference. The Jewish copyists had worked with great care. Over the 1,000 years one or two words had been wrongly written here and there, and some small changes made. The scroll proves beyond doubt that the Hebrew Bible on which all modern translations are based has hardly changed at all since the time of Jesus."[23]

"It is a matter for wonder through something like a thousand years the text underwent so little alteration. . . . Herein lies its chief importance [of the DSS], supporting the fidelity of the Masoretic tradition."[24]

How about those conspicuously "Christian" passages such as Isaiah 53 that biblical critics had accused Christians of inserting into the Old Testament? All of these texts were present with not one of them missing! Every OT passage suspected by critics is included in our oldest scrolls.

The author of GB had no idea that his charge of rabbinic corruption of the OT would be so thoroughly undermined by a discovery in 1947. The match-up between old and new scrolls was so close that no doctrine was affected. The GB's accusation that rabbis or Christians changed the texts can finally be dismissed.

Islamic Support of the GB

Despite the GB's obvious fallacies, some Islamic scholars defend its authenticity on the basis of the following evidence,[25] either real or so-called:

- "The GB was found in the cache of DSS documents." Yet all of those manuscripts have been carefully documented by a wide range of scholars. None has identified the GB.
- "The GB was accepted in 325 AD at the Council of Nicaea which destroyed the GB."
- "The writings of church father, Irenaeus, refer to the GB in the second and third centuries."
- Three official church documents cataloguing which writings are regarded as scripture and which are not; (a) the Glasian (sic) Decree of 496 AD includes *Evangelium Barnabe* in the list of forbidden books; (b) *Stichometry* of Nicephorus mentions the Epistle of Barnabas in Serial No. 3, Line 1, 200;

Muslims often confuse the GB with the *Epistle of Barnabas*, a genuinely Christian work written around 200 AD that teaches Jesus' sacrificial death, resurrection and Lordship.

(c) the list of Sixty Books include "Travels and Teaching of the Apostles" (Serial No. 17), "Epistle of Barnabas" (Serial No. 18) and "Gospel According to Barnabas" (Serial No. 24). These are presented by Rahim, pp 42-43.[26]

- A Greek fragment kept in an Athens museum (Rahim, 43)[27]
- "The Pope kept a copy of the GB in his private library" (Rahim, 42). [Rahim provides no evidence for this.]
- "During Emperor Zeno's rule in 478 AD, the remains of Barnabas were discovered and a copy of the GB, written in his own hand, was found on his breast. This is recorded in *Acta Sanctorum*, Bolund Junii, Tome II, 422-450, published in Antwerp in 1698" (Rahim, 43).[28]

Muslims often confuse the GB with the *Epistle of Barnabas*[29], a genuinely Christian work written around 200 AD that teaches Jesus' sacrificial death, resurrection and Lordship.

Muslims Who Reject the GB

To assume that it's only Christians who reject the GB would be a mistake. Many Muslim scholars have discredited this work such as J. Slomp:

> ". . .there is no question that [the Gospel of Barnabas] is a medieval forgery . . . It contains anachronisms which can date only from the Middle Ages and not before, and shows a garbled comprehension of Islamic doctrines, calling the Prophet "the Messiah", which Islam does not claim for him. . . ."[30]

After reviewing the evidence in an article in *Islamochristiana*, J. Slomp concluded:

> "In my opinion scholarly research has proved absolutely that this 'gospel' is a fake. This opinion is also held by a number of Muslim scholars."[31]

> "In their introduction to the Oxford edition of The Gospel of Barnabas, Longsdale and Ragg conclude that 'the true date lies. . . nearer to the sixteenth century than to the first.[32] Likewise, in his classic work, Jomier proved his point by showing beyond any

doubt that the G. B. V. contains an Islamicised late medieval gospel forgery.'"[33]

Conclusion

Putting theology aside for a moment, any Christian or Muslim reading the *Gospel of Barnabas* is immediately confronted with its credibility. It is an embarrassment to the intelligence of both Christians and Muslims. The author makes mistakes that are so outrageous they would have brought laughter to those living in Jesus' day and derision to those living in Muhammad's (p) for calling him "the Messiah!"

A Problem that Runs Deeper than the GB

Let's pause for a moment. If I were a Muslim, what would keep me from throwing in my enthusiastic endorsement for the GB, an enchanting work that on the whole supports my religious faith? Not only is it riveting reading that pulls at my heart strings by its charm, it touches my conscience with its copious biblical citations. More importantly, this Injeel confirms everything I've been taught in my madrassas and weekly sermons. Finally, we have a source from outside the Qur'an explaining how Christians arrived at their mistaken exaggerated claims about Jesus. So why not cast my vote in its favor?

> Muslims should reject *The Gospel of Barnabas* becauseit is neither a gospel ("good news") nor penned by the biblical Barnabas.

As much as I might want to believe it as a Muslim, I could not allow my desire to override my judgment, intellect and conscience. Muslims should reject *The Gospel of Barnabas* because it is neither a gospel ("good news") nor from the pen of Barnabas. It is a late forgery dressed up as the original Injeel.

May I offer a candid opinion? Are we missing the larger story? This single forgery reveals a deeper problem, a root issue of which the GB is only symptomatic. The GB is the product of a mindset that enshrines the last literary work as the benchmark by which all earlier scriptures are judged.

That starting norm permits its adherents in taking liberties of retrofitting early scriptures to conform with the last. This undermines the continuity of divine revelation, thus collapsing the entire edifice. Sooner or later, the final Book's initial triumph over its predecessors will boomerang on itself. Until then, its confidence is short-lived, like a branch boasting it can destroy the trunk while sustaining its own vitality. Despite the GB's charm, as a Muslim I would ask myself if my religion requires such a precarious replacement. Must the integrity of my Book be sustained by a forgery?

My interest is not to aggravate you, Muslim reader, but spare you the poisonous claims of a counterfeit gospel. This spoof had a threefold aim: distort (Scriptures), deceive (readers) and displace (the Gospel).

I quickly came to the following conclusion: This work is sacrilegious to the core. If the television series, *Saturday Night Live,* ever presented a biography of Jesus it could be the *Gospel of Barnabas.* Discarding all rules of history, it portrays Jesus as a Monty Python in a gospel of trivialization, one recovering its sanity only with the arrival of the Prophet. Its absurdities of history, chronology and geography have had only minimal impact on the spell it casts on millions of Muslims. Anyone with an appetite for mockery need look no farther than the GB. It is the *National Lampoon* of religious literature.

Who actually authored the GB?

> "The book is a rewrite of the Biblical Gospel most likely by a Muslim who wanted to portray Jesus as a Muslim who taught Islam and predicted the coming of Muhammad (p). This type of rewriting has been done elsewhere by Muslims in *The Gospel According to Islam.* This type of behavior is disgraceful, and it is disgraceful for Muslims to continue to publish, promote and distribute this false Scripture."[34]

Beware. Trifling with foundational realities is never inconsequential. Forgeries cast evil power over cultures. Continuing to publish a work known to be fraudulent shows feverish desperation for legitimatizing a religion.

The author of *Barnabas* launched a campaign of misinformation that was aimed at debunking the deity of Jesus, the Trinity and the doctrine of atonement while heralding the coming of the greater messenger, Muhammad (p). This frontal assault on the NT in the name of history has far reaching consequences. Who stands to lose the most? Muslims like the young woman cited earlier who raved about it to me. She and others are placing their faith in a man-made substitute "Gospel." It openly and unabashedly blasphemes God by "cutting and pasting" explicit passages that are applied to Jesus and then, without an iota of warrant, attributes them to Muhammad (p). Such manipulation robs Muslim people everywhere of knowing the Good News of God's saving purposes.

Who are Our True Friends?

The healthy are to look out for the best interests of the vulnerable, sometimes at cost to themselves. If I start to stray, I learn who my real friends are. They are the ones who will pull me aside to give me a reality check. "J. P., look out." So, good Muslim people, I urge you. Look out! Why bank your future on a lie? Don't give another second to this forgery. Get a true Injeel that was inspired by the Spirit of truth, one written by eyewitnesses and not a man claiming to live in the first century who quoted a poet from the fourteenth!

Come home to the true Messiah. You and I both know, that wasn't Muhammad (p).

9:1: Why has the history of Isa (Jesus) changed and we [Muslims] believe different facts from the Christians?

I love this question for its neutrality! It honestly acknowledges that our Books present us with two different sets of historical facts about Jesus. Commendably avoiding a rush to judgment on the merits of one over the other, you raise the question of why these discrepancies exist in the first place. Upon reading your question, I was sure that I did *not* know the answer and became very motivated to find it.

What kind of answer should we be looking for? How about an *objective* one that your unbiased question deserves. Let's go where the data leads, not the dogma. Dogma is a positive word if data leads there. The dogmatic answer that I hear most often in my current circles goes something like this. "The history of Isa has changed and we Muslims believe different facts from the Christians because they have embellished the history of Jesus. Islam is here to correct it with a pure history that is stripped of overstatement and exaggeration." Have you ever heard that before? A typical example is by Muhammad 'Ata'ur-Rahim from his Preface in *Jesus, Prophet of Islam*:

> "An eminent scholar of Christian history admits that present-day **Christianity is a 'mask' on the face of Jesus,** peace be on him, but goes on to say that a mask worn for a long time acquires a life of its own and it has to be accepted as such. **The Muslim believes in the Jesus of history and refuses to accept the 'mask'.** This, in a nutshell, has been **the point of difference between Islam and the Church** for the last fourteen hundred years."[35]

There you go. That is a dogmatic statement, even citing an "eminent" Christian scholar for support. But does the data lead to it? That is the question. **Every God-seeker, whether a devout Christian or Muslim, desires to unmask the real Jesus.**

Historic Shift: From "Both Books" to "Which Book?"

Before delving into our Book's differences, let's note when this dispute about contradictions began. As I understand it, it did not flare up to a significant degree until after the passing of Muhammad (p). He strongly believed that all Scriptures originated from one Source, a conviction that guaranteed their across-the-board agreement. So regardless of when each Book appeared, perfect synchronism would exist between them. That conviction removed any qualms over advising Muslims to ask "people of the Book" to explain or elaborate on biblical texts.[36] Upon his death, however, Muslims began reading the Injeel for the first time. When they did, they discovered numerous disparities between the Books involving both doctrine and history. And since the crux of the Christological debate involved Jesus' crucifixion – "Did he or did he not die?" – to render one Book true called the other into question. Understandably, arguments escalated with this shift from "Both Books are true" to "Which Book is true?" The data of contradiction challenged the dogma of synchronization.

Let's start by identifying as closely as possible the differences in our respective Jesus-histories. Then we can take the next step.

PART 1: WHAT DIFFERENCES?

Comparisons of Jesus in the Injeel and al-Qur'an

What historical differences about Jesus are we talking about? Are they trivialities like hair color or weightier matters impacting who he was and what he did? To find out, the chart below places the two sets of "facts" about Jesus side-by-side in corresponding fashion, a "Parallel Bible and Qur'an" if you will, providing us an objective tool to precisely compare similarities and inconsistencies. Since both Books present Jesus as the Messiah, that theme will serve as a useful framework.

The Messiah's Family Lineage
The Messiah's Birth and Childhood
The Messiah's Nature, Identity and Mission
The Messiah's Forerunner (John the Baptizer [Yahya])
The Messiah's Public Ministry
The Messiah's Death, Resurrection and Ascension
The Messiah's Return

NOTE: The following Qur'anic references to Isa have been sought to the best of my ability. I invite Muslim readers to fill in any gaps I may have unintentionally overlooked. Also, given its length, readers may wish to jump to a summary chart following, "Two Jesus Histories at a Glance."

PARALLEL HISTORIES OF JESUS Injeel & Qur'an		
INJEEL Only	**Common to Both**	**QUR'AN Only**
1. MESSIAH'S FAMILY LINEAGE		
Two genealogies, one from each parent, established Jesus' ancestry: *Messianic lineage* back to Abraham through Judah and David through his legal father and his *human lineage* through his mother back to Adam (Matt 1:1-17; cf Lk 3:23-38; Gen 49:10; 2 Sam 7).	Son of Mary (Lk 2; Surah 3:44-47; 4:156, 171; 19:2-35; 21:91; 46:15, etc.)	Jewish, Levite tribe through Imran (S. 3:35-37)

PARALLEL HISTORIES OF JESUS
Injeel & Qur'an

INJEEL Only	Common to Both	QUR'AN Only
2. MESSIAH'S BIRTH AND CHILDHOOD		
Mary, the Mother of Jesus		
Silence about her birth and childhood Father: **Heli** (Lk 3:23) Jewish tribe: **Judah** (Matt 1:1-17; Lk 3:23-37), of David's dynasty[37] Raised in **Nazareth**, a small Galilean village		Father: **Imran** or Amran (S. 3:35-37) Jewish tribe: **Levi**, that of priests **Her mother dedicated her unborn child to God's service.** Mary was purified by Allah (S. 3:42). Raised in **Jerusalem Temple** (S. 3:35) under priest Zechariah's supervision, (S. 3:35-37; 44). **Supernaturally fed** from God (S. 3:37)
Jesus' Birth		
PART 1: ANNOUNCEMENT & PREGNANCY	**PART 1: ANNOUNCEMENT & PREGNANCY**	**PART 1: ANNOUNCEMENT & PREGNANCY**
Joseph and Mary engaged to be married and morally chaste. **First, Angelic Visit to MARY in Nazareth** **Later, Angelic Visit to JOSEPH** *Mary's fiancé (Matt 1:18-25), discovers her pregnancy despite their chastity. Decided to divorce quietly to save her from shame (Matt. 1:19).* The child would be **male** **Name him "Jesus"** (Lk 1:31; 2:21). His birth **associated with John the Baptizer** [Yahya]	Angel Gabriel[38] announced to the virgin Mary that God chose her to be Jesus' mother (S. 3:42). Mary asks how she could be pregnant as a virgin. Jesus was conceived by the Holy Spirit without the aid of a man (Lk 1:38, :26-56; Matt 1:18; S. 3:47; 19:22-23; 21:91) [39] The mode of Jesus' birth proves God's power (Lk 1:37) "for whom nothing is impossible." "Allah creates what He wills. When He has decreed something, He says to it only: 'Be!' – and it is." (S. 3:48; see 19:20-21) [40]	Announcement of "glad tidings" made to Mary alone; Joseph is not mentioned. The announcement was made by one angel (S. 19:17-21) or multiple angels (S. 3:42, 45). Emphasis on the mode of conception as the creative power of God.

PARALLEL HISTORIES OF JESUS
Injeel & Qur'an

INJEEL Only	Common to Both	QUR'AN Only
Emphasized the Son's **unique mission & identity**		
Angel to Joseph		
Joseph, Mary's fiancé (Matt 1:18-25), discovers her pregnancy despite their chastity. Decided to divorce quietly to save her from shame (Matt. 1:19). The angel intervenes:		
"Do not divorce Mary. . ." because her child is a divine miracle fulfilling **God's promise of "Immanuel, God with us"** (Isa 7:14, Matt. 1:23)		
Name him "Jesus" [*Yeshua*, the LORD saves] (Matt. 1:24-25).		
Joseph marries Mary but refrained from conjugal relations until after Jesus's birth (Matt. 1:24-25)		
PART 2: JESUS' BIRTH	**PART 2: JESUS' BIRTH**	**PART 2: JESUS' BIRTH**
(Lk 2:1-20)	Jesus born as prophesied (Lk 2:1-20; S. 19:22ff).	*When?* Undisclosed
When? **Caesar Augustus' reign** during his census (Lk 2:1); **Quirinius' first** census (5 B.C.), Syrian Governor		*Birthplace* – Mary leaves home to a **faraway place in an eastward direction** (S. 19:6). Jesus born in a **desert under a palm tree.** (S. 19:20-23)
Birthplace – **Bethlehem of Judea,** the City of David because Joseph was of the House of David (Lk 2:4)		*People Present* – **Only Mary**
Circumstances – Mary delivered baby in **livestock stable;** Bethlehem inns were full. Used a feeding trough for cradle (Lk 2:7)		*Circumstances.* Mary **nearly died** in labor. **Baby Jesus consoled her** and **shook figs** from the palm tree for her nourishment and **caused springs to quench her thirst** (S. 19:23-25).
People Present – Mary, **Joseph** and **local shepherds** who arrived after an angelic announcement of the Savior's birth (Lk 2:8-20).		The virgin birth essential belief on the straight path (S 19:19-36)

PARALLEL HISTORIES OF JESUS
Injeel & Qur'an

INJEEL Only	Common to Both	QUR'AN Only
PART 3: JESUS' INFANCY		**PART 3: JESUS' INFANCY**
Jerusalem Temple Jesus' parents fulfilled requirements of the Law. He was circumcised on 8th Day (Gen 17:12) and dedicated as firstborn son (Lev 12:3; Lk 2:21-38)		From his cradle, Jesus **defended Mary's reputation** (S. 3:46-49; 5:110; 19:27-29) and preached his first message (S. 19:27-33, 36)
		Jesus' Cradle Sermon
Prophetic Word confirmed Jesus as the Messiah, a Light for all nations; his mission of peace will involve conflict causing his mother's grief. (Lk 2:34-35)		He would **permit actions previously forbidden to Jews** (S. 19:49-50)
		Warned Christians against worshiping him – "I am Allah's servant" (S. 19:29; S. 19:34-35; 37-39)
Anna, an elderly prophetess, associated Jesus with the **redemption of Jerusalem"** (Lk 2:36-38)		Appointed as Prophet and **received the Book** (S. 19:29)
Family returned to Nazareth about the time Yahya was born (Lk 1:36, 56)		Pronounced **God's benediction upon his own death and resurrection** (S. 19:32. See S. 3:47; 3:55)
	Jesus' Childhood	
Visited by Magi – While a toddler, a **unique star led Magi (astrologers) from the East (Persia or Arabia) to pay him homage as the One "born King."** Alarmed King Herod the Great who feigned desire to worship him (Matt 2:1-12).		**Breathed life into clay bird** (S.5:109-110; 3:48)
Family escapes to Egypt after angelic warning; Herod ordered **all boys** under age three **slaughtered in Bethlehem** (Matt 2:13-23). Family **remained in Egypt** until Herod died.		
Hometown in Nazareth, Galilee – Jesus lived in **obedient submission to his parents** (Lk 2:39-40; Matt 2:19).		

PARALLEL HISTORIES OF JESUS
Injeel & Qur'an

INJEEL Only	Common to Both	QUR'AN Only
Age 12 – Jesus **visits the Jerusalem Temple; engages in religious discussion with rabbis. Joseph died** sometime after Jesus turned 12.		

3. JESUS' NATURE, IDENTITY AND MISSION

WHO IS JESUS?	WHO IS JESUS?	WHO IS JESUS?
Identified in his Nativity	*Title & Capacities* (not restricted to infancy)	**Identified in his Nativity**
HIS MISSION		**HIS MISSION**
Savior for all (Lk 2:11, 32, cf. Matt 28:18; 1 Cor 3:8; Jas 2:14-17; Rev 19:8).	"Messiah" [*al-Masih*] (S. 3:45; 4:170, 171 and Matt 16:16)	**Messenger to the children of Israel** as their example (cf. S. 3: 49) and **confirm the Tawrat** (S. 3:3-4; 61:6). He would clarify differences (S. 43:52-64) and permit some actions previously forbidden (S. 19:49-50). Later, his mission extended beyond Israel (S. 43:5946).
His name will be **"Jesus"** ("the LORD saves") because he will save people from their sins (Matt 1:20-23)	"Messenger of God" [*rasula 'Mah*][42] (S. 4:169-170 and Mk 9:7)	
Light of revelation to the Gentiles" (Lk 2:32)	"The Prophet of God" [*Nabiya 'llah*] (S. 9:31 and Matt 14:15; 21:46; Lk 7:16; 24:19; Jn 4:19; Acts 7:37)	**Predicted Muhammad's (p) arrival** ("giving glad tidings of a Messenger to come after me, whose name shall be Ahmad" (S. 61:6 Khan tr.)..
To Israel first	"Servant of God" [*abdu 'llah*] (S. 9:31; 4:171 and Phil 2:6-8)	
HIS NATURE	"The Word of God" [*Kalimatuhuu*] (S. 4:170-171) "His Word" [not "a *Word from God* alone but *the Word of God*"[43]]; Jn 1:1, 14 [*Logos*] Rev 19:13. This "expression is uniquely used [in the Qur'an] of Jesus Christ," Abdul-Haqq); (S. 3:39): the angels to Zachariah that his son, Yahya, will witness to a *kalimatim-minallaah*, "a Word from Him"; (S. 3:45): the angels to Mary speak of Isa as a *kalimatim-minhu*, "a Word from Him"	**HIS NATURE**
Human, Holy Son of Mary		**Only human,** like Adam, "created from dust" and by God's command, "Be!" (S. 3:59), Son of Miriam (S. 3:44; 4:170) and no more (S. 5:15, 72; 9:30). Only a messenger (S. 5:75).
Divine – Son of God (Lk 1:32, 35)[41] – The long-awaited **"Immanuel**, God with us" (Isa 7:14; Matt 1:23).		Isa's life was predestined as a sign and mercy (S. 19:30). The full truth about him must await until after people die (S. 4:159).
	"The Word of Truth" [*Qaula 'l-Haqq*] (S. 9:85 and Jn 1:14, 17; 14:6; 18:37)	

PARALLEL HISTORIES OF JESUS
Injeel & Qur'an

INJEEL Only	Common to Both	QUR'AN Only
	"The Spirit of God" [*ruhun minhu*] (S. 4:171) "a Spirit from him"[44] (Jesus addressed in Hadith traditions, *Ya Ruhallah*, "O Spirit of Allah")[45] and 1 Cor 15:45 (*rauch*) **"Straight Path"** (to God's Mercy and Grace) (S. 4:174; cf 3:51, 6:153, 19:36, 43:61, 64; 46:30, 48:2, 20; 60:1 67:22 and Jn 14:6; Acts 4:12)	**His Attributes & Achievements** (S. 3:42-51) Venerated in this world and the next. Among those brought near to God (S. 3:45) Righteous **like other prophets** (S. 3:46); Endowed with judgment, tenderness and purity (S. 19:12-14) **Infant preacher** (S. 3:46) and miracle worker (S. 3:49) Confirmed the Tawrat of Moses **His Uniqueness:** A Sign (S. 23:50; 43:61). "Endowed more lofty than other prophets" (S. 2:253).

4. MESSIAH'S FORERUNNER, JOHN THE BAPTIZER (Yahya)

JOHN'S BIRTH	JOHN'S BIRTH	JOHN'S BIRTH
Mother: **Elizabeth** For doubting God's promise of a son, JB's father, Zachariah, was **mute until his birth 9 months later** (Lk 1:20) Approximately 6 months older than Jesus (Lk 1:36) **Filled with the Holy Spirit while in his mother's womb** (Lk 1:15)	Parents were devout believers (Lk 1:7, 13), old and childless. His father, Zachariah (Zakariyya), a priest serving in the Temple, prays secretly (S. 19:2) for an heir (S. 3:38; 19:3-6; 21:88) God answers (S. 21:88-89) [48] him through an angel (multiple angels, S. 3:39) bringing glad tidings of a son (Lk 1:61; S. 3:39; 21:90). Zachariah doubted God's promise in light of their advanced ages, asks for a sign (Lk 1:18; S. 3:40; 19:8). God corrects his doubt with	Mother: Unnamed **Zechariah prays for an heir** "of the family of Jacob" (S. 19:6) God answers Zechariah's doubt: "Easy for me; I created you, though you were nothing before" (S. 19:8-9) Zachariah became **mute for 3 full days and nights** (S. 19:10)

PARALLEL HISTORIES OF JESUS Injeel & Qur'an		
INJEEL Only	**Common to Both**	**QUR'AN Only**
	temporary muteness, since it was delivered through an angel(!). Unable to speak, he communicates by resorting to gestures (Lk 1:7, 22; S. 19:10)	
	God named him John (Lk 1:31; S. 19:7)	
JB'S IDENTITY & MISSION	**JB'S IDENTITY & MISSION**	**JB'S IDENTITY & MISSION**
"Prophet of the Most High" (Mk 1:2; Lk 1:76).	"a Prophet" (S. 3:39)	Emphasis on character: "among the righteous" (S. 6:85). Endowed with insight, mercy and able to sympathize with human beings (S. 19:12)
His role linked to Jesus. His appearance signaled "the beginning of the gospel of Jesus Messiah" (Mk 1:1)	He would be noble and chaste, manifesting righteous character (S. 6:85), wisdom, one of the righteous (Lk 1:15; 80) 49	
Rugged attire/diet like Elijah (Mk 1:8)		JB's role: Receive a Book by the angel: "Yahya, take the Book with power" (S. 19:12 RQ). "It was said to his son: "O Yahya (John)! Hold fast the Scripture [the Tawrat]. And We gave him wisdom while yet a child."
Forerunner to the Messiah (Lk 1:17; Jn 1:6-8; 3:28) "to prepare the way for the coming of the Lord" (Mk 1:2; Jn 1:23), i.e., Jesus.		
Served God's larger covenant with Abraham (Lk 1:72)		If JB was the forerunner to the Messiah, it is never mentioned. I found no unique connection to Jesus.
Culminated prophetic succession up to Messiah (Mal 3:1; Mk 1:2-3)		
(5) JB compared to Jesus: **"Jesus is Greater!"**		
Despite JB's enormous popularity, (Matt 3:4-5; Mk 1:5; Lk 3:15-17), he exalted Jesus to different class than himself. "After me comes one more powerful than I, the straps of whose sandals I am not worthy to stoop down and untie" (Mk 1:7).		

PARALLEL HISTORIES OF JESUS
Injeel & Qur'an

INJEEL Only	Common to Both	QUR'AN Only
Jesus Superior because: **Greater baptism** – *I baptize you with water [external], but he will baptize you with the Holy Spirit [internal]"* (Mk 1:7; Jn 1:27; 3:30-36). **'Greater Anointing** – "I saw the e Spirit come down from heaven as a dove and remain on him . . .I have seen and testify that this is God's Chosen One" (Jn 1:32, 34). **Greater Origins** –Jesus was born after John yet existed before him. "He who comes after me has surpassed me because he was before me" (Jn 1:15, 30, 26, etc.)		
### JB'S ACTIONS *Preacher–* Called Jews and *non-Jews to repent* through baptism in the Jordan River[47] for the forgiveness of sins (Matt 3:5-10; Mk 1:4; Lk 3:3-14; Jn 3:23). Fearlessly confronted King Herod's immorality. *Confirmed Jesus as the Messiah* – "Are you the Promised One?" Sought confirming evidence. Jesus answered with reports of his miraculous signs of Messiahship (Lk 7:18-23) *Publicly Identified Jesus as the Sin bearing Messiah* (Jn 1:29; Lk 3:16-18) *Baptized Jesus* – Reluctant to do so because Jesus was the greater figure. His reticence was overcome in obedience to God's will (Mk 1:9-13)		### JB'S ACTIONS **Received a Book** (Tawrat of Moses?) (S. 19:12)

PARALLEL HISTORIES OF JESUS
Injeel & Qur'an

INJEEL Only	Common to Both	QUR'AN Only
Exalted Jesus over Himself – Once his preparatory work was complete, he receded into the background so that Jesus would be prominent.		

JB'S DEATH & COMMENDATION		**JB'S DEATH & COMMENDATION**
Most religious authorities rejected JB (Lk 7:30) as they did Jesus as Messiah.		**Received special benediction:** "Peace on his day of birth, death and resurrected alive" (S. 19:17; cf with Jesus, S. 19:29) [50]
King Herod Antipas imprisoned JB for preaching against his flagrant immorality (Mk 6:17-20; Lk 3:19-20). On Herod's birthday gala, Salome, his step-daughter, danced before him and his guests. He offered to give her anything she wished. On her mother's advice, she asked for JB's head on a platter (Mk 6:21-29) – a wish he granted.		
JESUS' OPINION OF JB		
Jesus singled out JB for special distinction. As forerunner to the Promised One (Lk 7:26-27), **he was the greatest of all prophets.** Yet the least in the kingdom of God would be greater than him (Lk 7:28-29).		

5. MESSIAH'S PUBLIC MINISTRY

Jesus' Baptism, Anointing with the Spirit and Desert Temptations

Age 30 – Jesus baptized and anointed by the Holy Spirit (Matt 3:13-17; Mk 1:9-11; Lk 3:21-23; Jn 1:32-34).	**Al-Masih** – Only Isa is called Messiah in the Qur'an. (S. 3:45; 4:157, 171-2; 5:17, 72, 75; 9:30-31).	Isa's baptism unmentioned. Yet he was anointed or "aided with the Holy Spirit" for his teaching and miraculous ministry (S. 2:87; 252-3; 5:110).

PARALLEL HISTORIES OF JESUS
Injeel & Qur'an

INJEEL Only	Common to Both	QUR'AN Only
Messiah (*anointed one* — title, not a name) – "The Arabic word Masih comes from the Hebrew word *Mashiakh*. The English equivalent comes from the Greek word *khristos* (Christ)...This title means *he who was anointed with oil as God's appointment as prophet, priest, and king.* Oil is several times connected with God's Spirit (**T,** 1 Sam 16:13, Isa 61:1, Zech 4:11-14). In the Tawrah, prophets, priests, and kings were anointed with oil to show God's appointment to their jobs, but only the Messiah had all three roles in one person. As a *prophet*, he delivered Allah's message (Matt 13:57; 21:11, 46). As a *priest*, he interceded (which requires a close relationship to Allah, sinlessness, and Allah's permission: (Heb 6:20). Also as a priest, he offered sacrifice: (Heb 9:26; 10:5, 12). As a *king* he was to be obeyed. (Rev 17:14)." (RQ, 748) Fasted 40-days alone in the desert where he countered Satanic temptations designed to sabotage his divine mission (Matt 4:1-11; Mk 1:12-13; Lk 4:1-13).		The Qur'an hints at these Messianic functions: "As a *prophet*, Isa delivered God's message (S. 19:30; 3:49). As a *priest* he interceded (S. 2:255; 3:49; 5:110; 19:19; 3:45) and offered sacrifice (S. 3:55; 5:117; 37:107). As a *king*, he was to be obeyed (S. 3:50-51; 43:61-64)." (RQ, 748)

Jesus' Apostles

Jesus appointed 12 Apostles by name ("the Twelve"):	Disciples are Allah's helpers who have submitted to God's messenger (S. 3:52-53; 61:14). They believed in him when others disbelieved and God gave them his favor.	The term "Christians" occurs more than 600 times in the Qur'an.

PARALLEL HISTORIES OF JESUS
Injeel & Qur'an

INJEEL Only	Common to Both	QUR'AN Only
Andrew, James, brother of John; James (the less); John, Judas Iscariot (betrayer), Judas Thaddaeus, not the betrayer), Matthew (also called Bartholomew), Nathaniel, Peter, Philip, Simon the *Zealot*, Thomas (Matt 10:1-4; Mk 3:13-19; Lk 6:12-16) Jesus accompanied by women: Mary, Miriam, Mary Magdalene, Salome (mother of James and John) (Matt 27:56; Mk 15; Matt 20:20-21)		Jesus apostles called *Al-Hawartyyun* (the white garbed?) (5:111-112), [51] sometimes called "the Twelve" (S. 3:52-53; 5:111-115). None is named personally. God inspired them to place faith "in Me and My Apostle." They answered, "We have faith, and do thou bear witness that we bow to God as Muslims" (S. 5:114, Youssef Ali). God "put into the hearts of his [Isa's] followers compassion and kindness..." (S. 57:27). Helpers in the cause of Allah (S. 61:14) who claim to be Muslims (S. 5:111). Muslims admonished to avoid friendship with Jews and Christians (S 5:51; 57-9), w/ exception of converts to Islam (S. 82-85)
The Apostles View of Jesus "The Christ [Messiah], the Son of the living God" (Matt 16:16).		**The Apostles View of Jesus** God's Messenger – They professed, "We are Muslims" (5:111) and follow "the Messenger" (3:53)

PARALLEL HISTORIES OF JESUS
Injeel & Qur'an

INJEEL Only	Common to Both	QUR'AN Only
	Jesus' Miracles	

SPECIFIC MIRACLES

Nature. Turned water to wine, Jesus' first miracle (Jn 2:6-10); Extraordinary catches of fish (Lk 5:4-6; Jn 21:6); Walked on the sea (Matt 14:25-27, 29); Calmed raging seas (Matt 8:23-26; 14:32)

Healing. Nobleman's son (Jn 4:46-53); Centurion's son (Matt 9:5-13); fever (Matt 8:14-15); paralytic (Mk 2:3-12); man's withered hand (Matt 12:10-13); sick man (Jn 5:5-9); woman's incessant flow of blood (Matt 9:20-22); deaf and mute boy (Mk 7:32-35); woman of infirmity (Lk 13:11-13); dropsy (Lk 14:2-4); a severed ear of his enemy during Jesus' arrest (Lk 22:50-51) and many unnamed diseases (Matt 4:23-24; 14:14; 15:30; Mk 1:34; Lk 6:17-19).

Raising the Dead. Matt 9:18; 11:5; 19:23-25; Lk 7:12-17; 8:40-56; Jn 5:21; 11:11-5)

Exorcism. Cast out demons and evil spirits (Matt 8:28-32; 9:32-33; 15:22-28; 17:14-18; Mk 1:23-27)

Provision. Tribute money for taxes (Matt 17:27); Fed crowd of 1,000's from boy's lunch basket (Matt 14:15-21; 15:32-38)

Jesus' body transfigured (Matt 17:1-8)

Jesus performed miracles to relieve human pain and manifest God's compassion

Jesus had power to heal the sick, many ailments beyond human ability to cure.

Restores sight to the blind (S. 5:110; Matt 9:27-30; Mk 8:22-25; Jn 9:1-41) and lepers to health (Matt 8:1-4; 11:5; Lk 17:11-19).

Raised dead to life (Matt 9:18; 11:5; 19:23-25; Lk 7:12-17; 8:40-56; Jn 5:21; 11:11-53; S. al Imran 3:49)

Jesus possessed miraculous knowledge of hidden matters, especially what people were thinking. He knew what was *in* man (i.e., true condition of human nature) (Jn 2:24-25; Jer 17:10; Jn 6:64; 9:4; 12:25; 1 Cor 4:5; S. 3:48-49; 52; 5:110, 112; 19:19, 20, 24, 30-33)

Jesus' enemies dismissed his miracles as originating from outside of God (Matt 9:34; Mk 3:22; S. 5:110)

"Jesus mission with many manifest signs, being strengthened by the Holy Spirit." Summary by A. Injeel. Allen's Dictionary of Islam (1st edition, 1885)

SPECIFIC MIRACLES

Spoke twice as an infant

– His day of birth and from cradle (S. 3:46-49; 5:110; 19:24); what he says (S. 19:30-33)

Shook a Palm Tree to feed his mother (S. 19:23-25)

Created life – Breathed life into a clay bird and made it fly (S. 5:109-110; 3:48)

The Heavenly Table – (Uncertain meaning). Table spread with food (S. 5:112-115). Jesus' disciples ask him to "make a table descend upon us from heaven."[52]

Snatched from Crucifixion (?) – Most Muslims understand S. 4:157-158 to teach that Isa was miraculously rescued from the cross and taken to heaven. Belief in his death is the minority opinion.

PARALLEL HISTORIES OF JESUS Injeel & Qur'an		
INJEEL Only	**Common to Both**	**QUR'AN Only**
MODE OF MIRACLES **Jesus' direct command,** not through incantation, magic or prayer request. As the Son of God, Jesus replicated miracles he saw his Father doing to express their indivisible unity (Jn 5:19-20).		**MODE OF MIRACLES** **By prayer request** (e.g. the heavenly table, S. 5:112-114). Jesus performed miracles (S. 3:43-46) by God's permission (S. 3:49).
Jesus' Sinless Character		
Lived entire life without any moral defect. **Called "the Holy One of God"** (Mk 1:24), the guileless one (Isa 53:9; 1 Pet 2:22) **Holy in his nature,** not through an experience by which he *became* pure. Jesus was holy as the eternal Word of God (Jn 1:1) and conceived by the Holy Spirit (Lk 1:28- 31, 35; Matt 1:23) Subjected to severe temptations, afflictions and testing to complete his mission (Matt 4:1-10; Heb 4:15), yet without sinning (Jn 8:46; Acts 4:27; 2 Cor 5:21; Heb 1:9; 4:15; Reve 3:7).[53] Jesus' life a "moral miracle," humanity's only sinless one (Jer 17:8-10; Ps 51:5; Lk 11:13; Mk 7:21; Rom 3:23, etc.), Jesus lived fully obedient to his Father (Ps 40:8; Jn 4:34; 15:10)	Lived a life without sin	Lived without sin **in the same way as did all righteous prophets** (S. 3:46; 6:85) *All Prophets Sinless?* On the one hand, **all prophets are sinless** (S. 3:46; 6:84-86). [54] "Each one of them was one of the righteous" including Isaac, Jacob, Noah, David, Solomon, Job, Joseph, Moses, Aaron, Zachariah, Yahya, Elijah and Jesus (S. 6:84-85). On the other hand, prophets, like the rest, need God's forgiveness for their own moral flaws (S. 40:55; 47:19; 48:1-2).

PARALLEL HISTORIES OF JESUS Injeel & Qur'an		
INJEEL Only	**Common to Both**	**QUR'AN Only**
Jesus' Authority to Forgive People's Sins		
Authority to Forgive belongs only to God – (Tawrat, Exo 34:5-7; Num 14:17-20; Neh 9:16- 17; Ps 103:1-18; Isa 43:25; Mic 7:18- 20; Injeel, 1 Jn 1:8-9)	*Jesus is full of mercy* (Lk 23:34; Heb 2:17)	
Fulfilled Scriptures – Jesus fulfilled promises of the New Covenant of forgiveness and new hearts (Jer 31:31- 34; Matt 1:20-21; Jn 1:29; Matt 26:27-28; Heb 8:8-12)		
Notable Examples of Jesus forgiving others – Zacchaeus (Lk 19:1-10); Women of ill-repute (Jn 4); Jesus' Executioners (Lk 23:24);		
Jesus' Stories (parables) Illustrated God's Forgiveness – The unmerciful servant (Matt 18:23-35), the lost son (Lk 15:11-32; Lk 7:36-50)		
Jesus' Authority to forgive sins a sign of his Deity – (Matt 9:1-8; Mk 2:1-2; Lk 5:17-26)		

6. MESSIAH'S DEATH, RESURRECTION AND ASCENSION

Jesus' Death

JESUS' DEATH		JESUS' DEATH
Fact of History		**An Uncertainty**
<u>6 Months Prior</u>		See Question 9.2 for discussion.
Jesus begins **predicting his death** (See Question 9.2)		Jews boast of killing Jesus – S. 4:157
Days before his final week, Jesus **raised Lazarus from death** (Jn 11). News traveled throughout Jerusalem, setting off alarm bells among his enemies (Jn 12:17-19).		

402

PARALLEL HISTORIES OF JESUS Injeel & Qur'an		
INJEEL Only	**Common to Both**	**QUR'AN Only**
Events of the Final Week (Sequence is approximate) **Arrest warrant** for Jesus circulated in Jerusalem (Jn 11:57; 12:10) *Sunday.* Jesus **entered Jerusalem in a manner announcing himself as Messiah and King** (Matt 21 and parallels; Jn 12:14-16). *Monday.* Jesus **drove out moneychangers at the Temple** (Matt 21:12-13 and parallels). His arrest is delayed because of his immense popularity (Mk 11:18; Lk 19:47-48) *Tuesday.* Jesus taught openly at the Temple. **Condemned religious leaders** for their self-righteousness, religious hypocrisy, legalism and injustice (Matt 23:1-36) Jesus mentored his disciples: **Predicted future events:** (a) his **death,** (b) **Jerusalem's destruction / its Temple** (Matt 23:37f; Lk 19:41f) and (c) his **Second Coming** (Mk 13:1f). Jesus **anointed** in Bethany (Matt 26:6f; Jn 12:2f); **foretells his death** (Matt 26:1f) Jesus **anointed** in Bethany (Matt 26:6f; Jn 12:2f); **foretells his death** (Matt 26:1f) **Judas bargained** with religious authorities to **betray** Jesus (Matt 26:3f; 14f).		**4 Critical Passages**[56] Miriam 19:33 [Jesus from the cradle said] "Peace upon me the day I was born, and the day I die, and the day I shall be raised up alive."[57] Al-Nisa 4:155-156 (Palmer) [Traditional Muslim view] "And for their [the Jews] saying, 'Verily, we have killed the Messiah, Jesus the son of Mary, the apostle of God,' ... but they did not kill him,[58] and they did not crucify[59] him, but *a similitude*[60] *was made for them.* And verily, those who differ about him are in doubt concerning him; they have no knowledge concerning him, but only follow an opinion. They did not kill him, for sure! Nay, God raised him up unto Himself; for God is mighty and wise! And there shall not be one of the people of the Book but shall believe in him before his death; and on the day of judgment he shall be a witness against them." [61] "That the Jews intended to crucify him, but *God deceived them, for they did not crucify Jesus, but only his likeness.*"[62] (Hadith) Al-Maidah 5:117 (Shakir[63,64])

PARALLEL HISTORIES OF JESUS
Injeel & Qur'an

INJEEL Only	Common to Both	QUR'AN Only
Thursday. Morning – Jesus returned to the Temple to **teach publicly** (Lk 21:37f) while his disciples prepared the Passover meal in "Upper Room" (Lk 22:7f; 14f; Mat 26:26f; Mk 14:22f). *Evening* – Jesus **shared Passover meal with the Twelve** and **instituted the "Lord's Supper (Table)"** (Jn 13:1f). He washed their feet in selfless love (Jn 13), predicted Judas' betrayal (Jn 13:18f; Matt 26:20f) and apostles' abandonment at his imminent arrest (Lk 22:31-34; Jn 13:36f). Despite these dire projections, he exudes joy and comforts them with **promises of his resurrection** and subsequent **return to his Father's right hand** (Jn 14:1f).		[Jesus to God] "I did not say to them aught save what Thou didst enjoin me with: That serve Allah, my Lord and your Lord, and I was a witness of them so long as I was among them, but when[65] *Thou didst cause me to die,* [66] Thou wert the watcher over them, and Thou[67] art witness of all things." In a Sunni Hadith, Muhammad (p) regarded *belief in Isa's crucifixion to be clearly anathema.*[68] Al- Imran 3:47-50 (Palmer) "But they (the Jews) were crafty, and God was crafty, for God is the best of crafty ones! When God said, 'O Jesus! I will make Thee die and take Thee up again to me and will clear thee of those who misbelieve,[69] and will make those who follow thee above those who misbelieve, at the day of judgment, then to me is your return." When God said, 'O Jesus! I will make Thee die and take Thee up again to me and will clear thee of those who misbelieve,[69] and will make those who follow thee above those who misbelieve, at the day of judgment, then to me is your return."

PARALLEL HISTORIES OF JESUS Injeel & Qur'an		
INJEEL Only	**Common to Both**	**QUR'AN Only**
CONDEMNED BY JEWISH COURT Jesus **interrogated before Annas,** a deposed High Priest (had served from 6-15 A.D.) who still exercised great influence. Then **interrogated before Caiaphas the sitting High Priest** (18-36 AD) who had predetermined the outcome (Matt 26:5). **Peter denied Jesus** (Matt 26:69-72; Lk 22:55-58; Jn 18:15-17) *Early Friday Morning.* **Jewish Trial** –Jesus officially tried by the Sanhedrin ("the Council") that had convened to condemn him. False witnesses called (Mk 14:55- 64; Lk 22:54, 63-66). Cross-examination: *Caiaphas:* "Are you the Christ, the Son of the Blessed One?" *Jesus:* "I am; and you shall see the Son of Man sitting at the right hand of Power, and coming with the clouds of heaven" (Mk 14:61-62; cf Matt 26:63-64) *Verdict:* "Tearing his clothes, the high priest said, 'What further need do we have of witnesses? You have heard the *blasphemy*; how does it seem to you?' And they all *condemned Him to be deserving of death*" (Matt 26:65-66; Mk 14:63-64; Lk 22:66-71) **Peter's 3rd denial** (Matt 26:73-4; Lk 22:59-60; Jn 18:26-27). His remorse (Lk 22:60- 62). **Judas commits suicide** (Matt 27:3-10)		

PARALLEL HISTORIES OF JESUS
Injeel & Qur'an

INJEEL Only	Common to Both	QUR'AN Only
Roman Praetorium in Jerusalem **Pilate's wife warned through a dream** of Jesus' innocence (Matt 27:19). Pilate tries to free Jesus by **offering them Barabbas**, a notorious criminal, to be crucified instead. The crowd, manipulated by religious leaders, demanded release of the criminal and crucifixion of Jesus (Matt 27:20-23; Mk 15:6-14; Lk 23:18-23; Jn 18:40). Jesus **mocked, "crowned" with thorns** (Matt 27:27-30; Mk 15:16-19; Jn 19:1-3) and **scourged with whips** laced with bone pieces and metal spikes (Mk 15:16-20; Jn 19:1-3). **Pilate interrogates Jesus** (Jn 19:12-15) in a final attempt to free him, offering the crowd one last chance (Jn 19:4-6). **Pilate washed his hands** publicly to declare his own innocence of shedding innocent blood (Matt 27:24-25). **Inscription** on the cross: "Jesus of Nazareth, King of the Jews" (Matt 27:37; Jn 19:19-22) **Pilate released Barabbas** (Lk 23:24-25)		

PARALLEL HISTORIES OF JESUS Injeel & Qur'an		
INJEEL Only	**Common to Both**	**QUR'AN Only**
CRUCIFIXION Jesus was led to the crucifixion site just outside the Jerusalem wall about 500 yards beyond the Antonia Fortress. Faltering under the weight of the 50-pound crossbeam (*patibulum*), **Simon of Cyrene** was forced to carry it (Matt 27:32; Mk 15:21-22; Jn 19:17). Jesus tells **women mourners to weep for themselves** and their children for what lay ahead for the city (Lk 23:27-31) **Crucifixion** – 9:00 AM – 3:00 PM **Soldiers gamble for Jesus' clothing** (Matt 27:35-36; Jn 19:23-24). **Jewish leaders mock** Jesus & stir crowd (Matt 27:39-44; Lk 23:35- 37). **Darkness covers the land** (Matt 27:45-47; Mk 15:23-28; Lk 23:32-34) **Jesus died** – 3:00 PM (Matt 27:50; Mk 15:37; Lk 25:46; Jn 19:30). His death set in motion **extraordinary events** and a myriad of human responses (Matt 27:51-56; Mk 15:39-41; Lk 23:45-49). **Soldier pierces Jesus' side, confirming his death** by the outflow of water and blood (Jn 19:31-37).		

PARALLEL HISTORIES OF JESUS Injeel & Qur'an		
INJEEL Only	**Common to Both**	**QUR'AN Only**
## JESUS' BURIAL Joseph of Arimathea, a respected **member of the** Council, received Pilate's permission to remove the corpse **for burial. Nicodemas, a leading Pharisee,** assisted. Women helped prepare the burial ointment (Lk 23:55-56; Matt 27:59-60; Mk 15:46; Lk 23:53; Jn 19:41-42). Jesus' body laid in a Jerusalem tomb near the crucifixion site (**Matt 27:57-61**). At the request of Jewish leaders, Pilate posted **Roman guards at his tomb** and **sealed its entrance** with a heavy stone (Matt 27:62-65) **Saturday** – Body of Jesus remained in the tomb		
### Jesus Raised back to Life, Appears to People and Ascends to Heaven		
## RESURRECTION *Sunday Morning* The soldiers guarding the tomb testify to an **early-morning earthquake** dislodging the heavy stone sealing it. **The body of Jesus was gone**. Explanations not forthcoming and keenly aware their lives were on the line, the soldiers **rush with the news to the Jewish authorities** who had hired them (Matt 28:2-4). The Jewish leaders **paid the soldiers** handsomely to **spread a rumor** that the disciples had stolen the body during the night. They would commit this perjury with the understanding that the		## RESURRECTION **Ambiguous** – Isa's resurrection that followed his death was foretold. His birth, death and resurrection are essential beliefs for those on the straight path (S. 35:5; 19:33; 4:117; S. 5:117).

PARALLEL HISTORIES OF JESUS Injeel & Qur'an		
INJEEL Only	**Common to Both**	**QUR'AN Only**
religious leaders would bribe their Roman superiors. This cover-up became **the earliest explanation why the tomb of Jesus was found empty** (Matt 28:11-15).		

Jesus' Tomb Found Empty

Women first visiting the tomb found it empty (Mk 16:1-4). An angel announced "Jesus is risen!" and reminded them of his prediction (Mark 16:5-7; Lk 24:4-8). They leave with awe and fear (Mk 16:9).

Jesus meets with some of these (Matt 28:8-10, 11-18) including **Mary Magdalene** (Mk 16:9; Jn 20:11-17).

They inform Jesus' disciples of their encounter (Mk 16:10-11; Lk 24:9-11; Jn 20:18), but **their story is met with suspicion.** A woman's testimony was regarded less than equal to that of a man in that day and culture.

Two of the Twelve, **Peter** and **John**, run to check it out for themselves. Reaching the tomb, they looked in to find it uninhabited as the women said, but not empty. **Jesus graveclothes** remained – both the **head cloth** and **burial shroud** (Lk 24:12; Jn 20:2-10). These pieces sat conspicuously on the stone slab in the exact spot where the body had been laid late Friday afternoon. The shroud retained its form like an empty cocoon, undisturbed as if the body had simply vanished. If the body had been stolen, how did human hands manage to extract it so cleanly? John believed.

PARALLEL HISTORIES OF JESUS Injeel & Qur'an		
INJEEL Only	**Common to Both**	**QUR'AN Only**
Sunday Afternoon Jesus joined Cleopas and another disciple while walking on a road lamenting recent events. He revealed his identity to them (Lk 24:13-35; Matt 16:12). Cleopas informs the disciples (Lk 24:33-35; Jn 20:19). Later it is learned that Jesus also met with Peter (1 Cor 15:5; Lk 24:34). *Sunday Evening* For the first time, Jesus appeared to the apostolic group (minus Thomas) all at once (Matt 16:14; Lk 24:36-44; Jn 20:19-20). Jesus offered proofs that he was alive. Afterwards, they run to tell Thomas who immediately dismissed the story, refusing to believe without seeing and feeling the marks left by the nails and the sword. (Jn 20:24-25). *One Week later* Jesus appeared again to the whole apostolic group, this time with Thomas [pre]sent.70 His doubts instantly collapsed in the face of empirical evidence (Jn 20:24-29). Over the next 40 days, Jesus physically appeared many times to his disciples, teaching and providing **convincing proofs** he was alive (Acts 1:3). *Eyewitness Summary* Those encountering Jesus alive included (1) **over 500 disciples simultaneously** (1 Cor 15:5), possibly referring to Galilee (Matt 28:10-20);		

PARALLEL HISTORIES OF JESUS Injeel & Qur'an		
INJEEL Only	**Common to Both**	**QUR'AN Only**
(2) **seven disciples** in a fishing boat (Jn 21:1-14);		
(3) **Peter** when Jesus reinstated him (Jn 21:15-17) and predicted the manner by which Peter would die as a martyr for him (Jn 21:18-19);		
(4) **James,** (not the apostle) **Jesus' natural half-brother** who first regarded Jesus as misguided. All that changed upon seeing Jesus alive after his crucifixion (1 Cor 15:7; see James 1:1; Acts 15:13);		
(5) **the Apostles** (Acts 1:3-11; 10:41); and finally,		
(6) **Saul, Christianity's Public Enemy #1** who persecuted the earliest church. His tirades ended abruptly upon meeting the risen Christ months after his resurrection (1 Cor 15:8; Acts 9:1-8; 1 Tim 1:13-16).		
Unanimous Testimony – **Jesus rose from the dead!** (Matt 16:21; Lk 24:6; Jn 10:18; 1 Ths 4:14)		
ASCENSION INTO HEAVAN	**ASCENSION INTO HEAVAN**	**ASCENSION INTO HEAVAN**
As **foretold by Jesus** (Jn 6:62; 7:33; 14:28; 16:5; 20:17), he physically ascended back into heaven **in the presence of his disciples 40 days after his resurrection.** This occurred on **the Mount of Olives** (Mk 11:1; Lk 24:50-51; Acts 1:3, 9, 12).	Jesus ascended into heaven – Raised Up ((Mk 11:1; Lk 24:50-51; Acts 1:3, 9, 12; S. 3:55-58; 4:157-159) Isa is the only one to ascend into heaven where He is given a high place (S. 3:54-55). Jesus has been brought close to Allah (S. 3:45-51).	While there are differences of opinion on which level of Paradise Jesus now is, interpreters agree that "Jesus is now in one of the stages of celestial bliss."[71]

411

PARALLEL HISTORIES OF JESUS
Injeel & Qur'an

INJEEL Only	Common to Both	QUR'AN Only
FINAL STATUS		**FINAL STATUS**
Jesus is the **preeminent Lord,** enthroned on God's right hand w/ **supreme power and authority** (Lk 24:26; Eph 1:20-21; 1 Pet 3:22).		Isa is the **penultimate prophet** pointing ahead to **Muhammad (p) the preeminent Prophet.**

Jesus Sends the Promised Holy Spirit from Heaven

INJEEL Only	Common to Both	QUR'AN Only
Pouring Out. The Father and Messiah **sent the promised Holy Spirit on his original 120 followers** (Jn 16:7; Acts 2:33). *Going Out.* The Holy Spirit **propelled Jesus' mission forward.**		Isa, God's **penultimate prophet,** points to the arrival of **Muhammad (p), his preeminent Prophet.** The Spirit (*Ruh*), known only to God (S. 17:85), is identified variously: • The archangel Gabriel (at Jesus' conception), angel of revelation – S. 16:102; 26:192-94 (*the Trustworthy Spirit*); cf 70:4? At the Last Judgment, he will stand silently in line with the most noble angels – S. 78:38 • Breath of life; God's animating spirit breathed into Adam at creation; the soul – S. 15:29; 17:85; 32:9; 38:72 • Source of strength from God to believers at his command during hard times perhaps as proofs, signs or guidance – S. 58:22 • Divine inspiration or revelation that "comes down" by God's command – S. 16:2; 40:15; 42:52; 97:4

PARALLEL HISTORIES OF JESUS Injeel & Qur'an		
INJEEL Only	**Common to Both**	**QUR'AN Only**
		Is the Spirit deity? No. Obviously not if it is Gabriel since angels are created beings, not deity. Likewise, being sent down at Allah's command distinguishes it from God who would not order himself. As to the breath of life from Allah, the question is left unanswered.
WHAT IS THE GOSPEL?		**WHAT IS THE GOSPEL (INJEEL)?**
"Gospel" (Gk, *euangelion*) means *good news*, not good views. It is a front-page headline, not an opinion piece.		The Injeel is "the Book given directly to Isa" (S. 5:46) by God who taught it to him along with the Tawrat and wisdom (S. 3:48; 5:110). "We gave him [Isa] the Injeel" (S. 5:46; 3:3, 65; 5:46-47, 66-68; 57:27)
Content –Jesus' victory over sin, death and Satan by which he reconciled people to God and inaugurated God's kingdom of righteousness, peace and joy(Mk 1:14).		*Consistency* – As the Injil confirmed the Tawrat, so the Qur'an confirmed the Injeel. (S. 3:3-4; 5:48)
The Gospel's 5 Anchor Points		*Value* – Gives "guidance" (*huda*) and "light" (*nur*) (S. 5:46). As "sent down" from Allah, Christians must follow it (S. 5:47) as their solid foundation for eternity (S. 5:68-9), but most of them disobey it to their eternal detriment (S. 5:65-66).
ONE – Gospel Events		
Acts 10:34f: "Jesus went around doing good and healing all who were under the power of the devil."		
Luke 4:36 – "With authority and power he ordered impure spirits and they come out!"		*Message* – It predicts "glad tidings of a Messenger whose name shall be Ahmed" (S. 61:6; 5:19; 7:157).

PARALLEL HISTORIES OF JESUS
Injeel & Qur'an

INJEEL Only	Common to Both	QUR'AN Only
Romans 4:25: "He [Jesus] was delivered over to death for our sins (God's sacrifice) and was raised to life for our justification (God's pardon)." See 1 Cor 15:1-3		*Isa's Role* – A prophet to the Prophet (p). What Yahya had been to Jesus in the NT, Jesus was to Muhammad (p) in the Qur'an: the herald foretelling the arrival of the final Messenger.
TWO: Gospel Witnesses – The credibility issue		*Necessity* — For rejecting this gospel (including later revelation or *Furqan*), Christians will meet severe punishment (S. 3:3-4; 5:65, 85-6; 9:29ff).
• *Witness of the Old Testament*		
Luke 24:44-46: Jesus: "Everything must be fulfilled that is written about me in the Law of Moses, the Prophets and the Psalms ... This is what is written: The Messiah will suffer and rise from the dead on the third day."		**The Injeel Advances Islam's Ultimate Triumph over all Religions**
Acts 3:18: "This is how God fulfilled what he had foretold through all the prophets, saying that his Messiah would suffer."		*Parable of the Sapling* – S. 48:28-29. Islam's immense growth is likened to a strong plant from a fragile sapling. That expansion portends Islam will ultimately supersede all previous religions.[4] What does it mean?[5] The Injil testifies to the prevailing religion of Islam. Just as Isa receded before the greater Prophet, so the Injeel seems to advance Islam as the greater religion and provide incentive for its spread (S. 9:111)[6]
Romans 1:1-3 – "The gospel of God— the gospel he promised beforehand through his prophets in the Holy Scriptures regarding his Son, who as to his earthly life was a descendant of David, and who through the Spirit of holiness was appointed the Son of God in power by his resurrection from the dead: Jesus Christ our Lord."		
• *Eyewitness Testimony to Jesus' Resurrection*		
Acts 1:3: "After his suffering, he presented himself to them and gave many convincing proofs that he was alive."		
Acts 2:32: "God has raised this Jesus to life, and we are all witnesses of it."		

PARALLEL HISTORIES OF JESUS		
Injeel & Qur'an		
INJEEL Only	**Common to Both**	**QUR'AN Only**
Acts 3:15: "You killed the author of life, but God raised him from the dead. We are witnesses of this."		
Acts 10:39-41: "We are witnesses of everything he did in the country of the Jews and in Jerusalem. They killed him by hanging him on a cross, but God raised him from the dead on the third day and caused him to be seen ... by witnesses whom God had already chosen—by us who ate and drank with him after he rose from the dead."		
THREE: Gospel Affirmations – Who is Jesus today?		
• *The Savior with authority to forgive sin and bestow salvation*		
Luke 24:46-47: "Jesus told them, This is what is written: 'The Messiah will suffer and rise from the dead on the third day, and repentance for the forgiveness of sins will be preached in his name to all nations, beginning at Jerusalem.'*		
• *The Lord with authority to demand submission*		
Acts 2:36: "Therefore let all Israel be assured of this: God has made this Jesus, whom you crucified, both Lord and Messiah."		
Philippians 2:5-11: "Christ Jesus: Who, being in very nature God, did not consider equality with God something to be used to his own advantage; rather, he made himself nothing by taking the very nature of a servant, being made in human likeness. And being found in appearance as a man, he humbled himself by becoming obedient to death—		

PARALLEL HISTORIES OF JESUS		
Injeel & Qur'an		
INJEEL Only	**Common to Both**	**QUR'AN Only**
even death on a cross! Therefore God exalted him to the highest place and gave him the name that is above every name, that at the name of Jesus every knee should bow, in heaven and on earth and under the earth, and every tongue acknowledge that Jesus Christ is Lord, to the glory of God the Father."		
FOUR: Gospel Promises — In the name of Christ, God offers all people remission of sins and the gift of the Holy Spirit, forgiveness of the past and a new life in the present through His indwelling Spirit.		
Acts 2:38-39: "Brothers, what shall we do?" Peter replied, "Repent and be baptized, every one of you, in the name of Jesus Christ for the forgiveness of your sins. And you will receive the gift of the Holy Spirit. The promise is for you and your children and for all who are far off—for all whom the Lord our God will call."		
Rev 11:15: Certain hope for the future – "The kingdoms of this earth have become the kingdom of our Lord and of his Christ, and he shall reign forever and ever."		
FIVE: Gospel Demands – People must turn away from their sins and commit their lives totally to Christ		
Acts 3:19: Repent, then, and turn to God, so that your sins may be wiped out, that times of refreshing may come from the Lord.		

PARALLEL HISTORIES OF JESUS
Injeel & Qur'an

INJEEL Only	Common to Both	QUR'AN Only
The Advancing Gospel of the Kingdom of God *1 Thes 1:5:* How the Gospel advances— "Our gospel came to you not simply with words, but also with power, with the Holy Spirit and with deep conviction." *13:31-33,3 Parable of the Mustard Seed* — Jesus likened the spread of the kingdom to a mustard seed, at the time the smallest known seed. From out of that tiny kernel grew a humongous shrub reaching up to 10 feet high. It proved to be an apt metaphor, capturing the astounding growth of the Good News from his mere twelve apostles to the millions who would receive Christ throughout the world. *Romans 1:16-17:* Universal scope – "I am not ashamed of the gospel, because it is the power of God that brings salvation to everyone who believes..."		
7. MESSIAH'S RETURN		
The Messiah will return to earth as Judge. He will come quickly (Rev 6:12-17; Mk 4:22; Matt 25:34-41) "Then will appear the sign of the Son of Man in heaven. And then all the peoples of the earth will mourn when they see the Son of Man coming on the clouds of heaven, with power and great glory." (Matt 24:30) "For the Lord himself will come down from heaven, with a loud command, with the voice of the archangel and with the trumpet call of God..." (1 Thess 4:16; see vv 14-18)		Isa knows the Hour or is a sign of Judgment Day (S. 43:61). Isa will bear witness against unbelievers on Resurrection Day (S. 4:159).

417

This chart demonstrated the spot-on accuracy of your question. Our two Books indeed present us with two sets of "facts" about Jesus. For your convenience, I have condensed these below.

TWO JESUS' HISTORIES AT A GLANCE 20 Point Comparison		
	INJEEL	**QUR'AN**
Messiah?	Yes	Yes
Lineage	Judah, tribe of kings, a Messianic requirement	Levi, tribe of priests
Mary's Father	Heli	Imran (Amran)
Mary's Home	Humble village of Nazareth, Galilee	Jerusalem Temple under priest Zachariah's supervision
Gabriel Announced Jesus' Birth to	Mary first, later to Joseph, her fiancé.	Mary
Introduced by the Angel as	*Immanuel,* "God with us" "the holy Son of God" Emphasis: Jesus' *identity*	"Messenger and slave of God" Emphasis: Jesus' *mode* of conception: "Be!"
Name & its Significance	"Jesus," [*Yeshua*] "Yahweh saves," named by God to define his mission	"Isa" Meaning unspecified
Birthplace	Bethlehem, City of David, in a stable for livestock	Unspecified area in the East, under Palm tree
Time of Birth	During reigns of Rome's Caesar Augustus, Governor Quirinius of Syria and Herod the Great in Jerusalem	Unspecified
People Present at Nativity	Mary, Joseph and nearby shepherds sent by an angelic host announcing the Savior's birth	Mary and her infant
Divine Protection of the Babe from King Herod	Herod's plan to murder Jesus along with all male toddlers in Bethlehem was prevented by angelic warning to Joseph	N/A
Mission of John the Baptist (Yahya)	Prepared Israel for Messiah's arrival	Received a Book

TWO JESUS' HISTORIES AT A GLANCE 20 Point Comparison		
	INJEEL	**QUR'AN**
Ranking of John the Baptist (Yahya)	Subordinate to Jesus "unworthy to loosen his sandals"	Received God's equal benediction
Jesus' First Miracle	Age 30	Spoke from the cradle in infancy and created a live bird from clay as a boy
Performed Miracles	By direct command	By prayer
Death?	Definitely. His death, burial and return to life three days later confirmed by a wide range of eyewitness testimonies	Unclear. Three explicit references to Isa's death offset one disputed reference to his crucifixion.
Ultimate Responsibility for Jesus' Death	God	God
Purpose Served by Jesus' Death	Salvation Reverse Sin's Effects & Death	Unspecified
When Jesus Ascended into Heaven	40 days after Jesus died	Prior to his crucifixion (majority Muslim view) or after dying in an unspecified manner (minority view)
Coming Back at the End of the Age	Yes	N/A

This side-by-side comparison is the big first step in answering your question. It has identified the places in which our respective Jesus portraits overlap, their unique details and narratives and some contradictions. These variations range from biographical incidentals (Mary's hometown) to defining events impinging on core beliefs (Jesus' death and resurrection).

Now – finally! – we are ready for the next step. *Why* are they so different? How can the same historical Figure almost come out as two completely different persons?

419

PART 2: WHY THE DISCREPANCIES?

When contradictions surface between our venerated Books, what can we do? Rather than become defensive, the Preface of the present work suggests a constructive path: *investigate* them. Where shall we begin? Let's inquire to see if their respective storylines can be traced back to earlier sources feeding them.

A. Sources for Jesus in the Injeel

Where did the Injeel draw its information about Jesus? The answer boils down to two fundamental sources: eyewitness reports from his chosen companions and the ancient Scriptures. We previously discussed the first of these in Chapter 7. Now let's turn to the latter. Should we even expect earlier Scriptures to shape the Jesus we meet in the Injeel? Jesus thought so. He prepped us to see the connecting links between the Books and the Man:

Ancient Scriptural writings took several forms but all contributed to the Injeel's portrait of Jesus. Some came as God's specific **promises** ("I will/will not do"), some as **predictions** ("This will/will not happen"), some as **qualifications** required for specific offices (e.g. priests, kings, the Messiah), and some as ancient **foreshadowings** that reached their concrete embodiment in Jesus (rituals, festivals, institutions and historical events). Occasionally God's promises took the form of an oath, "to swear" (Gen 26:3; 1 Chron 16:15-18; Neh 9:15). These categories may overlap, but what is clear is that God's Word advanced history toward accomplishing his goal.[72]

> "Everything must be fulfilled that is written about me in the Law of Moses, the Prophets and the Psalms." (Luke 24:44)

OT references to Jesus are not all prophecies, yet still pointed to him. They come in various forms:

What follows is an extensive list from the sacred repository linking the Text to the Man. Using the same Messianic categories as before, we'll simply change the lens from the cradle-to-grave eyewitness reports of Jesus' life to the ancient Scriptural soil out of which it grew.

SOURCES FOR JESUS IN THE INJEEL

Original Source Old Testament Promises, Predictions & Foreshadowings	New Testament Completion

1. MESSIAH'S ANCESTRAL LINEAGE

	Original Source	New Testament Completion
Evil's Final Destruction **Seed of the Woman would "bruise" or "crush" the Serpent's "head"**	Immediately following Adam and Eve's sin, God addressed the Serpent: And I will put *enmity* between you [the *Serpent*] *and the woman*, and between *your offspring [seed] and hers*; he will crush his head, and you will strike his heel. (Gen 3:15)	But when the set time had fully come, God sent his Son, *born of a woman*, born under the law, to redeem those under the law, that we might receive adoption to sonship. (Gal 4:4, 4 BC) The God of peace will soon *crush Satan under your feet*. (Rom 16:20) The reason the *Son of God appeared was to destroy the devil's work*. (1 Jn 3:8, AD 90)
Through "seed" of Abraham	I will surely bless you [Abraham] and make your descendants as numerous as the stars in the sky . . . and *through your offspring [seed] all nations on earth will be blessed*, because you have obeyed me. (Gen 22:18, c.1800 BC) God swore this promise with an oath upon seeing Abraham's willingness to sacrifice his son. (Gen 22:15-18; 26:3; Isa 45:23) God's promise of blessing was *first* given to Abraham's *ethnic* offspring and *then*, through them, to *all* nations (Gen 12:1-3; 7; 15:9-21, 17:1-22). Its centrality to the entire biblical story is evidenced by its five repetitions in Genesis alone – 12:3; 18:18; 22:18; 26:4; 28:14. "It points back to the promise of Genesis 3:15 as well as forward to Christ and the salvation which he secures."[73]	Since the children have flesh and blood, he too shared in their humanity . . . For surely it is not angels he helps, but *Abraham's descendants*. (Heb 2:14-16, AD 60) There is *neither Jew nor Gentile*, neither slave nor free, nor is there male and female, for you are all one in Christ Jesus. *If you belong to Christ, then you are Abraham's seed, and heirs according to the promise*. (Gal 3:28-29) See Matt 1:1; Heb 11:8-9, 17-19; Acts 3:25; Gal 3:16

SOURCES FOR JESUS IN THE INJEEL		
	Original Source Old Testament Promises, Predictions & Foreshadowings	**New Testament Completion**
Through "Seed" of Isaac	But God said to Abraham, " . . . it is *through Isaac* that your offspring will be reckoned." (Gen 21:12, c. 1760 BC) . . .your wife Sarah will bear you a son, and you will call him Isaac. *I will establish my covenant with him* as an everlasting covenant for his decedents after him. (Gen 17:19; 26:3-4)	By faith Abraham, when God tested him, offered Isaac as a sacrifice. He who had embraced the promises was about to sacrifice his one and only son, even though God had said to him, "It is through Isaac that your offspring will be reckoned." Abraham reasoned that God could even raise the dead, and so *in a manner of speaking he did receive Isaac back from death.* (Heb 11:17-19, AD 64) See Matt 1:2; Lk 3:34
Through Jacob	. . . .*all peoples on earth will be blessed through you [Jacob] and your offspring.* (Gen 28:14, 1760 BC); See Gen 46:2-4 I see him, but not now I behold him, but not near. *A star will come out of Jacob; a scepter will rise out of Israel.* (Num 24:17, 19)	This is the genealogy of Jesus the Messiah the son of David, the son of Abraham: . . .Isaac the father of *Jacob*, Jacob the father of Judah . . . (Matt 1:1-2, 5 BC) See Luke 3:34; Rev 22:16
Descendant of Judah	*The scepter will not depart from Judah*, nor the ruler's staff from between his feet. . . (Gen 49:10, 1689 BC) *NOTE: The scepter (the symbol of government) was taken away when Judea paid her first taxes to Rome. Then in Bethlehem of Judea, Yeshua was born.*[74]	For it is clear that *our Lord descended from Judah*. . . (Heb 7:14, AD 64; see Matt 1:2-3; Lk 3:33)
Descendant of David & Heir to his Throne **Perpetual Dynasty**	When your [David] days are over and you rest with your ancestors, *I will raise up your offspring to succeed you,* your own flesh and blood, and I will establish his kingdom. . .and *I will establish the throne of his kingdom forever.* (2 Sam 7:12-13, 1042 BC) "The days are coming," declares the LORD, "when *I will raise up for David a righteous Branch, a King* who will reign wisely and do what is just and right in the land." (Jer 23:5); See 1 Chron 17:4-14; 1 Ki 8:15, 24; Isa 9:6-7; 11:1-5	This is the genealogy of Jesus the Messiah the **son of David** (Matt 1:1, 6) *From this man's [David's] descendants* God has brought to Israel the Savior Jesus, as he promised. (Acts 13:22-23, AD 45) . . . who as to his earthly life was *a descendant of David*. . . (Rom 1:3-4, AD 60)

SOURCES FOR JESUS IN THE INJEEL

Original Source Old Testament Promises, Predictions & Foreshadowings	New Testament Completion

1. MESSIAH'S BIRTH

Will Come 483 years (69 x 7) after rebuilding Jerusalem's wall	Know and understand this: From the time the word goes out to restore and rebuild Jerusalem until the Anointed One, the ruler, comes, there will be seven 'sevens,' and sixty-two 'sevens.' It will be rebuilt with streets and a trench, but in times of trouble. (Dan 9:24-26)	*But when the set time had fully come, God sent his Son . . . (Gal 4:4-5)* In those days Caesar Augustus issued a decree that a census should be taken of the entire Roman world [for taxation]. (Lk 2:1, 5 BC) See Matt 2:1, 16, 19; Lk 1:26- 35; 3:1, 23
Have Eternal Existence	But you, Bethlehem Ephrathah, *Though* you are little among the thousands of Judah, *Yet out of you shall come forth to Me The One to be Ruler in Israel, Whose goings forth are from of old, From everlasting.* (Mic 5:1-2 NKJV)	*In the beginning was the Word,* and the Word was with God, and the Word was God. He was **in** *the beginning with God.* . .And the Word became flesh and dwelt among us, and *we beheld His glory,* the glory as of the one and only of the Father, full of grace and truth. (Jn 1:1, 14; 8:58) See Eph 1:3-4; Col 1:15-19; Rev 1:18
Born of a Virgin	Therefore the LORD himself will give you a sign: *The virgin will conceive and give birth to a son,* and will call him Immanuel. (Isa 7:14, 742 BC)	This is how the birth of Jesus the Messiah came about: His mother Mary was pledged to be married to Joseph, but *before they came together, she was found to be pregnant through the Holy Spirit.* (Matt 1:18, 21, 4 BC)
Born in Bethlehem of Judea	But you, *Bethlehem Ephrathah. . .out* of you will come for me one who will be ruler over Israel, whose origins are from of old, from ancient times. (Mic 5:1-2, 710 BC)	Jesus was *born in Bethlehem in Judea. . .* (Matt 2:1, 4 BC) See Lk 1:34-37; 2:4-7
Be the Son of God	I will declare the decree: The Lord has said to Me, "*You are My Son,* Today I have begotten You." (Ps 2:7; Prov 30:4) For to us a child is born, to us *a son is given,* and the government will be on his shoulders. And he will be called Wonderful Counselor, Mighty God, Everlasting Father, Prince of Peace. (Isaiah 9:6)	*The* Holy Spirit will come upon you, and the power of the Highest will overshadow you; therefore, also, that *Holy One who is to be born will be called the Son of God.* (Lk 1:35; See Matt 3:17)

SOURCES FOR JESUS IN THE INJEEL

	Original Source Old Testament Promises, Predictions & Foreshadowings	New Testament Completion
Have God's own Name Applied to Him	This is *the name* by which he will be called: *'The LORD Our Righteous Savior.'* (Jer 23:5-6) And he will be *called* 'Wonderful Counselor, Mighty God, Everlasting Father, Prince of Peace.' (Isa 9:5-6)	She will give birth to a son, and you are to give him the name *Jesus*, because he will save his people from their sins. (Matthew 1:21) *NOTE: The name Jesus means "The LORD saves!"* Therefore *God exalted him* to the highest place and *gave him the name that is above every name, that at the name of Jesus* every knee should bow, in heaven and on earth and under the earth, and every tongue acknowledge that *Jesus Christ is Lord,* to the glory of God the Father. (Phil 2:9-11)
Great Persons to Adore Him	May the *kings of Tarshish and of distant shores bring tribute to him.* May the kings of Sheba and Seba present him gifts. May *all kings bow down to him* and all nations serve him. (Ps 72:10, 52 BC)	*Magi from the east* came to Jerusalem and asked, "Where is the one who has been born king of the Jews? We saw his star when it rose and have come to worship him." . . . they saw the child with his mother Mary, and *they bowed down and worshiped him.* Then they opened their treasures and presented him with gifts of gold, frankincense and myrrh. (Matt 2:1, 2, 11, 4 BC)
2. MESSIAH'S FORERUNNER		
Preceded by One who would Announce Him	*I will send my messenger, who will prepare the way before me. Then suddenly the Lord you are seeking will come.* . .(Mal 3:1, 397 BC; See Isa 40:3-5)	And he [John the Baptizer] will go on before the Lord . . . *to make ready a people prepared for the Lord.* (Lk 1:17, 7 BC) See Matt 3:1-3; Lk 3:2-6

SOURCES FOR JESUS IN THE INJEEL

Original Source Old Testament Promises, Predictions & Foreshadowings	New Testament Completion
3. MESSIAH'S LIFE & MINISTRY	

	Original Source	New Testament Completion
Be Anointed with the Spirit of God	*The Spirit of the LORD will rest on him*—the Spirit of wisdom and of understanding, the Spirit of counsel and of might, the Spirit of the knowledge and fear of the LORD . . . . (Isa 11:2, 713 BC) . . . therefore God, your God, has set you [Christ] above your companions by *anointing you with the oil of joy.* (Ps 45:6-8)	As soon as Jesus was baptized, he went up out of the water. At that moment heaven was opened, and he saw *the Spirit of God descending like a dove and alighting on him.* (Matt 3:16, AD 30) For the one whom God has sent speaks the words of God, for *God gives the Spirit without limit.* (Jn 3:34, AD 30) You know . . . how *God anointed Jesus of Nazareth with the Holy Spirit and power.* . . (Acts 10:38)
Entered Public Ministry Identified as the "Anointed One"	*The Spirit of the Sovereign LORD... has anointed me* to proclaim good news to the poor. He has sent me to bind up the brokenhearted, to proclaim freedom for the captives and release from darkness for the prisoners, to proclaim the year of the Lord's favor to comfort all who mourn. . . (Isaiah 61:1-3, 698 BC)	*Jesus' First Sermon* – Unrolling the scroll, he found the place where it is written: "*The Spirit of the Lord is on me, because he has anointed me* to proclaim good news to the poor". . . Then he rolled up the scroll, gave it back to the attendant and sat down. . . . He began by saying to them, *"Today this scripture is fulfilled in your hearing."* (Luke 4:18-21, AD 30)
Begin His Ministry in Galilee	In the past he humbled the land of Zebulun and the land of Naphtali, but in the future *he will honor Galilee of the nations,* by the Way of the Sea, beyond the Jordan—The people walking in darkness have seen a great light; *on those living in the land of deep darkness a light has dawned.* (Isa 9:1-2, 740 BC) See Isa 8:23-9:2	*Jesus withdrew to Galilee. He went and lived in Capernaum,* which was by the lake in the area of Zebulun and Naphtali— to fulfill what was said through the prophet Isaiah. . . (Matt 4:12, 16, 23, AD 30)
Be a Prophet like Moses	The LORD your God will raise up for you a *prophet like me [Moses] from among you, from your fellow Israelites.* You must listen to him. (Deut 18:15, 18)	But this is how God fulfilled what he had foretold through all the prophets, . . . that he *may send the Messiah,* who has been appointed for you— *even Jesus.* . . . as he promised long ago through his holy prophets. For Moses said, "*The Lord your God will raise up for you a prophet like me. . .*" (Acts 3:20-22, AD 33)

SOURCES FOR JESUS IN THE INJEEL

	Original Source Old Testament Promises, Predictions & Foreshadowings	New Testament Completion
Have Humble Beginnings	He grew up before him like a tender shoot, and like a root out of dry ground. He *had no beauty or majesty to attract us to him*... (Isa 53:2)	*"Isn't this the carpenter?* Isn't this Mary's son and the brother of James, Joseph, Judas and Simon? Aren't his sisters here with us?"* (Mk 6:3, AD 32) Jesus replied, "Foxes have dens and birds have nests, but *the Son of Man has no place to lay his head."* (Lk 9:58, AD 32)
Be Meek and Lack Ostentation	He *will not shout or cry out,* or raise his voice in the streets. (Isa 42:2)	A large crowd followed him, and he *healed all who were ill. He warned them not to tell others about him.* This was to fulfill what was spoken through the prophet Isaiah: "... He will not quarrel or cry out; no one will hear his voice in the streets." (Matt 12:15-16, 19, AD 31)
Have Ministry of Binding up the Brokenhearted	He has sent me to *bind up the brokenhearted ... to comfort all who mourn ...* to bestow on them a crown of beauty instead of ashes, the oil of joy instead of mourning, and a garment of praise instead of a spirit of despair. (Isa 61:1-2)	*"Come to me, all you who are weary and burdened, and I will give you rest.* Take my yoke upon you and learn from me, for *I am gentle and humble in heart, and you will find rest for your souls.* For my yoke is easy and my burden is light." (Matt 11:28-30)
Be Tender and Compassionate	He tends his flock like a shepherd: He *gathers the lambs in his arms and carries them close to his heart; he gently leads those that have young.* (Isa 40:11, 712 BC) *A bruised reed he will not break, and a smoldering wick he will not snuff out.* In faithfulness he will bring forth justice; (Isa 42:3, 11; 712 BC)	A large crowd followed him, and he *healed all who were ill.* This was to fulfill what was spoken through the prophet Isaiah: "*A bruised reed he will not break,* and a smoldering wick he will not snuff out, till he has brought justice through to victory." (Matt 12:15, 20, AD 31) *For we do not have a high priest who is unable to empathize with our weaknesses,* but we have one who has been tempted in every way, just as we are—yet he did not sin. (Heb 4:15, AD 64)
Have Ministry of Healing	Then will the *eyes of the blind* be opened and the *ears of the deaf* unstopped. Then will the *lame leap* like a deer, and the *mute tongue* shout for joy. (Isa 35:5-6, 712 BC)	Jesus replied, "*Go back and report to John (Yahya) what you hear and see:* The *blind* receive sight, the *lame* walk, those who have *leprosy* are cleansed, the *deaf* hear, the *dead* are raised, and the good news is proclaimed to the poor. Blessed is anyone who does not stumble on account of me." (Matt 11:4-6, throughout the Gospels; AD 31)

SOURCES FOR JESUS IN THE INJEEL

Original Source Old Testament Promises, Predictions & Foreshadowings	New Testament Completion
Rejected by His Brothers	I am a *foreigner to my own family,* a stranger to my own mother's children; (Ps 69:8) See Isa 53:2-3; 63:3-5	He came to that which was his own, but *his own did not receive him.* (Jn 1:11, AD 30) Jesus' brothers said to him, "Leave Galilee and go to Judea... *For even his own brothers did not believe in him.*" (Jn 7:3, 5, AD 32) See Mark 3:21; 6:3
Enter Jerusalem on a Donkey	Rejoice greatly, Daughter Zion!...See, *your king comes to you,* righteous and victorious, *lowly and riding on a donkey,* on a colt, the foal of a donkey. (Zech 9:9, 487 BC)	This took place to fulfill what was spoken through the prophet [Zechariah]: "Say to Daughter Zion, 'See, your king comes to you, gentle and riding on a donkey, and on a colt, the foal of a donkey.'" *They brought the donkey and the colt and placed their cloaks on them for Jesus to sit on.* ...The crowds that went ahead of him and those that followed shouted, "Hosanna to the Son of David!"... When Jesus entered Jerusalem, the whole city was stirred and asked, "Who is this?" (Matt 21:4-5, 7, 9-11, AD 33; See Mk 1:1-11)
Enter the Temple with Authority	Then *suddenly the LORD you are seeking will come to his temple;* (Mal 3:1, 397 BC) Has *this house, which bears my Name,* become a *den of robbers* to you? (Jer 7:11)	When *Jesus entered the temple courts, he began to drive out those who were selling.* "It is written," he said to them, *"My house* will be a house of prayer'; but you have made it 'a den of robbers." (Lk 19:45-46; See Matt 21:12-24)
Be the Greater Temple	"I will shake all nations, and what is desired by all nations will come, and I will fill this house [Temple] with glory," says the LORD Almighty. *"The glory of this present house will be greater than the glory of the former house,"* says the LORD Almighty. "And *in this place I will grant peace,"* declares the LORD Almighty. (Hag 2:7, 9, 520 BC)	*The Word became flesh* and made *his dwelling* [skene, *"tabernacle"] among us.* We have seen his glory... (Jn 1:14) "*Destroy this temple, and I will raise it again in three days."* They replied, "It has taken forty-six years to build this temple, and you are going to raise it in three days?" *But the temple he had spoken of was his body.* (Jn 2:19-21)

SOURCES FOR JESUS IN THE INJEEL

Original Source Old Testament Promises, Predictions & Foreshadowings	New Testament Completion
4. MESSIAH'S SUFFERING & DEATH	

	Original Source Old Testament Promises, Predictions & Foreshadowings	New Testament Completion
Time of Messiah's Death **"Cut Off and have nothing" 69 x 7 years after Rebuilding of Wall of Jerusalem**	*After the sixty-two 'sevens,' the Anointed One [Messiah] will be put to death* ["cut off"] *and will have nothing. The people of the ruler who will come will destroy the city [Jerusalem] and the sanctuary. The end will come like a flood: War will continue until the end, and desolations have been decreed.* (Dan 9:26-27, 537 BC) *NOTE: The Messiah would be "cut off" before the Romans would destroy the Temple in Jerusalem, which occurred in AD 70.*	With a loud cry, Jesus breathed his last. (Mk 15:37, AD 33) As he approached Jerusalem and saw the city, he wept over it and said, *"If you, even you, had only known on this day what would bring you peace—but now it is hidden from your eyes. The days will come upon you when your enemies will build an embankment against you and encircle you and hem you in on every side. . .because you did not recognize the time of God's coming to you."* (Lk 19:41-44, AD 33) See Matt 24:2; Mk 13:2; Lk 21:6
Approach Holy God Only through Blood Sacrifice	For the life of a creature is in the blood, and I have given it to you to make atonement for yourselves on the altar; *it is the blood that makes atonement for one's life.* (Tawrat, Lev 17:11)	The law [of Moses] requires that nearly everything be cleansed with blood, and *without the shedding of blood there is no forgiveness.* (Heb 9:22, AD 64)
Be a Priest	The Lord has sworn and will not change his mind: *"You are a priest forever, in the order of Melchizedek."* (Ps 110:4)	Son though he was, he learned obedience from what he suffered and, once made perfect, he became the source of eternal salvation for all who obey him and was *designated by God to be high priest* in the order of Melchizedek. (Hebrews 5:8-10) We have this hope as an anchor for the soul, firm and secure. It enters the inner sanctuary behind the curtain, where our forerunner, Jesus, has entered on our behalf. *He has become a high priest forever,* in the order of Melchizedek. (Heb 6:19-20. See Heb 7:15-17; 9:12)

SOURCES FOR JESUS IN THE INJEEL

	Original Source Old Testament Promises, Predictions & Foreshadowings	New Testament Completion
Be the Passover Lamb	*Each man is to take a lamb for his family, . . .* [It] must be year-old *males without defect.* "On that same night I will pass through Egypt and . . . I will bring judgment on all the gods of Egypt. I am the LORD. The blood will be a sign for you on the houses where you are, and *when I see the blood, I will pass over you.* (Tawrat, Exo 12:3-5; 12-13)	The next day John saw Jesus coming toward him and said, "Look, *the Lamb of God, who takes away the sin of the world!*" (Jn 1:29); See Matt 26:2, 18, 26-29; 1 Cor 5:7-8
Be Sinless & without Guile	. . . he had *done no violence, nor was any deceit in his mouth.* (Isa 53:9, 712 BC)	*He committed no sin, and no deceit was found in his mouth.* (1 Pet 2:22, AD 60)
Bear Reproaches Due Others	*The insults of those who insult you fall on me.* When I weep and fast, I must endure scorn; when I put on sackcloth, people make sport of me. Those who sit at the gate mock me, and *I am the song of the drunkards.* (Ps 69:9-12). See Isa 53:11-12	For even *Christ did not please himself* but, as it is written: "The insults of those who insult you have fallen on me." (Rom 15:3, AD 60)
Be Hated without a Cause	*Those who hate me without reason* outnumber the hairs of my head; many are *my enemies without cause,* those who seek to destroy me. (Ps 69:4) This is what the Lord says—the Redeemer and Holy One of Israel—to him who was *despised and abhorred by the nation.* (Isa 49:7, 712 BC)	If I had not done among them the works no one else did, they would not be guilty of sin. As it is, they have seen, and *yet they have hated both me and my Father.* But this is to fulfill what is written in their Law: 'They hated me without reason.' (Jn 15:24-25, AD 33)
Be Rejected by Jewish Rulers	*The stone the builders rejected has become the cornerstone;* (Ps 118:22)	Jesus said to them, "Have you never read in the Scriptures: '*The stone the builders rejected has become the cornerstone;* the Lord has done this, and it is marvelous in our eyes'"? (Matt 21:42, AD 33). See Jn 7:48

SOURCES FOR JESUS IN THE INJEEL

	Original Source Old Testament Promises, Predictions & Foreshadowings	New Testament Completion
Be Plotted Against by Jews & Gentiles Together	Why do the *nations conspire and the peoples plot in vain?* The kings of the earth rise up and *the rulers band together against the LORD and against his anointed.* (Ps 2:1-2)	Indeed *Herod and Pontius Pilate met together with the Gentiles* and the people of Israel in this city to conspire against your holy servant Jesus, whom you anointed. (Acts 4:27, AD 33)
Would Suffer Willingly	He was oppressed and afflicted, yet *he did not open his mouth; he was led like a lamb to the slaughter,* and as a sheep before its shearers is silent, so *he did not open his mouth.* (Isa 53:7, 710 BC)	Then the high priest stood up and said to Jesus, "Are you not going to answer? What is this testimony that these men are bringing against you?" *But Jesus remained silent.* (Matt 26:63, AD 33) When he was accused by the chief priests and the elders, he gave no answer. Then Pilate asked him, "Don't you hear the testimony they are bringing against you?" *But Jesus made no reply, not even to a single charge*—to the great amazement of the governor. (Matt 27:12, 14, AD 33) When they hurled their insults at him, *he did not retaliate;* when he suffered, *he made no threats.* Instead, *he entrusted himself* to him who judges justly. (1 Pet 2:23, AD 60)
Be Betrayed by a Friend	Even *my close friend,* someone I trusted, *one who shared my bread, has turned against me.* (Ps 41:9; See Ps 55:13-15)	*Jesus:* 'But this is to fulfill this passage of Scripture: 'He who shared my bread has turned against me.' I am telling you now before it happens, so that when it does happen you will believe that I am who I am.' After he had said this, *Jesus was troubled in spirit* and testified, 'Very truly I tell you, *one of you is going to betray me.*' (Jn 13:18-21, AD 33) See Matt 26:21-25, 47-50; Acts 1:16-18
Be Forsaken by His Own Disciples	"Awake, sword, against my shepherd, against the man who is close to me!" declares the LORD Almighty. *"Strike the shepherd, and the sheep will be scattered. . ."* (Zech 13:8, 48 BC)	[At Jesus' arrest] Then all the disciples *deserted him and fled.* (Matt 26:15, AD 33; See Matt 26:31, 52)

SOURCES FOR JESUS IN THE INJEEL		
	Original Source Old Testament Promises, Predictions & Foreshadowings	**New Testament Completion**
Be Sold for 30 Pieces of Silver	I told them, "If you think it best, give me my pay; but if not, keep it." *So they paid me thirty pieces of silver.* (Zec 11:12, 487 BC)	"What are you willing to give me if I deliver him over to you?" So *they counted out for him thirty pieces of silver.* From then on Judas watched for an opportunity to hand him over. (Matt 26:15, AD 33)
Have His Price Thrown into Temple Treasury	And the LORD said to me, "Throw it to the potter—the handsome price at which they *valued me!" So I took the thirty pieces of silver and threw them to the potter at the house of the LORD.* (Zec 11:13, BC 487)	When Judas, who had betrayed him, saw that Jesus was condemned, he was seized with *remorse and returned the thirty pieces of silver to the chief priests and the elders.*
Be Struck on the Cheek	They will *strike Israel's ruler on the cheek with a rod.* (Mic 5:1, 710 BC; See Mic 4:1-5)	"I have sinned," he said, "for I have betrayed innocent blood." So they (chief priest) decided *to use the money to buy the potter's field as a burial place* for foreigners. That is why it has been called the Field of Blood to this day. (Matt 27:3, 7, AD 33) *They took the staff and struck him on the head again and again. (*Matt 27:30, AD 33)
Be Spat upon & Beaten	*I offered my back to those who beat me,* my cheeks to those who pulled out my beard; I did not hide my face from *mocking and spitting.* (Isa 50:6, 712 BC)	Then some began to *spit at him*; they blindfolded him, *struck him with their fists,* and said, "Prophesy!" And the guards took him and beat him. (Mk 14:65, AD 33) See Matt 26:67; 27:30 Then Pilate took Jesus and had him *flogged.* (Jn 19:1, AD 33)
Be Executed by Crucifixion by having His Hands & Feet Pierced	Dogs surround me, a pack of villains encircles me; *they pierce my hands and my feet. All my bones are on display; people stare and gloat over me.* (Ps 22:16-17); See Zech 12:10	There *they crucified him*, and with him two others—one on each side and Jesus in the middle. (Jn 19:18, AD 33) See Matt 27:35; Lk 24:39; Jn 19:34-35; Rev 1:7 Unless I [Thomas] *see the nail marks* in his hands and put my finger where the nails were, and put my hand into his side, I will not believe. (Jn 20:25, AD 33)

SOURCES FOR JESUS IN THE INJEEL

	Original Source Old Testament Promises, Predictions & Foreshadowings	New Testament Completion
Feel Forsaken by God	*My God, my God, why have you forsaken me? Why are you so far from saving me, so far from my cries of anguish?* (Ps 22:1-2)	About three in the afternoon *Jesus cried out in a loud voice, **"Eli, Eli, lema sabachthani?"*** (which means "My God, my God, why have you forsaken me?"). (Matt 27:46, AD 33)
Be Mocked	*All who see me mock me;* they *hurl insults, shaking their heads.* "He trusts in the LORD," they say, "let the LORD rescue him. Let him deliver him, since he delights in him." (Ps 22:7-8)	Those who passed by *hurled insults at him,* shaking their heads and saying, "You who are going to destroy the temple and build it in three days, save yourself! Come down from the cross, if you are the Son of God!" In the same way the chief priests, the teachers of the law and *the elders mocked him.* *"He saved others,"* they said, *"but he can't save himself!* He's the king of Israel! Let him come down now from the cross, and we will believe in him. He trusts in God. *Let God rescue him now if he wants him,* for he said, 'I am the Son of God.'" In the same way the rebels who were crucified with him also *heaped insults* on him. (Matt 27:39-44) See Matt 26:67
Be Thirsty during His Execution	*My mouth is dried up* like a potsherd, and my tongue sticks to the roof of my mouth; (Ps 22:15)	Jesus said, *"I am thirsty."* (Jn 19:28)
Be Given Gall and Vinegar to Quench His Thirst	*They put gall in my food and gave me vinegar for my thirst.* (Ps 69:21)	There they offered Jesus *wine to drink, mixed with gall;* but after tasting it, he refused to drink it. (Matt 27:34, AD 33)

SOURCES FOR JESUS IN THE INJEEL

	Original Source Old Testament Promises, Predictions & Foreshadowings	New Testament Completion
Suffered to an Extreme Degree	*I am poured out like water, and all my bones are out of joint.* My heart has turned to wax; it has melted within me. My mouth is dried up like a potsherd, and my tongue sticks to the roof of my mouth; you lay me in the dust of death. (Ps 22:14-15)	*Jesus* [On eve of his death]: "Father, if you are willing, take this cup from me; yet not my will, but yours be done." And *being in anguish,* he prayed more earnestly, and *his sweat was like drops of blood falling to the ground.* (Lk 22:42, 44, AD 33)
Be Executed without a Bone Broken **Be the One Whose Death would Atone for the Sins of Mankind**	...slaughter of the *Passover lamb....* *Do not break any of the bones.* (Tawrat, Exo 12:3, 21, 46, 1400 BC) He [God] protects all his bones, *not one of them will be broken.* (Ps 34:20) *Surely he took up our pain and bore our suffering,* yet we considered him punished by God, stricken by him, and afflicted. But he *was pierced for our transgressions, he was crushed for our iniquities;* the punishment that brought us peace was on him, and by his wounds we are healed. We all, like sheep, have gone astray, each of us has turned to our own way; and *the LORD has laid on him the iniquity of us all...* he poured out his life unto death, and was numbered with the transgressors. For *he bore the sin of many, and made intercession for the transgressors.* (Isa 53:4-6, 12, 710 BC)	But when they came to Jesus and found that he was already dead, *they did not break his legs...* These things happened so that the scripture would be fulfilled: "Not one of his bones will be broken" (Jn 19:33, 36, AD 33) The Son of Man did not come to be served, but to serve, and *to give his life as a ransom for many.* (Matt 27:34, AD 33) Mk 10:45; Jn 1:29; 3:16; Acts 8:30-35 For you know that it was not with perishable things such as silver or gold that *you were redeemed from the empty way of life* handed down to you from your ancestors, but *with the precious blood of Christ, a lamb without blemish or defect.* (1 Pet 1:18-19) *God made him who had no sin to be sin for us,* so that in him we might become the righteous-ness of God. (2 Cor 5:21) You see... *Christ died for the ungodly.* Very rarely will anyone die for a righteous person, though for a good person someone might possibly dare to die. But God demonstrates his own love for us in this: *While we were still sinners, Christ died for us.* (Rom 5:6-8)
His Garments Parted and Lots Cast for His Robe	They divide my clothes among them and *cast lots for my garment.* (Ps 22:18)	When they had crucified him, *they divided up his clothes by casting lots.* (Matt 27:35, AD 33)
Be Considered a Transgressor	He poured out his life unto death, and was *numbered with the transgressors.* (Isa 53:12, 712 BC)	They crucified *two rebels with him,* one on his right and one on his left. (Mk 15:27-28, AD 33); See Matt 27:3; Lk 23:32

SOURCES FOR JESUS IN THE INJEEL

	Original Source Old Testament Promises, Predictions & Foreshadowings	New Testament Completion
Intercede for His Executioners	For he *made intercession for the transgressors.* (Isa 53:12, 712 BC)	They crucified him there. Jesus said, *"Father, forgive them,* for they do not know what they are doing." (Lk 23:34, AD 33)
Be Pierced with a Sword	They will look on me, the one they have *pierced*. . . (Zec 12:10, 487 BC)	Instead, one of the *soldiers pierced Jesus' side with a spear,* bringing a sudden flow of blood and water. . . (Jn 19:34, 37, AD 30)
Buried With the Rich	He was *assigned a grave* with the wicked, and *with the rich in his death.* . . (Isa 53:9, 712 BC)	. . .there came a *rich man from Arimathea, named Joseph,* who had himself become a disciple of Jesus. . .he asked for Jesus' body, and Pilate ordered that it be given to him. *Joseph took the body,* wrapped it in a clean linen cloth, and *placed it in his own new tomb that he had cut out of the rock.* (Matt 27:57-60, AD 33)
Be Mediator of the New Covenant	*God's first covenant with Moses and Israel: See Exo 19:1-6; 24:1-8* "The days are coming," declares the LORD, "when *I will make a new covenant* with the people of Israel and with the people of Judah. It will not be like the covenant I made with their ancestors when I took them by the hand to lead them out of Egypt, because *they broke my covenant,* though I was a husband to them," declares the LORD. "This is the covenant I will make with the people of Israel after that time," declares the LORD. *"I will put my law in their minds and write it on their hearts. I will be their God, and they will be my people.* . .*For I will forgive their wickedness and will remember their sins no more."* (Jer 31:31-37)	*Jesus' Death Satisfies & Completes Sacrificial Requirements* For if there had been nothing wrong with that *first covenant,* no place would have been sought for another. But God found fault with the people. . . (Heb 8:7-8) . . .*He has appeared once for all at the culmination of the ages to do away with sin by the sacrifice of Himself.* (Heb 9:26) But *when Christ came as high priest* of the good things that are now already here, he went through the greater and more perfect tabernacle that is not made with human hands, that is to say, is not a part of this creation. He did not enter by means of the blood of goats and calves; but *he entered the Most Holy Place once for all by his own blood, thus obtaining eternal redemption.* (Heb 9:11-12) For this reason *Christ is the mediator of a new covenant,* that those who are called may receive the promised eternal inheritance— now that he has died as a ransom to set them free from the sins committed under the first covenant. (Heb 9:15)

SOURCES FOR JESUS IN THE INJEEL

	Original Source Old Testament Promises, Predictions & Foreshadowings	New Testament Completion
5. MESSIAH'S RESURRECTION & ASCENSION		
Be Raised from the Dead	Therefore my heart is glad and my tongue rejoices; my body also will rest secure, because *you will not abandon me to the realm of the dead, You make known to me the path of life;* (Ps 16:9-11) See Ps 2:7-8 Yet it was the LORD's will to crush him and cause him to suffer, and though the Lord makes his life an offering for sin, **he will see his offspring and prolong his days**, and the will of the LORD will prosper in his hand. (Isa 53:10, 712 BC)	[Sunday following his crucifixion] "Why do you look for the living among the dead? He is not here; he has risen!" *Jesus himself stood among them* [the Eleven] and said to them, "Peace be with you. Why are you troubled, and why do doubts rise in your minds? Look at my hands and my feet. *It is I myself! Touch me and see;* a ghost does not have flesh and bones, as you see I have." (Lk 24:6, 34, 38, AD 33) See Matt 28:1-20; Acts 2:23-26; 10:40-42; 13:33-35; 1 Cor 15:4-6
His Body Would Not Undergo Corruption	*[The LORD will not] let your faithful one see decay.* (Ps 16:8-11)	Seeing what was to come, he [David] spoke of the resurrection of the Messiah, that *he was not abandoned to the realm of the dead, nor did his body see decay.* (Acts 2:31, AD 33)
Ascended to Right Hand of God	When you *ascended on high*, you took many captives; you received gifts from people, even from the rebellious— *that you, LORD God, might dwell there.* (Ps 68:18; See Ps 68:19)	While he was blessing them, he left them and was *taken up into heaven.* (Lk 24:51, AD 33) See Acts 1:9-4; 7:55
Sits at God's Right Hand	You make known to me the path of life; *you will fill me with joy in your presence, with eternal pleasures at your right hand.* (Ps 16:11) The LORD says to my Lord: *"Sit at my right hand* until I make your enemies a footstool for your feet." (Ps 110:1)	After he had provided purification for sins, *he sat down at the right hand of the Majesty in heaven.* (Heb 1:3, AD 60)

SOURCES FOR JESUS IN THE INJEEL

	Original Source Old Testament Promises, Predictions & Foreshadowings	New Testament Completion
Giver of the Holy Spirit	*I will pour out my Spirit on all people.* Your sons and daughters will prophesy, your old men will dream dreams, your young men will see visions. Even on my servants, both men and women, I will pour out my Spirit in those days. (J. P.l 2:28-29) *I will sprinkle clean water on you, and you will be clean;* I will cleanse you from all your impurities and from all your idols. *I will give you a new heart and put a new spirit in you; I will remove from you your heart of stone and give you a heart of flesh. And I will put my Spirit in you* and move you to follow my decrees and be careful to keep my laws. (Ezek 36:25-27)	*Christ promised the Holy Spirit* *I am going to send you what my Father has promised*; but stay in the city until you have been clothed with power from on high. (Lk 24:49) And I will ask the Father, and *he will give you another Advocate to help you and be with you forever—the Spirit of truth.* (Jn 14:16) Do not leave Jerusalem, but *wait for the gift my Father promised,* which you have heard me speak about. For John baptized with water, but in a few days *you will be baptized with the Holy Spirit.* (Acts 1:4) *Christ sent the Spirit* (Acts 2) *All of them were filled with the Holy Spirit.* . . (Acts 2:4) Exalted to the right hand of God, he has received from the Father the promised Holy Spirit and has *poured out* what you now see and hear. (Acts 2:33) Peter replied, "Repent and be baptized, every one of you, in the name of Jesus Christ for the forgiveness of your sins. And *you will receive the gift of the Holy Spirit.* The promise is for you and your children and for all who are far off—for all whom the Lord our God will call." (Acts 2:38, 39)
Intercedes in Heaven for Us	It is he who will build the temple of the LORD, and he will be *clothed with majesty and will sit and rule on his throne. And he will be a priest on his throne.* (Zech 6:13, 519 BC)	Therefore, brothers and sisters, since we have confidence to enter the Most Holy Place by the blood of Jesus, by a new and living way opened for us through the curtain, that is, his body, and since *we have a great priest over the house of God, let us draw near to God* with a sincere heart and with the full assurance that faith brings. (Heb 10:19-22) See Heb 7:25-8:2 It is God who justifies. Who then is the one who condemns? No one. Christ Jesus who died— more than that, who was raised to life—*is at the right hand of God and is also interceding for us.* (Rom 8:33-34, AD 60)

SOURCES FOR JESUS IN THE INJEEL

	Original Source Old Testament Promises, Predictions & Foreshadowings	New Testament Completion
Be the Cornerstone of God's Messianic Community	So this is what the Sovereign Lord says: "See, *I lay a stone in Zion, a tested stone, a precious cornerstone* for a sure foundation; the one who relies on it will never be stricken with panic." (Isa 28:16, BC 712; See Psa 118:22-23)	You also, like living stones, are being built into a spiritual house to be a holy priesthood, offering spiritual sacrifices acceptable to God through Jesus Christ. For in Scripture it says: "See, *I lay a stone in Zion, a chosen and precious cornerstone,* and the one who trusts in him will never be put to shame." Now to you who believe, *this stone is precious.* But to those who do not believe, . . . "A stone that causes people to stumble and a rock that makes them fall." (1 Pet 2:5-7, AD 60) See Matt 21:42; Eph 2:20e
Reign as King	I have installed my king on Zion, my holy mountain. (Ps 2:6) *Of the greatness of his government and peace there will be no end.* He will reign on David's throne and over his kingdom, establishing and upholding it with justice and righteousness from that time on and forever. (Isaiah 9:7)	Pilate then went back inside the palace, summoned Jesus and asked him, "Are you the king of the Jews?" Jesus answered, "You say that I am a king. In fact, the reason I was born and came into the world is to testify to the truth. Everyone on the side of truth listens to me." (Jn 18:33, 37, AD 33) On his robe and on his thigh he has this name written: '*King of kings and Lord of lords.*' (Rev 20:16-17)
6. MESSIAH'S SALVATION PROVIDED FOR ALL		
Be Sought After by Gentiles as well as Jews	In that day the Root of Jesse [Messiah] will stand as a *banner for the peoples; the nations will rally to him,* and his resting place will be glorious. (Isa 11:10, 713 BC) See Isa 42:1	Some *Greeks . . . at the festival came to Philip . . . with a request. "Sir," they said, "we would like to see Jesus."* (John 12:21-23)
Be Accepted by the Gentiles	It is too small a thing for you to be my servant to restore the tribes of Jacob and bring back those of Israel I have kept. *I will also make you a light for the Gentiles, that my salvation may reach to the ends of the earth.* (Isa 49:6) See Isa 11:10; 42:1-4; 49:1-6	The circumcised believers [Jewish Christians] who had come with Peter were astonished that *the gift of the Holy Spirit had been poured out even on Gentiles.* (Acts 10:45, AD 41); See Acts 13:46-48; Matt 12:18-21; Rom 9:30; 10:20; 11:11; 15:10 *Jesus unites believing Jews and Gentiles* (non-Jews): See Eph 2:11-18; 3:6; Gal 3:8, 29; 4:28; Acts 2:38-39; Rom 9:8; Heb 11:39-40

SOURCES FOR JESUS IN THE INJEEL		
	Original Source Old Testament Promises, Predictions & Foreshadowings	**New Testament Completion**
Be Seen by Israel as Pierced	*They will look on me, the one they have pierced, and they will mourn for him* as one mourns for an only child, and *grieve bitterly for him* as one grieves for a firstborn son. (Zech 12:10; See Ps 22:17)	One of the soldiers pierced Jesus' side with a spear, bringing a sudden flow of blood and water. The man who saw it has given testimony, and his testimony is true. He knows that he tells the truth, and he testifies so that you also may believe. . .as another scripture says, "They will look on the one they have pierced." (Jn 19:34-37) Lk 24:39; Rev 1:7 "Look, he is coming with the clouds," and "every eye will see him, *even those who pierced him"; and all peoples on earth "will mourn because of him.*" (Rev 1:7)
7. MESSIAH'S RETURN		
Jesus will Come Again	"See, *I will create new heavens and a new earth. The former things will not be remembered,* nor will they come to mind. But be glad and rejoice forever in what I will create, for I will create Jerusalem to be a delight and its people a joy. I will rejoice over Jerusalem and take delight in my people; *the sound of weeping and of crying will be heard in it no more. . . .*The wolf and the lamb will feed together, and the lion will eat straw like the ox, and dust will be the serpent's food. They will neither harm nor destroy on all my holy mountain," says the Lord. (Isa 65:17-25; See also Isa 11:3-10)	Just as people are destined to die once, and after that to face judgment, so Christ was sacrificed once to take away the sins of many; and *he will appear a second time,* not to bear sin, but *to bring salvation to those who are waiting for him.* (Heb 9:27-28; See 2 Pet 3:4, 9, 13; 1 John 2:25; Jas 1:12; 2:25) *Resurrection of the dead:* See Jn 5:28-29; 1 Thess 4:15-18 *Then I saw "a new heaven and a new earth,"* for the first heaven and the first earth had passed away, and there was no longer any sea. . . . Look! *God's dwelling place is now among the people, and he will dwell with them.* They will be his people, and God himself will be with them and be their God. *He will wipe every tear from their eyes. There will be no more death' or mourning or crying or pain, for the old order of things has passed away.* (Rev 21:1-4)

Summary of Injeel*'s Sources*

As you can see, the Injeel draws from the Old Testament to a remarkable degree. **Every major aspect of Jesus' life in the Injeel is traceable back to the Tawrat of Moses, the Prophets and** the Psalms. **That dependence illustrates how one Testament completed the other.** It comes down to this. If the Injeel's history of Jesus was somehow orphaned from the Old Testament, Jesus would be incomprehensible, the Injeel could not have survived and there would be no Christianity. Does that sound dogmatic? Yes! Does the data lead us there? Without question.

B. Sources for Jesus in the Qur'an

Let's turn our attention now to the Qur'an's portrait of Jesus. Since your question asks why the history of Jesus has *changed*, we will narrow our search to its biographical information that is missing in the Injeel. I began this inquiry having some basic assumptions.

My Three Starting Assumptions

> I assumed that any new information about Jesus in the Qur'an would be found nowhere else as a testimony of its independence from any prior outside sources.

First, I assumed the Qur'an would exhibit the same level of interdependence with the Injeel that the Injeel had with the Old Testament. That expectation was based on the Qur'an's own claim to continue the Scriptural heritage preceding it, "making no division between them" (Al-Baqarah 2:136), believing every part to be "the Word of God" (Al-Ankabut 29:46) and thus equally immutable since "nothing can change the Word of God" (Al-Anaam 6:34, 115; Yunus 10:64).

Second, I assumed that Qur'anic information about Jesus that is missing in the Injeel would be found nowhere else, testifying to the Qur'an's independence from earlier outside sources. The Qur'an introduces six such episodes that will be identified and examined later in this chapter.

> I assumed the Qur'an would exhibit the same level of interdependence with the Injeel that the Injeel had with the Old Testament.

This expectancy was based on mainstream Islamic teaching that these historical occurrences came directly by divine revelation transmitted from God through the angel to the Prophet (p). When I ask Muslims where these episodes originated, they unanimously say, "They came straight from God (where else?)." That implies these episodes would have been unfamiliar to anyone living prior to seventh-century Arabia.

Third, I assumed that the Qur'an's dependence upon the Bible would have a point of departure. Based partly on your question, "the history of Jesus changed" as opposed to the history of Moses or David, etc. and partly on our widely known Christological differences, I began with a hunch that I would discover the Qur'an to have consistently aligned itself with the Tawrat of Moses, the Prophets and the Zabur of David until reaching the Injeel when suddenly it would veer sharply from it. That is, the arrival of Jesus would have brought doctrinal and historical variances forcing a dramatic departure.

Now let's see where the data led. Here's what I found.

Actual Findings

First, rather than interdependence with the canonical New Testament, I found the Qur'an's history of Jesus displays an amiable independence from it. By *amiable*, I mean that the Qur'an everywhere respects the Old and New Testaments. By *independence*, I am referring to an absence or near absence of citation from these books as well as a surprising disregard for its historically shaped portrait of Christ. So my first assumption was difficult to maintain. While acknowledging common ground, the Qur'an introduced considerable biographical, historical and theological information that is missing from, and often at odds with, the Injeel.

Second, five of the Qur'an's six unique Jesus stories were not independent at all. Instead, they echoed previous non-canonical writings known today as Christian Apocrypha. These writings consisted of two major collections originating in the second century

Five of the six unique episodes in the Qur'an's history of Jesus correlated with the non-canonical collections of writings known today as Christian Apocrypha.

and later – Christian Infancy Gospels (IG) and polemical Gnostic 'Gospels'. While not citing from these verbatim, their echoes are unmistakable. By asking this question of each one, *Could Muhammad's (p) peers have recognized this story when he introduced it?,* yielded a yes answer in five of the six episodes. They were familiar stories long before the seventh century. So I was equally mistaken in this second premise.

Since our approach is to follow the data rather than the dogma, it will help to examine these more closely before moving on to the findings of my third assumption.

First, how did these episodes of Jesus' life become so enormously popular in the years between the writings of the Injeel and the advent of the Qur'an? A brief synopsis of Christian Apocrypha will help Christians and Muslims understand why.

Christian Apocryphal Jesus-Histories

Second Century and Later

"Apocrypha," refers to what is "hidden" or "doubtful." The Christian Apocrypha are sometimes called today "the lost books" of the Bible that were discovered in Egypt during the last century. None of these became part of the New Testament canon, i.e. the twenty-seven books of the Injeel, and yet they enjoyed wide popularity from the second century and following. It is a common mistake to lump all the Apocryphal Gospels together, particularly equating two sub-collections within it: (1) Christian "Infancy Gospels" (IG) and (2) Gnostic anti-Christian polemical writings. Since both are represented in the Qur'an's Jesus-stories, [75] some preliminary background about each group will help.

Group 1: Christian Infancy Gospels

The Infancy Gospels are writings about Jesus and Mary, primarily focusing on their respective nativities and childhoods, that arose in the second and third centuries. Four of these deserve special mention for providing some of the pieces of information about Mary and Jesus that are missing in the Injeel but included in the Qur'an. I've listed them in their probable order of appearance:

- *Infancy Gospel of James* (*Protoevangelium of Jacobi* or *James the Less*). Written in the mid-second century, it had the greatest influence. Its unknown author was definitely not the Apostle James who had been dead for a century (62 A.D.). It focuses much on Mary, emphasizing her exceptional purity and devotion. It tells the stories of her birth and childhood, betrothal to Joseph, Jesus' birth in Bethlehem, visit of the Magi, John the Baptist's [Yahya] escape with his mother from Herod and the murder of Zacharias the priest by Herod's deputies. It both harmonized and embellished the two Gospel accounts of Matthew and Luke.
- *Infancy Gospel of Thomas* (not to be confused with *The Gospel of Thomas*) arose in the mid to late-second century. Its author, "Thomas the Israelite" (probably a Gentile as he showed little knowledge of Jewish life), emphasized the miraculous side of Jesus' boyhood, starting with his infancy and continuing through age twelve.[76]
- *Arabic Gospel of the Infancy* (or *Syriac Infancy Gospel*) introduced a lively series of miracles performed by Jesus starting from his cradle up through age twelve. Its author, likely from eastern Syria, borrowed, adapted and augmented the two earlier IGs mentioned above. While some Islamic scholars argue that it was not translated until the post-Islamic era, most scholars assign it to the fifth or sixth centuries.[77] As a reproduction and harmonization from the earlier IGs, its date is of secondary importance since its ideas were already widely circulated in that oral culture.
- *Infancy Gospel of Matthew* (later titled *The Gospel of Pseudo-Matthew*) dated around 600 to 625 AD. Similar to the *Arabic*

Gospel of the Infancy, it reproduces and harmonizes the earlier Infancy Gospels of *James* and *Thomas*.

The Christian Infancy Gospels shared these characteristics:

(a) Their authors lived *after* the first century, a historical disadvantage that rules them out as eyewitnesses of Jesus. Consequently, they mixed historical material from the canonical Gospels (Injeel) together with later embellishments, sometimes introducing historical details that were at odds with the Injeel.

(b) None of them showed interest in Jesus as an adult, ending their narratives at age 12.

(c) They attempted to promote Christianity in the world, often by combining Scriptures with legendary content. Blending the sacred with the sensational and the factual with the fictional, these hybrids became enormously popular. While some of their non-biblical claims *may* have happened, others were clearly dubious. Some Buddhist traditions from the Pali canon that circulated in Persia were imported into the IGs as well.

(d) They are often mistaken as being Gnostic. They weren't.

(e) Their Christology, i.e. beliefs about Jesus, was closer to the New Testament than to the Qur'an.[78]

Anti-Christian Gnostic 'Gospels'

In contrast to the Infancy Gospels, the Gnostic school stood against orthodox Judeo-Christian doctrines, attempting to replace them with semi-Christian alternatives that were heavily weighted with Hellenistic and pagan philosophy. From ancient manuscripts that were discovered in Nag Hammadi in Egypt, we know much about their teaching. Gene Edward Veith summarizes them:

"Gnostic myths *reject the objective, created order* in favor of an inner-directed secret knowledge. Since the *creation is evil, so is the Creator*, so the Gnostics turn the Old Testament upside down: God is attacked as a cruel, oppressive deity, while the serpent in the garden and Satan himself are seen as the good guys." [79]

Their assault did not stop with the Old Testament:

"*Christ is not God in the flesh,* who died on the Cross *but a mystical*

443

avatar who gives knowledge to the spiritual elite. Since the physical body doesn't matter, sexual immorality is not problematic, and gender distinctions are illusions."[80]

"Today this heresy, gaining entry through academia, has made a ferocious comeback in Western society. It infects the post-modern worldview 'which *rejects objective truth in favor of the notion that truth is nothing more than a construction of the mind,* [which] is itself intrinsically Gnostic.' It echoes the ancient Serpent's pitch to Eve, 'Did God really say?' and leads to the same fatal end. In this worldview, you can construct 'truths' of your own to advance your power agenda. There really is no difference between fact and fiction. It is all fiction."[81]

Writings from both of these collections circulated widely throughout Persia, Styria and Arabia and beyond. The chart below provides a quick comparison of how each collection related to the twenty-seven authoritative "books" written in the first century that became the canonical New Testament.

RELATIONSHIP TO THE CANONICAL INJEEL Infancy Gospels VS Gnostic Gospels	
Infancy Gospels	**Gnostic Gospels**
Supplements the New Testament	Replaces Old & New Testaments
Strengthens the existing Church	Supersedes Christianity
Christology Supports the New Testament	Christology Rejects the New Testament

This brief background prepares us to explore the Qur'an's fascinating Isa scenes.

Six Isa Episodes in the Qur'an Not Found in the Injeel

The Qur'an provides six noteworthy vignettes in Jesus' life that have endeared its readers for their human interest and captivated them by their literary rarity. They are as follows:

Key

1. Mary raised in the Jerusalem Temple (Al-Maidah 5:115; Mariam 19:22-26)
2. Mary Miraculously Nourished at Jesus' birth (Al Maidah 5:110 and Mariam 19:22-32)
3. Jesus spoke as an infant (Al-Imran 3:46-49; Mariam 19:24, 29-33)
4. Jesus gave life to a clay bird (Al-Imran 3:48-49 and Al-Maidah 5:110)
5. Table with food descended from heaven (Al-Maidah 5:112-115)
6. Jesus' death an Illusion (possibly) (Al-Nisa 4:156)

These intriguing scenes evoke the interest of many Christians including mine. Their absence from the Injeel naturally raises curiosities of origin that, in turn, put us on a quest in search from where they may have arisen. In the interest of space, the following chart summarizes its results, matching each episode with an earlier source.

GENRE	TITLE	1	2	3	4	5	6
Buddhist Pali Canon	*Nidanakatha Jatakam* (c. 80 BC) *The CariyaPitakam*; *Buddha Carita; Lalita Vistar*		X	X			
Christian Infancy Gospels	*Infancy Gospel of James*	X	X	X			
	Infancy Gospel of Thomas			?	X		
	Arabic Gospel of the Infancy		?	X	X		
	Infancy Gospel of Matthew	X	X	X			
Gnostic Polemical Writings	Basilides						X
	Second Treatise of the Great Seth						X
	Apocalypse of Peter						X
	Acts of John						X
	Mani/Manichaeism						X

1. Mary's Childhood

The Injeel and the Qur'an both extol Mary's character and yet present two sets of facts about her. When visited by the angel Gabriel, she was young and engaged to be married:

> "In the sixth month of Elizabeth's pregnancy, God sent the angel Gabriel to *Nazareth*, a town in Galilee, to a *virgin pledged to be married* to a man named *Joseph, a descendant of David.* The virgin's name was Mary." (Luke 1:26-27)

The Qur'an begins Mary's story by introducing her aged parents, Imran and Anna:

> "Behold! *A woman of Imran said: 'O my Lord! I do dedicate unto Thee what is in my womb for Thy special service:* So accept this of me: For Thou hearest and knowest all things.' When she was delivered, she said: 'O my Lord! Behold! I am delivered a female child!. . .I have named her Mary, and *I commend her and her offspring to Thy protection* from the Evil One, the Rejected.'" (AlImran 3:35-36, Youssef Ali)

The wife of Imran dedicated her unborn child to the service of God, that is, in the Jerusalem Temple. Expecting a boy, she was surprised to discover a baby girl.

> "Right graciously did the Lord accept her. He made her grow in purity and beauty. *To the care of Zakariyya was she assigned.* Every time that he entered (her) chamber to see her, *he found her supplied with sustenance.* He said: 'O Mary! Whence (comes) this to you?' She said: *'From God; for God provides sustenance to whom He pleases, without measure.'"* (AlImran 3:37, Youssef Ali)

Mary was raised in the Temple at Jerusalem under the care of Zacharias the priest and, to his surprise, was fed supernaturally. Since these details are not found in the Injeel, are they found elsewhere prior to the seventh century?

According to *Infancy Gospel of James*, Mary's mother, childless and desperately advanced in years, begged God for a child and made the promise to God that she would dedicated the child she bore to him. God granted her request and Anna kept her promise. When Mary turned three, Anna took her to the Temple in Jerusalem to live serving God. The Jewish priests gladly received Mary and appointed Zechariah to be her guardian. Then we learn:

> "Mary was *in the Temple* of the Lord like a dove being fed, and *she received food from the hand of an angel.*"[82]

Later, *Matthew's Infancy Gospel* adapted this story.

2. Mary Miraculously Nourished at Isa's Birth

In Mariam 19:22-32, the Qur'an introduces a tender story of Isa's nativity. After a grueling labor under a barren palm tree, Mary, alone with her newborn and still reeling with *physical and emotional exha*ustion, hears a voice (either from Gabriel or Isa) instructing her to cease her gri^{ev}ing in light of the Lord's immediate provision:

> "The Lord h*as created below you a stream.* Shake the trunk of the palm tree and it will drop upon you fresh ripe dates. Eat, drink and rejoice" (19:24-26, Majid Fakhry).

While not in the Injeel, does this touching episode have antecedents elsewhere? From the mid-to-late second century, we read an unmistakable parallel in The Infancy Gospel of James.83 When Jesus was only three days old,

> "The *infant Jesus,* who was resting with smiling face at his mother's bosom, *said to the palm, 'Bend down, tree, and refresh my mother with your fruit.'* And immediately, at this voice, the palm bent down its head to the feet of Mary, and they gathered fruit from it by which

all [Mary, Joseph and Jesus] were refreshed. . . [Then] '*Open a water course beneath your roots which is hidden in the earth, and from it let flow waters to satisfy us.*' and the palm raised itself at once, and fountains of water, very clear and cold and sweet, began to pour out through the roots."[84]

Later the same story is repeated and further embellished in *The Infancy Gospel of Matthew*[85].

It has clear antecedents in *The Arabic Gospel of the Infancy,* which itself was derived from the earlier work of *James*.[86] But where did second-century *James* get it? This story can be traced back beyond the first century to earlier Buddhist Pali Canon, *Maha-Vamso* written during the reign of King Vattagamani of Ceylon about 80 BC, where a similar story was written about Buddha's birth[87] and was perhaps the original source of the story.[88]

3. Jesus Spoke as an Infant

The Nativity story of baby Jesus talking in Al-Imran 3:46-49 and Mariam 19:24, 29-33 again holds especially high interest. The angel Gabriel informed Mary that she would bear a son, a messenger of God. Like other prophets, he would speak for God, but unlike them, his prophetic career would begin in his infancy (Al-Imran 3:46). This miracle was so extraordinary that it was recalled decades later when Jesus faced a challenge calling for renewed confidence. God pointed him back to this cradle miracle as a reminder of his unprecedented power (Al-Maidah 5:110).

Since the Injeel does not record this event, I was interested to learn what kind of situations demanded a talking infant. The Qur'an provides two.

The first situation overlaps with the previous episode, occurring while Mary agonized in her birth pangs beneath a palm tree. All alone, clinging desperately to its trunk and wishing death upon herself, Isa (more likely than Gabriel) addressed her. Instead of normal bellowing sounds of infancy, the babe consoled his mother with mature reason and compassionate provision as we just read (Mariam 19:24-26 Haleem).

Babies depend on their nurturing mother for life. And yet, here it is the mother who draws sustenance from her infant.

The second incident followed closely. Having her immediate physical and emotional needs met, members of Mary's family, in view of her status as a single mother and who are ignorant of Isa's virgin birth, hurl against her innuendos of moral impropriety.

> "O Mary! Indeed you have brought a thing Fariyy [a mighty thing]. O sister of Harun [Aaron]! Your father was not a man who used to commit adultery, nor your mother was an unchaste woman." (Mariam 19:27-33, Noble Qur'an)

Their stinging insinuation called for refuge from their moral slander. Who will speak in Mary's defense to counter their moral outrage? Only she and her baby are present.

> "Then she pointed to him. They said: 'How can we talk to one who is a child in the cradle?'
>
> He [Isa] said: 'Verily, I am a slave of Allah, He has given me the Scripture and made me a Prophet; And He has made me blessed wheresoever I be, and has enjoined on me Salat, and Zakat, as long as I live. And dutiful to my mother, and made me not arrogant, unblest. And Salam be upon me[89] the day I was born, and the day I die, and the day I shall be raised alive!" (Mariam 19:29-33)

So in two related incidents, baby Jesus speaks to save the life of his mother and then rescues her reputation.

Source

Was this episode new information when it was spoken by the Prophet in the seventh century? It actually traces back to the *Infancy Gospel of*

449

James, then the *Arabic* rendition and finally in *Matthew's* account. We may trace it even farther back to the infancy stories of Buddha. Since it partially overlaps with the previous story of the bending palm tree, it is not necessary to repeat its citations.

4. The Child Jesus Life to a Clay Bird

According to the Injeel, Jesus performed his first miracle around age thirty (Jn 2:11), that is, after reaching adulthood.

The Qur'an presents Jesus performing a miracle during childhood. He is said to have created a clay bird and then breathed life into it (AlImran 3:48-49 and Al-Maidah 5:110). This is indeed an incredible act, for who other than God can bring an inanimate object to life?

Was this occurrence new information in the seventh century? In the *Infancy Gospel of Thomas* from the second century, we read:

> "When this child Jesus was five years old, he was playing at the ford of a stream. He made pools of the rushing water and made it immediately pure; he ordered this by word alone. *He made soft clay and modeled twelve sparrows from it.* It was the Sabbath when he did this. There were many other children playing with him. A certain Jew saw what Jesus did while playing on the Sabbath; he immediately went and announced to his father Joseph, 'see, your child is at the stream, and has taken clay and modeled twelve birds; he has profaned the Sabbath.' Joseph came to the place, and seeing what Jesus did he cried out 'Why do you do on the Sabbath what is not lawful to do?' *Jesus clapped his hands and cried to the sparrows, 'Be gone.' And the sparrows flew off chirping.* The Jews saw this and were amazed. They went away and described to their leaders what they had seen Jesus do."[90]

How does *Thomas' Infancy Gospel* portray the boy Jesus? He was a youth who was unable to reign in his powers. In contrast to the Injeel in which Jesus was "obedient to his parents" (Luke 2:51) and "grew in wisdom and stature and in favor with God and man" (Luke 2:52), Thomas depicts Jesus as a bully who wielded colossal powers.

> "While occasionally he used his powers to heal, this boy Jesus more

often *wielded them to maim or kill anyone who upset him.* He would
fly off the handle at the slightest provocation. For example, when a
boy accidentally ran into him, *Jesus struck him dead!*

... This Jesus *cursed his teachers and brought grief to Joseph* who finally
ordered Mary: *"Do not let him go outside the door, because anyone
who angers him dies."*[91]

This legend of the clay bird was then picked up by the *Arabic Gospel
of the Infancy* where it was told twice (chs. 36 and 46). Barnstone
summarizes the *Arabic Gospel*:

"'The Children Who were Changed into Goats,' is typical of many
morality miracles attributed to Jesus. *The child Jesus causes a terrible
event – he maims, blinds, or kills.* Then, after the faithful offer prayers
to the all-powerful, all-knowing child, *he restores the victim* to his or
her previous condition. He heals or restores life.[92]

The *Arabic Gospel* was made available to Muhammad (p) or the
compilers of the Qur'an who selectively incorporated its legends.[93] This
Christian author was eager to enhance Jesus' image by embellishing
the canonical Injeel. It had the opposite effect. His legends, while
wildly popular, trivialized him as a vindictive human being.

5. The Descent of the Lord's Heavenly Table – God's Provision and Warning for Christians

In Al-Maidah 5:112-115, Jesus' apostles request him to send
down a table.

"'O Jesus son of Mary! Can your Lord *send down to us a table set from
heaven?'* After Jesus had prayed for such a miracle Allah is said to
have sent one down with *dire warnings against any unbelief on their
part thereafter.*"

I could find no prior source for this event,[94] so I looked for clues in
Al-Maidah 5 to better understand its meaning. The disciples had

' asked Jesus for physical nourishment, but what
ıs an authenticating sign "to know that you [Isa]
.he truth and that we ourselves be its witnesses"
ɔ, Khan). Jesus prayed for God to send down a table
ɾood) – as "a festival and a sign from You; and provide
ᴡıth sustenance" (S. 5:114). God answered Jesus' prayer but
attached a stern warning to his disciples. If they fell into unbelief,
severe torment would befall them.

Such passages, whether found in the Bible or the Qur'an, often
suggest there is more to a story than meets the eye. In the present
case, the severity of God's warning to the Christians seemed
disproportionate to a request for food or for a sign. Is there a backstory
to this? What kind of "unbelief" must they avoid? Aya 116 answers.
Christians are warned against turning Prophet Jesus into God and
then incorporating him and Mary into the Trinity. Such a sin is
heinous indeed! This warning would apply to some tangential cases
involving heretical offshoots practicing Mariolatry, but thankfully not
orthodox Christianity. For our purposes, the disciples' request for a
heavenly table, it seems, would have been completely new information
to the seventh century.

6. Jesus' Death a Divine Trick?

The fourfold Gospel account in the Injeel unanimously presents Jesus' death by crucifixion as medical fact.

In contrast, according to most Muslims, Al-Nisa 4:156 describes Jesus' death as some kind of illusion in which God caused an exact likeness of Jesus to be transferred to another man, perhaps a bystander, who bore Jesus' punishment at the hands of mistaken executioners.

Again, we raise the question of whether this scenario was unknown prior to its being passed through the angel Gabriel to the Prophet (p). Had

> According to most Muslims, Al-Nisa 4:156 describes Jesus' death as some kind of illusion . . .God caused an exact likeness of Jesus to be transferred to another man, perhaps a bystander, who bore Jesus' punishment at he hands of mistaken executioners.

anyone else reported such a dramatic last-minute switch of iden.
by which God saved one innocent man by condemning another? 1.
answer is yes.

Basilides

This teaching arose from the anti-
Christian Gnostic schools starting
with Basilides inAlexandria, Egypt
from A.D. 125-150. His second
century version of Jesus' death as cited
by Irenaeus went like this:

> "He [Jesus] suffered not; but Simon a
> Cyrenian was compelled to carry the
> cross for him; and he through error
> and ignorance was *crucified, being transfigured by him, that it might
> be thought he was Jesus himself.*"[95]

"He [Jesus] suffered not;
but Simon a Cyrenian
was compelled to carry
the cross for him; and
he through error and
ignorance was crucified,
being transfigured by him,
that it might be thought
he was Jesus himself."
Basilides, Second century

This Cyrenian named Simon was a historical figure drawn from the
Injeel's original account who assisted in carrying Jesus' cross to the
crucifixion site (Matt 27:32; Mk 15:21; Lk 23:26). Basilides' use of
eyewitness testimony stops there.

The Second Treatise of the Great Seth

About a century later, a similar illusion story by another Gnostic
teacher took the name "Seth" and enlarged on Basilides' account.
Before reading his crucifixion story it will help to meet him first.

In the Tawrat Genesis 4, we meet the **biblical Seth** who was an
impressive figure – Eve's son born to replace Abel after being murdered
by his brother Cain. While Cain's family line spawned violence,
Seth and his family built altars, "calling on the name of the LORD"
(Genesis 4:25-26). From his lineage would come notable heroes of
faith like Enoch who "walked with God" (Gen 5:22), Noah, the
ark builder and Abraham, the friend of God. So the biblical Seth of
Genesis was honorable and God-fearing. This **third century "Seth"**
is quite another figure. Where the first had built altars, he built

ıer "wolves in sheep's clothing," he **stole the good**

, about Jesus' crucifixion? In *The Second Treatise*
, Jesus himself narrated the experience.

> ıy death, which they think happened, [happened] to them in
> their error and blindness, since *they nailed their man unto their
> death . . . It was another,* their father, who drank the gall and the
> vinegar; *it was not I.* They struck *not me* with the reed; it was *another,
> Simon,* who bore the cross on his shoulder. It was *another* upon
> whom they placed the crown of thorns . . . And *I was laughing at
> their ignorance.*"[96]

Like Basilides' earlier account, Jesus was not crucified but rescued from it by a bystander named Simon who after carrying the cross for Jesus, to his surprise, found himself being nailed to it. The real Jesus was off to the side relishing with delight over their show of ignorance. Muslim reader, you may be wondering – I hope you are – how the Gnostic school could concoct such a travesty. Figuring it out is quite simple. Their crucifixion story was made to fit their creation story. Here's what I mean.

Seth and the entire Gnostic school had contempt for biblical truth, its prominent people like Abraham and, most of all, its God. Why so? According to them, the Creator made[6] the physical universe evil, inherently and irretrievably so. It was evil from the start. Human suffering was unrelated to human sin. The Fall of humankind was inconceivable in an originally flawed world. *God* handed us a poorly made world to begin with, interweaving two irresolvable forces into every particle of the universe. Adam was the victim, God was the Culprit and the Serpent was the Savior! Salvation for Adam was to *swallow,* not resist, the Serpent's bait: "You can be like God. Eat the fruit and you will realize the divinity within you." It sounds like a page right out of a New Age Playbook.

Tales from the Gnostic schools were popularized in Arabia through Mani (Manichaeism) long before Muhammad's (p) day.

Seth's "Jesus" looked like a man, talked like a man, ate like a man but was not a man. The Serpent had awakened Adam to the truth about himself – he was Divine, not human. And if his humanity was unreal, his death on the cross must be as well. For if he was not human, how could he die? This secret knowledge ("gnosis") meant for Jesus salvation *from* the cross. What did he find so funny about his crucifixion? It was the executioners imagining they had killed him! The joke was on them!

If space allowed, a third name could be added to Basilides and Seth, **Mani the Persian** (A.D. 216-277), another Gnostic who taught a docetic view of Jesus' crucifixion. Mani craftily integrated Gnostic and orthodox Christian phraseology, igniting a movement of congregations eerily resembling Christian churches. Through them he spread Gnostic ideas in Persia, Egypt, Syria and eventually reaching China.

> While portrayed positively, the Isa emerged as a composite figure, a montage of fragments drawn from folk tales beginning in the second century.

The point is this. Tales from the Gnostic schools were popularized in Arabia through Mani (Manichaeism) long before Muhammad's (p) day. They are too plenteous to ignore. When Muslims say that Al-Nisa 4:156 teaches someone other than Jesus died on the cross through a divine trick by which a Jesus look-alike died in his place, how can informed readers, even those sympathetic to Muslims, *not* associate them with these alternate crucifixion accounts, ones wrenched from history and refashioned by teachers like Basilides and Seth and then spread to the ends of the earth by the Manicheans?

Summary – My Personal Assumptions Proven Wrong

As with any kind of research, starting assumptions and final conclusions are seldom identical. Evidence leading elsewhere calls for appropriate adjustment. That was the case with all three of my assumptions. Here's what I found.

First, the Injeel's identification of Jesus as the Messiah arose from two chief influences: eyewitness testimonies of the events themselves and dozens of promises, predictions and foreshadowings written earlier in the Old Testament. These included his genealogy and birth, his home village, where he launched his ministry, his anointing at baptism, his miraculous signs, his piercing teachings, details of his suffering and death for Adam's lost race, the resurrection of his body followed by his ascension into heaven.

The Qur'an also identifies Isa as the Messiah but its understanding of him was shaped by traditions originating much later than Jesus' generation. It either ignored or was unaware of information supplied by the biblical canon. It does confer upon Jesus honorific titles. Our present focus, however, is historical and not doctrinal. I was unable to find historical anchors or Scriptural citations to support them. The Isa of the Qur'an, while portrayed positively, emerges more as a composite figure, a montage of popular fragments drawn from folk tales beginning in the second century. His **childhood** conforms to second-century *Infancy Gospels*, some rooted in earlier legends of Buddha's birth. His **crucifixion** in Al-Nisa 4:156 point to the Gnostics who denied his humanity and therefore the possibility of his death. These earlier sources all shared one common liability: physical absence from the events about which they described. None could furnish eyewitness testimony about Jesus since they were written much later and from outside Palestine.

WHY TWO JESUS HISTORIES?
Where the Data Leads

Why then do Christians and Muslims have two strikingly divergent histories of the same person? Based on this data, the answer is twofold, one obvious and the other mysterious.
First, the obvious reason for our two sets of facts about Jesus boils down to *sources*.

This explanation follows an archaeological principle: *Where we dig will determine what we'll find.* If I plant my shovel in Texas, am I more likely to unearth arrowheads or Egyptian pottery? So my initial answer to your question is that Christians and Muslims present us with different "finds" because they dug from different "fields."

Muslims may be wondering if earlier sources should even factor into the question since the Prophet (p) only served as the conduit through which truth passed rather than as a composer of God's message. If you recall, that was my starting premise but the data could not sustain it. For that view to work, these episodes would have to be unfamiliar to anyone living prior to the seventh century. Still, some Muslims may interpret my observations as an attack which is *not* my intention. We should note that St. Clair-Tisdall, whose seminal work traced many of the stories that wound up in the Qur'an to Christian heretical sects:

> "was quick to stress that he was not accusing Muhammad of unoriginality, rather the analogy would be the way in which a house builder has to use existing stones. Muhammad's aim was to draw in and unite followers of these other faiths."[97]

Sources alone cannot explain the reason for our two sets of "facts" about Jesus. We must find a deeper cause.

Second, the mysterious cause for our two sets of facts about Jesus involved an unknown criterion by which some sources were chosen to the exclusion of others. Someone had to sift through the artifacts and the oral stories of Jesus to determine which of them should and should not be incorporated in the Qur'an. By simply tracing these six episodes back to their sources still leaves important questions unanswered.

- Within the broad spectrum of this Jesus material being circulated in seventh-century Arabia, who or what guided the selection process determining what to include in the Qur'an? That question I cannot answer.
- How can we explain the preference of Infancy Gospels and Gnostic works from the second and third centuries over the earliest reports of Jesus from the canonical Scripture? Again, I cannot answer that.

One factor I considered to explain this preference for later episodes was simply a matter of availability. That is, the Christian gospel may not have reached Arabia by the time of the Prophet (p). Again the data failed to support it. Specifically, this becomes apparent in the **manner in which** the Qur'an adapted the content of its original source.

For example, the Qur'an incorporated the popular story of Jesus speaking from the cradle from the *Infancy Gospel of Matthew*. While only an endearing second-century legend, its Christology was perfectly aligned with the Injeel. It read:

> "Jesus spoke when he was in the cradle, and called out to his mother Mary: *'Verily I am Jesus, the Son of God, the Word,* whom thou hast given birth to according to the good tidings given thee by the Angel Gabriel, and *my Father hath Sent me for the Salvation of the World.'*"[98]

Yet when the Qur'an borrowed this tale, it dramatically altered baby Jesus' message about himself:

> He [Isa] said: 'Verily, *I am a slave of Allah,* He has *given me the Scripture and made me a Prophet. . .'* (Mariam 19:29-33)

This modification from "I am . . . the Son of God" to "I am a slave of Allah" suggests the challenge to be not one of ignorance of the original Gospel but a preference for a different one. What makes us think so? While incorporating this tale as sacred history, a conscious decision was made to modify it in a way that diminished its Christology.[99] Prior criteria guided not only which sources were selected but how they got reshaped in the Qur'an.

Sources alone, then, cannot adequately explain the different set of facts about Jesus between our Books. The same source can yield dramatically different messages. This modified cradle message had to be recast to conform to another framework and, in doing so, took liberty to create a new identity for the Child in the cradle. This modification reveals a criterion that prevailed over the source. **The definitive answer to your question rests here.** Once an innocent tale was freely borrowed, the criterion exchanged one Babe, "the Son of God" for another, "a Slave of God" (Mariam 19:30).

This illustrates how Christology in the Injeel is tied to actual events that were interpreted through previous Scriptures. Teachings about the incarnation *followed* history and were demanded by it. By contrast, the Qur'an, for whatever reason, untethered to the biblical past, assumed greater liberty to recreate its own version in the service of its own theological purpose.

From the introduction, you may recall how theologian Muhammad 'Ata'ur-Rahim explained the reason for our two different Jesus histories. Christianity, he said, wears a mask denying the Jesus of history that remained until removed centuries later by the Islamic Jesus of history. Nothing is wrong with such dogmatic positions if that's where the data leads. In the present case, it led elsewhere. Here it brought us to second-century tales about Jesus by the *Infancy Gospels* combined with the absurd blasphemies of the Gnostics. They dressed Jesus up in their full costume, brazenly masking over the Son of Mary, Son of God. This semi-historical figure became the Islamic Jesus. Christians refuse to accept the mask.

My Third Starting Assumption Also Proved Wrong

Let's return now to my third starting assumption that the Qur'an would agree with the earlier Books up to the time of Jesus and then part ways. I expected it to be in lockstep with the Old Testament history starting with Adam and Eve, then finally arrive at the Injeel only to find its doctrines about Jesus unacceptable and make a fast exit. This idea of parting ways also proved false! Departures require an original union. My biggest surprise was that the Qur'an, while mentioning familiar names and events from the Old Testament, was just as unfamiliar with the message of Moses in the Tawrat as it was with Jesus in the Injeel. Even its account of Adam and Eve in the Garden veered dramatically from Genesis, weaving a strikingly different story.

Literary sources will often behave similarly with family genealogies. Just as families bear a unique set of traits distinguishing them from other families, so our two Books inherit characteristics from their predecessors. In turn, the Injeel and the Qur'an pass on to their respective readers unique biographical and theological traits of the person and work of Jesus precisely because each bore those traits prior to Jesus.

Each retained its family history without co-mingling. From start to finish, beginning with Adam and Eve in the Garden and running through Jesus' childhood and then all the way to his cross, we find two markedly different accounts. Of my three starting premises, this third surprised me most. While acquainted with many Old Testament episodes, the Qur'anic drew from its own family tree – Jewish commentaries *about* Scripture rather than the sacred writings themselves.

To be candid, I was struck to learn that information about Jesus found was not as new as I once imagined it to be. Prior to this study, the Qur'an's Isa was a unique figure to me. Now it has become apparent that he bears striking resemblance to the pre-adolescent Jesus portrayed tenderly in the Infancy Gospels and the "crucified" Jesus we meet in the unsympathetic Gnostics.

So to answer your question, the data leads to the following. Two histories of Jesus arose from two predecessors:

- The Injeel's Jesus is inseparable from the Old Testament and eyewitnesses. His life meshed with ancient expectations (as opposed to popular ones) and shaped who Jesus was and did. He was no populist Messiah.
- The Qur'an's Isa is inseparable from the Apocryphal Gospels of the second century. Preexisting doctrinal criteria shaped its Jesus-history.

You've asked a great question and I hope this helps clear it up.

CHAPTER 10

CONFUSION OVER
JESUS' DEATH

Question 10: "If Jesus was sent to die on the cross, why did he never say that since this is the heart of Christianity?"

Q 10.1: "At the crucifixion, God died. How can that be?"
Q 10.2: "If Isa is God, how can he be killed?"

୬

Your intriguing question asks not whether Jesus was actually crucified, but why he never mentioned it. Your logic makes sense: If Jesus believed his death was linked to his mission, he would certainly have spelled that out beforehand. But you're assuming that Jesus was silent about it which deserves a closer look.

> How important is it, really, if Jesus simply died on the cross but never brought it up in the context of his mission?

But first, let's put this into perspective. How important is it, really, if Jesus simply died on the cross but never brought it up beforehand in the context of his mission? A comparison of four possible scenarios might help sort this out for us.

Story Line 1: Jesus predicted his death by crucifixion, his burial and his bodily resurrection to life on the third day. He *was* crucified, buried and raised to life on the third day.

Story Line 2: Jesus never predicted his death. Yet he *was* crucified, buried and raised to life on the third day.

Story Line 3: Jesus predicted his death by crucifixion but *was not* crucified.

Story Line 4: Jesus never predicted his death by crucifixion, and he *was not* crucified.

Obviously, only one of these rundowns could have actually occurred. I may be wrong, but by the wording of your question I would hazard a guess which of these you think Christians and Muslims would choose. Christians, you would say, based on the Injeel, would gravitate to Story Line 2. Muslims, based on the Qur'an, would lean toward Story Line 4.

Does it Matter?

Each scenario leads to a different outcome. Let's consider their implications.

Story Line 1: If true, Jesus' death on the cross was a revelation of divine love and central to his saving mission. It displayed the extent of God's power and the depth of his love.

Story Line 2: If true, Jesus' death on the cross was a historical fact but not a revelation of divine love. The absence of forethought exposes it as an unintended tragedy over which God triumphed, proving his power over death but nothing more.

Story Line 3: If true, Jesus' miscalculation would strike a lethal blow to *both* of our faith traditions. For Christians, no-death equals no-salvation. For Muslims, false prophecy equals false prophet. His gross misjudgment disqualifies him either as a world Savior or an infallible Prophet.

Story Line 4: If true, Jesus' death was inconsequential to his mission on earth. This scenario could play out in one of two ways. Either Jesus simply vanished from public life and died later of natural causes or he was spared death altogether by a miraculous transport from earth into heaven. In either case, in matters of human salvation, his death was beside the point. Furthermore, this scenario renders the Injeel's testimony of his crucifixion and resurrection as a hoax.

This broad range of impact regarding Jesus' death calls for our close attention to all the details surrounding it. Only then can we hope to arrive at the correct scenario. Your insightful question weds the historical event to its prominence that you correctly assume Jesus would have voiced beforehand. Will Jesus' public crucifixion *align* with his private forecasts lending it *weight?* Synchronizing these two elements, of course, requires more than your question admits. So let's begin with your assumption that Jesus was silent about his death. Did he predict it beforehand, and, if so, did he connect it to his mission?

Once determined, we will explore how each of the four Story Lines aligns with the Injeel and the Qur'an.

PART ONE: Did Jesus Predict His Death?

During his last six months Jesus spoke of his approaching death on at least twenty separate occasions. These spread across all four Gospel accounts and multiple times in each: Matthew (10), Mark (8), Luke (7) and John (17).[1] *That* Jesus foretold his death is important. *What* he said about it equally so. The following statements were usually made while he was alone with his twelve apostles.

> During his last six months Jesus spoke of his approaching death on at least twenty separate occasions.

What did Jesus say about his death? In approximate chronological order, he made the following statements.

Six Months before Jesus' Death

Prediction #1: Essential to his Messianic Mission – Matthew 16:21

Jesus timed the breaking news of his death to coincide with the revelation of his Messiahship. After two-and-a-half years of ministry among the villages and cities of Galilee, the name "Jesus of Nazareth" became widely talked about. With this immense popularity came confusion over who he was. To settle it once and for all, Jesus took his apostles to a private place where he asked them this question: 'Who do you say that I am?' Simon Peter answered,

> "**'You are the Christ [Messiah], the Son of the living God.'** And Jesus said to him, 'Blessed are you, Simon Barjona, because flesh and blood did not reveal this to you, but My Father who is in heaven.'" (Matthew 16:13-16)

Jesus spoke of his death in the language of "must" rather than "maybe."

Once this divine truth was spoken through the fisherman, the Twelve must have been intoxicated with excitement. Peter's answer was spot on. Yet the apostles had a flawed understanding of Messiah. Like most of their contemporaries living under crushing Roman domination, they looked for a militant Liberator, a view based on a partial selection of Old Testament passages. Before they had a chance to celebrate, Jesus corrects their misunderstandings of what "being Messiah" would require:

> "From that time Jesus began to **show** His disciples that He **must** go to Jerusalem, and **suffer many things** from the elders and chief priests and scribes, and **be killed**, and **be raised up** on the third day." (Matthew 16:21, emphasis mine)

In describing this ordeal, Jesus didn't speak in generalities. He "*showed* them[2] exactly what lay ahead, taking time to spell it out in plain terms.

Their reaction was immediate. It felt to them as if Jesus punched them in the stomach. *The religious authorities kill the Messiah? Preposterous!* This was not the Rambo Messiah they imagined. Peter spoke for them all, pulling Jesus aside and even "began to rebuke him!" He said, "Never, Lord! This shall never happen to you!"

Muslims, you are not alone in your repugnance towards Jesus' cross. The first opposition to it came from his closest followers! What counts, however, is not what *we* think, but what *God* thinks! Jesus answered Peter with blunt force:

> "Get behind me, Satan! You are a stumbling block to me; *you do not have in mind the concerns of God, but merely human concerns.*" (Matthew 16:22-27)

"From that time Jesus began to show His disciples that He must go to Jerusalem, and suffer many things from the elders and chief priests and scribes, and be killed, and be raised up on the third day."
Jesus, Matthew 16:21

Specific Details

1. *Its necessity.* Jesus used the language of "must" rather than "maybe." His death was not tentative. Never does he say, "The way things are turning out, who knows, I might get killed!" For Jesus, the driving force behind his fate was not historical circumstances, the will of the Jews or the people's choice. It was his God-ordained destiny (Lk 4:43; 9:22, 44; 12:50; 13:32-33; 24:7, 26, 44), one pre-scripted by God's prophets centuries earlier. They pointed to the arrival of a sin-bearing Messiah on humanity's behalf (Isaiah 53). Secondary factors should not be confused with the root cause. Jesus marched to that drum, advancing ever closer to actualize it. Like a moving train to Jerusalem, nothing would be able to stop Almighty God's sovereign purposes. Once the clock strikes a certain hour, Jesus declares, "It *will* happen. Get ready!"

Muslims, you are not alone in your repugnance towards Jesus' death. The first opposition to it came from Jesus' closest followers!

2.   *Its cruelty.* Jesus would "suffer many things." Cruel acts would be perpetrated against his body, mind and dignity. It will hurt. This sounds too obvious, but the fusion of natures embodied in the Messiah took nothing away from Jesus' humanity. When punched in the face, it would sting. When pounded with a wooden staff, pain would course through his entire body.

3.   *Its perpetrators.* Jesus' death will come at the instigation of the Jewish authorities presiding in Jerusalem – "the elders and chief priests and scribes."[3] This too was part of the earlier Script warning that the gracious Cornerstone of God's salvation would become "the stones the builders rejected" (Psalm 118:22; Isaiah 28:16).

4.   *Its reversal.* Jesus' death would be temporary. His grave would give him up, not at the Last Day like the general population, but he would "be raised"[4] on "the third day" following his death.

Prediction #2: Triggered by Betrayal – Matthew 17:22-23

> "As they were meeting in Galilee, Jesus told them, "The Son of Man is **about to be betrayed into the hands of men**. They will kill Him, and on the third day He will be raised up." And they were deeply distressed."[5] (Matthew 17:22-23 HCSB"

New Detail

Jesus would be delivered over to the power of the State through an act of betrayal. The initial anger felt by the apostles towards Jesus' death now deepens to "distress." Its very thought makes them sad.

Prediction #3: An Unexpected Path – Matthew 20:17-19[6]

> "As Jesus was about to go up to Jerusalem, He took the twelve disciples aside by themselves, and on the way He said to them, '**Listen! We are going up to Jerusalem**. The Son of Man will be handed over to the chief priests and scribes, and they will condemn Him to death. Then they will hand Him over to the Gentiles to be mocked, flogged, and crucified, and He will be resurrected on the third day." Matthew 20:17-19 HCSB

New Details

1.   *To Jerusalem!* Jesus told them, "Listen!" (*idou*),[7] using a term of surprise to convey this counterintuitive journey. That shocker was Jesus' chosen destination: *Jerusalem*, the city plotting his ordeal! He navigated towards his peril, not his preservation. In a save-your-own-skin world, what could have sounded more preposterous? It would have surprised no one had he said, "We're going to Lebanon," the country due north in the opposite direction. Not Jesus.

2.   *Nightmare.* Jesus adds critical details to the ordeal awaiting him. Jewish authorities would instigate his demise, condemning him before delivering him into the custody of the State for prosecution and execution, but the Gentiles would inflict the torture. Crucifixions were common occurrences in Jesus' day. He spells out for them specific forms of inhumane torture: (a) "Mockery," "to make fun of by pretending that he is not what he is or by imitating him in a distorted manner."[8] The wisest man alive would become open season for jesters. (b) "Scourging" with *flagellums*, whips made of leather soaked in brine and laced with pieces of bone and spiked metal balls would be inflicted on the back of his naked body. These cut open the body by tearing the flesh of the victim fastened to a post. If those weren't enough, next came (c) "Crucifixion" in which the victim's naked body is rough handled onto a vertical stake, nailed and publicly hung in broad daylight. Originally performed only on corpses, in Jesus' day it was on living victims. From crucifixion we get the word "excruciating" to describe pain that is unbearable. His enemies will be unsparing. Jesus will undergo the nightmare of his life.

Prediction #4: Cross before the Crown – Luke 17:24-25

On his way to Jerusalem, some Jewish scholars asked Jesus when God's kingdom would arrive. They were right to expect the kingdom of God, (Daniel 7, etc.), but the kingdom they had in mind was one to be ruled by a grand earthly Messiah who, all at once, would liberate their nation and enforce world peace. Jesus corrects their view:

"The coming of the kingdom of God is not something that can be observed, nor will people say, 'Here it is,' or 'There it is,' because *the kingdom of God is in your midst."* (Luke 17:20-21)

Jesus explained how God's kingdom had *already* arrived in its initial stage the moment he began his ministry. Its Messiah-King, standing before them, had been performing miraculous signs confirming this. While most of the authorities discredited his claims, the facts spoke for themselves. Beyond any doubt, God's kingdom had already begun, breaking through the long reign of darkness with truth, grace and power. Then Jesus took his disciples aside and gave them a preview of the grand finale at his Second Coming:

> "A time will come when you will long to see one of the days of the Son of man and will not see it. They will say to you, "Look, it is there!" or, "Look, it is here!" Make no move; do not set off in pursuit; for as the lightning flashing from one part of heaven lights up the other, so will be the Son of man when his Day comes. But *first he is destined to suffer grievously and be rejected by this generation."* (Luke 17:24-25 New Jerusalem Bible)

New Details

Jesus divided the coming of his kingdom into two stages – humble service and final glory.

1.   Jesus reigns in two phases. Jesus divided the coming of his kingdom into two stages – humble service and final glory. The Jewish experts erred by being so bent on the latter that they had missed the former. Each phase would achieve a different kind of peace.[9]

2.   Jesus' rejection by religious rulers validated, not sabotaged, his Messiahship. Scriptures had destined the Messiah to first suffer grievously and "be rejected (*apodokimazo*) by this generation." The term means "to judge someone or something as not being worthy or genuine, thus something to be rejected."[10] Thus, Jesus' rejection by Jewish leaders, rather than invalidating his claims as Messiah, was an essential element to which he was "destined." Before coming as the glorious Son of Man in power at the end of time with unmistakable visibility (Daniel 7:13-14), he must first appear "in plain clothes," a man among men, as God's Suffering Servant who would win human hearts in ways military power could never do (see Hebrews 9:27-28). These two contrasting advents were separated in time, distinguished in purpose, varied in manner and equal in necessity.

Prediction #5: Achievement for Mankind – Matthew 20:28

Jesus' rejection by Jewish leaders, rather than invalidating his claims as Messiah, was an essential element to which he was "destined."

Finally reaching the outskirts of Jerusalem, Jesus turns to his disciples for a teaching moment. He gave them a counter-intuitive lesson on the telltale signs of real power and, out of that, the significance of his death:

"But Jesus called them over and said, "You know that the rulers of the Gentiles dominate them, and the men of high position exercise power over them. It must not be like that among you. On the contrary, whoever wants to become great among you must be your servant, and whoever wants to be first among you must be your slave; just as *the Son of Man*[11] *did not come to be served, but to serve, and to give His life a ransom for many.*" (Matthew 20:28 HCSB, emphasis added)

New Details

1.   Jesus shifted the focus away from the *mode* of his death to its *purpose* and from what *he* stood to lose to what *others* stood to gain. Perhaps right here his disciples begin to see why their Master headed to Jerusalem instead of fleeing to Lebanon. At the forefront of his mind was not his personal demise but the new freedom that would be afforded humanity.[12]

2.   Jesus called attention to the voluntary nature of his death. "The Son of Man came to *give his life* rather than having it forcibly snatched from him. Let's be clear. This was more than lack of resistance to the scheming leaders. Jesus was *initiating* the events about to transpire as a revelation of his Father's love. The decision was his. For what reason?

"The voluntary death of the Son of Man will be a 'ransom' (*lutron*), the price paid for the release of a slave."[13]

> "This saying tells us why Jesus died. His life was not taken but given, and given as a ransom, a price paid to redeem captives. Here, for the first time, He adds the element of vicarious substitution to an announcement of His coming death. He will ransom the slaves of sin, purchasing their freedom by His death in their stead."[14]

Prediction #6: Defeat of Satan's Kingdom

The death that would bring good news of salvation for humanity would spell the end for Satan and his kingdom.

> "'*The hour has come* for the Son of Man to be glorified. . . . *Now my soul is troubled, and what shall I say?* 'Father, save me from this hour'? *No, it was for this very reason I came to this hour. Father, glorify your name!.* . . Now is the time for judgment on this world; *now the prince of this world will be driven out.* And I, when I am lifted up from the earth, will *draw all people to myself.*" He said this to show *the kind of death he was going to die.*" (John 12:23, 27-28, 31-33)

> "'And I, when I am lifted up from the earth, will draw all people to myself.' He said this to show the kind of death he was going to die."
> Jesus, John 12:32-33

Jesus knew that the causes behind his death were more than a political conspiracy or power-play. His battle was not against flesh and blood, but invisible principalities and powers. For "now the prince of this world will be driven out."

> "Jesus unveiled this mystery, that his death would unseat the Ruler of darkness (Satan) by dethroning him from power ("will be driven out"). The Cross sealed his fate, for "*now* [present] the prince of this world *will be* [future] driven out." In the Garden of Eden, it was Satan speaking through the Serpent who gained the upper hand and took mankind down. Now the same Ruler of Darkness worked behind the scenes to bring about Jesus' demise." Jesus knew what his

enemy did not:

> "The devil initiated Jesus' death, but, ironically, that death spelled for the devil the beginning of the end."[15]

Jesus later supplemented this truth, claiming that through his cross "the prince of this world *now* stands condemned" (John 16:11). Not only would his death spell the future overthrow of Satan's reign but the personal sentence of doom hanging over his head.

New Details

1.   *Jesus dreaded his ordeal.* Against the Pollyanna view of Jesus waltzing his way to the Cross, this sobering passage reveals some of the mental agitations stirring beneath his resolute obedience. We too easily equate human determination with pleasantry. There is nothing casual in Jesus' attitude. As his "hour" approached, an inner turbulence became increasingly noticeable. With eyes wide open, he knew what lay ahead and, that God would not intervene to bail him out of it. Nor is there the slightest hint of him fancying his imminent ordeal as a nice symbolic metaphor of sacrifice but as the lethal instrument of physical torture that it truly was.

2.   *Jesus overcame his dread.* By drawing inspiration from two deep convictions, Jesus was able to push through his upcoming grim reality. First, that his death was central to his mission, "for this very reason I came to this hour." Second, that in the end, his death would *glorify* "the Son of Man." We wonder how such a ghastly ordeal could possibly result in divine glory.

> "The devil initiated Jesus' death, but, ironically, that death spelled for the devil the beginning of the end."
> Susan R. Garrett

Jesus' death would end Satan's domain, the triumph awaiting Jesus' final return at the end of the age (Daniel 7; Revelation 12:10).

3.   *The Great Paradox – the Cross's Drawing Power.* Bad news for Satan meant good news for humanity. It would set us free from all the powers of evil: "When I am lifted up from the earth, will draw all people to myself."

The Night before Jesus' Crucifixion

Prediction #7: Jesus Identified Himself as the Passover Lamb to be Slain–Matthew 26:1-2; Luke 22:14; Matt 26:26-30

Jesus prearranged his death to coincide with the Jewish Passover when thousands of lambs would be slain.

> "You know that after two days the Passover is coming, and *the Son of Man is to be handed over for crucifixion."* (Matthew 26:1-2; see 17-18)

> "When **the hour** came, Jesus and his apostles reclined at the table. And he said to them, *'I have eagerly desired to eat this Passover with you before I suffer.'"* (Luke 22:14-15)

> "As they were eating, Jesus took bread, blessed and broke it, gave it to the disciples, and said, 'Take and eat it; *this is My body."* Then He took a cup, and after giving thanks, He gave it to them and said, "Drink from it, all of you. For *this is My blood* that establishes the covenant;17 it is shed for many for the forgiveness of sins.'" (Matthew 26:26-30 HCSB)

New Details

1.   *Backdrop – Significance of Passover*

> "Passover is the annual festival commemorating God's miraculous deliverance of the Israelites from Egyptian bondage. Exodus 12 records the deaths of all firstborn males in Egypt, except for those born to Israelites whom God spared or 'passed over' when the avenging angel saw the blood of the lamb on their doorposts."[16]

2.　　*Passover's new Lamb and the cost of freedom.* Jesus presented himself as the Passover sacrifice, the final Lamb to be slain (see 1Cor 5:7-8; 1Peter 1:18-19; Rev 5:6-12). On the eve of his death, he instituted his Supper to remind believers in every age of the high cost of freedom. For Israel's liberation from slavery, it required the life of an innocent animal: "When I see the blood, I will pass over you. No destructive plague will touch you..." (Tawrat, Exodus 12:13). For liberation from the sins of the world, the price was even higher: Jesus' broken body and spilled blood (Matt 26:30). "For this is My blood that establishes the covenant; it is shed for many for the forgiveness of sins" (Matt 26:30).

What connected these two events? Aphrahat, a third century Syriac Christian, wrote:

"At Passover, the Jews escaped from the slavery of Pharaoh; we [Christians] were liberated from Satan's thrall on the day of crucifixion. They sacrificed a lamb and were saved from the destroyer by his blood; we were saved from the corrupt deeds which we had done by the blood of the beloved Son; they had Moses as a guide, we have Jesus as Chief and Savior."

Prediction #8: Jesus Identified His Betrayer and Set him Loose– Matthew 26:20-25; John 13:27, 30

"Now when evening came, Jesus was reclining at the table with the twelve disciples. As they were eating, He said, "Truly I say to you that one of you will betray Me." "Being deeply grieved, they each one began to say to Him, "Surely not I, Lord?" "And He answered, *'He who dipped his hand with Me in the bowl is the one who will betray Me. The Son of Man is to go, just as it is written of Him; but woe to that man by whom the Son of Man is betrayed! It would have been good for that man if he had not been born.'"* (Matthew 26:20-25)

"As soon as Judas took the bread, Satan entered into him. So Jesus told him, 'What you are about to do, do quickly.' As soon as Judas had taken the bread, he went out. And it was night." (John 13:27, 30)

New Details

1.　*Jesus' suffering begins.* Aware that the Messiah's suffering would be triggered by the betrayal of a close companion (Psalm 55:13-15), Jesus painfully but clearly exposed him as Judas Iscariot.

2.　*Two contrasting destinies.* Jesus identified himself with Judas as co-sufferers under God's decree with two profound differences: motive and fate. Jesus suffered by obeying God as a force for good. Judas suffered as an accomplice of evil. His complicit role with the evil One, while unwittingly playing into God's larger plan, evoked "woe," recognizing the harrowing torment awaiting him in judgment.

3.　*Jesus let evil play out.* Rather than stopping the works of darkness, Jesus set it loose.

Prediction #9: Intercessor for the Undeserving – Luke 22:37

Jesus linked his death to prophecies that placed it among outcasts.

> "For I tell you that this which is written must be fulfilled in Me, 'And *He was numbered with transgressors*'; for that which *refers to Me has its fulfillment.*" (Luke 22:37)

Which specific prophecy is Jesus referring to that is being fulfilled? One that includes two actions the Messiah would make on behalf of undeserving people: dying for their sins and interceding for their forgiveness. Isaiah 53:12 includes both actions:

> "Because He poured out Himself to death, and was *numbered with the transgressors;* yet He Himself bore the sin of many, And *interceded for the transgressors.*" (Isaiah 53:12)

At the most unthinkable moment, Jesus made good on this prophecy – while they hung him out to dry. Yet he prayed for them,

> "Father, forgive them, for they do not know what they are doing." (Jesus from the cross, Luke 23:34)

New Details

The habit for which Jesus became famous in life – befriending sinners – he continued in death.

1.   During his life, Jesus was called "friend of sinners" by association. He dined with outcasts, a bold act of inclusion in his culture, restoring dignity to the ones whom society had written-off as no-good. Without validating sin, he recuperated sinners. Remarkably, the epitome of purity entered human shame, bore its guilt and interceded for its salvation.

2.   Jesus' death proved to sinners that he did not 'bait and switch" by earning their favor in life just to ditch them when his life was on the line. By completing his mission, he perfected their confidence in his one-time death and ongoing intercession. Citing this verse shows that Jesus did not view himself as a martyr dying for those deemed noble but as a Savior for all, from top to bottom.

Prediction #10: Defining Moment – Desperate Prayer and Valiant Obedience – Matthew 26:36-45; Hebrews 5:7-8

"Then Jesus came with them to a place called Gethsemane, and said to His disciples, 'Sit here while I go over there and pray.' And He took with Him Peter and the two sons of Zebedee, and began to be grieved and distressed. Then He said to them, '*My soul is deeply grieved, to the point of death*; remain here and keep watch with Me.'

"And He went a little beyond them, and *fell on His face* and prayed, saying, '*My Father, if it is possible, let this cup pass from Me; yet not as I will, but as You will.*' And He came to the disciples and found them sleeping, and . . .

"He went away again a second time and prayed, saying, '*My Father, if this cannot pass away unless I drink it, Your will be done.*' Again He came and found them sleeping, for their eyes were heavy. And He left them again, and went away and *prayed a third time, saying the same thing* once more." (Matthew 26:36-45)

"During the days of Jesus' life on earth, he offered up *prayers and petitions with fervent cries and tears* to the one who could save him from death, and he was *heard* because of his reverent submission. Son though he was, he learned obedience from what he suffered and, once made perfect, he became the source of eternal salvation for all who obey him..." (Hebrews 5:7-9)

New Details

1.   Last chance to escape. Life's toughest battles are often fought, not in the physical realm, but on the private battlefield of the soul. It is a spiritual battle over control and is as comfortable as passing a kidney stone. Yet out of it, one emerges either freed or crippled. This pre-crucifixion prayer between Father and Son became Jesus' defining moment. The man we see here shatters

> Rather than begging God to save him, Jesus offered his sin-free life to rescue a sin-laden world.

the fiction that his humanity was fake. This was no avatar! Curiously, Muslim friends of mine interpret this prayer as Jesus begging God to save *him* from the Cross and that God granted his request. They often point to Hebrews 5:7 to show how God answered Jesus' prayer by saving him from death. It says: "During the days of Jesus' life on earth, he offered up prayers and petitions with fervent cries and tears to the one who could save him from death, and he was heard because of his reverent submission." Let's pay close attention to what it says.

Jesus addressed his prayed to the God who "could save him from death" (Heb 5:7). Indeed! This verse, however, only affirms Almighty God's capacity without referencing his actual course of action. Muslims and Christians agree that God *can* perform many acts that he leaves undone. Here he answered Jesus' prayer, not by the act of prevention – "save him *from* death" – but something far better. He saved him *through* it by an immeasurably greater miracle that delivered him *forever* out of the grave. Until that ultimate victory came, however, God did not turn a deaf ear to Jesus' situation at hand. While Jesus' Gethsemane prayer was met with God's silence, it was not with his inattention. Jesus was "*heard* because of his reverent submission" (Heb 5:8).

How vivid Jesus' Garden reverence became as he pleaded with God, asking if any other path than the "cup" of crucified suffering might open up to him, an Option B, *anything* else. His request was met with dead silence, for that cup was meant to be, the reason for which he came, making its consumption Jesus' most consequential obedience.

This prayer lasted an hour, not long for someone accustomed to praying all-night. Why so short? Its brevity arose, not because the *Father* gave Jesus what he asked for and, once getting it, Jesus dashed into the night. Just the reverse. Jesus gave the Father *his* desire: "Not my will, but Yours be done!" Not what I want, but what you want, Father" (Mark 14:36)! That's the "reverent submission" God *heard!*

I respect my Muslim friends for pointing out Hebrews 5: 7 and encourage them to keep reading to the very next verse:

> "Son though he was, he learned obedience from what he suffered and, once made perfect, he became the source of eternal salvation for all who obey him" (v 8-9).

We are thankful that the God who *could* have saved Jesus from death chose not to. Instead, he used the reverent submission of One destined for the Cross, saying "Yes!" in a colossal act of obedience for our salvation.

2.   *Whatever it takes.* Some of our African brothers call this the "GG Prayer," shorthand for the Garden of Gethsemane where Jesus poured out his soul. It's the *whatever it takes* prayer. Anytime God calls his people to tasks requiring extraordinary cost or sends

"When Jesus' followers saw what was going to happen, they said, 'Lord, should we strike with our swords?' And one of them struck the servant of the high priest, cutting off his right ear. But Jesus answered, 'No more of this!' And he touched the man's ear and healed him." Jesus, Luke 22:49-51

them to places where the stakes are high, this GG prayer becomes the template of preparation. Like a bootcamp for the soul, it is designed to bring us to an internal place where divine purpose and personal desire are one.

3.   *Composure through surrender.* Paradoxically, souls reaching the place of alignment with God by saying "Yes, Lord" rise from prayer with new freedom previously not thought possible. Jesus emerged from this crucible with bolstered readiness for what lay ahead, now in terms of minutes rather than days.

Immediately following this Garden travail, Jesus meets the armed posse come for him. Surprisingly, it is Jesus who takes command. At his arrest, he exuded inexplicable composure, the mental presence of someone buoyed by a conviction, amid the human bluster of the moment, that God's ancient purpose was unfolding. Both they and he were carrying out God's will. The difference was that only one of them knew it. They operated on the delusion that they sat in the driver's seat. Fully submitted to his Father, Jesus commandeered it all.

Predictions #11: "Sheathe Your Sword! You're Incurring Backlash and Fighting God" – Matthew 26:51-56

> "When Jesus' followers saw what was going to happen, they said, *'Lord, should we strike with our swords?'* And one of them struck the servant of the high priest, cutting off his right ear. But *Jesus answered, 'No more of this!'* And he touched the man's ear and healed him." (Luke 22:49-51)

> "Then Jesus said to him, *'Put your sword back into its place; for all those who take up the sword shall perish by the sword.* Or do you think that I cannot appeal to My Father, and He will at once put at My disposal more than twelve legions of angels? *How then will the Scriptures be fulfilled, which say that it must happen this way?'*

> At that time Jesus said to the crowds, 'Have you come out with swords and clubs to arrest Me as you would against a robber? Every

day I used to sit in the temple teaching and you did not seize Me. But *all this has taken place to fulfill the Scriptures of the prophets.'"* (Matthew 26:51-56)

Jesus forbade his disciples from defending him. Why did he order Peter and the other apostles to sheathe their swords while his enemies wielded theirs? He gave them four reasons.

First, Jesus didn't need their weapons: "Don't you think that I cannot appeal to My Father, and He will at once put at My disposal more than twelve legions of angels?" (Matt 26:53).

Second, Jesus wished to avert a bloodbath of carnage: "Those who take up the sword shall perish by the sword" (Matt 26:51).

Third, protection of Jesus would place the apostles in opposition to God: For "all this has taken place to fulfill the Scriptures of the prophets" (Matt 26:56). The Messiah's death was foreordained as was his ensuing resurrection. Drawing their swords would only forestall the inevitable.

> Why did Jesus order Peter and the others to sheathe their swords since his enemies wielded *theirs*?

Fourth, Jesus' rule was *God's* rule, not militant earthly realms like that of Caesar: "My kingdom is not of this world. If it were, my servants would fight to prevent my arrest by the Jewish leaders. But now my kingdom is from another place" (John 18:36). A spiritual kingdom conquers only with spiritual weapons, a repeated NT theme (e.g. 2 Cor 10:4).

New Details

Not once do we see the scuttles inflicted by his opponents or the flaring emotions of his apostles cloud the clarity of his focus. He came not to preserve his life, but to give it! Former Scriptures *must* be fulfilled.[18]

The one who had said, "No one takes my life from me; I lay it down freely," begins his descent. Ironically, the roles blur between those being controlled and those taking charge.

Conclusion of Jesus' Predictions

Did Jesus predict his death by crucifixion? These eleven episodes occurring over the final six months of Jesus' ministry, while varied in settings, nuance and detail, all tend to prove the same point that Jesus expected to meet with an early death and that he said so.

PART 2: Did Jesus Tie His Death to His Mission?

Five Evidences

Let's move closer to the gist of your question. I agree with you that if Jesus linked his death to his mission, he surely would have said so. It's inconceivable that it would have caught him off guard or, even more implausible, that he would have received that "little detail" at the back end of his mission ("Oh, by the way. . .!").

Did Jesus regard his death as an integral part of his mission? Evidence affirming so arises from his predictions just noted. The particular elements attesting this position are not equal. Two carry the greatest weight while the rest are vital, yet supportive.

These two foremost indicators showing that Jesus bundled his death with his mission are seen in his first steps towards Jerusalem and his final step in the Garden. The first revealed his understanding of it; the last proved his commitment to it. We might think of these as two bookends holding the rest in place. Please consider:

The foremost clue that Jesus joined his suffering to his mission is his clear understanding that it had to be so because Scripture demanded it. From the time his Messiahship was revealed to his apostles after which he steered them to Jerusalem, Jesus explicitly embedded his suffering into his mission (Matt 16:21; 20:17-19). For Jesus it could be no other way. His death was mandatory precisely because ancient Scripture made it so. On that basis, he always wrapped his suffering in imperative language – it "must" happen and never tentatively speculating, it "might" happen. The binding nature of Scripture justified its necessity, requiring the Messiah to suffer on behalf of others before entering into his final glory.

Second, Jesus' belief translated into action. His walk proved his talk from the moment he "set his face like flint" towards Jerusalem, knowing full-well executioners awaited him there who were already trimming the gallows. Only someone sold-out to a mission would commit themselves to a journey so absurd on its face.

The third sign came when Jesus voluntarily embraced the grand purpose of his death by counting our plight greater than his cost. The act of dying was not an end in itself. Nor was it about himself. When Jesus died, the God of the Universe had you and me in mind. Jesus shifted his focus from his own grueling loss of life to the eternal gains God was offering everyone else. His life was not taken from him, but freely given, a pure gift (John 10:10).

Fourth, Jesus presented his sacrificial death as God's final solution for human sin, the means by which lost people could be found and brought home to the waiting Father. By associating his own death with God's Passover Lamb, Jesus put an end to all other atoning sacrifices. It was no coincidence that within forty years after speaking these words, the altars in the Jerusalem Temple that for centuries had dripped with the blood of animal sacrifices would itself be brought to utter ruin. That altar – and all others – have no abiding relevance. His final sacrificial death had enduring efficacy, establishing God's new and lasting covenant for the forgiveness of sins.

Fifth, any remaining vestige of doubt whether or not Jesus tied his death to his mission is removed by revisiting the vivid scene in the Garden of Gethsemane. The most explicit evidence Jesus knew deep-down in his bone marrow of the inseparability of the ordeal awaiting him the next day and the mission assigned from ancient times surfaced here on the eve of his crucifixion.

Jesus "got the picture." His body language screamed *crucifixion*-awareness. Waves of panic formed their chokehold. They seized his breath, drenched his clothes in sweat and finally stripped away his stamina, dropping him in a heap onto the hard clay. Such a grim scene, however, says nothing of Jesus' *mission*-awareness. But then he prays. "Papa [*Abba,* literally!], do you have a Plan B? Is this galling cup really necessary?" In other words, "Can people recover their lost dignity, mend their botched relationships, reverse the ill-effects of their sinful choices, set themselves loose from Satan's grip, lighten their souls of a million regrets and love you deeply with all of their hearts *through any other way?*" These questions gushed out of Jesus not once, even twice, but three times. His prayer does not end with a wimpy question mark, but an exclamation mark of affirmation: "No, Papa? No? Then so be it! Stick to your plan! And count me in! Not my will, but yours be done!"

Here, in this intimate audience with the Almighty One, Jesus weds his Cross to his mission with unmistakable candor and culminating splendor.

So did Jesus regard his death as integral to his mission? His detailed explanation upon taking his initial steps to Jerusalem revealed exactly that understanding. His final step in Gethsemane proved that conviction. These two bookends seal it. To Scripture's eternal mandate was joined Jesus' internal compliance.

A wise old saying goes, "The fox knows many things, but the hedgehog knows one big thing. Imitate the hedgehog." Was there "one big thing" Jesus knew that eluded all the foxes?

Jesus saw beyond the cross to the crown. A silver lining ran through all his dire predictions: His endgame did not stop at his crucifixion. Jesus, not them, knew the one big thing that would come next: *I will rise up on the third day!* Here is mission accomplished. How were the powers of darkness overthrown? By letting them mount their full fury, unleash their worst and then run their victory lap. The reign of darkness will be overthrown by Christ's victory over sin and death. Knowing that "one big thing" thrust him forward: "As the time approached for him to be *taken up to heaven,* Jesus resolutely set out for Jerusalem" (Luke 9:51). By it Jesus endured his crucible with a poise that baffled everyone.

Back to Your Question

Your question touches on a profound subject – the death of Jesus – so important, in fact, that in Parts One and Two, I've attempted to step out of the way to let him speak directly. I think you'll agree: His words are powerful. No one spoke like Jesus, God's living Word.

Part 3 speaks to the question of perspective: How important is it, really, if Jesus simply died on the cross but never brought it up in the context of his mission? What impact might this have on Christianity and Islam?

PART 3: Which Story Line Matches Up with the Injeel and Qur'an?

In light of Jesus' predictions and their connections to his mission, which of the four Story Lines matches most closely with the Injeel and the Qur'an?

Story Line 1: **Jesus foretold his death by crucifixion, his burial and bodily resurrection on the third day. He *was* crucified, buried and raised to life just as predicted.**

Aligned with the Injeel? – Yes. This squares with Jesus' predictions in every detail. His expectations arose from God's salvation announced in ancient Scriptures making Jesus' death and resurrection a revelation of his love and power.

Aligned with the Qur'an? – Maybe. Jesus' prediction of his own death and the belief that it would comply with Allah's will aligns with three passages.

(1) Mariam 19:33 records Isa's first message spoken from the cradle in which he predicted both his death and ascension.

(2) Allah informs Isa in Al-Imran 3:54-55 that his death was not carried out in opposition to his will, but in alignment with it:

'O Isa! I will make Thee die[19] and take Thee up again[20] to me and will clear thee of those who misbelieve...[21]

(3) In Al-Maidah 5:17 Isa addressed Allah in a way that showed his awareness that his death was divinely caused, thus fulfilling an undisclosed divine purpose: "... when[22] Thou didst cause me to die.[23]

Story Line 2: Jesus never predicted his death. Yet he *was* crucified, buried and raised to life on the third day.

Aligned with the Injeel? – No. This ignores Jesus' many predictions of his death and suggests it caught Jesus by surprise. It also bypasses earlier prophecies upon which Jesus based his predictions. This in effect reduces the crucifixion to a human injustice stripped of its saving value and the resurrection to a cliff-hanger comeback.

Aligned with the Qur'an? – No. Isa predicted his death and resurrection as an infant in Mariam 19:33: "Peace be upon me the day I was born, the day I will die, and the day I will be resurrected alive!" Furthermore, this scenario feeds the myth that Isa's life was taken from him by evil men who exerted themselves over the will of Allah, a contradiction of Allah's promise to Isa in Al-Imran 3:54-55: "Isa, I will make you die and raise you up to me." It also counters Isa's retrospective view of his death in Al-Maidah 5:117 as having already occurred in the past: "I was a witness over them while I remained among them, and when you made me die [*tawaffa*]..." The term *tawaffa*, interpreted "to cause to die," strongly suggests that God had a direct hand in it. After considering alternate definitions, Abdul Mannan Omar in *Dictionary of the Holy Qur'an, Arabic-English* defends "caused him to die," citing Lisan al-Arab:

> "*Twaffahu Allahu* means Allah took his soul or caused him to die. When God is the subject and a human being the object and the root is *Waw, Fa, Ya* and this is a verb then it has no other meaning than that of taking away the soul and causing to die. Not a single instance from the Holy Qur'an or the sayings of the Holy Prophet can be shown which can provide an argument that this expression can be used in a sense other than to cause any one to die by taking away his soul."[1]

Comparative Significance of Scenarios 1 & 2

Does it matter really if Jesus voluntarily gave his life to fulfill a divine purpose or if his death resulted from a random injustice? Some Christians have opted for Scenario 2 hoping to exonerate God of any blame for Jesus' death. Well-meaning, perhaps, but this view does just the opposite. The Injeel supports Scenario 1 over Scenario 2 for good reason. If God was in a holding pattern, uninvolved until *after* he witnessed the human rejection of the Son, then we are left with a God of remarkable power to raise the dead, but lacking prescience, even caught off-guard by the cruelties inflicted on his Son.

Did God predict and plan Jesus death on the Cross? The Table in Question 9.1, "Sources for Jesus in the Injeel" shows from the earlier Books how God knew in advance the cost of bringing redemption. While mystery prevails over how God functions over human moral agents, this we do know. **Subtracting divine forethought from the message of the Cross leaves us with a different God, not the Sovereign of the universe who meets us in the Injeel.** Story Line 2 categorizes the cross as a catastrophe of divine negligence, not an act of unfathomable love. Fortunately, such is not the God of the previous Books. His love was proven on the cross by one thing: he *meant* to do it!

HOW DEEP THE LOVE OF GOD
Jesus' Death Exposed More than Human Injustice

"This man [*Jesus*] *was handed over to you by God's set purpose and foreknowledge*; and you, with the help of wicked men, put him to death by nailing him to the cross." (Acts 2:23)

"But *God demonstrates his own love for us* in this: While we were still sinners, *Christ died for us*." (Romans 5:6-8)

"God is love. *This is how God showed his love among us*: He sent his one and only Son into the world that we might live through him. *This is love*: not that we loved God, but that *he loved us and sent his Son as an atoning sacrifice for our sins*." (1 John 4:8-10)

"As to this salvation, *the prophets who prophesied of the grace* that would come to you made careful searches and inquiries, seeking to know what person or time the Spirit of Christ [Messiah] within them was indicating as *He predicted the sufferings of Christ [Messiah] and the glories to follow*." (1 Peter 1:11)

"You were not redeemed with perishable things like silver or gold from your futile way of life inherited from your forefathers, but with *precious blood,* as of a *lamb* unblemished and spotless, *the blood of Christ. For He was foreknown before the foundation of the world,* but has appeared in these last times for the sake of you who through Him are believers in God, who raised Him from the dead and gave Him glory, *so that your faith and hope are in God*." (1 Peter 1:18-21)[24]

Story Line 3: Jesus predicted his death by crucifixion but *was not* crucified.

Aligned with the Injeel? No.

Aligned with the Qur'an? No.

***Story Line 4:* Jesus never predicted his death by crucifixion, and he *was not* crucified.**

If Jesus was spared death altogether and taken straight to heaven, would it matter? Certainly, it would, for Jesus! All charges against him along with the death sentence would be dropped. Immediately, he would enjoy unprecedented closeness to God making him the honored beneficiary of his escape from death. Would it matter for anyone else? Apparently not. His end-of-life rescue would benefit no one but himself.

Aligned with the Injeel? *No.* This view flies in the face of Jesus' many predictions and raises a host of questions making it untenable. What then of the New Testament accounts? Was Jesus even arrested and tried? Where does history end and illusion begin? If they innocently mistook Jesus to be dead, how does one account for the unanimous reports of his death by Roman and Jewish authorities at the time? And if the apostles intentionally fabricated the story, why did they die as martyrs for preaching it? Are liars and martyrs cut out of the same cloth?

Aligned with the Qur'an? Yes and no. (a) Yes, according to the Muslim Majority View of Al-Nisa 4:156. Appealing to this reference, most Muslims view the crucifixion as a tragic event that happened to someone other than Jesus. Two readings in the English from reputedly literal interpreters are as follows:

> "... they [the Jews] did not kill him, and they did not crucify him, *but a similitude was made for them...*" The Koran, E Palmer

> "... but they killed him not, nor crucified him, but *the resemblance of Isa (Jesus) was put over another man (and they killed that man)...*" Khan

There are compelling reasons Muslims might want to reconsider this Majority View. First, the text does not say that Jesus was not killed, only that the Jews did not kill him, a true statement. They conspired, but the actual execution was performed by the Romans. Second, anyone can trace this view back to its original source – not to the Qur'an of the seventh century, but Basilides in the second. He is the first known teacher who reduced Jesus' crucifixion to an illusion that caused a travesty of justice for an innocent bystander from Cyrene. (See Chapters 9 and 11.)

In an attempt to show independent historical support for this Majority View of Al-Nisa 4:156, Islamic apologists often present Basilides as an early *Christian* leader. This is an egregious error since it is well-known that his Gnostic school was an *enemy* of orthodox Christianity. Even if he had been a Christian, he still lived almost a century after Jesus died, handicapping his testimony with a significant chronological challenge.

Basilides' teachings were amplified a century later in *The Second Treatise of the Great Seth* and again by Mani, the "prophet of Babylonia," both discussed elsewhere.[26] Each was a bona fide heretic by both Christian and Islamic standards.

(b) No, this scenario is out of step with Al-Nisa 4:156 according to the Minority Muslim View. It rejects the illusion theory and ascribes historical accuracy to Jesus' death. Recently during a private conversation with a well-educated imam from Iraq, I heard this statement: "Prophet Muhammad (p) did not give his life for others. Only Prophet Isa." Thinking I must have misheard him, I apologized and asked if he would repeat it. Sure enough, he meant every word.

While catching me off-guard, his comment excited me. I had never heard any Muslim, much less a Ph.D. in Islamic studies, make such an admission. Later I read a historical study by Todd Lawson, *The Crucifixion and the Qur'an: A Study in the History of Muslim Thought*.[27] This scholarly work documents belief in the reality of Jesus death on the cross in early Islamic tradition.

He concludes:

> "The Qur'an itself is *neutral* on the subject of the historicity of the crucifixion and may indeed be read to *affirm* it." (emphasis mine)

My initial excitement over this discovery was short-lived. Lawson points out that much of the Muslim objection of the crucifixion is less about history than about the atonement that the Injeel teaches.

> "...many of the problems usually associated with an interpretation of 4:157-8 are seen to be the result of an *Islamic rejection of Christian soteriology* – the theory of *the doctrine of salvation*."[28]

While the house of Islam lacks consensus on the historical question of Jesus' death – most answer *No, he did not* while a relative handful argue *Yes, he did* – Muslims unanimously deny its atoning value. Lawson concludes:

> "It is interesting to speculate whether or not it would have been necessary for Muslims to deny the crucifixion of Jesus if that event were a doctrinally neutral issue. In other words, it would seem that a simple crucifixion, which did not carry with it such un-Islamic concepts as vicarious atonement, could easily be accepted."

Is anything gained from the Minority View acknowledging a historical fact but rejecting its saving benefits? Such recognition is a commendable step in the right direction, especially where there's pressure to believe otherwise. To my knowledge, outside of Muslim and Gnostic (who rejected Jesus' humanity) circles, Jesus' death is universally accepted with the exception of *fictional* writings published and popularized many centuries later.[30] To that, we might add another advantage for those Muslims who concede the history of his death but deny the soteriology – *curiosity*. My guess is that many of you who say, "Yes, I believe Jesus underwent death by Roman crucifixion, but it had nothing to do with human salvation," have secretly wondered:

- Why the cross for *this* Prophet, upon whom the Qur'an heaped more eminent titles than any other? As an act of Allah's will, what purpose did it serve?
- How do we reconcile Jesus' sublime entrance into our world with his ghastly exit from it?
- Perhaps the most challenging: If Jesus' death was not about atoning the sins of others, what horrendous evils did he commit during his lifetime to earn for himself such a savage sendoff?

Jesus Meets Human Need, not Demands

Where does this leave us? *Most* people, not just Muslims, find the message of the Cross galling. Despite this offensive reality, as Jesus' disciples we are tasked with passing it on to others. That includes all of it, both its what and why. Belief in the *what* — *that* Jesus died, is important; belief in the *why* – that he died *according to the Scriptures*, is the Gospel of salvation. Why can't we Christians back off and just give people the silence they desire? The answer becomes clear in this scene at the Cross:

> "The chief priests, the teachers of the law and the elders mocked him. 'He saved others,' they said, 'but he can't save himself! He's the king of Israel! *Let him come down now from the cross, and we will believe in him.* He trusts in God. Let God rescue him now if he wants him, for he said, 'I am the Son of God.'" (Matthew 27:41-43)

Why didn't Jesus give the crowd what it wanted and match its terms of acceptance: *Let him come down now from the cross, and we will believe in him?* He could easily have pulled it off, calling 10,000 angels to his rescue. Two reasons prevented him. First, Jesus remained on the cross because of *who* he wasn't and who he was. He was *not* a politician currying votes. He was God's Messiah reconciling a sinful humanity with a holy God.

> "We all, like sheep, have gone astray, each of us has turned to our own way; and the LORD has laid on him the iniquity of us all."
> Prophet Isaiah 53:6

Second, Jesus refused their demands for another reason. Had he given them what they wanted, he would have robbed them of what they needed. They wanted a roaring Lion wielding a sword, not a dying Lamb removing sins. They demanded a political Messiah imposing a militant path to national ascendency over Rome. By refusing, Jesus gifted them with something far superior. One of executioners took all this in – the shrill crowd and its demanding charade and Jesus fixed to the cross as unyielding Truth, silent except for his intercessory prayer for the whole sorry lot, "Father, forgive them. They don't know what they're doing." That soldier became the first answer to the Lamb's prayer and went home a changed man (Matt 27:54; Lk 23:34).

Again, where does this leave us? As Christians desiring friendship with Muslims, we are naturally inclined to avoid the offense of the cross message. In doing so, we would be doing you no favors! We would be insincere friends acting out of fear rather than love. As God's Lamb, Jesus died to rid us of an oppressor far closer to home than our political enemies:

> "We all, like sheep, have gone astray, each of us has turned to our own way; and *the LORD has laid on him the iniquity of us all.*" (Isaiah 53:6)

Why did some people under-rate Jesus? Blind to their true condition, Jesus' enemies couldn't recognize who he was. By over-inflated their own standing before God, they misjudged his:

> "*. . . we considered him punished by God, stricken by him and afflicted. But he was pierced for our transgressions, he was crushed for our iniquities; the punishment that brought us peace was upon him, and by his wounds we are healed.*" (Isaiah 53:4-5)

They all returned to their homes with bad news, "Jesus of Nazareth died." Tragically, they missed the Good News, "He died *for me.*"

> "For what I received I passed on to you as of first importance: that Christ *died for our sins according to the Scriptures,* that he was *buried,* that he was *raised on the third day according to the Scriptures . . . .*" (1 Corinthians 15:3-7)

"For what I received I passed on to you as of first importance: that Christ died for our sins according to the Scriptures, that he was buried, that he was raised on the third day according to the Scriptures . . . ."
Injeel,
1 Corinthians 15:3-7

Belief that Jesus actually died is a step in the right direction. No person needs to stop there.

> "If you *declare with your mouth, "Jesus is Lord,"* and believe in your heart that God raised him from the dead, you will be saved.* For it is with your heart that you believe and are justified, and it is with your mouth that you profess your faith and are saved. As Scripture says, "Anyone who believes in him will never be put to shame." For there is *no difference between Jew and Gentile*— the same Lord is Lord of all and richly blesses all who call on him, for, *"Everyone who calls on the name of the Lord will be saved."* (Romans 10:9-13)

Options Open to Muslims

Muslims and Christians, contemplating the four possible scenarios of Jesus' death, face the same two questions. Which of these best matches up with sacred Books and recorded history?

And upon which of them should we stake our future? On the joint testimonies from the Injeel and the Qur'an, both of whom align Jesus' death with God's purpose, one clearly spelled out in the Injeel as *God's* way of removing human sin and establishing peace with himself? Or should we rely on oppositional reports presenting Jesus' death as only an illusion by men who were nowhere near the event in time or place and flagrantly defied Christian and Islamic orthodoxy.

Jesus' crucifixion was not the death of God, even for a weekend.

I invite Muslim readers to prayerfully weigh the testimony of Story Line 1, God who proved his self-giving love and resurrection power – one who planned early against heretics who came late.

Question 10.1: "At the crucifixion, God died. How can that be?"

Q 10.2: "If Isa is God, how can he be killed?"

These penetrating questions remind me of the wisdom I once read on a university whiteboard:

> "God is dead."
> –Nietzsche
> "Nietzsche is dead."
> –God

Jesus' crucifixion was not the death of God, even for a weekend. God is absolute, unchanging and cannot die.[31] So how is it possible for Jesus to have a divine nature and yet die? The answer is found in Jesus' two complete natures as God and man as explained in Chapter 3. An ancient Christian thinker wrote:

> "In the same way we say that he 'suffered and rose again.' We do not mean that God the Word suffered in his Deity . . . for the Deity is impassible [incapable of being harmed] because it is incorporeal [lacking material substance]. But the body which had become his own body suffered these things, and therefore he himself is said to have suffered them for us. The impassible was in the body which suffered."[32]

In more up-to-date language, Abdu Murray aptly captured the thought:

> "In the Christian view, Jesus did not die as God or in his divine nature. That nature transcends his physical body and did not cease to exist just because Jesus' brain activity may have stopped for a time. Rather, *Jesus physically died as a man.*[34]

> "The physical death would not necessarily result in the death of the transcendent any more than the sudden loss of every Qur'an in the world would mean that the message itself would somehow cease to exist."[35]

In his humanity, Jesus suffered, bled and died, but His divine nature was not subject to change.

> "In the beginning was the Word, and the Word was with God, and

the Word *was* God. He was with God in the beginning. Through him all things were made; without him nothing was made that has been made.... The Word *became* flesh and made his dwelling among us. We have seen his glory, the glory of the one and only Son, who came from the Father, full of grace and truth." (John 1:1-3, 14)

At the crucifixion, only that which was temporary died. Divine nature cannot be altered in any way, much less cease to exist. Hearing me explain this, Akbar, a thoughtful Muslim, responded:

"What you say of Jesus is true of anyone. The Qur'an teaches that when we die, our bodies decay while our spirit continues to exist. At the last Day, our bodies will raise for Judgment. There is no difference."

His insight deserves a thoughtful response. Is there a difference between humanity's spiritual-physical separation at death and that of Jesus? Is it fair to equate the undying divine Word with the surviving human spirit? Akbar is correct that both the Word and the human spirit persist beyond the grave. But he argued that this commonality challenged the unique Deity of Jesus. Here's where the equation breaks down. Man's spirit was *derived* from God at human creation, that is, entering man (Adam) from outside himself.

"Then the *LORD God* formed a man from the dust of the ground and *breathed into his nostrils the breath of life*, and the man became a *living being*." (Genesis 2:7)

God's breathing his Spirit into us made us spiritual creatures. It did not make us God. By contrast, as we read in John 1:1 that "The Word *was* God" – His divine nature was intrinsic to him, not derived from outside himself. Nor was there a time when he received his life as a product of creation. Instead, "through him all things were made" (John 1:2).

Your excellent question has an answer: Jesus' crucifixion was not the death of God, even for a weekend.

CHAPTER 11

PREVIOUS SCRIPTURES, AL-QUR'AN & PROPHET MUHAMMAD (P)

Question 11: Why don't Christians believe in the Qur'an (Muslim holy book) when it acknowledges, affirms and reveres Jesus, son of Mary?

Q 11.1: "Was the prophet Mohammad in the Bible?"
Q 11.2: Christians believe in Moses in a line of prophets. Why don't they believe that Muhammad (p) is a continuation of the same message after Jesus?
Q 11.3: Why in your religion don't you acknowledge or admit Muhammad (p) as the last prophet (messenger) of God?

DISCLAIMER

This question-set asks how Christians respond to Islam's primary sources. If this chapter doesn't help you, please skip it. I don't know how to do this section without the unintended consequences of offending the very readers for whom I cherish. Despite this risk, your questions invite our perspectives on matters of Muslim veneration, making comparisons with earlier revelation and asking for our honest evaluation. On the plus side, they bring great promise, opening a door for both Christians and

Muslims to expand ourselves by enlarging our horizons as we explore new terrain. My answers, admittedly limited as coming from outside the Muslim fold, are not made off-the-cuff but have been formed after applying my reasonably best efforts to consider the broad scope and tenor of Islamic writings.

Q-11 focuses on Islam's Book, Al-Qur'an. The next three consider Islam's Prophet, Muhammad (p), each addressing one specific aspect of his relationship to Jesus. Q-11.1 wants to know if his coming is predicted in the Earlier Books. Q-11.2 inquires of his continuity with those former Books. Q-11.3 considers the Prophet's finality as the culminating seal of the prophetic line.

Question 11: Why don't Christians believe in the Qur'an (Muslim holy book) when it acknowledges, affirms and reveres Jesus, son of Mary?

The premise to your question seems clear. Since the Qur'an venerates Jesus as the Injeel's central Figure, should not Christians respond in kind by embracing it as the last Book?

Twenty years ago, I read the Qur'an from cover to cover for the first time. To my astonishment, Jesus is frequently mentioned and was "held in honor in this world and in the Hereafter" (Al-Imran 3:145 Kahn). Titles attributed to him, I discovered, were nothing short of stunning.

Remarkably, the Qur'an's Jesus is the son of Mary[1] who was born of a virgin,[2] the Messiah (*al-Masih*),[3] the Messenger of God (*rasula 'Mah*),[4] the Prophet of God (*Nabiya'llah*),[5] the servant of God (*abdu 'llah*),[6] Word of God (*kalimatu 'llah*),[7] the Word of truth (*Qaula 'l-Haqq*),[8] a Spirit from God (*Ruhun min Allah*),[9] a giver of life to the dead and miracle-worker,[10] who ascended into heaven,[11] a true man like Adam in every respect[12] except for sin[13]

496

and, despite his moral perfection, became the conveyor of God's mercy![14] How extraordinary![15]

In light of this unparalleled esteem for Jesus, your question makes perfect sense. Why are Christians so reluctant to accept a Book that places Jesus on this high a pedestal?

Let's begin by considering what it means to honor – "acknowledge, affirm and revere" – a historical figure such as Jesus?

A conversation I had years ago with a Muslim neighbor puts this into perspective. Maher from Khartoum, Sudan was a distinguished gentleman in his sixties with a quiet gravitas. He was well-educated and an excellent father. Our kids played soccer together. One day he pointed out to me the considerable overlapping beliefs our religions shared about Jesus. With a note of jubilation, he said:

> "J. P., Christians and Muslims believe in the same God. We Muslims believe the same teachings about Jesus that you do except only two: that he was the Son of God and that he was crucified. Other than that, we agree. That's all!"

I mention this because almost every Muslim I meet echoes Maher's sentiment. Christians genuinely appreciate Muslim goodwill behind such expressions. Certainly, I have never heard a devout Muslim *dis*honor Jesus. So what is the problem? It is this. While not dishonoring Jesus, to his devout followers they still fall far short of rendering tribute that matches his signature tour de force.

What if?

Maybe a comparison will help. Think for a moment about Dr. Jonas Salk (1914-1995), the scientist who invented the groundbreaking polio vaccine. Before his invention, thousands suffered. In 1953 there were more than 57,000 cases of polio in the U.S. In 1955 when the vaccine was approved that number fell to 28,985 and by 1957 it had decreased to 5,894. By 1963, it dropped to less than a thousand. The great mind also had a big heart. Dr. Salk never patented his discovery because he wanted it to be distributed freely to everyone. For that, he became a national hero who in 1955 was awarded a special citation from President Dwight Eisenhower. By 1959, 90 other countries used Salk's vaccine. Today in the U.S., cases of polio are extremely rare. Dr. Salk earned his place in medical history and is remembered as the man who stopped polio. Those are the facts.

Now imagine a modern biography was published about the life of Dr. Salk in which the author left out his signature life-saving discovery. Instead, he homed in on the difficult conditions of his childhood, coming from a poor family in New York City. He heaps praise on the doctor for surmounting arduous hardships, achieving academic accolades and extols him as a moral example worthy of imitation. Finally, in the last chapter, this biographer denies that Salk made any contribution to the groundbreaking vaccine. Instead, he advises that unfounded rumors to the contrary should be ignored.

What's your call? Would you award it with a 5-star rating? Does its author truly acknowledge, affirm and revere the great scientist? How do you think the doctor's friends and family would rate it? How about the beneficiaries who are fortunate enough to live after Salk's discovery? Could we justify awarding this biography anything higher than two stars?

Does this fictional biography fairly apply to the Qur'an's portrayal of Jesus? I want to respectfully argue for its fairness on this basis. While honoring Jesus, the Qur'an short-changes him by downplaying his supreme contribution to humanity and diminishing his identity.

1. The Qur'an Radically Abbreviates Jesus' Life

I read the Qur'an's 93 references to Jesus with keen interest. I didn't expect it to repeat Jesus' actions and sayings that we find in the Injeel, for sequels need not retell events, but they normally take up where the earlier work left off. As a book claiming that all divine revelation must confirm prior revelation, I naturally looked for those connectors, places in which the Qur'an builds on the Injeel's foundational truths of Jesus. Frankly, that did not happen. In all due respect, I came away with a gnawing sense that its coverage of Jesus is disproportionate and incomplete. Let me explain.

A striking feature of the Qur'an, at least to me, is the sheer number of people cited by name from the biblical Books – forty-two! – starting logically with Adam, humanity's common father. [16] That is remarkable! But even more surprising is that thirty-seven of these come from the Old Testament, leaving only five from the Injeel! In other words, the Qur'an skips over most of the Injeel.

Moreover, what completely captured my attention was that out of those five individuals from the Injeel, each was is in some way connected to Jesus' Nativity. Its cast of biblical characters stops with Yahya, the Baptizer, whose role in the Injeel was preparing Israel to receive the coming of the Messiah and then to *announce* him to them. [17] In other words, **the Qur'an's coverage of Jesus practically ends with his debut.** While reserving for Jesus alone the highest titles of honor, it presents him as a prophet with power to perform healing miracles, even raising the dead, but without even a hint about how or why only he could pull off such feats.

Does this uneven coverage even matter? Indeed, it does. It brings the meaning of the virgin birth, a miracle so revered in the Qur'an, to a virtual dead-end. When I ask Muslims what the virgin birth tells us about who Jesus was, I typically get a blank stare. I don't blame them. The material omitted by the Qur'an leaves its readers guessing, perhaps that the Virgin Birth simply demonstrates God's creative power. Of course, no one would argue with that. Yet it leaves bigger questions unraised. How many other eminent prophets of God were born without a human father? Zero. Why Jesus alone? What greater purpose was served by a supernatural birth? Was there a connection between his mode of conception and the miracles that he would later perform?

By restricting its major coverage of Jesus to the sliver of his nativity and practically skipping over the rest severs his life from his birth and deprives Muslims of the necessary information by which to answer those questions. Its missing parts also explain Maher's dismissive comment cited earlier: "We agree about Jesus on everything except for two things: Son of God and that he was crucified."

It is precisely these two matters that deprive Jesus of his unique identity and his historic contribution. Let's turn to them now.

2. The Qur'an Honors Jesus without Recognizing his Full Identity

Our culture's anti-supernatural leaning scoffs at the virgin birth of Jesus. Liberal Christianity considers it an embarrassment on the New Testament. I am thankful for the Qur'an's clear presentation of it as history and not legend. Along with Bible-believing Christians, you believe in an Almighty Creator who is able to say "Be!" and it is! For us, Jesus' virgin birth is no cause for embarrassment, but an evocative miracle of irrepressible wonder. This private marvel was twice told both in the Injeel and twice again in the Qur'an. A serious discussion on this question is long over-due. Can we accept Jesus' supernatural conception while normalizing his identity after entering the world in that fashion?

Our anti-supernatural leaning culture scoffs at Jesus' virgin birth. Even liberal Christianity considers it an embarrassment on the New Testament. I am thankful for the Qur'an's clear presentation of it as fact and not legend.

By opening with this miracle, the New Testament opens the door to a whole new world altogether. For Jesus:

". . .stands on the threshold of the New Testament, blatantly supernatural, defying our rationalism, informing us that all that follows belongs to the same order as itself and that if we find it offensive there is no point in proceeding further."[18]

Jesus is who he is. By assigning him a place with other prophets, none of whom entered the world without male involvement, introduces a medical anomaly without the benefit of a rationale. The Qur'an commendably admits to an unprecedented miracle but then retreats to the limits of human intellect.

"This miracle eliminates any possibility of understanding or grasping the nature of God in Christ in a purely intellectual fashion. It leaves only a spiritual understanding in which God's purposes are understood in God's own way."[19]

500

As a Christian who has read the Qur'an carefully, I agree with you that it "reveres" Jesus. But it does so in a way that strips him of who he is. One's identity, unlike his or her character, endures as a stubborn reality. For example, comparing a person as a kindergartener and later as a senior adult should reflect a developing character but with the same set of fingerprints.

What determines identity? Where does it originate? Is it not derived from parents and expressed through names? J. P. Knight contains both my personal and family names, each an essential element in defining who I am. At birth my parents named me J. P. to distinguish me from my two older siblings while Knight was inherited from my father, who received it from *his* father. Both names are necessary to identify me. No one is named just "Bob." Bob who?

Let's apply this to Jesus. The Qur'an states that he was conceived not by normal biological means but through a divine miracle of the Spirit. Thus, it acknowledges that Jesus entered the world without the *normal* marital union, but *not* without a sacred fusion. Mary as a virgin was incapable of producing Jesus on her own. Making this a miracle was the absence of *male* involvement but not of a second party altogether. That is a fact from which neither the Injeel nor the Qur'an shies away. The Qur'an in Al-Tahrim 66:12, with surprising boldness, uses even more explicit language than the Injeel, so much so that most English translations gloss over it.

Why mention this? Because the angel Gabriel, at the time of his announcement to Mary, tied both the newborn's nature and identity to the second party. He said:

> "You will conceive and give birth to a son, and you are to call him Jesus. He will be great and will be called the Son of the Most High. . . *The Holy Spirit will come on you*, and the power of the Most High will overshadow you. *So the holy one to be born will be called the Son of God*." (Luke 1:32, 35)

So this coming child would receive his unique character as "the holy one" and identity as "the Son of God" directly from "the Most High" through his Spirit. By contrast, the Qur'an restricts Jesus' personhood to his mother's side, calling him only "the son of Mary."

The irony is, that it celebrates the spectacular mode of his birth while stopping short of recognizing the Person produced by it. Islamic tradition is reticent, to put it mildly, to recognize what is written plainly in its own Book, namely, that the contributing Party[20] was the necessary factor making Jesus more than simply unique among all men, but of a different classification altogether.

Jesus, then, is more than the "son of Mary." The Injeel identifies Jesus both as the son of Mary *and* the Son of God, fully incorporating both sets of traits he received through his unprecedented conception. It is puzzling that, on the one hand, the Qur'an adamantly denies Jesus' unique divine Sonship while, on the other, celebrating the miraculous union creating it. And on what basis? As we saw in Chapter 2, the grounds for rejecting the Son of God had no bearing on the Injeel's message whatsoever. An artificial crisis has severed an indivisible union between the eternal Father and Son. Consequently, while honoring Jesus in comparison to other men, it stops short of recognizing what such a union demanded. That portrayal offers Muslims an incomplete Jesus, lacking all the elements of what made him *Him*.

> Was there a correlation between what we see throughout the life of Jesus and the contributing Spirit of God at his conception? . . . Does anyone connect the dots between that outwardly visible range of authority with the transcendent nature it required?

Is it taboo for us to humbly contemplate this unprecedented wonder we call the virgin birth? If off-limits, why its inclusion in sacred Scripture? Is it outrageous to consider the union by which Jesus was conceived and ask what patterns of behavior and traits we might expect to visibly manifest throughout his life? Could there be a correlation between that unique union and those titles and attributes making him the most unique Prophet in your Book and ours? Let me suggest an answer.

First, in matters of physical appearance, it is likely that Jesus grew up being told, "You take after your mother's side of the family. You don't look anything like Joseph." While not in the Injeel, it must have been so. His humanity, all of it, came through Mary.

Second, by the same token, Jesus displayed traits, actions and words bearing no resemblance whatsoever to either Mary or Joseph his stepfather. Many of his moral choices and overall demeanor arose independently of them. If not from them, then from whom? Is it farfetched to see a correlation between the extraordinary elements of Jesus' life and God's contributing holy Spirit who conceived him? Does anyone connect the dots between his outwardly visible range of authority with the transcendent nature it required?

What traits are we talking about? What did Jesus do that betrayed his unique origins? We could begin with his *moral character.* We see a man of extraordinary moral fiber. Isn't absolute power supposed to corrupt absolutely? Since when do we see unchallenged dominion and pure goodness manifested in one person? We see the same man wield raw power and apply healing mercy to restore vibrant life.

What about his *range of knowledge*? We see a man describe the celestial world of angels and the divine throne with hometown familiarity – without resorting to visions, trances or mantras. We see a man who could read people's inner-thoughts such as the Samaritan woman who relayed to her friends, "He told me everything I ever did!" (John 4:39).

How about his *creative command over nature*? We see a man who could say "Be!" and clammy ashen bodies suddenly pulsated with new life. As the Creator spoke the Cosmos into existence, Jesus just spoke the word and the dead son of a nobleman returned to normal life. Another time, Jesus joined a group of mourners who had gathered at the tomb of a man who had been dead for four days. Yes, four days decaying in a tomb! Calling him by name, Jesus ordered him to come out. The shrouded man immediately stood to his feet and walked out. That night he and his family and friends dined in his home with Jesus. We see lepers medically repaired and socially restored.

These feats over nature were neither rare nor performed privately. We see cripples doing jumping jacks, the deaf hearing and singing, the blind suddenly roaming about safely and fearlessly. We see a man who said of his own death, "Destroy this temple and I will raise it up in three days."

Who else in either the Bible or the Qur'an dared take divine authority to declare sins committed by others forgiven?

Finally, who else from a young age would address, not Joseph, but Almighty God, as "My Papa?"

Does anyone ask, *Did Mary do those things?* None of the above.

So why Jesus and only him? The Injeel provides the only sane answer. What Jesus *did* matched who Jesus was. His performance matched his personhood. More accurately, his personhood *enabled* his performance. All of this is captured in Jesus' conception. While Mary gave him birth, she did not produce him by herself.

The fruit of Nazareth's most sacred union became more than another prophetic voice, but a unique Person, unlike any other, blessed and holy. Throughout his life, Jesus bore her likeness with its human charm and grace. And the whole time, every step of the way he bore the unmistakable imprint of the God of the universe through the Spirit who conceived him.

> "The virgin birth at the opening and the empty tomb at the close of Jesus' life bear witness that *this life is a fact marked off from all the rest of human life.*"[21]

> "The virgin birth at the opening and the empty tomb at the close of Jesus' life bear witness that this life is a fact marked off from all the rest of human life."
> Karl Barth

> "Jesus' life is different in origin for his sonship is related to the direct work of God through the Holy Spirit, and in purpose for *he came to reveal the nature of God and bring salvation to the world.*"[22]

All of this presents Jesus' dual nature as a mystery rather than a contradiction. It makes us bow in humility, riveted in adoration to something too wonderful for words.

Maybe you're still skeptical that the Injeel suddenly innovated the Son of God. Lest suspicion persist, God set the stage for this mystery seven centuries prior to Mary's generation by "sending his Word that will not return void" (Isaiah 55). A Son would come from Galilee, of the lineage of David, to whom was given names considered outlandish for any prophet, yet befitting this newborn Son: *Wonderful Counselor,*

The fruit of Nazareth's most sacred union became more than a another prophetic voice, but a unique Person, unlike any other, blessed and holy.

Father of Eternity, Mighty God and Prince of Peace (Isaiah 9:6). This identity would not *double* the number of Gods, but through the divine Agency of the Holy Spirit through a pure virgin (Isaiah 7:14), a Son, like none other, would enter this world under the banner "Immanuel, God with us." Only One so endowed could rescue humanity, accomplishing what no mere human being could pull off: an acceptable sacrifice for sin.

Which leads to my neighbor Maher's second objection.

3. The Qur'an Honors Jesus without his Signature Achievement

The Qur'an offers four passing references to Jesus' death or crucifixion which, according to most Muslims, simply declare it never happened. By divine miracle, he escaped the cross, implicitly accusing the Injeel of false testimony.

We must never, of course, confuse accusation with demonstration. That God is capable of pulling off an illusion is not the question. But the absence of corroborating evidence for the illusion theory, both during and after the crucifixion, should give pause to anyone holding that view. For example, we search the Qur'an in vain for just one member in the impressive cast of people surrounding Jesus' death who could vouch for its denial. Both his friends and foes crowded the awful scene.

Can a mother not recognize her firstborn? Did God dupe her along with the rest, the pure virgin he honored to bear his Messiah?

- Where is Pontius Pilate and other notables from the political world?
- Where are official records from religious authorities documenting a surprising last-minute disappearance of Jesus, just when they thought they had him? Any word from members of the Sanhedrin, the Supreme Court who condemned Jesus?

- Where are those notable Jewish authorities who became followers of Jesus – Joseph of Arimathea, a member of the Sanhedrin or Nicodemus, a ruling scribe — who joined hands to lovingly wrap his body in linen strips soaked in seventy-five pounds of spices (John 19:40)? Have they come forward to break the secrecy?
- Where are the brave loyal women who stood at the foot of the Cross, near enough to hear his labored breathing or even speak to him?

Among them stood Mary, his own mother. Let's reenact the scene. Did God dupe her too, the chaste virgin of his sacred choosing to usher his Messiah into the world? Can a mother *not* recognize her firstborn son? How about John, the young man at her side. From the cross, Jesus tenderly addressed each of them. To Mary, he said, "Woman, here is your son," and to John "Here is your mother" (John 19:27). With those words Jesus entrusted the "disciple he loved" with the guardianship of his mother most blessed. From that day forward she moved in with his family. Muslim reader, I ask you. If the man on the cross was anyone other than Jesus – a look-alike, whether Simon of Cyrene, Judas the betrayer, or anyone else – would they have made loving provision for his mother? Could those words have come from the lips of anyone except Jesus? Can something so sacred as the mother-son bond be interlaced with trickery in God's name?

> If the man on the cross was anyone other than Jesus – a look-alike, whether Simon of Cyrene, Judas the betrayer, or anyone else – would they have expressed such concern making provision for his mother?

Consider those involved with Jesus after the crucifixion, the chorus of witnesses whose lives were put right-side up after seeing him in the days immediately following his death. Is there any evidence that one of them later backtracked his or her story?

- Where are Jesus' apostles who with wonder placed their hands on his healed scars, feeling for themselves the reality of a body

If the man on the cross was anyone other than Jesus – a look-alike, whether Simon of Cyrene, Judas the betrayer, or anyone else – would they have expressed such concern making provision for his mother?

in glorified form, who spoke and ate with him over a 40-day period?

• Where are those men and women who became awestruck upon gazing skyward as Jesus disappeared in the clouds?

• Where are the 120 disciples, male and female, crowded in a room when the Holy Spirit was sent down upon each of them?

• Where is the numberless host of Christ-followers who refused to say "Caesar is Lord" but at great cost to themselves, confessed "Jesus is Lord" on the basis of his death, resurrection and ascension?

• Where is Stephen, the first to wear a martyr's crown?

• Where are Paul, Luke, John Mark, Barnabas, Philip, Silas or Timothy?

Does it seem odd that a public event so newsworthy as the death of Jesus, even attracting hundreds of people with a wide range of biases – disciples, Jewish authorities, government officials and even philosophers – *that not a single person ever called Jesus' death into question, voiced a dissenting opinion or retracted their testimony?*

If the view of the majority of Muslims held true, then surely one such eyewitness could be found saying that Jesus' death on the cross was fake news. *Actually, some did,* in fact, call it a false news story, a divine trick. Who were they? Absentees, all of them! The earliest we know of was Basilides, living far away in Egypt and probably not yet born when Jesus died, no less. A century later came Seth. After him Mani. **What do they all tell us? Nothing at all**

Does it seem odd that a newsworthy public event like the death of Jesus, one that attracted hundreds of people from diverse backgrounds, friends and foes alike – disciples, Jewish authorities, government officials and even philosophers – that not a single one of them ever called Jesus' death into question, posited a dissenting opinion or retracted their testimony?

about *Jesus* but volumes about *themselves.* They shared in a hatred towards everything biblical, blaming God for an evil world. It comes as no surprise that they rewrote the Jesus Story to fit their arrogant philosophies. Muslim reader, on the scales of credibility, why give their speculations equal weight with those who surrounded him when he breathed his last?

Where Does this Leave Us? Two Observations, One Question

First, those of us embracing the teachings of the Injeel will honestly read the Qur'an and come away feeling somewhat like the family of Dr. Salk. A tribute devoting disproportionate attention to Jesus' birth that says little about his life and negates his death and resurrection is hard for us to consider fitting. In contrast to the many witnesses marshalled in the Injeel, it offers us a cryptic denial without a scintilla of support.

Second, let's be fair. We believe the Prophet (p) intended to honor Jesus, not sink him! The Qur'an, in all fairness, presents a significant contrast to our make-believe biographer who robbed Dr. Salk of the accolades he deserved. The contrast between them is motive. Where Dr. Salk's biographer intended to diminish the scientist, **the Qur'an sought to honor Jesus by rescuing him from the indignity of crucifixion.**

Which leads us to this final question: *If Jesus' death was erased from human memory, would it diminish or elevate his place in history?*

The Jesus Answer
Badge of Honor or Mark of Shame?

Since Jesus is the one to actually experience his traumatic death, it seems only right that he should have the last word about it. Previously we heard his many predictions of it beforehand. Most people are unaware, however, that his most extensive teaching on the subject came *after* its occurrence in Luke 24:36-53. It calls for our full attention.[23]

Let's set the scene. It's Sunday night, the third day after Friday's crucifixion and burial of Jesus. The apostles are still in Jerusalem huddled in a room behind locked doors.

Three days earlier, they had watched Jesus, their beloved leader, subjected to crucifixion, the most dreaded form of State-sanctioned capital punishment ever invented. This spectacle of shame lasted from nine in the morning until three o'clock. They winced at every sight and sound, especially as professional executioners anchored his body to the bark of a wooden crossbar by driving metal spikes through his wrists and feet to inflict maximum pain. This procedure prevented writhing victims from becoming unfastened when jerked skyward in the beam's vertical sheath. Then, what spikes were to physical agony, the upraised body became to social anguish. Shame had no covering, hoisted high in full display for all to see. Flanked by coarsened murderers, Jesus was drenched in blood. Verbal mockery and vicious sneers came from all sides.

Jesus' loyal followers blended anonymously into a crowd of gawkers. How they wanted to see a miraculous comeback, and with good reason to expect it. For three years they watched him, a fusion of composure, mercy and unmatched power. He was untouchable by man, woman or jinn.

Surely, he would pull something off at the last minute. But now, oddly enough, he put up no resistance, none whatsoever! The longer the clock ticked away, the more jarring his passivity became. Religious leaders were having a field day: "He saved others; let Him save Himself if this is the Messiah of God, His Chosen One" (Injeel, Lk 23:35). Soldiers joined in the taunts: "If You are the King of the Jews, save Yourself!" (Injeel, Lk 23:37). And then it was over.

> The Qur'an sought to honor Jesus by rescuing him from the indignity of crucifixion.

"And all the crowds who came together for this spectacle (*theoria*), when they observed what had happened, began to return, beating their breasts." (Luke 23:49 NASB)

"Spectacle," from *theoria*, captures the impact of this theater on those present.[24] It pierced their hearts and dashed their hopes. Like movie-goers expecting to watch Bruce Willis in *Diehard*, all that was showing was *Schindler's List*. Only worse. What a colorless assault on goodness, truth and beauty, a nightmare. That was Friday.

Now Sunday's come and almost gone. One haunting question hung in the air: *Was Jesus really God's conquering Messiah or have we made a colossal mistake?* What happened next erased that question forever.

> "Jesus himself stood among them and said to them, 'Peace be with you.'" (Luke 24:36)

He appeared out of nowhere. They see him. But that can't be him. Yes, he looks like Jesus, but it can't be! Memories of Friday were still fresh. His shroud-wrapped body would barely be dry of its fluids. There must be another explanation. *Are we seeing things? Is this a hallucination?*

> "They were startled and frightened, thinking they saw a ghost." (Luke 24:37)

Muslim reader, Jesus begins to put everything into place. Looking retrospectively at his death, he placed it within the great drama of God's unfolding Story. Jesus gets to the nub of the Qur'an's tribute to the never-crucified Messiah. *Does the denial of Jesus' death truly honor or diminish him and his place in history?*

5 LANDSLIDE VICTORIES
How Jesus Viewed His Death *Afterwards*

It was the News Flash of the Ages. Jesus throws entirely new light on his recent demise. With his own death behind him, he paradoxically uncovers five undying realities about his present condition, future destiny and humanity's hope.

1. NEVER-ENDING LIFE – "I'm Alive and Well"

> "Jesus said to them, "Why are you troubled, and why do doubts rise in your minds? *Look at my hands and my feet. It is I myself ! Touch me and see*; a ghost does not have flesh and bones, as you see I have." When he had said this, he showed them his hands and feet.

And while they still did not believe it because of joy and amazement, he asked them, "Do you have anything here to eat?" *They gave him a piece of broiled fish, and he took it and ate it in their presence.*" (Luke 24:38-42)

Dead bodies, after multiple days and without modern machines, do not return to life. **Except here.** The crucified man stood before them alive. How then can anyone explain it? The details of Jesus' appearance rule out commonplace explanations.

First, could his resurrection be explained as a spiritualized metaphor? Not on the basis of the details. The conspicuous absence of a body in his tomb provoked search parties, not sermonizing. No one suspected a resurrection but a theft. *Who took him? Where's his body?* Fortunately, it wasn't found! Body-vocabulary is reserved for the dead, not the living. Between "Where's J. P.?" and "Where's J. P.'s body?" lies a world of difference for J. P. The one standing before them now was infinitely better than a body wrapped in its soiled shroud. It was *Him* fully alive! Yes, physically. Jesus invited them to a multi-sensory experience, placing their hands on the fresh contours of his scars. Next was a face-to-face encounter complete with conversation and shared meal! Who attends their own funeral dinner? And since when do ghosts eat, especially fish, leaving its bones sitting on the plate? Seeing was believing and seeing brought their search party to an end. Skepticism drowned in a tide of overwhelming tangible evidence. Poetry was out; the five senses were in.

Second, could his resurrection be explained as a hallucination? All of them saw him together. Besides, had they hallucinated and started preaching the resurrection, anyone could have gone to the tomb and produced the real body. An absurd theory.

Third, could his resurrection be explained as the product of the apostles' great faith? According to this theory, "Whatever the apostles *thought* they saw sprang from their faith, not a

> "After his suffering, he presented himself to them and gave many convincing proofs that he was alive. He appeared to them over a period of forty days and spoke about the kingdom of God."
>
> Injeel, Acts 1:3

real physical body. Strong belief made them gullible to suggestion, imagining they saw a stupendous miracle. They were convinced, but deluded. This so-called resurrection was nothing more than a mental trick conjured by a predisposition to believe." This explanation faces a serious glitch. All the evidence tells an exactly opposite story. Between Friday and Sunday, *what faith?* The disciples failed to exhibit an ounce of it – not until Jesus appeared to them, that is. Once seeing him, faith was not even necessary. Sight rendered it irrelevant. What they saw with their own eyes and touched with their own hands ruled faith out.

Why did this matter? Belief commonly refers to an acceptance of something unseen. By contrast, belief in this case took in the full view of its object and aided through multisensory verification. Why was this tangible confirmation necessary? The day would come when these men would face hungry lions for proclaiming Jesus' resurrection. It was essential for the first preachers to stand on a platform of firsthand certainty derived from empirical knowledge. They knew that they knew that they knew!

Fourth, could his resurrection be explained as the apostles getting caught up in the excitement of the moment? Human memory can be short-lived. Even a group experience may fade over time causing some to second-guess themselves. Not in this case! There would be more than this single appearance. Jesus sustained their certainty, reappearing to them on multiple occasions over a longer span, each time drilling deeper his living facticity:

> "After his suffering, he presented himself to them and *gave many convincing proofs that he was alive. He appeared to them over a period of forty days* and spoke about the kingdom of God." (Acts 1:3, emphasis mine)

The New Testament confirms the physical nature of Jesus' resurrection. He exited his grave in a manner that defies alternative explanations. This was no cutesy metaphor, no hallucinatory mind-trick, not a product of faith and not an impulsive conclusion of men and women caught in the excitement of a single experience. Though his body was in its glorified state (not subject to death), Jesus was physically alive!

Christianity's most crucial fact is celebrated by millions every Easter. If it was the apostles' great faith that caused the body of Jesus to reappear, we have a false gospel, a dead hope and cathedrals built on toothpicks. But it was not! With such concrete proof of the Living One, their bewildering doubt gave way to rallying certainty.

2. SURE FOUNDATION – "My death proves God does what he promises, providing a solid foundation for your faith"

"'Everything must be fulfilled that is written about Me in the Law of Moses, the Prophets and the Psalms.'" (Luke 24:44)

Jesus' shameful death did not reveal him to be a dismal failure, but the lead part in God's great drama of salvation history. By doing so, he gave us a place to pin our hopes: the truthfulness of God's Word.

Now that Jesus has been fully restored and back in the seat of power, at whom will he point the finger of blame for his death? Anyone who has been robbed of justice knows the visceral feelings it kindles. Given Jesus' innocence and the failure of the system to render him justice, we wait for him to get it off his chest. Who will he call out by name from the instrumental causes behind his demise. For starters, he'll lash out against the Sanhedrin's corruption and Governor Pilate's miscarriage of justice. He might even top it off with, "And God, where were you in all of this!"

We hear none of that and here's why.

His cross was a fulfillment, not a fluke. He explained: "'Everything **must** be fulfilled that is written about Me in the Law of Moses, the Prophets and the Psalms." Believing that the Scripture's organic unity went hand-in-hand with its binding nature, Jesus skipped over all secondary causes to unveil the real trigger behind his recent ordeal. Evil had impelled men to scrape the underbelly of depravity to rid the world of him – just as they had with earlier prophets who they ridiculed, skinned and butchered. Little did they realize that for centuries, God had been planting imperishable seeds deep into the

513

hearts of his Messengers, truths that became inscribed in "the Law, the Prophets and the Psalms." Once sown, seeds of truth would germinate and, in time, sprout. While evil men could eliminate the prophet, they could not uproot the seed. Spanning generations, what had long seemed dormant – even dead – suddenly sprouted up. Truth, in time, required fulfillment. By the simple term "must"[25] a term of demand, a divine insistence, pressing for realization, obligatory, indispensable, not maybe, possibly, perhaps, as the case may be, if possible, weather permitting. Buried grains of truth, building and building for centuries, finally burst through earth's crust at the cross.

By doing so, he laid a solid foundation on which humanity can safely stand: the unfailing truthfulness of God's Word.

Jesus took them right to Scripture to show that the last word is not man's unimaginable cruelties but God's imperishable truth! Truth reigns!

"In the fullness of time, God sent forth his Son, born of a woman, born under the Law, to redeem those under the Law" (Gal 4:4). Thank you, Caiaphas. Thanks, Herod. Thanks, Pilate. You all played right into God's hand.

Was this a novel conclusion, a spur of the moment epiphany? Was Jesus putting a positive spin on his misfortune, a happy face on the Grim Reaper? Not at all. It was rooted deep "in the Law of Moses, the Prophets and the Psalms." That weekend's events joined in lockstep with God's ancient plan. Jesus tells us that, rather than a random collection of moral stories, the biblical story is "about me" – His miraculous coming, sinless life, sacrificial death and triumphant ascension. How thrilling it must have been to see the range of Scriptural pieces come together one piece at a time.

> "Then he opened their minds so they could understand the Scriptures. He told them, "This is what is written: *'The Messiah will suffer and rise from the dead on the third day. . .'"* (Luke 24:44-47, emphasis mine)

But to what end? What difference going forward would his death make?

3. PEACE WITH GOD IN JESUS' NAME – "My death offers New Beginnings to people everywhere"

Next, Jesus told them why his death was front and center to his mission:

"*Repentance for the forgiveness of sins will be preached in his name to all nations,* beginning at Jerusalem. You are witnesses of these things." (Luke 24:47-48)

Jesus achieved what no religion can do: bring us close to God by removing what kept us from God!

That reason was you and me. Muslim reader, you might be asking yourself: *Why was Jesus' death necessary? Isn't God's forgiveness a foregone conclusion? He's merciful and compassionate. And I'm a decent human being. Of course, God will forgive me.*

The Man with nail-scarred hands says otherwise. In this third revelation, Jesus says that "forgiveness of sins" is given "in his name." Why *his* name and not another? Because no sinful person can die for the sins of another. Forgiveness is found in Jesus' name because, as the Lamb of God, he had no moral blemish of his own. He alone could take our place. God foretold his coming through Prophet Isaiah:

"But he was pierced for our transgressions, he was crushed for our iniquities; the punishment that brought us peace was on him, and by his wounds we are healed. We all, like sheep, have gone astray, each of us has turned to our own way; and the LORD has laid on him the iniquity of us all." (Isaiah 53:5-6)

Jesus offers God's clemency to us "in his name," making the gift of our forgiveness the direct result of his costly suffering.

By what sign does God demonstrate his acceptance of Jesus' sacrifice? The same passage answers:

"It was the Lord's will to crush him and cause him to suffer, and though the Lord makes his life an offering for sin, *he will see his offspring and prolong his days*, and the will of the Lord will prosper in his hand. *After he has suffered, he will see the light of life* and be satisfied;

Jesus' comeback from the dead was God's immediate reward conferred on Jesus for fully giving himself on our behalf.

Notice also that it is not nice Jesus, the Sin-bearer, at odds with the cruel Father who is on the verge of decimating the human race! Jesus did not come into the world to twist the arm of a reluctant God — "Please, please, please, God. Don't be so mean!" Muslim reader, if you discard everything else in this book, please do not miss this: God is the emphatic subject. "It was the LORD's will to crush him."

> "The LORD has laid on him [Jesus] the iniquity of us all" (53:6). "All this is from God, who reconciled us to himself through Christ...God was reconciling the world to himself in Christ, not counting people's sins against them" (2 Cor 5:18-19).

God is pleased with his sin-bearing Servant! The same God who sent him to Calvary did not leave him there. Through his dying and his rising, God offers every man, woman and child the best gift imaginable:

> "by his knowledge my righteous servant will justify many, and he will bear their iniquities." (Isaiah 53:10-11)

Muslim readers, this, *not* a Book, is the true Gospel (Good News). Through his death Jesus achieved what no religion can provide: bring us near to God by removing the sinful barrier. Now we know why, at his arrest on Friday, Jesus became so passive and did not fight back.

> "Christianity is a love story. It is about love lost at Eden and love restored at Calvary."[6]

When Jesus returns, we too will see his scars. How will we broach the subject? Will anyone dare say to him, "Your crucifixion was irrelevant. I'm just fine without it thanks to my many good deeds?" The Injeel warns that the spectacle of Jesus' wound in that day will not evoke glib talk: "They called to the mountains and the rocks, 'Fall on us and hide us from the face of him who sits on the throne and from the wrath of the Lamb!'" (Rev 6:16)

In this third eye-opening revelation, Jesus offers God's clemency to us "in his name," making the gift of *our* forgiveness the direct result of *his* costly suffering.

Good news is meant to be shared. Here is where **Jesus' ultimate honor became viral.** This message would be heard, starting at Ground Zero, the site of his crucifixion in Jerusalem. Even Jesus' executioners were offered forgiveness and a second chance. It would ignite a moral revolution spreading to every nation and tribe in Adam's broken family. The landscape of warring nations and clashing ethnicities would see grace-filled communities rise up, havens where petty provincialisms and untamed nationalisms will diminish in a fellowship of the forgiven and the forgiving.

4. ABIDING NEARNESS – "I am with you forever through the Holy Spirit."

Fourth, Jesus informs them of one remaining promise that would soon be fulfilled.

> "*I [Jesus] am going to send you what my Father has promised;* but stay in the city until you have been clothed with power from on high." (Luke 24:49, emphasis added)

> "*But you will receive power when the Holy Spirit comes on you;* and you will be my witnesses in Jerusalem, and in all Judea and Samaria, and to the ends of the earth." (Acts 1:8, emphasis added)

Jesus instructed them to stay put in Jerusalem. "It is near! Wait for this gift my Father promised." The disciples did just that (Acts 1 and 2) and the world was forever changed (the Book of Acts).

5. CELESTIAL ENTHRONEMENT & FINAL RETURN – "I am coming back!"

> "After he said this, *he was taken up before their very eyes*, and a cloud hid him from their sight. They were looking intently up into the sky as he was going, when suddenly two men dressed in white stood beside them. 'Men of Galilee,' they said, 'why do you stand here looking into the sky? *This same Jesus, who has been taken from you into heaven, will come back in the same way you have seen him go into heaven.*" (Acts 1:9-11, emphasis mine)

This climactic revelation brings Jesus earthly mission full-circle. The Father received him back in heaven. There he will remain to intercede for us until his return in the clouds for his waiting family.

Rethinking the Qur'an's Tribute to Jesus

Conquering kings of old time returned with their armies in a parade of victory with spoils of war in tow. We just heard from Jesus himself, on the third day of his entombment, who stood before his stunned apostles as Victor with his spoils of war trailing in the form of five permanent blessings ready to be doled out on all who follow him.

In light of these, what are we to make of the Qur'an's laudatory tribute to the life of Jesus while virtually dismissing his death altogether? Does its denial, at least by the majority of Muslims, truly honor Jesus or diminish him and his place in history? Both the Qur'an and Injeel honor Jesus as one who is near to God in heaven, yet for different reasons. The Qur'an lauds Jesus by *sparing* him the indignity of the crucifixion. The Injeel lauds Jesus *through* his chosen path of suffering for others:

> "Instead of the joy set before him, he endured the cross, scorning its shame, and sat down at the right hand of the throne of God" (Hebrews 12:2).

Eternal praise awaits Jesus in heaven as angels numbering in the tens of thousands and the redeemed family join in celebration:

> *"Worthy is the Lamb, who was slain,* to receive power and wealth and wisdom and strength and honor and glory and praise!" (Revelation 5:11-12, emphasis added)

Such acclaim is merited and timeless.[29] It answers friends like Maher, our Sudanese neighbor, who gladly accepted the virgin-born miracle worker preaching from the cradle, even commanding the palm tree to bend into submission, but who completely bypassed the greater honor of the crucified Son of God who robbed the grave on behalf of all.

Question 11.1: "Was the prophet Mohammad in the Bible?"

This question often comes up in conversation. It is a belief supported by the Qur'an:

> "And (remember) when *Isa* (Jesus), son of Maryam (Mary), said: "O Children of Israel! I am the Messenger of Allah unto you, confirming the Taurat [(Torah) which came] before me, and *giving glad tidings of a Messenger to come after me, whose name shall be Ahmad.*" Al-Saff 61:6, Kahn[30]

Since Muhammad (p) was born six centuries later than Jesus and claimed to be his successor, it's natural to expect Jesus to predict his arrival in much the same way that the earlier prophets had foretold his coming as Messiah. At the very least, we should find clues or hints of another major prophet who would appear on the distant horizon.

In the name of friendship, it would be more convenient for Christians to sidestep this question. Your inquiry deserves a straightforward answer, however, so I will stick to the basic facts.

Scriptures nowhere foreshadow, predict or intimate a future prophet to appear after Jesus. Nor do we find the names of Muhammad (p) nor Ahmad anywhere mentioned in the Tawrat, the Prophets, Zabur nor the Injeel. Finally, any signs suggesting that either name had been redacted from a biblical text are absent. Evidence to the contrary is presented exclusively by Islamic authors and lacks any independent verification.

To support this aya, two options are open to Islamic apologists. Either they must charge previous Books with corruption or artificially insert predictions about Muhammad (p) into selected biblical texts. Three of the most commonly cited are below.

1. Song of Solomon 5:16

At a debate recently, a man from the audience used this verse as proof that Muhammad's name was in the original Hebrew but scrubbed from English translations. Here it is with the word in question italicized:

> "His mouth is sweetness itself; he is *altogether lovely*. This is my beloved, this is my friend, daughters of Jerusalem." (Song of Solomon 5:16)

I could not recall this particular verse, but was familiar with Song of Solomon, a poetic book on God's affirmation of the exquisite beauty of marital love. I wondered why Muhammad (p) would appear in a book about the intimate relations between a man and wife. So without reading it, I asked the man to tell me what the book was about. "It doesn't matter. That verse uses Muhammad's name!" Since it is a short book, I asked "Have you ever read it?" He did not answer.

I share this, Muslim reader, to show what I often find to be different ways of reading Scripture between our two traditions. For Christians, sound interpretation requires us to begin with the larger context rather than individual words. How can we know the meaning of any word until we know how it's used in a sentence? For example, consider the common English word, "well." What does it mean?

> "Well, I don't know." "Are you feeling well?" "Have you checked your oil well lately?" "Not only did my friends leave me, my dog did as well."

Even with a dictionary, no one can understand the meaning of "well" without knowing how it is used in a sentence. This basic rule guiding our everyday conversations also applies to literature. Ascribing a word from the book of Song of Solomon to Muhammad (p) without consulting the passage leaves the man's argument open to question. Simply looking up the verse would have shown him that inserting the name of any future human figure distorts its plain meaning. Arguments from the Hebrew text are relevant as well. [31]

2. John 14:15-17; 16:7, 13 The Paraclete Jesus Predicted

During his final days on earth, Jesus' predicted the coming of a *parakaletos*, often translated "Advocate," who would follow him.

> "But very truly I tell you, it is for your good that I am going away. Unless I go away, the Advocate [*parakaletos*] will not come to you; but if I go, I will send him to you." (John 16:7)

Muslims often argue that the Advocate referred to here is Muhammad (p). Yet to introduce the name of any human being into this promise, prophet or otherwise, is precarious for a number of reasons. First, Jesus had already identified who he was:

"I will ask the Father, and he will give you another Advocate [*parakaletos*] to help you and be with you forever—the Spirit of truth." (John 14:15)

Moreover, as the Spirit [*pneuma,* "wind," "breath"], this *parakaletos* or Advocate, would be invisible and capable of indwelling believers: "The world cannot accept him, because it neither sees him nor knows him. But you know him, for he lives with you and will be in you." (John 14:15-17; see also 15:26-27; 16:13-14)

Third, the promised *parakaletos* had already arrived prior to the conclusion of the Injeel, more precisely, just ten days after Jesus ascended into heaven. That early descent renders later claimants as redundant at best. The Holy Spirit's coming was sudden in appearance, sovereign in timing and unmistakably dramatic:

"Suddenly a sound like the blowing of a violent wind came from heaven and filled the whole house where they [120 disciples of Jesus] were sitting... *All of them were filled with the Holy Spirit...*" (Acts 2:2, 4)

Peter identified the source of that power that had just come upon them:

"Exalted to the right hand of God, he [Jesus] has received from the *Father the promised Holy Spirit and has poured out what you now see and hear.*" (Acts 2:33)

The factors mentioned above prevent anyone other than God's Spirit as the *parakaletos.* The first to claim this title for himself was **Mani** (Manicheanism), "the Prophet of Babylonia," born several centuries (216 AD) before Muhammad (p). He became an immensely influential Gnostic teacher, calling himself the "Paraclete."

Why rule out him or any other prophet? Because (a) Jesus clearly identified the *parakaletos* as the Spirit of truth (b) whose attributes of invisibility and inter-penetrability exclude any human being and (c) who descended from heaven within two weeks after Jesus promised, "If I go, I will send him to you."

Passages like this one that allegedly point to any person, whether Mani or Muhammad (p), succeed only by being shoehorned into the contexts. Islamic theologians are divided in their interpretations.[32] Mani hated the book of Acts for good reason. It recorded the historic coming of the *Paraclete*, the Holy Spirit, and thus stole his thunder and exposed his pretense.

3. Deuteronomy 18:17-18 – "the Prophet like Moses?"

Moses predicted the coming of a future prophet, one like himself:

> "The LORD said to me: *I will raise up for them a prophet like you from among their fellow Israelites*, and I will put my words in his mouth. He will tell them everything I command him. I myself will call to account anyone who does not listen to my words that the prophet speaks in my name." (Deuteronomy 18:17-18)

This future prophet will embody at least five identifying characteristics in common with Moses. This prophet would:

(1) Be of Jewish descent: "from among their fellow Israelites." (2) Receive the very words of God: "I will put my words in his mouth." (3) Faithfully teach everything God tells him to say: "tell them everything I commanded him." (4) Expect obedience: "I will call to account anyone who does not listen. . ." (5) Reveals the name of God: "the prophet speaks in my name."

Let's begin by observing how Jesus met all five criteria. He was (1) born into a Jewish family (Matt 1:1); (2) Received God's words (John 7:16); (3) Perfectly obeyed in word and life (John 8:26-29; 12:49; 14:30; 17:4); (4) Summoned obedience from people (John 3:18-21; 14:15, 23); (5) Spoke in God's Name that he revealed as the Father (John 17:6; see 5:31-32, 37, 43; 7:28; 8:45; 12:49- 50; 17:25-26).

Perhaps you are thinking that these five qualities of the "prophet like Moses" characterize any authentic divine Messenger (see the Prophet Test, Chapter 7).

Expectation of "a prophet like you" causes us to look beyond the marks of *any* true prophet to ascertain what was *unique* to Moses as a divine spokesman. Let's let Scripture answer Scripture. The Tawrat itself provides two conspicuous aspects distinguishing Moses' prophetic vocation. The first of these is direct encounter, the absence of a mediating angel or vision to convey God's message:"And he [the LORD] said, "Hear my words: When there are prophets among you, I the LORD make myself known to them in visions; I speak to them in dreams. Not so with my servant Moses; he is entrusted with all my house. *With him I speak face to face*— clearly, not in riddles; and *he beholds the form of the LORD.*" (Numbers 12:6-8 NRSV)

The second distinguishing mark was the *physical* effect that these face-to-face encounters with the Almighty had upon Moses. His face radiated the LORD's glory with such intensity that required a veil as a shield of protection for the people:

". . .whenever Moses entered the Lord's presence to speak with him, he removed the veil until he came out. And when he came out and told the Israelites what he had been commanded, they saw that *his face was radiant.* Then Moses would put the veil back over his face until he went in to speak with the Lord." (Exodus 34:34-35)

Jesus' last words from the cross were not "I am finished," the cry of dereliction, but "It is finished" (John 19:30), the declaration of completion. His agonizing work of redemption was over!

"When Moses came down from Mount Sinai . . ., he was not aware that *his face was radiant because he had spoken with the Lord.* When Aaron and all the Israelites saw Moses, *his face was radiant, and they were afraid to come near him.*" (Exodus 34:29-30)

Many faithful prophets followed Moses. However, these two aspects that distinguished Moses from the rest find their counterpart *only* in Jesus of Nazareth.

On a number of occasions, Jesus testified to seeing the Father face-to-face. For example, referring to himself: "Not that anyone has seen the Father, except the One who is from God; He has seen the Father" (John 6:46).

Nothing so vividly identified Jesus as the "prophet like Moses" as the visual radiance transforming his appearance before the eyes of three of his leading disciples while they were on a mountain praying. Jesus was always the miracle-worker, the one performing them. This time was different. Here it was God who performed it, Jesus who received it and three disciples who witnessed it. What happened?

> "There *he was transfigured before them.* His clothes became dazzling white, whiter than anyone in the world could bleach them. And there appeared before them Elijah and Moses, who were talking with Jesus." (Mark 9:2-3)

Unlike miracles of restoration done *by* Jesus that brought sick people back to health, here was a miracle of identification done *to* Jesus. Not only did Jesus' face beam like Moses as he had emerged from the Tabernacle. From head to toe, his whole body flashed with blinding intensity! On top of that, two bigger-than-life figures from the past suddenly appeared: Moses, himself the Lawgiver and Elijah the flaming prophet. After a brief conversation with Jesus about his "exodus," they disappeared to another world, leaving Jesus standing alone. Finally, as if dazzling radiance and multi-realm conversations weren't enough, clinching the spot for Jesus as the one to whom Moses pointed was this audible identification and command from above:
"This is my Son, whom I love. *Listen to him!*" (Mark 9:7)
The "prophet like Moses" could be none other than Jesus himself.

Question 11.2: "Christians believe in Moses in a line of prophets. Why don't they believe that Muhammad (p) is a continuation of the same message after Jesus?"

Your question rests on a solid premise that the existence of one God leads to a corresponding single line of divine revelation of unbroken prophetic continuity.[33] Since Muslims and Christians share this starting point[34] the issue here lies only with its range. How far does it go? Does it stretch all the way from the Tawrat to the Injeel, stopping there, or also extend to the Qur'an that came through Muhammad (p)?

My answer to this important question emerges at multiple levels. I find myself in a quandary, feeling torn between my deep respect for my Muslim friends who enrich my life and my unquestioned allegiance to Jesus anticipated in the Tawrat and revealed in the Injeel. I can proceed because of a deep conviction that he not only shares but infinitely transcends the love I feel towards them.

Is there evidence of continuity that links the Injeel and the Qur'an? Indeed!

Points of Continuity

Along with many Christians, I acknowledge with appreciation Muhammad's (p) positive view towards the previous Scriptures.[35] I also admire the circumspect lifestyles I see in many of my Muslim friends in their disciplined pursuits to keep God at front and center in their lives. We also celebrate the multiple beliefs that surface in the Qur'an, doctrinal teaching that Christians and Muslims share (see text box). There remain for us reasons we keep Muhammad (p) at bay and view him as a figure of discontinuity with the Books preceding him. The first two of these have less to do with anything perceived to be absent in Muhammad (p) and more with what we find sufficient in Jesus our Messiah.

1. Lacking in Expectation

Why not Muhammad (p)? The simplest answer is that we were given no reason to expect another prophet. While a handful of prophets do appear in the Injeel, in the history of redemption, prophetic voices dominated the era leading up to and paving the way for God's coming Messiah.

"*God, after He spoke long ago to the fathers in the prophets* in many portions and in many ways, *in these last days has spoken to us in His Son,* whom He appointed heir of all things, through whom also He made the world. And He is the radiance of His glory and the exact representation of His nature, and upholds all things by the word of His power." (Hebrews 1:1-3)

"God, after He spoke long ago to the fathers in the prophets in many portions and in many ways, in these last days has spoken to us in His Son" (Hebrews 1:1). In the history of redemption, prophetic voices dominated the era leading up to and paving the way for God's coming Messiah.!

The prophets pointed to the Messiah as the grand finale arriving at the end of their expectations. Had Jesus alerted us of another prophet who would appear later on the horizon, believe me, we would be vigilantly looking. Such was not the case.

2. Satisfaction that Resists Supplements

A second reason that Christians find themselves disinclined toward other prophets is an existential suffusion that renders Jesus attractive to us and other figures unnoticed.

Satisfies our deepest hunger

Jesus' popularity spiked one day after feeding 5,000 famished people from a boy's small picnic basket. The crowd went bonkers and wanted to make him a king. Jesus knew who he was, already a king, but reigning over a different kind of kingdom than the one that they had in mind. No sooner than he refused their request, his popularity took a nosedive. Once realizing Jesus didn't come to be their food bank, the crowd thinned. Observing their backside as they walked away, Jesus asks his disciples, "Are you leaving as well?" Peter's answer is the reason I'm telling you this:

> "*Lord, to whom shall we go? You have words of eternal life.* We have believed and have come to know that *You are the Holy One of God.*" (John 6:68-69)

When times get tough, and they do, we're not prone to run *from* but *to*

BELIEFS MUSLIMS & CHRISTIANS SHARE Partial References
(1) *One God who created and transcends the world* — Surat 7:11-19, 54; 15:16-19; 16:35-40; 21:20; 32:4; 42:11; 57:4; 82:1-2; 89:21
(2) *Creator of humanity – Adam* — Surat 2:30-38; 7:10; 15:26; 16:38-40; 17:70; 22:5-6, 36; 23:12-14; 32:7-9; 40:64-67; 42:11; 55:14; *Eve:* Surah 2:35a; 4:1; 13:5
(3) *Existence of angels* (seen throughout)
(4) *Reality of Satan, our adversary* — Surat 2:34, 8:48; 18:50; 35:5; 4:120; 7:20 25; 38:71-77
(6) *Final Resurrection* — Surat 16:38-40; 22:5-6
(7) *Final Judgment* — Surat 22:5-7; 29:19-21; 36:77-80; 80:18-22
(8) *Heaven* — Surat 10:4; 14:28, 48; 29:19; 82:1-2; 89:21; 104:1; 7:43; 35:33-35; 36:55-58; 43:71-73; 47:15; 52:19-24; 55:46-76; 56:12-38; 43:71-73; 47:15; 52:19-24; 55:46-76; 56:12-38
(9) *Hell* — Surat 3:176-181; 23:104; 25:11, 27-28; 36:64; 54:48; 59:93-4; 70:10; 80:34-36

Jesus. Because of who he is, "the Holy One of God" and what he alone can give, "eternal life," we're not going anywhere. There is something deep down that Jesus satisfies. He meets our deepest hunger in a lasting way:

> "Do not work for the food which perishes, but for *the food which endures to eternal life,* which the Son of Man will give to you, for on Him the Father, God, has set His seal." (John 6:27)

Provided Full Satisfaction for our Sin

Jesus' last words from the cross were not *"I* am finished," the cry of dereliction, but *"It* is finished" (John 19:30), the declaration of completion. The ordeal is done, the victory won! His agonizing work of redemption was over! The infinite debt of human depravity alienating us all from God and from our fellow human beings has now been paid-in-full. No longer do we search for a scapegoat to slaughter. Jesus was God's Lamb offered once, and once was enough! His single offering for our sins was proven acceptable to God by his resurrection the dead. Now through faith in that miracle of supreme love, we can bury our hatchets of bitterness from which we are set free!

Fulfilled the Law's requirements

Who among us ever kept all of God's Ten Commandments without fail? Only one, Jesus, who came and lived subject to the Law just like you and me. Unlike us, not once did he break even one of them!

> "But when the fullness of the time came, God sent forth His Son, born of a woman, *born under the Law, so that He might redeem those who were under the Law,* that we might receive the adoption as sons." (Galatians 4:4-5)

Being born "under" the demands of God's Law meant that Jesus was not issued a Grace Card exempting him from the same divine standards expected of others. He lived in the same rough-and-tumble world as ours. He wasn't born in a Sunday School or madrassas. And yet, while facing temptations common to man, Jesus never deviated from doing the right thing. That fact alone certainly set Jesus apart, but in and of itself benefits no one else except by presenting others with an exemplary model. Through the earlier Books we learn of God's original plan to bless all nations through Abraham (Tawrat, Genesis 12:1-3). He would funnel that blessing narrowly through Abraham's descendants. To them was given a moral Law known as the Ten Commandments.[36] Through Moses' lips the Lawgiver spoke to Israel:

> "I have set before you life and death, the blessing and the curse. So *choose life* in order that you may live . . . by *loving the LORD your God,* by *obeying* His voice, and by *holding fast* to Him; for *this is your life.*" (Deuteronomy 30:19-20)

Israel failed to keep this covenant of law, placing them under a curse. Before casting blame, non-Jews without the Ten Commandments are not off the hook and find themselves in the same sinking boat. To govern his world and educate the individual conscience, God has imbedded his moral law into the very cells of the human heart.[37] Unfortunately, every one of us has at times turned a deaf ear to God's inner voice, thus placing ourselves under the same curse.

> "*Christ redeemed us from the curse of the Law, having become a curse for us*—for it is written, "Cursed is everyone who hangs on a tree"— in order that *in Christ Jesus the blessing of Abraham might come to the Gentiles,* so that we would receive the promise of the Spirit through faith." (Galatians 3:13-14; cf. Tawrat, Deuteronomy 21:3)

In his moral life, Jesus succeeded where we all failed. Through his death, he took the hit for our failure! **Through both the obedience he performed and the demise he endured, Jesus fully satisfied the demands of the Law.**

Back to the question. Muhammad's (p) shift away from a reliance upon Christ's death towards the law of human merit reintroduced a system of human failure and shame, the very thing from which Christ's blood has rescued us.

Space forbids mention of other aspects of the existential suffusion Jesus provides.[38]

3. Introduced Doctrinal Novelty into the Previous Books

The third reason that we do not find continuation looks specifically at the *teachings* of Muhammad (p). Your term, "continuation" is key and evokes a word-picture of boys on the shore of a lake skipping rocks across its surface. Each young man represents a point of origin, a single source guiding the stone's projectile and supplying its energetic thrust. Let's say we want to know how many boys are playing. Unfortunately, we can't see them, for a huge boulder stands between us blocking our view. All we can see is the lake, not the boys themselves. Still we can get an accurate count by watching the rocks being thrown and tallying the number of their trajectories skipping across the water. We've got this!

The logic of this unscientific model may help answer your question. Just by paying attention to the number of doctrinal trajectories (i.e. patterns of continuation), we should be able to tally the points of origin that propelled the Tawrat, Prophets, Psalms, Injeel and Qur'an. It seems reasonable to expect that if all the Books originated from the same source, there should be only one "Thrower."

First, what should we look for to determine continuity between these Books? Does a consistent trajectory from one era to the next require rote repetition?

Mahmoud, a close Muslim friend from North Africa, asked a probing question: "J. P., was Jesus' message about God different than that of Moses?" This was no trick question, but it caused me to stop and consider. If I say "Yes, Jesus' message was different," then Jesus could be wrongly perceived as introducing novelty. If I say "No, his message was the same as Moses," then his message could mistakenly be viewed as redundant and unnecessary. So what is the right answer?

Doctrinal consistency requires more than simple repetition. Truth is not pickled in formaldehyde, to use Charles Kraft's apt word picture of dead tradition. Two reasons make it so. First, while God's nature is constant, his self-disclosure is gradual and his purposes unfolding. Second, God has sequentially arranged (roughly) the collection of sixty-six biblical Books to advance a single drama towards a saving goal. Earlier Books set the stage and prepared the way for later ones so that, together, God's actions in the final Books complete the expectations of preceding ones. Altogether they form a totality expressing a wide range of operations by one God.

So was Jesus' message about God different than Moses'? No, it was not different, but it was much richer and fuller. Jesus never negated Moses. He *fulfilled* him, bringing his law to completion. The Injeel then continues on the same path without deviation, especially where the earlier Books predict specific future events.

So back to our question. If not simple repetition (kept in formaldehyde) what tell-tale signs distinguish consistent doctrine? We should look for two things: agreement of core themes and a connected narrative. Genuine doctrinal continuity, then, must manifest both a consistent theology and a connected storyline. Let's begin with the first.

Establishing doctrinal continuity logically divides our search into two sequential pairings: from the Tawrat to the Injeel and then from the Injeel to the Qur'an. This simple exercise can help us fix the range of God's continuing revelation.

First Pairing – From the Tawrat to the Injeel

If we start with the Tawrat and read through the Injeel, will we find a single trajectory on both counts of thematic congruence and storyline? Indeed. On the wings of one propulsion by the Spirit of God, the earlier Books led narrowly to the message of salvation finally revealed in the Injeel.[39] Notice, for example, how the earlier Scriptures prepared one young man, Timothy, to receive the Injeel's message of salvation.

> *". . .from childhood you have known the sacred writings which are able to give you the wisdom that leads to salvation through faith which is in Christ Jesus"* (2 Timothy 3:15-16)

The connection between early and late Scriptures is plain – enough so that the Books of Moses, David and the Prophets were Timothy's primer to faith in Jesus.

Let's return to our analogy. A consistent message ties early Scriptures

Notice how his prior knowledge of the Earlier Books prepared one young man, Timothy, to receive the salvation message in the Injeel: ". . .from childhood you have known the sacred writings which are able to give you the wisdom that leads to salvation through faith which is in Christ Jesus" (2 Timothy 3:15)

to later ones forming a straight path back to one unseen "Thrower" on the shore. From that single Source came a coherent message — first stoking expectation through promises and then experiencing the joy in the arrival of their fulfillment. The God of Abraham, Moses, the Prophets and David propelled forward a single message throughout, a drama culminating in Jesus of the Injeel (See the table in Chapter 9, "Sources for Jesus in the Injeel").

This brings us to the relationship of the Qur'an to the Injeel.

Second Pairing – From the Injeel to the Qur'an

> "The Gospel of Jesus is new, but not a novelty! Jesus was the missing piece completing the previous Books, anticipated by its prophets whose arrival was met with celebration and not regarded as a stranger."
> Rick Brown

What happens when Muhammad (p) joins in? Will the themes and storyline introduced in the Qur'an form a seamless sequel to its literary predecessors? Or will it show us that "another thrower" has arrived on shore, introducing themes of his own with an independent narrative and set of practices? By tracing the teachings and practices of the Qur'an to the same thematic and narrative trajectory as the Injeel and its former Books, can we follow it back to the same Source?

As noted previously, we celebrate many doctrinal agreements between the Qur'an and the Scriptures, not to mention how the Qur'an explicitly sanctions the earlier Books, confirming without any caveats the collection of writings Christians call the Bible. But here's the rub. It introduces a new pattern of thought, not concerning *which* Books receive its endorsement, but by modifying the *content* they contained.

The following chart highlights where consistency ends and divergence begins.[41] Biblical references are cited in the Endnotes.[42]

BIBLE				QUR'AN
Old Testament			New Testament	Muhammad
Torah	Prophets	Psalms	Gospel	
<--------------- c. 1500 years ------------->				23 years
Humanity is created in the image of God.				No
The Fatherhood & Son of God				No
God dwells with his people.				No
Priesthood & Sacrifice of Atonement for Sin				No
Covenants of Noah, Abraham, Moses, & David				No
One Story of Redemption				No

To reach our goal in determining the range of continuing divine revelation by following consistent thematic patterns, what do we learn?

First, we see a striking similarity flowing through the Earlier Books from the Tawrat to the Injeel even though they cover 1500 years through multiple human authors. The author summarizes:

- There is weight to the testimony of all the prophets. That is, the long-inspired message given to Moses in around 1400 B.C. and that in the Injeel remains the same.
- This demonstrates that our Scriptures have not been changed.
- The Gospel of Jesus is new, but not a novelty! Jesus was the missing piece completing the previous Books, anticipated by its prophets whose arrival was met with celebration and not regarded as a stranger.[43]

Second, what do these comparisons tell us about the ongoing continuity between the Earlier Books and the Qur'an? They demonstrate two significant facts. First, that the Qur'an takes a dramatic departure from the Injeel. Second, and perhaps more importantly, that departure is not from the Injeel alone. It circumnavigates the entire Biblical continuum extending from Moses to Jesus.[44] At nearly every turn on matters of vital importance throughout the biblical storyline, Muhammad (p) introduced innovation. Perhaps this was not Muhammad's (p) intent. I found no evidence in the Qur'an to suggest it was. Nevertheless, on matters of vital importance, we find discontinuity.

Three specific areas, then, prevent Christians from discerning a line of continuity between Jesus and Prophet Muhammad (p): (a) lacking in expectation, (b) satisfaction that resists supplements and (c) his introduction of doctrinal novelty into the previous Books.

Question 11.3: Why in your religion don't you acknowledge or admit Muhammad (p) as the last prophet (messenger) of God?

Your question provides a fitting sequel to the preceding one. Where it focused on Muhammad's (p) prophetic continuity with Jesus and Moses, yours asks why Christians withhold their support of his unique position as "the last" messenger in that lineage. That culminating place catapults him to the "seal of the prophets" (*khatimu 'N-Nabiyin*, Al-Ahzab 33:40), fully aware that "the succession of prophets has been completed in me."[45] That designation lifted the Man and his Book to the distinguished place of final divine authority:

> That culminating place catapults Muhammad (p) to the "seal of the prophets" (khatimu 'N-Nabiyin, Al-Ahzab 33:40), fully aware that "the succession of prophets has been completed in me."

> "Sunni and Shia theology alike understood it to mean that Muhammad ended the series of Prophets, that he had accomplished for all eternity what his predecessors had prepared, that he was God's last messenger delivering God's last message to mankind."[46]

So to answer your question, Muslim reader, I respectfully see two overarching reasons preventing us from acceding that place to your

Prophet (p). While acknowledging his many excellent qualities and contributions, such a consent would be for us intellectually indefensible and relationally irreconcilable. Please hear me out.

As I understand Islamic teaching, the finality as "seal of the prophets" endows the revelation given to Muhammad (p), the Qur'an, with a three-fold superiority above all previous Books.

> The finality as "seal of the prophets" endows the revelation given to Muhammad (p), the Qur'an, with a three-fold superiority above all previous Books.

First, in relation to its origins, the Qur'an is timeless. It did not originate in the seventh century but existed eternally and was believed to be either uncreated or at least originated previously to the former Books (Sunni understanding). The greater point is that it came down straight from God without a scintilla of human influence, including that of Muhammad (p). Its infallibility rests on that uncreated attribute, impervious to even the minutest changes and, in contrast to the earlier Books, will never be replaced or supplemented.

Second, in relation to its scope, the Qur'an is universally binding. Unlike previous Books and their prophets that were confined to localities, the Qur'an speaks always, to all peoples living in all places.

Third, in relation to the preceding Books, the Qur'an is God's agent of clarification and correction. The final Book serves as the last Word on behalf of all earlier Books. It will thoroughly cleanse the errors of the Tawrat, the Prophets, the Psalms and the Injeel. Why so? Because over time, either through the mistakes of the innocent or the revisions of the mischievous, corruption crept into those divine Originals. One infallible standard, and only one, can restore them to their pristine purity: the Qur'an – timeless, universal and corrective.

Christian acknowledgement, then, of Muhammad (p) as God's "last *prophet*" carries with it our endorsement of this threefold superiority of the Qur'an as God's last Book. On that basis, I have taken the liberty to rephrase your question:

> Why don't Christians acknowledge the Qur'an as God's finishing revelation that infallibly completes the message and corrects the inaccuracies that have crept into preceding Scriptures?

Time Out

This question touches us all deeply. (1) We "People of the Book" are called that for a reason. Jews and Christians, revering Scripture as God-breathed, may be startled to discover its need of purging from human corruption. And they may need special grace to learn that the appointed Agent assigned to that task appeared on the calendar many centuries later and on an atlas from a distance of 800 miles. People of the Book must take a deep breath. (2) Muslims too deeply revere their Book, yet can enter this conversation buoyed in the conviction that, as God's uncreated Word, it was dictated directly to the Prophet (p). That should allay any fears and infuse confidence that it can withstand honest scrutiny that such a claim invites. For all of us, it calls for rigorous honesty, patient consideration and charitable discourse.

> Your question is commendable. Asking Christians to explain their reluctance to recognize Muhammad (p) as the "last Prophet (messenger) of God" is both fair and courageous.

IS THE QUR'AN GOD'S FINAL AGENT TO CORRECT ERRORS IN EARLIER BOOKS?
6 Difficulties Preventing Christian Endorsement

Muslim friend, your question is commendable. Asking Christians to explain their reluctance to recognize Muhammad (p) as God's "last Prophet" is both fair and courageous. Fair because scrutiny is a double-edged sword that cuts both ways. Muslims seldom hesitate to inform me (politely) how men have introduced doctrinal corruption into the Injeel and, for that reason, it must be cleansed by the Qur'an. So that oft-heard accusation against one Book and the exoneration of Another invites scrutiny that is bi-directional. Your question demonstrates exemplary courage

> Three impressive claims for the Qur'an – that it is eternal, universal and the perfecter – confront Christians with five intellectual difficulties preventing their endorsement.

in the pursuit of truth by soliciting honest feedback from an outsider about the Book you revere.

Scrutinizing is one thing, however, and scurrilously denigrating quite another. After investing a fair amount of time studying the Book you cherish, I am keenly aware of the limits of my knowledge of it. As a Christian, I know what it feels like when critics from outside the Christian Faith criticize the Bible without having an adequate understanding. I find it annoying. For that reason, I will present my difficulties as honest inquiries in the form of questions rather than dogmatic statements.

That said, these three impressive claims for the Qur'an – that it is eternal, universal and the perfecter – confront Christians with six *intellectual* difficulties preventing their endorsement.

1. How can the Qur'an correct a Book it doesn't know?

My initial difficulty in recognizing the Qur'an as the Injeel's correcting agent is that I found little to indicate that Muhammad (p) was familiar with it. During my first reading, the question crossed my mind several times whether he had read the Injeel or the other previous Books. Everything I read answered in the negative. It was like reading the description of a large city written by someone peering in from its City Limits signs, no closer. Similarly, when I ask Muslims if they have read the Injeel they often say yes. But when probed a little deeper, most of them had only read snippets quoted in Islamic publications that often take them out of context and used to support Islamic doctrines. The ability to bring responsible correction to any subject, it would seem, requires a firsthand knowledge of it.

By contrast, the Bible used by the first Christians was the Old Testament. Jesus and his apostles knew it thoroughly. They never stopped at its edges but showed intimate familiarity with it all the way through. Revering it as the Word of God, they dared not malign or disparage it. It was considered vital that Christian doctrines were in step with Biblical revelation in its entirety.

I could find no such familiarity of the Injeel in the Qur'an. One encouraging sign is a growing interest in the Bible that I see among today's Muslims.

2. How can the Qur'an rewrite events of the past?

My second difficulty in accepting the Qur'an's infallible credentials to correct earlier Books lies in its claim to rewrite past historical events which, by nature, are irreversible. Of course, historical records are subject to revision, but only when warranted by credible evidence. We fully concur with this aya:

It was like reading the description of a large city written by someone peering in from its City Limits signs, no closer.

"I shall turn away from My Ayat those who behave arrogantly on the earth, without a right, and *(even) if they see all the Ayat (proofs, evidences, verses, lessons, signs, revelations, etc.), they will not believe in them.*" (Al-Aaraf 7:146 Khan)

Similarly, for Christians those *ayat* that God presented visibly for the people of the Book are more than words on a page. They are the mighty deeds that God performed in history. The Qur'an obviously recognizes this law by its use of the term *khabar* to describe that which cannot be abrogated. It means:

"A narration about an event that has happened is called a report, or *khabar*. In the Quran *such a report cannot be abrogated because it would mean the event did not happen and imply that it is a lie.*"[47]

The term correctly recognizes the irreversibility of historical events. The problem is that *khabar* protection applies narrowly to events recorded in the Qur'an alone, excluding those in the earlier inspired Books. Since the Qur'an identifies God as the common Source for *all* Scripture, why not cast the net of *khabar* over the whole range of revelation? Islam, however, abrogates earlier sacred records by nullifying or radically revising many events predating it. How is this

"When I act, who can reverse it?" God, Prophet Isaiah 43:13

possible? Aren't historical events stubborn things that refuse to go away? Can we dial back the clock?

Does Hoping So Make It So?

Let's pretend that on a Thursday night my teenage son borrows my new Ford pickup, wrecks it, drives it home and parks it in our garage. Can I walk into my garage Friday morning and find it in the same new condition it had been on Wednesday? Only in my dreams! We cannot undo past events, even recent ones.

If this is true of actions committed by men, how much more with those performed by Almighty God who said:

"When I act, who can reverse it?" (Isaiah 43:13).

> The Qur'an confronts Christians with a choice between two conflicting written accounts of a first-century set of events.

The answer, obviously, is no one! Our chief reluctance to embrace the Qur'an lies here. Our acceptance of it would be an insincere pretense because it would require us to deny the *ayat* of divine actions upon which the Gospel rests, stupendous acts befitting the Almighty One. The Gospel was a real-life *happening*, not a theological essay.

The Qur'an confronts Christians with a choice between two conflicting written accounts of a first-century set of events. One of them provides detailed reports of the public suffering, death, resurrection and ascension of Jesus the Messiah. Its ringing certainty is heightened by its straightforward reporting.

It was not trying to produce great literature, but, under the Spirit's guidance, reports its news matter-of-factly. Enhancing its credibility were its multiple eyewitnesses who produced written documents tightly tethered in unanimous agreement to all the essential elements. But later, the Qur'an presents a second written account that wraps the very same event in a garment of ambiguity and historical uncertainty. An unbiased reader would find it short on factual details and long on speculation.

This is understandable, coming over 500 years later. That second report challenges the veracity of the first. Shouldn't it be the other way around? Why would the burden of proof not be placed upon the absent witness from afar? For Christians to switch their long-held belief in the Injeel's historical record for this later report would not simply be emotionally repelling but intellectually illogical. Faith severed from its historical cause is simply a leap in the dark.

Faith for us is far more than believing in one supreme Being, but in a personal God who entered our world in history at a specific time and place. It *followed* his mighty workings. On top of that, previous Scriptures anticipated them so we could positively identify this Messiah when he arrived. Together, God's Word joined with his works, formed a perfect union, lifting faith from the realm of possibility to a logical necessity and moral obligation. Emotionally, for us to opt for the second report is no more likely than for devout Shi'as to regard Hussain ibn Ali's courageous opposition against the tyranny of Yazid a childish fable.

> Faith, if not rooted in reality, is delusion.

What if the shoe was on the other foot?

Let's pretend its AH 700/AD 1400 and a stranger marched into the city of Medina with this public announcement:

> Together, God's Word and works make faith in God possible.

> "Salaam, citizens of Medina! God has spoken to me through an angel who revealed that the Hijrah to Yathrib was a mere fantasy, the battles of Badr and the Trench were only legends added centuries later and even the life of the Prophet (p) himself was a phantom with reality in appearance only."

Would the citizens of Medina fall for this? How do you think they would respond? My guess is that intelligence would prevail over accusation. The Medinan citizens would challenge the stranger to substantiate his absurdities. "Sir, you *say* that these landmarks of recorded history never happened and a historical figure of monumental influence never lived. The burden of proof is on you!" The Medinans would dismiss this "prophecy" as a hoax and later historians would regard this foreigner as out of his mind or under a jinn's evil spell.

Muslim readers, how does that pretend story differ from this summons addressed to Christians?

> "O people of the Scripture (Jews and Christians)! Now has come to you Our Messenger (p) making (things) clear to you, after a break in (the series of) Messengers, lest you say: 'There came to us no bringer of glad tidings and no warner.'" (Al-Maidah 5:19 Khan)

Our reluctance to follow Muhammad (p) does not stem from unbelief, but from prior belief. For us, God's "glad tidings" of salvation stand anchored to the "glad happenings" performed by a Man who out-lived, out-loved and out-died his contemporaries.

As Christians we ask, making *what* clear to us? What additional glad tidings in the form of signs are needed in addition to those already revealed in the Injeel? Shouldn't Christians share the same right as the Medinans to demand of Islam compelling reasons to part ways from the one who gave himself for us? Certainly Muslims can understand our reluctance to dismiss the proofs validating Jesus in light of Surat such as Al-Baqarah 2:86-87. Should we equate grand claims with credible support? Just because the shoe is on the other foot does not alter the logic.

And for what compelling reason? Our reluctance to follow Muhammad (p) does not stem from *un*belief, but from *prior* belief. For us, God's "glad tidings" of salvation are anchored in the "glad happenings" performed by a Man who out-lived, out-loved and out-died his contemporaries.

"And having disarmed the powers and authorities, he [God] made a public spectacle of them, triumphing over them by the cross."

Injeel,
Colossians 2:15

"For God did not appoint us to suffer wrath but to receive salvation through our Lord Jesus Christ. *He died for us so that . . . we may live together with him.*" (1 Thessalonians 5:9-10)

Clearly, Jesus' literal death is what frees us from God's future wrath. Extracting it would cancel the eternal hope it secured. The Qur'an agrees with the Injeel that "the Jews did not kill Jesus" and that his death came by God's initiative, not man's. God outwitted the best of human intelligence.

> "None of the rulers of this age understood it [God's wisdom], for if they had, *they would not have crucified the Lord of glory.*" (1 Corinthians 2:8)

> "And having *disarmed the powers and authorities,* he [God] made a public spectacle of them, *triumphing over them by the cross.*" (Colossians 2:15)

God's superior wisdom over man's was seen, not by establishing the means of human salvation through a popular act, but by an irreversible one.

Past actions are irreversible and cannot budge any more than a wrecked Ford truck can self-repair.

3. How can it claim infallibility if it contains important details needing correction?

My third difficulty in accepting the Qur'an as an infallible guide are simple mistakes that appear to discredit that claim. While many of these involve minor details with little

Faith is not gullibility and virtue is not mental laziness. Investigating the content of new messages expresses the premium value hat a person places on truth.

impact on a particular message, that is not the point. The issue is its claim of absolute inerrancy.

Muslims, as noted earlier, often raise questions about the Injeel's integrity. As Christians, we welcome these. For example, in the Injeel citizens from the city of Berea were commended precisely for delaying their acceptance of the Gospel until they had examined it against previous Scripture (Acts 17:1012). Faith is not gullibility and virtue is not mental laziness. Investigating the content of new messages expresses the premium value that a person places on truth.

Pointing out alleged fallacies in the Qur'an is a worn path, even an old minefield. Nothing said here hasn't already been said a hundred times. Should we even proceed with this? Only to a point.

It is kind of like the game of American football, a good, clean, hard-hitting sport when played by the rules. Players caught breaking those rules get penalized. One such infraction called "piling on" occurs after the ball-carrier has already been tackled and the referee's whistle has blown. If a player hurls himself on the pile of bodies just to make the other team "feel it" a little more the Referee "throws the flag" and penalizes the offending team 15-yards for "unnecessary roughness." Piling on is overkill. I introduce it here because I see a parallel with this book. The gravity of issues between our Books calls for us to be hard-hitting on truth but not on each other! There is a place to honestly examine the warrant for the claims we make. In writing this book, I have no interest in "piling on" with excessive argument. Only two historical inconsistencies should sufficiently question the claim of infallibility.

The Qur'an Shows Chronological and Geographic Confusion

Al-Qasas 28:38 presents us with a command by Pharaoh during the time of Moses:

> *Fir'aun (Pharaoh)* said: "O chiefs! I know not that you have an ilah (a god) other than me. So kindle for me (a fire), *O Haman, to bake (bricks out of) clay,* and set up for me a *Sarhan (a lofty tower,* or palace) in order that I may look at (or look for) the Ilah (God) of *Musa* (Moses); and verily, I think that he [Musa] is one of the liars."

(Al-Qasas 28:38 Khan; see also Al-Mumin 40:36-37)

Christians have no reason to quibble with this excellent object lesson on the folly of the Pharaoh's arrogance. It's the details that we find problematic – a tower of clay bricks, a pharaoh during the time of Moses and Haman's tower – cobbled together into a single episode when they were separated by centuries and continents.

- The Tower of Babel was built prior to Abraham's day (c. 2000-1800 BC) and recorded in Genesis 11:1-7. It was one of the many vaunted staircases that was believed to link earth to heaven. Like the aya in the Qur'an, it was constructed of clay bricks that were baked in kilns (common to ancient Babylon) and thus not to be confused with the pyramids of Egypt built from stone.
- The Pharaoh who opposed the God of Moses lived around lived around 1400 BC.
- Haman lived in the Persian capital of Susa and ministered as chief officer in the court of King Xerxes I who reigned between 486-465 BC. Like the aya, Haman did in fact erect a lofty tower, a seventy-five foot gallows to be exact (Esther 3:14). But its purpose was not to provide anyone with a glimpse of God but to hang an innocent man as a first step of annihilating all the Jews (Esther 3:1-6).

The drawback for us is this. How can the Pharaoh ruling in Egypt during Moses' day (1400 BC) command Haman, a court minister who lived way over in Persia almost a millennium later, to build a ziggurat tower of clay bricks drawn from Babylonia in Abraham's day (c. 2000-1800 BC)? The value of its moral lesson cannot cancel out the fact that Al-Qasas 28:38 gives no indication that it should be interpreted allegorically. It narrates a scenario as straightforward history that would have been impossible to occur.

A simple chronological discrepancy makes absolute infallibility difficult to accept.

The Qur'an Confuses Details about the Plagues of Egypt

Moses had reached his eighty-third birthday when he freed the Children of Israel from centuries of Egyptian bondage. Even a man with vigorous youth could not imagine he could deliver over a million slaves from Pharaoh who refused to release them. To change his mind, God sent multiple plagues on Egypt and its people. Exodus chapters 7 – 11 records the devastating toll from these ten cataclysmic scourges: blood (rivers), frogs, gnats, flies, livestock, boils, hail, locusts, darkness and finally the firstborn. Finally, Pharaoh summoned Moses and said, "Up! Leave my people, you and the Israelites! Go worship the LORD as you have requested" (Exodus 12:31). The Qur'an, however, when describing this event, presents the Flood as the first plague:

> "So We let loose upon them *the flood* and the locusts, the lice and the frogs, the blood, distinct signs; but they waxed proud and were a sinful people." (Al-Aaraf 7:130, Arberry)

There also seems to be confusion about the number of plagues – sometimes only nine (Al-Isra 17:103; Al-Saffat 37:112) versus five, the first believed to be the Flood (Al-Aaraf 7:133).

Reconciling a claim of infallibility with a confusion about obvious details of history and chronology presents an obstacle for our acceptance.

4. Does the perfect transmission of an ancient Book prove its divine origin?

Another difficulty Christians have in recognizing the Qur'an as the Injeel's correcting agent is the dubious yardstick used by Islamic apologists to prove its divine origin, one that purportedly invalidates the Injeel and exonerates the Qur'an. This measuring device sets the existence of "only one Qur'an, perfectly preserved" over against multiple Injeels with their variant readings. Chapters 7 and 8 addressed the Injeel's manuscripts. Let's focus here on the preservation yardstick. Three brief citations are representative of a torrent of others like them:

"The Qur'an's text is entirely reliable. It has **not been altered, edited, or tampered with since it was revealed**. . .All Muslims know **only one Qur'an, perfectly preserved** in **its original words** since the Prophet's death, when Revelation ended."[26]

Abdullah Yusuf Ali states emphatically:

"So well has it been **preserved**, both in memory and in writing, that the Arabic text we have today is **identical to the text as it was revealed to the Prophet**. Not even a **single letter has yielded to corruption** during the passage of the centuries."[27]

Alhaj A. D. Ajijola, writes: "The Qur'an is **fully preserved** and **not a jot or tittle has been changed or left out**."[28]

As a Christian reflecting on these accolades celebrating the Qur'an's perfect transmission through the centuries, I offer two respectful observations hoping to continue the conversation – one about their implications and the other a personal concern. First, this claim is admirably bold. My purpose here is not to challenge its accuracy but to consider what it implies. That is, even if true, what would it prove? Undoubtedly, Islamic apologists would concur with the following conclusions by scholar Daniel Brubaker:

- That the Qur'an passed through subsequent generations unscathed, its Arabic texts protected from omissions, additions, alterations of words or phrases. As such, today's generation is provided with an exact reproduction of the original.
- That the message of Muhammad (p) it its totality is authenticated for future generations with unfailing precision.
- That this successful transmission of the original Arabic Quranic text in its pristine form over a fourteen-century period and distributed throughout the world constitutes a magnificent achievement.

None of these is up for debate. The value of faithful transmission is obviously enormous. Here's what I find missing. All three citations focus exclusively on the Qur'an's *ongoing* perpetuity yet say nothing about its *original* status.

The logic breaks down for us in equating "only one Qur'an perfectly preserved" with "it must be the Word of God." How can the yardstick of impeccable transmission, as valuable as it is, be used to accurately measure divine origin? Is it the tell-tale sign authenticating God's Word?

Let's consider *The Book of Mormon*. If today's version is identical to the one first published by Joseph Smith in 1830, would Muslims regard it as God's infallible Word and embrace Joseph Smith as your prophet by virtue of its unchanged condition? I seriously doubt it! Why not? *Because if it was heresy back then, it remains heresy today!* Time does not straighten a crooked stick. Old heresies are not wine that improve with age (presumably, since I don't drink). When Muslims appeal to the Qur'an's perfect textual transmission as proof of its divine origins, they seem, at best, to be using a flawed yardstick. That is my point.

This is not to deny the paramount value of faithfully transmitting texts. What I'm trying to say is that its value is in direct proportion to the status of the original. If proven to be from God, its preservation matters supremely. But if the original failed, its transmission is inconsequential. Transmission only conforms to its source document, saying nothing about its transcendence or lack thereof.

My second response is more personal. To be candid, many of us are concerned for our Muslim friends in face of the ultimate downside of attributing divine origin to a Book on the basis of "only one Qur'an perfectly preserved." That position places one's faith on a shaky foundation that could quickly prove hazardous to it. What happens if solid research on the Qur'an's early transmission history presents incontrovertible documentation that challenges the assumption of its perfect uniformity? That day seems to have already arrived. By citing hundreds of scribal corrections and manuscript dissimilarities, Daniel Alan Brubaker's recent publication, *Corrections in Early Qur'an Manuscripts: Twenty Examples*,[8] is one of a growing number of scholarly studies in this field. The author does not attack Islam in spirit or letter nor does he draw theological conclusions. He simply intends to "deal in reality" (p. xxii) in addressing assumptions of uniformity among its earliest extant parchments.

The New Testament, as presented in Chapter 7, uses a different yardstick to verify divine speech. Of first importance was Who wrote the rules by which to deem it true or false. That took us back to the Torah itself, specifically, the Prophet Test to identify authentic inspired Scripture.

5. How can the Qur'an be the uncreated heavenly Original when it cites earlier literature?

This difficulty does not address the Qur'an's infallibility per se, but its eternal origins[48] as the "mother of all books" that is believed to secure it. Specifically, if the Qur'an's infallibility rests upon its transcendent origins, that it descended to earth in pristine purity and absolutely free from human influence, my fourth difficulty lies in the many clear allusions to earlier literary works that it incorporates. It is my understanding, especially from conversations with Sunni Muslims, that Islam bases its claim for the Qur'an's infallibility on the following three sub-claims.

Islam's Claims for the Qur'an

#1: Of all the revealed Books, the Qur'an is both first and last. That is, it existed *first* in heaven prior to any previous Book and appeared *last* in historical sequence (Sunni view). It is thus the pure words of Allah, untainted by human influence. Several ayat are used to support this view.

> "This Quran could not have been composed by any except Allah; but it is a confirmation of that which was revealed before it, and an explanation of the scripture; there is no doubt thereof; sent down from the Lord of all creatures." (Yunus 10:37)

Allah's eternal Word is "glorious," a term of sublimity as originating purely from God apart from human intervention:

> "Nay, it is a *glorious*[49] *Quran,* upon a *Preserved Tablet.*" (Al-Buruj 85:21-22 Nasr)

Many equate the "Preserved Tablet" with the Qur'an's designation as "Mother of the Book:"

> "And with Him [Allah] is *the Mother of the Book* (Al-Lauh Al-Mahfuz)." (Al-Raad 13:39 Kahn)

> "[This Qur'an] is in *the Mother of the Book* (i.e. Al-Lauh Al-Mahfuz) *with Us*, indeed exalted, full of wisdom." (Al-Zukhruf 43:2-3 Kahn)

This maternal designation that is fused with the Preserved Tablet is believed to set the Qur'an apart as "the source of all revelation, from which the Quran and all other revealed Books are derived."[50]

#2: The Qur'an clarifies and completes all previous revelations. As Mother and Preserver of all revelation, it is enshrined with a privileged authority over previous Scriptures. Khan's English version of Yunus 10:37 brings this out:

> "This Quran . . . . is a *confirmation* of (the Revelation) which was before it [i.e. the Taurat (Torah), and the *Injil* (Gospel)], and a *full explanation* of the Book (i.e. the laws decreed for mankind – wherein there is no doubt – from the Lord of the Alamin (mankind, jinn, and all that exists)." (Yunus 10:37 Khan, emphasis added)

According to this aya, the Qur'an seems to play two roles in relation to earlier Scriptures.

Confirms previous Scriptures. To "confirm" something means to establish its truth, accuracy, validity or genuineness. Christians appreciate the Qur'an's repeated exoneration of Biblical revelation (Al-Baqarah 2:41, 89, 91, 97, 101; AlImran 3:3, 81; Al-Maidah 5:48; Al-Anaam 6:92; Yunus 10:37; Al-Fatir 35:31; Al-Ahqaf 46:3).

Completes previous Scriptures. Moreover, the Qur'an takes on a second role of bringing "full explanation" to earlier revelation. This is a little puzzling in that when we compare individual events found in both books, the fuller account is almost always the biblical one (see Appendix). One example is the Creation, a cardinal doctrine for Muslims and Christians. While agreeing with a six-day creation, only the Tawrat provides detailed information of what God made on each day.

Corrects previous Scriptures. In addition to these two roles, is there a third? I am not sure how, but Muslims often inform me that the Qur'an's second role expands from merely *completing* the earlier Books to *perfecting* them. By this is meant that it identified and then corrected their historical inaccuracies and doctrinal perversions. It is endowed with final authority to declare some portions of the Old and New Testaments as valid and others invalid. But how is this possible? This third role, it would seem, confronts the Qur'an with a moral dilemma. **How can it purge the Bible of its errors after certifying its accuracy? Should not its role be either to purge it *or* to certify it, but not both?** Can it in good conscience "confirm" as true a text that is corrupted? By the same measure, from what will it "cleanse" from a Book that it confirms to be sound? And after initially confirming it as God's Word, then to alter it borders dangerously close to blasphemy by attributing profane qualities to that which is sacred? Despite this conundrum, I have yet to meet a Muslim who denies the Qur'an's role in correcting the errors of earlier Books. This takes us to the next question of criteria used to determine corruption.

Criteria used to Identify Corruption

Please help us understand the criteria by which the Qur'an decides what in the earlier Books stays and what goes. There must be more going on here that meets the eye. Tarif Khalidi, esteemed professor of Arabic and Islamic studies at the American University in Beirut, provides a clue. After describing Jesus as he is portrayed in Islamic tradition and the Qur'an, he says:

> How can the Qur'an purge the Bible of its errors after certifying its accuracy? Should not its role be to either purge or to certify it but not both?

"Here, then, is the true Jesus, "cleansed" of the "perversions" of his followers, a prophet totally obedient to his Maker and offered up as *the true alternative to the Jesus of the Incarnation, Crucifixion, and Redemption.*"[51]

If Khalidi expresses Islamic orthodoxy (likely), the criteria determining which passages about Jesus are targeted for purging become clear. Ironically, it is not the legendary-laden folklore derived from late Sources (see "Similarity Test" below). Rather, teachings that must be laundered out of the Injeel are those rooted in history. That includes Jesus entering the world as the divine Word incarnate, vindicated as such by signs and miracles, being crucified on our behalf as a sign manifesting God's love and raised on the third day to offer eternal life through redemption. **In short, the purge has nothing to do with the Injeel's historical integrity but Islam's predetermined roster of doctrinal contraband.** It targeted narrowly the Biblical canon ranging from Scriptural prophecy to its historical fulfillment supported by eyewitness testimony. To most Christians, this sounds less about the Gospel's cleansing and more about its evisceration and replacement.

#3: The Qur'an can prove its claims Christians and Muslims agree that these claims for the Qur'an are behemoth in size. Like water seeking its own level, *towering claims call for towering evidence.* What matching basis supports the Qur'an's authority to act as Mother and Arbiter of all previous revelation?

> Christians and Muslims agree that these claims for the Qur'an are behemoth in size. Like water seeking its own level, towering claims call for towering evidence.

Some in Muhammad's (p) day were skeptical about his revelations, even charging him with repeating stories from popular "tales" circulating in Arabia:

> "Those who disbelieve say: 'This (Qur'an) is nothing but a lie that he (Muhammad (p), p) has invented, and others have helped him at it'. . . And they say: 'Tales of the ancients which he has written down, and they are dictated to him morning and afternoon.'" (Al-Furqan 25:4-5 Khan)

The Prophet (p) answered their skepticism with a bold challenge by which to prove the Qur'an's divine origins once and for all. Like Moses who instituted "the Prophet Test" in the Tawrat to verify if God had spoken (see Chapter 7), so Muhammad (p) implemented what might be called "the Similarity Test," showing the Qur'an to be incomparable.

"Or do they say: 'He (Muhammad (p) [p]) has forged it?' Say: '*Bring then a Surah (chapter) like it,* and call upon whomsoever you can besides Allah, if you are truthful!'" (Yunus 10:37-38 Khan)

"And if you (Arab pagans, Jews, and Christians) are in doubt concerning that which We have sent down (i.e. the Qur'an) to Our slave (Muhammad (p) Peace be upon him), then *produce a Surah (chapter) of the like thereof and call your witnesses (supporters and helpers) besides Allah,* if you are truthful. But if you do it not, and you can never do it, then fear the Fire (Hell) whose fuel is men and stones, prepared for the disbelievers." (Al-Baqarah 2:23-24)

The Prophet (p) genuinely believed such a search would come up empty:

Say: "If mankind and the jinn were together to produce the like of this Qur'an, they could not produce the like thereof, even if they helped one another." (Al-Isra 17:88 Khan)

As a devoted follower of Jesus, I appreciated this permission allowing us to investigate this matter for ourselves. Reputable scholars[52] have taken up the Prophet's challenge by carefully examining the Qur'an to see if passages "like it" had existed prior to or during Muhammad's (p) time.[53]

The Similarity Test

Students who read both the Qur'an and the Bible quickly discover that the Qur'an recasts biblical events, often introducing details missing from the Bible. In addition to passages of this nature pertaining to Jesus previously noted (Q 9.1: "Sources for Jesus in the Qur'an"), I have selected the following six for inquiry:
1.   Adam and Eve's banishment from Paradise and the fall of Iblis
2.   Cain's murder of his brother Abel
3.   Abraham delivered from a fire
4.   A mountain to split if in contact with Qur'an
5.   Golden calf lowed
6.   Queen of Sheba visits Solomon and Hoopoe bird

Since these episodes contain information that cannot be found in the earlier Scriptures, the Similarity Test challenges inquirers to find literature resembling them from the pre-Islamic period. I began with the assumption that they would not. As new revelation coming directly from heaven through the angel to the Prophet (p), it would be free of human influence, unlike any other literature past or present.

What I learned. I found that in all six cases, these episodes were in circulation well-before Muhammad's (p) time. Most came from Judaism through the Talmud and others derived from a blend of Gnostic, Buddhist and Persian writings. A classic *Dictionary of Islam* examined incidences from Jewish history that are cited in the Qur'an, presenting an exhaustive list tracing their derivation to Talmudic Judaism rather than the Old Testament.[54]

These literary matches can be easily verified by interested students. In the interest of space, the following chart serves as an overview.

Chart A: Qur'anic Use of Earlier Literary Sources							
GROUPS	TITLE	1	2	3	4	5	6
Jewish Apocrypha Mishnah, Haggadic **Midrash** **(commentary on Hebrew Scriptures)** **Targums**	*Targum of Jonathan Ben Uzziah, Mishnah Sanhedrin* 4.5, (2ⁿᵈ century)		X				
	The Life of Adam and Eve 13:1-16:3 (c. 100 BC – AD 100); Latin text *"Vita Adae et Evae"* (c. AD 400) – Commentary on Genesis 1-4	X					
	Midrash Rabah			X			
	Targum Jonathan Ben Uziel			X			
	2 Enoch 29:45 includes Satan's refusal to bow down to Adam	X					
	Pirke Rabbi Eliezer, Midrash					X	
	II Targum of Esther						X
	Abodah Zarah, Targum on Judges 5:5				X		
Gnostic Gospels	*Gospel of Bartholomew*	X					
	Second Treatise of the Great Seth						
	The Sethian-Ophites	X					
	Apocalypse of Peter	X					
	Acts of John	X					
	Mani/Manichaeism	X					

Brief summaries are provided below.

SIMILARITY TEST	
The Qur'an's Dependence on Talmud Judaism	
AL-QUR'AN **Uncreated Original**	**ORIGINAL LITERARY** **SOURCES**
ADAM & EVE STORY Iblis refuses to bow down to Adam; Adam and Eve fall from heaven to earth (S. 2:30, 34; 7:11-18; 15:28-44; 17:61-65; 18:50; 20:116-117; 38:71-85) **Biblical Account:** Adam and Eve lived in the Garden of Eden located on Earth rather than in heaven. Surrounded by orchards of delicious fruit, God designated one tree in the middle as off-limits: the Tree of the Knowledge of Good and Evil. Violation would result in death. Satan tempted them to doubt God's Word. They listened and succumbed. For their transgression, Adam and Eve were "sent out" from God's presence in the Garden, not cast down to Earth. Neither the angels nor Satan were commanded to do homage to Adam. (Gen 3:23-24)	Iblis refuses to bow down to Adam; Adam and Eve fall from heaven to earth *100 BC; The Life of Adam and Eve* 13:1-16:3 (Latin text *"Vita Adae et Evae"* c. 400 A.D 55 *First Century C.E. — 2 Enoch* – its Jewish version including Satan's refusal to bow down to Adam56 (1st century) *Late Second Century C.E.–The Sethian-Ophites* [57] (late 2nd century) *Third Century C.E.–The Gospel of Bartholomew* 4:51-55
HABIL AND QABIL (S. 5:27-32) *a) The Raven, Cain and the burial of Abel's body* "God sent a raven to scratch up the ground and show him how to cover his brother's corpse..." (S. 5:31 Haleem) *b) Moral Value of Protecting Life*[a] "Because of that We ordained for the Children of Israel that if anyone killed a person not in retaliation of murder, or (and) to spread mischief in the land it would be as if he killed all mankind, and if anyone saved a life, it would be as if he saved the life of all mankind." (S. 5:32 Khan)	**HABIL AND QABIL** First Century AD — **The Raven scratching the earth** — *Targum of Jonathan Ben Uzziah*. Jewish Midrash – *The Pirke Rabbi Eliezer,* Second Century AD — **Protecting life citation:** *Mishnah Sanhedrin* 4.5, Jewish Targum "Therefore but a single person was created in the world to teach that if any man has caused a single life to perish from Israel, he is deemed by Scripture as if he had caused a whole world to perish; and anyone who saves a single soul from Israel, he is deemed by Scripture as if he had saved a whole world."[59]
Biblical Account: Abel and Cain (Gen 4:1-16)	

SIMILARITY TEST The Qur'an's Dependence on Talmud Judaism	
AL-QUR'AN Uncreated Original	**ORIGINAL LITERARY SOURCES**
ABRAHAM DELIVERED FROM THE FIRE (S. 19:42-50; 21:57-71; 26:69-86; 29:16-17; S. 37:83-98; 43:26-28; 60:4) Part 1 – Abraham Demolished Idols (S. 21:57-66; 37:83-96); Part 2 – Abraham Delivered from the Fire (S. 21:67-71; 37:97-100) **Biblical Account:** None	Second Century AD — *Midrash Rabah* – story included with Jewish folktales; *Targum Jonathan Ben Uziel* [60]
A MOUNTAIN WOULD SPLIT ASUNDER IF IN CONTACT WITH THE QUR'AN: "Had We sent down this Qur'an on a mountain, you would surely have seen it humbling itself and rending asunder by the fear of Allah." (S. 59:21 Khan) **Biblical Allusion** (?): The Mountain shook when God gave the Ten Commandments at Mt. Sinai (Jud 5:5): "The mountains quaked before the Lord, the One of Sinai, before the Lord, the God of Israel."	Mt. Sinai quaked when 10 Commandments given Second Century AD–*Abodah Zarah*, Jewish Targum to Judges 5:5
THE GOLDEN CALF LOWED (S. 20:88-909; 71:47) **Biblical Account:** The Golden Calf (Exo 32) No mention of lowing	Lowing of the Golden Calf First Century AD — *Pirke Rabbi Eliezer*, included in the Midrashic work
QUEEN OF SHEBA'S VISIT TO SOLOMON & THE HOOPOE BIRD (S. 27:16- 46) **Biblical Account:** Queen of Sheba's visit to Solomon; The Queen lauded Solomon's wisdom. No mention of a hoopoe bird (1 Ki 10:1-13; 2 Chron 9:12)	Second Century AD — *II Targum of Esther* (popular in seventh century Arabia)

Conclusions

The unique events or details added to biblical events that I previously believed to have originated in the Qur'an were composed long before the time of the Prophet (p). Citations such as these make it difficult for us to reconcile the Qur'an's infallibility when argued on the basis of its eternal existence.

This, Muslim reader, is not meant to be confrontational. We look forward to conversations where you can help us understand how the Qur'an as the "mother of all books" can claim dissimilarity with previous literature in light of its incl^{usi}on from a wide range of Jewish61 Talmudic and Zoroastrian sources from Persia. Some Muslims argue that this broad inclusion simply demonstrates that all religions reach their culmination in Islam. That is for another discussion. Here we focused narrowly upon the test established by the Prophet (p) by which to authenticate the Qur'an as pure divine revelation, namely its independence from existing literature in the seventh century. On that score, we found multiple borrowings in the form of unmistakable allusions or near-verbatim excerpts.

> We look forward for opportunities for Muslims to help us better understand what is meant by the Qur'an's dissimilarity as the "mother of all books" in the face of apparent borrowing from a wide range of prior sources.

Others may contend that Muhammad's (p) challenge was for a person to find a whole book like the Qur'an. Of course, there is none. Even if there was, what would that prove? Joseph Smith could have issued the same challenge for the *Book of Mormon*. Should we consider the absence of a replica as proof of its divine origin?

In summary, please help us understand how the Qur'an is considered by many people to be eternal and free of human involvement in light of these findings.

6. How can it add to a complete Gospel?

The sixth difficulty Christians have is not with any deficiencies thought to exist in either the Prophet or his Book, but is based on the conviction that the Jesus Gospel is God's completed revelation that fully addresses the human condition. The theme of salvation will be addressed more fully in Volume 2, but it applies to your question.

Why Jesus Is Enough

Jesus is God's cure for the fundamental ailment afflicting us all:

> "Surely the arm of the Lord is not too short to save, nor his ear too dull to hear. *But your iniquities have separated you from your God; your sins have hidden his face from you, so that he will not hear.*" (Isaiah 59:1-2)

What is the solution for this out-of-sync condition ailing our species? It is the Gospel of the Messiah! The first time we hear it communicated to a non-Jewish audience was a historic occasion when Peter, a Jewish apostle, delivered it in the home of a Roman Gentile.

> "Then Peter began to speak: 'I now realize how true it is that God does not show favoritism but accepts from every nation the one who fears him and does what is right.'"

> "You know the message God sent to the people of Israel, announcing the good news of peace through Jesus Christ, who is Lord of all. You know what has happened throughout the province of Judea, beginning in Galilee after the baptism that John preached— how God anointed Jesus of Nazareth with the Holy Spirit and power, and how he went around doing good and healing all who were under the power of the devil, because God was with him.

> We are witnesses of everything he did in the country of the Jews and in Jerusalem. They killed him by hanging him on a cross, but God raised him from the dead on the third day and caused him to be seen. He was not seen by all the people, but by witnesses whom God had already chosen—by us who ate and drank with him after he rose from the dead. He commanded us to preach to the people and to

testify that he is the one whom God appointed as judge of the living and the dead.

All the prophets testify about him that everyone who believes in him receives forgiveness of sins through his name.'" (Acts 10:34-43)

The Gospel that Changed History

This gospel of God's saving acts displays his love, reveals his character and applies his creative might on behalf of all people for all times in all places.

Its Source is God, not man – "*God* sent. . .*God* anointed. . .*God* raised him from the dead. . .*God* commanded. . .*God* appointed"

Its Attitude is winsome – "announcing the good news"

Its Fruit is restored relationships – "of peace"

Its Provider is the Savior – "through Jesus Christ [Messiah]"

Its Invitation is wide – "Lord of *all* . . . God does not show favoritism . . . *Everyone* who believes in him receives forgiveness of sins"

Its Power is liberating – "He went around doing good and healing all who were under the power of the devil"

Its Sacrifice was total – "They killed him by hanging him on a tree"

Its Triumph was irreversible – "God raised him from the dead on the third day"

> What counts is not the final Book, but the everlasting Man: "Jesus Christ is the same yesterday and today and forever."
> (Hebrews 13:8)

Its Advanced billing prepared the way – "All the prophets testify about him"

Its News is trustworthy – "We are witnesses of everything he did"

Its Means of propagation is honorable – "God commanded us to preach to the people and to testify"

Its Command is urgent – "He is the one whom God appointed as judge of the living and the dead"

Its Promise is sure – "Everyone who believes in him receives forgiveness of sins through his name"

This Gospel covers any and every circumstance imaginable. That is because it is the story of the unconquerable love of God!

> *Who shall separate us from the love of Christ?* Shall trouble or hardship or persecution or famine or nakedness or danger or sword? . . . "No, in all these things we are more than conquerors through him who loved us. For I am convinced that neither death nor life, neither angels nor demons, neither the present nor the future, nor any powers, neither height nor depth, nor anything else in all creation, will be able to separate us from the love of God that is in Christ Jesus our Lord."(Romans 8:31-39)

What counts is not the final Book, but the everlasting Man: "Jesus Christ is the same yesterday and today and forever." (Hebrews 13:8)

Summary

Your question about why we withhold our endorsement of your Final Book given to the "last Prophet" shows immense courage, candor and it deserves our honest answer. Respectfully, our reservations are these:

1. How can it correct a Book about which it is unfamiliar?
2. How can it rewrite events of the past?
3. How can any book claim infallibility while containing details in need of correction?
4. By what logic is the perfect transmission of an ancient book thought to prove its divine origin?
5. How can a Book exist first when it cites earlier literature?
6. How can anyone add to a Gospel that is already complete?

THE AUTHOR AND HIS REASONS FOR WRITING

I heard about some horse-riding stables located out in the western part of the USA with a billboard that read:

> "WE'VE GOT A HORSE FOR YOU!
> For fat people, we've got fat horses.
> For skinny people, we've got skinny horses.
> For people who have never ridden a horse before,
> We've got horses that have never before been ridden!"

Muslim friend, this book project is for me a horse that has never before been ridden. Despite getting bucked off many times, I wouldn't trade it for anything. I'm also keenly aware of others with far greater qualifications for such a project. I claim no expertise on Islam but am an interested and invested student. It begs the question. What motivations are behind the writing of this book? It really boils down to three discoveries I've made along my journey beginning with my personal heritage, valued friendships and a post-graduate study.

1. Through my heritage, I was introduced to the Gospel of God's holy love.

While today's Western culture bears many marks of a secular wasteland and hedonistic playground, within it resides a lively substratum of deep piety that goes largely undetected by most media outlets. In that substratum was the home of my upbringing. Prayer was fervent, the study of Scripture frequent, attendance in public worship without fail, the Ten Commandments observed and conversation free within the boundaries of respect. The formation of social circles enriched the daily humdrum of life with pleasure, encouragement and counsel. In that environment, the awareness of God was normal with a normalizing effect by defining the norms of vibrancy. From this heritage, I learned the paramount importance of seeing God rightly through the infallible lens of Scripture. And through that lens, I met a God of holy love.

God is holy.[1]

God's holiness (*qadesh*) describes his separateness from all creation, but covers more than transcendence or power. It is:

> "his total and unique moral majesty. *When people fear before God (e.g. Judg 6:22; 13:22) it 'is not the consciousness of . . . humanity in the presence of divine power, but the consciousness of . . . sin in the presence of moral purity.'"*[2]

> From this heritage, I learned the paramount importance of seeing God rightly through the infallible lens of Scripture. And through that lens, I met a God of holy love.

Prophet Isaiah is a case in point. Upon seeing a vision of God's throne surrounded by seraphs (burning ones) covering their faces, he heard them cry out:

> "Holy, holy, holy[3] is the LORD Almighty; the whole earth is full of his glory." (Isaiah 6:3)

These flaming voices could easily have cried "Mighty, mighty, mighty" or "Distant, distant, distant." But a revelation of the thrice-holy God became a moral blast that blew him away:

> "Woe to me!" I cried. "I am ruined![4] For I am a man of unclean lips, and I live among a people of unclean lips, and my eyes have seen the

King, the Lord Almighty." (Isaiah 6:5)

The means by which God rid Isaiah of his moral pollution is striking:

> "Then one of the seraphim flew to me with a live coal[5] in his hand, which he had *taken with tongs from the altar.* With it he touched my mouth and said, 'See, this has touched your lips; *your guilt is taken away and your sin atoned for.*'" (Isaiah 6:6-7)

This "live coal" purging the prophet's speech was taken "from the altar," the place of sacrifice.[6] While perhaps foreign to Islam, the altar was the place established by the thrice-holy God whereby sinful humans could enter his presence, receive forgiveness, and restore fellowship. Had God *not* been holy, this merciful provision would have been pointless. Anyone could simply have waltzed into his presence at their convenience. The biblical text stipulates a different mode of entry. It runs throughout the Earlier Books, starting within the Tabernacle in the Tawrat and culminates outside Jerusalem through Jesus' death in the Injeel.[7]

So God's intrinsic holiness permeates all his work. He is majestic in creation, unchangeable in character, perfect in justice, faithful in promise and measured in revelation. He demands holiness of his people (Lev 19:2ff).

God is love.

In addition to God's holiness, I learned that: "God is love" (1 John 4:8). Not to be confused with human sentimentality, the love of God is demonstrative action. It is free from every contaminant known to pollute the purity of love. As an attribute, it was present from the beginning. It was on creative display at the genesis of life, evident in his call to Abraham and his descendants to bless *all* families of the earth (Gen 12:1-3), revealed at the

> The claim, "God is love," is followed by the act, "God showed his love among us."

giving of commandments for the preservation of human society, and confirmed by his ongoing faithfulness to every covenant promise made to Abraham. The pinnacle of God's revelation of love, however, arrived in the Injeel:

> "*God is love.* This is how God *showed* his love among us: He sent his one and only Son into the world that we might live through him. *This is love: not that we loved God, but that he loved us and sent his Son as an atoning sacrifice for our sins.*" (Injeel, 1 John 4:8-10)

Note the sequence here. The claim, "God is love," is followed by the act, "God showed his love among us." Human words such as "I love you" seldom come with guarantees. Likewise, occasionally we meet someone who regards him or herself as a "loving person" while living a narcissistic life. Not so with God. For him, action and claim form a perfect match. The giving of his Son was not God acting in desperation, but God being himself.

The merging of these attributes, "God is holy" and "God is love," ushers us to the place where human sin was nailed and divine mercy unleashed.

Recipients of this love, those truly transformed by it, are the ones who never confuse its Subject and its object. Its *Subject* is God whose loving claim was proven by its extravagant act, the giving of his Son on our behalf. Its *object* is one who, regardless of where he or she lands on the sliding-scale of moral goodness, knows himself to be inwardly desperate, realizing that the sin that was nailed to the Tree was his own. That recipient receiving such "grace," the free gift of a new start, cannot possibly remain the same. They begin treating others as God in Jesus treated them.

"God is love. . .*We love because he first loved us.*" (1 John 4:16, 19)

In a world calloused, calculating and often cold, the ripple effect is incalculable.

The giving of his Son was not God acting in desperation, but God being himself.

My heritage introduced me to hymns celebrating God's holy love. One of those, "Amazing Grace," was more than a popular song. It was the spiritual autobiography of John Newton, formerly a British captain of an African slave-ship. Upon receiving God's holy love, the change in his life was dramatic. Newton joined William Wilberforce in the crusade to abolish the slave trade in England. In the year of his death in 1807, the British Parliament finally abolished it. His own epitaph can be read today on his granite tombstone:

> John Newton, minister,
> Once an infidel and libertine,
> A servant of slaves in Africa,
> Was, by the rich mercy of our
> Lord and Savior Jesus Christ
> Preserved, restored, pardoned
> And appointed to preach the faith he
> Had long labored to destroy.[8]

The foundational motivation for this book is the desire to keep this divine love moving from one person to another. But that does not answer why this book addresses Muslims specifically.

2. Through valued friendships, I've learned how Muslims and Christians are more alike than we are different.

The second motivation for this book is a relatively newfound respect and love for Muslim people. Six years ago, my wife and I sold our home, moved across the state and bought a little bungalow in an amazing, global-rich neighborhood. To the left of us live Egyptians, to the right Mexicans and behind us Iraqis. Directly across the street are Palestinians, African Americans, Lebanese and more Lebanese. Fanning out from there is block after block of all of the above. So we are planted in the heart of the USA, the land of Chevrolet and apple pie – and yet, in a city where a Kansas boy and an Oregon girl reside as ethnic and religious minorities. So what has living in this neighborhood taught us about Arabic culture? Some really good things! We've discovered firsthand so many notable qualities that we've come to greatly admire:

- *High value of hospitality and a desire to share generously with others.* My summer afternoon strolls along sidewalks almost always take me to someone's front porch! Such openness has won my heart. On top of that, a week hardly goes by without sharing a meal or receiving a delicious dish.

- *Respect and care for parents,* a value we share in observance of the fifth commandment: "Honor your father and your mother."

- *Healthy curiosity with a zest for learning.* We've seen this admirable quality in formal studies and spontaneous conversations. For instance, one of my neighbors asked me for an Arabic Bible, indicating her desire to gain a firsthand knowledge of the earlier Books.

- *Respect for modesty,* a high value also shared by our holy Scriptures[9] and in short supply in today's culture.

- *Desire to integrate truth and life.* Carving out time five times each day for prayer counters our culture's tendency to compartmentalize life between secular and sacred.

- *Enjoys talking about God.* Of all these, this trait I probably admire most. For example, late one night recently I was invited to a neighbor's home. I arrive to find five Muslim university students studying law, pharmacy and engineering all sitting on couches, sharing tea, having a good time and talking theology! And they invited me to join in the conversation. Muslims have reintroduced God into the conversation in places where rampant secularism has imposed an unwritten gag-order.

> What an extraordinary gift is the recognition of our shared humanity!

We've learned that we are alike in many ways. Christians aren't from Mars and Muslims from Venus. We both belong on this native soil, breathe the same air and, if pushed back far enough, arrived here through a common ancestor by the same Creator who is forever praised. What an extraordinary gift is the recognition of our shared humanity!

This recognition heightens the impulse to initiate friendship in a post-9-11 world. My guess is that it is not easy being a Muslim today. Daily being singled out on news outlets that is seldom positive would challenge anyone. Perhaps there are times when you feel yourself being watched by others with suspicion. In this contentious climate, it would be easy to play it safe, grow inward and withdraw from the wider society. I pray that this book interacting with your questions can move today's conversations beyond politics!

A third motivation for this book came from beyond the God of my heritage and our newfound friends. It arose from my firsthand reading of your holy Book, the Qur'an.

3. Through a post-graduate study, I discovered that Islam and Christianity are more different than they are alike.

My guess is that it is not easy being a Muslim today. Daily being singled out on news outlets that is seldom positive would challenge anyone. In this contentious climate, it would be easy to play it safe, grown inward and withdraw from the wider society.

Many Muslims tell me that deep down our religions are the same. Let me tell you how I arrived at a different conclusion.

After twenty years of pastoring in major American metropolitan areas—Portland, Oregon, Seattle, Washington and Austin, Texas—we witnessed a burgeoning influx of immigrants arriving from around the world. Along with them came their religions. Over time, the religious landscape took on a different shape as temples and mosques dotted the scene and their members became more mainstream in American life.

With this cultural shift, new questions arose. We often found ourselves perplexed by the religious multiplicity of our global culture. Some have privately wondered, am I responsible to share Jesus' saving message with the soft-spoken Hindu family that just moved in next door? Or with the devout Muslim internist at our hospital? Or the circumspect Buddhist lab partner at my med-school? Or, should we consider their sincere devotion to their religious faiths to place them beyond the need for the gospel of salvation through Jesus' death and resurrection?

To avoid charges of bigotry, many Christians muted their witness. At the same time, religious pluralism gathered steam in American culture through academia. It promoted the idea that beneath the surface, all religions share fundamental agreement about God's nature, humanity's condition and its saving remedy. None is superior to another. "Deep down we're all saying the same thing." Perhaps attempting to promote a society of tolerant coexistence, a worthy goal to be sure, did it do so at the expense of truth by ignoring contradictions on major doctrines?

To the question of religious sameness, most people I encountered answered something like this: "Of course, they're alike" or "No way!" To my follow-up question how they arrived at their conclusion, they varied from "O, just a hunch" to "I read their Books in a world religions class." When pressed, most in the latter group had only read anthologies, collections carefully selected from the sacred writings in support of the editor's answer to the question. Sadly, I was no better. If I told a Buddhist that Jesus is the only way of salvation and he asked me if I had read the Buddhist Scriptures, I'd be sunk! Not necessarily mistaken, just naïve in his eyes. How can we overcome this religious stalemate? Why not subject the pluralist premise of sameness to an objective study by leaping over ignorant hunches and cherry-picked anthologies to actually compare the full texts of sacred writings at their respective fountainheads? I returned to graduate school to do just that. For my major thesis, I chose four major world religions – Hinduism, Buddhism, Christianity and Islam – selecting only one doctrine, the afterlife, and ran it through the grid of their hagiographa.

Drawing from classic texts revered by these faiths, I compared heaven in Christianity with Hindu *Moksha*, Buddhist *Nirvana* and Islamic *Paradise*. Specifically, I looked to see how each religion answered three fundamental afterlife questions:

(1) What happens to people when they die and to what do they aspire? This differentiated "moksha," "nirvana," "heaven," and "paradise."
(2) By what path must people take to arrive at the desired place?
(3) How confident are people of reaching their aspired goal?

I limited my comparisons to the best English translations of their earliest holy Books and steered clear of later theologians. For Hinduism I read *The Rig Veda, The Thirteen Principal Upanishads* and *The Gita*. For Buddhism (Theravada, earliest tradition), the *Buddhist Scriptures (Tripitaka)*. For Islam, the Qur'an, and for Christianity, the New Testament (Injeel).

Outcome

The specific conclusions of that study are beyond this book. The bottom line is this: On the question of deep doctrinal similarity, the texts did nothing to support the pluralist premise. On the question of the afterlife, while each religion outside of Christianity affirmed its reality, none offered anything remotely close to confident hope. Where the two Eastern religions assigned hope to the basket of vices, Islam viewed it as ardent desire in anticipation of the Day of Reckoning. The data led conclusively to this politically *in*correct conclusion. While many religions exist, there is only one Gospel, the grand announcement of a *living* hope based upon the risen Christ.

> "God has given us new birth into **a living hope through the resurrection of Jesus Christ from the dead**, and into an inheritance that can never perish, spoil or fade." (1 Peter 1:3-4)

Jesus' death and resurrection secured for his followers three priceless gifts: *Pardon* (removal of sins), peace (right standing with God) and *paradise* (future place in heaven):

> "He was delivered over to death for **our sins** and was raised to life for **our justification** [pardon]. Therefore, since we have been justified through faith, we have **peace with God** through our Lord Jesus Christ.... And we rejoice in **the hope** of the glory of God." (Romans 4:25-5:2)

That study changed the course of my life, especially by widening the embrace of people from other faiths in light of the Gospel. But it does not explain this book's particular interest in Muslim people.

Where did I get my heart for this book?

That study introduced me to the message of the Qur'an which, in turn, created the need for this book.

Of the religions of my study, Islam held the greatest interest for me. Where the Eastern religions of Hinduism and Buddhism appeared centuries prior to the coming of Jesus, Islam came after him and, to some extent, rooted itself in the Tawrat and Injeel. Reading it moved me deeply. Its passionate call for singular devotion to the one God was compelling. As a non-Muslim, parts of its message eluded my understanding. To be candid, when it came to its coverage of the Gospel, my responses went from confusion to anger which finally co-mingled with grief. Let me explain.

Afterlife in al-Qur'an

Correct me if I'm wrong, but my reading of the Qur'an shaped this brief summary of the Islamic doctrine of the afterlife. I will paint these with broad strokes for brevity.

First, the absolute certainty and precise nature of the afterlife incentivize Muslims to live beyond the present world in preparation for the next. Chief among these incentives are entry into Paradise, the Garden of delight, and avoidance of Hell, the abode of eternal Fire.

Second, while retaining many doctrines from the earlier Books such as divine Creation, universal Resurrection and final Judgment, the Qur'an omits, beclouds or explicitly denies the Messiah's death as a divine provision of salvation as promised by the earlier Prophets.

Third, this absence forces Muslims to shift their reliance of final salvation from God's historic work through Jesus to their own diligent efforts. Sufficient merits must accrue by which to gain Allah's final approval. Paradise awaits those who, by adhering to the dictates of Qur'anic law, have earned enough merits that will outweigh their misdeeds on life's final moral scale.

Fourth, the Injeel's buoyant hope dissolves in the Qur'an, reemerging as fervent desire and intense yearning. Devout Muslims have an unquestionable zeal for God and righteousness, but without the benefit of knowing the gift of righteousness God has already provided for them through the Messiah. This leaves Muslims to live with a "wait and see" assurance making the present age one of suspense awaiting to hear God's final verdict.

Muslim reader, my distilled summary of Islamic hope directly resulted from reading your Book for myself multiple times. If it oversimplifies the matter, I beg your forgiveness and invite your correction. It's here to help you see what led to the myriad of reactions evoked by my reading of the Qur'an. *Initial bewilderment* – Can historic events of Jesus' death and resurrection simply vanish by the stroke of a pen? What new evidence warrants it? *Growing indignation* – Who dares defy God by vandalizing the NT's greatest treasure, God's supreme demonstration of love and power? *Moral Obligation* – Should Christians sit idly by and not stand up to defend the Gospel in the face of such defiance? Then something happened to shift my disposition from attack to advocacy.

I stated befriending Muslim people.

Suggesting that my angry feelings over a gospel substitute vanished or even subsided would overstate the matter. More accurately, it became swallowed up in grief over the very people I had come to know and love and, most importantly, who were most directly affected by the change. Now the challenge shifted from who would rise to Christianity's defense to who would step-up to defend Muslim people bereft of God's gift of salvation. Especially when many have silently given up on God while continuing to practice their religion because they know of no other option. Their crisis of faith is grievous and unnecessary. Faith feeds on truth, rising to the level of revelation. By removing that revelation, Islam deprives Muslims of the historic basis for vibrant belief rooted in God's action:

> "Through Jesus you believe in **God, who raised him from the dead** and glorified him, and **so your faith and hope are in God**." (1 Peter

1:21)

All I've tried to do in writing this book is to reinsert the faith-building elements that your religion removed. It is important to me that you are clear about these motivations.

Think of it like this. Let's say you have a precious grandmother whom you adore whose loving husband suddenly passed away. No amount of money could possibly compensate for her loss, but how thankful she was for the lavish life insurance policy he left her to more than cover for her needs. When she examined the policy, to her dismay, she found that its provisions had been redacted. Someone had taken a black Magic Marker, struck through them, making them unreadable! Although she had every right to redeem that policy and receive a significant amount of money, she assumed that it was obsolete. She returned the perfectly good policy back into its file where it sat unclaimed. She began a job search to pay her rent and make ends meet. A year later you discover this injustice.

As her grandchild, what's your reaction? You are livid. *What an injustice! She's the very one for whom the policy was purchased. Who would commit such an evil?* Who's to blame, your grandmother? Certainly not! She's the victim, not the villain.

After reading the revised Gospel in the Qur'an, I became that grandchild. I learned that someone had, in effect, taken a black Magic Marker and struck through the clearest display of God's most magnanimous action on behalf of the human race by Jesus' death and resurrection.

How could this happen? Why would anyone rob major populations of that which was rightfully theirs? Especially in light of its cost to the Giver on behalf of its intended recipients?

This reality is hardly imaginary. Over a billion people around the globe miss out, misbelieving Jesus' suffering as fantasy. The repercussions? Like the deceived grandmother needlessly paying her own way, Muslims are left on their own to earn the soul-rest Jesus offers: "**Come to me,** all you who are weary and burdened, and **I will give you rest.**" (Matthew 11:28)

Would Jesus withhold that invitation from Muslims, loving them less that others? The absurdity of the question answers itself. Meeting hundreds of Muslim people and the privilege to call many of them my valued friends has made this more than an academic issue.

I hope this helps you understand the shift I've experienced from primarily defending Christianity to advocating for Muslim people.

How rich the Bedouin's wisdom: "The greatest sin in the desert is to know where the water hole is and to not share it." Having freely received a treasured eternal gift, passing it on to you is an unspeakable delight. I know a few Christians who have never shared the Gospel with a Muslim and then blame them for not knowing it! Shame on us!

Marquis, one of my former students, said it best: "Muslims, you deserve the right to receive an unadulterated presentation of the Gospel – even if you choose to reject it."

> "God actually did demonstrate his solidarity with humanity by visibly entering our world and defeating death itself, allowing us to understand life in a wholly new way, with redemptive love able to overcome human wickedness and reveal the true face of God." Lamin Sanneh, a Muslim reflection on the cross

Rethinking the Stumbling Block

Each day over the past decade, thousands of Muslims have been coming to faith in Jesus. Doing so meant overcoming the stumbling-stone of the cross. In one way or another, every one of them came to see Jesus' death in a new light.

The Cross cannot Save

It is a great paradox. God used Jesus' public crucifixion as an instrument to attract people to him! Seems impossible, I know. This spectacle of torment was so abhorrent that it caused people to turn and run. An instrument to draw people to Jesus? Jesus made it clear that the attraction was *not* the cross:

> "'And **I**, when **I** am lifted up from the earth, **will draw all people to myself.**' He said this to show the kind of death he was going to die." (Injeel, John 12:32-33).

Did you catch that? The wooden crossbeams drew no one. During Jesus' time, crucifixions were daily occurrences and had the opposite effect – repelling, not attracting. The drawing force was not the cross, but the Man on it. It was *Jesus*. He was the attraction: "And *I*, when *I* am lifted up. . . will draw" (emphasis mine).

What special allure could Jesus possibly exert while "lifted up" in public shame that he did not have while performing miracles from a boat, teaching on the Temple steps or healing in the synagogues?

Lamin Sanneh's story might help. A devoted Muslim from Gambia, Africa almost against his will, harbored a secret intrigue with the crucifixion, specifically the identity of its victim:

> "As hard as I tried, I could not run from the questions: Who died on the cross? If we don't know his name, how can we know the God who put him there? But suppose Jesus did die on the cross, and suppose God intended it to be so; how would that change our knowledge of God?"[10]

This question took Sanneh, a noted scholar of history, beyond mere academic concerns of historicity to reflections of meaning amid life's tragedies:

> "I reflected on the suffering and the heartbreak which are part of life, hopes that are often dashed to pieces, for even in my relative youth I had known tragedy in my family and in that of others, such being the precarious nature of life in an Africa just emerging from its middle ages. It seemed to me that deep down at the center and core of life, the cross and its anonymous burden was declaring something about the inner integrity and mystery of life which rang true to all authentic experience."[11]

"I felt truly unshackled, released from the crippling incapacity to seek to please God. . .I came to see that only God can give us the grace to accept his unconditional love for us. . ." Lamin Sanneh, a disciple of Jesus

These reflections led Sanneh to a startling conclusion:

"If we can put a face and a name to the anonymous victim of the Qur'anic crucifixion, we could do worse than let that victim be Jesus. Of all the characters mentioned in the Holy Book, Jesus was the one for whom the cross was most intended, and therefore of all individuals, the one who came closest to it, whatever the effectiveness of the divine rescue. In such a case, it would follow that God actually did demonstrate his solidarity with humanity by visibly entering our world and defeating death itself, *allowing us to understand life in a wholly new way, with redemptive love able to overcome human wickedness and reveal the true face of God.* Seen in the light of the cross of Jesus Christ, all of human nature, indeed all of history, appears to gather at one sharp, poignant place. It all began to make sense to me. The need for the cross seemed so compelling and true to the way life is."[12]

Lamin Sanneh was no John Newton, the captain of the African slave ship who wrote "Amazing Grace." Sinners like Newton obviously need salvation. But Sanneh? How can we explain why such a devoutly religious man and scholar felt pulled toward the One on the cross for something amiss within his own soul?

"I came upon the fantastic teaching of God's justification by faith. I was stunned by God's magnanimity, more so because I had no personal cultural pedigree in Christianity. . . ."[13]

Sanneh the devout Muslim and Newton the profligate slave trader shared something in common: an overwhelming poise in the certain embrace of God's amazing grace. Sanneh's reliance for salvation shifted from his own flawed attempts to win God's approval through his own works to the perfect obedience of another, Jesus the Righteous One, whose final "Yes" to God completed his work for the sake of our righteousness. Sanneh's personal relief was beyond calculation.

"I felt truly unshackled, released from the crippling incapacity to seek to please God. . .I came to see that only God can give us the grace to accept his unconditional love for us. . ." Lamin Sanneh, a disciple of Jesus

"[Those] who have never known a religion of strict rules and regulations, what it felt like to be crushed beneath the burden of having to obey God's inscrutable ordinances and how, by contrast, the intervention and interposition of Jesus on the cross felt like a godsend . . . I felt truly unshackled, released from the crippling incapacity to seek to please God . . . I came to see that only God can give us the grace to accept his unconditional love for us, since culture, experience, and habit will instill in us a cultivated indifference to revealed truth. . . ."[14]

This book aims to share the hope with Muslims everywhere, whether like Lamin Sanneh or John Newton, that you may overflow with hope and assurance for eternity with God, and that you may experience the freedom of knowing Jesus, the One who endured and overcame death for our salvation!

Guiding Principles for Writing this Book

Muslim reader, thank you for reading *Questions Muslims Ask Christians*! No doubt, along the way you experienced a wide range of emotions. I prayerfully hope that your questions were answered, if not satisfactorily in every case at least as a genuine attempt to do so. Your comments, questions and corrections will greatly improve future editions.

In *content,* I've strived for accuracy, fairness and clarity. In *tone,* a humility appropriate to the Subject of God and Scripture, hopefully stimulating, not squelching, conversation. Who respects a tirade? Jesus taught a better option, keeping conversations on the up-and-up, infusing them with life-giving words. Two guardrails, he said, will keep us on the right track.

First, speak out of the overflow of a good heart:

"The mouth speaks what the heart is full of. A good man brings good things out of the good stored up in him, and an evil man brings evil things out of the evil stored up in him." (Matthew 12:34-35)

Jesus instructs us to communicate with noble intentions. Our hearts, that is, must be in the right place. If good speech depends on good hearts, it follows that the best preparation for engaging ideas is performed privately before an audience of One with this simple prayer: "Search me, O God, and know my heart; test me... see if there is any offensive way in me, and lead me in the way everlasting" (Zabur, Psa 139:23-4).

Muslim reader, much valuable information you find on these pages has been culled from books on my library shelves. But if you came across truths or insights having fresh poignancy, there's a good chance they emerged from that private chamber on my knees. All glory be to God.

Such preparedness also minimizes unnecessary offence. Love is honest but not rude. It shuns the "billy goat" approach that prides itself on butting heads rather than filling them.

Instead, we "speak the truth in love" (Injeel, Ephesians 4:15).

Second, say only what we mean.

> "But let your statement be, 'Yes, yes' or 'No, no'; anything beyond these is of evil." (Injeel, Matthew 5:37)

> "You will know the truth, and the truth will set you free." (John 8:32)

Simplicity, says Jesus, signals a noble soul while its opposite, embellishment, evil duplicity. The corrupt uses words to conceal truth where the noble uses them to express it. Good people are not infallible, but correctible. Evil people are neither.

Throughout these pages, I have endeavored to write only what I believe to be true and refrain from glossing over our differences even for the sake friendship.

APPENDIX
Reading Aid

BIBLICAL PEOPLE IN THE QUR'AN
WHERE YOU CAN FIND THEM

"So if you are in doubt about what We have revealed to you,
ask those who have been reading the scriptures before you.
The Truth has come to you from your Lord,
so be in no doubt and do not deny God's signs."
(Yunus, 10:95, Haleem)

Listed in approximate order of appearance in the holy Books

BIBLICAL NAMES & PASSAGES THAT MENTION THEM T = Tawrat; Z = Zabur; I = Injeel	BIBLICAL NAMES IN THE QUR'AN & PASSAGES THAT MENTION THEM M = Meccan; Y = Yathrib (Medinan)
Adam (*of the earth*) – **T**: Gen 1:26-5:5; **I**: Lk 3:38; Ro 5:14; 1 Cor 15:22, 45; 1 Tim 2:13-14; Jude 10	**Adam – M:** 7:11, 19-27-35, 172; 17:11, 61, 70; 18:50, 56; 19:58; 20:115-123; 36:60; **Y:** 2:30-41; 3:33-34, 59; 5:27
Enoch (*dedicated*), father of Methuselah – **T**: Gen 5:8-24; **I:** Heb 11:5	**Idris – M:** 19:56-57; 21:85; 96:4
Noah (*rest*) – **T**: Gen 5:1-9:29; 1 Chron 1:1; Isa 54:9; **I:** Matt 24:37-8; Lk 3:36; 17:26-7; Heb 11:7; 1 Pet 3:20; 2 Pet 2:5	**Nuh – M:** 7:59-64, 69; 9:70; 10:71-73; 11:25-49, 89; 14:9; 17:3, 17; 19:58; 21:76-77; 23:23-30; 25:37; 26:105-122; 29:14-15; 37:75-83; 38:12-14; 40:5, 31; 42:13; 50:12; 51:46; 53:52; 54:9-15; 71:1, 21-28; **Y:** 3:33; 4:163; 22:42; 33:7; 57:26; 66:10 **Nuh's wife – Y:** 66:10
Sons of Noah: Shem (*name; renown*)**, Ham** (*become hot*) **& Japheth** (*make wide*), **T**: Gen 5:32; 6:7; 7:13; 9:18, 23-27; 10:1, 21-31; 11:10-11; 14:2; 1 Chron 1:4, 17, 24; **Z**: Psa 78:51; 105:23, 27; 106:22; **I**: Lk 3:36	**Nuh's sons – M:** 11:42-43; 1-41; 21:76

577

Job, prophet known for patience – **T:** Job 1-42; Eze 14:14, 20; **I:** Js 5:11	**Ayub – M:** 6:84
Terah, father of Abraham – **T:** Gen 11:24	**Azar – M:** 6:74
Abraham (*father of multitudes*) – **T:** Gen 11:26-25:8; Exo 2:24; 3:6-16; 4:5; 6:3-8; 32:13; 33:1; Lev 26:42; Nu 32:11; Dt 1:8; 6:10; 9:5, 27; 29:13-20; 34:4; Josh 24:2-3; 1 Ki 18:36; 2 Ki 13:23; 1 Chron 1:1, 27-34; 16:16; 29:18; 2 Chron 20:7; 30:6; Ne 9:7; Isa 29:22; 41:8; 51:2; 63:16; Jer 33:6; Eze 33:24; Mic 7:20; **Z:** Psa 47:9; 105:6, 9; 105:42 ; **I:** Matt 1:1-2, 17; 3:9; 8:11; 22:32; Mk 12:26; Lk 1:55, 73; 3:8, 34; 13:16, 28; 16:22, 29-30; 19:9; 20:37; Jn 8:33-58; Acts 3:13, 25; 7:2-17, 32; 13:26; Ro 4:1-18; 9:7-8; 11:1; 2 Cor 11:22; Gal 3:6-29; 4:22; Heb 2:16; 6:13-15; 7:1-10; 11:8, 17-19; Js 2:21-22; 1 Pet 3:6	**Ibrahim – M:** 6:74-84, 161; 11:69-76; 12;6, 38; 14:35-41; 15:51-60; 16:120-123; 19:41-50, 58; 21:51-73; 26:69; 29:16-27, 31-32; 37:83-113; 38:45; 42:13; 43:26-28; 51:24-34; 53:37; 87:19; **Y:** 2:124-140, 225-260; 3:33, 65-68, 84, 95-97; 4:54, 125, 163; 9:70, 114; 22:26, 43, 78; 33:4; 57:26; 60:4
Ishmael (*God hears*), oldest son of Abraham – **T:** Gen 16:1-16; 17:1-25; 21:8; 25:9, 12-17; 28:9; 36:3; 37; Judg 8:24; 1 Chron 1:28-31; 2 Chron 19:11; 23:1; Ezra 10:22; **Z:** Psa 83:6	**Ismail – M:** 6:86; 19:54-55; 21:85; 38:48; **Y:** 2:125-129, 133; 4:163
Lot (*covered*), nephew of Abraham – **T:** Gen 11:27-13:14; 14:12-16; 19:1-36; Deut 2:9, 19; **Z:** Psa 83:8; **I:** Lk 17:28-34; 2 Pet 2:7. **Lot's wife** (nameless): Gen 19:26	**Lut – M:** 6:86; 7:80; 11:70-89; 15:59-61; 21:71, 74; 26:160-161, 167; 27:54-56; 29:26-33; 37:133; 38:13; 50:13; 54:33-34; **Lut's wife:** 26:170; **Y:** 22:43; 66:10
Isaac (*he laughs*), second son of Abraham – **T:** Gen 17:19-21; 21:3-25:11; ("the God of Abraham, the God of Isaac and the God of Jacob," Exo 3:15 — repeated often); Exo 33:1; Lev 26:42; Nu 32:11; Deut 1:8; 6:10; 9:5, 27; 30:20; Josh 24:3-4; 1 Ki 18:36; 2 Ki 13:23; Jer 33:26; Amos 7:9, 16; **Z:** Psa 105:9; **I:** Matt 1:2; 8:11; 22:32; Mk 12:26; Lk 3:34; 13:28; 20:37; Acts 3:13; 7:8, 32; Ro 9:7, 10; Gal 4:28; Heb 11:9, 17, 18, 19-20	**Ishaq – M:** 6:84; 19:49; 21:72; 29:27; 37:112-113; **Y:** 2:133; 4:163
Jacob (*he supplants*), son of Isaac – **T:** Gen 25:29-28:5; God changed his name to "Israel" – Gen 32:28-32; 33:20; 35:10; 37-47; 49:33; Exo 1:1, 5; 2:24; Exo 3:6: "I am the God of your father, the God of Abraham, the God of Isaac and the God of Jacob" – frequently repeated; Lev 26:42; Nu 23 & 24; 32:11; Josh 24:4, 32; 1 Sam 12:8; 2 Sam 23:1;1 Ki 18:31; 2 Ki 17:34; 1 Chron 16:13, 16; Isa 2:3-6; 8:17; 9:8; 10:20-21; 14:1; 17:4; 27:6-9; 29:22-23; 40:47; 41:8, 14, 21; 42:24; 43:28; 44:1-21; Jer 2:4; 5:20; 10:16, 25; 30:7, 10, 18; 31:7, 11; 33:26; 46:27-28; 51:19; Lam 1:17; 2-3; Eze 20:5; 28:25; 37:25; 39:25; Hos 10:11; 12:2, 12; Amos 3:13; 6:8; 7:2, 5; 8:7; 9:8; Obad 1:10, 17-18; Mic 1:5; 2:7, 12; 3:1-9; 4:2; 5:7-8; 7:20; Nah 2:2; Mal 1:2; 2:12; 3:6; **Z:** Psalms 14, 20, 22, 24, 44, 46 47, 53, 59, 75, 76, 77, 78, 79, 81, 84, 85, 87, 94, 99, 105; **I:** Matt 1:2, 15, 16; 8:11; 22:32; Mk 12:26; Lk 1:33-34; 13:28; 20:37; Jn 4:5-6, 12; Acts 3:13; 7:8-46; Ro 9:13; 11:26; Heb 11:9, 20, 21	**Yaqub – M:** 6:84; 12:18; 19:49: 21:72; 29:27 **Y:** 2:132-133; 4:163 "Twelve sons of Yaqub" [*Asbat*]: **M:** 2:140; **Y:** 3:84; 4:163
Joseph (*he adds*), son of Jacob – **T:** Gen 37-50	**Yusuf – M:** 6:84; 12:4-102; 40:34

Pharaoh – T: (*P & Abraham*) Gen 12:15f; (*P & Joseph*) 37:36-41:17; (*P & Moses*) Exo 1- 6; Deut 6:21-22; 7:8, 18; 11:3; 29:2; 34:11; 1 Sam 2:27; 6:6; (*P & Solomon*) 1 Ki 3:1; 7:8; 11:1;	**Fir'aun – M:** 7:103-137, 141; 28:6-9, 37; 10:75-92; 20:24; 40:24, 36-37; 44:17-33; 68:9; 73:16; 85:17-20; 89:10-14; **Y:** 2:49-50; 3:11
Potiphar (see Joseph & Pharaoh)	**Al-Aziz –** royal title of Egyptian high nobles; used of Potiphar in reference to prophet Yusef (**M:** 12:30, 51); also the sixth beautiful divine name, "exalted in Might," **M:** 59:23
Moses (*draw out [of the water]*) – **T:** Exo 2:10-Deut 34:5; Josh 1- 4; 8:31-35; 9:24; 11:12-23; 12:6; 1:8, 12; Ju 1:16, 20; 3:4; 4:11; 18:30; Ezra 3:2; 6:18; 7:6; Ne 1:7-8; 8:1, 14; 9:14:10:29; 13:1; Isa 63:11-12; Jer 15:1; Dan 9:11, 13; Mic 6:4; Mal 4:4; **Z:** 77:20; 90:1; 99:6; 103:7; 105:26; 106:16, 23, 32-33; **I:** Matt 8:4; 17:3-4; 19:7-8; 22:24; 23:2; Mk 1:44; 7:10; 9:4-5; 10:3-5; 12:19, 26; Lk 2:22; 5:14; 9:30-33; 16:29-31; 20:28, 37; 24:27, 44; Jn 1:17, 45; 3:14; 5:45-6; 6:32; 7:19-23; 8:5; 9:28-29; Acts 3:22; 6:11, 14; 7:20-44; 13:39; 15:1, 5, 21; 21:21; 26:22; 28:23; Ro :5:14-15; 10:5, 19; 1 Cor 9:9; 10:2; 2 Cor 3:7, 13-15; 2 Tim 3:8; Heb 3:1-16; 7:14; 8:5; 9:19; 10:28; 11:23-24; 12:21; Jude 9; Rev 15:3	**Musa – M:** 6:84, 91, 154; 7:103-160; 10:75-89; 11:17, 97, 110; 14:5-8; 17:2, 101-104; 18:60-82; 19:51-53; 20:9-98; 21:48; 23:45-49; 25:35-36; 26:10-68; 27:7-14; 28:3, 48, 75; 29:39; 32:23; 37:114-122; 40:23-37, 53; 41:45; 42:13; 43:46-55; 46:12, 30; 51:38-40; 53:36; 79:15-26; 87:19; **Y:** 2:51-71, 87, 92, 108, 136, 246, 248; 3:84; 4:153, 164; 5:20-26; 22:44; 33:7, 69; 61:5
Jethro (*dedicated*), Moses' father-in-law; also called *Hobab* (Judg 4:11) & *Reuel* (Ex 2:18) – **T:** Exo 18:1-12	**Shuaib – M:** 7:85-93; 11:84-95; 29:36-37
Aaron (*shining light*), brother of Moses – **T:** Exo 4 – 7; Lev 1-3 and 6-8 (Aaron's sons, priests); Nu 3-4; 17; 33:39; Deut 9:20; 10:6; 32:50; Josh 21:4,m 10: 21:13, 19; 24:5, 33; Judg 20:28; 1 Sam 12:6, 8; 1 Chron 6; 15:4; 23:13, 28, 32; 24:1, 19, 31; 2 Chron 13:9-10; 26:18; 29:21; 31:19; 35:14; Ezra 7:5; Neh 10:38; 12:47; Mic 6:4; **Z:** Psa 77:20; 99:6; 105:16; 115:10, 12; 118:3; 133:2; 135:19; **I:** Lk 1:5; Acts 7:40; Heb 5:4; 7:11; 9:4	**Harun – M:** 6:84; 7:122, 142; 7:150; 10:75; 19:83; 20:30, 90, 92; 21:48; 23:45; 25:35; 26:12; 26:48; 28:34; 37:114-120; **Y:** 4:163
Miriam, sister of Moses – **T:** Exo 15:1-21; Nu 12:1-15; 20:1; 26:59; Deut 24:9; 1 Chron 4:17; 6:3; Mic 6:4	**Mariam; Miryam – M:** 19:27-34; 35-45; 28:13; **Y:** 66:12
Heber–T: Gen 46:17; Nu 26:45; Ju 4:11-21; 5:24; 1 Chron 4:18; 7:31-32; 8:17	**Hud – M:** 7:65-72; 11:50-59; 26:124-138; 46:25
Samuel (*heard by God*) the seer – **T:** (birth, childhood, divine call) 1 Sam 1-4; 7; 1 Chron 6:27-33; 7:2; 9:22; 11:3; 26:28-29; 2 Chron 35:18; Jer 15:1; **Z:** Psa 99:6; **I:** Acts 3:24; 13:20; Heb 11:32	**Smameel – Y:** 2:247
Goliath (*conspicuous*), giant that David killed – **T:** 1 Sam 17:1-58	**Jahut – Y:** 2:249-251
Saul (*tall*), Israel's first king – **T:** 1 Sam 9:1-2 Sam 1:27; **I:** Ac 13:21	**Talut – Y:** 2:246-249

David (*beloved*), father of Solomon; Israel's second king – **T:** 1 Sam 16:13-1 Ki 2:10; 1 Chron 9:22-29:30; Isa 7:2, 13; 9:7; 16:5; 22:9, 22; 29:1; 37:35; 38:5; 55:3; Jer 13:13; 17:25; 21:12; 22:2-4, 30; 23:5; 29:16; 30:9; 33:15-26; 36:30; Eze 34:23-24; 37:24-25; Hos 3:5; Amos 6:5; 9:11; Zech 12:7-12; 13:1; **Z**: Psalms 3 – 9, 12-27; Prov 1:1; Eccl 1:1; Song or Songs 4:4; **I:** Matt 1:1, 6, 17, 20; 9:27; 12:3, 23; 15:22; 20:30-31; 29:9, 15; 22:42-45 (parallels in Mk and Lk); Lk 1:27, 32, 69; 2:4, 11; 3:31; 6:3; 18:38-39; 20:41-44; Jn 7:42; Acts 1:16; 2:25-34; 4:25; 7:45; 13:22, 34-36; 15:16; Ro 1:3; 4:6; 11:9; 2 Tim 2:8; Heb 4:7; 11:32; Rev 3:7; 5:5; 22:16	**Daud, Dawud** – **M:** 6:84; 17:55; 21:78-80, 105-106; 27:15-16; 34:10-13; 38:17-26, 30; **Y:** 2:251; 4:163; 5:78
Solomon (*peace*), David's son and Israel's third king – **T:** 1 Ki 1:1-11:43; 1 Chron 22 – 2 Chron 9:31; 2 Sam 5:14; 12:24; Ezra 2:55, 58; Neh 12:45; 13:26; Jer 52:20; **Z:** Psalms 72 and 127; Prov 1:1; 10:1; 25:1; Eccl.; Song of Songs; **I:** Matt 1:6-7, 29; 12:42; Lk 11:31; 12:27; Jn 10:23; Acts 3:11-12; 7:47;	**Sulayman** – **M:** 6:84; 21:78; 21:79; 21:81; 27:15-21; 34:12-14; **Y:** 2:102; 4:163
Queen of Sheba – **T:** 1 Ki 10; 2 Chron 9; **I:** Matt 12:42; Lk 11:31	**Malkat Saba; Bilqis** – **M:** 27:29
Elijah (*My God is the Lord*), prophet – **T:** 1 Ki 17-2 Ki 2:11; Mal 4:5; **I:** Matt 11:14; 16:4; 17:3-12; 27:47-49 (w/parallels); Lk 1:17; 4:25-26; 9:8-33; Jn 1:21, 25; Ro 11:2; Js 5:17	**Ilyas** – poss. **M:** 37:123-132; 6:85
Elisha (*my God saves*), prophet; servant of Elijah – **T:** 1 Ki 19:16-2 Ki 3; **I:** Lk 4:27	**(Elisaie) Alyasa** – **M:** 6:86; 38:48
Michael (*Who is like God?*), angel – **I:** Rev 12:7	**Mikaeel** – **M:** 19:54
Jonah (*dove*), prophet swallowed by the great fish – **T:** Jonah 1-4; 2 Ki 14:25; **I:** Matt 12:39-41; Lk 11:29-32	**Yunus** –**M:** 6:86-87; 10:97-98; 37:139-148; **Dhu Al-Nun** ("he of the fish," 21:87-88); **Y:** 4:163; **Sahib al-hut** ("he of the whale," 68:48-50)
Ezekiel (*dedicated*), prophet/priest – **T:** Eze 1:3; 24:24 (poss the name of Obadiah)	**Hizqeel/Dhul-kifl** – **M:** 21:85; 38:48
Cyrus the Great – Persian monarch – **T:** Isa 45:1-4	**Dhul-Qarnayn** – **M:** 18:33 [or identified as Alexander the Great; see below]
Ezra (*help; my helper*), priest/scribe – **T:** Ezra 1; 7-10; Neh 7:73; 8:1-18; 12:1-36; **Z:** Psalms 88-89;	**Uzair** – **Y:** 9:30
Haman (*solitary; rioter*, Medo-Persian)– **T:** Esther 3–6	**Haman** – **M:** 28:6, 8, 38; 29:39, 40:24, 36-37, 46
Zachariah (*God remembered*), father of John the Baptist; priest – **I:** Lk 1:5-80	**Zakariyya** – **M:** 3:37-41; 6:85; 19:2-15; 21:90
John the Baptizer (*God's grace*), Messiah's forerunner – **T:** prophesied in Isa 40:3-5; Mal 3:1; 4:5-6; **I:** Matt 3:1-4:12; 9:14-17; 11:2-18; 14:2-10; 16:13-14; 17:10-13; 21:25-32; Mk 1:1-14; 6:14-29; 8:27-28; 11:30-32; Lk 1:13-80; 3:2-20; 5:33; 7:18-35; 9:7-9, 18-20; 11:1; 16:16-17; 20:4, 8; Jn 1:6, 40; 3:23; 4:1; 5:33-36; 10:40-41; Ac 11:16; 13:24-25; 19:4	**Yahya** – **M:** 6:85-86; 19:7-15; 21:90; **Y:** 3:38-40

Mary (*myrrh; bitter*), mother of Jesus – **T:** prophesied in Isa 7:14; **I:** Matt 1:16-2:24; 13:55; Mk 6:3; Lk 1:27-2:5-39; Jn 19:25; Acts 1:14	**Mariam – M:** 10:68; 19:30-34; 21:91; 23:50; 61:6, 14; **Y:** 2:136; 3:35-36; 4:163; 9:30-31; 33:7; 66:12. *Note.* She is called the daughter of Imran in 66:12 and 3:35-36. "There is a similarly-named person in the Tawrah (Exo 6:20, Nu 26:59) called Amram, who is the father of Harun, Musa, and Miriam (same spelling in Arabic as Mariam.) If the same person is intended, this may refer to Mariam's descent from the priestly line of Harun, as her relative Elizabeth was descended from Harun, son of Amram (Injil, Lk 1:5, 36)." (RQ, 747)
Gabriel (*strong man of God*), an angel sent from God – **T:** Dan 8:16; 9:21; **I:** Lk 1:19, 26	**Jibrael – M:** 26:193; 53:6-7, 13-18; 81:19-21; **Y:** 2:97-98; 66:4
Jesus (*God saves*) – see Table in Chapter 9	**Isa** – see Table in Chapter 9
Jesus' followers – those called to follow and serve Jesus Christ; Christians in general, usually called *believers* or *disciples*. **Apostles** refer to Jesus' uniquely appointed representatives who he chose, trained and sent out with authority; designated "the Twelve" (Mat 19:28; Jn 6:70, etc.) and included Paul (Acts 26:12-18; 1 Cor 15:3-10; Gal 2:8).	**Al-Hawariyyun** (the white-garbed), Al-Nasara (Derived from Nazareth, Jesus' hometown or from "ansar" [helpers/servants, **M:** 61:14; **Y:** 3:52

Some persons are mentioned but unnamed in the Qur'an: Eve, Jochebed, Noah's wife, Sarah, Zipporah, Elizabeth, Korah, Joseph's brothers, Potiphar. Some are identified in Islamic tradition.

Cain (*acquisition*) – **T:** Gen 4:1-17, 24-25; **I:** Heb 11:4; 1 Jn 3:12; Jude 11	**Qabil – Y:** 5:27-31; Islamic tradition
Abel (*breath; vapor; fragile*)– Gen 4:1-17, 25; 4:25; **I:** Matt 23:35; Lk 11:51; Heb 11:4; 12:24	**Habil – M:** 19:56-58; 21:85; **Y:** 5:27-31; Islamic tradition
Hagar (*flight, immigrant, fugitive*) – **T:** Gen 16; 21:8-17; 25:12; 1 Chron 1:29; **I:** Gal 4:21-25	**Hagar – Y:**14:37(?); frequently mentioned in Hadith
Isaiah (*the Lord saves*), prophet – **T:** 2 Ki 19:2-20; 2 Ki 20:1-16; 2 Chron 26:22; 32:20, 32; Isa 1:1; 2:1; 6:1; 7:3, 13; 8:1; 13:1; 20:2-3; 37:2; **I:** Matt 3:3; 4:14; 8:17; 12:17; 13:14; 15:7 Lk 3:4; 4:17; Jn 1:23; 12:38-41; Acts 8:28-30; 28:25; Ro 9:27-29; 10:16-20; 15:12	**Ashi'ya** – appears frequently as a prophet in Islamic tradition (Muhammad Ibn Ishaaq [ra])
Jeremiah (*the Lord will exalt*), prophet/priest – **T:** 2 Ki 23:31; 24:18; 2 Chron 35:25; 36:12, 21-22; Ezra 1:1; Neh 10:2; 12:1, 12, 3; Jer 1:1-11 (called by God); 7:1; 10:23; 11:1, 18; 12:1; 14:1; 18:1, 18; 19:14; 20:1-7; 21:1-3; 24:3; 25:1-13; 26:1-8; Dan 9:2; **I:** Matt 2:17; 16:14; 27:9	**Aramayah** – appears in Islamic tradition (Wahb ibn Munabbih; Hisham ibn Muhammad ibn Saib al kalbi)

HISTORICAL FIGURES NAMED IN THE QUR'AN BUT NOT THE BIBLE	
Alexander the Great – prophesied about in **T:** Daniel 11:3	**Dhul-Qarnayn** ("he of the two horns" – horns symbolic of power) – greatest king of the Greeks – **M:** 18:83, 36, 94 [see Cyrus the Great]
Nations or national leaders: **Gog & Magog** – *Gog*, **T:** 1 Chron 5:4; Eze 38:2-3, 14, 16, 18, 21; 39:1, 11; **I:** Rev 20:8. *Magog*: **T:** Gen 10:2; 1 Chron 1:5; Eze 38:2; 39:6; **I:** Rev 20:8	**Ya'juj & Muj'us** – **M:** 18:94; 21:96

For this section, I am indebted to several reference works, especially the *Reference Qur'an*, biblical lectionaries and Qur'anic indexes. For the benefit of providing historical context by distinguishing early and late surahs, I've simply cited points of agreement between two recognized sources: Mohammed Marmaduke Pickthall, *The Glorious Qur'an* (Elmhurst, NY: Tahrike Tarsite Qur'an, Inc., 2000) and Muhammad Taqi-ud-Din Al-Hilali and Muhammad Muhsin Khan, *Interpretation of the Meanings of the Noble Qur'an* (Maktaba Dar-us-Salam, 1996).

WORKS CITED

Al-Fadi, Abd. *The Person of Christ in the Gospel and the Quran*, electronic edition. Undated.

Al-Jibouri, Yasin T. (ed.). *Najhul-Balagha, Peak of Eloquence*. Elmhurst, NY: Tahrike Tarsile Qur'an, Inc., undated.

Aland, Kurt and Barbara. *The Text of the New Testament*. Grand Rapids, MI Eerdmans, 1995.

Alexander Roberts (ed.), *Ante-Nicene Fathers*, Vol. 1. Irenaeus: *Against Heresies*, The Gnostic Society Library, http://gnosis.org/library/advh1.htm.

Anderson, M. "The Trinity: An Appreciation of the Oneness of God with Reference to the Son of God and the Holy Spirit for Christians and Muslims," http://Injeel.answering-islam.org/Mna/trinity.html#02-theExpression, 1996.

Aslan, Reza. *No god but God: The Origins, Evolution, and Future of Islam*. NY: Random House, 2005. *Zealot: The Life and Times of Jesus of Nazareth*. NY, NY: Random House, 2013.

'Ata'ur-Rahim and Ahmad Thomson, *Jesus, Prophet of Islam*, Revised Ed. London, UK: Ta-Ha Publishers, 1995.

Bannister, Andrew. *An Oral Formulaic Study of the Qur'an*. Lexington Books, 2014.

Barnstone, Willis (ed.). "The Second Treatise of the Great Seth." *The Other Bible: Jewish Pseudepigrapha, Christian Apocrypha, Gnostic Scriptures*. NY, NY: Harper & Row, 1984.

Bauckham, Richard. *Jesus and the Eyewitnesses: The Gospels as Eyewitness Testimony.* Grand Rapids: Eerdmans, 2006.

Bediako, Kwame. *Christianity in Africa: The Renewal of a Non-Western Religion.* Maryknoll, NY: Orbis Books, 1995.

Berger, Klaus. *Jesus and the Dead Sea Scrolls.* Louisville, KY: John Knox Press, 1995.

Bettenson, Henry and Maunder, Chris (eds.). *Documents of the Christian Church,* 3rd Edition. NY: Oxford University Press, 1999.

Beverly, James A. and Evans, Craig A. *Getting Jesus Right.* Lagoon City, Brechin, Ontario: Castle Quay Books, 2015.

Biblical Archaeological Review, 25th Anniversary publication, 1996.

Block, Darrell L., Enns, Peter and Kaiser, Walter C. Jr. and Berding, Kenneth and Lunde, Jonathan (eds.), *Three Views on the New Testament Use of the Old Testament.* Grand Rapids: Zondervan, 2008.

Brotzman, Ellis R. *Old Testament Textual Criticism.* Grand Rapids, MI, 1994.

Brown, Colin. *Miracles and the Critical Mind.* Grand Rapids: Eerdmans, 1984.

Brown, Michael L. *Answering Jewish Objections to Jesus, Vol 2: Theological Objections.* Grand Rapids, MI: Baker Books, 2000.

Brown, Rick. "Muslims Who Believe the Bible," *Mission Frontiers,* July-August 2008. Pasadena, CA: USCWM.

Brubaker, Daniel Alan. *Corrections in Early Qur'an Manuscripts: Twenty Examples.* Lovettsville: Think and Tell Press, 2019.

Bruce, Alexander B. *The Training of the Twelve.* Edinburgh, England: T & T Clark, 1871.

Bruce, F. F. *The New Testament Documents: Are they Reliable?* 5th edition. Grand Rapids, MI: Eerdmans Publishing Co, 1943, 1988. Also http://Injeel.ncbible.info/MoodRes/Transmission/NTDocuments-Reliable-Bruce.pdf

Campbell, I. D. *Opening up Matthew.* Leominster: Day One Publications, 2008.

Carson, D. A. *The Gagging of God: Christianity Confronts Pluralism*. Grand Rapids, MI: Zondervan, 1996.

Catechism of the Catholic Church, English tr. Collegeville, MINN: The Liturgical Press, 1994.

Chambers, Oswald. *Approved Unto God* in *The Complete Works of Oswald Chambers*. Grand Rapids, MI: Discovery House, 2000, orig 1936. *The Secret of the Burning Heart in The Complete Works of Oswald Chambers*. Grand Rapids, MI: Discovery House, 2000; orig 1930.

Charles, Joshua. *Liberty's Secrets: The Lost Wisdom of America's Founders*. Washington D.C., WND, 2015.

Cragg, Kenneth. *The Call of the Minaret*, 3rd ed. Oxford: One World, 2000.

Cullmann, Oscar cited in Slomp, Jan. "The Gospel of Barnabas in Recent Research." *ChristlichIslamische Gesellschaft* e.v., Injeel.chrislages.de.

Daryabadi, Abdul Majid. *The Glorious Qur'an: Text, Translation & Commentary*. Leicester, UK: The Islamic Foundation, 2008.

Dabiq ISIS Journal, "Break the Cross," Issue 15, 1437 Shawwal.

Doyle, Tom. *Dreams and Visions*. Nashville, TENN: Thomas Nelson, 2012.

Dugard, Martin and O'Reilly, Bill. *Killing Jesus – A History*. NY, NY: Henry Holt and Co., 2013.

Elias, Abu Amina. "Was Jesus Christ crucified or someone else?" May 1, 2013. http://abuaminaelias.com/islam-is-mercy-for-the-entire-universe-believers-and-unbelievers-even-animals/.

Evans, Craig A. *Fabricating Jesus: How Modern Scholars Distort the Gospels*. Downers Grove, ILL: InterVarsity Press, 2006.

Field, Benjamin. *The Student's Handbook of Christian Theology*. NY, NY: The Methodist Book Concern, 1887.

Flint, Annie Johnson(1866-1932). "He Giveth More Grace." copyright 1941, 1969. *Sing to the Lord*. Kansas City, MO: Lillenas Publishing House, 1993.

Farquhar, J. N. *The Crown of Hinduism*. New Delhi, India: Oriental Publishers, 1913, 1971.

Frydland, Rachmiel and Klayman, Elliot (ed.). *What the Rabbi's Know about the Messiah*. Columbus, OH: Messianic Literature Outreach, 1991.

Gairdner, Injeel. Injeel. T. *God as Triune, Creator Incarnate, Atoner*. Madras Allahabad Calcutta Rangoon Colombo: Christian Literature Society, 1916.

Gariepy, Henry. *Songs in the Night*. Grand Rapids, MI: Eerdmans, 1996.

Gilcrist, John. *The Origins and Sources of the Qur'an*. http://truthnet.org/islam/source.htm.

Giovanneti, Bob. *The Birth of Jesus*. NY, NY: Centennial Media, 2017.

Green, Samuel. "The Gospel of Barnabas," answeringislam.com, 2004.

Greeson, Kevin. *The Camel*. Arkadelphia, AR: Wigtake Resources, 2007.

Hamilton, Victor P. *Handbook on the Pentateuch*. Grand Rapids, MI: Baker, date unspecified.

Harrison, Everett F. *A Short Life of Christ*. Grand Rapids, MI: Eerdmans, 1996.

Hengel, Martin. *The Son of God*. Eugene, OR: Wipf & Stock Publishers, 1976.

Hill, C. E. *Who Chose the Gospels?* NY, NY: Oxford University Press, 2012.

Hills, A. M. *Fundamental Christian Theology*, Vol 1. Pasadena, CA: C. J. Kinne, 1931.

Hilscher, Solomon S. *The Eternal Evangel*. NY: Broadway, c. 1910.

Holmes, Michael Injeel. (ed.). *The Apostolic Fathers in English*. Grand Rapids, MI: Baker, 2006.

Institute of Islamic Information and Education. "The Authenticity of the Qur'an." http://Injeel.iiie.net/index.php?q=node/46

Ishaq, Ibn. *The Life of Muhammad, Sirat Rasul Allah*, Guillaume (intro). Karachi, PAK: Oxford University Press, 1967 (1955).

Jamieson, R., Fausset, A. R., & Brown, D. *Commentary Critical and Explanatory on the Whole Bible*, Vol. 2. Oak Harbor, WA: Logos, 1997.

Jenkins, Philip. *Hidden Gospels: How the Search for Jesus Lost its Way*. NY, NY: Oxford University Press, 2001.

Jesus-Islam. Injeel.jesus-islam.org/Pages/ WhyhaveChristianshiddenthegospelofBarnabas.aspx.

Jeyachandran, L. T. "The Trinity as a Paradigm for Spiritual Transformation. Ravi Zacharias (Ed.), *Beyond Opinion: Living the Faith We Defend*. Nashville, TENN: IVP Academic, 2010.

Johnson, Robert Clyde. *The Meaning of Christ*. Philadelphia: The Westminster Press, 1958.

Kelly Monroe, (ed.). Sanneh, Lamin. "Jesus, More than a Prophet." *Finding God at Harvard: Spiritual Journeys of Thinking Christians*. Grand Rapids: Zondervan, 1996.

Khalidi, Tarif (Ed. and tr.). *The Muslim Jesus: Sayings and Stories in Islamic Literature*. Cambridge, MASS: Harvard University Press, 2001.

Kinlaw, Dennis. *This Day with the Master*. Grand Rapids, MI: Francis Asbury Society, Zondervan, 2002.

Knight, J. P. "Hope Against Hope: Hinduism, Buddhism, Christianity & Islam." Unpublished Th.M. Thesis, Calvin Theological Seminary, Grand Rapids, MI, USA, 2000.

Lange, J. P., & Schaff, P. *A Commentary on the Holy Scriptures: Matthew*. Bellingham, WA: Logos Bible.

Larkin, William J. *Cornerstone Biblical Commentary: The Gospel of Luke and Acts*. Carol Stream, ILL: Tyndale Publishers, 2006.

Lateran Council IV: DS 800. *Catechism of the Catholic Church*. Collegeville, Minnesota: The Liturgical Press, 1992.

Lawson, Todd. *The Crucifixion and the Qur'an: A Study in the History of Muslim Thought*, 1st Asian edition. NY, NY: One World, Oxford, 2011.

Lenski, R. C. Injeel. *The Interpretation of St. Luke's Gospel*. Minneapolis, MN: Augsburg Publishing House, 1961.

Lewis, C. S. http://Injeel.biblia.work/sermons/christperson-of/. *Mere Christianity*. London, C. S. Lewis Pte. Ltd, 1952.

Licona, Michael R. *The Resurrection of Jesus: A New Historiographical Approach*. Downers Grove, ILL: IVP Academic, 2010.

Mangalwadi, Vishal. *Truth and Transformation: A Manifesto for Ailing Nations*. Seattle, WA, YWAM Publishing, 2009.

Martin, Ralph P., (ed) *Interpretation: A Bible Commentary for Teaching and Preaching. Ephesians, Colossians, and Philemon*. Atlanta, GA: John Knox Press, 1991.

McCumber, William E. *Beacon Bible Expositions*, Vol 1: *Matthew*. Kansas City, MO: Beacon Hill Press, 1975.

McFarland, Alex. *Ten Answers to Skeptics*. Minneapolis, MINN: Bethany House, 2011

McRay, John. *Archaeology and the New Testament*. Grand Rapids, MI.: Baker Books, 1991.

The Meaning of Life. "The History of the Gospel of Barnabas." http://Injeel.mlife. org/bible_kjv/historyofbarnabas.html

Miley, John. *Systematic Theology*, Vol. 1. NY, NY: Hunt & Eaton, 1892.

Millard, Alan. *Treasures from Bible Times*. Belleville, MI, 1985.

Miller, Stephen M. *The Complete Guide to the Bible*. Phoenix, AZ: Stephen M. Miller, 2007.

Milton, John P. *Our Hebrew-Christian Heritage*. Madison, WIS, Straus Printing Co., 1973. *God's Covenant of Blessing* (Madison, WIS, Straus Printing Co., 1965.

Morethandreams.org.

Motyer, J. Alec. *The Prophecy of Isaiah*. Downers Grove, ILL: InterVarsity Press, 1993.

Murray, Abdu. Grand Central Question: *Answering the Critical Concerns of the Major Worldviews*. Downers Grove, ILL: InterVarsity Press, 2014.

Njozi, Hamza Mustafa. *The Sources of the Qur'an: A Critical Review of Authorship Theories*. Riyadh, Saudi Arabia: International Islamic Pub House, 2005.

Orthodoxy. https://oca.org/orthodoxy/the-orthodox-faith/doctrine-scripture/the-symbol-of-faith/nicene-creed.

Packer, J. I. and Oden, Thomas C. (eds.). *One Faith*. Downers Grove, ILL: InterVarsity Press, 2004.

Parsons, Martin. *Unveiling God*. Pasadena, CA: William Carey Library, 2005.

Peebles, Bernard M. (ed.), Chase, Frederic Injeel. Jr. (tr.), *The Fathers of the Church*, Vol 37: *Saint John of Damascus: Writings*. Washington, D.C.: The Catholic University of America Press, 1958.

Peter the Venerable, Irvin M. Resnik (tr.), *The Fathers of the Church*, Vol. 16. Washington D.C.: The Catholic University of America Press, 2016.

Phillips, Abu Ameenah Bilal. *The Fundamentals of Taweed*. Riyadh, Saudi Arabia: International Islamic Publishing House, 2005.

Ragg, Longsdale and Laura (tr.). *The Gospel of Barnabas*, Critical Ed. Oxford: Clarendon Press, 1907. Reprinted with notes and commentary by Yusseff, M. A Darya Ganj, New Delhi: Islamic Book Service, 2001.

Rahner, Karl. *The Trinity*. New York: Seabury Press, 1974.

Ramsay, William. *St. Paul the Traveler and the Roman Citizen*. Grand Rapids: Baker Books, 1982.

Roberts, Alexander (ed.). *Ante-Nicene Fathers,* Vol. 1. Irenaeus: *Against Heresies,* The Gnostic Society Library, http://gnosis.org/library/advh1.htm.

Rogers, Cleon L Jr. and Rogers, Cleon L. III. *The New Linguistic and Exegetical Key to the Greek New Testament*. Grand Rapids, MI: Zondervan, 1998.

Scott, Eugene. *A Philosopher Looks at Christ*. Westcott Publishing.

Seamands, John T. *Tell it Well*. Kansas City, MO: Beacon Hill Press, 1981.

Simmons, William A. *Peoples of the New Testament World*. Peabody, MASS, 2008.

Slomp, J. "The Gospel in Dispute," in *Islamochristiana*, Vol 4. Rome: *Pontificio Instituto di Studi Arabi*, 1978. Software, 2008.

St. Clair-Tisdall, Injeel. *The Original Sources of the Qur'an*. London, England, Society for Promoting Christian Knowledge, 1905. May be accessed electronically at: http://Injeel.muhammadanism.org/Tisdall/sources_quran/sources_quran.pdf

Stern, David Injeel (tr.). *Complete Jewish Bible*. Clarksville, MD: Jewish New Testament Publications, 1998.

Stott, John R. Injeel. *The Bible Speaks Today: The Message of Acts*. Downers Grove, IL: InterVarsity Press, 1990.

Strobel, Lee. *The Case for Christ*. Grand Rapids, MI: Zondervan, 1998.

Sweet, Leonard and Viola, Frank. *Jesus: A Theography*. Nashville, Thomas Nelson, 2012.

Targum of Esther, Isidore Singes, Cyrus Adler (Eds.), The Jewish Encyclopedia, Vol. 11. Funk & Wagnall Co, 1907.

Tennent, Timothy C. *Christianity at the Religious Roundtable*. Grand Rapids, MI: Baker Book House, 2002.

Thallus, Felix Jacoby. *Die Fragmente der Griechischen Historiker*. Vol 8, Fragment 1. Also Julius Africanus online translation: http://Injeel.newadvent.org/fathers/0614.htm.

The Protocols of the Elders of Zion review. https://InjeelInjeel.ushmm.org/wlc/en/article.php?ModuleId=10007244.

Thielicke, Helmut. *I Believe: The Christian's Creed*. Carlisle, Cumbria: CA, 1968.

The Qur'an Dilemma. USA: TheQuran.com, 2011.

Toby Jepson, Injeel.debate.org.uk/topics/history/qur_hist.htm

Tozer, *The Pursuit of God*. http://Injeel.ntslibrary.com/PDF%20Books/ Tozer_Pursuit_of_God.pdf, 1948.

The Knowledge of the Holy, http://Injeel.heavendwellers.com.

Vincent, M. R. *Word Studies in the New Testament,* Vol. 1. New York: Charles Scribner's Sons, 1887.

Westcott, B. F. *The Gospel According to St. John.* Grand Rapids, MI: Eerdmans, 1881, 1973.

White, James R. *What Every Christian Needs to Know about the Qur'an.* Minneapolis, MINN: Bethany House, 2013.

Wilson, Marvin R. *Our Father Abraham: Jewish Roots of the Christian Faith.* Grand Rapids, MI: Grand Rapids, MI: Eerdmans, 1989.

Wordpress, https://biblethingsinbibleways.wordpress.com/2013/12/29/was-god-known-as-father-in-the-old-testament/.

Wright, N.T. *What Saint Paul Really Said: Was Paul of Tarsus the Real Founder of Christianity?* Grand Rapids, MI: Eerdmans, 1997.

Wycliffe Translation, https://InjeelInjeel.wycliffe.org/about/whInjeel. United Bible Societies, 1996, electronic ed.

Wynkoop, Mildred Bangs. *A Theology of Love,* Second Ed. Kansas City, MO: Beacon Hill Press, 1972, 2015.

MAPS

"Early Civilizations of the Middle East." Washington D.C.: National Geographic Society, 1978.

"Lands of the Bible Today," produced by William T. Peele, Chief Cartographer of the Cartographic Division, National Geographic Society, 1976.

STUDY BIBLES

Archaeological Study Bible. Grand Rapids, MI: Zondervan, 2005.

Faithlife Study Bible, (Dt 6:4). Bellingham, WA: Logos Bible Software.

McGrath, Alister. (ed.). *The NIV Thematic Reference Bible.* Grand Rapids, MI: Zondervan, 1996.

NIV Cultural Backgrounds Study Bible. Grand Rapids, MI: Zondervan, 2016.

Smith, F. LaGard. *The Daily Bible in Chronological Order, NIV.* Eugene, OR: Harvest House, 1984.

Cabal, Ted (Ed.). *The Apologetics Study Bible.* Nashville, TENN: Holman Bible Publishers, 2007.

The New Open Bible, New American Standard Bible Study Edition. Nashville: Thomas Nelson, 1990.

ENGLISH QUR'ANS

Ali, Abdallah Yousuf (tr.). *The Glorious Kur'an: Translation and Commentary* (1938, 1934).

Arberry, A. J. (tr.). *The Koran Interpreted.* NY, NY: Touchstone, 1955.

Haleem, M.A.S. Abdel (tr.). *The Qur'an.* NY, NY: Oxford University Press, 2010.

Khan, Muhammad Muhsin (tr). *The Noble Qur'an.* Riyadh, Saudi Arabia, 1996.

Nasr, Seyyed Hassein (ed.). *The Study Qur'an.* NY, NY: Harper One, 2015.

Palmer, E. Injeel. (tr.). *The Koran*, Kessinger Publishing. Undated.

The Arabic-English Reference Qur'an: The First Translation of the Qur'an from the Original Arabic into Modern English with References to the *Tawrah*, Zabur, and *Injil*. Version 3.0. The Reference Qur'an Council, 2015.

DICTIONARIES AND ENCYCLOPEDIAS

Allen, Injeel. Injeel. *The Dictionary of Islam*, First Edition. London, England, 1885 on Global Mapping International CD Rom, 2006.

Beitzel, B. J. and Elwell, Injeel. A. *Baker Encyclopedia of the Bible*, Vol. 2. Grand Rapids, MI: Baker Book House, 1988.

Cross, F. L., & Livingstone, E. A. (Eds.). *The Oxford Dictionary of the Christian Church* (3rd ed). New York: Oxford University Press, 2005.

Fenlason, A. C. "Prophets." Mangum, D. and Brown, D. R. and Klippenstein, R and Hurst, R. (Eds.). *Lexham Theological Wordbook*. Bellingham, WA: Lexham Press, electronic edition, 2014.

Geisler, Norman. *Baker Encyclopedia of Apologetics*. Grand Rapids, MI: Baker, 1999.

Hoad, J. Injeel. L in Wood, D. R. Injeel., Marshall, I. Injeel., Millard, A. R., Packer, J. I. & Wiseman, D. J. (Eds.), *New Bible Dictionary*, 3rd ed., "Promise." Leicester, England; Downers Grove, IL: InterVarsity Press, 1996.

Jackson, Samuel M. (ed.), *The New Schaff-Herzog Encyclopedia of Religious Knowledge,* Vol. II. Grand Rapids, MI: Baker Book House, 1952.

Kittel, G., Bromiley, G. Injeel., & Friedrich, G. (Eds.), *Theological Dictionary of the New Testament*, Vol. 2. Grand Rapids, MI: Eerdmans, 1964, electronic ed.

Louw, J. P., & Nida, E. A. *Greek-English Lexicon of the New Testament*, Vol 1. 2nd ed. New York: Barry, J. D., Heiser, M. S., Custis, M., Mangum, D., & Whitehead, M. M. (2012).

Myers, A. C. *The Eerdmans Bible Dictionary*. Grand Rapids, MI: Eerdmans, 1987.

Omar, Abdul Mannan (tr.), Musnad Imam Ahmad Bin Muhammad bin Hanbal (subject codifier and Ed., *Encyclopedia of Islam), Dictionary of the Holy Qur'an: Arabic Words-English Meanings with Notes*. Hockessin, DE: NOOR Foundation, 2010.

Wolf, Injeel., R. L. Harris, G. L. Archer Jr., & B. K. Waltke (Eds.). *Theological Wordbook of the Old Testament* (electronic ed.). Chicago: Moody Press, 1999

ENDNOTES

1
Thanks to Fouad Masri for this wonderful Bedouin saying.

2 Many excellent printed Bible translations are available through bookstore chains such as Barnes and Nobles. A popular English version is the *New International Version (NIV)*. BibleGateway.com has over 200 online Bibles in 72 languages. For Arabic, *The Sharif Bible: The Holy Bible in Modern Arabic* is recommended.

CHAPTER 1: Monotheism

1 A. Injeel. Tozer, *The Knowledge of the Holy*, accessed online at http://Injeel. heavendwellers.com.

2 Literally, "united one" or absolute unity.

3 R. E. Clements cited in Brian Edgar, *The Message of the Trinity* (Downers Grove, IL: InterVarsity Press, 2004), 71.

4 Brian Edgar, *The Message of the Trinity* (Downers Grove, IL: InterVarsity Press, 2004), 72-76.

5 Victor P. Hamilton, *Handbook on the Pentateuch* (Grand Rapids, MI: Baker Book House, date unspecified), 201.

6 Edgar, *Trinity*, 71.

7 Edgar, *Trinity*, 71.

8 God's omnipresence had also been David's source of personal comfort: "Where can I go from your Spirit? Where can I flee from your presence? If I go up to the heavens, you are there; if I make my bed in the depths, you are there. If I rise on

the wings of the dawn, if I settle on the far side of the sea, even there your hand will guide me, your right hand will hold me fast." (David, Psalm 139:7-10)

[9] Bernard M. Peebles (ed.), Frederic Injeel. Chase, Jr. (tr.), *The Fathers of the Church, Vol 37: Saint John of Damascus: Writings* (Washington, D.C.: The Catholic University of America Press, 1958), 173.

[10] For the role of the scribes in ancient society, see William A. Simmons, *Peoples of the New Testament World* (Peabody, MASS, 2008), 76-88.

[11] I am indebted to my friend, Steve Barber, for this insight.

[12] Kent Dobson, *Teachings of the Torah* (Grand Rapids, MI: Zondervan, 2014), 234.

[13] Unknown source.

[14] Isaiah 13:10 declares judgment against these nature deities upon which the nations depended: "The stars of heaven and their constellations will not show their light. The rising sun will be darkened and the moon will not give its light." See comment on this verse, *NIV Cultural Background Study Bible*, 1137.

[15] Eric Lewellen, "Miracles," D. Mangum, D. R. Brown, R. Klippenstein, and R. Hurst (eds.), *Lexham Theological Workbook* (Bellingham, WA: Lexham Press, 2014, electronic ed.).

[16] "Far from being His domicile, the mountain functions only as Yahweh's temporary abode." Hamilton, *Pentateuch*, 194.

[17] Hamilton, *Pentateuch*, 196.

[18] "Making an Idol," *NIV Cultural Background Study Bible* (Grand Rapids, MI: Zondervan, 2016), 1010.

[19] "Making an Idol," *Cultural*, 1010.

[20] "Making an Idol," *Cultural*, 1010.

[21] Cecil A. Boyle's Collection, http://oaks.nvg.org/pakistan-proverbs.html.

[22] A. Elwell & B. J. Beitzel, "Witness, Altar Of," *Baker Encyclopedia of the Bible*, Vol. 2 (Grand Rapids, MI: Baker Book House, 1988), 2154–2155.

[23] Augustine cited in Hamilton, *Pentateuch*, 203.

[24] John R. Injeel. Stott, *The Bible Speaks Today: The Message of Acts* (Downers Grove, IL: InterVarsity Press, 1990), 276-79.

[25] Stott, *Acts*, 276.

[26] Isaiah 65:2-3; see Deut. 9:7, 18, 22; Psa. 106:28-29; Hosea 8:5.

[27] Stott, *Acts*, 278.

[28] James Orr, *The Problem of the Old Testament* (NY, NY: Charles Scribner's Sons, 1907), 31-32. Cited in Daniel P. Fuller, *The Unity of the Bible* (Grand Rapids, MI: Zondervan, 1992), 22.

[29] He may have quoted Al-Kafirun 109:6 as support: "To you be your Way, and to me mine" (Ali).

[30] Implicit in the NT teaching that Jesus Christ is only Savior continues the OT revelation that God alone can save. See Acts 4:12; 5:31; Eph. 5:23; Heb 7:25, etc.

[31] Beitzel and Elwell, "Promise," Baker, 1766.

[32] Validation encompasses more than prophetic fulfillment. The influence of the previous Books in the Injeel is astoundingly high. It cites 265 separate passages, some multiple times that total 365 actual citations. In addition to these must be added allusions to the previous Books. *The Greek New Testament,* 891-900, lists over a thousand such OT passages to which the Injeel alludes. Enns, *Three Views,* 178.

[33] Enns, *Three Views*, 179.

[34] Milton, *Covenant*, 19.

[35] Oliver Wendell Holmes, Sr. cited by Alex McFarland, *Ten Answers to Skeptics* (Minneapolis, MINN: Bethany House, 2011), 49.

[36] Michael L. Brown, *Answering Jewish Objections to Jesus*, Vol 2: *Theological Objections* (Grand Rapids, MI: Baker Books, 2000), 14.

CHAPTER 2: Son of God

[1] In another place, "God never had a child" (Al-Muminun 23:91) and "They say: (Allah) Most Gracious has begotten a son!" (Mariam 19:88).

[2] "The idea that Allah had sexual relations with a woman and fathered a son by her is not supported at all in any of the books." *The Reference Qur'an* (RQ), n 863, p 119.

[3] Crowds, Al-Zumar 39:3-4: "If Allah had wanted to choose a boy, he would have chosen what he will from what he created. May he be glorified! He is the one, conquering Allah. He created the heavens and the earth in truth. . ." Al-Anaam 6:100-101 RQ: "He is the creator of the heavens and the earth. How could he have a boy, since he has no girlfriend? He created everything, and knows everything. He is Allah, your Lord. He is the only god, the creator of everything. So worship him. . . . "God never had a child." Al-Muminun 23:91

[4] Abdallah Yousuf Ali (tr.), *The Glorious Kur'an: Translation and Commentary* (1938, 1934).

[5] Gerhard von Rad, *Commentary on Genesis* cited in John Milton, *Our Hebrew Christian Heritage*, 44.

[6] See Ali Yusef's comment in Part 1.

[7] J. P. Louw & E. A. Nida, *Greek-English Lexicon of the New Testament*, Vol 1 (New York: United Bible Societies, electronic ed. of the 2nd edition, 1996), 590.

[8] M. Anderson, "The Trinity: An Appreciation of the Oneness of God with Reference to the Son of God and the Holy Spirit for Christians and Muslims," 1996, http://Injeel.answering-islam.org/Mna/trinity.html#02-theExpression.

[9] Michael L. Brown, *Answering Jewish Objections to Jesus,* Vol 2: *Theological Objections* (Grand Rapids, MI: Baker Books, 2000), 38.

[10] Anderson, "Trinity."

[11] Peter refers to this event in 2 Peter 1:16-18.

[12] "This word denotes the form regarded as the distinctive nature and character of the object, and is distinguished from σχῆμα [*schema*] the changeable, outward fashion: in a man, for instance, his gestures, clothes, words, acts. The μορφή [*morphe*] partakes of the essence of a thing; the σχῆμα is an accident which may change, leaving the form unaffected." M. R. Vincent, *Word Studies in the New Testament*, Vol. 1 (New York: Charles Scribner's Sons, 1887), 99.

[13] I. D. Campbell, *Opening up Matthew* (Leominster: Day One Publications, 2008), 104-105. Also, "The light, then, it would seem, shone not upon Him from without, but out of Him from within; He was all irradiated, was in one blaze of celestial glory." R. Jamieson, A. R. Fausset & D. Brown, *Commentary Critical and Explanatory on the Whole Bible,* Vol. 2 (Oak Harbor, WA: Logos Research, 1997), 107.

[14] Lange, J. P., & Schaff, P., *A Commentary on the Holy Scriptures: Matthew* (Bellingham, WA: Logos Bible Software, 2008), 307.

[15] Martin Dugard and Bill O'Reilly, *Killing Jesus – A History* (NY, NY: Henry Holt and Co., 2013), 74-78.

[16] See https://biblethingsinbibleways.wordpress.com/2013/12/29/wasgod-known-as-father-in-the-old-testament/

[17] Thanks to John Ho for that insight.

[18] Posturing oneself as good through cunning is the weapon of evil. Jesus easily saw through Satan's guises (John 8:44; Revelation 3:9). Later calling him the "Father of lies," Jesus defined the essence of evil and its mode of operation (Tawrat, Genesis 3:4-5; Job 1:11; 2:5). Deceit is Satan's weapon of choice whether by whispered innuendos into the human soul or false prophets who bombard the airwaves with false messages (Tawrat, Deut. 13:5; Prophets, Jeremiah 23:26; 28:15; 29:21; Ezekiel 13:6-10; Injeel, 2 Peter 2:1-3, 18-19). They typically present themselves as humanity's caring allies.

[19] It is clear from Mark 1:24 that the demonic world was well-aware of Jesus' identity as Son of God. Here Satan intended either to inject doubt into Jesus' mind of that identity or to entice him in using it strictly for himself and, by so doing, divert him from his God-given mission to give his life for others.

[20] Martin Hengel, *The Son of God* (Eugene, OR: Wipf & Stock Publishers, 1976), 22.

[21] Genesis 6:2, 4; Job 1:6; 38:7; 2:1; Psalm 29:1, 89:7; Psalm 82:6; Deuteronomy 32:8ff.

[22] Hengel, *Son of God*, 22. For instance, Psalm 2:7 reads "He (Yahweh) said to me, 'You are my son, today I have begotten you.'" Scholars have rightly stressed that the "today" excludes all physical concepts of begetting.

23 David's successor was also enthroned by divine choice: "Of all my sons—and the LORD has given me many—he has chosen my son Solomon to sit on the throne of the kingdom of the LORD over Israel." (1 Chronicles 28:5)

24 Saul's actions exposed his excessive concern for human approval, his disregard of the holy (2 Samuel 6:1-5) and substituted obedience to God's way with that of his own (1 Samuel 13:10-13; 15:10-21, 28). His insecurity led him to treachery at a level that can only be described as cut-throat (1 Samuel 22:16-19; See Psalm 52). For these reasons, God rejected him (2 Samuel 7:16-17).

25 Smith, F. LaGard, *The Daily Bible in Chronological Order*, New International Version (Eugene, OR: Harvest House, 1984), 261.

26 Anderson, "Trinity."

27 Michael Brown writes, "The verses preceding this glorious prophecy refer to the fall of Assyria, the great enemy of the Jewish people seven hundred years before Jesus. So the birth announcement could refer to a Davidic king born in that general time frame. But no king born at that time fulfilled what was promised. . . . Both Jews and Christians have argued that this is a Messianic prophecy, plain and simple, since the prophets always saw the Messiah coming on the immediate horizon of history. In this vein, the [Jewish] Targum explicitly calls the child born 'Messiah.' These prophetic words, spoken over a Davidic king born in Isaiah's day, were never fulfilled. They only reached their goal when the Messiah came into the world. . . . These verses had their immediate, incomplete application in the days when they were spoken, and they have their final, complete application in the Messianic era, an era that began when Jesus came into the world." Brown, *Answering Objections*, 47.

28 Brown, *Answering Objections*, 47.

29 The Gospel according to Mark begins with the same announcement, "The beginning of the gospel of Jesus Christ [Messiah], the Son of God" (Injeel, Mark 1:1).

30 This helpful outline is taken from: *The New Open Bible, New American Standard Bible Study Edition* (Nashville: Thomas Nelson, 1990), 1059-60.

31 "Lord and Messiah" – The Messiah's divinity had been hinted at in the OT: Isa 9:6; 40:3; Jer 23:6; Mal 3:1. Applications in the Injeel include these pairings – Ro 10:13f/J. P.l 2:32; Jn 12:40-41/Isa 6:10; Ro 9:33/Isa 8:14; Eph 4:8/Ps 68:18.

[32] Even the Jewish High Priest referred to the Messiah as "the Son of the Blessed One" (Mark 14:62) and asked Jesus point blank: "Are you the Son of God?" (Luke 22:70).

[33] David was buried in Jerusalem (I Kings 2:10).

[34] The Book of Hebrews in the Injeel also associates the Son of God with the royal title (Hebrews 1, 5:5-6).

[35] Galatians 4:4-7; Matt 12:50; John 3:16-18; 5:23-24; 6:40; 11:26-27; 14:1-2; 20:31; Romans 8:13-17; Ephesians 1:5-6

[36] Brown, *Answering Objections*, 47.

CHAPTER 3: Jesus' Two Natures

[1] Yusef Ali, *The Glorious Qur'an*.

[2] Josephus, *Against Apion* 1.12 quoted by Marvin R. Wilson, *Our Father Abraham: Jewish Roots of the Christian Faith* (Grand Rapids, MI: Eerdmans, 1989), 60.

[3] Marvin R. Wilson, *Our Father Abraham: Jewish Roots of the Christian Faith* (Grand Rapids, MI: Eerdmans, 1989), 123.

[4] Wilson, *Our Father Abraham*, 123. This reference is drawn from the Babylonian Talmud (*Sukkah* 42a).

[5] Wilson, *Our Father Abraham*, 299.

[6] Wilson, *Our Father Abraham*, 123.

[7] Wilson, *Our Father Abraham*, 299.

[8] Wilson, *Our Father Abraham*, 123.

[9] The book of Deuteronomy's broad influence is indicated by: (1) The New Testament has more quotations from Deuteronomy then from any other book of Moses. (2) Among the Dead Sea Scrolls at Quran, more separate copies of the scroll of Deuteronomy were found than of any other Mosaic writing. (3) As an adult, Jesus, at the beginning of his ministry, quotes three times from this book in mustering spiritual support in response to the three temptations of Satan (Matthew 4:1-11). Wilson, *Our Father Abraham*, 123.

[10] Josehus, *Antiquities* 19.343-344. Cited in William J. Larkin, *Cornerstone Biblical Commentary: The Gospel of Luke and Acts* (Carol Stream, ILL: Tyndale Publishers, 2006), 494.

[11] Larkin, *Luke*, 494.

[12] Dennis Kinlaw, *This Day with the Master* (Grand Rapids, MI: Francis Asbury Society, Zondervan, 2002), June 14 entry.

[13] These may be sent to myquestions@4ethne.org.

[14] A. C. Myers, *The Eerdmans Bible Dictionary* (Grand Rapids, MI: Eerdmans,1987), 386.

[15] J. P. Louw & E. A. Nida, *Greek-English Lexicon of the New Testament: Based on Semantic Domains*, Vol. 1 (New York: United Bible Societies, 1966, electronic edition of the 2nd edition), 584.

[16] Jesus repeatedly emphasized the impossibility for human beings to cross the boundary separating heaven and earth, for they are confined by earthly nature. Yet as the Son of Man, He contrasted his nature to men by placing himself in a different category: "No one has ever gone into heaven except the one who came from heaven—the Son of Man" (Injeel, John 3:13).

[17] Merrill C. Tenney's commentary in Frank E. Gabelein (Ed.), *The Expositor's Bible Commentary*, Vol 9: *John-Acts* (Grand Rapids, MI: Zondervan, 1981), 34.

[18] Cyril, "Second Letter to Nestorius," February 430 C.E., quoted in Henry Bettenson and Chris Maunder (eds.), *Documents of the Christian Church*, 3rd Edition (NY: Oxford University Press, 1999), 52.

[19] Gregory of Nazianzus, Bishop of Constantinople, 380 C.E., *Epistle*, quoted in Bettenson and Maunder, *Documents*, 49.

[20] Leo, Bishop of Rome, 440-461 C.E., *The Tome of Leo, Epistle xxviii (to Flavian)*, June 13, 449 C.E., quoted in Henry Bettenson and Chris Maunder (eds.), *Documents of the Christian Church*, 3rd Edition (NY: Oxford University Press, 1999), 54-56.

[21] Ronald Nash cited by James A. Parker III, "The Incarnation: Could God Become Man Without Ceasing to be God?" Ted Cabal (ed.), *Apologetics Study Bible* (ABS) (Nashville, TENN: Holman Bible Publishing, 2007), 1777.

[22] Macarius the Egyptian (301-391 A.D.), *50 Spiritual Homilies*, cited in Horatius Bonar, *Words Old and New* (Carlisle, PA: Banner of Truth Trust, 1866), 18.

[23] Cyril, "Second Letter to Nestorius," Bettenson and Maunder, *Documents*, 52.

[24] Cyril's Exposition IV from his "Second Letter to Nestorius," Bettenson and Maunder, *Documents*, 52.

[25] Injeel.Injeel.T. Gairdner, *God as Triune, Christ Incarnate, Atoner* (Calcutta, India: Christian Literature Society for India, 1916).

[26] Anderson, "Trinity."

[27] John T. Seamands, *Tell it Well* (Kansas City, MO: Beacon Hill Press, 1981), 200-214.

[28] Seamands, *Tell it Well*, 200.

[29] Anderson, "Trinity."

[30] John T. Seamands, *Tell it Well* (Kansas City, MO: Beacon Hill Press, 1981), 200-214.

[31] Mae Elise Cannon, *Just Spirituality: How Faith Practices Fuel Social Action* (Downers Grove, ILL: InterVarsity Press, 2013), 19.

[32] J. I. Packer, http://Injeel.biblia.work/sermons/christperson-of/.

[33] Leo, Bishop of Rome, 440-461 C.E., *The Tome of Leo, Epistle xxviii (to Flavian)*, June 13, 449 C.E., quoted in Henry Bettenson and Chris Maunder (eds.), *Documents of the Christian Church*, 3rd Edition (NY: Oxford University Press, 1999), 54-56.

[34] See filiations_religion_id=0&affiliations_year=2010&region_name=All%20 Countries&restrictions_year=2015.

[35] Farquhar, J. N., *The Crown of Hinduism* (New Delhi, India: Oriental Publishers, 1913), 1971.

[36] Farquhar, *Crown*, 423.

[37] Farquhar, *Crown*, 424.

[38] Harnack, *History of Dogma*, i. 75, cited in Farquhar, *Crown*, 426.

[39] Farquhar, *Crown*, 430.

[40] Farquhar, *Crown*, 431.

[41] Oswald Chambers, *Approved Unto God in The Complete Works of Oswald Chambers* (Grand Rapids, MI: Discovery House, 2000, orig published 1936), 14.

[42] Oswald Chambers, *Approved unto God*, 14.

[43] Farquhar, *Crown*, 432.

[44] John T. Seamands, *Tell it Well* (Kansas City, MO: Beacon Hill Press, 1981), 200-214.

CHAPTER 4: Jesus' Humanity

[1] Nabeel Qureshi, *Legacy Conference*, Grand Rapids, MI, 2016.

[2] S. MacLean Gilmour, *Introduction and Exegesis*, George A. Buttrick (Ed.), *The Interpreter's Bible, Vol VIII: Luke and John* (Nashville, TENN, 1952), 313.

[3] Gilmour, *Luke*, 314.

[4] William McCumber, *Beacon Bible Expositions*, Vol I: *Matthew* (Kansas City, MO: Beacon Hill, 1976), 146.

[5] A similar question was asked Prophet Muhammad (p) in *The Heights*, Al-Aaraf 7:187-188.

[6] While limits to his knowledge were temporarily placed on Jesus by virtue of his incarnate life on earth, they did not strip him of divine knowledge in carrying out that assignment. For example: "Knowing their thoughts, Jesus said, 'Why do you entertain evil thoughts in your hearts?'" (Matthew 9:4); "He knew all people. He did not need any testimony about mankind, for he knew what was in each person" (John 2:24-5); "Now we can see that you know all things" (John 16:30); "Peter was hurt because Jesus asked him the third time, "Do you love me?" He said, 'Lord, you know all things; you know that I love you'" (John 21:17); "Christ, in whom are hidden all the treasures of wisdom and knowledge" (Colossians 2:3); "Christ Jesus, who has become for us wisdom from God" (1 Corinthians 1:30).

7 Psalms 18:11; 68:4-5; 104:3; Isaiah 19:1; Ezekiel 1:4, 28; Daniel 12:7. At Jesus'
parousia (second coming) – Matt 24:30; 26:64; Mk 13:26; 14:62; Luke 12:54;
21:27; 1 Thess 4:17; Revelation 1:7; 14:14-16. .

8
Source unknown.

CHAPTER 5: Jesus' Deity

1 Abdallah Yousuf Ali, translator. *The Glorious KUR'AN. Translation and
Commentary.* (1938, 1934) Comment on Al-Maidah 5:77.

2 It would be hard to overestimate the importance of this question, even while
recognizing that New Testament preaching sets out to prove Jesus' Messiahship
more than his deity. See, for example, Acts 17:3: "He reasoned with them from
the Scriptures, explaining and proving that the Messiah had to suffer and rise
from the dead. 'This Jesus I am proclaiming to you is the Messiah...'" At the same
time, Peter's message to an audience of non-Jewish inquirers made it clear that
Jesus was more than Messiah: "... announcing the good news of peace through
Jesus Christ [Messiah], who is **Lord of all**" (Acts 10:36, emphasis mine). The
deity of Jesus initially stands in the background behind his Messianic position:

"The Bible is more focused upon proving that Jesus is the Messiah than on
proving that Jesus is God. While some NT passages clearly declare that Jesus
preexisted as deity, dozens demonstrate that Jesus of Nazareth is the long-awaited
Davidic Messiah-King of Israel. In other words, Jesus is the only one anointed
with the Holy Spirit by God the Father and thereby uniquely authorized and
empowered to bring about God's kingdom on earth. He is the Anointed One
(Hebrew = Messiah; Greek = Christ). While his messianic identity includes
His divine preexistence, this isn't the primary emphasis of the NT. That's why
all four Gospels speak of Jesus' anointing (baptism) with the Holy Spirit as
the beginning of His ministry as the Christ" (Matt 3:13-17; Mk 1:9-11; Luke
3:21-22; John 1:32-34)." Walter Russell, "What Does It Mean to Say, 'Jesus is
Messiah?'" *Apologetics Study Bible*, 1286.

3 Some things, even if true, should be left unsaid. Would a truly humble person go
around telling people "I am humble?" Boasting of one's virtues is like using a bar
of soap: the more you use it, the less you have it. Jesus wisely refrained from saying
"I am sinless!" Matthew 11:29-30 was no exception to this rule when Jesus said,
"I am gentle and humble in heart." There he was not patting himself on the back

but inviting the "weary and burdened," those feeling rejected by religious leaders, to come to him where they would "find rest for their souls."

4 D. A. Carson cited by Mark Durie, *Liberty to the Captives* (Deror Books, 2010), 81.

5 *A Critical and Exegetical Commentary on the Gospel of John* cited by Durie, *Liberty*, 81.

6 Mark Durie, *Liberty*, 81.

7 This resolve fulfills Isaiah's prophecy of the "Servant of the LORD" as one who first listened to God and then "will not falter or be discouraged" (Isaiah 42:4) and who "set my face like flint" (Isaiah 50:2) towards completing his mission. This obedience is remarkable for its sacrifice (Isaiah 50:4-6; 53:10).

8 Centuries prior to Jesus' birth, God prophesied the coming of this Servant through Isaiah in what are called Servant Songs. All four describe the life and ministry of Jesus with remarkable detail: Isaiah 42:1-4; 49:1-6; 50:4-9 and 52:13-53:12.

9 This Branch will rule over God's people in the future (Jer 23:5; 33:15-16; Isa 4:2; 11:1-5; Zech 3:8; 6:12-13).

10 The Bible is obviously silent here, but even Muhammad did not claim to be sinless (Yunus 10:3; 48:2). Islamic theology, by contrast, teaches the sinlessness of all the prophets, including Adam despite Al-Aaraf 7:23.

11 For other examples, see Matthew 9:2-8 and Luke 7:48-49.

12 Exodus 34:6-8; Psalm 51:4; 103:3; Isaiah 4:3-5, etc.

13 We should note that even when God's severe judgment becomes necessary, it is to bring about beauty and cleansing "by a spirit of judgment and by a spirit of burning" (Isaiah 4:4) so that his glory may return (Isa 4:5-6).

14 Jesus' identification of himself as the Son of Man is seen in the parallel accounts of Mark 8:27 ("Who do men say that I am?") and Matthew 16:13 ("Who do men say the Son of Man is?").

15 "Whereas Jesus accepted the title 'Messiah' when others ascribed it to Him, He persistently claimed that of 'Son of Man.'" A. Injeel. Argyle, "The Evidence for the Belief that our Lord Himself Claimed to be Divine," *The Expository Times:*

International Journal of Biblical Studies, Theology and Ministry, Vol 61:5, May 1, 1950.

[16] A third category for Daniel's Son of Man might be added, "Representative Man," one representing the collective people of God. Following the total destruction of the final pagan king, we read: "Then the sovereignty, power and greatness of all the kingdoms under heaven will be handed over to the holy people of the Most High. His kingdom will be an everlasting kingdom, and all rulers will worship and obey him" (Daniel 7:26-27). Here the people of God are mysteriously subsumed in the single Figure introduced earlier in verse 13. The Son of Man represents the people of God so that his rule becomes their rule, his victories their victories and his sufferings their sufferings. The lone Figure coming with the clouds so identifies himself with the holy people on earth that their inheritance is interchangeable. Surprisingly, when the world kingdoms are "handed over to the holy people of the Most High," we expect a plural pronoun to follow, "their kingdom will be an everlasting kingdom, and all rulers will worship and obey them (verse 27. And yet, it returns to the singular Figure introduced previously in verses 13-14.

[17] Compare the similarity with John 1:1, 14 under a different title when the eternal "Word" united with "flesh."

[18] We often hear of the Son of Man coming "on" the clouds, leading some to mistakenly view the clouds as his means of transportation or support. In reality, he will come "with" or "in" the clouds signifying a greater truth.

[19] For an excellent study, see Eugen J. Pentiuc, "The Aramaic Phrase Bar 'enos 'Son of Man' (Dan 7:13-14) Revisited" (NY, NY: Greek Orthodox Archdiocese of America, 2017).

[20] I am indebted to Pentiuc for these citations. "Aramaic Phrase Bar 'enos 'Son of Man.'

[21] "The allegories in Dan, of which this is the first, are veiled descriptions of the great successive empires of history: Neo-Babylonian, Medan, Persian, Greek (Alexander's Asiatic kingdom governed by his successors). The allegory is here borrowed from ancient speculations on the ages of the world, the symbolism being used of metals in descending scale of value. Last of all comes the messianic kingdom. The empires of earth collapse and give place to a new kingdom which, being founded by God, is everlasting: the 'kingdom' of heaven cf. Mat 4:17. Jesus

will later call himself 'Son of Man' (Dan 7:13 and Mat 8:20); he will also refer to himself (cf. Mat 21:42-44; Lk 20:17-18) as the keystone formerly rejected, (Ps 118:22), and as the foundation stone of Isa 28:16, with a clear allusion to the stone which breaks away from the mountain and crushes him on whom it falls, Dan 2:34, 44-45." Note, *The Jerusalem Bible*, 1425.

22 George Eldon Ladd, *A Theology of the New Testament* (Grand Rapids, MI: Eerdmans, 1974), 157.

23 See also Mk 12:38-40; Lk 12:1-3; Jn 3:20-21; 1 Cor 4:5, etc.

24 Toshiko Kaneda, Senior Research Associate and Carl Haub, Demographer Emeritus, https://InjeelInjeel.prb.org/howmanypeoplehaveeverlivedonearth/, accessed Sept 28, 2018.

25 "Christ died for all people but that does not automatically bring salvation. People are not saved unless they believe. His coming is both positive and negative. The person who exercises faith is not condemned and need not fear judgment. But the one who persists in unbelief is condemned already. Why so? Because he has "not believed in the name of God's one and only Son." A rejection of the God's Son is a rejection of the Father who sent him." Morris, *John*.

26 Morris, *John*.

27 F. F. Bruce (ed.), *The New International Commentary on the New Testament*, Leon Morris, *The Gospel According to John* (Grand Rapids, MI: Eerdmands, 1971), 233.

28 Holtzmann cited by Leon Morris, *John*, 232. Some people will be condemned, but that was not the purpose of his coming (Jn 3:19). See also Matt 27:42; Mk 8:35; Lk 19:10, etc.

29 See also Matt 10:32-33; Lk 12:8-9; Mark 8:38; Lk 9:26; John 9:39; 12:48.

30 *Catechism of the Catholic Church*, 177. See Matt 12:32; Jn 3:18; 12:48; 1 Cor 3:12-15; Heb 6:4-6; 10:26-31.

31 Scott, *Philosopher*.

32 All of these references, of course, point back to the time-period preceding his earthly lifespan of thirty-three years (John 8:58; Hebrews 1:12; 7:3, 24; 13:8; Psalm 102:27; Revelation 1:8; 5:13; 22:13). His eternal nature placed him before

the creation of the world (John 1:1-2; John 17:5, 24; 1 John 1:1-3; 2:13; Micah 5:2; Colossians 1:17; 2 Timothy 1:9; 1 Peter 1:20).

[33] A hadith states "that the *Haqiqatu' l-Muhammadiyah* or the *Nuri-Muhammad*, "the essence, or light of Muhammad," was created before all things which were made by God." Allen, Injeel. Injeel., *The Dictionary of Islam*, First Edition (London, England, 1885 on Global Mapping International CD Rom, 2006), 234.

[34] See Matthew 13:26, 31; John 4:24-26; 6:63; 7:15-18; 12:48-50; 13:13; 14:6.

[35] See Matt 5:21-22, 27-28; 12:41-42, 17:5; Mark 2:5, 10; 8:38; 9:7; 10:15; Luke 4:18; 9:35.

[36] "The name of Jesus represents His character. It is another way of referring to the mind and heart of Jesus. This phrase appears often in John (cf. 14:13–14, 26; 15:16; 16:23–26). The more like Christ one is, the more likely the prayers are to be answered in the affirmative. The worst thing God could do spiritually to most believers is answer their selfish, materialistic prayers.: R. J. Utley, *The Beloved Disciple's Memoirs and Letters: The Gospel of John, I, II, and III John*, Vol. 4 (Marshall, Texas: Bible Lessons International, 1999), 129.

[37] Argyle, "Evidence."

[38] C. S. Lewis, *Mere Christianity*, 1943, pdf., Scan and OCR by Copper Kettle aka T.A.G, 2003-12-21. Yekaterinburg. https://InjeelInjeel. truthaccordingtoscripture.com/ documents/apologetics/mere-christianity/ Mere-Christianity.pdf.

[39] Exodus 25:23-30; Hebrews 9:3

[40] Exodus 30:1-37; Hebrews 9:9

[41] Exodus 26:31-33; Hebrews 10:19-20

[42] Exodus 25:17-22; 26:33-34; Hebrews 9:3, 5.

[43] Hamilton, *Pentateuch*, 236.

[44] See Exodus 16:10; 34:5; 40:34-35; Isaiah 40:5, etc.

[45] Morris, *John*, 103.

[46] *NIV Cultural Background Study Bible*, 178.

[47] Mrs. Charles E. Cowman, *Streams in the Desert* (Grand Rapids, MI: Zondervan). Date and page unknown.

[48] Hamilton, *Pentateuch*, 236.

[49] Morris, *John*, 103.

[50] Augustine, *Homilies on the Gospel of John*, 114.

[51] Augustine, *Homilies on the Gospel of John*, VIII.3; XVII.16.

[52] Thanks to my good friend, Dany Gomiz, for this apt comparison.

[53] In rare instances, Jesus refused requests to reveal his divine nature through explanation or demonstration. King Herod tried his best to pry answers out of Jesus, demanding him to "reveal your glory!" Knowing that he was more interested in seeing a magic show than to worship, Jesus gave him the judgment of silence. In a tantrum, Herod sent Jesus back to Pilate for crucifixion.

[54] Not once did he claim to be the Father who sent him nor the Spirit who had not yet been given. He was one member of the Godhead, not the whole.

[55] Tenney, *John-Acts*, 66.

[56] "Jesus was the Son, not the slave of God. Yet as the perfect agent of the divine purpose and the complete revelation of the divine nature." Tenney, *John-Acts*, 64.

[57] "Equality in nature, identity of objective, and subordination of will are interrelated in Christ." Tenney, *John-Acts*, 64.

[58] *Apologetics Study Bible*, 1580.

[59] Tenney writes, "Jesus considered the 'works' he performed as one of the strongest witnesses to his claims (Jn 5:36; 14:10-11). They were not abnormal activities or special occasion miracles but were rather the usual mode of Jesus' actions when confronting a challenging situation." Tenney, *John-Acts,* 69.

[60] The Father also testified about Jesus at his baptism (Matt. 3:17; Mk 1:11; Lk 3:22) and later at the Mount of Transfiguration.

[61] Athanasius, *On the Incarnation*, 18, quoted in Colin Brown, *Miracles and the Critical Mind* (Grand Rapids: Eerdmans, 1984), 4.

[62] See Chapter 9, the table, "Sources for Jesus in the Injeel."

[63] When Jesus asked John to baptize him, he protested on the basis that he, not Jesus, who was a candidate for the baptism of repentance: "John tried to deter him, saying, 'I need to be baptized by you' (Matthew 3:13-15). Jesus insisted on it because his baptism was not for himself but his mission to redeem fallen people. Stepping into the humbling waters of baptism became his opening act in that merciful identification.

[64] This indictment, directed at religious leaders in Jerusalem who conspired against Jesus, applies universally. The Injeel does not pin the blame of Jesus' death on them, but upon the wrongs of humanity as a whole.

[65] Source unknown.

[66] Other divine attributes include claims of omnipresence (Matthew 18:20; 28:20), co-Creator and eternal (John 1:1-4), etc.

[67] For a complete list of miracles performed by Jesus, see chart in Question 9.1, "Facts about Jesus Life."

[68] A. M. Hills, reference unknown.

[69] Tenney, *John-Acts*, 69.

[70] Tenney, *John-Acts*, 69. This applies to people (Jn 3:19-21; 7:7; 8:34, 41), Satan (Jn 8:41) or God (Jn 4:34; 5:20; 6:28-29; 9:3-4; 10:37).

[71] Brown, *Miracles*, 5.

[72] Justin Martyr, *Dialogue with Trypho*, 69, quoted in Colin Brown, *Miracles*, 4.

[73] These include: *Dynamis*: "Power, Deed of Power" – Literally, the ability to perform an activity. . .Something God brings into the world to reveal his purposes and to carry them out. Miracles. (Matthew 13:54; Mark 6:14; Acts 8:13; 1 Corinthians 12:10). God's action in the Gospel: (2 Thessalonians 1:11; 2 Corinthians 13:4; Hebrews 1:3; 1 Peter 1:5; Revelation 19:1). Often linked with "authority" [*exousia*] (Luke 9:1; Revelation 12:10). *Semeion*: "Sign, Indicator, Miracle" – An event that signifies something; an object or occurrence that makes a particular insight or perception possible (Mark 13:4; John 2:6-11; Acts 6:8). *Teras*: "Potent, Omen, Wonder" – An unusual sign that foretells coming events (always paired with signs and used in the plural). (Acts 14:3) *Ergon*:

"Deed, Accomplishment, Work" – An action or activity performed by a person but includes miracles. John 10:25Eric Lewellen, "Miracles," D. Mangum, D. R. Brown, R. Klippenstein, and R. Hurst (eds.), *Lexham Theological Workbook* (Bellingham, WA: Lexham Press, 2014, electronic ed.).

[74] Tenney, *John-Acts*, 69.

[75] F. LaGard Smith, commentary in *The Daily Bible* (Eugene, ORE: Harvest House, 1984), 1397.

[76] C. S. Lewis, cited on http://Injeel.biblia.work/sermons/christperson-of/.

[77] See also Jn 1:18; Lk 24:52; Acts 10:36; 1 Tim 3:16, etc.

[78] For an excellent survey of the worship of Jesus in the Injeel, see Sam Shamoun, "The New Testament on the Worship given to Jesus – Its Significance and Implications for the Deity of Christ," http://Injeel.answering-islam.org/Shamoun/worship.htm.

[79] Jackson (ed.), *New Schaff-Herzog Encyclopedia*, 51..

[81] Samuel M. Jackson (ed.), *The New Schaff-Herzog Encyclopedia of Religious Knowledge,*, Vol. II (Grand Rapids, MI: Baker Book House, 1952), 51.

[82] Samuel M. Jackson (ed.), *The New Schaff-Herzog Encyclopedia of Religious Knowledge,*, Vol. II (Grand Rapids, MI: Baker Book House, 1952), 51.

[83] Richard P. Bailey, "Chart of Prophets in the Bible," October 2011.

[84] Many thanks to the *RQ* for their careful study (61, 116, 131, 142, 342, 574).

CHAPTER 6: Trinity

[1] "Prayer for Higher Understanding," https://prayer.knowing-jesus.com/Prayers-for-Understanding.

[2] Kinlaw, *This Day with the Master*, March 29.

[3] G. L. Borchert, *John 12-21*, Vol. 25b (Nashville, TENN: Broadman & Holman, 2002), 117-118.

[4] Cited in M. N. Anderson, *The Trinity*, electronic edition, 1996.

5 The exception to this is to begin with the ways by which God disclosed himself prior to Jesus in the Old Testament to demonstrate a pattern of consistency of God coming in a relatable form or that shows plurality in the divine Being.

6 John A. Sbuhan, *How a Sufi Found His Lord*, 4th Ed. (Lucknow, India: Lucknow Publishing House, 1952), 60.

7 Without using the actual term, the Qur'an makes three clear references to the Trinity.

8 "Nowhere in any of the books is Allah ever referred to as three." *RQ.*

9 See Injeel, Matthew 24:36, 1 Corinthians 2:11

10 Another translation reads: "When God says, 'Jesus, son of Mary, did you say to people, 'Take me and my mother as two gods alongside God''?' he will say, 'May You be exalted! I would never say what I had no right to say. . .I told them only what You commanded me to: "Worship God, my Lord and your Lord" (emphasis added). M.A.S. Abdel Haleem (tr.), *The Qur'an* (NY, NY: Oxford University Press, 2010 edition).

11 *Sahih Al-Bukhari*, Volume 6, Book 60, *Hadith 201 and 202* cited by James R. White, *What Every Christian Needs to Know about the Qur'an* (Minneapolis, MINN: Bethany House, 2013), 82.

12 White, *Qur'an.*, 84.

13 From the definition of the triune God by the National Association of Evangelicals Statement of Faith: J. I. Packer and Thomas C. Oden (eds.), *One Faith* (Downers Grove, ILL: InterVarsity Press, 2004), 58.

14 Ravi Zacharias in a recorded lecture to American university students in 2001 on the Hindu religion. Unfortunately, I no longer in possession of the source.

15 Douglas K. Blount, "The Trinity: Is It Possible That God Be Both One and Three?" *Apologetics Study Bible*, 1459.

16 Blount, "One and Three?", *ASB*, 1459.

17 Adapted from the late Nabeel Qureshi, *Legacy Conference* 2016, for whom I have great respect.

[18] Battle for the Heart video series.

[19] Solomon S. Hilscher, *The Eternal Evangel* (NY: Broadway, c. 1910), 168.

[20] Nabeel Qureshi lecture, *Legacy* 2016.

[21] "*Echad* can describe united action of many individuals in a cause (Judges 20:8; 1 Sam 11:7), speaking with one voice (Exodus 24:3)), the reunion of two nations (Ezekiel 37:17, 22) and Abraham as "the one" from whom all the people descended (Isaiah 51:2; Malachi 2:15), the one father of the nation. Prophet Zechariah uses the term for the one God ruling universally in the coming age: "The Lord will be king over all the earth; in that day the Lord will be (the only) one, and His name (the only) one" (Zechariah 14:9 NASB). Wolf, Injeel. R. L. Harris, G. L. Archer Jr., & B. K. Waltke (Eds.), *Theological Wordbook of the Old Testament* (electronic ed., p. 30; Chicago: Moody Press, 1999) 61.

[22] Tozer, *Holy*, 56.

[23] *Webster's Third New International Dictionary of the English Language Unabridged*, Vol 2.

[24] Tennent, *Roundtable*, 157.

[25] Surat 2:263, 267; 3:97; 4:131; 6:133; 10:68; 17:8; 22:64; 27:40; 29:6; 31:12, 26; 25:13; 39:7; 47:31; 57:24; 60:6; 64:6.

[26] How "that he [Allah] should have a son" (Al-Anaam 6:101) compromises divine transcendence is based on a gross misinterpretation that the Son of God was the offspring of the male God and female consort (see Al-Zumar 39:4, the so-called Satanic verses)! God forbid We previously saw that the Qur'an's rejection of the Trinity was partly based on mistaken perversions thought to be associated with Jesus' sonship and how Jesus was a prophet who Christians later deified. James R. White carries these lines of thought into later Islamic commentary (tafsir). "But the Qur'an connects its condemnation of God having a "consort" and offspring with the Christian belief that Jesus is God's Son... [There is] abundant evidence that Christians had long before professed belief that the relationship between the Father and the Son was not marked by a female deity and offspring. The Son of God, the second person of the Trinity, had eternally borne that relationship to the Father. He did not become the Son at a point in time. The Father/Son terminology refers to a relationship that has always been. There is no female deity, no multiple gods or celestial pregnancies or anything even remotely like

this. And yet, when we turn to some of the most respected and widely consulted commentaries (tafsir) of the Qur'an, we repeatedly find these misconceptions relating to the trinity tied directly to the interpretation of the text." James White, *Every Christian Needs to Know*, 84.

[27] Tozer, *Holy*, 39.

[28] In a debate, "Is God Triune or Absolutely One" at Wayne State University between Shabir Ally and the late Nabeel Qureshi (April 8, 2015), Qureshi argued in favor of the trinitarian position. I am indebted to his serious reflections on this question which I have adapted.

[29] Tozer, *Holy*, 39.

[30] L. T. Jeyachandran, "The Trinity as a Paradigm for Spiritual Transformation," chapter 11 in Ravi Zacharias (Ed.), *Beyond Opinion: Living the Faith We Defend* (Nashville, TENN,), 241.

[31] Tennent, *Roundtable*, 153.

[32] Jeyachandran in Ravi Zacharias, *Beyond Opinion*, 246.

[33] Tennent, *Roundtable*, 155.

[34] A. Injeel. Tozer, *The Pursuit of God* (Chicago: Moody Press, 2016), 13.

[35] Haleem, *The Qur'an*, 444.

[36] Brian Edgar, *The Message of the Trinity* (Downers Grove, IL: InterVarsity Press, 2004), 70.

[37] Edgar, *Trinity*, 77-78.

[38] Vanhoozer, *First Things*, 29.

[39] Ralph P. Martin, ed., *Interpretation: A Bible Commentary for Teaching and Preaching. Ephesians, Colossians, and Philemon* (Atlanta, GA: John Knox Press, 1991), 48.

[40] Translator's note: "The pagan Arabs gave part of their crops and livestock to their deities (6:136)."

[41] "Oh, the depth of the riches of the wisdom and knowledge of God! How unsearchable His judgments, and His paths beyond tracing out!" (Romans 11:33-34).

[42] "As the heavens are higher than the earth, so are *My ways higher than your ways and My thoughts than your thoughts.*" (Isaiah 55:9)

[43] Karl Barth quoted by Martin Parsons, *Unveiling God* (Pasadena, CA: William Carey Library, 2005). He adds, "By contrast, "unbounded monotheism does not draw a sharp distinction between God and all else. It is therefore possible to conceive of semi-divine beings who have various degrees of divinity." This "pantheistic" view has no place in biblical Christianity." 24.

[44] "This is what the high and exalted One says — He who lives forever, whose name is holy: I live in a high and holy place. . ." (Isaiah 57:15). "God, the blessed and only Ruler, the King of kings and Lord of lords, who alone is immortal and who lives in unapproachable light, whom no one has seen or can see. To Him be honor and might forever. Amen." (Injeel, 1 Timothy 6:15 TNIV)

[45] *The Call of the Minaret*, 3rd ed., Oxford: One World, 2000, p 288. Quoted in Martin Parsons, *Unveiling God: Contextualizing Christology for Islamic Culture* (Pasadena, CA: William Carey Library, 2005).

[46] Reza Aslan, *Zealot: The Life and Times of Jesus of Nazareth* (NY, NY: Random House, 2013), 6.

[47] Reza, *Zealot*, 6.

[48] Reza, *Zealot*, 7.

[49] Reza, *Zealot*, 7.

[50] A. M. Hills, *Fundamentals of Christian Theology* (Pasadena, CA: 1931), 234.

[51] Nabeel Qureshi, *Legacy* 2016.

[52] D. A. Carson, *The Gagging of God: Christianity Confronts Pluralism* (Grand Rapids, MI: Zondervan, 1996), 254.

[50] A. M. Hills, *Fundamentals of Christian Theology* (Pasadena, CA: 1931), 234.

[53] Benjamin Field, 39-90.

[54] Translations of Yahweh are written in all caps as LORD.

[55] The plural forms in this verse, Genesis 1:26, do not prove the Trinity but they indicate distinction within the divine Being. See also Genesis 19:24; Psa 45:7; Psalm 110:1; Hosea 1:7, etc.

[56] Benjamin Field, 39-90. Where Fields uses the term "Jehovah," I have substituted "Yahweh." These are interchangeable without altering meaning.

[57] Singular, not "names" but "in the name – the one undivided name – of the three Divine Persons." Field, *Student Handbook*, 91.

[58] Henry Gariepy, *Songs in the Night* (Grand Rapids, MI: Eerdmans, 1996), 5.

[59] "He Giveth More Grace," Annie Johnson Flint (1866-1932), copyright 1941; renewed 1969, Lillenas Publishing House, Sing to the Lord, 1993, 101. Language has been updated. Drawn from Isaiah 40:29.

[60] Tom Doyle, *Dreams and Visions* (Nashville, TENN: Thomas Nelson, 2012) xv.

[61] Morethandreams.org.

CHAPTER 7: Credibility of the Injeel

[1] The Bible contains 66 books (39 OT, 27 NT) that, for ease of use, were subdivided into chapters and verses. So, for example, Matthew 1:15 refers to Matthew (book), 1 (chapter) and 15 (verse).

[2] Gary DeLashmutt, "How is the Bible Different from Other Scriptures?" (Columbus, OH: Xenos, date unknown).

[3] Joseph P. Knight, "Hope Against Hope: Hinduism, Buddhism, Christianity & Islam." Unpublished Th.M. Thesis, Calvin Theological Seminary, Grand Rapids, MI, USA, 2000.

[4] Gordon R. Lewis, "What Does It Mean That God Inspired the Bible?" *Apologetics Study Bible*, 1812.

[5] Cleon L. Rogers Jr. and Cleon L. Rogers III, *The New Linguistic and Exegetical Key to the Greek New Testament* (Grand Rapids, MI: Zondervan, 1998), 506.

[6] Gary DeLashmutt, *Xenos Christian Fellowship*, see https://Injeel.xenos.org/teachings/.

[7] *Peter the Venerable*, Irvin M. Resnik (tr.), *The Fathers of the Church*, Vol. 16 (Washington D.C., The Catholic University of America Press, 2016), 127, 147.

[8] *Peter the Venerable*, 128.

[9] *Peter the Venerable*, 128. Prophets such as Isaiah foretold both universal events and those pertaining to certain nations: Babylonia (Isa 13:19), Moab (Isa 25:10; 15:1; 16:2-7), Damascus (Isa 17:1), Egypt (Isa 19:1-24), Edom (Isa 11:14), Arabia (Isa 21:13) and Tyre (Isa 23:13). Others in this category include Jeremiah and Daniel. 153.

[10] *Peter the Venerable*, 148,

[11] A. G. Herbert wrote, "It is common for the word 'Revelation' to be used to mean both the Divine acts and the interpretation of their meaning. But . . . it is better and clearer to keep the word revelation for the former, and Inspiration for the latter, provided it is understood that the two are inseparable." *Throne of David*, 247.

[12] Herbert, *Throne of David*, 250-251.

[13] Herbert, *Throne of David*, 248.

[14] Old Testament prophets also used the phrase "it is written" to establish their message upon God's prior revelation in the Law of Moses (Joshua 8:31; 1 Kings 2:3; 2 Chronicles 23:18; 31:3; Ezra 6:18; Nehemiah 8:15; Isaiah 65:6; Daniel 9:13).

[15] Matthew 4:4, 6, 7, 10; 21:13; 26:24, 31 (parallels in Mark and Luke); John 6:31, 45; 8:17; 12:14.

[16] Acts 1:20; 7:24; 13:33; 15:15; 23:5; Romans 1:17; 2:24; 3:4, 10; 4:17; 8:36; 9:13, 33; 10:15; 11:8, 26; 12:19; 14:11; 15:3, 9, 21; 1 cor. 1:19, 31; 2:9; 3:19; 9:9; 10:7; 14:21; 15:45; 2 Corinthians 8:15; 9:9; Galatians 3:10, 13; 4:22, 27; Hebrews 10:7; 1 Peter 1:16.

[17] Michael Licona interviewed by Caleb Lindgren, "Why Don't the Gospel Writers Tell the Same Story?", *Christianity Today*, May 2017, 45.

[18] This is discussed in response to Question 10.3.

[19] See John 1:1-4, 14. .

[20] R. K. Harrison, "Fulfillment," *Evangelical Dictionary of Biblical Theology* (Grand Rapids, MI: Baker Book House, electronic ed., 1996).

[21] J Injeel. l. Hoad, in D. R. Injeel. Wood, I. Injeel. Marshall, A. R. Millard, J. I. Packer, & D. J. Wiseman (Eds.), *New Bible Dictionary*, 3rd ed., "Promise" (Leicester, England; Downers Grove, IL: InterVarsity Press, 1996), 963.

[22] Milton, *Hebrew-Christian Heritage*, 11.

[23] The Tawrat Exodus 3:4ff, 7:1, 8:1; the Ten Commandments, Exodus 20:1ff; the sacrifice of atonement, Tawrat Leviticus 17; the Prophets Jeremiah 1:2, 4, 2:1, 7:1; Isaiah 3:16; Ezekiel 1:3; Hosea 1:1; J. P.l 1:1; Amos 1:1; Obadiah 1:1; Micah 1:1; Habakkuk 1:1; Zephaniah 1:1, etc.; David's Zabur, 2 Samuel 2:1, 7:8-17; 24:11-14; Inspired prayers and praises in Psalms 2; 3:4; 12:6-7; 105:5; 108:7; 110:1-7; 115:4-18; 117:2; 118:5-9; 21-24; 119:11, 18, 24, 27, 42-48, 71-72, 89-90, 105, 160; Proverbs 1:20-33; 8:1ff, 21-36, etc.

[24] Paul D. Feinberg, "Does the Bible Contain Errors?" *Apologetics Study Bible*, 1412.

[25] On another occasion, Faizur called this passage into question on a different basis, contending Matthew could not have been the author because in this verse he referred to himself by his name. Had it truly been Matthew writing, he would refer to himself by using personal pronouns, "I" or "me." Other conclusions may be drawn, however. Had Matthew wanted to draw attention to himself, he certainly would have injected the personal pronouns pointing to himself. The purpose of his Gospel account was to draw attention to Jesus throughout his book and whose command in 9:9, "Follow Me!" changed his life.

[26] Fethullah Gulen, *Questions and Answers about Islam*, Vol. 1., https://Injeel. scribd. com/document/30367673/M-Fethullah-Gulen-Questions-and-Answers-AboutIslam-Vol-1.

[27] Abdullah Yusuf Ali, *The Holy Qur'an* (Madinah: King Fahd Complex for the Printing of the Holy Qur'an, 1413 AH), v.

[28] Alhaj A. D. Ajijola, *The Essence of Faith in Islam* (Lahore: Islamic Publications, 1978), 79.

[29] Darrell L. Bock, "Is the New Testament Trustworthy?" *Apologetics Study Bible*, 1452.

[30] F.F. Bruce, *The New Testament Documents: Are They Reliable?*, 5th Edition (Leicester, England: Inter-Varsity Press, 1988, 1943), 7-8.

[31] Bruce, *New Testament Documents,* 7-8.

[32] See James A Beverly and Craig A. Evans, *Getting Jesus Right* (Lagoon City, Brechin, ON, CAN, 2015), 16f.

[33] Samuel Byrskog, Story as History – History as Story, 64, in Richard Bauckham, *Jesus and the Eyewitnesses: The Gospels as Eyewitness Testimony* (Grand Rapids: Eerdmans, 2006), 8-9.

[34] Bauckham, *Eyewitnesses,* 9.

[35] Bruce, *New Testament Documents*, 90. His chapter on "The Writings of Luke" substantiates his assessment of Luke.

[36] Luke 1:1-4 underscores the author's credible sources (already discussed).

[37] Sir William Ramsay, *St. Paul the Traveler and the Roman Citizen* (Grand Rapids: Baker Books, 1982), 8.

[38] Ramsay, *Traveler*, 8.

[39] Comparisons between the martyrdom of Imam Ali (p) whose brave army fought at his side and Jesus' solitary death at the abandonment of his apostles appear on the surface to indict the apostles. But that would fail to account for these contrasting factors. **(1) Earlier prophecy in Zechariah 13:7 had predicted their abandonment.** Well-aware of this, Jesus told them in advance that they would all forsake him (Injeel, Matthew 26:31; Mark 14:27). Upon hearing it, they were the ones to protest, not Jesus. He gave them this heads up as a matter of fact – not to invite their sympathy for his fate nor to lay on them a guilt trip. **(2) It was Jesus who protected the apostles and not the other way around.** We see this in his prayer for them immediately preceding his arrest: "While I was with them, I protected them and kept them safe by that name you gave me. None has been lost except the one doomed to destruction..." (John 17:12 NIV). Then at his arrest, Jesus surprised his captors by his willing personal compliance while requesting the apostles' release. "I told you that I am he. If you are looking for me, then let these men go." This happened so that the words he had spoken would be fulfilled: "I have not lost one of those you gave me" (John 18:8-9). **(3) Most importantly, had they succeeded in shielding Jesus from his enemies,**

he would have failed his mission. He entered this battle to give his life, not save it. Their "help" would have been a nuisance. His saving mission was not a team effort. They were beneficiaries, not his accomplices. So, while both Imam Ali (p) and Jesus sacrificed themselves for others, the comparison between them and those defending them is false. Ali and his army died fighting as martyrs, Jesus alone gave his life as Savior.

[40] Between Day 1 and Day 50, Peter's multiple encounters with Jesus contributed to his change. Day 3, Sunday at the empty tomb — That afternoon, Peter entered Jesus' tomb along with John and found it empty. However, Jesus' grave clothes were still lying on the stone burial slab undisturbed, just missing the body. That evening, Peter was present when Jesus appeared to the apostles. Jesus continued to appear to them, teaching and eating with them over several weeks. In one of the intervening days, Jesus confronts Peter for his denials and restores his shepherding role. He also predicts Peter's faithfulness to the end, even to a martyr's death (John 21:15- 23). Day 40 outside Jerusalem – Peter, along with the others, watched Jesus physically return into heaven. Before leaving, Jesus commissions them as witnesses.

[41] Feinberg, "Errors?", *ASB*, 1412.

[42] Jean-Pierre Isbouts, *Atlas of the Bible* (Washington D.C.: National Geographic Partners, 2018), 5.

[43] "Early Civilizations of the Middle East," *National Geographic* (Washington D.C.: National Geographic Society, 1978. "Lands of the Bible Today," produced by William T. Peele, Chief Cartographer of the Cartographic Division of the National Geographic Society), 1976.

[44] Co-sponsored by the Jerusalem Institute for Holy Land Studies and the Biblical Archaeology Society, 1981.

[45] "Tells" are mounds that had formed where ancient cities once thrived and were later abandoned, usually due to war.

[46] Another term for Jerusalem of ancient times. It was first a Jebusite city (Prophets, Judges 19:10-20) until conquered by David in the 10th century BCE (Prophets, 2 Samuel 5:7-9). Its borders were enlarged in the 8th century BC during the reign of King Hezekiah of Judah. During the 8th and 7th centuries BCE it enjoyed a period of prosperity as attested by the prominent structures. Then in 586 BC,

it was totally destroyed by the Babylonians until reoccupied seventy years later under the decree of Persian emperor Cyrus.

[47] Destroyed in AD 70 by the Romans

[48] Alexander B. Bruce, *The Training of the Twelve* (Edinburgh, England: T & T Clark, 1871), 515.

[49] Walter C. Kaiser, Jr., *Apologetics Study Bible*, 1148.

[50] The following are taken from multiple sources: Stephen M. Miller, *The Complete Guide to the Bible;* Walter Kaiser, (ed), *Hard Sayings of the Bible; Biblical Archaeological Review*, 25th Anniversary publication, 1996; Toby Jepson, Injeel. debate.org.uk/topics/ history/qur_hist.htm; *Xulos Christian Fellowship.*

[51] Code of Hammurabi – The world's oldest surviving set of laws, 283 to be exact, can be seen at the Louvre Museum in Paris. They are chiseled onto a stone pillar and date several hundred years before Moses. Some of these laws are similar to the laws that Moses gave to the Israelites (Miller, 56). Those similarities, we should note, apply only to civil law ("If you do this, you will suffer that") and not with the Ten Commandments that were given directly to Prophet Moses by God. Those are without precedent in the ancient world.

[52] The existence of two Jerichos goes back to the time when Joshua and his army destroyed the ancient city. He placed a curse on anyone who would rebuild it (Prophets, Joshua 6:26). So the old city was left in rubble and a new Jericho was built adjacently.

[53] Basilides (AD 125-150), cited in Toby Jepson, http://Injeel.debate.org.uk/topics/ apolog/crucifix.htm and Alexander Roberts (ed.), *Ante-Nicene Fathers,* Vol. 1. *Irenaeus: Against Heresies,* The Gnostic Society Library, http://gnosis.org/library/ advh1.htm. See "Sources for Jesus in the Qur'an," Question 9.1. For a newer solid translation see Alexander Roberts & James Donaldson (eds.), *Irenaeus of Lions, Against Heresies* (Ex Fontibus, 2015), 103-105.

[54] Tacitus, *Annales*, xv. 44, cited in Bettenson and Maunder, *Documents*, 2.

[55] The Delphi Inscription also "fixes the date of Gallio's proconsulship at AD 51-52, providing a way of dating Acts18:12-17, and as a result, much of the rest of Paul's ministry." *Apologetics Study Bible,* "Selected Important New Testament Archaeological Finds."

[56] John McRay, *Archaeology and the New Testament* (Grand Rapids, MI.: Baker Books, 1991), 227.

[57] An "aedile" is an official in ancient Rome put in charge of public works and games, police, and the grain supply (*Merriam Webster Dictionary*).

[58] Norman Geisler, *Baker Encyclopedia of Apologetics* (Grand Rapids, MI: Baker, 1999), 47.

[59] F.F. Bruce, *The New Testament Documents: Are They Reliable?*, 5th Edition (Leicester, England: Inter-Varsity Press, 1988, 1943),17.

[60] F. G. Kenyon, *Our Bible and the Ancient Manuscripts* (Eyre & Spottiswoode, 1958) cited in F. F. Bruce, New Testament Documents, 20.

[61] Bruce, *New Testament Documents*, 16-17.

[62] Kurt and Barbara Aland, *The Text of the New Testament* (Grand Rapids, MI Eerdmans, 1995), 291-292. Cited in fn. by White, 277. Cited in Strobel, *Case for Christ*, 277.

[63] Lee Strobel, *The Case for Christ* (Grand Rapids, MI: Zondervan, 1998), 71. Cited by White, 277.

[64] Nasr explains, "Although *Book* is used in the singular here, it refers to all previous revealed books, that is, to "scripture" used as a collective noun. After the positive command, a warning is issued against disbelieving in five specific things: *God, His angels, His Books* (all revealed scriptures, including the Quran)k, *His messengers* (all prophets, minor and major), and the *Last Day* (the Resurrection and Final Judgment)." Seyyed Hossein Nasr, *The Study Quran*, 254.

[65] Kevin Greeson, *The Camel* (Arkadelphia, AR: WIGTake Resources, 2007), 140.

[66] Yasin T. Al-Jibouri (ed.) with commentary by Martyr Ayatollah Murtada Mutahhari, Imam Ali ibn Abu Talib, Najhul-Balagha, *Peak of Eloquence* (Elmhurst, NY: Tahrike Tarsile Qur'an, Inc., undated), 157.

[67] This is for argument's sake. Evidence for such corruption is nonexistent to my knowledge.

[68] Accessed September 1, 2015 at https://InjeelInjeel.wycliffe.org/about/whInjeel

[69] Kwame Bediako, *Christianity in Africa: The Renewal of a Non-Western Religion* (Maryknoll, NY: Orbis Books, 1995), 62.

[70] Accessed September 1, 2015 at http://Injeel.biblica.com/en-us/bible/ bible-faqs/ why-are-there-so-many-versions-of-the-bible-in-english/

CHAPTER 8: Consistent Message within the Injeel

[1] C. E. Hill, *Who Chose the Gospels?* (NY, NY: Oxford University Press, 2012), 211.

[2] Quoted in F. F. Bruce, *The New Testament Documents: Are They Reliable?* (Grand Rapids, MI: Eerdmans, 1954), 28.

[3] *NIV Cultural Background Study Bible*, 1484.

[4] Oscar Cullmann, cited in Jan Slomp, "The Gospel of Barnabas in Recent Research," Christlich-Islamische Gesellschaft e.V., Injeel.chrislages.de.

[5] Bob Giovanneti, *The Birth of Jesus* (NY, NY: Centennial Media, 2017), 8.

[6] Baukman, *Eyewitnesses*, 475

[7] Baukham, *Eyewitnesses*, 411.

[8] C. S. Lewis, *Mere Christianity* (London, C. S. Lewis Pte. Ltd, 1952).

[9] Darrell L. Bock, "Is the New Testament Trustworthy?" *Apologetics Study Bible*, 1452.

[10] This is difficult, for we find groups of prophets, false prophets and some who are called prophets by others who may not be true prophets.

[11] A. C. Fenlason, "Prophets." D. Mangum, D. R. Brown, R. Klippenstein, & R. Hurst (Eds.), *Lexham Theological Wordbook* (Bellingham, WA: Lexham Press, electronic edition, 2014).

[12] A. C. Myers, *The Eerdmans Bible Dictionary* (Grand Rapids, MI: Eerdmans, electronic edition, 1987), 851–852.

[13] Reza Aslan, *Zealot: The Life and Times of Jesus of Nazareth* (NY, NY: Random House, 2013).

[14] Wissam Youssif, *Islam in Christ's Eyes: A Scriptural Study on the Origins of Islam and the Christian Response* (Lubbock, TX: Sunset Studies, 2017), 49ff.

[15] "Thought to myself" – Paul was convinced his hostility against Christians was God's will.

[16] *Dabiq*, once the flagship journal of ISIS, attempted to discredit this vision as an apparition of demonic origin on the basis that Jesus in Matthew 24:5 warned that "many will come in my name, saying, 'I am the Christ,' and they will lead many astray." *Dabiq*, "Break the Cross," Issue 15, 1437 Shawwal. In that passage, however, Jesus was explicitly referring to his Second Coming, his glorious return to earth at the end of time to establish his kingdom. Such a time, he warned, would be preceded with the appearance of imposter messiahs. While we should ignore them, this has no relevance to Saul's personal conversion and commissioning.

[17] As seen elsewhere, Christianity's core teachings that are often attributed to Paul actually find their source in the Tawrat, Prophet and Psalms.

[18] The Injeel chides immature Christians for pitting Christian leaders against each other. "For I have been informed . . . that there are quarrels among you. . . .Each one of you is saying, 'I am of Paul,' and 'I of Apollos,' and 'I of Cephas,' and 'I of Christ.' Has Christ been divided?" (1 Corinthians 1:11-13). This practice must stop: "Now I exhort you, brethren, by the name of our Lord Jesus Christ, that you all agree and that there be no divisions among you" (verse 10).

[19] Youssef, *Gospel of Barnabas*, 1.

[20] Editor's citation, M. A. Yusseff, *Gospel of Barnabas*, 255.

[21] Aslan, *Zealot*, 188.

[22] Aslan, *Zealot*. For a well-reasoned and informed critique of this work, see James A. Beverly and Craig A. Evans, *Getting Jesus Right* (Lagoon City, Brechin, Ontario: Castle Quay Books, 2015).

[23] See N.T. Wright, *What Saint Paul Really Said: Was Paul of Tarsus the Real Founder of Christianity?* (Grand Rapids, MI: Eerdmans, 1997).

[24] According to Aslan, "Paul holds particular contempt for the Jerusalem-based triumvirate of James, Peter, and John, whom he derides as the 'so-called pillars of the church' (Galatians 2:9)." Aslan, *Zealot*, 185.

[25] William Barclay cited in Everett F. Harrison, *A Short Life of Christ* (Grand Rapids, MI: Eerdmans, 1996, 136).

[26] Everett F. Harrison, *A Short Life of Christ* (Grand Rapids, MI: Eerdmans, 1968), 136.

CHAPTER 9: Competing Histories of Jesus

[1] Longsdale and Laura Ragg (tr), *The Gospel of Barnabas, Critical Edition [GB]* (Oxford: Clarendon Press, 1907). Reprinted with notes and commentary by M. A. Yusseff (Darya Ganj, New Delhi: Islamic Book Service, 2001).

[2] *GB*, 1.

[3] Commentary by M. A. Yuseff, GB, 204.

[4] *GB*.

[5] *GB*, xv.

[6] Acts is the fifth of the twenty-seven books of the New Testament. It records Jesus' ascension into heaven, the sending of the promised Holy Spirit and the expansion of the Church from the city of Jerusalem all the way to Rome.

[7] *GB*, xv-xvi.

[8] Muslim readers, you can go straight to the Injeel, Acts 15, to get the real story that GB discombobulates.

[9] The GB introduced the idea that three Books descended in succession upon Moses, David and Jesus.

[10] So convincing was this illusion, even the apostles were under its spell. The GB blames God, perhaps inadvertently, for their subsequent preaching of the cross. GB, 225.

[11] Matthew 4:6-7; Luke 4:10-11.

[12] 1 Timothy 2:5-6; 1 John 2:22-23; Acts 8:1, 4-5. The unanimous message of Christians is "Jesus has risen."

[13] "Whoever wrote this book did not know the Greek meaning of the word 'Christ' is 'Messiah.' Barnabas was a Hebrew who lived on the island of Cyprus, a Greekspeaking island, and travelled around the 1st century Greek-speaking world! He was Hebrew and knew Greek and could not have made this mistake with such a famous word." Samuel Green, "The Gospel of Barnabas," 2004.

[14] Samuel Green, "The Gospel of Barnabas," 4. Green cites J. E. Flectchure, "The Spanish Gospel of Barnabas", *Novum Testamentum*, vol. XVIII, 1976, 314-320. Also, Iskandar Jadeed, *The Gospel of Barnabas – A False Testimony*, Switzerland: *The Good Way*, 6, undated.

[15] Barnabas fails the apostolic test of accompanying Jesus from his baptism up until the time of his ascension. So, we might ask, could he possibly be an eyewitness?

[16] *GB*, 89.

[17] Samuel Green, "The Gospel of Barnabas," 2004.

[18] For this specific dependence of the GB on Dante, see: Injeel.jesus-islam.org/Pages/WhyhaveChristianshiddenthegospelofBarnabas.aspx.

[19] Ragg, *GB*, xlviii.

[20] Ragg, *GB*, 54.

[21] Ellis R. Brotzman, *Old Testament Textual Criticism* (Grand Rapids, MI: Baker Book House, 1994), 90. "The paleographic study of the manuscripts, the dating of the pottery and the coins discovered . . . in the caves, and carbon-14 analysis of samples of the linen coverings of the manuscripts all coincide in establishing a general date of the last two centuries B.C. and the first century A.D. for the scrolls and their placement in the caves. . ."

[22] Brotzman, *Textual Criticism*, 95.

[23] Alan Millard, *Treasures from Bible Times* (Belleville, MI: Lion Publishing, 1985), 162.

[24] Millar Burrows, *Burrows on the Dead Sea Scrolls* (304) cited by Bortzman, *Textual Criticism*, 95.

²⁵ Samuel Green substantially counters each of these claims.

²⁶ Green writes, "In this case Rahim accurately represents the sources. Barnabas is mentioned in them, and it is recorded that there was a Gospel and an epistle (letter) in this name. However, evidence is required to establish that the *Gospel of Barnabas* mentioned in the same lists. In 1859, a 4th century A.D. copy of the *Epistle of Barnabas* was discovered [*Early Christian Writings*, ed. Betty Radice; London: Penguin Books, 1987, pp. 155-158.]. "So what does the *Epistle of Barnabas* show? If it confirms the teaching of the *Gospel of Barnabas that Muslims* promote, then this would provide good evidence that this book is indeed the same Gospel mentioned in these lists. But it doesn't. The *Epistle of Barnabas* is a thoroughly Christian document, though it is not to be regarded as scripture. It teaches Jesus' sacrificial death, resurrection and lordship. For to this end the Lord endured to deliver up His flesh to corruption, that we might be sanctified through the remission of sins, which is effected by His blood of sprinkling (*Epistle of Barnabas,* ch. 5). "Therefore, the related evidence from the *Epistle of Barnabas* suggests that the *Gospel of Barnabas* mentioned in these lists was still a Christian document which taught the death, resurrection and lordship of Jesus. It is therefore a different book to the one that Muslims are promoting."

²⁷ Only one fragment of a Greek version of the Gospel of Barnabas can be found. It is in a museum in Athens, which is all that remains of a copy which was burnt. Here is a translation of the text from the fragment. *'Barnabas the Apostle said that in evil contests the victor is more wretched because he departs with more of the sin.'*

So does this citation validate the GB? Not at all. Green explains: "The problem with this evidence is that the text on this fragment is not the text of the Gospel of Barnabas! This sentence bears no resemblance to any sentence in the Gospel of Barnabas. The fragment is from a different book altogether. Therefore, this fragment does not provide any evidence for the antiquity of the Gospel of Barnabas. Again Rahim's scholarship is found wanting."

²⁸ Green: "When this claim is investigated it is found to be false. The *Acta Sanctorum* (*Acts of the Saints*) is available in major libraries and the internet [Joannes Bollandus, et al, *Acta Sanctorum*. Reprint. Originally published: *Antuerpiae: Apud Ioannem Meursium*, 1643-. *The Acta Sanctorum* online]. . . . What it actually says is: "The relics of Barnabas the Apostle were found in Cyprus under a cherry tree, having upon his breast the Gospel of St. Matthew copied by Barnabas' own hand. [emphasis mine]" Again we see Rahim's poor scholarship.

The story of Barnabas says he was found with the Gospel of Matthew [and] not the Gospel of Barnabas."

[29] Michael Injeel. Holmes (ed.), *The Apostolic Fathers in English* (Grand Rapids, MI: Baker, 2006), 177f.

[30] Muslim scholar Cyril Glasse, cited by Fouad Masri, *Sahara Challenge*, Section 10 (Crescent Project, 2006), 86.

[31] J. Slomp, "The Gospel in Dispute," in *Islamochristiana* (Rome: Pontificio Instituto di Studi Arabi, 1978), vol. 4, 68.

[32] Longsdale and Luara Ragg, *The Gospel of Barnabas* (Oxford: Clarendon Press, 1907), xxxvii.

[33] J. Jomier, Egypte: *Reflexions sur la Recontre al-Azhar* (Vatican au Caire, avil 1978), cited by Slomp, 104.

[34] Green, "Barnabas," 11.

[35] Muhammad 'Ata'ur-Rahim and Ahmad Thomson, *Jesus, Prophet of Islam*, Revised Ed. (London, UK: Ta-Ha Publishers, 1995), ix.

[36] Yunus 10:94-95: "If you are in doubt concerning that which We reveal to you, then question those who read the Scripture before you. Verily the Truth from the Lord has come to you so be not of the waverers. Don't doubt the signs of God."

[37] The Injeel gives us two genealogies of Jesus, one of them through his legal father (Matthew) and the other through his mother (Luke). Why are these so important? "In societies organized around kinship, genealogies . . . serve as public records that document history, establish identity and/or legitimate office. The key to legitimacy and identity is a direct, irrefutable familial tie with the past . . . The registration of families . . . [was] important in ancient Israel because the right to hold important offices was hereditary privilege. For example, the priesthood was assured to the sons of Levi (Tawrat, Exodus 6:16-26), while kingship was reserved for the descendants of Judah (Genesis 49:10) and more specifically for the son of David (2 Samuel 7:1216; Psalm 89:29; Isaiah 9:7; 11:1-3)." *Archaeological Study Bible* (Grand Rapids, MI: Zondervan, 2005), 1559.

[38] Mariam 19:17 used the angel Gabriel interchangeably with the Spirit: "We sent her our Spirit [Ruh] who appeared to her as a complete man."

[39] Both accounts of Jesus' conception in the Qur'an vividly describe the supernatural means by which Jesus was conceived (Al-Anbiya 21:90-91; Al-Tahrim 66:12). Yuseff Ali translates Al-Tahrim 66:12: "And Mary the daughter of Imran, who guarded her chastity; and We breathed into (her body) of Our spirit: and she testified to the truth of the words of her Lord and of his Revelations, and was one of the devout (servants)." The Arabic term here for "body" is *fajh*, a term referring to the female generative organ (*farjaha*).

[40] "Allah is able to create anything from nothing. In the case of Isa's conception, Allah breathed of his Spirit into Mary (21:91, 66:12) and through that, Allah created a sperm or chromosomes or something from nothing." RQ, fn, 344.

[41] Matthew 1 and Luke 1. For unique details, see "Son of God." Jesus was unique and holy. "Where John the Baptist was made pure, Isa was pure from the womb" (RQ).

[42] This is the same title Muhammad assumed for himself.

[43] John Gilchrist in "Three Unique Titles Applied to Jesus in the Qur'an," writes: "This clearly implies, not that the Word was revealed to Jesus or that he was created by the Word, but rather that he himself is the Word of God. The title relates to his person and not to any feature or circumstance of his life." He cites William Goldsack: "The Arabic shows that it means 'The Word of God', not merely 'a Word of God'. (*Kalimatullaah, not kalimatimmin kalimaatullaah*). Thus we see that Jesus is the word or expression of God, so that by Him alone can we understand the mind and will of God. No other prophet has been given this title, because none other is, in this sense, the special revelation of God's mind and will. . . The fact is that this title of the Lord Jesus can only be understood by a reference to the Gospel wherein it is clearly stated that Jesus the Word of God is divine, and existed with God before His birth into the world" (Goldsack, *Christ in Islam*, p. 14-15). Gilchrist concludes: "The Word did not come to Jesus from above, rather he himself is that very Word which came from heaven to earth." John Gilchrist, "Three Unique Titles Applied to Jesus in the Qur'an," http://Injeel.answering-islam.org/Gilchrist/Vol2/5c.html.

[44] Yusuf Ali says it is "the divine spirit" and that it is "as incomprehensible as God himself." The language he uses is unambiguous the Spirit from God is clearly believed by him to be from the realm of deity and not from the created order. He

is, according to this interpretation, practically synonymous with the Holy Spirit in the Christian Bible." Cited by John Gilquist, "Titles."

[45] Goldsack wrote: "The titles given to other prophets, such as 'Friend of God', 'Chosen of God', 'Prophet of God' may be applied to frail beings like ourselves, but the name 'Spirit of God' given to Christ by Muslims clearly hints at a higher station and a nobler dignity, and witnesses with no uncertain sound to His superiority over all other prophets. Such a person may well be called the 'Son of God', and Christians often wonder why their Muhammadan brethren so object to the latter title, when they themselves have given Jesus a title not less high." William Goldsack, *Christ in Islam*, p. 21 cited by Gilquist, "Titles".

Quoting such distinguished commentators as Imam Razi and Baidawi, Goldsack observes: "Candid Muhammadan writers freely admit that this title 'Spirit of God' carries with it some specialty such as can be predicated of no other prophet" (Goldsack, *Christ in Islam*, p. 21). Gilchrist makes this astute connection: "It is very interesting to note that the very expression applied to Jesus in Al-Nisa 4.171, *ruhun minhu*, appears in exactly the same form in Al-Mujadilah 58.22 where we read that God strengthens true believers with "a spirit from him". The Muslim translator Yusuf Ali appends the following comment to this verse: "Here we learn that all good and righteous men are strengthened by God with the holy spirit. If anything the phrase used here is stronger, "a spirit from Himself". Whenever anyone offers his heart in faith and purity to God, God accepts it, engraves that Faith on the seeker's heart, and further fortifies him with the divine spirit which we can no more define adequately than we can define in human language the nature and attributes of God. " (Yusuf Ali, *The Holy Qur'an*, p. 1518). This is a remarkable comment which clearly contains a veiled implication that the *ruhun minhu* is the very Spirit of the living God, uncreated and eternal in essence."

[46] cf. Al-Anbiya 21:91, "made her son a sign to all the universe."

[47] Baptism was practiced in Judaism at the time of Jesus. However, it was only for Gentiles, not natural born Jews who were already considered part of Abraham's covenant. Yet JB directed his preaching to include the Jews as well as Gentiles (Luke 3:14), warning them against false reliance upon their ethnic heritage for salvation. They too must present fruits of repentance (Luke 3:10-13) and be baptized. See Matthew 3:7-10; Luke 3:7-9.

[48] "We made his wife fertile" (Al-Anbiya 21:88-89).

[49] Yahya would be wise, sympathetic, dutiful – Mariam 19:12-15.

[50] Abdallah Yousuf Ali commented, "This is spoken as in the life-time of Yahya. Peace and God's Blessins [sic] were on him when he was born; they continue when he is about to die an unjust death at the hands of a tyrant [King Herod Antipas]; and they will be especially manifest at the Day of Judgment." *The Glorious Kur'an*, 770.

[51] "The reference is to the twelve disciples that Isa sent out as apostles. The Arabic word is of uncertain meaning. Some have suggested that it refers to their arguing, and others to their wearing white robes, or workers in bleaching clothes." *RQ*, 143.

[52] "The religious leaders (Imams)," according to Abd al-Fadi, "have disagreed in describing the descent of the 'table'; also how it looked and what was on it. Qatada, quoting from Jabir and Yasir ibn Ammar and Muhammad (p), said, 'The table was sent down spread with bread and meat. The disciples had asked Isa for food they could eat and which would not cease.' He said to them, 'I will do this for you and it will remain, if you do not hide it nor cheat. If you do you will be punished. But before the day had passed they cheated and hid food, so the 'table' was taken up and they were transformed into monkeys and pigs." *Person of Christ, Miracles*. The Qur'an itself, we should add, does not include this reference of severe punishment.

[53] Sinless perfection not only singled Jesus out, it was a necessary qualification in fulfilling his primary roles: to sacrifice for sin (the righteous for the sinful), to Judge with authority to forgive the sins of others. By his sinless sacrifice for the failures of others, Jesus established the New Covenant prophesied by the prophets (Jer 31:3134). Judgment belongs exclusively to the Messiah because he alone is righteous. Just judgment rests upon undeviating submission to God (Jn 5:30; Zech 9:9; Isaiah 59:1418; 42:1-4; Matt 12:18-21). Compromising his goodness would have contaminated His sacrifice for sin and clouded his judgment. Purity alone sees with perfect clarity.

[54] The Qur'an regards Jesus as righteous, but not uniquely so. His moral distinction seems to be shared equally with the company of the righteous (Al-Anaam 6:82-86). These include Ibrahim, Ishaq and YTaqub, Nuh, Dawud, Sulayman, Ayyub, Yusuf, Musa and Harun. Also Zakariyya, Yahya, Isa and Ilyas. Ismail, Alasa (Elijah), Yunus (Jonah) and Lut (Lot).

[55] Jesus Instituted "Lord's Supper (Table)" that memorialized his saving death for all time." Matthew 26:27-8: "Then he took the cup, gave thanks and offered it to them, saying, "Drink from it, all of you. This is my blood of the covenant, which is poured out for many for the forgiveness of sins.

[56] Joseph L. Cumming (Yale University), "Did Jesus Die on the Cross? The History of ReflectionontheEndof HisEarthlyLifeinSunniTafsirLiterature,"May2001. Accessed at http://enrichmentjournal.ag.org/201203/201203_056_Jesus_Son_ of_God.cfm This Christian scholar from Yale University presented this paper at an open forum at the Al-Azhar University in Cairo. I highly recommend it for its tone and content.

[57] "In a footnote about this verse, Abdullah Yusuf Ali wrote: 'those who believe the [Christ] never died should ponder over this verse.'" Cited in *RQ*, 344.

[58] "Several explanations have been proposed for this statement in light of Al-Baqarah 2:154. The first is that Isa's body died, but the spiritual nature of Isa did not die. (See also *Injil*, Matthew 27:46). The second is that although the cross was the punishment of criminals, Isa was not a criminal. Allah did not allow Isa to be left on the cross, where the birds would eat his body, but his body was taken down and buried (See *Injil*, Matthew 27:59). The third is that the Jews did not murder Isa because Isa submitted to Allah's will and lay down his life voluntarily for people. (See *Injil*, John 10:15, 17, 18)." RQ, 115.

[59] "There is no contradiction between this verse and 19:33, which talks specifically about Isa's death, because this verse only says that the Jews did not kill him. It does not say that the Romans did not kill him. Thus there is no contradiction within the Qur'an itself, or between the Qur'an and the previous books, which affirm that the Romans killed him. See the *Injil* Matthew 20:19, 27:26-35. For those who claim that Isa has not died yet, 5:117 is clear, where Isa speaks of his death in the past tense, and is clearly alive, for dead people do not speak at all. Furthermore, it is recorded in the Qur'an, so this happened before the Qur'an was written. In addition, 3:55 affirms this, for Allah tells Isa that he will make him die, and then that his followers will be above the disbelievers until the day of resurrection, not after." RQ, 116.

[60] "This phrase does not say someone was made to look like him /*shubbiha bihi*/ or /*tashaabaha alayhim* (2:70)/ but /*shubbiha lahum*/ (it seemed so to them). The Jews indeed thought that they had ended Christ's message and influence by

killing him, but when Allah resurrected him from death to life and then raised him to himself. Allah got the great victory (verse 158) see 3:55." RQ, 116.

[61] This declaration is softened by its wording and context. The Jews, it says, did not kill or crucify Jesus, which is true since it was the Romans who performed the actual execution. As for context, Jesus' crucifixion is not the main subject of Al-Nisa 4 but the indictment of the Jews over a litany of offenses: they "broke the covenant," murdered their prophets, became so incorrigible that God "stamped disbelief on their hearts" and accused Mary of a great scandal (156). Last mentioned was their boast, "we killed the Messiah, Isa Son of Miriam, Allah's messenger." This aya clarifies their boast by the words, "though they did not kill him nor crucify him" (157). But Allah raised him up to himself" (158).

[62] A. Injeel. Allen, *Dictionary of Islam* (1885)

[63] M. Injeel. Shakir, (tr.), *Holy Qur'an* (Elmhurst, NY: Tahrike Tarsile Qur'an, Inc., 1986), 78.

[64] "Isa speaks of his death in the past tense. Since he speaks, he is alive, and since this conversation is recorded in the Qur'an, it happened before the Qur'an was recorded." *RQ*, 144.

[65] See previous footnote. *RQ*, 144.

[66] See *RQ*, fn 143 on S. 3:55.

[67] See footnote 60, *RQ*, 116.

[68] *Sahih Al-Bukhari*, Vol. 9, *Hadith* no. 532b.

[69] "3:55 and 5:117 say that Allah made Isa die... [The] verse (19:33) confirms that Isa died, for if he did not die, then he would have to be giving money to poor people in heaven, where he is now (4:158). Does Allah have poor people in heaven that need money?" *RQ*, 344.

[70] Sometimes called, "Doubting Thomas." One of Jesus' original 12 apostles who doubted his physical resurrection after seeing the crucifixion (Matthew 28:9-10; Luke 24:36-48). The reason Jesus appeared to him was not simply to answer his personal crisis of faith, but to fit him for his apostolic assignment as witness to his resurrection. Thomas must see Jesus alive with his own eyes and not simply report what he had been told. It must have worked. Thomas travelled all the way

to India faithfully proclaiming the good news of Jesus' resurrection for which he died a martyr!

[71] Allen, *Dictionary of Islam*, 230.

[72] The following citations have been adapted from two principal sources: David Injeel. Stern (tr.), *Complete Jewish Bible* (Clarksville, MD: Jewish New Testament Publications, 1998), xxxix. Rachmiel Frydland, Elliot Klayman (ed.), *What the Rabbis Know about the Messiah* (Columbus, OH: Messianic Literature Outreach, 1991), 87-96.

[73] B. J. Beitzel and Injeel. A. Elwell, "Promise." *Baker Encyclopedia of the Bible*, Vol. 2 (Grand Rapids, MI: Baker Book House, 1988), 1766-1768.

[74] "The word 'scepter' in Hebrew, as used here, refers to tribal identity. A 'staff' denotes a judge's staff and refers to judicial authority. The prediction is that the Messiah would come before Judah would lose its tribal identity (lost in A.D. 70 with the destruction of the temple) and judicial authority (lost in A.D. 6 OR 7 when the Romans replaced Herod Archelaus with a Roman Governor). Based on these two elements, the Messiah needed to come by the first century." Michael Rydelink, "What does the Hebrew Bible Say About the Coming Messiah?" *Apologetics Study Bible*, 1351.

[75] Two collections of writings are called "Apocrypha" (meaning "hidden" or "doubtful") and both are differentiated from the canonical Books of the Bible. The exception is the Roman Catholic Church which regards the earlier collection as part of the canon. Those need not be debated here. It is the later collection written during the second and third centuries that are cited in this chapter and called "Christian Apocrypha."

[76] Excellent scholarly reviews from a Christian perspective on the Infancy Gospels, see http://Injeel.earlychristianwritings.com/infancythomas.html. The reviewer summarizes the present work: "There is nothing particularly Christian about the stories attributed to Jesus; rather, the stories elaborate on the missing years of Jesus with reference to Hellenistic legend and pious imagination."

[77] For a sixth-century date, see J. K. Elliott, *The Apocryphal New Testament: A Collection of Apocryphal Christian Literature in an English Translation* based on M. R. James (NY, NY: Clarendon Press, Oxford, 1993), 86. Barnstone maintains that: "the fact that the work was translated into Arabic made it available to

Mohammed (or whoever compiled the Koran), who in turn adopted its legends in the Koran. The stories entered Persian legends and reached India as well." Willis Barnstone (ed.), *The Other Bible*, Introduction, 407.

[78] All four of these Infancy Gospels held to an orthodox biblical view of Jesus. For example, in *James*, Jesus is called the "Lord Jesus Christ" and Mary's midwife was healed when she "worshiped him as King born unto Israel." *Thomas* refers to Jesus as "the Lord Jesus Christ" and concludes his work with a benediction to him: "To him be glory forever and ever. Amen." The *Arabic Infancy Gospel* affirms the incarnation, including his baptism when the Father opens the heavens saying "This is My beloved Son" and sending the dove of the Holy Spirit. He calls Jesus the "Son of God" and "Savior of the world." In *Matthew*, the angel and shepherds call Jesus the "Savior of the world who is Christ the Lord" (ch 13).

[79] Gene Edward Veith, "Know Nothings," *World*, July 3, 2004, 50.

[80] Gene Edward Veith, "Know Nothings," *World*, July 3, 2004, 50.

[81] Veith, *World*, 51.

[82] *The Infancy Gospel of James*, cited in Willis Barnstone (ed.), *The Other Bible: Jewish Pseudepigrapha, Christian Apocrypha, Gnostic Scriptures* (NY, NY: Harper & Row, 1984), 387.

[83] Buddhist Pali Canon, *Nidanakatha Jatakam* (Group 1, pp. 50-53). "In the Buddhist Pali Canon there are two stories that are remarkably similar to the nativity story and, as Buddhist monks were known to have penetrated Persia and what is today Afghanistan (statues of Buddha, usually defaced, still exist there), the transfer of the story into Christian heretical sources is easily explained. The Buddhist MahaVamso states that these Pali books were reduced to writing during the reign of King Vattagamani of Ceylon about 80 BC." John Tisdall.

Two separate stories describe fruit trees being made to bow down for food during the infancy of the Buddha. For the first, see *Nidanakatha Jatakam* (Group 1, pp. 50-53). For the second, The *Cariya-Pitakam* (Group 1, Poem 9). The Qur'anic narrative is clearly a blend of details from all these sources.

[84] *The Infancy Gospel of Pseudo-Matthew*, Willis Barnstone (ed.), *The Other Bible: Ancient Esoteric Texts*, 396. This reference work includes translations of large portions of Jewish Pseudepigrapha, Christian apocrypha and Gnostic Scriptures along with the editor's introductions. Most of the works cited here are taken from

this encyclopedic source. In the interest of space, I will cite the name of the work, TOB, and page number.

[85] *The Infancy Gospel of Pseudo-Matthew*, Alexander Roberts, Sir James Donaldson, Arthur Cleveland Coxe (ed.), *Ante-Nicene Fathers*, Vol 8, 1886, http://gnosis.org/library/psudomat.htm.

[86] *Historia Nativitat Mariae* (20th Group). Tisdall summarizes this work: "A typical apocryphal Christian work known only from an Arabic text and probably of Coptic origin. Right at the beginning *there* is the declaration mentioned in the last Group that Jesus spoke from the cradle to the effect that he was the Son of God whom his Father had sent for the salvation of the nations." Where did Muhammad (p) discover it? Tisdall offers a plausible scenario: "It is wellknown that during his lifetime Muhammad (p) was sent two girls as a present from the governor of Egypt one of whom, Miriam, became his close companion and is said to have become one of his wives. She bore him a son, Ibrahim, who died in infancy. Such connections with the land of Egypt would have given Muhammad (p) access to such legendary Christian material." *The Origins and Sources of the Qur'an.* http://truthnet.org/islam/source.htm.

[87] *Buddha Carita* (Book 1, passage 34), *Lalita Vistara*.

[88] Woodberry.

[89] "A person who pronounces peace upon himself must have authority to do so." Fn in *RQ*, 344.

[90] "The Infancy Gospel of Thomas," *TOB*, 399.

[91] "The Infancy Gospel of Thomas," *TOB*, 401.

[92] Willis Barnstone (ed.), Introduction to "The Arabic Infancy Gospel: The Children Who were Changed into Goats," *TOB*, 407.

[93] John Tisdall, *Origins and Sources*.

[94] This account is not found in any Christian book. Tisdall writes, "The word used in Al-Maidah 5:115 for table, *maidah majidah*, is derived from a similar Ethiopic word used by the Abyssinian Christians for the Lord's Table, the main sacrament of the Christian Church. "The story is probably derived from a perversion of the story of the Last Supper and the challenge of the disciples for a table to be sent

down from heaven is also most likely derived from these words of the Israelites during the exodus which are recorded in very similar terms: "They spoke against God, saying, 'Can God spread a table in the wilderness?'" (Psalm 78.19)

[95] Irenaeus summarizes and refutes Basilides position in Irenaeus, *Against Heresies*, Book I, Chapter 24, sections 3-7. http://Injeel.earlychristianwritings.com/basilides.html. For a solid translation in modern English, see Alexander Roberts and James Donaldson (eds.), Irenaeus of Lyons, *Against Heresies* (Ex Fontibus Co, 2015), 103-4.

[96] Translated by Roger A. Bullard and Joseph A. Gibbbons, *Second Treatise of the Great Seth*, Wikipedia.

[97] Thanks to Andrew G. Bannister for this observation, *Oral-Formulaic Study*, 27.

[98] Tisdall, *Origins and Sources*.

CHAPTER 10: Confusion over Jesus' Death

[1] Thanks to Nehls for this observation.

2 MATTHEW 16:21; 20:17-19; 26:1-2; 26:12; 26:17-18; 26:20-25; 26:26-28; 26:31- 32; 26:45; 26:51-56; MARK 8:31-9:1; 9:30-32; 14:8; 14:21; 14:22-25; 14:27; 14:34-42; 14:49; LUKE 9:21-22; 9:43-45; 22:14-20; 22:21-22; 22:27; 22:39-44; 22:52-53; JOHN 2:18-22; 3:13-15; 7:1-9; 7:32-34; 8:28-29; 10:10-18; 12:7; 12:20-25; 12:27-28; 12:31- 36; 13:31-33; 14:28-31; 16:16-22, 32-33; 17:1-5; 18:10-11; 19:10-11.

[3] Mark: "He was stating the matter plainly" (Mark 8:32). Luke: "Let these words sink into your ears. . ." (Luke 9:44).

[4] This historical reality is grounds neither for anti-Semitic sentiment nor violence against Jews. The pogroms against them during various periods of church history are biblically indefensible and antithetical to the spirit of Jesus. See Luke 23:34; Acts 3:17-18; 13:26-27; Romans 10:1-3; 11:11-32, etc.

[5] Jesus never predicted his death without including his resurrection. The verb to "be raised" is always in the passive voice denoting the action happens to the subject, not by it. In other words, Jesus' lifeless body would not raise itself, but be raised by Another.

[6] The disciples distress, no doubt, naturally arose over the loss of one they adored. At another level, they mourned because their cherished expectations of Messiah were unraveling. They had always believed he would be a Ruling Conquer. That, however, was only half right. Jesus was completing the picture that the Son of Man came first to be a suffering Figure.

[7] Luke explicitly emphasizes fulfillment: "See, we are going up to Jerusalem, and everything that is written about the Son of Man by the prophets will be accomplished. For he will be delivered over to the Gentiles and will be mocked and shamefully treated and spit upon. And after flogging him, they will kill him, and on the third day he will rise" (Luke 18:31-33 ESV).

[8] Translated "Behold" in the King James Version. I don't use it because it sounds churchy and no longer conveys startling realities.

[9] Rogers and Rogers, *Linguistic and Exegetical Guide*, 45.

[10] Genesis 3:15, Psalm 22; 118:22; Isaiah 8:14; 52:13-53:12; Zechariah 12:10; Luke 2:34; Matt 21:42-46; Acts 2:23.

[11] Louw & Nida, *Greek-English Lexicon of the New Testament*, 364.

[12] "The Son of Man" in the earlier Books can simply refer to a human being (Psalm 8:4), God's title of address for a prophet (Ezekiel 2:1) or the title of a heavenly ruler who received a kingdom from God (Daniel 7:13). William McCumber writes, "By Jesus' time, Son of man was popularly conceived as a power figure, but He merged the ruler concept with a sufferer role. He is the King whose rule and conquest are by suffering love." William E. McCumber, *Beacon Bible Expositions*, Vol 1: *Matthew* (Kansas City, MO: Beacon Hill Press, 1975), 154.

[13] "This saying tells us how Jesus lived. He filled His days with service to human need. His power was exercised to confer benefits, not to exact them. He lived for what He could give, not for what He could get." McCumber, *Matthew*, 154.

[14] "For many" (*anti pollon*). "Anti" means "for" or "instead of. There is the notion of exchange and substitution." "Pollon" or "many" is a Semitic way of expressing "all." Rogers and Rogers, *Linguistic and Exegetical Guide*, 45.

[15] McCumber, *Matthew*, 155.

[16] Susan R. Garrett, "The Meaning of Jesus' Death in Luke," *Word & World* (St. Paul, MN: Word & World, Luther Seminary, 1992), 16.

[17] McCumber, *Matthew*, 198.

[18] Prophet Jeremiah had foretold of this new covenant: "Look, the days are coming"—this is the Lord's declaration —"when I will make a new covenant with the house of Israel and with the house of Judah. This one will not be like the covenant I made with their ancestors when I took them by the hand to bring them out of the land of Egypt—a covenant they broke even though I had married them"—the Lord's declaration. "Instead, this is the covenant I will make . . ."

[19] Matthew 20:28; 26:52-54; Genesis 3:15; Exodus 12:3, 6, 7, 13; Isaiah 53:5, 6, 7, 12;; John 1:29; Mark 10:45; 1 Peter 2:24; Revelation 5:9-10.

[20] "This word in Arabic /tawaffa/ means 'to cause to die.' Some translators ignore the clear statement of the Qur'an that Isa died and instead translate common beliefs. The clearer commentary on the Qur'an is the Qur'an itself, not what others say about it. This verb, in its various forms, occurs 25 times in the Qur'an. Twice (here and 3:55) refer to Isa, and everywhere else (2:234, 240, 3:198, 4:15, 97, 6:60, 61, 7:37, 126, 8:50, 10:46, 104, 12:101, 13:40, 16:28, 32, 70, 22:5, 32:11, 39:42, 40:67, 777, 47:27), is in the context of death. Even today, it is used euphemistically to mean 'to pass away,' and the word 'obituaries' is from the same root." *The Reference Qur'an*, fn 532, 66.

[21] "This word refers to Isa's ascension, not his resurrection. *Injil*, Acts 1:2, 9-11, 22, 1 Timothy 3:16. Since he was raised up to be with Allah, he is with Allah now." RQ, 67.

[22] "3:55 and 5:117 say that Allah made Isa die. . . [The] verse (19:33) confirms that Isa died, for if he did not die, then he would have to be giving money to poor people in heaven, where he is now (4:158). Does Allah have poor people in heaven that need money?" *RQ*, 344.

[23] "Isa speaks of his death in the past tense. Since he speaks, he is alive, and since this conversation is recorded in the Qur'an, it happened before the Qur'an was recorded." *RQ*, 144.

[24] See *RQ*, fn 143, 3:55.

[25] Like the Messiah, those who receive His salvation will actively follow him in a similar pattern of suffering and glory. For believers' expectation of suffering, 1 Peter 1:6 and glory, 1 Peter 1:3-5.

[26] Basilides, cited in Irenaeus, *Against Heresies*, Book I, Chapter 24, sections 3-7.

[27] See Chapters 9 and 11.

[28] Todd Lawson, *The Crucifixion and the Qur'an: A Study in the History of Muslim Thought*, 1st Asian edition (NY, NY: One World, Oxford, 2011).

[29] Lawson, *The Crucifixion and the Qur'an*, 23.

[30] *Encyclopedia of the Quran* cited by Lawson, *The Crucifixion and the Qur'an*, 23-4.

[31] For an insightful critique of these, see Philip Jenkins, *Hidden Gospels: How the Search for Jesus Lost Its Way* (NY, NY: Oxford University Press, 2001).

[32] See Chapter 3, *FTQ* 6.

[33] Cyril, "Second Letter to Nestorius," 52.

[34] Leo, cited in Bettenson and Maunder, *Documents*, 54-56.

[35] Abdu Murray, *Grand Central Questions: Answering the Critical Concerns of the Major Worldviews* (Downers Grove, ILL: InterVarsity Press, 2014), 220.

[36] Murray, *Grand Central Questions*, 220.

CHAPTER 11: Previous Scriptures, Al-Qur'an & Prophet Muhammad (p)

[1] AlImran 3:45

[2] AlImran 3:47

[3] AlImran 3:45

[4] Al-Nisa 4:169, the same title Muhammad assumed for himself.

[5] Al-Tawbah or Al-Baraah 9:31

[6] Al-Tawbah or Al-Baraah 9:31

[7] AlImran 3:45 = Injeel, John 1:14. "This title is the special kalimah for Jesus Christ." *Dictionary of Islam*, 229.

[8] Al-Tawbah or Al-Baraah 9:85

[9] Al-Baqarah 2:87; Al-Nisa 4:171 = Injeel, Luke 4:18; Acts 10:38. Al-Baizawi says it is "a spirit which proceedeth from God." Allen, *Dictionary of Islam*, 229.

[10] AlImran 3:49

[11] AlImran 3:57

[12] AlImran 3:59 = Hebrews 4:15 (Please help me understand. The contemporary view of Muhammad's (p) sinlessness is confusing when compared to what he claimed about himself (Al-Mumin or Al-Ghafir 40:55, 57; Muhammad 47:19. In Al-Fath 48:2 he prayed for forgiveness).

[13] AlImran 3:46, 55; Mariam 19:19 = Injeel.

[14] Mariam 19:21 = Injeel.

[15] Allen's classic work, *The Dictionary of Islam* (1885), takes notice: "Islam admits of the miraculous conception of Christ, and that He is the 'Word' which God 'conveyed into Mary'; and whilst the other five great prophets are but 'the chosen,' 'the preacher,' 'the friend,' 'the converser with,' and 'the messenger of' God, Jesus is admitted to be the 'Spirit of God.' He is the greatest miracle worker of all the prophets; and while Muhammad is dead and buried, and saw corruption, all Muslim divines admit that Jesus 'saw no corruption,' and still lives with a human body in Paradise." 234.

[16] For the list of biblical names cited in the Qur'an, see the Introduction.

[17] But even that might be saying too much. I don't see the Qur'an connecting Yahya to Isa in any direct way. Like Jesus, we read only of his nativity where he predicted that he would be blessed on the day of his death.

[18] Donald Mcleod cited in Brian Edgar, *The Message of the Trinity* (Downers Grove, ILL: InterVarsity Press, 2004), 127.

[19] Brian Edgar, *The Message of the Trinity* (Downers Grove, ILL: InterVarsity Press, 2004), 127.

[20] Spiritual, not biological. See Chapter 2.

[21] Karl Barth, *Church Dogmatics*, I/2, 182, cited in Edgar, *Trinity*, 127.

[22] Edgar, *Trinity*, 127.

[23] For Jesus' predictions about his death, see Chapter 9.

[24] R. C. Injeel. Lenski, *The Interpretation of St. Luke's Gospel* (Minneapolis, MN: Augsburg Publishing House, 1961), 1156.

[25] "This word expresses the 'character of necessity or compulsion' in an event." Kittel, G., Bromiley, G. Injeel., & Friedrich, G. (Eds.), *Theological Dictionary of the New Testament*, Vol. 2 (Grand Rapids, MI: Eerdmans, 1964, electronic ed.), 21.

[26] Referring to his death, Jesus said that he *"must go to Jerusalem and undergo great suffering"* (Matt 16:21; Mk 8:31; Lk 9:22); "it *must* happen in this way" (Matt 26:54); "*must* endure much suffering and be rejected" (Lk 17:25); "this scripture *must* be fulfilled in me" (Lk 22:37); "the Son of Man *must* be handed over" (Lk 24:7); "everything *must* be fulfilled" (Lk 24:44); "the Son of Man *must* be lifted up" (Jn 3:14). Emphasis added in all.

[27] Prophets J. P.l 2:28-32; Jeremiah 31:33-34; Ezekiel 36:26-27; 39:29. This was fulfilled in Injeel, Acts 2:16-21

[28] Reminiscent of the Ten Commandments given through Prophet Moses in the earlier covenant at Mt. Sinai (Tawrat, Exodus 20:2).

[29] Other passages in the Injeel on the question of whether Jesus' death on the cross was a mark of shame or honor: John 7:39; 12:16, 23; Acts 3:13-15; 1 Pt 1:21; Heb 2:19, etc.

[30] Translator Muhammad Khan explains the name Ahmad as "the second name of Prophet Muhammad (p) . . . and it (Ahmad) literally means: 'One who praises Allah more than others." Pickthall translates this verse, Jesus came "bringing good tidings of a messenger who cometh after me, whose name is the Praised One" (i.e., either Ahmad or Muhammad (p)).

[31] Dave Miller, Ph.D. deftly addresses the linguistic issues. He writes, "The meaning of the Hebrew *ma-kha-madeem* is different from the meaning of the word "Muhammad" in Arabic. According to Sheikh Abd al-Azîz, Grand Mufti

of Saudi Arabia, the word "Muhammad" is derived from the Arabic root word *hamd* meaning "praise." It is the emphatic passive participle of that root and can be translated as "the Oft-Praised One" (n.d.). However, the Hebrew term (*makh-mahd*) in the passage under consideration has a completely different meaning. It refers to "grace, beauty" (Gesenius, 1847, p. 464), "a desirable thing, delightfulness" (Brown, et al., 1906, pp. 326-327), "a pleasant thing" (Payne, 1980, 1:295), or "precious" (Holladay, 1988, p. 190). English translations render the term "altogether lovely" (NKJV, NIV), "wholly desirable" (NASB), and "altogether desirable" (ESV, RSV). No reputable English translation would render the underlying Hebrew as "praised one," let alone as "Muhammad." All Muslims have done is happen upon a Hebrew word that phonetically sounds somewhat like "Muhammad" and have erroneously concluded the word must be referring to him. Such handling of linguistic data is irresponsible—if not deceptive." Dave Miller, "Does Song of Solomon Mention Muhammad?" Accessed at: http://ap.lanexdev.com/APContent.aspx?category=8&article=4749.

[32] For example, in the section, "Biblical Prophecy on the Advent of Muhammad (p)," Khan writes: "Muslim theologians have said that "another Comforter" is Muhammad (p), the Messenger of Allah; and him to 'abide forever' means the perpetuity of his laws and way of life (Shari'a) and the Book (Qur'an) which was revealed to him" (Kahn, *The Noble Qur'an*, 840). This view is challenged by Seyyed Hossein Nasr, editor of the elegantly written *The Study Qur'an*: "Such an interpretation is, however, complicated by the next verse, 14:17, where the Advocate or Paraclete is said to be 'the Spirit of truth, whom the world cannot receive, because it neither sees him nor knows him. You know him, because he abides with you, and he will be in you,' and by 14:26, where the Advocate is again equated with the Holy Spirit." Seyyed Hassein Nasr (ed.), *The Study Qur'an* (NY, NY: Harper One, 2015), 1366.

[33] Continuity in the earlier Books should not be confused with the succession of prophets in the form of being passed down biologically (i.e. father to son) like we find with Davidic kings ruling over Israel (David, Solomon, Rehoboam, etc.) or the priests serving at the sanctuary (Aaron and sons). Prophets were individually chosen by God to deliver messages to the people. They were directly summoned by God: "The word of the LORD came to . . ." So the "line of prophets," in which Moses was a significant part, though not biologically determined, did indeed carry a continuing message calling for faithfulness to God's covenant and moved the plan of God forward.

[34] Christians affirm and celebrate the continuity of divine revelation. The record of God's actions and words through the ages form one story, an organic whole. The Bible divides into two "Testaments" or covenants, the Old and the New, forming one Bible of many inspired by one God. We believe neither Testament can be understood without the other.

[35] The Qur'an teaches: (1) *God's command to believe all the Scriptures & warns against rejecting them;* (2) *Four main books of Scripture:* Tawrat of Moses, Zabur of David, Injeel (Gospel) of Jesus, Qur'an of Muhammad (p); AlImran 3:84; 2:285; Warnings: AlImran 3:3-4 (3) *Al-Qur'an confirms previous Scriptures* – Al-Baqarah 2:97; Al-Maidah 5:46; Yunus 10:37; Yusuf 12:111. Rick Brown, "Muslims Who Believe the Bible," *Mission Frontiers,* July-August 2008 (Pasadena, CA: USCWM), 19-23.

[36] Tawrat, Exodus 20 and Deuteronomy 5

[37] Injeel, Romans 2:12-16

[38] John 7:37-39; Hebrews 9:26; 10:19; Colossians 2:8-9, 13-15, etc.

[39] These need not be repeated here. See Question 9.1, "Sources for the Injeel."

[40] Most devout Christians would agree that the primary source for a full-orbed faith is "all Scripture" and not just our favorite portions. As God's primary means of speaking to us, it should never take for granted.

[41] http://engagingwithislam.org/wp-content/uploads/2014/02/TPPG_table.gif

[42] (1) *Humanity created in the Image of God* – Torah – Genesis 1:26-28; Leviticus 19; Prophets – Isa 10:2 (God's holy character to be reflected in his people); Micah 6:8; Psalms – Psalm 8; Gospel – Matt 7:12 – love God and others; Jn 13:34-35; 1 Cor 13:12-13; 2 Cor 3:18; Col 3; Gal 5:22-24; Qur'an? No, nothing compares with God.

(2) *The Fatherhood and Son of God* – Torah – Exodus 4:22 (Israel); Prophets – Kings of Judah called sons of God. These were all failed kings – 2 Samuel 7:14; 1 Chronicles 28:5-6. Isaiah 9:6 predicted a King who would not fail; Psalms – Psalm 8; 110; Gospel – Son-King who did not fail: Luke 2:10- 13; Mark 8:29; 10:45; 15:25-26; The Lord's Prayer, "Our Father" Luke 11:2-4; Galatians 4:4; Qur'an? No

(3) *God dwells with his people* – **In contrast to the distant deities of other nations: Torah** – Genesis 2-3; God walked with Adam & Eve in Eden; Exodus 34 (tent of meeting); Deut 4:7; 12:1-15, 17-22, 26-28; Lev 17:1-7; Prophets – 1 Kings 8:38-40; Psalms – Psalm 23:6; Gospel – Philippians 2:5-11; Luke 4:18-21; John 1:14; Qur'an? No

(4) *Priesthood & Sacrifice for Atonement for Sin* – **(directly linked to the preceding: a holy God's nearness to sinful persons requires an atoning act)** – Torah – Exodus 19:6-7; Leviticus; Prophets – Isaiah 1:18; 9:6-7 (Prince of Peace); 53:12; Zabur, Psalms – Psalm 22; Gospel – John 10:11; Matthew 9:12-13; Revelation 5:9-10; Acts 2:36; 1 Peter 2:8-9, 20-24; 1 Corinthians 1:18; Qur'an– No

(5) *Covenants of Noah, Abraham, Moses & David* **(All these emphasize that God initiates pledges and faithfully keeps his covenant promises): NOAH –Torah,** Genesis 8:21-22; Sign, Gen 9:12-17; Isaiah 24:5; Injeel, Hebrews 11:7; 1 Peter 3:20; Qur'an? No.

ABRAHAM – Promised him: (a) he would father a great nation through which someday all nations would be blessed: Genesis 12:1-3; 15:5; 17:4-6, 16; 22:17; Hebrews 11:11-12; (b) the land of Canaan, Gen 17:8; 15:18-21; Exodus 6:4; Joshua 1:3; Nehemiah 9:8; Acts 7:5; (c) a unique relationship with God, Genesis 17:8; Gen 26:24; Deut 29:13; Matt 22:32; Acts 7:32; Qur'an? No.

MOSES (at Mt. Sinai) – Exodus 20; (related to Abraham's covenant – Deut 29:12-13; Exodus 2:24; 6:4-8; Deut 7:8); Required obedience to the law (Exodus 24:7; 34:27- 28; Deut 4;13), holiness (Deut 14:2; Lev 11:45; 20:26) and wholehearted devotion (Exodus 34:14; Deut 4:23); Qur'an? No.

DAVID – Establish David and his descendants on Israel's throne forever – 2 Samuel 7:11-16; 6:21; 23:5; 1 Kings 8:16; Psalm 78:70; Jeremiah 33:17; Qur'an? No.

(6) *One Story of Redemption* – (narrow selection): (a) Creation: Genesis 1 & 2; (b) Adam and Eve's willful transgression and its consequences: Genesis 3-11; (c) First promise of Redeemer, Genesis 3:15; (d) Table lists 70 nations of the world favorably (Gen 10) and yet fallen (Gen 11); (€) On their behalf, God selects none of the 70 nations to bless the others but creates one through Abraham and elderly Sarah through whom "all the families of the world will be blessed" (Gen 12:1-30). God loves and blesses both of Abraham's sons, Ishmael, son of Hagar

and Isaac son of Sarah through whom redemption in a Messiah would come. God blesses Ishmael with 12 tribes and kings would become joyous recipients of that redemption. (f) The Messiah winning the obedience of nations would come through the tribe of Judah (Gen 49:10). The Messiah is the Seed of Abraham (collective noun) in whom all who believe in Him receive Abraham's covenant blessings (Galatians 3). The entrance of the nations into Abraham's covenant was a mystery that was

finally opened through Messiah Jesus (Colossians 1:25-27; 2:2-3). (g) Jesus offered himself in death for the sins of all humanity whose sacrifice was vindicated by his resurrection. Jesus brought the New Covenant of the Spirit prophesied by Jeremiah and Ezekiel. Qur'an? No.

[43] Rick Brown, http://engagingwithislam.org/wp-content/uploads/2014/ 02/ TPPG_table.gif.

[44] Rick Brown, http://engagingwithislam.org/wp-content/uploads/2014/ 02/ TPPG_table.gif.

[45] Nasr references two primary sources: Imad al-Din Abu'l-Fida Ismail ibn Umar ibn Kathir (d. 774/1373), Tafsir al-Qur'an al-azim and Abu Abd Allah Muhammad ibn Ahmad al-Qurtubi (d. 671/1172), al-Jami li-ahkam al-Qur'an. Nasr, *The Study Qur'an*, 1032. Ignac Goldziher wrote, Ignac Goldziher, "Sects." *Introduction to Islamic Theology and Law*, Andras and Ruth Hamori (tr.) (Princeton, NJ: Princeton University Press, 1910), 220-221.

[46] Ignac Goldziher, "Sects." *Introduction to Islamic Theology and Law*, Andras and Ruth Hamori (tr.) (Princeton, NJ: Princeton University Press, 1910), 220-221.

[47] *The Qur'an Dilemma* (USA: TheQuran.com, 2011) 574.

[48] Belief in the eternality of the Qur'an is not held universally among Muslims. Upon mentioning it recently in conversation with a devout Shi'a as Islamic dogma, she objected to it and inquired about its Qur'anic citation.

[49] By "glorious" (*majid*) according to some "indicates the utmost in nobility, magnanimity, and grace. Others say that it indicates the uncreatedness of the Quran." Nasr, *Study Qur'an*, 1498.

[50] Nasr, *Study Qu'ran*, 1499.

51 Tarif Khalidi (Ed. and tr.), *The Muslim Jesus: Sayings and Stories in Islamic Literature* (Cambridge, MASS: Harvard University Press, 2001), 15.

52 A seminal work frequently cited is Injeel. St. Clair-Tisdall, *The Original Sources of the Qu'ran* (London, England, Society for Promoting Christian Knowledge, 1905. It may be accessed electronically at http://Injeel.Muhammadanism.org/Tisdall/ sources_quran/sources_quran.pdf); Two other Christian scholars draw from and augment this work. http://truthnet.org/islam/source.htm; Nehls, "The Sources of Islam," answeringislam.org. Reasons for Christianity's universal rejection of the Apocrypha from the second and third centuries have been previously given. What is the Muslim attitude towards them? How do Islamic apologists justify their inclusion in the Qur'an? (1) For a scholarly Muslim perspective of the Qur'an's use of apocryphal sources, see Tarif Khalidi (Ed. and tr.), *The Muslim Jesus: Sayings and Stories in Islamic Literature* (Cambridge, MASS: Harvard University Press, 2001), 7-9. In addressing the apocryphal material in the Qur'an, he does not deny it but emphasizes today's academic trend: "old polemics have been replaced with a new synthesis." Its inclusion, he believes, is justified by an increasing appreciation for the apocrypha of late due to the scientific study of folklore and the discovery of Gnostic texts at Nag Hammadi. By citing these, in his view, the Qur'an was "echoing a living Christian tradition, not an imaginary one." He disregards their heretical status in Christianity and even their doctrines that contradict orthodox Islam. He does not address our present discussion of the impact of outside sources on the Qur'an's eternal origins.

(2) Abul Hasan Ali Nadwi who writes the Introduction to *The Glorious Qur'an: Text, Translation & Commentary* by Abdul Majid Daryabadi (Leicester, UK: 2008), p xxiii xxiv states that Daryabadi's exegesis "provides a conclusive answer to those Jewish and Christian critics of Islam who claim that the Holy Qur'an draws its material from the Scriptures and apocryphal writings of Judaism and Christianity...These critics are unable to appreciate the fact that the Holy Qur'an has been revealed to confirm the Scriptures of old and to restate and uphold the spirit of their true teachings, which, by itself, involves refutation of such accretions, alterations and additions as have found a place in the Scriptures of Judaism and Christianity." While stating that "the Qur'an is a repository of the Divine Message revealed in the earlier Scriptures is an article of faith for Muslims," he asserts that "their scribes, translators and commentators" have inserted into their Scriptures "spurious matter." How does he determine what is "spurious?" He states, "Whatever in these Books finds confirmation by the

Holy Qur'an is undoubtedly correct; everything else is a later addition mixed up with Divine revelation." Three observations deserve notice. First, there's no indication that the author is aware that Christianity does not regard both Apocryphal writings and the Scriptures as divinely inspired books. Secondly, he does not deny the Qur'an's use of the Apocrypha. Third, none of his criticism is against the Apocrypha's in-your-face contradictions with the Qur'an and earlier Scriptures, including their blasphemies, but focuses entirely upon the Scriptures.

(3)Another Muslim perspective, while polemical in tone, is still valuable: Hamza Mustafa Njozi, *The Sources of the Qur'an: A Critical Review of Authorship Theories* (Riyadh, Saudi Arabia: International Islamic Pub House, 2005), esp. 63-82.

[53] Islamic defense advocating the divine origins for the Qur'an that I have found typically runs along different lines than the validating criteria issued in these ayat. More common are its perfect preservation, its unsurpassed style considering Muhammad (p) as unlettered and uneducated, the Prophet's integrity and its historical content and scientific information. For example, see "The Authenticity of the Qur'an" essay published by the Institute of Islamic Information and Education at http://Injeel.iiie. net/index.php?q=node/46.

[54] *Dictionary of Islam*, 235-243. "Whilst, therefore, Muhammad took little of his religious system from Christianity, he was vastly indebted to Judaism both for his historical narratives and his doctrines and precepts. . .The teachings of Jesus form no part of his religious system. . . A Jewish Rabbi, Abraham Geiger, in A.D. 1833, wrote a prize essay. . . In this treatise it is clearly demonstrated how much the whole system of Islam is indebted to Talmudic Judaism for its teachings. Its narratives, its doctrines, and its theological terms, are chiefly derived from those of the Talmud."

[55] Andrew Bannister, *An Oral Formulaic Study of the Qur'an* (Lexington Books, 2014), 6. The author places this story of Adam's Fall that we find echoed in the Qur'an as early as 100 BC with its oldest extant text AD 400. This work drawn from his Ph.D. thesis highlights the oral culture Muhammad (p) lived and excelled in.

[56] Ibn Ishaq, Sirat Rasul Allah, *Guillaume*, 62, cited by Nehls, *Sources*.

[57] The Qur'an drew this version of "the fall" from the Sethian-Ophites probably without knowing it. It's account of Adam and Eve descending from heaven to earth made it into the Quran and not the Genesis account in which they

were driven out of the Garden. Christians and Muslims would both find this Gnostic work to be outrageous heresy. It is rooted in polytheism. This tale is about competing gods, the Creator God having a mother (Sophia) who helped Adam and Eve 'combat the tyranny of God' (659). The "fall" fit into its view of a "Upper Mother (god)" and "Lower Mother." Angels seduced Eve and produced sons through her, producing angels. Sophia rejoiced when they ate of the forbidden fruit. "Ialdabaoth...cast Adam and Eve out of Paradise, since they had transgressed his commandment... Thus they were . . . cast down into the lower world by him" (662). God is the villain and Satan the hero. The Serpent plays a positive role by providing Adam and Eve with secret knowledge to combat an evil God. "by being free from their Creator God, they could find the light in their souls and return to the true Father" (*The Other Bible*, 659-660).

[58] We wholeheartedly embrace this eloquent statement on the value of life taught here in the Qur'an.

[59] Mishnah, *Sanhedrin* 4.5, https://InjeelInjeel.scribd.com/document/75763369/Sanhedrin-4-5.

[60] The story of Abraham's deliverance from the fire is based on a mistranslation of Genesis 15:7 from Hebrew into Aramaic. "It confused two words, the Babylonian city of Ur with "fire." Non-canonical Jewish writers then spun tales such as this one until they discovered the error. Yet it was imported into the Qur'an." Tisdall, *Sources*.

[61] "In the Arabian Peninsula there were many Jewish communities living in the diaspora after the destruction of Jerusalem in 70 A.D. Many of these were guided by legends (Hagadda, etc.) and Talmudic writings, rather than the Torah. Many Jews at the time believed that the Talmud had been added to the "preserved tablets" (i.e. to the Ten Commandments, which were kept in the Ark of the Covenant and were believed to be replicas of the heavenly book). Mohammed added to this the Quran. There are several traditions from Judaism that were accepted by Mohammed and incorporated in Islam." Nehls, "The Sources of Islam."

[62] Paul S. Minear, *The Obedience of Faith* (London, 1971) cited in Leon Morris, *The Epistle to the Romans* (Leicester, England: Inter-Varsity Press, 1988), 63.

EPILOGUE

[1] "God's 'name' is qualified by the adjective 'holy' in the Old Testament [Tawrat] more often than by all other qualifiers put together." J. Alec Motyer, *The Prophecy of Isaiah* (Downers Grove, ILL: InterVarsity Press, 1993), 76-78.

[2] Motyer, *Isaiah,* 77.

[3] "Hebrew uses repetition to express superlatives or to indicate totality. (Gen 14:10 "pits, pits" is rendered "full of pits" and 2 Ki 25:15 "gold, gold" is rendered "pure gold". Only here is a threefold repetition found. Holiness is supremely the truth about God, and his holiness is in itself so far beyond human thought that a 'super-superlative' has to be invented to express it." Motyer, *Isaiah,* 77.

[4] "Nidmeti" (ruined) is from *dama* (to be silent), which is used of the silence following disaster or death (Jer 14:17; 47:5; Psalm 49:12, 13, 20,21). "Silenced" would be telling in this context, i.e. excluded from the heavenly choir, forbidden even to join from afar in adoration, but the silence of death must be included too. The explanation of this judgment is that what we might reckon the lightest of sins (unclean lips) is linked with what we might accept as the least threatening of privileges (see. . .the LORD) but the mixture is deadly. Isaiah adds the fact that he accepted unclean speech in society and made no attempt to separate himself from it (live among) as an aggravation of his guilt." Motyer, *Isaiah,* 77.

[5] "In the OT fire is not a cleansing agent but is symbolic of the wrath of God (Gen 3:24; Nu 11:1-3), his unapproachable holiness (Ex 3:2-6; 19:18-25) and the context of his holy law (Dt 4:12, 33, 36)." Motyer, *Isaiah,* 77.

[6] "The perpetual fire (Lv 6:12-13) on the altar went beyond symbolizing divine wrath, for the altar was the place where the holy God accepted and was satisfied by blood sacrifice (Lv 17:11). It holds together the ideas of the atonement, propitiation, and satisfaction required by God and of the forgiveness, cleansing and reconciliation needed by his people. All this is achieved through substitutionary sacrifice and brought to Isaiah, encapsulated in the single symbol of the "live coal." Motyer, *Isaiah,* 78.

[7] "Jesus also suffered outside the city gate to make the people holy through his own blood" (Hebrews 13:12).

[8] Story told by Henry Gariepy, *Songs in the Night* (Grand Rapids, MI: Eerdmans, 1996), 107.

[9] For modesty, see Prophet Isaiah 3:16-24; Injeel, 1 Timothy 2:9-10; 1 Peter 3:3. In the attitude of humility and avoidance of excessive flamboyance, see Zabur, Proverbs 25:6-7; 29:23; Injeel, Luke 22:25-27; Romans 11:20-21; 2 Corinthians 10:13-16; 12:5-6; Philippians 2:5-8; 1 Peter 5:5.

[10] Lamin Sanneh, "Jesus, More than a Prophet," *Finding God at Harvard: Spiritual Journeys of Thinking Christians*, ed. Kelly Monroe (Grand Rapids: Zondervan, 1996), 192.

[11] Sanneh, *Finding God*, 192.

[12] Sanneh, *Finding God*, 192.

[13] Sanneh, *Finding God*, 160-180.

[14] Sanneh, *Finding God*, 192.

CONTACT INFORMATION

Thanks for reading my book! Your feedback is important to me! After you read it, or while you're going through it, I'd love to know what you think.

You can log-on to our website at **jpknight.com**.

Or if you want to keep it confidential, you can email your questions, comments or concerns to <u>myquestions@4ethne.org</u> and I'll do my best to respond.

Be looking for Volume 2 in 2021!
QUESTIONS MUSLIMS ASK CHRISTIANS
Conversations about Salvation and Life Practices

This sequel will focus on your questions regarding salvation and on a wide range of issues on practical living that would not fit in the present volume.

CPSIA information can be obtained
at www.ICGtesting.com
Printed in the USA
BVHW090107230221
600781BV00001B/5